A HISTORY OF
BRITAIN

A HISTORY OF
BRITAIN

THE BRITISH WARS
1603–1776

SIMON SCHAMA

M&S

National Library of Canada Cataloguing in Publication Data

Schama, Simon
A history of Britain

Vol. 2 published by McClelland & Stewart.
Including bibliographical references and index.
Contents: v. 1. The edge of the world?, 3000 BC-AD 1603. - v. 2.
The British wars, 1603-1776.
ISBN 0-563-38497-2 (v. 1). —ISBN 0-7710-7920-6 (v. 2)

1. Great Britain--History. I. Title.

DA130.S44 2000   941   C2001-902029-5

Frontispiece: *Oliver Cromwell*, by an unknown artist, c. 1650

This book is published to accompany the television series
A History of Britain first broadcast on BBC2 in 2000
Executive producer: Martin Davidson. Series Producer: Janet Lee
Producers: Clare Beavan, Ian Bremner, Martina Hall,
Liz Hartford, Mike Ibeji, Tim Kirby, Paul Tilzey
Series developed by Janice Hadlow

Published simultaneously in Great Britain by BBC Worldwide Ltd,
Woodlands, 80 Wood Lane, London W12 0TT

Commissioning editors: Sheila Ableman and Sally Potter
Project editor: Belinda Wilkinson
Copy editors: Esther Jagger and Margaret Cornell
Art director and designer: Linda Blakemore
Picture researchers: Deirdre OíDay, Charlotte Locchead, Miriam Hyman
Cartograhper: Olive Pearson

Set in Bembo by BBC Worldwide
Printed and bound in Great Britain by Butler & Tanner Limited, Frome
Colour separations by Radstock Reproductions Limited, Midsomer Norton
Jacket printed by Lawrence Allen Limited, Weston-super-Mare

McClelland & Stewart Ltd.
The Canadian Publishers
481 University Avenue
Toronto, Ontario
M5G 2E9
www.mcclelland.com

1   2   3   4   5   05   04   03   02   01

CONTENTS

For Martin Davidson and Janice Hadlow –
history-makers

*Narrative is linear. Action is solid. Alas for our chains and chainlets
of 'causes' and 'effects' which we so assiduously track through the countless
handbreadths of years and square miles when the whole is a broad,
deep immensity and each atom is 'chained' and complected with all …*

THOMAS CARLYLE, 'History' from *Fraser's Magazine*

Vico's fantasia *is indispensable to his conception of historical knowledge;
it is unlike the knowledge that Julius Caesar is dead or that Rome was not built
in a day or that thirteen is a prime number, or that the week has seven days;
nor yet is it like knowledge of how to ride a bicycle or engage in statistical research
or win a battle. It is more like knowing what it is to be poor, to belong to a nation,
to be a revolutionary, to fall in love, to be seized by nameless terror,
to be delighted by a work of art …*

ISAIAH BERLIN, *Giambattista Vico and Cultural History*

*Man is the only animal that laughs and weeps;
for he is the only animal that is struck with the difference
between what things are and what they ought to be.*

WILLIAM HAZLITT, *Lectures on the English Comic Writers*

PREFACE

If it's a truism that being British has never been a matter of straightforward allegiance, never was this more glaringly obvious than during the two centuries narrated by this book. Was this country an archipelago or an empire, a republic or a monarchy? 'Great Britain' began as a grandiose fantasy in the head of James VI of Scotland and I of England, and ended as a startling imperial reality on the bloodied ramparts of Seringapatam. The confident chroniclers of the mind-boggling transformation, from sub-insular realms to global empire, liked to imagine that this history was somehow pre-ordained, unfolding naturally from the imperatives of geography and from a shared sense of the inevitability of a parliamentary monarchy. But never was a nation's destiny less predictable, or *less* determined by the markers of topography, which said nothing about whether its bounds should be on the Tweed or the coast of Sligo, the Appalachians or the Bay of Bengal, nor whether those who decided such things should be thought of as the servants of the Crown or the representatives of the people.

It was these battles for allegiance – the British Wars, between and within the nations of our archipelago, and then beyond in the wider world, between different and fiercely argued ideas about our historical and political inheritance – that made us what we became. The creation of our identity was a baptism of blood.

But the slaughters were not always mindless. Crucially, for our future, they were often, even excessively, mindful. The Victorian historians, especially Macaulay, who believed the good fortune of British birth to be a reward won by the sacrifices of ancestors, are habitually berated in much modern scholarship for their detestably insular smugness, their fatuous error of reading history 'backwards' and their habit of projecting on periods – entirely innocent of parliamentary civics – their own nineteenth-century preoccupations. Read those books, it's said, and you are in a world drained of historical freewill, of the uncertainty of outcomes, a past ordered to march in lock-step to the drumbeat of the Protestant, parliamentary future. But a dip, or better yet, a prolonged immersion in the great narratives of the last century – Gardiner, Carlyle, and, to be sure, Macaulay – suggest, to this lay reader anyway, anything *but* imprisonment in a universe of self-fulfilling prophecies. At their most powerful, those wonderfully *complicated* texts deliver the reader into a world shaking with terror, chaos and cruelty.

But it is true, certainly, that many of the grand narratives assumed that the long story they told was one of a battle of beliefs, rather than a mere imbroglio of interests, and that the eventual, admittedly partial, success of the party of liberty represented a genuine turning point in the political history of the world. If to tell the story again, and yet insist that that much is true, is to reveal oneself as that most hopeless anachronism, a born-again Whig, so be it.

New York, 2001

1

'Great Britain?' What was that? John Speed, tailor-turned map-maker and historian, must have had some idea, for in 1611 he published an atlas of sixty-seven maps of the English counties, Wales, Scotland and Ireland, loftily entitled *The Theatre of the Empire of Great Britaine*. An energetic opportunist, Speed was taking advantage of King James's widely advertised desire to be known, not as the Sixth of Scotland and First of England, but as monarch of Britain. The fancy of a British history had been given fresh authority by William Camden's great compilation of geography, the antiquarian chronicle, *Britannia*, already in its sixth edition by 1607. On its frontispiece sat the helmeted personification of the island nation, flanked by Neptune and Ceres, together with an emblem of British antiquity – Stonehenge – thought to have been built by the Romano-British hero Aurelius.

But Camden's erudite work was originally in Latin, a volume for the shelves of a gentleman's library. Speed was after the public, sensing the excitement of even arm-chair travel, the need of the country to fix its place in the world, to contemplate, simultaneously, its past and its present. So the atlas, produced by John Sudbury and George Humble's print shop in Pope's Head Alley, London, was not just a compilation of topographic information but a busy, animated production, full of comings and goings. Sites of historic interest, like the battlefields of the Wars of the Roses, were indicated by miniature sketches of horsemen and pikemen doing their worst; the colleges of Oxford and Cambridge by gowned scholars and coats of arms; royal palaces like Nonesuch and Windsor by elaborate pictorial illustration. On the map of Kent, ships, loaded with cargo, sailed up the Medway before Rochester Castle. Fifty towns were mapped for the first time, given their own insets, streets, markets and churches laid out for the prospective traveller or the proud resident. In this enterprising determination to be the first to provide a popular atlas for the new reign and the new century, the ex-tailor had no scruples about taking his shears to his predecessors. At least five of his maps of the English counties were pilfered more or less directly from the

RE-INVENTING
BRITAIN

Landscape with St George and the Dragon, by Peter Paul Rubens, *c.* 1629.

great Elizabethan cartographer Christopher Saxton (who had provided Burghley with his own pocket atlas) and another five from the English map-maker John Norden. For the single map of Scotland, which made good Speed's pretention of a British atlas, he relied on an earlier version by the Flemish cartographer and map-maker Gerardus Mercator, as well as on arcane information (Loch Ness never froze, horse-men speared salmon in the rivers) and on shameless flattery (the people being 'of good features, strong of body and courageous mien and in wars so virtuous that scarce any service of note hath been performed but they were the first and last in the field'). His eastern Ireland was so accurate that he may have gone there in person, but the west was obviously an exotic mystery, peopled by the medieval chronicler Gerard of Wales's fantasy that off the coast 'lay islands, some full of angels, some full of devils'.

A roughly stitched thing of many odd cloths and fragments though it was, Speed's map of Great Britain was not entirely a fake. The comments he inscribes on the reverse of the maps may sometimes have been recycled platitudes about the clean-ness or foulness of the air. But just as often they spoke of a real journey, of a man who had taken his theodolite to the shires. There were days when he must have trotted out from some damply shadowed valley and found himself surveying the panorama of England. The landscape before him would not have been so very different from our own: crookedly framed fields (with far fewer individual strips than a century before), copses of standing trees, a distant flock of sheep, a wisp of wood smoke. At one such place – the vale of the Red Horse in southeast Warwickshire – the prosaic Speed felt moved to reach for the hyperbole of the pastoral poets. The county was sharply divided by the river Avon. To the north was the semi-industrialized Forest of Arden, a country populated not by love-lorn Rosalinds and Celias but by impover-ished charcoal-burners, woodland-gleaners, poachers and forge-workers on the verge of riot. But to the south was Feldon: 'champaign', rolling arable country, where the valley flats were planted with wheat and the gentle hills grazed by sheep. It was there, at just the point where the Cotswolds descend sharply, that Speed relates his rustic epiphany: 'The husbandman smileth in beholding his pains and the meadowing pastures with the green mantles so embroidered with flowers that from Edgehill we might behold another Eden.'

John Speed died in 1629, leaving behind his *History of Great Britaine*, his pretty maps, eighteen children and (presumably) exhausted wife, Susanna. Thirteen years later, on 23 October 1642, Charles I arrived at the same Warwickshire ridge from which the map-maker had been given a glimpse of bucolic paradise, took out his prospective glass and peered down at the Roundhead troops below. By nightfall there were sixty bodies piled up where the king had stood on the top of Edgehill, and Charles was kept from his sleep by the vocal agonies of the thousands of wounded, groaning in the razor-sharp cold. Next morning, across Speed's flower-embroidered meadow lay the corpses of 3000 men, their allegiances indistinguishable in their nakedness, bodies stripped for loot, fingers broken to extract rings. Eden had become Golgotha.

By the time that the first round of the British wars was over – in 1660 – at least a quarter of a million had perished in England, Wales and Scotland. They had been lost to disease and starvation as well as to battle and siege. Men had died of infected wounds more commonly than they had endured clean-cut deaths in combat. The scythe of mortality, always busy, never fussy, had swept up all kinds and conditions: officers and rank and file; troopers and musketeers; sutlers and camp whores; apprentices with helmets on their heads for the first time; hardened mercenaries who had grown rusty along with their cuirasses; soldiers who could not get enough to fill their stomachs or boots to put on their feet and peasants who had nothing left to give them; drummer boys and buglers; captains and cooks. Even if the father of modern demography, Sir William Petty (Charles II's surveyor-general in Ireland), grossly over-counted another 600,000 dead in Ireland and his total is divided by three, the toll of life, expressed as a proportion of the 5 million population of the British archipelago, is still greater than our losses in the First World War (1914–18).

In any case, the raw body count fails to measure the enormity of the disaster that reached into every corner of the British isles from Cornwall to County Connacht, from York to the Hebrides. It tore apart the communities of the parish and the county, which through all the turmoil of the Reformation had managed to keep a consensus about who governed and how they went about their duties. Men who had judged together now judged each other. Men and women who had taken for granted the patriotic loyalty of even those with whom they disagreed in matters of Church and parliament now called each other traitor. Ultimately, what had been unthinkable was thought and acted on. Men and women, for whom the presence of a king was a condition for the well-being of the commonwealth, were asked to accept that the well-being of the commonwealth required that he be killed.

The wars divided nations, churches, families, father from son, brother from brother. Sir Bevil Grenville died at the battle of Lansdown knowing that his brother Richard was a parliamentary commander (who switched sides not long after). Private Hillsdeane, dying at the siege of Wardour Castle in Wiltshire, let it be known that it had been his own brother who had shot him, though he forgave him for 'only doing his duty'. During the most brutal year of the Scottish civil wars, 1645, Florence Campbell learned that her brother Duncan had been killed by the victorious leader

Frontispiece to *The Theatre of the Empire of Great Britaine* (1616), by John Speed, engraved by Jodocus Hondius. Speed's imaginative depictions of ancient peoples set in classical niches reflect popular, contemporary myths about Britain's early history.

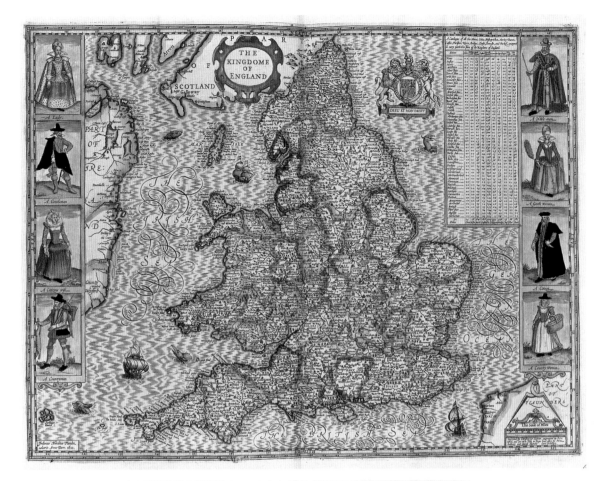

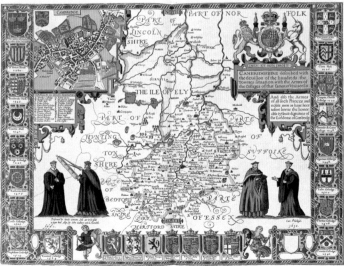

Two maps from an early edition of John Speed's *Theatre of the Empire of Great Britaine* (1610), both filled with colourful local detail, such as the country folk in *The Kingdome of England* (top), or the college dons in *Cambridgeshire* (bottom).

of the MacDonalds after the battle of Inverlochy. While her brother had been a loser, her husband and son, royalist MacLeans, fought with the winners. But in her wrathful grief Florence was all Campbell. 'Were I at Inverlochy,' she wrote, 'with a two-edged sword in my hand and I would tear asunder the MacLeans and the MacDonalds and I would bring the Campbells back alive.'

The house of Britain was not just divided, it was demolished. The grandiose buildings that proclaimed the wealth and authority of the governing classes and that awed the common people to defer to their senatorial power were, in many cases, turned into blackened ruins by the relentless sieges that became the dominant form of assault. Many of those houses were converted into fortified strongholds and garrisons and, like Basing House in Hampshire and Corfe Castle on the Isle of Purbeck, held out to the bitter end. The defenders died, sword in hand, framed in burning doorways and windows, going down in hand-to-hand combat, or starved into surrender like the beleaguered defenders of Wardour Castle who had been subsisting on eight ounces of cereal each and their small share of half a horse. If anything much was left when the sieges were done, the houses were 'slighted' – one of the great euphemisms of the war – to make sure they would never again be a threat.

Epidemics of smallpox and typhus raged opportunistically through populations weakened by shortages of food. Perhaps the most successful army of all was the army of rats, which brought another great wave of plague to add to the bellyful of suffering. For a few years the worst affected regions of the four nations came perilously close to a total breakdown of custom, compassion and law. Towns like Bolton, subjected to a massacre in 1644, lost *half* their population. At Preston in 1643 'nothing was heard but "Kill dead, kill dead"', horsemen pursuing the poor amazed people, killing and spoiling, nothing regarding the doleful cries of women and children'. After Aberdeen fell to the army of the Marquis of Montrose and Alasdair MacColla, the better-off citizens were made to strip naked before being hacked to death so that the blood would not stain the valuable booty of their clothes. For some victims the trauma would never go away. The septuagenarian Lady Jordan, according to John Aubrey, 'being at Cirencester when it was besieged was so terrified with the shooting that her understanding was spoyled, that she became a tiny child that they made Babies for her to play withall'.

Why had the nations of Britain inflicted this ordeal on themselves? For what exactly had the hundreds of thousands perished? As often as this question has been asked, it can never be asked enough. As often as historians have failed to provide an answer, we can never give up trying to find one. We owe it to the casualties to ask if their misery had meaning. Or were the British wars just a meaningless cruelty?

Did the Irish, Scots, English and Welsh of the seventeenth century suffer, as Victorian historians believed, so that their descendants might live in a parliamentary political nation, uniquely stable, free and just? Was their cause one of principle, an unavoidable collision between ultimately irreconcilable visions of Church and state? Or were the protagonists, high and low, the fools of history, jerked around by forces they only half-comprehended and whose outcomes they were blind to predict? Was the whole bloody mess an absurd misunderstanding that, by rights, ought never to have happened at all?

Victorian certainty about a providential purpose running through our histories has, it is safe to say, long been out of fashion, at least in the academic world. Reacting against the sentious, self-righteous view of the Victorians, some modern historical scholarship has argued that the bleaker, more complicated view happens to be the truth: that the British wars were eminently unpredictable, improbable and avoidable. Until the very last moment, late 1641 or 1642, the political class of England was united in a harmonious consensus that the country should be governed by a divinely appointed monarch assisted by a responsible parliament. If there were disputes they were containable. If there were matters that separated people they were as nothing compared to the interests and bedrock beliefs that bound them together. The king was no absolutist, the parliament no champion of liberty. They were all much of a muchness, and that muchness was Englishness: the sound, middling way. The Victorians, like the historian S. R. Gardiner, who blew up every petty squabble between the Stuarts and their parliaments into some great drama of political principle, were deluded by their two-party way of thought, their over-concentration on the sound and the fury of parliamentary debates and their need for a foundation epic. Thus, the argument goes, they read history backwards, so parliament, the beating heart of the nineteenth-century empire, would be thought always to have been the instrument of progress and the hallmark of the British 'difference', separating the nation from the absolutist states of continental Europe. It is this naively insular, nationalist, parliamentary narrative, with heroes like Pym and Hampden defending fortress England from sinking into European despotism, that has drawn the fire of scholars for the last half century. The very worst that can now be said of any account of the origins and unfolding of the civil wars is that it suffers from the delusions of 'Whig' history, in which the parties of 'progress' and 'reaction', of liberty and authority, are cleanly separated and programmed to clash. The truth was just the opposite, the critics insist. Crown and parliament, court and country, were not running on a collision course heading inevitably towards an immense constitutional train wreck. On the contrary, until the very last minute they were moving smoothly on parallel lines.

James VI of Scotland, by Adrian Vanson, *c.* 1585. An early court portrait of the young Scottish king that was probably sent to the Danish court to woo his future wife, Anne of Denmark.

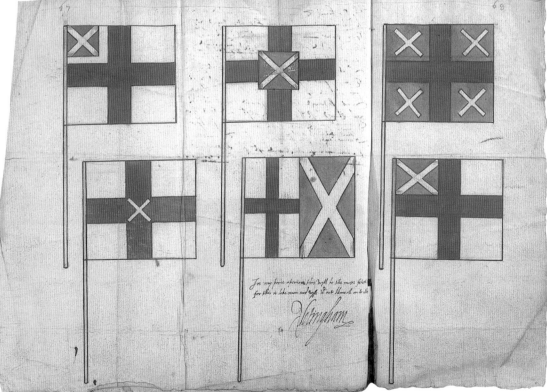

Top: Commemorative medal for James I's accession in 1603, with the king cast as a laurel-wreathed, Roman emperor.
Above: A variety of early designs for a union flag combining the colours of England and Scotland. When the first union flag was finally created in 1606, Scottish shipowners immediately complained that the cross of St George obscured the saltire of St Andrew.

The lights were green, the weather fair, the engine well oiled. When, in 1629, Charles I opted to govern without parliaments, no one, except a few self-righteous, self-appointed 'guardians' of English liberties, could have cared less.

But someone, somehow, seems to have thrown a switch. And, then, that utterly unpredictable, unlikely, what-shall-we-call-it? – a misfortune – took place. It was, I suppose, just about the biggest misfortune in our shared history. But there you are. Accidents happen.

Or do they?

For a time, it was rumoured that King James VI and I was about to change his name to Arthur. Well, why not? Hadn't Camden himself made it clear that 'Britain' was not some new invention at all but merely the *restoration* of an ancient unity, the realm of Brutus the Trojan and of King Lucius, who had been the first to be converted, and ultimately the heart of the great Arthurian-Christian British empire, which had extended from Iceland to Norway, from Ireland to Armorican Brittany. Certainly James himself believed that he was reuniting two realms that had been snapped apart, bringing about dreadful and unrelenting bloodshed. He was reminded by the court preacher John Hopkins of Ezekiel 37, in which the prophet had had a vision of two dry sticks, which he was commanded to put together; and when he did so, lo, they became one and a living thing too, a dream-parable of the reunion of the sundered Israel and Judah. John Gordon, a Scottish minister who had travelled down with James and who fancied himself a cabbalist, unlocked the esoteric signficance of the Hebrew etymology of Britannia, in which Brit-an-Yah – translation: 'a covenant (*Brit*) was there' – encoded God's command to reconstitute Britain from its fractured halves. James was ready and eager to oblige, right from the moment he received the sapphire ring taken from Elizabeth's finger. By the time that he reached Newcastle upon Tyne in April 1603, the king had already redesigned the coinage, styling his kingdom 'Great Britain' and himself as its very Roman-looking, laurel-wreathed emperor. Throughout his reign, one of his adopted persona would be the new Constantine, the first Christian Caesar, born (as it was commonly thought) in north Britain.

Francis Bacon, the philosopher of science, essayist and politician, who would do his utmost to promote the union of realms, feared that the king 'hasteneth to a mixture of both kingdoms and nations faster perhaps than policy will conveniently bear'. But there was no stopping James. Union meant security, wholeness, peace. Everything, everyone, had to be enfolded within the inclusive embrace of his come-together kingdom. The Great Seal would incorporate all the coats of arms of his three kingdoms (four, if you count, as James certainly did, the lilies of France). A new flag, embodying the union, which James often and over-optimistically compared to a loving marriage, would fuse in connubial bliss the crosses of St George and St Andrew. Many trial designs were made, one with the Scottish saltire and the cross of St George side by side, another with the saltire merely quartered with the red and white. But in the end, the first Union flag, featuring the red and white imposed on the blue and white, was adopted in 1606. Scottish shipowners immediately complained that their saltire always seemed obscured by the cross of St George. It was not a good sign for the prospects of the union that any semblance of equity between the two kingdoms was defeated by the laws of optics, which dictated that a saturated red would always seem to project beyond the recessive blue, dooming St Andrew's cross to be read as 'background'.

But never mind the flags: bring on the players. For those who offered themselves to be its publicists and showmen, the fantasy of the happy marriage of realms was a heaven-sent opportunity. Thomas Dekker, for example, East End slum-dweller, hack playwright, chronic debtor and jailbird, seized the moment as a godsend. Together with his much better placed colleague Ben Jonson, Dekker was charged with staging *The Magnificent Entertainment* for the city of London, by which the king would be formally greeted by his capital. Happy Britannia, of course, would be at the centre of it. 'St George and St Andrew, that many hundred years had defied one another, were now sworn brothers: England and Scotland being parted only with a narrow river.' Dekker knew exactly what to do. The two chevaliers, St Andrew and St George, would ride together, in brotherly amity, to greet the king: a real crowd pleaser, Dekker optimistically thought. And he would write a story of the nation in 1603, draped in mourning black and suffering from a melancholy ague, until a miraculous cure was effected by 'the wholesome receipt of a proclaimed king … FOR BEHOLD! Up rises a comfortable sun out of the north whose glorious beams like a fan dispersed all thick and contagious clouds.'

Unhappily for Dekker, the plague dashed the cup of success from his lips just as he was poised to taste it. ('But OH the short-lived felicity of man! O world, of what slight and thin stuff is thy happiness!') Between 30,000 and 40,000 died in the summer of 1603. The theatres were closed, the streets empty. So Dekker had to revert to plan B and squeeze some money out of misery rather than jubilation, making the most of the plague in a pamphlet, *The Wonderfull Yeare* (1603):

What an unmatchable torment were it for a man to be bard up every night in a vast silent Charnel-house; hung (to make it more hideous) with lamps dimly & slowly burning, in hollow and glimmering corners: where all the pavement

should in stead of greene rushes, be strewde with blasted Rosemary, withered
Hyacinthes, fatal Cipresse and Ewe, thickly mingled with heapes of dead men's
bones: the bare ribbes of a father that begat him, lying there: here, the Chaplesse
hollow scull of a mother that bore him: round about him a thousand Coarses,
some standing bolt upright in their knotted winding sheets, others half
mouldred in rotten Coffins ... that should suddenly yawne wide open, filling his
nostrils with noysome stench, and his eyes with the sight of nothing but
crawling wormes.

A year later, though, with the pestilence finally in retreat, Dekker and Jonson got to
stage their pageant after all. If anything, the postponement had only whetted London's
appetite for the kind of festivity not seen since the accession of Elizabeth a half
century earlier. Dekker was probably not entirely self-serving when he reported 'the
streets seemed to be paved with men ... stalles instead of rich wares were set out
with children, open casements [the leaded glass windows having been taken out]
filled up with women'. With this king, however, public enthusiasm created a problem
rather than an opportunity, since crowds made James decidedly nervous, wanting to
be off somewhere else, preferably on horseback in the hills near Royston, energetically pursuing the stag. But the allegorical outdoor theatre, full of music and gaudy
brilliance, disarmed, at least temporarily, the royal churlishness. In addition to the
brotherly Andrew and George, Old Father 'Thamesis', with flowing whiskers taken
from his emblem-book personification, offered a tribute in the form of 'an earthen-
ware pot out of which live Fishes were seene to runne forth'. And it was hard not to
be impressed by Stephen Harrison's immense wood-and-plaster triumphal arches, 90
feet high and 50 wide, punctuating the processional route. One of them was a three-
tower trellis structure, thick with greenery, purporting to show James's realm as a
perpetual 'Bower of Plenty' and featuring 'sheep browzing, lambes nibbling, Birds
Flying in the Ayre, with other arguments of a serene and untroubled season'. On the
arch, erected at Fenchurch, an immense panorama of London rose from a crenellated
battlement (as though seen from a distant tower), with the pile of old St Paul's in its
centre and looking a great deal more orderly than the chaotic, verminous metropolis
of 200,000 souls it really was. Below this Augustan vision of New Troy was none
other than Britannia herself, bearing the orb of empire on which was inscribed *Orbis
Britannicus Ab Orbe Divisus Est* (a British world divided *from* the world). Sharp-eyed
scholars of the classics – and perhaps there were some in the crowd – would have
recognized an erudite allusion to Virgil, in particular to the pastoral poems of the
Fourth Eclogue, in which the return of a new golden age was prophesied. Right at the

beginning of *Britannia*, William Camden had already identified Virgil's lines as a recognition of Britain's historic destiny as a place apart. And much, of course, had been made of the identification by some of the foggier classical geographers of the British archipelago as the legendary 'Fortunate Isles' of the western ocean. Until 1603 it was the English who had fancied themselves blessed by this priceless gift of insularity; Shakespeare's vision of 'This fortress built by Nature for herself/Against infection and the hand of war' confirmed the national faith in a divinely ordained immunity from the rest of the world's sorrows.

Now, however, this happy insulation was to be understood as *British*, extended to lucky Ireland and Scotland (notwithstanding the fact that, historically, Scotland had always enjoyed closer connections with Europe than England). In October 1604, to a deeply suspicious English parliament (which had already bridled at being informed by the king that its privileges were a grant from his majesty), James promised that 'the benefits which do arise of that union which is made in my blood do redound to the whole island'. When he spoke of his realm, he repeatedly referred to it, indivisibly, as 'the Ile'. His apologists conceded that there had been unfortunate disagreements, even bloodshed, between the neighbours on either side of the Tweed, but much of that could be attributed to the wicked Machiavellianism of interfering continentals (especially the French and the Spanish), who had deliberately set them at each other's throats. Now, in the person of James – in whom English, Welsh, French and Scots blood flowed and whom God had *already* blessed with two healthy sons – the long, miserable wars of succession were done with. 'The dismall discord,' Camden wrote, 'which hath set these nations (otherwise invincible) so long at debate, might [now] be stifled and crushed forever and sweet CONCORD triumph joyously with endless comfort.' Enter masquers, piping tunes of peace; roll on the Stuart Arcady.

As it turned out, the 'world divided from the world', the 'Britain apart' so cheerfully anticipated by Ben Jonson, Thomas Dekker, John Speed and William Camden, was the bringer not of concord and harmony but of havoc and destruction. The more strenuously that governments, both royal and republican, laboured to pull the pieces of Britain together, the more abysmally they fell apart. The obsession with 'union' and 'uniformity' that consumed both James and Charles I turned out to guarantee hatred and schism. In the first year of James I's reign no one (certainly not Jonson or Dekker) could have predicted this (although the high-handed remarks made by the king to parliament were not a good sign). It would take some time before the 'British problem' became dangerously apparent. The clearest warnings came from Charles I's Scottish friend and ally the Duke of Hamilton as late as 1637, when he counselled the king to back off from his obstinate plans to impose religious uniformity in

Scotland as well as England, lest a violent backlash north of the border spread throughout his other two kingdoms.

Ironically, then, the business of building a harmonized Britain was auto-destructive, creating discord both between the three kingdoms and within them. The historians who want us to think of the Stuart realm as an essentially docile polity, bound together by consensus, have contended that arguments about religion and politics, such as they were, could always be contained within the conventions and habits of the settled order of government and society. Stuart England (in common with so much of British history) was, in this view, ruled by a gentlemen's agreement. The governing classes were agreed on the powers and limitations of the monarchy, agreed that parliament's job was to supply the king with money, agreed on the fixed hierarchy of society and, under James, agreed on a broadly Calvinist religious consensus. When differences of opinion arose between parliament and Crown, most people wished them to be resolved rather than further polarized. But then again, perhaps the impression given by scholars that there was nothing so seriously amiss about the country as to push it towards disaster results from a narrowly English focus: historians have asked not so much the wrong questions, as the right questions about the wrong country. If the country concerned is England and the questions are about the governing communities of its counties, a case for the containment of conflict can be made (though not, I think, clinched). But if the country in question is not England but Britain – Scotland and Ireland in particular – then very serious trouble did not suddenly pop up in the 1640s to disturb the calm of the English political landscape. It had been there for at least two generations. It was not as if, somehow, the English political commotions were suddenly and unaccountably aggravated by conflicts rumbling away somewhere remote on the storm-lashed Celtic fringe. The trouble *was* Calvinist Scotland and Catholic Ireland and their deep religious appeal for some factions in Stuart England. Those religious entanglements, as we shall see, carried with them not just theological but also political and even foreign policy implications, which an imperially assertive England attempted to iron out through the imposition of a 'British' uniformity only at its own dire peril. The refusal of both Scotland and Ireland to do as they were ordered, except when coerced, brought about the British wars. Britain killed England. And it left Scotland and Ireland haemorrhaging in the field.

So if we return to those questions and put them to the *right* countries, a rather different accounting between long-term and short-term causes of the disaster becomes apparent. Ask yourself whether English Puritans were angry enough, or strong enough, by themselves, to bring down the Stuart monarchy and the answer is probably no, although they could certainly inflict punishing damage on its dignity and authority. Ask yourself whether Scottish Calvinists, in collusion with English Puritans (both of whom believed that kings were bound in a contract with their subjects), could bring down the Stuart monarchy and the answer is yes. When one of the militant Scottish Calvinist 'Covenanters', Archibald Johnston of Wariston, met Charles I at Berwick in the 1639 negotiations that ended the first Bishops' War, he interrupted the king so repeatedly and so offensively that the normally reserved Charles, unaccustomed to this kind of temerity, had to command Johnston, a common advocate, to hold his tongue. The Scots would inflict far worse indignities on Charles Stuart before they were through. Ask yourself whether an Irish-Catholic insurrection could create a situation in which the king of England were suddenly revealed not as the defender but the subverter of Church and state, and the answer would again be yes. Had James been, say, Dutch or German (as kings were to be in the future), with no strong feelings about Scotland, would there have been a civil war?

But James was a Scottish king, and it mattered. James VI of Scotland, already in his late thirties, became James I of Great Britain with the heartfelt gratitude of a man who for many years has had to endure a stony couch and is at last offered a deep and welcoming featherbed. The stony couch had been James's painful and protracted education as the king of Scotland. With the unedifying and dangerous example of his mother, Mary Stuart, very much on their minds, the Calvinist nobility who deposed her made sure that her infant son received a stern Calvinist education. In 1570 they consigned James to the frightening tutelage of George Buchanan, beside whom the fulminations of John Knox seemed light as a spring breeze. Buchanan's briskly undeferential attitude to kingship is best summed up by the story of his response to the Countess of Mar when she protested at his rough handling of the royal child: 'Madam, I have whipt his arse, you may kiss it if you please.' No one was under any illusion that Buchanan was himself any sort of arse-kisser; quite the contrary. His view of monarchs, forthrightly expressed in *De juri regni apud Scotos* (1579), written to justify the deposition of James's mother, was that they were appointed to serve the people, who were entitled to remove them if they failed to live up to the contract made with their subjects. It naturally followed from this theory of resistance that Kirk and Crown were separate and coeval powers and that royal meddling in the affairs of the Church would also be a warrant for removal. For the Presbyterian Kirk was inimical to any kind of royal governorship. It was a national Church with a single, uniform doctrine, but that doctrine was arrived at, and policed by, a general assembly constituted from delegates of its many congregations.

But James Stuart was, when all was said and done, his mother's son, and he was not about to spend the rest of his life as the doormat of Presbyterians. Unlike Mary, though, he would pave his road to sovereignty with arguments rather than adventures. His chosen tactics were more like Elizabeth's: subtlety, pragmatism and flexibility. From the time of his majority in 1587, James, whose intelligence and taste for learning were already evident, began to restore the authority of the Crown over both the general assembly (an institution created to govern the Kirk while a Catholic queen was on the throne) and the perennially factious nobility. Without any kind of standing army, his appeal was necessarily that of a Solomonic adjudicator, and James knew how to make his authority work through gestures heavy with symbolic meaning. To celebrate his majority, he made sure to provide liberal entertainment for the notoriously feud-prone Scottish nobility at Market Cross in Edinburgh. When the wine had them sufficiently relaxed, James asked them to walk hand-in-hand down the High Street to the royal residence, Holyroodhouse, where parliament sometimes met. They went like lambs, and did so dressed in the more formal costumes that the king had encouraged for parliamentary sessions. He also knew when division, as well as unity, might work in his favour. By making some small concessions to the Kirk, James managed to split his Presbyterian enemies into those who were prepared to work with him and hard-line Calvinists such as Andrew Melville, for whom any royal interference in the Kirk was a presumptuous abomination. Once strengthened by a 'royal party' inside the Kirk, he began to make further moves, determining, for example, the timing of general assemblies. By reinventing the episcopacy to look much less grandiose than its English counterpart James even managed, for five years at any rate, to reinsert bishops into the Kirk. In 1591 he felt strong enough to mint a gold piece bearing a Hebrew inscription referring to his Maker, 'Thee Alone Do I Fear' – a premature gesture, since the very next year Melville managed to get the Scottish parliament to do away with the bishoprics, and James was forced to consent. There was never a time when James would feel completely relaxed about his personal safety. Although he banned Buchanan's books, the old flogger continued to haunt his royal pupil, visiting his dreams as late as 1622 to inform James that 'he would fall into ice and then into fire' and that 'he would endure frequent pain and die soon after'. Not only Buchanan but the Ruthvens haunted him. It had been a Ruthven who had pointed a pistol at him *in utero*; a Ruthven descendant had held him hostage in 1582; and as recently as 1600 another of the family, the Earl of Gowrie, had abducted him, tied him up and threatened his life again. No wonder James was always a little jumpy.

For those who trade in thumbnail sketches of the British monarchy – blood-and-thunder Henry VIII, the Virgin Gloriana and the like – James I is bound to seem a baffling mixture of characteristics that have no business inhabiting the same personality: the hunt-mad scholar who would pursue Calvinist theologians and the stag with the same energetic determination; the slightly sloshed reveller, noisily demand-ing in the middle of an interminable masque and in his thick Scots accent to see the dancers, especially his queen 'Annie' (Anne of Denmark), who loved to perform in them; the long-winded, blustering master of disputation, battering preachers and parliamentarians over the head with his bibliography. But James's dominant charac-teristics (not least his sexual preferences) resist glib classification. Drunk or sober, shallow or deep, gay or straight, there certainly was no other prince who felt so repeatedly compelled to theorize about his sovereignty and to do so on paper. James, of whom it was accurately said 'he doth wondrously covet learned discourse', pub-lished no fewer than ten treatises dealing with various matters he considered weighty, including the evils of witchcraft and tobacco. Two of them, the *Basilikon Doron* (the 'Prince's Gift', written in 1598, but published in 1599, for his son Henry, and con-sisting for the most part, like its model, Charles V's advice to Philip II, of practical advice on the conduct of kingship) and *The True Law of Free Monarchies* (published in 1598), appeared in the immediate period before his arrival in England. At least until they attempted to read them (for neither work, while succinct, could be fairly described as a page-turner), his new subjects must have been eager to see if James's books provided any clues to the character of their king, because between 13,000 and 16,000 copies were sold in the first few months after his accession.

Both works have been misunderstood as the theoretical equivalent of a royal command to his subjects to begin practising their genuflections. It is certainly true James made no bones about the fact that his authority was based on appointment by God, to whom alone princes were ultimately and exclusively accountable. 'For Kings sit in the throne of God and thence all judgement is derived', as he would notori-ously put it. This was the sort of utterance calculated to set parliamentary teeth on edge and persuade champions of the supremacy of common law, such as Sir Edwin Sandys, Nicholas Fuller and Sir Edward Coke, that James had been infected by despotic European attitudes to sovereignty and now needed a crash course of remedial instruction on just how things were in England.

Coke and those who thought like him believed that the 'ancient constitution of England', its origins lost in the remote mists of time (like other fundamental customs such as the age of majority and the size of a jury) but already established by the time of the Anglo-Saxon heptarchy, had been embodied in a common law that was prior to, and took precedence over, the person of any individual sovereign. Sovereignty was, and had always been, that of the indivisible king-in-parliament. Brutal conquests, such as that inflicted on England, might have temporarily set this aside, but the 'ancient constitution' embedded in the very marrow of Englishness was somehow preserved in custom, waiting its opportunity to assert itself again in, for example, Magna Carta. Going on about 'memory' to James (whose own memory was considered elephantine) did not, of course, help make the case, especially to someone who had been brought up in the very different and much more Romanized Scottish law tradition. And in his account of Scottish kingship James had already dealt briskly with the fable of primitive parliaments preceding the institution of monarchy. 'Parliaments … were not installed before them (as many have foolishly imagined) but long after that monarchies were established were they created.' None of this needs have been a serious issue, though, since in *The True Law of Free Monarchies* James had also taken pains to concede that the origins of a monarchy had little to do with the way it should govern in a 'settled' state, by which he obviously meant contemporary Scotland and England. As far as he was concerned, there was nothing at all contradictory about insisting on his contractual responsibility, first and foremost to God, his only superior, and accepting as a fact of life a 'mixed' and balanced monarchy, in which some matters of government were the exclusive prerogative of the king and many others were not. To ignore the 'fundamental laws' of a realm was precisely to cross the line between legitimate kingship and tyranny, to violate rather than respect the compact made with God. It was when responsible royal government degenerated into the tyranny of an arbitrary will that the king could be shown to have violated his contract with God as well as with his subjects. Although a 'king is preferred by God above all other ranks and degrees of men … the higher that his seate is above theirs: the greater is his obligation to his maker … And the highest benche is the sliddriest to sit upon.'

It would be misleading then to think of James arriving in England as completely impervious to the balance between king, lords and prelates, and Commons, which was endlessly touted as the peculiar genius of the nation's polity. But equally there was no mistaking his determination to uphold his 'regality and supreme prerogative' against any kind of impertinences, real or imagined, by the Commons. For the moment, though, putting aside self-appointed tribunes like Coke (who was perfectly willing to accept a government appointment himself when the opportunity arose), relatively few of the governing class, much less the common people, were apprehensive that an alien despotism was about to trample the liberties of England underfoot. They accepted the basic truism that order, both political and social, was the indispensable condition of the peace of the realm and that it was the office of the king and his councillors to provide it. They got much more upset about English wealth and offices being handed over on plates of gold to freebooters from Caledonia. James had actually been at pains to preserve the eminent Elizabethans on the Privy Council:

the Lord High Admiral Howard of Effingham, hero of the Armada, and in particular the indispensable little hunchback Secretary of State, Robert Cecil, whom the king promoted to the earldom of Salisbury. Although six Scots had been appointed Privy Councillors, only two of them – Sir George Home (shortly to become the Earl of Dunbar) and Lord Kinloss – had any kind of high office. But because the king filled the more personal household staff of the Privy Chamber with Scottish friends and boyhood companions like the Duke of Lennox and the Earl of Mar (on whom he also showered lavish gifts and money), the impression was certainly given that access to the king could be gained only by way of these Scottish courtiers, especially the captain of the palace guard, Sir Thomas Erskine. More than one angry English suitor waiting for an audience with the king complained they had become 'lousy' sitting so long in Erskine's watchful presence. The Venetian ambassador reported in May 1603 that 'no Englishman, be his rank what it may, can enter the Presence Chamber without being summoned, whereas the Scottish lords have free entree of the privy chamber'. It was an exaggeration, but it was certainly a widely shared impression.

A Scottophobic backlash was inevitable. The ending of *Macbeth* (*c.* 1605-6), falsified Scottish history, the better to suggest that Malcolm Canmore had won the throne only with English help. Stage comedies, like Jonson's *Eastward hoe* (1605) (for which he did a little time in the Tower with his co-authors George Chapman and John Marston), featured impecunious Scottish nobles freeloading at the expense of the English. In 1612 the sensational trial of the Scottish Lord Sanquhar for commissioning two assassins to shoot the English fencing master who had accidentally put out one of his eyes some years before produced a vitriolic outpouring of Scottophobic doggerel, not at all appeased by the conviction and hanging of Sanquhar as if he were a common felon.

> They beg our Lands, our Goods, our Lives
> They switch our Nobles and lye with their Wives
> They pinch our Gentry and send for our Benchers
> They stab our Sergeants and pistoll our Fencers.
> Leave off proud Scots thus to undo us
> Lest we make you as poor as when you came to us.

Fights regularly broke out between Scots and English nobles at Croydon racetrack, and in the Inns of Court, where a Scot called Maxwell nearly started a riot by ripping out an Englishman's earring along with most of his ear. For a time the London Scots stayed close to their little colonies in Holborn and Charing Cross,

Frontispiece to *The Workes* ... by Prince James, 1616. James, who loved learned discourse, published no fewer than ten treatises on religion, politics and kingship.

especially avoiding the back alleys near theatres where they might be pounced on by 'swaggerers', who made roughing up Scotsmen their speciality. In more respectable theatres of opinion the hostility was just as fierce. Despite Francis Bacon's best propaganda, the king's project for a formal treaty of union ran into a storm of parliamentary protest that exchanging English for 'British' nationality would be the end of English law and the ancient constitution; would confuse foreigners when the English were abroad; and would open the country to hordes of impoverished, unwashed and greedy immigrants ('stinking' and 'lousy' were the usual insults of choice). By 1607 the union treaty had died the death of a thousand cuts, although James, bewildered and angry at the rebuff, continued to style himself 'King of Great Britain, France and Ireland' and ordered (at public expense) a new 'Imperial Diadem and Crown' of sapphires, diamonds and rubies.

How did the abortive union look from the other direction? A ban imposed by James on *anti-English* ballads, poems and pamphlets suggests (not surprisingly) that the affronted Scots gave as good as they got in the abuse department. But wounded feelings aside, Scotland – or rather, Lowland, Protestant Scotland – had little reason to feel disadvantaged by the 'dual government' set up by James as long as its religious independence remained unthreatened. In this last, crucial department the king moved, as was his wont, slowly and cannily, waiting until his deputy governors (the earls of Dunbar and Dunfermline) had demonstrated the benefits of cooperation thoroughly enough to large sections of the Scottish nobility. With his base of support secure, he felt strong enough to move directly against the most uncompromising Presbyterians. Bishops were reinstated in 1610, and the fulminating Andrew Melville, incarcerated in the Tower of London since 1607, was finally banished in 1611. In 1618 a general assembly at Perth agreed (with some serious contention) on practices that not long before would have been denounced as Catholic idolatry: kneeling at communion, the celebration of five holy days and the administration of the sacraments.

James could get away with the 'Five Articles' of Perth, which, characteristically, he did not enforce very energetically, because the balance sheet of costs and benefits brought to Scotland by the union of crowns looked, from Edinburgh or Perth or Stirling, fairly positive. Once a ferocious border policing commission (manned by both Scots and English) was in place and had started to catch, convict and hang the gangs of rustlers and brigands who had made the Borders their choice territory, cross-frontier trade took off. Fishermen, cattle-drivers and linen-makers all did well. Duty-free English beer became so popular in Scotland that the council in Edinburgh had to lower the price of the home product to make it competitive. The sections of Scots society, especially in the more densely settled areas of Midlothian and Fife, that had had enough of the rampages of feuding lords – small lairds, town burgesses, lawyers – all had little enough to complain of from a government that managed to be both distant and attentive. As for the great lords, with James handing over land and offices in England, Ireland and Scotland just as fast as he could, they knew better than to look a gift horse in the mouth.

But they were not all of Scotland. For as long as its histories had been written (starting with Tacitus), a profound division had been noticed between the lands south and north of the Forth and Tay: Lowland and Highland. In customs, language, faith and farming – everything that mattered – the two peoples were worlds apart. James himself made another distinction between the mainland Highlanders, who were 'barbarous for the most part and yet mixed with some show of civility', and the Hebridean islanders, who were 'utterly barbarous without any sort or show of civility'. Should the savages not avail themselves of the blessings of godly civilization, it was obvious that they should be uprooted, driven out and, if necessary, killed off. Worst of all were the primitive clan leaders, scarcely better, the king and his officers of state thought, than cattle rustlers and brigands – like the MacGregors of the west, or the Gaelic chieftains of Ireland like Con O'Neill – who continued to mislead their followers into outlawry and plunder. James's plans for the colonization of the Western Isles, begun before he came to England, involved leasing land to Lowland nobles who were expected to 'develop' them for pacification and profit, if necessary deporting populations and replacing them with more pliable immigrants. When those schemes failed to overcome local resistance he turned to the big stick, in 1608 mobilizing a pan-British armada, raised from English troops in Ireland and ordered to do what was necessary in Lewis and Kintyre to teach the obstreperous natives a lesson they would never forget. Most of the draconian brutalities later inflicted on the Highlanders and islanders by William III and the Hanoverians – including the banning of the plaid and the Gaelic language – were all anticipated, at least in theory, by the Scottish James VI.

To their credit, James's own Scottish councillors balked at a punitive onslaught on the islands, for they knew it would be ruinously expensive and ineffective, and would create a permanently disaffected population for the Spanish or French to exploit. At the same time, they brought round the Highland clan leaders by inviting them to a meeting on board a ship, ostensibly to hear a sermon, and then holding them hostage on the island of Mull until they had seen reason. The result was the Statutes of Icolmkill, by which the solution of 'indirect empire', which Britain would use again and again (from southern India to northern Nigeria), was first unveiled. Instead of direct proconsular rule in the manner of a Roman conquest, the local chieftains and magnates were co-opted into a decentralized system of government and awarded status and land in return for being responsible for the conduct and taxation of their own clansmen. Made cooperative, they were organized around allegiances to grandees – the Campbells, Mackenzies and Gordons among others – who undertook to keep their huge territories quiet. Just as would be the case in the tropical empires, the deal came with all kinds of ostensible commitments to moral reformation: the regulation of alcohol, the suppression of feuds and the removal of native children to the metropolitan mainland, where they would be intensively re-educated for their own good and that of their homeland. The laboratory for the British empire turned out to be the Hebrides, and it was (as it would so often be in the future) entirely the enterprise of the Scots.

Now that the Highlands and islands were, for the time being, self-governing, James's grand design of settling impoverished but hardy Protestant farmers from the overpopulated Lowlands among the 'heathen' Catholics of the mountains had to be rethought. And the solution was staring at everyone right across the North Channel in Ireland. There were already some Scots in northern and eastern Ireland, but after the rebel nobles Hugh O'Neill, Earl of Tyrone, and Rory O'Donnell, Earl of Tyrconnel, fled to Rome in 1607, their huge estates, forfeit to the Crown, suddenly became available for James and his government to play British emperor.

And play it he did, on a massive scale. Up to 1641 close to 100,000 Scots, Welsh and English immigrants were 'planted' in Ireland, the vast majority in the nine counties of Ulster (six of which now form Northern Ireland), but with sizeable populations also in Munster (originally 'planted' in the 1580s). The seventeenth-century colonization of Ireland was, with the possible exception of Spanish Mexico, the biggest imperial settlement of any single European power to date, and it utterly dwarfed the related 'planting' on the Atlantic seaboard of North America. To such as Camden, of course, Hibernia was no more than the 'western enclosure of Britain'. Since an act of 1541, the status of Ireland had changed from a lordship to a kingdom, whose ruler had the 'name, style, title and honour' of a king, and all the prerogatives of a 'king imperial'. In effect, the throne of Ireland was 'united and knit to the imperial crown of England'. In Elizabeth's reign there had been wild-eyed schemes from the likes of Sir Thomas Smith, ambassador and privy councillor, to Protestantize and civilize the island by massive immigration and settlement. And such men imagined the land, as imperial dreamers generally do, either as conveniently vacant or populated by so many grunting Calibans who, once educated out of sloth, superstition and crime, would be impatient to acquire (in some necessarily menial way to begin with) the blessings of metropolitan culture. But Ireland, of course, was neither vacant nor

Ceiling panels in the Banqueting House, Whitehall Palace, London, by Peter Paul Rubens, *c.* 1635: (above) *The Benefits of the Reign of James I*, with Peace and Abundance embracing at bottom left; (opposite) *The Union of the Crowns*.

inhabited purely by Gaelic-speaking peasants and cattle-rustling lords. In Leinster there were the 'Old English' descendants of the original Anglo-Norman settlers who had come over with Richard de Clare (Strongbow), in the time of the Angevins and who had mostly remained faithful to the Catholic Church. And over the centuries the frontiers, once so sharp between native Gaels and English intruders, had softened to the point of there being many intermarriages and shared estates, especially in the southeast. Although many Old English defined themselves through their loyalty to the Crown, they shared with the native Gaels some basic common causes – a common religion and resentment of the threat of massive immigration from England.

Both communities were brushed aside in defeat – the Gaels, of course, with more contemptuous brutality than the Old English. James's attorney-general in Ireland, the poet Sir John Davies, became eloquent on the subject of the murdering natives 'little better than cannibals'. The confiscated estates of the Earl of Desmond in Munster had been handed over to thirty-five English landlords in large lots of between 4000 and 12,000 acres. Ulster, though, was subdivided into smaller parcels of between 1000 and 2000 acres to 'undertakers' and ex-military 'servitors' who, in return for their lucky prize of land, contracted to set aside sums for the endowment of the Protestant Church of Ireland and for the schools and colleges that would plant the Reformed religion so deep that no Papist could tear it up. In another unique transfer, Derry was handed over to syndicates of the City of London, which prefixed its name on the ancient city. When James ran out of forfeited and confiscated lands, he continued the process of extraction by requiring all Irish landowners to prove title according to the rigorous standards of English law – a notoriously difficult if not impossible task for estates that had been granted countless generations before systematic records were made and preserved. But that, of course, was the point. Large tracts in Wexford, Longford, Waterford and Carlow were transferred by this route from Irish to planter ownership.

As far as the king was concerned, the whole project was a huge success, although regrettably slow to take root. When his 'undertakers' in Ireland seemed to be unconscionably timid about dispossessing the Irish, he threatened to seize back their land unless they carried out the evictions with greater speed and diligence. By 1620, large numbers of poor farmers had been transplanted from the over-populated, over-zealous Calvinist southwest of Scotland to a place where they could really get their teeth into a challenge, and James had found space and fortunes in Ireland for Scottish lords like James Hamilton, Earl of Abercorn, on whose loyalty he could now dependably count. Along with many of the planters themselves, James unquestionably believed in the socially and morally redemptive nature of the plantation. Free-wandering Irish herds and flocks would be rounded up inside winter stalls to provide heavy manure for the under-nitrogenated Irish pasture, milk yields would multiply, wheat would appear, markets would beckon, and farmers responding to them would be able to afford stone houses, glass windows, wooden floors. The picture-perfect landscapes of the Weald and the Wolds would magically become reproduced in Tyrone and Fermanagh. Towns, those nurseries of civility, would grow and prosper. Literacy in the only language that counted – English – would spread like wildfire, and the unintelligible gibberish of the indigenes would recede into bogland. Such was the vision of the new Hibernia.

In fairness, it should be said that not all the Old English or even the Gaelic Irish were as uniformly hostile to the newcomers and their innovations as nationalist history needs to believe. Just as Old English and Gaelic cultures had become intermixed over the centuries, so too cities like Dublin and Derry were places where newcomers and natives shared all kinds of commercial, legal and social interests. Institutions like Trinity College, Dublin, turned into extraordinarily flourishing centres of learning. None the less, the plantation, especially in Ulster, was from the start deformed by its neurotically defensive character: Britain's frontier against Rome and Madrid. And the natives continued to be restless. Stone houses may have arrived with the planters, but beyond their walls and fences the country proved obstinately unwelcoming to Protestantism and that, in turn, perpetuated the insecurity of the planters, who were forever on the lookout lest the Catholic population invite in the Spanish and make Ireland the next major theatre of the ongoing British wars of religion. Seeds were planted in Jacobean Ireland all right, but they would not produce the kind of harvest the inventors of Jacobean Britain had imagined.

But if there were a strong note of Discord among the Music of British Harmony, one would never know it in Whitehall. Although Rubens' paintings decorating the ceiling of Inigo Jones's glorious new Palladian Banqueting House, celebrating the virtues of James as the British Solomon, were commissioned by his son Charles in 1630 and completed in 1634, nine years after James's death, they are none the less a perfect picture of Jacobean wishful thinking: an orgy of royal good intentions, with Peace and Plenty caught in a tight clinch while the new Augustus presides over Wisdom dispatching War. In view of what had actually happened (and what would happen to demolish the reign of Charles I) the nearest painting to the entrance was the most optimistic: the most famous Solomonic story of all, recycled as an allegory of the birth of a new Britain. The all-wise monarch leans forward to deliver judgement on two mothers who hold up a baby. But a proposal to chop it into two would hardly fit the mood or the message. Instead, James is all benevolence; the

James VI of Scotland, I of England, by Juan de Critz, *c.* 1615.

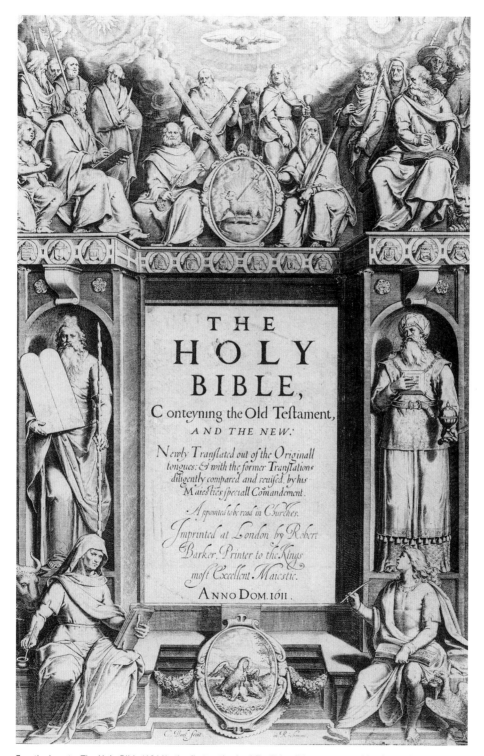

Frontispiece to *The Holy Bible* (1611), the first authorized English edition, sponsored by James I and bearing his name. An able scholar and theologian, the king also encouraged the development of the sermon.

women are, of course, the two kingdoms, and the chubby Rubensian baby is none other than Britain itself.

This hyper-inflated expectation of the blessings to be conferred by the new reign was not just the fantasy of the Stuart court. From his gentleman's manor of Arbury in Warwickshire John Newdigate, one of the thousands of readers of the king's *Basilikon Doron,* decided to write to him personally – 'my dear sovereign' – to express his pleasure that the country was now to be ruled by a Solomon and that his countrymen were rushing to witness for themselves, like the Queen of Sheba, the full measure of the king's wisdom and greatness. But, said Newdigate, warming to his subject, the king had a host of urgent matters to reform: the disgusting habit of men dressing in women's clothes, for example; gentlemen who spent their entire time in London being swallowed alive in costly lawsuits, while their estates and tenants languished in rustic decay; the loathsome parasites who bought monopolies from the Crown and proceeded to use them to fleece the defenceless; the heavy taxes and levies raised in his own county for foreign wars; and on and on. What Newdigate wanted from the king was not proclamations and legislation but reformation: a great cleansing of the country's impurities, not least at court itself. 'I hope your highness will … helpe many reform themselves to your couler,' wrote the optimistic Newdigate, adding, lest James was tempted to slack off, 'for all Solomon's wisdom and good beginning, perseverance was at sume times absent and the blessings of peace made him sinne.'

Grievously disappointed though they would be, there were many such as Newdigate who had the highest hopes of the new reign. Another godly gentleman who would become a parliamentary militant and survive into the Commonwealth, Robert Harley, of Brampton Bryan in Herefordshire, was happy enough to be included among the sixty-two gentlemen knighted by the king (as a Knight of the Bath, too) in his coronation honours. Such men as Harley and Newdigate had no idea, of course, just how much James despised Puritans, even while regarding them as a minority. Evangelicals, by contrast, James had a bit more sympathy for, even if they did sit 'Jack fellowlike with Christ at the Lord's Table'. Men like Harley and Newdigate looked at the godly Kirk in Scotland and thought James was bound to carry its virtues to England, while the king was, in fact, overjoyed to be leaving it behind. 'Puritan' was still a term of abuse applied to the 'hotter' Christians. But of all the divisions that bedevilled the Stuarts, that which came between those who passionately believed that the Church had not yet been properly reformed and that Edward VI's godly evangelism had been put on hold for half a century by his sister, and those who were satisfied with the Anglican status quo, was perhaps the most dangerous, because it presupposed two utterly incompatible temperaments and ideologies about the duties of the state. The bugbears of the hot gospellers – the sign of the cross in baptism, the use of the ring in the marriage sacrament, the wearing of the surplice by priests – might seem so much trivia (and, to their fury were defined by James as *adiaphora* or things 'indifferent', which lay within the purview of the king to retain or discard as he saw fit), but to the godly they were relics of abominable Catholic idolatry. They wanted them purged and the Crown instead to promote godly preaching and teaching.

It is ironic that the only lasting accomplishment to survive the extended theological debates between James and the unsatisfied reformers was the imperishably beautiful Bible that bears his name. For a Church atomized into innumerable individual readers of scripture, engaged in obsessive self-interrogation or shut up with their own family in a hermetically sealed household of godly morality, was, to James's way of thinking and to that of those ministers he specially favoured, like George Abbot or Lancelot Andrewes, entirely destructive of the unity of Church and nation. To Calvinists, for whom the world both now and hereafter was either black or white, Christ or Antichrist, appeals to 'unity' were at best a vain delusion, at worst a deliberate snare to inveigle the innocent into promiscuous communion with the sinful. Was it not obvious that the Almighty himself had no interest in the subject of 'union'? As Calvin and St Paul had both well understood, God had decreed that mankind was irremediably *divided* into the damned and the saved, or, as the rector of Holy Trinity Church in Dorchester, John White, forthrightly put it, according to a startled member of his congregation: 'Christ was not the Saviour of the whole world but of his elected and chosen people only.' They assumed that James's refusal of a more 'thorough' reformation was amoral spinelessness, when in fact it was a carefully thought-out theology, heavily rehearsed by him at the Hampton Court conference, convened in 1604 to consider these matters. James's preference for ceremony, sacrament and the 'decencies' of the Church was not just some middle way, arrived at by default to position himself between Catholicism and Puritanism. It embodied his active wish for the incorporation of Christians within a big-tent Church – attracting both loyal Puritans and loyal Catholics, separating them from their more extreme elements and offering the possibility (not the certainty) that sinful man might still achieve salvation through good works and observances. And there was the matter of rank and order, which James took very seriously indeed, and which he believed was properly embodied in the hierarchy of the Church, with himself, prince temporal and spiritual, at the top, the archbishops and bishops immediately below. Through his entire reign, in both Scotland and England, James never swerved from his conviction (not unlike Henry VIII's or Elizabeth's) that the combination of the royal supremacy and bishops was the strongest way to *resist* Rome. And he passed that belief on to his son, with, as it turned out, fatal consequences.

All this was incomprehensible to the evangelicals, for whom any fudging of pre-destination, any suggestion that good works might to the slightest degree affect the prospects of salvation, was the purest papism. In fact, many *Catholics* also (and happily) misunderstood such views as the expression of a secret wish to return home to the old Church. When James made peace with Spain in 1604, the rumours about the king's conversion and his restoration of England to Roman obedience seemed mirac-ulously imminent. The fact that the queen, Anne of Denmark, had already converted to Catholicism, did nothing to dampen these expectations. Had they read James's wonderful account of his own baptism they might have been better informed about his potential for conversion. 'At my Baptism I was baptised by a Popish Archbishop [his mother, Mary] sent word to forbear to use spittle ... which was obeyed being indeed a filthy apish trick ... And her very own words were "that she would not want a pocky priest to spit into her child's mouth".' Like his mother (but from the other confessional stance) James saw no reason why his queen should not practise a different private religion from the official Church, but at no time did he ever think of himself as anything other than an unequivocal Protestant. Blinded though they may have been to James's true position, it is understandable that loyal Catholics like Sir Thomas Tresham, out of prison and able to give his attention once more to his Northamptonshire house, Lyveden New Bield, designed to symbolize his faith, could now imagine that their days of persecution and recusant impoverishment were at last over.

Very soon they realized just how wrong they had been. Instead of offering them relief, James's regime, enthusiastically enforced by Robert Cecil and Archbishop Richard Bancroft, cracked down even harder on recusants and hidden Jesuits. Predictions of plots became self-fulfilling. It was from the bitterness of having been so thoroughly deceived that conspiracies to eliminate the king and his heretical min-isters were born. George Buchanan's Calvinist teaching of the legitimacy of resistance to an ungodly king was matched on the Catholic side by the Jesuit Juán de Mariana's doctrine of lawful insurrection against the tyranny of a heretical prince. That absolu-tion fed the ardour and optimism of Catholic conspirators and assassins. Even before the gunpowder plotters had designed their own coup, at least two violent plots had been exposed in 1604, one (a real stroke of genius, this) meaning to abduct the king and hold him hostage until parliament had agreed to demands to tolerate Catholicism in England. But the plan launched by Robert Catesby together with Tresham's son, Francis, Sir Everard Digby, Thomas Percy, Thomas Winter and Guido Fawkes, a soldier who had served the Spanish armies in the Netherlands, and blessed by a Jesuit, Father Thomas Garnet, was much the most dramatic. The idea was not just to destroy parliament on the opening day of its session, along with the king, Prince Henry and possibly even the four-year-old Charles, but to set their sister, Princess Elizabeth, on the throne in their place, since they supposed that she had been most influenced by her mother, the Catholic Queen Anne, and would at the very least be more inclined to tolerate them. How close it came to success was entirely another matter, since it seems possible that even before Lord Monteagle was advised by an anonymous letter (which probably came from Lady Monteagle's brother) not to attend the opening of parliament on 5 November 1605, Robert Cecil's intelligence network had penetrated the conspiracy. A search was made of the cellars beneath the Westminster house whose premises had been rented by one of the plotters, Thomas Percy. There they found Fawkes together with thirty-six barrels of gunpowder, enough to destroy the entire House of Lords immediately above the cellar.

The confederates came to famously gruesome ends: Catesby and Thomas Percy were tracked down to their safe house in Staffordshire and killed in the assault, Catesby dying holding a picture of the Virgin. Their bodies were exhumed from their graves so that their heads could be removed for proper display at the corners of the parliament building they had planned to detonate. Tresham died in the Tower of some monstrous urethral infection after a copious confession, his excruciating condition presumably making the customary rack redundant. Fawkes and the rest were hanged very briefly, then, still living, had their hearts cut out and displayed to the appreciative public.

More important than the plot itself were the effects it had on the prospects of the Stuart monarchy, which were all positive. Even though he always suffered from the conspiracy jitters (his father, Darnley, had, after all, also been the victim of a gunpowder plot), the king was careful not to go on an anti-Catholic rampage. In fact, he and his government were at pains to separate the 'fanatics' like Fawkes from loyal Catholics like the senior Tresham and to hope that they had been scared into settling for private ways of exercising their conscience. But 5 November became the Protestant holy-day *par excellence*, the new 'birth-day of the nation', with bonfires and bells celebrating the deliverance of not only the king himself but also the entirety of the English constitution. James had never seemed so English, so parliamentary as when he had come close to sharing a terrible incineration with the Lords and Commons. Catesby, Percy and Guy Fawkes had achieved something that James could never have done by himself: they had made him a popular hero. Declaring the Gunpowder Treason day a holiday, parliament outdid itself in eulogizing James as 'our most gracious sovereign … the most great learned and religious king that ever reigned'.

This did not mean, of course, that the next twenty years were a prolonged honeymoon. If anything, the longer the reign went on, the more out of love with each other James and the British became. Godfrey Goodman, Bishop of Gloucester, was just one of many contemporaries who noticed nostalgia for Elizabeth grow ever rosier as the lustre of the Jacobean court became tarnished by outlandish extravagance and scandal. The dimming of reputation, though, was not necessarily a prelude to constitutional crisis, not least because parliament met for only thirty-six months in total out of the twenty-two years of James I's reign, and this intermittent record seemed no more controversial than it had been in the reign of Elizabeth. Parliament did not yet think of itself as an 'opposition' nor even as an institutional 'partner' in government. The majority of its members, in both the Lords and Commons, accepted the king's view that their presence was required principally to provide him with the money needed to conduct the business of state. But – and it was an enormous qualification – they shared the inherited truism that they had a responsibility to offer the king counsel and to see that this revenue was not raised in a way that damaged the 'liberties' or the security of the people. This meant that, when the king did come to them for money, they felt duty bound to present him with a list of grievances. The litany of complaints had become a ritual, and the king was expected to respond, after cavilling about the infringement of his prerogatives, with concessionary gestures, such as the impeachment of some disposable officer of state or a few generalized expressions of love for the worthy representatives of the nation. Sometimes James could be relied on to make those gestures, but most often he had to be pushed. Not infrequently he behaved like a sulky adolescent forced to come home and ask his parents to bale him out from the creditors, gritting his teeth and rolling his eyes while they berated him for his wickedly irresponsible behaviour.

But then James's problems of the purse were self-inflicted. Compared with the famously tight-fisted Elizabeth he was a bottomless well of prodigality. From the very beginning of his reign he threw money at his Scottish companions and courtiers, provoking one parliamentarian to characterize the treasury as a 'royal cistern wherein his Majesty's largesse to the Scots caused a continual and remediless leak'. But James had come from a relatively poor country with limited resources (which had not, however, stopped him from piling up debts), and in England he obviously felt himself to be in hog heaven. Lands, monopolies, offices, jewels, houses were all showered on favourites, who then took their cue from the king by themselves spending colossally more than they could afford. The entire court culture was drunk on spending, and there was plenty to spend it on: elaborate masques (average cost £1400 a year) devised by Ben Jonson and Inigo Jones, in which mechanical contraptions were constructed to make men appear to be flying through the air or swallowed by the oceans; fantastic costumes, encrusted with carbuncle gems; immense dresses for the ladies, pseudo-Persian, billowing beneath the waist, or breasts revealed above, covered only with the most transparently gauzy lawn (a fashion that, to the horror of godly ministers, became ubiquitous at court). Feasting was Lucullan. In 1621 – a rocky year for Crown–country relations – one such banquet costing more than £3000 needed a hundred cooks for eight days to produce 1600 dishes including 240 pheasants. The Jacobean court's devotion to futile excess was perfectly epitomized by the novelty of the 'ante-supper' invented by the Scots lord James Hay, later Earl of Carlisle. Guests would arrive to ogle a vast table manificently set with food, the only point of which was to be inspected, tickling the saliva glands into action before the whole thing was removed, thrown away and replaced by identical food that had just come from the kitchens.

The craze for conspicuous waste was contagious. Anyone within the wide circle of the court (which James made a lot wider by creating no fewer than thirty-two earls, nineteen viscounts and fifty-six knight baronets, the last a wholly new invention) who wanted to be taken seriously needed to build on the spectacular scale demanded by fashionable taste and by a king who was constantly on the hoof between hunting lodges and who, even more than Elizabeth, expected to be entertained in palatial style. James made himself so much at home in his courtiers' houses that one desperate host wrote a letter to his bulldog, Mr Jowler, asking him, since he had the royal attention, if he would not mind urging departure on the king. Inevitably, the 'prodigy houses' that had been going up in the last decades of Elizabeth's reign became even more prodigious in James's time. With Britain at peace, its aristocrats travelled more freely and widely in Europe and brought back with them exuberantly Mannerist designs for stone-clad façades and intricately carved interior panelling. The show places of the Jacobean grandees, like Robert Cecil's Hatfield (the Hertfordshire estate given by the king in exchange for Cecil's sumptuous Theobalds), the Earl of Pembroke's Wilton in Wiltshire or the most prodigious monster of them all, the Earl of Suffolk's Audley End in Essex (on which James passed his famous backhand compliment, 'too big for a king but might do well enough for a Lord Treasurer'), boasted galleries as long as football pitches, and, now that the English glass industry had been properly established, great ranges of windows to light them. Even the furniture of the houses – beds, desks and cabinets – sprouted putti and sphinxes, obelisks and miniature temples. Draperies were required to be

Two grand prodigy houses of the Jacobean period: (top) a view of the east front of Wilton House, Wiltshire, show-place of the Earl of Pembroke; (above) the Great Hall at Audley End, Essex, with its bright ranges of glass and intricately carved panelling.

especially stunning and often renewed. Some £14,000 were spent just to furnish the Countess of Salisbury's (by definition temporary) lying-in chamber with white satin, embroidered with gold and ornamented with pearls. Nothing was too fantastic not to be diverting, especially the stunning gardens, which, since they now featured complicated riddles and allusions to the classics, embedded in statuary, fountains and grottoes, now required specialized hydraulic engineers, like the de Caus family, to design and maintain them.

All this was, of course, ruinously expensive, and many of the most ambitious builders were duly ruined. The most prodigal of all, the king (whose spending was at twice the rate of Elizabeth), drove successive treasurers to distraction attempting to find ways to support his extravagances. There were old ways and there were new ways, but none of them ever came up with enough money and all of them created resentment. The old ways featured the exploitation of 'Crown rights' like the 'purveyances', the right granted to the Crown to set prices for goods and services, ostensibly for the household, at well below market rates. Over time it seemed easier, especially to the Crown, to settle for money sums that represented the difference between purveyance prices and market prices, instead of the goods themselves. What had begun as something necessary to the dignity of the Crown had degenerated into a racket. That the honour of the Crown – still an important element in its authority – was shabbily compromised by James's creation of more than 800 new knights at £30 a head was obvious from all the jokes showing up in libels and ballads featuring figures like 'Sir Fabian Scarecrow', whose landlady coughed up the necessary for his knighthood.

None of these expedients was likely to endear the Crown to its subjects, especially out in the country, where knighthood and aristocratic hierarchy were still treated with reverence. Likewise, when the government sold tax 'farms' (the right, in return for an up-front sum, to run a tax-collection or customs operation as a private business), it seemed to be delivering the helpless consumer to a private individual who had an interest in maximizing his take in a period of continuing low wages and high prices. In many respects it was no worse than their experience in the last decade of Elizabeth's reign. But then there had been hope, by now gone, that James's government would be an improvement. By 1610 it was clear to Robert Cecil, now given the thankless job of Lord Treasurer in addition to being Secretary of State, that something had to be done to find a more dependable source of income for the Crown. In that year he did his best to sell a 'Great Contract' to parliament, in which the Crown would relinquish its feudal rackets, like purveyances and 'wardships' (the right to manage the property of a feudal minor), in return for a guaranteed annual revenue of

£200,000. The deal came to grief when, simultaneously, James decided to demand compensation for the abolition of wardship officers and parliament came to the conclusion that it had overpaid. In the general bitterness, the row over money turned constitutional. Dissolving the uncooperative parliament, James denounced the Commons who had 'perilled and annoyed our health, wounded our reputation, embouldened an ill-natur'd people, encroached on many of our privileges and plagued our purse'. Lord Ellesmere believed that the Commons' presumption in denying the king adequate funds had encroached on the 'regality supreme' of the Crown by parading a concern for 'liberty' that, if not checked hard and fast, 'will not cease until it break out into democracy'.

Without its life-line, the government staggered on, although Robert Cecil did not, dying of stomach cancer in 1612. He was hardly gone before the predictable attacks on 'Deformity', including one very pointed polemic by Francis Bacon, appeared. With Cecil collapsed both the moral and actual credit of the Crown. London brewers (hitting the king where it hurt) refused to supply any more ale without advance payment. A Dutch goldsmith, from whom James asked for a £20,000 loan on security of jewels he had bought from him, turned James down on the grounds that others had contributed to the purchase price! It did not help that the king now entrusted the Treasury to one of the Howard clan, the Earl of Suffolk, whose reckless prodigality at Audley End ought to have been an immediate disqualification. But the bigger the debt the more impressive the player, the king seems to have felt.

Little went right in the years ahead. In 1612 Henry, the Prince of Wales, the paragon of Protestant patriots, lauded as virtuous, intelligent, handsome on a horse and (compared to his father, old *Rex Pacificus*) refreshingly interested in bloodshed, died. The outpouring of sorrow at his huge funeral was genuine. In contrast to the defunct Protestant hero, his replacement as Prince of Wales, Charles, had been such a puny child that no one expected him to survive infancy, and even at the age of five he needed to be carried around in people's arms. He was tongue-tied (in glaring contrast to his father), solemn and very short. After Prince Henry died the golden suit of parade armour that had been made for him was passed down to the new Prince of Wales. It was too big for him. Much of his subsequent life would be spent trying to grow into its imperial measurements.

To compensate for a death, two great weddings were celebrated the following year, 1613. At the time there seemed reason only for rejoicing, but both unions turned out to be extremely bad news for the peace and good order of James's realm. The more auspicious of the two matches was the marriage of Princess Elizabeth to

Frederick, the prince-elector of the Rhineland Palatinate. If the court had had to suffer the loss of its own native Protestant son in Henry, the son-in-law, Frederick, seemed a reasonable replacement. The festivities, held in mid-February, were, as usual, rowdy and excessive, culminating in an elaborately staged mock naval battle on the Thames between 'Turks' and 'Venetians', during which the paper and paste-board port of Algiers went up prematurely in flames.

The second marriage crashed and burned even more spectacularly. The match was between Frances Howard, the daughter of the spendthrift Lord Treasurer, the Earl of Suffolk, and James's current favourite, Robert Carr (Scottish page of Lord Hay, the great party thrower), whose shapely length of leg caught James's eye when Carr was injured in the tilts. Carr, whom the Earl of Suffolk described as 'straight-limbed, well-favoured, strong-shouldered and smooth-faced with some sort of cunning and show of modsty, tho, God wot, he well knoweth when to show his impudence', had been promoted at dizzy speed, first in 1611 to the Viscountcy of Rochester, where he had been endowed with Henry II's immense pile of a castle, and then in November 1613 to the even grander earldom of Somerset. For the nuptials Ben Jonson produced a masque called *Hymenaei*, designed, in its rapturous extolling of marriage, to draw a veil over the unsavoury circumstances in which the union had come about. For Frances Howard had been married before, in 1606, at the age of thirteen, to the second Earl of Essex, then fourteen. But − so it was later claimed in the proceedings for annulment − the marriage had not gone well, at least not in bed. Not much was kept private in the world of the Jacobean court, especially since this kind of gossip was meat and drink for the printed *courants* or news-sheets, which, much as tabloids today, lived off stories of spooky astral occurrences and the juicy adulteries of the rich and famous. In Frances Howard they had a story beyond their wildest dreams.

Even before she had met Carr, stories of Essex's impotence were doing the rounds, along with rumours that Frances had obligingly unburdened Prince Henry of his virginity. In 1613, to the horror of his friend and political adviser Sir Thomas Overbury, Carr made it clear that he wanted to convert their affair into a marriage. It was a period when the power of the Howard clan was at its peak, and when the king found it virtually impossible to deny Carr anything, not even a wife, for even if the king were a sexually active gay, he seemed completely without jealousy where the heterosexual needs of his young protégés were concerned. And once she had made her mind up, Frances was simply unstoppable. Her marriage to Essex, she insisted, had never been consummated and not for want of her trying her best. (She was later accused of feeding Essex drugs to guarantee his impotence.) A commission of the Church was appointed to judge whether there was a case for divorce based on

Above: *Charles as Prince of Wales*, by Robert Peake, *c.* 1612–13.
Opposite: *Henry, Prince of Wales and Robert Devereux, Third Earl of Essex, in the Hunting Field*, by Robert Peake, *c.* 1605. Popular and gifted, Henry was regarded as the perfect Renaissance prince.

the claim of non-consummation, which (to the consternation of the Archbishop of Canterbury, who begged the king to be excused) involved the prelates of England solemnly listening to detailed evidence concerning the failure of the noble earl to introduce his member satisfactorily into the well-disposed orifice of the countess. A physical examination found that she was indeed virgo intacta (although it was later said that Frances had insisted on veiling her face during the inspection and had actually substituted a virgin hired for the imposture, which in light of her subsequent inventiveness cannot be entirely ruled out). When the reluctant Archbishop of Canterbury demurred over supplying the correct result, the king stacked the jury by adding bishops who were less exacting in their judgement. The Essex–Howard union was declared no union at all, and the new marriage sanctioned.

There was, however, one obstacle to the realization of marital bliss between Frances Howard and Robert Carr, and that was Sir Thomas Overbury, who annoyingly continued to refer to her as 'that base woman' and to counsel Carr to break off the alliance with someone he thought little better than a whore. To shut him up, Overbury was offered a foreign embassy, which, to general consternation, he declined. Declared an affront to the king's majesty, he was locked away in the Tower, where he died in September 1613.

For a while Frances and Somerset enjoyed a prolonged honeymoon. But about eighteen months after the wedding, in the summer of 1615, it emerged that Overbury had not simply died in the Tower but had been murdered, by the unusual method of a poisoned enema. The lowdown on Overbury's death had come from an apothecary's assistant, who, before dying, had confessed that he had been paid £20 by the countess of Essex to do the deed. An investigation produced an extraordinary story that the Lieutenant of the Tower had noticed that tarts and jellies and the like, delivered from the Countess for the prisoner, looked and smelled suspicious, especially when one of his own men had already confessed to attempting a poisoning. Scared of offending the most powerful woman in the country after the queen, the poor Lieutenant did what he could to protect the target of her fury by intercepting the lethal provisions and replacing them with food prepared by his own cook. But there was no intercepting (or even suspecting) an enema filled with mercury sublimate. Although Somerset himself had known nothing of the murder scheme, once confronted with the *fait accompli*, he made feverish attempts to cover up the traces of the crime, bribing where necessary, destroying documents where essential. With the appalled king pressing the investigation, going in person to the council and 'kneeling down there desired God to lay a Curse upon him and his posterity if ever he were consenting to Overbury's death', the plot unravelled. Once exposed, the sinister cast of plotters – a crook-back apothecary from Yorkshire who had supplied Frances with a whole range of poisons, including 'Powder of Diamonds', white arsenic, and something called 'Great Spider', and Anne Turner, dress-designer-cum-procuress, famous for popularizing yellow-starched fabrics, who passed the poisons to Overbury's gaoler – made the most lurid productions of John Webster seem understated by comparison. Confronted with the damning evidence, Frances broke down and pleaded guilty. Somerset, able with some conscience to plead not guilty of advance knowledge, was none the less convicted of having been at the very least an accessory after the deed. The commoners were, needless to say, given the horrible deaths reserved for poisoners; the nobles, of course, were spared by James and kept confined in the Tower, where Somerset contented himself with periodic exercises in interior redesign.

To those out in the shires whose theology divided the world into the legions of Christ and the battalions of Antichrist, the Howard–Somerset affair, featuring as it did all the prime transgressions – fornication, murder, criminal suppression of the truth, perhaps even witchcraft – was the clearest evidence that the court was indeed a Stuart Sodom, an unspeakable sink of iniquity. Puritan manuals on the right ordering of the commonwealth never tired of stressing the patriarchal family as the building block of a just and godly state. It was surely not accidental that the chief mover in bringing the king's attention to the likelihood of a hideous plot was himself an evangelical Protestant, Sir Ralph Winwood, the Secretary of State. To men like Winwood, the decency and integrity of the social and political order were at stake, for everything about that social order seemed to have been perverted in the Howard plot, involving as it did protagonists at the apex of the social and political pyramid. The proper deference of wife to husband had been demonstrably violated by the subjection of the pathetic Somerset to his frightening wife. Frances and her confederate Anne Turner seemed the incarnation of all the misogynist nightmares that haunted Jacobean culture: the insatiable, demonically possessed succubus, the fiend who destroyed through carnal congress. Could there be any doubt that the manner of poor Overbury's death must have been devised by the anally obsessed Devil? James himself seems to have concluded that Turner was, indeed, a sorceress.

Seen in this light, the grip that the Howards appeared to have on the government of England seemed evidence of a Satanic conspiracy to subvert the godliness and manliness of the aristocracy, whose privileges were still conditional on its status as an exemplary warrior caste. To soldiers like Barnaby Rich, writing in 1617, the atrophy had gone devilishly far, as it had with the Romans. No wonder the evil genius behind the Howard–Somerset plot had been the fashion queen, Mrs Turner, since 'our minds are effeminated, our martial exercises and disciplines of war are turned into womanish pleasures and delights … we are fitter for the coach than the camp'. As for the bishops, they too had also demonstrated the criminal worthlessness of their office by becoming party to infamy. (This was no surprise to Puritans, who made much of Mrs Overall, the notorious wife of the future Bishop of Coventry and Lichfield, who had run off with one of her many lovers in 1608.) The king won some credit from the critics of the court for his evidently sincere determination to get to the bottom of the crime. But the fact that he had forborne from punishing the principal malefactors with the full severity of the law while condemning their minions to death seemed further proof that James was impotent to prevent the descent of England into a pit of pagan immorality.

In the last thirty years of the twentieth century, it became a received wisdom that the Puritans were, especially by the 1620s, no more than a small if very vocal minority in England. (It is much harder to minimize the significance of ardent Calvinism in Scotland, which, of course, knew as much about the Howard affair as England.) And it is not to be imagined that episodes like the Howard scandal suddenly brought a majority round to thinking of the court as somehow irreversibly corrupt. But what it did do was reinforce the conviction of those who were already committed to the cause of moral cleansing (and who were doing something about it in their own households and local towns and villages) that the band of the Elect would, by definition, be a select but zealous troop. For the moment, the godly had to concentrate on local purifications, beginning, as always, with themselves and their immediate family and extending outwards into their community. A few would come to the conclusion that England was so far gone in abomination that to create a Zion apart required putting the distance of the Atlantic between them and Albion-Gomorrah. There was, to be sure, no strategy about any of this. It was not 'stage one' of some sort of timetable to create a true Jerusalem in England, but equally only the most myopic focus on the immediate circumstances of the outbreak of the civil war in 1641–2 could possibly write off the strength and spiritual intensity of the godly as of no consequence at all to the fate of Britain. Of course, the Puritans had no inkling whatsoever that the path ahead would involve an overthrow of the monarchy. But the agents of all such upheavals – in eighteenth-century France and early twentieth-century Russia, for example – are invariably zealous sects who believe themselves moved by some higher calling to a great and general scouring.

In the early years of the seventeenth century, the construction of Zion was a local business. But what the godly might achieve in places like the Dorset cloth town of Dorchester must have supplied for some, at least, practical evidence that with God's help his Faithful might yet prevail against the hosts of darkness. In 1613 – the year of

Top: *Frances Howard, Countess of Essex and Somerset*, by Isaac Oliver, *c.* 1600.
A fashionable beauty, Frances Howard was at the centre of two court scandals,
her divorce in 1612–13 and her trial for murder, 1615–16.
Above: *Robert Carr, Earl of Somerset*, by Nicholas Hilliard, *c.* 1611. Second
husband to Frances Howard, Carr was caught up in his wife's scandals.

the Howard-Somerset marriage – Dorchester, then a town of only 2000 souls, was ravaged by a terrifying fire, which destroyed 170 of its houses, miraculously taking just one life. To the Puritan rector of the Church of Holy Trinity, John White, who had been appointed to Dorchester in 1606, it was a communiqué from Sodom: a clear sign of God's wrath at the stiff-necked sinfulness of the people and their wickedly complaisant magistrates. Together with recent immigrants to the town of like-minded godliness, White set about, through preaching and teaching, to make a great and holy alteration. His targets were the usual suspects: fornication in general; adultery in particular; drunkenness; cursing, sports and pastimes (like bear-baiting and street theatre), which were especially vile when profaning the Sabbath but reprehensible at all times; chronic absenteeism from church; and casual rowdiness and violence. His enforcers were the constables (three of them), the part-time night-watchmen, the daytime beadles and the local justices, who were to send offenders to the stocks or, if necessary, to gaol. But White and his zealot friends also meant to make a positive change in the habits of the community by exhorting the flock to charity, even or especially at times of economic distress. The funds gathered from church collections were to be used to refashion the town: to create new schools and a house of learning and industry for children of the poor, and to care for the sick and old. Dorchester became a veritable fount of charity, not just for its own distressed, but also for any causes identifiable as morally deserving: victims of the plague in Cambridge and Shaftesbury, and victims of a fire (with which the locals had special sympathy) in Taunton, Somerset.

The fact that White and his fellow Puritans, a majority of whom came to dominate the town corporation, correctly believed themselves to be contending with a county society that was far from sympathetic to their goal of conducting a new godly reformation, only strengthened their passionate conviction that God's work had to be done. And between the year of the fire and 1640 they did accomplish an amazing change in the little town. Their moral police bore down on offenders with tireless zeal. Landlords who took advantage of their tenants' or their debtors' wives by forcing themselves on them were exposed, fined or pilloried. Compulsive swearers like Henry Gollop, who was presented to the magistrates for unleashing an awesome string of forty curses in a row, had their mouths stopped. Women who kept houses of assignation and alehouse-keepers, whose taverns were a place of constant riot, had their premises shut down or were evicted. Traditional festivals, which were notorious for promoting drunkenness and licentiousness, were expunged from the local calendar. Notorious absentees from church (especially among the young) were driven back there and sternly awaited every Sunday. Theatre disappeared. In 1615 an actor manager called Gilbert Reason came to town armed with a licence from the Master of the Revels in London entitling him to play before the townspeople. Dorchester's bailiff refused him in no uncertain terms, and when Reason replied that, since he was disregarding a royally authorized document, the bailiff was no better than a traitor, he found himself spending two days in gaol before being sent on his way. More sadly, a 'Frenchwoman' without hands, who had taught herself to do tricks with her feet (like writing and sewing) for a livelihood, was likewise sent packing.

In 1617 the killjoys were dealt an unexpected blow by the king's *Book of Sports*, which expressly allowed certain pastimes (like music) on Sunday evenings, while upholding the ban on bear- and bull-baiting and bowling. James's demand for a relaxation on censoriousness had been provoked by a stay in Lancashire en route back from Scotland, where he discovered that a particularly ferocious moral regime had been inflicted on innocent games and pastimes. But in Dorchester, the *Book of Sports* was heeded less than the vigilance of the local magistracy. The number of pregnant brides fell dramatically, as did the packs of beggars and unlicensed transients. Children were taken into the new schools and a 'hospital' established for the encouragement of sound work habits and piety. There were two new almshouses and a municipally funded brewhouse to employ the 'deserving' (that is non-begging) indigent. A house of correction was built with a homily carved over the door summing up the prevailing ethos in Dorset's little Jerusalem: 'Look in yourselves, this is the scope/Sin brings prison, prison the rope.'

In 1620 there was a new and urgent cause for which the godly in Dorchester were asked to empty their purses: Protestant refugees fleeing from an invasion of the Rhineland Palatinate by Catholic troops of the king of Spain. Some of the fugitives even came to settle in Dorchester, such was the international reputation of White, whose German assistant made sure the town was in close touch with events in continental Europe. Those events in the Rhineland, apparently remote from English and British concerns, became immediately a topic of supreme importance in the country's political and religious life, the subject of innumerable tracts, sermons and pamphlets, to the point where they changed Britain. By marrying his daughter Elizabeth to the apparently dull but safe Protestant Elector Frederick, James had unwittingly put his entire reputation as the king of peace in terrible jeopardy. The consequences of that marriage and the predicament in which it put the Crown would dog James until his death in March 1625 and would cast a long shadow over the beginning of his son's reign.

The problem could hardly have been anticipated, happening in the same place that even three centuries later Neville Chamberlain would notoriously describe as a

James VI of Scotland, I of England, by Daniel Mytens, 1621.

'far away country of which we know little': Bohemia. In 1618 the Protestant Estates rejected the Catholic nominee for their crown (the archduke who would become the Emperor Ferdinand) and made their point by throwing the envoys sent from the Emperor Matthias out of the windows of Hradčany Castle in Prague on to the substantial dung-heap below. Invitations went out to eligible Protestant candidates, and Frederick, certainly to his father-in-law's consternation, accepted the throne in August 1619. In November 1620 his army suffered a disastrous defeat at the hands of the Catholic Holy Roman Emperor at the battle of the White Mountain, and at the same time Spanish troops invaded his Rhineland home territory of the Palatinate. Frederick and Elizabeth – the Winter King and Queen, from their short stay in Prague – became the most famous and fashionable refugees of their age, travelling between England and France and finally settling in The Hague, where they established their own court in exile.

In the more Protestant centres of Britain, from London to Edinburgh (and certainly in Dorchester), a hue and cry went up for war against Spain and the Catholic powers. To the godly this was the battle of the Last Days, heralding the coming of the kingdom of the saints. Sides had to be taken. And the king, it was clear, would have to be pushed. But James's deep reluctance to turn warrior was not just a matter of ending his long and successful career as a pacifist; it was also a matter of bankrupting the realm. His trusted adviser, and later, from 1622, his Treasurer, Lionel Cranfield, who knew what he was talking about, coming as he did from a commercial and financial background, and who by dint of painstaking economies had managed to contain, if not reverse, the damage to the Exchequer from years of profligate spending, now warned of the fiscally catastrophic consequences of a war. But James was equally aware that to do nothing about the humiliating predicament of his daughter and son-in-law, to say nothing of the standing of the Protestant states of Europe, was to compromise beyond any possibility of recovery the authority of his government.

James felt personally betrayed by the Catholic offensive because for some time before 1620 he had been making overtures to Madrid for a marriage alliance between his son, Charles, and the daughter of King Philip III of Spain. In return for expressions of his own sincerity in seeking the match, James had been told not to worry about the Palatinate itself. Even after the occupation, the Spanish disingenuously claimed that their presence in the Rhineland was merely pressure to dislodge Frederick from Bohemia. Such was his aversion to conflict that, given this straw to grasp at, James was prepared to believe the transparent lie. He was abetted in this pathetic self-deception by his new favourite, George Villiers (the son of an impoverished Leicestershire knight), whose star had risen when those of Somerset and the

Howards had crashed. In rapid succession Villiers had been promoted to become Knight of the Garter, privy councillor, baron, earl, marquis and, finally, especially shocking since there had been no dukes in England since the execution of Norfolk in the reign of Elizabeth, Duke of Buckingham.

The last Spanish marriage – between Mary Tudor and Philip II – had not turned out well for anyone, so the gambit was from the beginning fraught with controversies that went to the heart of national and religious sensibilities. There were those, like the Puritan Sir Robert Harley in Herefordshire, who were old enough to remember the Spanish Armada. And Camden's immensely popular history of the reign of Elizabeth ensured that the epic of the wars against Spain was very much alive in Jacobean England. The Spanish court and government simply sat back and enjoyed the inexplicable desperation of the English, delighted that they were so keen to rule themselves out as adversaries in the wider European war. Their terms were aggressive. As a condition of the marriage they insisted (pushed by an equally overjoyed Rome) that the Infanta Maria be allowed not just a private chapel but a church that would be open to the public as well. Until they were into their adolescence, the responsibility for educating the children of the union would fall to the infanta, not the prince. And, most daring of all, they stipulated that English Catholics should now be allowed open freedom of worship. James must have known that to accept these terms would be to light a wildfire in both England and Scotland, but he was in absurd thrall to the beauteous Duke of Buckingham. In letters James addressed him as 'Steenie', a Scots endearment referring to his supposed resemblance to an image of St Stephen. In return Buckingham wrote back to his 'deare dade', knowing that no flattery would be too cloying for the besotted king, thus: 'I naturallie so love your person and upon so good experience and knowledge adore all your other parts which are more than ever one man had that were not onelie all your people but all the worlds besids sett together on one side and you alone on the other I should, to obey and pleas you, displeas, nay despise them.' Gouty old men should, of course, be wise enough in the ways of the world to discount sycophancy on this scale. But evidently James needed someone to lean on, both metaphorically and literally, and Buckingham, who had been entirely 'made' by the king as much as if he had fathered him, was obviously assigned the role of the perfect son: virile, clever and dynamic. He could do no wrong, especially when expanding on the wonderfulness of King James.

Charles might have been a tougher nut for Buckingham to crack, being so reserved in his demeanour and alienated from the unbuttoned bonhomie of his father, but a special feast that Buckingham gave for him took care of that. Together, Charles and Buckingham managed to persuade James – over what was left of his better judgement – that a way to nail the match was for them to go to Madrid, woo the infanta in person and confront the court there with a *fait accompli*. James was so anxious to avoid a war that he agreed to the hare-brained plan. In 1621 he had come through the fiercest political conflict of his whole reign when he had summoned parliament to provide a subsidy in the event of a war. The initial session in early 1621, with the prospect of doing damage to Spain in the offing, had turned into a virtual love fest, with parliament offering funds and James offering up the usual sacrifice of a minister for them to impeach (in this case, Lord Chancellor Bacon, who was accused of taking bribes) and conceding that he had brought some of the ruin on himself by being 'too bountiful' when he first came into the kingdom. By the end of the year, however, news of the serious consideration being given not to a war but to a Spanish marriage had soured relations. Parliament now adamantly refused to grant monies in advance of a commitment to go to war. In response, James turned furiously on them, denying their right to discuss matters such as a royal marriage and affairs of war and peace. 'You usurp upon our prerogative royal and meddle with things far above your reach.' This was, in fact, virtually the same position that Elizabeth had taken when she, too, had turned on parliament in 1566. But in the intervening period, History had happened, in particular, a richly developed historical discourse, which held that parliaments had, since time immemorial, been able to discuss such things and that their right to speak freely on matters of state was, in the words of their 'Protestation' of 1621: the ancient and undoubted birthright and inheritance of the subjects of England; and that the arduous and urgent affairs concerning the King, state and defence of the realm and of the Church of England, and the maintenance and making of laws and redress of mischiefs and grievances which daily happen in this realm are proper subjects and matters of counsel and debate in parliament.' James, who continued to insist that any such 'privileges' were a grant, not a right, may have been on more accurate historical ground, but he was, as his son also would be, the ideological loser of the argument. And losers turn petulant, especially Stuarts. The king's response was to have the offending page torn from the Journal of the House of Commons and the most offensive speakers locked up.

So perhaps it was the need to bring about an evacuation of the Palatinate without having to go to parliament for war funds that moved James to allow Buckingham and Charles to proceed with their adventure. Or perhaps James was just losing his grip, as an extraordinary letter to 'Steenie' and 'babie Charles' suggests, when he addressed them as 'my sweete boyes and deare ventrouse Knights worthy to be putt in a new romanse'. From the beginning, from when they chose the persuasive incognitos of 'Tom and Jack Smith' complete with false whiskers (which fell off en route),

Above: *George Villiers, First Duke of Buckingham*, studio of Peter Paul Rubens, *c.* 1620 (destroyed *c.* 1940).
Opposite, top: *Charles I, Prince of Wales* (detail), by Daniel Mytens, *c.* 1621.
Opposite, below: *The Return of Prince Charles and the Duke of Buckingham from Spain, 5 October 1623*, by Frederick Vroom, *c.* 1624.

to Charles's adolescent determination to climb the garden wall in Madrid to get a better view of the object of his adoration, the entire enterprise began to resemble one of the more puerile products of the Jacobean stage. The Spanish, at any rate, were hugely amused at the pit of embarrassment that Smith and Smith had so boyishly dug for themselves. For while Buckingham and Charles naïvely imagined that they were hastening a conclusion, the Spanish realized that they had been handed, in effect, two diplomatic hostages. If James had allowed such a thing, their reasoning went, he must be desperate for the marriage. And if he were desperate, then they would extract the most extortionate terms they could from his predicament. Not only would there now be a royally protected public Catholic church created for the infanta, but Prince Charles would also have to agree to take instruction from her chaplain. To their amazement this, too, was accepted by the prince, along with more or less anything else the Spanish could think of. Testing the limits of English tolerance, they now went one step too far. The marriage, they stipulated, was to be considered made on paper but strictly subject (for its actual realization and consummation) to the satisfactory completion of a one-year probationary period, to be served not just by Charles himself at Madrid but also by his father's government and kingdom. If during that period the terms of the treaty had been properly fulfilled, the infanta and her husband would be free to travel back to England; if not, well then not.

This last demand appalled King James, who now became genuinely (and rather touchingly) distraught at the possibility of not seeing his beloved 'Steenie' and his 'babie' for at least a year, during which time, God alone only knew, his aching old bones might have to be put in their tomb. Fortunately for James, Charles and Buckingham had also been affronted by the notion of their probation, and the heady romance of the Spanish affair had cooled. One of Charles's companions, the young Buckinghamshire gentleman Sir Edmund Verney, had struck a priest in the face when he attempted to administer the Catholic last rites to a dying page in the prince's retinue. The indignity of being captives rather than suitors began to seem like the humiliation it was. To secure their freedom Charles and Buckingham pretended to go along with the treaty, only to make it clear even before landing in England that they would repudiate it. By the time the party had got home, livid at the indignities, Buckingham had completely recast the prince's role (and his own) not as Spanish bridegroom but as Protestant hero. Instead of a wedding there would now be a war. There is nothing like a bad pre-nuptial agreement, it seems, to bring on an attack of belligerence.

When Charles returned home in October 1623, still a Protestant bachelor, the country exploded in relief, the likes of which had not been seen since the unmasking of the Gunpowder Treason. Once more, there were bonfires and bells. The spring session of parliament, summoned in February 1624 to provide a subsidy for the king, immediately turned into a concord between king and nation. Another minister (this time the relatively blameless and tireless, if well-rewarded, Lord Treasurer Cranfield) was duly served up for disgrace and ruin, and, now that the country was going to get its patriotic-Protestant war, parliament was prepared to give the king his money.

It was not quite the war they had bargained for. Memories of Elizabethan strikes against the Don, much glamorized by the passage of time and the embellishments of history, must have led many to assume that there would be swift and lethal raids and the capture on the high seas of Spanish treasure. But apparently there was to be a land campaign too, waged in the Rhineland by the mercenary general, Count Ernst von Mansfield, using troops impressed – that is to say coerced – from England. No one was chafing at the bit to sign up for this doubtful enterprise. Men sawed their fingers off or blinded themselves in one eye to avoid impressment, but 12,000 poor souls, digits and eyes intact, were plucked by the constables from alehouses and street corners and marched to Dover. By the time they could find a port willing to land them on the other side, at Flushing in Zeeland, the entire force had been so badly hit by the plague that bodies had to be thrown into the harbour every day, until just 3000 troops remained, scarcely enough to make any kind of military impact. So the Mansfield expedition ignominiously collapsed before it ever got under way.

It was to have been the last great campaign of the peacemaker king. But in March 1625, the king, who had become so stricken with gout that he could barely move at all, made his own peace with the Almighty. 'And Solomon sleeps with his fathers,' was the text of the funeral sermon preached by John Williams, Bishop of Lincoln, invoking the dusty cliché of Jacobean eulogies. But this time it was literal, since the great tomb of Henry VII in Westminster was opened and James's own remains were placed next to the founder of the Tudor dynasty. If he had had trouble making a union of his two realms in his life, at least he would manage one particular peaceful cohabitation in death. For although James was hidden from view, the tombs of his mother and his predecessor, Mary and Elizabeth, the one brilliantly coloured, the other virginally white, were made, by his order, to share the same space. Magna Britannia: R.I.P.

If James had been Britain's Solomon, could his son aspire to be its imperial Charlemagne? *Carolus Rex Magnae Britanniae* appears on a shield hung over an ancient oak in the most imposing of all of Van Dyck's equestrian portraits, in which the golden-spurred king rides forth in a pose unmistakably reminiscent of Titian's great equestrian portrait of the armoured Habsburg emperor, *Charles V on Horseback*, of 1548. Behind him is the sylvan glade of England, before him the cerulean sky of the new golden age over which he will preside, Roman Emperor and *miles Christianum*, Christian knight. Because he was so little, Van Dyck had to take liberties with the relative proportions of king and horse, so that Charles would seem a naturally commanding Caesar. Riding and ruling were supposed to be one and the same. Antoine de Pluvinel, the most famous riding instructor in all Europe, had published a widely read treatise that not only compared the stoical, perfectly calm control of a fiery charger to the ruler's government of his realm but actually argued as well for equestrian education in this style as a precondition of establishing proper princely authority. To command the great horse – impassive, fearless and still – as the statue of Marcus Aurelius on the Campidoglio in Rome made clear, was the mark of a true Caesar.

It is a certainty that Charles would have read deeply in the classics as part of his humanist education, and that the Stoics, Seneca in particular, would have been at the heart of such instruction. From an early stage the new king cultivated an aura of stoical self-possession, which made a startling contrast with the garrulous, expansive, disconcertingly unbuttoned informality of his father. Perhaps Charles, like so many others, had been impressed with the gravitas that ruled the Spanish court. At the Escorial sobriety ruled, and the king's presence was closed off from the common mob of courtiers by a solemn and elaborate fence of ritual. Sir Edmund Verney, who had not shown himself overly decorous by attacking a Jesuit, was now repaid by being awarded the office of Knight Marshal of the Palace, saddling him with the unenviable task of policing the court and its environs. It was Verney who had to see to the yards and corridors of the royal palaces, especially Whitehall, clearing them of the innumerable over-dressed louts, dunning tradesmen, doubtful men-at-arms and sundry petitioners who hung around the premises. There was, in any case, much in Charles's own reserved (not to say secretive) and rather prim manner that predisposed him towards solemnity. Of course, the more demure atmosphere he brought to the court could hardly have been thought a liability. A thorough cleansing of the Augean stables was, after all, what polite (not just Puritan) opinion had been clamouring for. And the substance of Charles's policies was not, in principle, so very different from that of his father, who had also refused to acknowledge the illegality of extra-parliamentary taxation, or the right of parliament to debate what it saw fit. When he bore down on parliament for presuming such things, he was doing no more than reiterating what he could be forgiven for thinking an accepted article of the Jacobean creed about sovereignty.

Charles I on Horseback, by Anthony van Dyck, *c.* 1637.

It was not so much what Charles said that got him and England into trouble as the way he said it. The violent ups and downs of James's political apprenticeship had educated him early and well in the need for timely, pragmatic concessions, and he was capable of alternating Caledonian wrath with equal bursts of ingratiating charm. Charles, though, set great store by consistency. Perhaps he had overdosed a little on Seneca and his seventeenth-century neo-Stoic admirers for whom there was no greater virtue in public men than constancy, for Charles was constitutionally incapable of seeing two (or more) sides to any matter. More seriously for the government of the realm, he was even more incapable of acting against his own decided convictions.

Charles would not, for example, do what kings of England had done since the days of Edward III and the 'Good Parliament' of 1376 and jettison a royal favourite for the sake of an improved working relationship between Crown and parliament. Cynicism and disloyalty shocked him deeply. Instead, Charles insisted on looking at the individual merits of the case. This was a terrible mistake. You will not find any chapters in constitutional histories devoted to the rituals of therapeutic disgrace, but creative scapegoating had, none the less, long been an integral element of English politics. Concentrating odium for unpopular policies on the head of a politician (which, of course, might fall as a result) preserved the fiction that the 'king could do no wrong'. By insisting from an honourable but obtuse loyalty (in the case of Buckingham and, later, Laud and Strafford) that there was no difference between the king's view and his servant's, he wrecked the convenience of impeachment. Blame had nowhere to go but back to HM himself.

None of this, of course, would occur or could even be explained to Charles himself even when, as in Buckingham's case, the favourite had reserved most of his energies for the accumulation of an immense empire of patronage rather than for the prosecution of the war he said he was so impatient to fight. In 1625 the doomed Spanish marriage project had been replaced by a successful French match (to Henrietta Maria, sister of Louis XIII), and, as part of the alliance, English ships and troops were supposed to join a French attack on Spain. But Cardinal Richelieu proved not much less manipulative than the Spanish and absorbed the English force into an attack on the Huguenot enclave of La Rochelle. When, in addition, it became apparent that Henrietta Maria was to enjoy the same conditions of freedom for Catholic worship that would have been guaranteed to the Spanish infanta and, even worse, that the recusancy laws were to be suspended as a condition of the marriage, it suddenly seemed that England was fighting a war *against*, rather than on behalf of, the Protestant cause.

The suspicion that the country had somehow been turned aside from a godly Protestant crusade to a sinister quasi-Catholic war, designed to insinuate popery back into the Church, was shared by the Puritans both in parliament and in the shires. Sir Robert Harley's letters to his third wife, Lady Brilliana (whose wonderful name had been taken from the seaport of Brielle or Brill, where the Dutch revolt had had its first success against Philip II, and where Brilliana's father had been commander), are heavy with mistrust and anxiety. What capped it for Harley was the appointment by Charles of Richard Montague as court chaplain. To men such as Harley, Montague was a notorious 'Arminian', which was little better than an outright Papist, perhaps even worse because of his pretence of remaining within the Church of England. In fact, Montague's brand of theology was no different from that preached and practised by ministers favoured by James, like Lancelot Andrewes and his successor, John Buckeridge. But the Puritans knew that in the cockpit of theological combat in the Dutch Republic the struggle (which had degenerated into a real civil war in 1618) between 'Arminians' and their more militant late sixteenth-century Calvinist adversaries was precisely over the crucial issue of predestination. The followers of the Dutch theologian Jacobus Arminius believed that salvation was not exclusively predetermined and that God might (not necessarily, but possibly) be persuaded to relent by the penitent good works of the sinner, and that therefore the boundaries between the saved and the damned were not hard and fast after all. Rightly or wrongly, they had been anathematized in Holland as little better than Catholics, and the same was true of their counterparts in England, including Montague and William Laud, whom Charles would appoint to be Bishop of London and then Archbishop of Canterbury. Like his father before him, Charles saw the anti-Calvinist theology as broadening the Church, conceivably even managing to bind up the wounds that had hurt it since the Reformation. To the godly, though, this was nothing but a counter-Reformation by the back door.

When Charles's first parliament convened in June 1625, summoned to provide funds for the war, it made clear – from the niggardly sums voted and the deliberately insulting grant of the usual customs duties, 'tonnage and poundage', not for life but for one year – that religious issues were going to be linked to the supply of revenue. A parliamentary commission of inquiry was appointed to investigate Montague, and the next on the list of targets was bound to be Buckingham, who had botched a raid on Cadiz so badly that suspicions were being voiced that his heart had never been in it. To persuade parliament otherwise, Buckingham abruptly switched tack to give them a war they might like – against, rather than on behalf of, the French and in support of the beleaguered Huguenots.

By the standards of past liability, Buckingham had already done enough to earn himself impeachment thrice over, but during Charles's second parliament, in June 1626, the king made it clear he would never countenance proceedings against his favourite. On 12 June, a tornado cut a path through southern England, opening the graves of plague victims who had been buried the previous year. The godly knew what this portended, but apparently the king did not. Faced with parliamentary refusal to vote subsidies for the new war unless Buckingham was impeached, Charles decided to levy a forced loan. This was bound to be inflammatory. The medieval tradition of 'benevolences' – money required without parliamentary sanction for the defence of the realm – had been outlawed in 1484 and abandoned since 1546, as it invariably raised serious constitutional questions about the king's exclusive right to judge when a war constituted an emergency or not. In 1614, however, James had revived benevolences, though they remained bitterly controversial. It was predictable that those whom Charles believed to be conspiratorial rabble-rousers, the orchestrators of 'popularity', should misrepresent the loan (as he thought) as an illegal confiscation. But the scale and breadth of outraged resistance must have startled him. Had not William Laud preached that since no power but God could judge the king, obedience to God extended, without demur, to obeying the king? The point, however, was not well taken. It was not just Puritans who denounced the loan as unlawful. The heart of the resistance came from sections of the political community on whom the king relied for stable government: the nobility and the gentry of the counties. Even so, not all the shires were equally incensed. It helped that the administrative arrangements for the loan were left to the counties themselves to organize, and the fact that £240,000 was raised, despite the hue and cry, suggests that by no means all of England and Wales was up in arms.

But some sections of the country were, indeed, belligerent in defence of the 'liberties' and property of the subject as never before. In Cornwall, for example, often thought of as loyal and royal, the MP William Coryton made it clear to the commissioners for the loan that he had consulted God, his conscience and historical precedent and had been instructed by all three that the loan was emphatically illegal. Coryton was imprisoned in the Fleet prison in London for his resistance. Some of the greatest and most powerful figures in the country became resisters: the Earls of Warwick, Essex, Huntingdon and Arundel. The twenty-seven-year-old Theophilus Clinton, Earl of Lincoln, an unlikely opposition hero, none the less mobilized resistance among seventy prominent gentry in the county and, when deposited in the Tower for his presumption, made sure his steward carried on the work of frustrating the commissioners. The spectacle of the mighty leading the charge in counties like

William Laud, by Anthony van Dyck, *c.* 1635.

Essex, Suffolk, Oxfordshire, Warwickshire, Northamptonshire and Buckinghamshire gave heart to godly preachers and men who would normally be thought of as pillars of stability. And the crisis provoked statements of shocking defiance and militancy. 'If it [the loan] goes forward,' wrote one Lincolnshire knight, 'we make ourselves and our posteritye subject to perpetual slavery without any recovery to be taxed at pleasure without any limits.' And in Yorkshire Sir John Jackson warned that 'if any of his men had give anie they should never hold land of him and iff anie of my tenants shall give, God's wounds I could or would hange them with my owne hands'.

The sound and fury did not die away once the money was collected. In the thirty-two contested elections for the parliament of 1628, opposition or submission to the forced loan became a critical issue in mobilizing the freeholders to defeat court-approved incumbents. Coryton and his friend, Sir John Eliot, who had also been jailed for resistance, were pressured by the government not to stand in Cornwall. But stand they did, turning their incarceration into a badge of honour and, more significantly, organizing like-minded gentry in a region supposedly warmly loyalist to ensure their triumphant return to parliament. Even more ominously for Crown control of politics, some of the more fiercely contested elections saw feisty mob scenes. At Cambridge Joseph Mead, the collector of political intelligence for his news 'separates', reported that in London not only had a linen draper, who had been in prison for resisting the loan, been elected, but the crowds had also been 'very unruly'. At Westminster supporters of the court-sponsored candidate, Sir Robert Pye, attempted to cry up his chances by parading the streets shouting, 'A Pye! A Pye! A Pye', but were met with derisive counter-cries of 'A pudding! A pudding! A pudding!' and 'A lie! A lie! A lie!' Many of the names that would become a fixture of parliamentary ideology and local political organization in the early 1640s – Francis Rous in Cornwall, John Pym at Tavistock – had their first political blooding in these elections, which were unlike anything that had yet been seen in English political life.

Of course, England was not yet on the verge of revolution, or even approaching it, but moments like the forced, loan crisis were, unquestionably, politically transformative. Rightly or wrongly, they fixed in the minds of an active, nationally educated political community the suspicion that this king was bent on breaching parliamentary defences of their property and their common law. It was an explosive apprehension, and from the most anxious it produced statements of unprecedented militancy about the limits of royal power. In Canterbury, for example, the city's MP Thomas Scott responded to the dean's sermon demanding unconditional obedience to the king with the statement that 'conscientious Puritans' (the word now self-attached as a badge of pride) were required to resist the abuses of unjust rulers: 'subjects may disobey and refuse an unworthy kinge his command or request if it be more than of duty we owe unto him.'

Standing firm in their belief in the supreme rationality of the English common law, the resisters were now taking to the courts to test both the legality of non-parliamentary taxation and the right of the government to imprison without showing due cause, something a Marlborough lawyer, Oliver St John, had said in 1614 violated the Magna Carta. In this case, the courts upheld the legality of the loan and thus the right of the Crown to confine resisters. And once the furore abated, the king should still have been able to contain the political fall-out, fierce though it was. But two events, both of them disastrous, made sure the book was not yet closed on the debate about taxation.

In October 1627 Buckingham turned in yet another hideous fiasco by failing – at huge expense – to take the French Atlantic fort of the Ilê de Rhé, not least because the organizational genius of the navy had failed to notice that the scaling ladders supplied for the siege were 15 feet too short to do the job. This single débâcle ate up £200,000 of the £267,000 collected by the loan. The duke was mercilessly pilloried by ballad-mongers and newsletter-writers. But even worse was to come. In March 1628 it was revealed that the terms of the judgement handed down in the challenge to the legality of the loan had been deliberately falsified by the attorney-general with the express knowledge and encouragement of the king. What the judges had ruled was that a forced loan was legitimate in this particular military emergency. What was published was a ruling that the king was entitled to make extra-parliamentary levies whenever he judged them to be appropriate to the kingdom's needs. It was a bombshell. Those who had believed the king found their trust badly shaken. Those who had taken the worst possible view of Charles's intentions, on the other hand, had a field day with the revelation. With the wind at their backs the guardians of the 'immemorial constitution' turned an argument over a specific measure into an all-out battle of constitutional principles. As a precondition of any further grants, they demanded a Bill of Rights declaring the illegality of non-parliamentary taxes, the prohibition of any imprisonment without trial by the king for unspecified 'reasons of state', and the unlawfulness of martial law and forced billets. The warriors for parliamentary liberties were, however, still in a minority in both the Commons and the Lords. The crisis was, in effect, a three-way showdown, with the party of moderate criticism in the middle, calling the tune. In the House of Lords the Earl of Warwick and Viscount Saye and Sele (both serious Puritans in their personal and religious life) decided, with a large measure of support, on the less confrontational form of a Petition of Right. A petition embodied the same points of substance as a bill, but crucially allowed

Charles to save face and protect James's compulsively reiterated principle (restated as recently as 1621) that such rights were granted by grace, not acceded to as of right.

This should have been the end of the crisis. The assassination of Buckingham in August 1628 was a body blow to Charles, but it neatly took the vexed question of what to do about the widely detested favourite out of the political equation. In shocked mourning, Charles was convinced that the parliamentary demonization of the duke had contributed directly to his death. (The assassin, John Felton, had, in fact, imagined that he was ridding the country, and his king, of a diabolical monster.) Smarting at being deprived of his effective power to wage war, Charles mounted a counterattack, asserting his control over matters not expressly specified in the Petition of Right. It's hard not to imagine the king burning the candle at both ends as he pored over the petition to find loopholes to exploit, a legitimate but politically fool-hardy impulse. He pounced on two significant omissions. First, he now claimed the right to go ahead and impose those 'tonnage and poundage' customs duties without waiting for parliamentary permission. Still more controversially, his appointment of Montague to the bishopric of Chichester and Laud to that of London said as loudly as possible that the king had no intention of conceding anything about his monopoly of wisdom and power in matters spiritual. Like his father, he thought of himself as God's 'lieutenant on earth'.

But the norms of politics and what could or could not be legitimately accepted as sovereign authority were changing under him even as Charles reiterated what he assumed to be the self-evident truths of his sovereignty. Yet even if he were incapable of compromising those principles, the arts of political management called for something other than noble obstinacy. The parliamentary moderates, who had cobbled together an artful resolution of conflict the previous year, were prepared to try again and were called to a negotiation with the king, however bleak the prospects. In the meantime, though, Charles had ordered a suspension of parliamentary proceedings to allow discussions to proceed without further public polarization. The order, of course, was construed as an enforced shut-down, and the militants in the House of Commons loudly advertised it as an infringement of their rights to debate. On 2 March 1629 the Speaker, Sir John Finch, attempted to adjourn proceedings in compliance with the king's order but was told that he was the Commons' servant, not the king's, and would not be allowed to suspend debates until a resolution attacking and condemning 'innovations in religion' and extra-parliamentary taxes had been read. In an awkward bind, Speaker Finch replied, rather pathetically: 'I am not the less the king's servant for being yours. I will not say I will not put it to the question but I must say I dare not.' He had no choice. Sir Miles Hobart had locked the door of

Siege of the Citadel of Saint Martin, Ilê de Rhé, after Jacques Callot, *c.* 1630.

the House and kept the key. With the king's officer hammering on the door and Denzil Holles, the member for godly Dorchester (and a big man), pushing the Speaker down in his chair and making sure he stayed there, the most eloquent leader of the radicals, Sir John Eliot, held the floor, warning that 'none had gone about to break parliaments but in the end parliaments have broken them.' Resolutions of startling fierceness were then read, declaring 'whoever should bring innovation of religion … advise the taking and levying of subsidies not granted by parliament' to be 'a capital enemy of the kingdom and Commonwealth and every subject voluntarily complying with illegal exactions a betrayer of the liberties of England and an enemy to the same'. Shouts of acclamation, 'Aye, Aye, Aye', rang through the battle-hot House. Two days later Hobart, Holles, Eliot and six others were arrested and sent to the Tower. Parliament dissolved on 10 March.

It is not much, is it, this shift from speaking to shoving and shouting? On the other hand, it's everything: a startling violation of decorum in an age when body language spoke volumes about authority and its vulnerability. Holles's roughness and his evident contempt for polite procedure presuppose a collapse of deference that was genuinely ominous for the status quo. And along with it came something equally pregnant with consequences for the future – the creation of a public sphere of politics, the birth, in fact, of English public opinion. Although debates in parliament were still largely supposed to be confidential, lengthy, detailed reports were being written by specialist scriveners, sometimes on commission, sometimes for a news-hungry market, and reproduced in multiple copies. Thus the great theatre of debate inside parliament became news, and for the first time it was possible to make a living from selling it. John Pory, who was also a geographer and foreign adventurer, had a network of correspondents through the country, and he collated their information into a newsletter, which he sold to subscribers for £20 a year. Ralph Starkey, another of these pioneers of the mail-order news business, offered a range of products and services, from '20 shillings a quire' for parliamentary reports to £10 a copy for the Black Book Proceedings of the Order of the Garter. The newsmongers recognized the importance of keeping it hot and juicily divisive. By hiring a team of copyists it took just a few days for a vendor of 'separates' to get the word out (on paper) of the latest debates. So the news business, in a recognizably modern guise, first saw the light of day during the battles between Crown and parliament in 1628–9. Its emphasis on conflict may not, as the revisionist historians reasonably insist, reflect any kind of actual polarization in the country at large, but it has always been the mischievous genius of news to shape politics even while pretending to report it. And the marked preference of the newsmen of early seventeenth-century England for offering a theatre of the bad and the good, the court and the country, may well have had the effect of making it happen by virtue of saying it was so. The circulation of newsletters did something else, too, of fundamental significance for the future: it connected events in London to a provincial public (and on occasion local events could be turned into 'national' news). Reports of speeches would not be printed until the Long Parliament in 1642, but the sixpenny 'separates' travelled along the king's highway, taking all kinds of liberties with his sovereign prerogatives.

News always needs heroes, and the heavy hand of royal government made sure it got them. For bad things had happened to the militant critics of the Crown. Denzil Holles, Sir Miles Hobart and Sir John Eliot were all in the Tower, and Eliot died there in 1632. In the circles of parliamentary opposition to Stuart absolutism, Eliot's fate made him the proto-martyr of their resistance. John Hampden, a Buckinghamshire gentleman and MP, was one of those who kept the torch burning by corresponding with Eliot, visiting him in the Tower and acting as guardian to his two teenage sons. Whether the opposition was dormant or secretly indignant made no difference to the king. Parliament would not be called again until 1640.

In the 1950s, the textbook assumption was still that this long period of non-parliamentary government was a bandage applied so tightly over an open wound as to ensure that the wound would fester, not heal, and that the body politic would become quietly but morbidly infected. The condition of England was said to be one of sullen acquiescence in 'ship money' and the quasi-Catholicization of the Church, while the gagged and bound champions of parliamentary freedom waited for the great day when they could recover the liberties of the nation. Not much of this story has survived drastic revision. A recent history of the personal rule goes so far as to argue that the 1630s were the 'halcyon days' of disinterested royal government, when an energetic administration responded to the wishes of an austere but public-spirited king.

Perhaps somewhere between these two poles (though not, I think, at the midpoint) lies the truth. The suspension of parliamentary government was certainly not thought of as some sort of royal *coup d'état* heralding the introduction of a Habsburg–Bourbon Catholic despotism. Long periods without parliament were not unknown in the English system, and Charles made it quite clear that he did not see this one as signifying the end of the 'king-in-parliament' tradition. Should parliament itself wish to return to what he called its 'ancient' and reasonable way of conducting business, especially the business of providing him with money to secure the nation's defence, it would be back in business. And, of course, the Jacobean and Caroline parliaments were not yet thought of as the elected tribunes of the people. Most of the members of the Commons had taken their seats as a result of consensual and uncontested selection in the counties and boroughs. Some of the most radical of their number, like John Pym, owed their place to a not merely exiguous but virtually non-existent electorate in a pocket borough owned by the Earl of Bedford. By and large, members of parliament were the same kind of people who were the natural governors of the county community as magistrates, deputy lord-lieutenants and sheriffs, and whatever their misgivings about the misuse of Crown prerogatives they still had no problem accepting its offices. It was thus perfectly possible for upright Puritans, like Sir Robert Harley, who had been incensed by the forced loan and by Arminian appointments in the Church, to fill the lucrative position of Master of the Mint, from 1626 to 1635 when he lost office.

On the other hand, neither was England between 1629 and 1640 quite the land of sleepy contentment and harmony that has lately come to dominate the revised histories. What had happened in 1628 and 1629 had happened. Barriers of politeness had been breached. Unforgivable and unforgettable things had been said on both sides. There had been excitement, agitation. Matters had turned physical. And even if those who had been exercised by the theatre of the extreme played out in those stormy years were only a tiny minority, they were a tiny minority with a long memory and access to the newsletters. If there was no sense of 'biding their time' (though this surely was the case for John Pym), neither would the deep grievances and arguments that had been aired at the end of the 1620s completely evaporate in some sort of cloud of resignation and goodwill. It's often said that had there been no furore in Scotland in 1637, the Long Parliament might never have happened. But that Scottish furore was not simply something that happened out of the blue, from causes utterly unrelated to Charles I's vision in the 1630s of a docile Britannia. On the contrary, what happened in Scotland, as we shall see, was, root and branch, sturdily connected to the royal trunk.

The problem with Charles Stuart was not his authoritarianism, his deviousness nor his political tin-ear, all of which have been overstated in the understandable interests of making the civil war seem more likely than it actually was. The problem with Charles Stuart was his good intentions, and the stubborn literalness with which he meant them to take effect. Conversely, in retrospect one can see quite clearly what enormous political assets his father's natural laziness and low threshold of distraction really were. (Uncannily, the same would be true of Louis XV and Louis XVI. Benign torpor should perhaps have been on the list of recommended virtues for successful princes.) James I's tendency to leave government to others, both in the Privy Council and in the shires, so that he could get off after the hare at Royston, was, since those others happened to be of the calibre of Robert Cecil and Francis Bacon and Lionel

Cranfield, the best thing he could have done for the country. Charles I, on the other hand, was positively driven by the itch to govern. To be fair, since he inherited James's gargantuan debts and a war to boot, he did not have much choice in the matter. But once England and Scotland settled back into a peace imposed on the king by fiscal stringency and political opposition, Charles was not one to spend the rest of his life hunting or posing for Van Dyck (though he was, in his way, partial to both). Just as it had for Augustus, for Constantine and, especially, for Alfred the Great, whose biography was commissioned by the king, Duty Called!

And that duty was to make a harmonious realm of Magna Britannia whether it liked it or not, especially in religion, where it seemed most divided. Charles conceived of his kingship in terms not so much of a political office and high judgeship (as James theorized) as of a triple calling: knight-commander-cum-Caesar, spiritual governor and father of the nation. In the first department he made St George something of a fetish, turning the saint's day into a national holiday and investing the Order of the Garter with immense significance. The badge itself, which he wore every single day, was personally redesigned to feature the enormous silver aureole (borrowed from the French order of Saint Esprit), which gave it the appearance of a numinous sacred emblem. Beyond this sense of chivalric Christian appointment, Charles (like many of his contemporaries in baroque Europe) evidently understood his place in the scheme of things as a Platonist. Plato's vision of a celestially ordered unity of the universe, governed by ineffable ideas and truths, which were beyond the reach or the earthly articulation of mere men but which could be apprehended through beauty by a discerning few, the guardians, had been grafted on to Christian theology to create a fresh justification for the priesthood. Charles undoubtedly thought himself to be guardian-in-chief of Great Britain, and the exacting self-discipline of the Platonic guardian – personal austerity, tireless dedication, emotional and sensual self-denial (not qualities for which his late lamented dad was famous) – was what he tried at all times to uphold and personify. What better aim could there be, given the unhappy experience of his first years on the throne, than to bring Harmony to England and Scotland – whether they damned well liked it or not?

In the Dutch and Flemish paintings Charles loved to collect (and for which he had stupendously good taste), Harmony was symbolically represented by the family, often playing music. It was a truism that the family was a commonwealth in miniature and at the same time a pattern for its proper rule. And, again in contrast to the rather slatternly chaos of his father's household, Charles meant his family to be an exemplary image of firm, but benevolent government. After a rough start, relations between king and queen became genuinely and reciprocally warm, and Charles's devotion to Henrietta Maria was passionate enough to blind him later to its very serious costs. Van Dyck's portraits of the royal family would be unique in the history of dynastic, even if they were just documents of private, sentiment. But as their prominent display in public spaces at Whitehall and Hampton Court makes clear, they were also a faithful visual translation of Charles's own ideology: that in the patriarchal family, with its strict but affectionate regulation of the relations between husband and wife, parents and children lay the foundation of all good order. In this, as in many other respects, his views were surprisingly close to those of the Puritans, and one of the reasons why Puritan nobles like Warwick were at such pains not to break with the king is because they saw in him someone as deeply committed to a moral vision of family and commonwealth as themselves.

But needs must, and needs could, disrupt the Caroline quest for Harmony, especially when it was the perennial want of money that was at issue. 'Ship money' would become reviled as one of the most notorious impositions ever laid on the country, a classic case of arbitrary and over-bearing government, but it was originally introduced as a response to the widely acknowledged neglect of the navy, painfully exposed in the Spanish and French wars, which had left English shipping vulnerable to Dutch privateers and pirates. Initially, only the coastal counties were required either to supply a ship or (as was more practical for most of them) pay the equivalent sum. So Charles was able to defend his imposition of ship money without parliamentary consent as legitimate, since it had been levied in defence of the realm. But an ongoing need for naval rearmament was not the same as if the country were facing a second armada, so there were some who thought this merely another edition of the forced loan. It was, though, only when the levy was extended to the inland counties in 1635 that concerted opposition started to gather momentum.

Money was raised. The wheels of local government cooperated with the Crown. The men who ran England and Wales – from lord lieutenants, through their deputies, to sheriffs, justices of the peace and constables and beadles – even if they had been critics in the stormy days of the 1620s, settled back into the role of political and social leaders of their communities, presiding at quarter sessions, leading the hunt, dominating the pews. But what does this resumption of local leadership really mean? That their criticisms had now been put to sleep by their self-interest or that they could without much difficulty administer justice and government without necessarily abandoning their strong reservations about the court?

Some of them, it is true, became partners in Charles's agenda of modernizing reform and renewal, which often resembles nothing so much as the Puritan programme in towns like Dorchester: extended poor relief, the suppression of unlicensed alehouses, the foundation of schools and colleges, and projects designed to improve agriculture like the Earl of Bedford's famous drainage of the Fens in the 1630s. But the intense hostility to the Dutch drainage programme on the part of the affected Fenland population is a good instance of the reaction of some local communities to the obsessive intervention of government in their own backyard, however well-intentioned. And the manner in which those 'improvements' were carried out was not always calculated to allay suspicions that, beneath grandiose declarations about the government promoting the welfare of the commonwealth, there lurked something that smelled of a scam. In the Fens the medieval Court of Sewers had been absurdly revived to move local populations off boggy land. Once conveniently vacated, the land could be transferred to the drainage syndicates, which profited from the enormous capital appreciation of the drained land.

To avoid this kind of odium, Charles's administration did its best to co-opt the county gentry and nobility in its projects. But there were still some schemes in which the intrusiveness of government was bound to be felt much more keenly than its good intentions, never more so perhaps than in the notorious project for the production and conservation of a strategic supply of gunpowder. This was not a trivial issue. The gunpowder shortage was a Europe-wide problem in an age of constant warfare, and a stockpile could make the difference between victory and defeat. What, then, could be a more laudable or necessary patriotic enterprise? In practice, though, what the scheme entailed was the creation of a national store of saltpetre. And the cheapest and most readily available source of nitrous saltpetre was the excreta of animals and humans. Only a monarch as solemnly bereft of a sense of humour as Charles I could possibly have asked his subjects, in all seriousness, to preserve a year's supply of their own urine as a major contribution to the national defence. (This would not, in fact, be the most outrageous attempt to turn body waste into munitions. During the Irish rebellion and wars of the Confederacy in the 1640s and 1650s, the remains of corpses were recycled into gunpowder – the most perfect example, I suppose, of a self-sustaining industry.) But the very energy of Charles's 'petre-men' quickly turned them into enemies of liberty and private property, as armed with warrants they entered barnyards and private households, digging up floors if necessary to get their hands on the precious and strategically important deposits of dove-droppings or sheep shit. Given the unusual working conditions of this assignment, it seems unlikely that, when confronted by householders understandably displeased at having their floors dug up without a by-your-leave, the petre-men would have made much of an effort to appease them.

Likewise, Charles's support for Archbishop Laud's programme for the Church was, while perfectly well intentioned, easily open to misinterpretation. The heart of Laudian doctrine was nothing more than the endorsement of ceremony and sacrament that had certainly been upheld by James I and his own favoured ministers and bishops, including Lancelot Andrewes. But James's Scottish apprenticeship had made him in practice, if not in principle, a grudging pluralist. He had spoken for uniformity (and in Scotland pushed it through in 1618), but in England he was more judicious and circumspect. Charles, on the other hand, saw in Laudian theology a way to bring the congregation of Christians together within an orderly hierarchy of the Church. The obsession with sermons and preaching, the privileging of individual reading of the scripture, the harping on the unbridgeable chasm between the saved and the damned he felt to be profoundly divisive. With the débâcle of Laudianism in 1640–41 came the assumption that somehow it was, indeed, an alien growth on the body of the native Church. But there were plenty of adherents in the 1630s who saw as a national duty, for example, Laud's levy for the repair and restoration of the ruinously neglected and profaned St Paul's Cathedral.

Herefordshire may have been home to the Harleys of Brampton Bryan, who turned their castle into a magnet for Puritan teachers and preachers and an asylum for those suffering from the enforcers of the Laudian Church. But it was also home to the Scudamores of Holme Lacy. The Scudamores had been in the business of supplying knights for the royal tilts right into the reign of James, and they took special pride in their horses, kept not just for the hunt but to be at the disposal of the king. As deputy-lieutenant for Herefordshire, the first Viscount Scudamore made public exhortations to the Herefordshire gentry to improve the quality and quantity of the horses they could bring to the service of the king. Arthurian chivalry was not, it seems, quite dead on the Welsh borderlands. But Scudamore was not just a loyal *preux chevalier*; he was also a genuinely learned country gentleman with an Oxford education. And like so many of the post-Baconian generation, he was an enthusiastic amateur scientist, a manipulator of nature. Scudamore's pride and joy was the Red Streak apple, said to produce the best and most commercially sought-after cider in England. All of Scudamore's passions – his veneration of the past, his vision of a Christian monarchy, his instinctive feeling for beauty – came together in a project that must have seemed as though it were the very justification for his authority in the Herefordshire countryside: the restoration of Abbey Dore.

The abbey was a Cistercian ruin. The Scudamores had acquired it along with its land in the mid-sixteenth century and had it reconsecrated, but by the time the viscount came to its rescue it was, like so many monastic wrecks all over Britain, at the point of collapse. The roof was so badly fallen in that the curate was forced to

The Scudamore's family chapel at Abbey Dore, with the royal arms of Charles I displayed on the chancel screen, between the arms of the Scudamores and William Laud.

read the service from the shelter of an arch to avoid rain falling on the prayer book. And when Scudamore went looking for the old stone altar slab he found it being used to salt meat and press cheese.

Scudamore, doubtless encouraged by Matthew Wren, Bishop of Hereford and one of the most ardent Laudians, evidently thought of himself as the Hezekiah of Herefordshire: the patron who would rebuild the ruined temple to the greater glory of God. The restoration of decayed churches and abbeys seems to have been a passion among the antiquarian community of the counties, so much so that the earliest date of the 'Gothic revival' might well be pushed back to the 1640s, when the antiquary and genealogist William Dugdale, in the depths of Puritan Warwickshire, began his monumental work of describing and chronicling all the church monuments of the country. Dugdale also produced the first great illustrated history of St Paul's Cathedral, a crucial weapon in Laud's campaign to cleanse and restore the polluted building and churchyard (freely used as a latrine) and to have the church thought of, as much as Westminster Abbey, as a national temple.

Scudamore busied himself locally much as Laud busied himself nationally. The desecrated altar was returned to Abbey Dore (according to a local story, crushing a servant who tried to make off with it, its surface running with blood). The beautiful green-glazed tiles of the medieval church scattered around farms and hamlets were reused where possible, replaced where not. And from the surviving *in situ* remnant of the crossing of the old abbey church, Scudamore had the Herefordshire craftsman John Abel (who had also designed a gloriously ornamental town hall at Leominster) carve a spectacular chancel screen in the authentic style of the Palladian revival, complete with Ionic columns. On Palm Sunday 1635, the date chosen not just for its place in the sacred calendar but as the anniversary of Scudamore's baptism, Dore was reconsecrated with a full day of prayers and processions, and much kneeling and bowing, the congregation commanded to remember that henceforth Dore was to be considered a 'Holie Habitation'.

Just across the county at Brampton Bryan Sir Robert and Lady Brilliana Harley would have seen the reconsecration of the Cistercian abbey as the most horrifying and damning evidence that the Popish Antichrist had already made a successful conquest of England, and that his Laudian minions were abusing their office to re-institute the full monstrous servitude of Rome. But to the Laudians, their work was not in any sense an act of spiritual or ecclesiastical subjugation. On the contrary, they saw the restoration of spectacle and mystery as a way of bringing back to the Church those who had been alienated by its obsession with the Word. To feast the eye rather than tire the ear was a way of appealing to all those whom the Calvinists had told were either damned or saved, a way of giving hope to sinners that they might yet be among the flock of those who would see salvation. So the restoration of propriety was not, in their minds, an affectation but a genuine mission. How could the flock be properly reminded of the redeeming sacrifice of the Saviour at a mean little table on which worshippers were accustomed to deposit their hats and from which dogs made off with the communion wafers? Reverence, order and obedience would make the congregation of the faithful whole again.

The Laudian emphasis on inclusiveness fitted neatly with Charles's own innocent concept of his monarchy as an office for the entirety of his subjects. The trouble, though, was that by entirety he meant Scotland as well as England. For if the object of the Laudian reforms was to create an orderly harmony within the Church of England, any kind of exceptions to its uniformity would, by definition, sabotage the whole project. Thus, thoroughly convinced of the rightness of his convictions, Charles planned to introduce the Laudian prayer book to Scotland. In 1634, a year after his coronation in Edinburgh, it must have seemed a good, a necessary project. How was he supposed to know that it was the beginning of his end?

2

The British wars began on the morning of 23 July 1637, and the first missiles launched were foot stools. They flew down the nave of St Giles's Cathedral in Edinburgh (the kirk of St Giles until the east and west walls had been removed to enlarge the church to proportions compatible with its new dignity), and their targets were the dean and the Bishop of Edinburgh. The reverend gentlemen had just begun to read from a new royally authorized Prayer Book. Even before the hurling of the stools, the attempt to read the liturgy had triggered a deafening outburst of shouting and wailing, especially from the many women gathered in the church. The minister John Row, who called the detestable object 'this Popish-English-Scottish-Mass-Service-Book', described keening cries of 'Woe, woe' and 'Sorrow, sorrow, for this doleful day, that they are bringing in Popery among us' ringing round the church. Terrified, the dean and bishop beat a swift retreat, but not before hands reached out in an attempt to strip the white surplices from their backs. In other churches in the city, such as the Old Kirk close by St Giles, the minister was barracked into silence; at Greyfriars the Bishop-designate of Argyll surrendered to a storm of abuse. In the afternoon the appearance of bishops and clergy was a sign for crowds to appear from nowhere, surrounding the nervous ministers, jostling and yelling their undying hatred of the 'Popish' liturgy.

The Prayer Book riots were not, of cou   spontaneous protest by the outraged common people of Scotland. The royal council had conveniently let it be known, months in advance, that the Prayer Book would be introduced by Easter 1637, which gave its opponents – Calvinist preachers and lords – time to organize their demonstration. Printing delays had postponed the date further, so that by July the trap was well set, and Archbishop Laud, his bishops, the council and the king innocently fell right in. They were caught completely off guard. As far as Charles I could see, Scotland was likely to be perfectly obedient to his ambition to create a single Arminian Church throughout Britain. Had not the Scottish parliament obliged him, if reluctantly, in

GIVE CAESAR HIS DUE?

Charles I in Three Positions, by Anthony Van Dyck, 1635–6.

The Prayer Book riots in St Giles's Cathedral, Edinburgh, 1637.

1633 when he had come to Edinburgh for his coronation (eight years after being crowned in Westminster)? To be sure, there had been some fuss in 1626 when he had revoked the land titles and grants of the Scottish nobility, but it was customary to do this every twenty-five years, before regranting them on terms spelled out by the new sovereign. What Charles had failed to notice was the intense resentment caused when it was made clear that some of those land grants transferred by the Reformation from Church to lay hands were now to be given back to establish endowments for the bishops. And the king had been much too complacent about the apparent lack of resistance to his 'book of canons', introduced in 1636, restricting preaching and giving dominant authority to the bishoprics.

But then Charles talked to all the wrong people in all the wrong places, to deracinated silk-coated London-Scottish noblemen like the Duke of Hamilton, or to his tough-minded treasurer in Edinburgh, the Earl of Traquair, who for the most part told him what he wanted to hear. The king had been born in the ancient royal abbey town of Dunfermline, but he was an absentee monarch who knew virtually nothing about the reality of Scotland and fatally misjudged the depth and breadth of its impassioned Calvinism. What he ought to have done was go to one of the little granite-grey towns of the southwest, such as Irvine, on a Monday marketday, and hear the full trumpet

blast of preachers like Robert Blair or David Dickson thundering against the iniquitous destruction of the godly Church by such as Archbishop Laud and his corrupt and
tyrannical lackeys, the bishops. The mere notion that the Church of Rome (as the
Arminians argued) was a 'true', if misguided, Church and not actually the abominable
institution of Antichrist, sent them into a paroxysm of wrath. Hard-pressed by the
official Church, often stripped of their livings, such men had become itinerant preachers, taking refuge with their equally fierce Presbyterian Scots brethren in Ulster, across
the North Channel. There, they were embraced into like-minded communities of
psalm-singers and scripture-readers. Despairing of the realm of the Stuarts, some of the
godly ministers had even decided to build their Jerusalem in Massachusetts and had
got as far as Newfoundland before being blown back by a tempest, which, needless to
say, they interpreted as God's design that they should, after all, do his work at home.
Back in Scotland they turned into so many Jeremiahs and Ezekiels, calling on God's
children to resist such abominations as surplices and kneeling and stone altars as if they
were the desecrations of Sodom.

Charles, however, was incapable of appreciating the power of Scottish Calvinism's
clarion call for a great purification. As far as the king was concerned, Scotland was not
all that different from England, and if the one had been bent to the royal will by well-
intentioned firmness, so might the other. But the Scottish Reformation, of course, had
been nothing at all like the slow, staccato progress of England's conversion to
Protestantism. Its Calvinism had struck in great electrifying bursts of charismatic conversion, backed up by teachers, lecturers and ministers, and only forced into reluctant
and periodic retreat by James I, who, unlike his son, had known when to stop. It was
an irony in the great holy shouting match of 1637-8, that *both* sides imagined they represented continuity not change. Charles and Laud thought they were building on the
Five Articles of Perth of 1618 and that the protesters were Presbyterian rebels who
sought to overthrow the whole royal supremacy of the Church. But ministers like
Samuel Rutherford, whose preaching at Anwoth had been so offensive that Bishop
Sydserf of Galloway had him banished to the safely conservative confines of Aberdeen,
believed that they were merely upholding a much more ancient covenant between
Scotland and God. That covenant was in every respect like the one made between God
and Israel but had specific roots in the (fictitious but immensely influential) history of
Scotland's conversion in the third century AD. According to those histories, the
Church had been received by the *community* before ever the first king, Fergus, had
begun his reign in the year 310. His sovereignty, then, had been conditional on acceptance of the covenant made between God and Scotland, the *original* godly nation –
before England and even before Rome.

Top: *Charles I and Henrietta Maria*, by Daniel Mytens, 1630–2.
Above: *Five Children of Charles I*, after Anthony van Dyck, 1637. From left to right: the Princesses Anne and Elizabeth, Prince Charles, the heir apparent, and baby Prince James in the arms of his sister, Princess Mary.

The National Covenant of Scotland, 1638.

This is what the likes of Blair and Dickson and Rutherford and countless other ministers preached, and this is what their flock fervently believed. Laud and the bishops were the filthy priests of Baal, who presumed to come between them and their covenant with the Almighty. For the moment, the king himself was given the benefit of the doubt, being led astray by 'evil counsel'. The Prayer Book riots in July 1637 and the still more startling events that followed were not meant to herald the overthrow of the house of Stuart. On the contrary, they were intended to reaffirm its sovereignty in Scotland but only on the understanding that that kingdom could not, and would not, be treated as a mere appendage of England. The hope, especially among the more moderate nobility, was that the unenforceability of the Prayer Book would persuade the king to listen to wise advice and retreat from his policy of 'innovations'. In fact, the Duke of Hamilton, who replaced Traquair as the king's principal commissioner in Scotland, warned the king in June 1638 to back away from further confrontation. Hamilton even had the prescience to predict to Charles that if he persisted trouble would not be confined to Scotland but would inevitably spread to all three of his kingdoms.

What Hamilton had witnessed since arriving in Scotland was the first revolutionary upheaval of seventeenth-century Britain. Even the organizers of the Prayer Book riots had been taken aback at the force and overwhelming popularity of the protests. Town officers did nothing about apprehending the rioters, other than briefly detaining a few of the serving women and apprentices who had made the loudest noise. But through the winter of 1637–8, the moment was seized to mobilize a great petitioning movement against the bishops, which caught up ministers, nobles, lairds and townsmen in its crusading fervour. A dissident group on the royal council in Scotland produced a 'Supplication' to the king, urging him to abandon the Laudian Church and replace it with a godly Presbyterian order. Charles's response was to assume that only some sort of foreign, probably French, influence could explain this temerity, to order the council out of the continuously riotous Edinburgh and to threaten to treat as traitors those who persisted in their opposition.

Instead of cowing the resistance, this response turned it into a revolution. On 28 February 1638 a 'National Covenant' was signed in a solemn, four-hour ceremony at Greyfriars Church, Edinburgh, full of prayers, psalms and sermons exhorting the godly to be the new Israel. Later that day it was exhibited at the Tailors' Hall on Cowgate, where it was signed by ministers and representatives from the towns. The next day the common people, including a substantial number of women, added their signatures, and copies were made to be sent throughout Scotland. Although the covenant at first sight seems to be written in the language of conservatism, claiming to protect the king's peace, it had been drafted in part by the uncompromising Calvinist lawyer Archibald Johnston. Johnston was the kind of dyspeptic, self-mortifying zealot who lay awake at night, tortured by the possibility that he might have one grain of impurity too many to qualify for the Elect, and who, on getting into bed with his teenage wife Jean, immediately assured God (out loud) that he preferred His face to hers. For Johnston, the covenant was 'the glorious marriage day of the kingdom with God', and he, like Samuel Rutherford, had no hesitation in assuming that kings could be lawfully called to account and if necessary removed if ever they should violate *that* marriage bed.

For countless thousands of Scots, signing the covenant was just an extension of the vows they took 'banding' them with God in the Kirk, but the document itself rapidly assumed the status of a kind of patriotic scripture, a way of determining who was truly Christian and who not, who was a true Scot and who not. Belatedly, Hamilton attempted to organize a 'King's Covenant' as a moderate riposte, and he managed to secure some 28,000 signatures, proof that, as in so many other crucial turning points in Scotland's history, the country was divided rather than united in its response. But it seems extremely unlikely that Charles himself ever thought of the 'King's Covenant' as anything more than a tactical manoeuvre while he mobilized enough force to bring the Scots to heel. And by late 1638, most of Scotland was already borne aloft in the whirlwind. A righteously intoxicated general assembly in Glasgow, where Johnston served as chief clerk, went the whole distance, effectively severing all connections between the English government and the Scottish Church: it abolished bishops and the rest of the Laudian establishment. Then the Scottish parliament, which first met in August 1639 and reconvened without royal permission in June 1640, introduced three-yearly parliaments, whether or not they were called by the king.

None of the Covenanters could have been under much illusion about what Charles I's response to the Glasgow assembly would be. Their own view was that they threatened nothing, presumed no interference in the affairs of England (although, as part of the international Calvinist defence against the Counter-Reformation, they could not but hope that they might set an example for Presbyterians south of the border). If, on the other hand, the king of England came in arms to undo their godly Reformation, they would, of course, defend it with their lives. And proper precautionary measures were quickly taken through the winter and spring of 1638–9 to see to this defence. The veteran soldier of the religious wars in Europe, General Alexander Leslie, was made commander of their forces; money was borrowed from the banker William Dick to buy munitions and powder from the Dutch; castles and strongholds were transferred from royal to Covenanter authority; and the local networks that had produced signatures for the petitions and covenant – the towns and villages of Scotland – were now mined to produce money and men. Charles and Laud had really managed something quite unique: they had contrived to unite two parties, the Kirk and the lords, who were more naturally accustomed to quarrelling. And two sets of loyalties, the Church and the clan, could be used to produce a godly army. By the spring of 1639 that army numbered at least 25,000 and perhaps as many as 30,000 men.

On the other side of the border it proved much harder to get an army together, let alone a force that could be relied on to strike terror into the hearts of the Scots (or at least persuade them to abandon the Covenant). Sir Edmund Verney, who by now was much more the country gentleman than the courtier, enjoyed nothing more than to tend his estate at Claydon in Buckinghamshire, and to keep company with his wife Mary and their rapidly expanding family. But he was still officially Knight Marshal, a member of the Privy Chamber, and therefore duty bound, however reluctantly, to answer the royal summons to attend the king at York, 'as a cuirassier in russett armes, with guilded studds or nayles, and befittingly horsed', despite his deep misgivings about the wisdom and propriety of the king's and Laud's policies. His eldest son, Ralph, was even less happy about his father (who was, in any case, in poor health) risking his life to enforce contentious doctrines of which he himself rather disapproved and which were best left to the divines to thrash out. Ralph could hardly have been reassured by his father making his will before leaving Claydon, nor by letters, which his father worried might be opened before reaching him, describing military disaster in the making: 'Our Army is butt weake; our Purce is butt weaker; and if wee fight with thes foarces and early in the yeare wee shall have our throats cutt.' The learned Thomas Howard, Earl Marshal Arundel, seemed to be better equipped to collect art and antiquities than to lead an army, for he led the king on to fight without warning him of the dire condition of the troops. 'I dare saye ther was never soe Raw, soe unskilfull and soe unwilling an Army brought to fight,' wrote Sir Edmund witheringly of Arundel.

My lord marshall himselfe will, I dare saye, bee safe, and then he cares not what becomes of the rest; trewly here are manny brave Gentlemen that for poynt of honor must runn such a hazard as trewly would greeve any heart but his that does it purposely to ruine them. For my owne parte I have lived till paine and trouble has made mee weary to doe soe; and the woarst that can come shall not bee unwellcome to mee; but it is a pitty to see what men are like to be slaughterd here unless it shall pleas god to putt it in the king's Hearte to increase his Army

Thomas Howard, Second Earl of Arundel and Surrey, by Peter Paul Rubens, 1629.

or staye till thes may knowe what they doe; for as yett they are like to kill theyr fellows as the enemye.

Verney was not exaggerating. The machinery of mustering the trained bands in the Midlands and northern counties to make up the English army was showing signs of imminent breakdown. It was proving difficult, and in some cases impossible, to raise the ship money that had been extended into the inland counties. County commissioners for troops and sheriffs for ship money were disappearing or protesting the impossibility of delivering funds. The men themselves – trained bands of literate artisans, such as clothiers – often failed to show up at the mustering places, and replacements had to be rounded up from wherever the impressment officers could find them. They, too, failed to understand why they were being called on to fight this 'bishops' war'. The trained bands were supposed to be called out strictly in defence of the realm against invasion, and it was known, not least from the propaganda the Covenanters were already circulating south of the border, that the Scots had explicitly disavowed any such aim. The reluctance of the trained bands was shared by many of their social superiors and officers. The king sensed this strained loyalty but only made matters worse by demanding of his officers an oath of loyalty, which the Puritan nobles, Viscount Saye and Sele and Lord Brooke (of Oxfordshire and Warwickshire respectively), point blank refused. The dissident nobles were immediately imprisoned in York for their shocking rejection of the royal command, thus covering themselves with glory among the godly. As for the rank and file, it was, as Sir Edmund Verney noted, a surly, underpaid (in many cases unpaid), poorly armed, wretchedly led force that trudged north from York towards the border.

At Kelso, just inside Scottish territory, all of Verney's pessimism seemed borne out. A small force of cavalry, led by the Earl of Holland and including Sir Edmund himself, was confronted by what seemed at first a manageably modest Scots army. But as Holland got his men into battle order the Scots army seemed to grow before their eyes, pikemen and dragoons and horse becoming more and more numerous until it was appallingly obvious that any kind of engagement would end in a calamitous rout. Hastily, Holland withdrew his troops to camp where they (necessarily) exaggerated the size of the waiting enemy. Charles, whose own mood had gone from supercilious complacency to grim irritation at the news of discontent and desertion, now thought better of an impetuous campaign. The Scots' request to clarify their own position (for they did not at any time consider themselves rebels) was accepted, and a meeting of delegations organized at Berwick-on-Tweed in June 1639. Charles himself appeared at this meeting, where he had his first chance to encounter the full, glaring Calvinist hostility of Archibald Johnston. As usual, the king's idea of diplomacy was to chide the Scots for their 'pretended' assembly and to concede nothing, except that the issues might be aired and, it was hoped, resolved by the calling of a Scottish parliament rather than on the field of battle. Pending that resolution, both armies were to be disbanded. Johnston suspected that this was merely a ploy on the part of the king to play for time, and he had the bad manners to say so, more or less to his face. But suspicious or not, a 'Pacification' was duly signed. The ink was hardly dry before Johnston's scepticism was vindicated as Charles made it known that he would expect a new general assembly to be called that would nullify all the reforms of Glasgow.

In Scotland in July that year there were near riots when the terms of the Pacification became known, since it was felt not unreasonably that an opportunity to defeat the king had been frittered away and that the Scots were now locked into a truce, pending the onset of a round of more serious warfare. And perhaps, for a time, Charles may have been smilingly deluded, imagining that he had got the better of the Scots tactically and would shortly get the better of them militarily, too. For he was now listening to the counsellor he thought would without question bring him victory, vindication and retribution against the Covenanters: Thomas Wentworth, his Lord Deputy in Ireland. Wentworth had been a kind of miracle for the king. From being one of his most aggressive critics in parliament, he had become the most unflagging and uncompromising upholder of the absolutism of the Crown. Psychologically, Charles must have felt that the flinty, saturnine Wentworth was truly one of his own: a man who understood that the destiny of the Crown was to apply the balm of royal adjudication to nations hurting from confessional wounds. Except that the Wentworth medicine invariably had a nasty sting to it. Those who begged to differ with the Lord Deputy found themselves smartly disadvantaged: their land title investigated, their property taken, themselves in prison. But the policy of 'thorough' had kept Ireland quiet, and that in itself was a recommendation for his understanding of the obscure and irate war of the sects – Old English Catholics, Ulster Presbyterians, Gaelic Irish. As far as Charles could see, Wentworth had kept the royal ship of state sailing high above the fray like some celestial galleon in a court masque. So when he gave the king advice about the Scottish crisis, Charles paid attention. Call a parliament, Wentworth advised. Without it, your army will never be well supplied nor the country truly disposed to fight the war. And fear not. Parliaments, however truculent they might seem, are manageable, especially when the defence of the realm can be legitimately invoked. To show the king what could be done, in March 1640 Wentworth called an Irish parliament at Dublin, which behaved like a lamb, the Old English voting with enough New English to produce solid majorities and fat little subsidies for the Crown. Strategy two was admittedly a little trickier. Wentworth was proposing to use an Irish army to deal with the Scottish rebellion. The only problem was how disciplined troops in numbers sufficient to make any impact on the Scottish war could be expeditiously raised. Needless to say, they could hardly be drawn from the New English and Scottish Presbyterians of the Ulster plantation, whose sympathies were all with the Covenant.

A solution was at Charles's right hand in the shape of Randal Macdonnell, the Marquis of Antrim. He was a unique figure in northern Ireland, a native Irish Catholic, but one who had profited from Wentworth's bargain, by which his own fortunes were expanded to the degree to which he made room for planters on his enormous estates. At the same time, Antrim had become a familiar, if not entirely trusted, figure in the inner circles of Charles's court. So when he offered to raise his own native Irish army to be put at the king's disposal Charles was tempted to take the proposal very seriously, even though Wentworth had deep misgivings about what he considered to be a low, barbarian Catholic force, 'with as many "Os" and "Macs" as would startle a whole council board', claiming to do the work of the king. Should the gamble not pay off, he had an all too clear vision of how the idea of a semi-private Catholic army deployed against the godly Covenanters would play in England!

From the beginning then, even Wentworth could see that the two arms of the king's strategy – a parliament and a native, predominantly Catholic-Irish army – might turn out to be in glaring contradiction to each other. But the king was not thinking logically. In fact, he was not thinking at all, just dreaming dreams of vindication and victory: the Grand Harmonization of Britannia virtually within reach.

Step one was the calling of a parliament in April 1640. Encouraged by Wentworth and Laud, Charles was confident that the interrupted but unresolved crisis with Scotland would ensure an assembly that, as in Ireland, would discuss only the matters proposed by the king and, after such discussion, produce adequate supplies for his armies. He also seems to have felt that his eleven years of personal rule had actually made this docility more, rather than less, likely, since the country had been exposed to the wisdom, energy, benevolence and disinterested justice of his sovereignty. And since he believed that the Covenanters had been in touch with the king of France, all he would have to do would be to flourish evidence of this revival of the notorious 'auld alliance' and the country would rise to the defence of the realm. Shades of the Plantagenets and the Bruces (albeit with the odd outcome of the Stuarts fighting against, rather than for, the independence of Scotland)!

It must have come as an unpleasant shock, then, when this new parliament, far from putting old, imagined grievances aside, immediately resurrected them. Virtually the first order of the day was their summoning of the records of the proceedings against Sir John Eliot, whose death in the Tower of London had not been forgotten but had been religiously remembered as a martyrdom suffered for the people's liberty. However extreme, this was precisely the way in which the fate of Eliot and a whole pantheon of victims of Laud's Court of High Commission and of Star Chamber appeared in the newsletters and 'separates' that were distributed around the provinces. For the newsmongers Eliot made wonderful copy, and there was a steady supply of victims and heroes to join him, men whose stories were celebrated in the newsletters as chapters in a scripture of godly liberty. Some of them like the obdurate, steely lawyer, William Prynne, had done everything they could to court persecution. Prynne's *Histrio-Mastix* had been a scathing attack on the court and in particular on the masques in which the king and queen liked to appear as dancers. More danger-ously, in the course of the polemic Prynne had asserted a doctrine of resistance (shared by both ultra-Catholic and Calvinist theorists) by which a prince plainly resolved to violate God's laws might be set aside. For his sedition Prynne was sentenced in 1634 to have his ears sliced off, pay a fine of £5000 and spend the rest of his life in the Tower of London. In London and in strongly Puritan communities like Dorchester the irascible, unstoppable Prynne became an immediate saint, his epistle broadcast through the network of the godly from Ulster to Scotland. In 1637 the government blunderingly reinforced and perpetuated his popularity by dragging Prynne out of the Tower to stand in the pillory along with Dr Henry Burton – the Puritan rector of St Matthew, Friday Street, London – who had preached sermons on a popish plot and the evils of the Church, and John Bastwick, another active sympathizer, who likewise refused to remain silent. Both the new malefactors had their ears cut off – no deter-rent to Burton who defiantly continued to preach while profusely bleeding, or so the Puritan Apocrypha had it.

Nehemiah Wallington, a devout wood-turner living in the parish of St Andrew's Hubbard, Eastcheap, believed every word of the gospel according to Prynne and began a 2000-page account of the sins and events of his times, including an encomium to the earless martyrs, Burton and Bastwick. In Wallington's tight little universe nothing could possibly happen without some sort of providential meaning. A boating accident was God's punishment for the profanation of the Sabbath; a storm that broke the stained-glass windows of a church His judgement on gaudy idolatry. Prynne, Burton and Bastwick had obviously been called to preach against the uncleanness of the times, and their torments were a sign that great days of reckoning were nigh. In this fevered world miracles, portents and signs abounded. A conversation set down in Wallington's book suggests just how intensely he and his fellow Puritan artisans felt the coming of the battle between the children of God and the legions of Antichrist. No sooner had one of these heretics finished denouncing the three as 'base schismatical jacks' who deserved hanging for troubling the kingdom, than he suddenly fell into a terrible sweat with blood pouring from his ears. Wallington's sense that Prynne, Burton and Bastwick were fighting the good fight, *his* fight, was brought home all too directly when he was named, along with the three others in a charge of seditious libel and ordered to answer for it before the court of Star Chamber in 1639. But his own ears survived the ordeal, and he lived to join the triumphal celebrations in the streets of London that greeted the liberation of Bastwick, ordered by parliament at the end of 1640.

The gallery of resistance heroes took in all social types and conditions, from dissident minor clergy like Peter Smart, who had lost his position as prebend at Durham Cathedral and had been fined £500 for attacking Bishop Neile's innovations in ceremony, to the Buckinghamshire gentleman and MP John Hampden (the guardian of Eliot's children) who had refused to pay the 20 shilling ship-money assessment on one of his estates and had gone to court to test its legality. Although the King's Bench had found against Hampden in 1638, it had done so by only seven votes to five, and both the impassioned arguments of his lawyer, Oliver St John, and the dissenting judgement of Judge George Croke added to what was rapidly becoming a canon of virtue: men who exemplified the counsel given in one of John White's sermons at Holy Trinity, Dorchester, that 'obedience to the will of God discharges a man from performing the will of the ruler'.

Unlike Prynne or White, John Hampden was not some abrasive and unworldly hothead but a well-respected county figure whose strength and clarity of opinion about the illegality of non-parliamentary taxes made essentially moderate gentlemen from the same county, like the Verneys, think very seriously about the constituitional price to be paid for obedience to the king. The Buckinghamshire members elected to parliament in 1640 no longer looked like a bunch of backwoods provincial knights and burgesses concerned first and foremost with parish-pump affairs and loyally willing to do the king's business. From militant Puritans, like Bulstrode Whitelocke, to Hampden himself and the Verneys, there was at the group's core a highly literate and politically articulate group, intensely tuned to national politics – indeed, who made no distinction at all between the affairs of the county and those of the nation. There were, of course, shades of opinion between them. While he felt the times did call for reform, Sir Edmund was less impatient for it than his son, Ralph, who would make a chronicle of the doings of the Long Parliament and who evidently felt that one of the great moments in the country's history was at hand. But father and son were not (yet) estranged. Hampden's case may have changed nothing on the law books in respect of the legality of non-parliamentary taxes, but it had changed a lot of minds. The very conditions of the personal rule had ensured that the king and his councillors would keep themselves ignorant of the many ways in which a genuine public opinion in England was in the process of being formed. And like so much of the radicalization of English politics, the catalyst travelled south in the form of broadsheets printed in Scotland by the busily righteous Covenanter press. Occasionally, there are documentary glimpses of just how quickly a politicized reading public was forming. At Radwinter in Essex an unknown man marched up to the curate in a Laudian church and threw a Puritan pamphlet on his desk, saying, 'There is reading work for you, read that.' In Stepney in 1640 another minister found a man reading the printed proceedings of parliament in his churchyard. But until it was much too late, in the winter of 1641–2, the royal government thought no more of these 'ephemera' than of the vulgar gossip of the impotent common people.

They were fatally deluded. The talk-filled, rumour-ridden, preachy, preternaturally suspicious, gossipy world of news was already giving the rough kiss of life to institutions that had been politically inert for generations. For the first time in living memory, elections for knights of the shire were being contested in the counties, sometimes hotly. The government did everything it could to influence the poll to produce members who would be as tractable as Wentworth's Irish parliament in Dublin, but where it faced money and local power from a determined opposition it almost invariably lost. In Dorset, for example, a great campaign was waged to elect Dudley Carleton, son of the English ambassador to the Dutch court at The Hague, in place of Denzil Holles, but it failed, and Holles was returned, more determined than ever to bring court and council to a reckoning before the representatives of the 'country'. The regime fared no better in the boroughs. In Cornwall, where loyalty to the king was usually thought fierce, government support was the kiss of death to all eight candidates recommended by it. And the elections in 1640, for both the April and November parliaments, began to turn up men from a much broader social circle (and much more strongly partisan religious colouring) than the usual gentlemanly MP. In counties like Warwickshire and Oxfordshire the Puritan nobles – Brooke, and Saye and Sele – spent money and knocked heads together to secure the election of godly members, many of them famous local resisters of ship money. In December 1639 Brooke apparently even had the audacity to try to bring to Warwick, Samuel Rutherford, the Covenanter preacher, whose *Lex rex,* published just five years later, made it clear that he thought political authority was 'a birthright of the people, borrowed from them; they may let it out for their own good and resume it when a man is drunk with it'.

By the 1630s Puritanism was not just a manner of worship. It was an entire subculture, which began in the cradle of the family hearth, embraced and enclosed men, women and children within its godly vision and conditioned the way they saw the political world. Crucially, for the future of Britain, that unity of vision cut across the old lines of social rank and deferential hierarchies. Puritan aristocrats like Brooke felt themselves to have far more in common with humble preachers and teachers than with their fellow nobles. These families raised their children on a common literature, sent them to the same kind of schools and to exemplary godly colleges like Emmanuel and Sidney Sussex in Cambridge, and ensured that they made godly marriages, perpetuating the cohesion of their tight little world and sealing it off, they hoped, from infection by worldly pragmatism and temptation. And, most important, they did business together, not exclusively to be sure, but often decisively, and those businesses could sometimes germinate something other than just money. In fact, they could lose money and still be profoundly fruitful for the common enterprises of the children of God. Throughout the 1630s, for example, virtually all those who would shape the destinies of political Puritanism in parliament – John Pym, John Hampden, his lawyer Oliver St John, Sir Arthur Haselrig, Lord Brooke, Viscount Saye and Sele, the earls of Bedford and Essex and, ubiquitously, Robert Rich, the colossally important and powerful Earl of Warwick – were all involved in ventures to create settlements in the Caribbean and New England. The Providence Island Company in the Caribbean, which was eventually destroyed by the Spanish (thus confirming the Puritan view of the world as a crusade between Christ and Antichrist), was the most intensively organized of their ventures. But the two lords/nobles also created the Saye-Brooke settlement on Long Island Sound, and most of them (especially Warwick) were in regular correspondence with the most promising colony of all, planted on Massachusetts Bay and including at least a dozen of the Dorchester godly in its complement of emigrants in March 1630. It had been John White who had preached the farewell sermon at Plymouth's 'New Hospital'. The deliberation on the government of those settlements in New England was, for the founding fathers back home, akin to a seminar on political theory, a learned speculation on the possibility of the shared Christian life. Across the Atlantic, in a cleaner, godlier world, schools and colleges would thrive, a true Zion would plant its seed. And those days and years of long-distance stewardship could only have encouraged them to think in like manner of making in England itself, should God so will it, a new Jerusalem.

These men were very much a minority, but being of the Elect they expected to be a minority: the redemption caucus. They gloried in their slightness of numbers as if they were the self-purifying troop of Gideon's army. (The analogy was often invoked.) Modern history is full of such intensely motivated minorities with a self-conscious martyr complex and a talent for collective self-promotion. With the right

Top: In *The First Act* of a satirical play, *c.* 1630, William Laud dines off the ears of Prynne and a fellow sufferer.
Above, left: *John Pym*, by Samuel Cooper, *c.* 1630.
Above, right: *Robert Rich, Second Earl of Warwick* (detail), studio of Daniel Mytens, *c.* 1630.

independent historical conditions, where their adversarial regimes have been weakened, such little legions of the righteous can move mountains. And that was precisely what happened in the astounding unravelling of the Stuart monarchy between 1640 and 1642.

Right from the opening of the 'Short Parliament', from 13 April to 5 May 1640, it was apparent that those who saw themselves appointed by God to deliver the country from the Antichrist had managed to persuade a much larger and more moderate phalanx of members, both in the Lords and in the Commons, that their view of the endangered liberties of the subject was historically accurate. The diaries and correspondence of peers and gentry, by no means all of them hot Presbyterians, are full of commonplace remarks to the effect that thorns had to be removed from the feet of the kingdom before it could walk; that ulcerous veins needed cleansing before the body (politic) could be healed. Edward Hyde, later the die-hard royalist Clarendon, along with his friend and patron, Viscount Falkland of Great Tew, and the legal scholar John Selden, were at this time, like so many of their fellows, convinced of the imperative necessity of reform and of a government that could rest securely on the confidence of parliament And although the notion of the outright abolition of the episcopacy, following the Covenanters, was still a shockingly radical proposal in England, there was a surprising degree of agreement that they needed taking down a peg from their Laudian loftiness. Bishops like John Williams of Lincoln, who, in the tradition of George Abbot, Laud's predecessor at Canterbury, had always seen Rome rather than Geneva as the enemy, who claimed to be the true custodians of the Tudor Reformation and had been prosecuted and imprisoned for their outspokenness, were now very much listened to.

The likelihood, then, that parliament would tamely hand over to the king the money he needed to resume the Scottish war and crush the impertinent and rebellious Covenanters was precisely nil. Charles grandly offered to forgo ship money (no hardship since by 1639 it had proved virtually impossible to collect) if parliament voted him twelve subsidies (later reduced to four). This was immediately treated as a bad joke. Relatively moderate members of the Commons, like Sir Harbottle Grimston, a great friend of the Verneys, insisted on the redress of grievances (not least the status of the courts of Star Chamber and High Commission), before any thought of a money bill could be entertained. On 17 April John Pym embarked on a lengthy frontal attack on the infamies he said had been perpetrated by the administration during the eleven years of personal rule, concentrating especially on the affronts done to religion by the Laudian 'innovations'. It was Pym, more than any other of the Commons' tribunes, who would contribute to the sense, both in April and in

News transmitted from London to Lord Conway, 1640. A scribal report of news covering events in the Short Parliament of 1640.

November 1640, when another parliament was called, that something like a national emergency was at hand, with the allied forces of popery and despotism planning an assault on the liberties of the English subject. And increasingly, inside the House and on the streets of London, where men like Nehemiah Wallington were all ears, John Pym was believed.

Fuming with frustration, the king dissolved parliament barely three weeks after it had been called. This was a tactical blunder of monumental proportions, since nothing is quite so inflammatory as the abrupt interruption of raised expectations. Both Wentworth (whose idea the parliament had been) and Edward Hyde immediately understood the decision as the political disaster it undoubtedly was: a priceless opportunity to settle problems within the traditional framework of king-in-parliament carelessly thrown away. But Charles had heard all the ranting and raving in 1629, and it had gone away when parliament did. He still blindly assumed that his real problem was Edinburgh, not Westminster, and that unless he destroyed the Covenanters – and swiftly, too – the contagion of their Calvinism and their apparently contractual notions of monarchy would spread like the plague south to England. He was, in fact, quite right (Pym was in treasonable correspondence with the Covenanter leaders, as were also Saye and Sele). But he chose the worst of all possible options: to fight the Scots without any idea of whether his army (which had looked so shaky the year before) was in any condition to follow him. At the back of Charles's mind, of course, was Wentworth's contingency plan to use the Irish to do the job for him, and in the course of the summer campaign against the Scots he appointed Wentworth Commander-in-Chief, having already raised him, in January 1640, to the earldom of Strafford, an honour that turned out to be a poisoned chalice. To discount the effect that Strafford's Irish strategy would have on the anti-Catholic propaganda fast spreading through London, presupposed a truly breathtaking obtuseness on the king's part. He had not listened to the sensible people in Scotland in 1638, and he was not listening to the sensible people now. The only person he was listening to, other than himself, was his Catholic queen.

What immediately followed in the summer of 1640 was a breakdown of deference of frightening magnitude. With no pay and none in the offing, the soldiers who were mustered in the Midlands and north imposed themselves on their billets in a bad temper and with growling bellies. In a number of towns, such as Hereford, the citizens rose in indignation and ran them out of town. Looking for someone to blame for their real distress, the rank-and-file soldiers turned on their own officers, especially any of them tainted as Catholics or Irish. Ugly scenes became commonplace. In Wellington, Somerset, a lieutenant suspected of being a Catholic was cut to pieces and the dead body robbed. In Faringdon, Oxfordshire, another officer was beaten senseless by soldiers from

Dorset (including a number from Dorchester), and when he was found to be receiving medical attention was pulled through the streets and beaten again, this time fatally. What was left of the mangled corpse was set in the stocks for posthumous abuse. As for their religious dependability as an anti-Calvinist army, the soldiery showed exactly what they thought of that by smashing communion table rails, altars and stained-glass windows and ripping surplices off clergy when they found them. Young Edmund Verney wrote to his father that he had to go to church three times in a day to assure his men that he was no papist, 'But once that day I a little nodded at church and had it been a minute longer truely I doe thinke I had been pulled by the nose, for the souldyers pointed extreamely at me.' To any foreign observer it must have seemed for all the world that the English troopers were the allies, not the enemies, of the Covenanters. 'Whereas before our soldiers would go against Scotland,' noted Nehemiah Wallington, 'now not any that I know of in this land would go.'

The disorder was rapidly spiralling out of control. The trained bands opened the gaols where men who had refused to pay the 'coat and conduct' money for their supply had been incarcerated. Other sections of society, equally alienated by the government, took the opportunity to make their point violently against those who enclosed common land or had chased them out of the forests. None of these aggrieved populations was logically connected, but it didn't matter – they were all hunting for someone to blame – and together they persuaded the men responsible for keeping law and order intact, the justices of the peace and the constables, that royal government as it had been constituted over the past eleven years was a broken reed.

In the circumstances it was hardly surprising that the war was a humiliating fiasco for the English. The commander of the Covenanters, General Leslie, knew exactly what he was doing, crossing the Tweed into England on 20 August and aiming for Newcastle to cut off the coal supply to the metropolitan heart of England. Leslie had now given the lie to the Scots' claims of fighting a defensive war, a nicety swept aside in the reality of the conflict. At Newburn, where the English army attempted to make a stand on the banks of the Tyne, Leslie's army, commanding the higher northern bank, raked the English with fire, sending the survivors reeling back to York, while the Scots occupied Newcastle and then Durham. The day after the ignominious defeat at Newburn, a group of inner-core parliamentarians – Oliver St John, Pym, Saye and Sele, Warwick and Brooke – and the earls of Essex and Bedford met at Bedford House in London to draft a petition, in the name of the twelve peers, calling for a new parliament. Manuscript copies were widely circulated around the city and provinces. Charles attempted to find some other way, any other way, to finance another campaign without calling a parliament, but a meeting of nobles made him understand that the war was lost and, since the Scots were demanding an indemnity as the price for evacuating England and releasing the coal supply, only a parliament could possibly supply those funds. On 24 September 1640, pre-empting another grand meeting of the lords, which would certainly have reiterated the demand for a parliament, the king conceded. It would meet on 3 November and would remain in session, in one form and another, until it had ended the life of Charles I and the monarchy along with it.

For Nehemiah Wallington the autumn of 1640 was the time of rosemary. Bunches of the grey-green herb, together with conquerors' garlands of bay, showered down on the heads of Burton, Prynne, Bastwick and Bishop Williams, who had been liberated – Bastwick from Scilly, the rest from the Tower – and paraded triumphantly through the packed streets of London. Rosemary was for remembrance, and how this parliament remembered! Almost immediately it continued the note struck in April by establishing forty committees of investigation into those responsible for illegal and arbitrary acts: ship money, the prerogative courts of Star Chamber and the Church's High Commission. But there were two designated villains on whom parliament concentrated its prosecutorial wrath: Strafford and Laud. Attacking the king by proxy, through his chosen counsellors, was of course a time-honoured way of making the Crown reverse course while still preserving intact the dignity and independence of its sovereignty. In both houses of parliament in 1640 there was a substantial majority for impeaching both men as well as the next rank of councillors, such as Lord Keeper Finch, and courtiers, such as Bishop Wren of Ely, as a way of marking the irreversible end of the Laudian Church and the years of personal rule. But beyond that, there was a serious division about what the impeachment, especially of Strafford, was supposed to accomplish. For men like Viscount Falkland and Edward Hyde the impeachment was essentially therapeutic and restorative. By concentrating the odium for unpopular government, the king had been given a chance to embrace a reformed version of his government, one that would rule together with a responsible parliament and through councillors who enjoyed the confidence of parliament. Their reform programme was corrective: the elimination of what they considered to be either imprudent and alien innovations (the Laudian Church regime and extra-parlimentary taxation) or obsolete institutions that had been shamelessly abused for power and gain (the prerogative courts, the forest regime and the knighthood fines). Clear them away, and you gave the monarchy a fresh start.

But for the most visible, audible and energetic group – Pym, Oliver St John, Sir Arthur Haselrig from Leicestershire, Brooke, Saye and Sele – who took control of the parliamentary agenda from the beginning, this was not, and would never be, enough.

Only Zion sufficed. The destruction of Laud would be a pyrrhic victory unless it got rid of the institution of the episcopacy altogether and replaced it by a godly Presbyterian Church, much as the Scots, whom they now treated openly as allies, had done. (When the king at the opening of parliament rashly referred to them as 'rebels' he was forced to retract the forbidden word a week later.) On 11 December a petition (petitioning having become a major weapon in the mobilization of opinion) on behalf of the City of London demanding the abolition of the episcopacy, 'root and branch', was presented to parliament. Pym was much too astute to press the issue on the Commons, knowing how divisive it would be and wanting to protect a tactical majority for Strafford's impeachment. The radical controlling minority also had something much more far reaching in mind when they considered the restructuring of the constitutional relationship between Crown and parliament, in effect, a Scottish programme for England – beginning with a triennial act, requiring the summoning of parliament every three years. When Charles signed the triennial act on 15 February 1641, he completed a circle of pure political futility. The war he had launched to suppress the Covenant and its works had succeeded only in transplanting it to England. Pym and his like-minded colleagues also wanted to make membership of the government not merely subject to parliamentary veto but directly *accountable* before the Lords and Commons and incapable of acting contrary to the expressed will of its majority. No longer would parliament be little more than a tax-sanctioning or denying body. Henceforth the Lords and Commons, as much as the king, would set the agenda. Henceforth it would be a legislator. No one was pretending yet that it could legislate without the king, but no one imagined that the king could legislate or choose his councillors in defiance of parliament. Pym was being spoken of (if Charles had any sense) as a possible future member of the Privy Council.

Huge amounts of ink and paper have been used to insist that this kind of alteration was no revolution at all. But to treat it as a mere adjustment absurdly shortchanges its overwhelming novelty. It's quite possible, as a fresh generation of historians has bravely reminded us, to be so frightened of committing Whiggery, of reading history backwards that we fail to give disruption its due. The fact that the authors and instruments of these profound changes had, until the last minute, little inkling of their long-term consequences does not for a minute dilute their significance. Revolutions invariably begin by sounding conservative and nostalgic, their protagonists convinced that they are suppressing, not unloosing, innovation. There's nothing so inflammatory as a call for the return of an imagined realm of virtue and justice.

To look at the doings and utterances of the Long Parliament, and at the immense political upheaval unfolding in the streets of London and on its printing presses, is to be convinced that its protagonists were correct in their belief that they were engaged in a battle of principles over both Church and state and that the outcome would be as momentous as the crisis that produced Magna Carta, a document often on their lips. This was not, of course, the birth of parliamentary democracy (not even the most Whiggish of the Victorian historians ever supposed so), but it was, unquestionably, the demolition of absolute monarchy in Britain. And it was the prospect of this that filled the hearts of men such as the Earl of Warwick, Sir Robert Harley, Oliver St John and Oliver Cromwell MP with racing excitement.

This revolution had no manifesto until the Grand Remonstrance of November 1641. Instead, it had a trial. Almost invariably great political upheavals require an arch-malefactor against whom the righteous can define themselves in new community, and the Scottish peace negotiators, received warmly by the parliamentary leaders even though their armies were occupying much of northern England, made it quite clear that they wanted Strafford's head for threatening their own revolution with an invasion of Irish Catholics. Robert Baillie, a relatively moderate Scots Calvinist, had no hesitation in referring to Laud and Strafford as 'incendiaries' who, if left at liberty or even alive, would never stop until they had reduced the country to a papist despotism. And Pym himself had enough respect for Strafford's formidable abilities to know that his own reconstruction of English politics could move safely ahead only when the earl was permanently out of the way. Moreover, Strafford's peculiar success in impartially alienating each of the three Irish communities (something he was rather proud of) now left him with no friends.

All the same, he would not be an obliging scapegoat. To stereotype Strafford as 'Black Tom Tyrant', the thuggish bully of the personal rule, was to make a terrible mistake. This was, after all, still the Thomas Wentworth who in the late 1620s had mounted a passionate attack against the forced loan, a man who had at least as deep an understanding of the law as the barrister John Pym. Strafford knew that Pym needed a full public show trial, duly observant of the procedures of the law, to uphold the superiority of justice over force, and he also knew that his prosecutors would have the greatest difficulty in turning criticisms of his administration in Ireland into acts of treason. Alone in the Tower, pondering his chances, Strafford nursed precisely the touching faith in the impartiality of the law and of English justice that his vilifiers claimed he had so consistently abused. How could he possibly be condemned, he must have asked himself, for violations of laws not yet passed when the alleged violations were committed, for acts of state that, at the time, were perfectly in keeping with the king's expressed will?

Through the seven weeks of the trial in the House of Lords, from March to April

Top: *Thomas Wentworth and his Secretary, Sir Philip Mainwaring*, by Anthony van Dyck, *c.* 1634.
Above: *The True Manner of Sitting of the Lords and Commons*, engraved by Wenceslaus Hollar, 1641.

1641, Strafford, not looking at all the part of Tom Tyrant, grey-whiskered and obviously sick, his head covered in a fur-lined cap, conducted his own defence with compelling logic, tearing apart all the inconsistencies and weaknesses in the evidence
presented by his prosecutors. It was easy enough to demonstrate that he had walked
roughshod over all kinds of persons and interests in Ireland – the Irish Catholics, by
continuing to dispossess their lands (not that anyone in the English parliament minded
that); the Old English, by seeking to expand the plantations into Connacht and tres-
pass on the Pale; most damagingly, the Ulster-Presbyterian Scots and English, by
strengthening the episcopal Church of Ireland and regulating their trade – but none
of it amounted to treason. On the contrary, it had all been done to maintain the king's
authority as loyally, impartially and firmly as was within his legitimate power as Lord
Deputy. The only count among the twenty-eight charges remotely capable of making
the case for treason was number twenty-three, which rested on a remark, said to have
been uttered by Strafford, that he would send an Irish army to 'reduce this kingdom'.
It had never been a secret that this had been part of the strategy to achieve victory
over the Scots, and Strafford reasonably argued that at the time, in the spring and
summer of 1640, the two nations had still been at war. The gravamen of the charge,
suggested by the New English planter from Antrim, Sir John Clotworthy, was that by
'this kingdom' Strafford had actually meant England, not Scotland, and that he had
sought to destroy parliament and the liberties of the people through an armed *coup
d'État*. That would, indeed, have constituted treason. Strafford continued to deny that
he had ever intended such a thing for England and to attack the credibility of verbal
testimony, at which point a written note containing the same ominous phrase was
introduced in evidence by Harry Vane the younger, who had discovered in the papers
of his father, the Secretary to the Council, the records of the meeting in which Strafford
had suggested bringing over the Irish army. But it was not in Strafford's hand, merely a
note claimed to be a verbatim, contemporary record, and by mid-April it was far from
clear that the Vane note, by itself, would be enough to convict as long as the trial continued to be conducted according to the regular conventions of impeachment.

But Strafford's trial was, of course, not at all a normal judicial event, more a public
theatre of disgrace and retribution. Every day the House of Lords and the streets and
courtyards around it in Westminster were packed with huge crowds, hungry for news
of the day's events. Handbills, broadsides and improvised petitions created a sea of
paper for the crowd to wade through. Ballads were sung; sermons were preached
against the pope-friendly Strafford. Nehemiah Wallington, who was among an
immense throng flocking to the House of Lords at the beginning of May to petition
for the death of the earl, said he had never seen so many people in all his life, 'and

when they did see any lord coming they all cried with one voice, "Justice! Justice!"' What Wallington was witnessing, again without knowing it, was another element of modern politics, the fever of the crowd, beginning to make itself felt.

Without any precocious understanding of the concept, Pym, St John, Haselrig and the rest intuitively understood the need for 'revolutionary justice', that baleful euphemism for crowd-pleasing demonstrations of political annihilation. So in mid-April, Pym changed the form of prosecution from an impeachment, a judicial process that required a decisive burden of proof, to an act of attainder, which was passed in a legislative process and needed no more than a body of suspicious evidence to constitute a presumption of guilt. Attainder effectively converted a trial into a hearing on the security of the state. Oddly enough, an act of attainder actually solved the problem of conscience for some like Viscount Falkland who, while unable to agree that the evidence against Strafford rose to the severe standards required for a conviction for treason, was prepared to vote for attainder by the weight of suspicion. Falkland and those like him believed that Strafford had, in fact, become a conspirator against the liberties of the country, and they were happy to be relieved of the bother of worrying precisely how this came to happen.

The only problem with an act of attainder was that it required the king to sign it. A day after it went through the Commons by 204 to 59 votes, Charles had written to Strafford. promising that he would not abandon him or repay his loyalty by allowing his loss of life, honour and fortune. And on 1 May 1641 Charles, who had been ostentatiously cordial and friendly towards Strafford throughout the proceedings, told the Lords that his conscience would not allow him to sign. Once again the king had managed to act directly against his own best interests. The whole point of the proceedings had been to deflect popular hatred and rage from the king himself (and from the queen, whose Catholic circle was becoming a daily target for the anti-popery lobby) and to safeguard the constitutional possibility of a new beginning. But Charles, and especially Henrietta Maria, believed they had other cards to play: a soft-line strategy, suggested by the Earl of Bedford, which involved bringing Pym in to the Privy Council, and a hard-line strategy, which involved getting his own loyal troops to the Tower and encouraging a move by some officers in the army to free Strafford, if necessary by force. In the end, it was Strafford himself who saw clearly where this was heading – towards chaos and bloodshed – and who decided on an extraordinary act of pre-emptive self-sacrifice. On 4 May he wrote to the king asking him to sign the act.

May it please your Sacred Majesty … I understand the minds of Men are more and more incensed against me, notwithstanding Your Majesty hath Declared that in Your Princely opinion I am not Guilty of Treason, and that You are not satisfied in Your Conscience, to pass the Bill.

This bringeth me in a very great streight, there is before me the ruine of my Children and Family, hitherto untouch'd … with any foul crime: Here before me are the many ills, which may befall Your Sacred Person and the whole Kingdom, should Your Self and parliament part less satisfied one with the other, than is necessary for the preservation both of King and People; Here are before me the things most valued, most feared by mortal men, Life and Death.

To say Sir, that there hath not been strife in me, were to make me less man, than, God knoweth, my Infirmities make me; and to call a destruction upon my self and my young Children … will find no easy consent from Flesh and Blood … So now to set Your Majesties Conscience at liberty, I do most humbly beseech Your Majesty for prevention of evils, which may happen by Your refusal, to pass this Bill.

On 10 May Charles signed the act, it's said with teary eyes, and almost without notic-ing what he was doing signed another, much more revolutionary bill presented to him, which prohibited the dissolution of parliament without its own consent. At the same time he wrote a letter to the House of Lords urging clemency, 'mercy being as inher-ent and inseparable to a King as Justice', and for Strafford to remain in prison for the rest of his life. 'This if it may be done without the discontentment of my People, would be an unspeakable contentment to me.' The Prince of Wales delivered the letter the following day, and on the day after that, 12 May, Strafford went to the block, protest-ing: 'In all the honour I had to serve His Majesty, I had not any intention in my heart, but what did aim at the joint and individual prosperity of the King and his People.' From his window in the Tower, Laud watched the execution. He never forgave Charles the betrayal, noting in his diary that the king 'knew not how to be, or to be made, great'. But then Charles never forgave himself. He truly believed that his own execu-tion, eight years later, was God's proper judgement on him for consenting to the death of a loyal servant.

Strafford was right to think that his death would be a national catharsis: a chance for the country to vent its anger on a convenient scapegoat but also an opportunity for the king, if he was shrewd, to cut his losses and stabilize his position. There was no doubt that the brutal business of the attainder had made some who were originally among the government's fiercest critics profoundly uneasy. Was one kind of arbitrary power to be exchanged for another?

Once both the earl and the institutional symbols of the old regime – the prerogative courts, ship money, communion rails – had been swept away in the summer of 1641, many on the benches of both the Lords and the Commons, and many more among the county communities of gentry and justices, began to ask themselves why the self–appointed tribunes like Pym continued to bang on relentlessly about tyranny and conspiracy. Although the Root and Branch Petition to abolish the episcopacy was steered through two readings in the Commons by Sir Robert Harley (to the proud delight of Lady Brilliana), it stalled badly in the Lords. Harley had to content himself with becoming the new *Thomas* Cromwell, overseeing a survey of the condition of parish churches (an ominous inquiry) and in Herefordshire pulling down the cross at the local Wigmore church in September 1641, causing it 'to be beaten to pieces, even in the dust, with a sledge and then laid … in the footpath to be trodden on in the churchyard'. To overcome the opposition of the Lords, compromises were made, disappointing the more intensely Calvinist Scots. If this were Presbyterianism, it was a very English kind: committees of nine laymen to replace the bishops, Church government by the hunting classes. Even so, there were many among the hunting classes who wanted none of it, who were prepared to see an end to the surplices and kneeling, and perhaps even see crucifixes trodden in the churchyard, but who thought bishops – plain and modest bishops, not the lofty, over-ornamental, theologically obscure, philosophically grandiose, Laudian bishops – were a proper part of the Church of England.

Others reacted to the outbreak of iconoclasm with deep horror. It was in the summer of 1641 that William Dugdale, the Warwickshire antiquary and genealogist, became convinced that there would shortly be a great and terrible obliteration. As he wrote in the introduction to his wonderful history of St Paul's Cathedral: 'Prudently foreseeing the sad effects thereof which by woeful experience were soon after miserably felt often and earnestly incited me to a speedy view of what Monuments I could find – the Principal Churches of the Realm, to the end that by Ink and Paper, the Shadows of them with their Inscriptions might be preserved for Posterity, the Things themselves being so near to Destruction.' And off Dugdale went, sketching and transcribing, poring through muniments and cartularies, spending furtive mornings in front of tomb effigies and stained-glass windows, working just as fast as he could to outpace the image-breakers, haunted by Lord Brooke's threat to St Paul's that he hoped 'to see no one stone left upon another of that building'.

Not everyone was quite so frantic. Noticing the backlash against the anti-bishop campaign, which by December included a decision to impeach twelve of them, a group of more moderate reformers, among them Edward Hyde, saw that Charles had a precious opportunity to exploit the divisions. It was their instinct (borne out by events twenty years later) that a non-absolutist but non-emasculated monarchy, the governor of the Church and the army, still possessed of legitimate prerogatives, including the right to choose its own government and to summon and dismiss parliaments, truly represented the wishes of the majority of the political nation. And it was from the clarity and strength of their convictions that constitutional royalism – hitherto a Stuart oxymoron – was born.

But Charles was not thinking with either clarity or strength of purpose about how the monarchy could best be renewed. He was thinking, when he was thinking at all, about how its full sovereignty might be restored. His most trusted advisers had been taken from him or had departed in the interests of self-preservation. Strafford was dead. Laud was in the Tower and most likely would follow him. Lord Keeper Finch (who had been Speaker during the stormy debates of 1629) and Secretary of State Windebanke had both fled to Europe to escape arrest. More than ever Charles depended on the queen for counsel, and her instincts were militantly against compromise. Any show of moderation that Charles now affected was just that. Not for a moment had he abandoned his deeply held conviction that the divine appointment of kingship required him to be faithful to the plenitude of its power. A mean little kingship seemed to him unworthy of the name, a kingship that said yea to whatever a parliament might propose was not the crown he had received from his father, nor one he could pass on to his son without the deepest sense of shame and betrayal. So when he travelled to Scotland in August 1641, ostensibly to conclude a peace settlement with the Covenanters, Charles was actually casting about for some way to use the Scots against the English as he had once hoped to use the English against the Scots. Even there, though, Charles was incapable of deciding between persuasion and plotting, between a campaign to win over aristocratic generals, like James Graham, Earl of Montrose, and the physical seizure of Covenanter leaders, like Archibald Campbell, eighth Earl of Argyll. It was, in any case, all moot. For while Charles imagined that he might order the affairs of one of his kingdoms to settle the disorder of a second, a third, Ireland, now exploded in violent rebellion.

It was as much of a jolt as the Covenanter rebellion had been four years earlier. The fall of Strafford's 'thorough' government, both Charles and the English parliament must have imagined, had probably removed most of the grievances of which those who counted in Ireland had complained. But as usual in the politics of Stuart Britain, everyone was looking the wrong way, addressing the problems of the last crisis, not the next one. To the Catholic communities of Ireland, especially the native Irish, the destruction of the Wentworth regime was a cause of apprehension, not of rejoicing. Bullying, grasping and thuggish though his administration had been, its tough

Driuinge Men women & children by hund:
reds vpon Briges & casting them into Riuers,
who drowned not were killed with poles &
shot with muskets.

G

An anti–Catholic propaganda print dramatising the massacre of Irish Protestants, *c*. 1640–1.

independence (and willingness quite often to co-opt the native Irish in its schemes) was immeasurably better than what seemed most likely to replace it: the unrestricted domination of the New English and Scots Presbyterians. As recently as 1639 Wentworth's 'Black Acts' had been directed at the Protestant, rather than the Catholic, communities. Now that he was gone, the situation seemed especially ominous to the Catholic gentry of Ulster. They looked across the North Channel and saw the Covenanter conquest and settlement of the western Highlands and islands by the Earl of Argyll and could only imagine that it would be their turn next. For years they had been forbidden to increase their own land holdings while the Protestant New English and Scots had been encouraged to settle in ever greater numbers, and in responding to Wentworth's challenge to turn their own estates into models of 'improvement' they had incurred huge debts, building themselves grandiose English houses and attempting to introduce fine livestock and tillage. Now the improbable victory of the English parliament over the king, symbolized so dramatically by the execution of Strafford, had robbed them of any prospect of harvesting the fruits of all this hard work and money by securing their position in a rapidly changing Ireland. Instead, they were facing the nightmare of Presbyterian encirclement. And for the moment the Catholic Old English, in the middle of the conflict, had shown no wish to swerve from loyalty to the English state. So Ulster lords, like Phelim O'Neill, who claimed descent from the great leader of the Nine Years War, Hugh O'Neill, Earl of Tyrone, now turned to armed resistance as a last line of self-defence. When Phelim O'Neill captured Charlemont Castle early in the rebellion, he settled all kinds of scores by killing his chief creditor there, a Mr Fullerton.

Paradoxically, then, the leaders of the Irish rebellion thought that by planning to seize strongholds, including Dublin Castle, towards the end of October 1641 they were actually coming to the aid of the beleaguered king. At least at the beginning their action was presented not as a proto-nationalist, but as a fervently loyalist revolt. On 4 November O'Neill even went so far as to claim that he had had the commission of the king himself for his military action. It was an outrageous fabrication, probably targeted at the Old English (always the most genuinely loyal of the three communities), who, as yet, had stood aloof from the rebellion. O'Neill may have been hoping that by purporting to do the king's work he could draw the Earl of Ormonde, the most powerful of the Old English (a Protestant but very definitely not a Presbyterian), into the revolt. Instead, the ruse did massive damage to Charles's credibility in England. To many of the godly he now seemed beyond all doubt to be conniving at an Irish-Catholic plot.

Paranoia is the oxygen of revolution. But in November 1641, to men such as Harley and Wallington, Pym and St John, there seemed a great deal to be paranoid about. The king was still in Scotland and was reported to have attempted to overthrow the Covenant by a coup. News was beginning to pour across the Irish Sea, not just of castles and fortifications being over-run, but of much darker things – massacres visited by the Catholic rebels on isolated Protestant towns and villages of the New English. By the time it was recycled for the Irish insurrection, anti-Catholic atrocity propaganda had become a formulaic part of the cultural war dividing Europe. The same pornography of violence, graphically illustrated with woodcuts and 'eye-witness' reports, which had been used to describe the behaviour of the Spanish in the Netherlands or of Wallenstein's troops in Germany, was rehearsed all over again: babies impaled on pikes; the wombs of pregnant women sliced open and the foetuses ripped out; skewered grandpas; decapitated preachers. Which is not to say that monstrous killings did not actually occur. At Portadown there was, unquestionably, terrible butchery: a hundred New English were herded on to the bridge, stripped and thrown into the river to drown. Those who looked as if they were swimming were clubbed or shot until they disappeared in the bloody water.

Little of this was countenanced by the military leadership of the rebellion, but they had only tenuous control over some sections of the Catholic rural population, which had suffered for generations at the hands of the planters and in some parts of Ireland now took the opportunity to make their point in blood. If they were not encouraged, neither were they stopped. The more isolated the plantations and villages – in Munster, for example – the more likely the target. Something like 4000 people lost their lives directly as a result of this violence and countless more as a result of being evicted, stripped naked and sent starving and unprotected into the cold, wet Irish winter. Among them were relatives of the Wallingtons, the family of Nehemiah's sister-in-law, the Rampaignes, rich farmers in Fermanagh. Attempting to flee to the coast, they were tracked down and Zachariah Rampaigne was killed in front of his children. The survivors had to protect themselves as best they could. Before long, of course, murderous retaliation would be inflicted on innocent Catholic populations, and the miserably unrelenting cycle of murder and counter-murder that stains Irish history would be well under way.

In England the Irish rising was immediately seen as an integral element in a pan-British conspiracy, ultimately aimed at itself. Wallington quoted in one of his note-books the proverb 'He that England will win / Must first with Ireland begin'. Worse even than that, the rebellion brought back Elizabethan memories of Ireland being used as a back door to England by the armed league of Catholic powers. Whether England liked it or not, its fate now seemed to be tied up with the international wars of religion, a suspicion confirmed when Owen Roe O'Neill, nephew of the Earl of Tyrone, who had fled to Rome in 1607 and had served for thirty years in the armies of the king of Spain, crossed from Flanders in the spring of 1642 and took command of the rebel forces. It was not long before a papal nuncio, Cardinal Giovanni Rinuccini, arrived to press an all-out Counter-Reformation agenda on the rebels: the restoration of the Church as it had been before the Henrician Reformation.

This was a tragic turning-point in the life of the Old English Catholic community in Ireland. It was now in the same quandary over allegiance that had been so disastrous for its English counterpart during the Spanish-papal offensive in the 1580s. It seemed impossible to make men like Owen Roe O'Neill grasp that it had been historically feasible, especially under Strafford, to live a life of loyal Catholicism, practising their faith quietly and being tacitly tolerated as long as they kept clear of sedition. But the collapse of the protecting authority of the Crown had suddenly taken away this vital living space. They were now between the rock of the Roman Church and the hard place of the Presbyterians. So in December 1641 some of the leading Old English entered into an agreement with the Irish rebels. By the following spring they were being asked, more pressingly, to contribute men and money, and with some trepidation many of the Old English peers (though not the Protestant Ormonde) actively joined the revolt. One of them, John Preston, became the Confederation's commander in Leinster. They may have consoled themselves with the thought that even in the spring of 1642 and the years ahead, the official line of the confederation, affirmed on its flags, was one of intense loyalism to Charles I. But that was not the way it was seen in England, either by the king or by his opponents. And once Robert Monro, a Scottish Presbyterian veteran of the Thirty Years War, took command of the Protestant forces, commissioned by the intensely Protestant Scots parliament, the polarization of Ireland into two armed religious camps was tragically complete. At Newry, where sixty men and women and two priests were murdered, Monro, who had been much affected by the atrocity literature, showed that he was perfectly capable of unloosing a massacre every bit as ugly as Portadown. 'Anti-Christ marcheth furiously,' wrote Wallington, and this was good news for it meant that the unsparing, long-heralded battle between the angels and demons could at last get under way.

Charles returned to London towards the end of November 1641 as news of the Irish slaughter, real and fictitious, was arriving, each day apparently bloodier than the last. A bill proposing to place control of a militia in the hands of parliament had already had a reading in the House of Commons, and Pym must have assumed that the Irish rebellion would work to complete, irreversibly, a momentous transfer of power from king to parliament. All sorts of demands – that Catholics be removed from the army, that parliament now have a decisive say in foreign policy – were being voiced. And, as a prelude to the capture of sovereignty, a Grand Remonstrance, drafted by the militants, was to capture history. The document represented a complete rewriting, for the present and for posterity, of the reign of Charles I, recording that from the beginning he had planned to violate the liberties of his subjects and impose on them a monstrous and detestable despotism. It recapitulated what had been done by the people's representatives to withstand that conspiracy and what still needed to be done.

The Grand Remonstrance became another immense public event in the life of an already feverishly politicized London. Wallington watched daily as troops of gentry and yeomen from Essex, Kent and Sussex clattered on horseback through the streets of the city towards Westminster, where they surrounded the parliament chambers. The showers of paper propaganda had turned into a virtual blizzard. But it was precisely this sense of being held hostage to the people – gentry and farmers in the provinces, artisans and apprentices in London – that turned a considerable number of both the Lords and Commons against the Remonstrance. Sir Edward Dering from Kent spoke for many when he expressed amazement at the 'descension from a parliament to a people … when I first heard of a Remonstrance, I presently imagined that like faithful councillors we should hold up a glass unto His Majesty … I did not dream that we should remonstrate downwards, tell stories to the people and talk of the King as a third person. I neither look for a cure for our complaints from the common people nor do desire to be cured by them.' Together with the sense that the gratuitously abusive tone of the Remonstrance had been deliberately calculated to put an accommodation with the king out of reach, it managed to pass the Commons by a majority of only eleven votes.

The discomfiture of Pym naturally presented an opportunity to a moderate group, with Edward Hyde as its presiding talent, to rally a reform-minded but non-Presbyterian party to the support of what he had been led to believe was a reasonably chastened king. Accordingly, Hyde drafted a response to the Remonstrance, which took the tone that royalist ideology would sustain throughout the civil war, namely that it was the king, and not a minority of Puritan zealots, who truly represented the well-being and interests of the people at large; that it was he, and not they, who was the true reformer. Those like Hyde who hoped to see the king wrap himself in the mantle of a non-Laudian, non-absolutist monarchy took heart from the warm reception that Charles, a figure who seemed more wronged than wrongful, had received on his journey back from Scotland to London. The narrow vote over the Remonstrance confirmed Hyde in his optimism that the tide of militancy could be pushed back.

But there was no political situation so fabulously promising for the revival of the king's fortunes that Charles could not still manage to undercut it by his ultimate belief in the arbitration of force. He had been persuaded by Hyde and Viscount Falkland, his new Secretary of State, and by the vote on the Remonstrance, that Pym and his fellows were indeed an isolated group within the Commons, who, once neutralized, could be brought back to the kind of parliament he cared to deal with and which would vote him money for an army to go to Ireland. But what he meant by neutralization was something more than just parliamentary defeat. So in December 1641 Charles, enthusiastically abetted by Lord George Digby, whose family castle at Sherborne was just a few miles from the Puritan citadel of Dorchester, systematically set about planning a *coup d'État*. The Earl of Essex's men – mostly trained bands from the City – who were guarding the approaches to parliament were replaced by Westminster troopers from the dependably royalist Earl of Dorset's regiment. For the first time the mutually derogatory epithets of 'Roundheads' (for the departing apprentices) and 'Cavaliers' (for the incoming guards) became part of the vocabulary of reciprocal hatred. Some sort of civil war had already started. The Warden of the Tower, right in the centre of the most riotously pro-parliamentary streets of the city, was likewise replaced with the notoriously brutal soldiers of Colonel Lunsford's regiment.

And all this, of course, was exactly what Pym wanted. Since Charles's return from Scotland it had been Pym, not the king, who had been forced on the defensive. The failure of the Remonstrance had made this worse. But now, Charles's transparent and laborious plans for a strike against the integrity of parliament itself had miraculously played right into his hands. Had he himself written the script by which the king suddenly stood revealed not as a reasonable reformer but as a military conspirator Pym could hardly have improved on Charles's own performance. (The queen, as always, helped.) On 3 January 1642 five members of the Commons – Pym, Hampden, Holles, Haselrig and William Strode – together with Viscount Mandeville, were formally charged with impeachment by the Attorney General in the House of Lords. Their immediate arrest (carefully following the procedure used against Strafford and Laud) was demanded. Both houses of parliament made it clear that they would not surrender the accused, but articles charging the six with subverting the fundamental laws of the realm were now made public. If by now Pym, Holles and the rest were not sure of what was coming, the forced search of their houses gave them a pretty good idea. Charles must have felt confident – with control of the areas around both parliament and the Tower – that everything was in place for his strike.

Forewarned by spies at court, Pym and his friends were themselves playing with fire. They could have disappeared to safety on the night of 3–4 January, but they actually wanted the king to come and get them, exposing himself, unequivocally, as the violator of the independence of parliament. So on the morning of 4 January there they were in the Commons, informed by Lady Carlisle and other spies, of the king's progress from Whitehall. Once they were sure he was on his way, they made their departure. At the last minute William Strode, in a fit of misplaced bravura, nearly wrecked the strategy by announcing that he would rather like to stay and confront the king in person, and he had to be dragged off to the barge waiting to convey the members downstream to the City.

The famous scene played itself out: intruding tyrant versus absent champions of the people. No king had ever before presumed to intimidate the Commons with a display of armed force. The king arrived with a small personal guard, George Digby making sure that the door was left open with a clear view of the soldiers standing guard outside. Before long, the courtyard outside the parliament house was packed with anxious crowds. Doffing his hat in a gesture of respect, Charles asked politely for the use of the Speaker's chair, duly surrendered to him. He then asked for the accused to be delivered up. Silence. When Charles asked Speaker Lenthall to point out Pym and the others, Lenthall replied in the precise terms that Denzil Holles had forced on the terrified Finch in 1629: he had 'neither eyes to see nor tongue to speak in this place but as the House is pleased to direct me'. As it had always been, this was a drama of long political memories. Charles replied that he had eyes to see for himself and what he saw was that 'the birds are flown'. A huge caesura, full of silent rage, foolishness and foreboding, hung over the house. The embarrassed king, roiling in chagrin, departed whence he came, shouts of 'Privilege, privilege' following him through the door.

It was an unmitigated fiasco. The gamble had been worthwhile only if Charles could be absolutely sure of success. In abject failure he now stood nakedly exposed (just as Pym had wanted) as something worse than a despot – a blundering despot. With the abortive arrest of the MPs disappeared the last possibilities of constructing something like a moderate consensus for a reformed but sovereign monarchy. When the king demanded that the city yield up the accused, parliament responded by appointing a professional soldier and veteran of the European wars, Philip Skippon, to command the London militia and by declaring that anyone assisting the assault on parliament and its members was guilty of capital treason. London was, in any case, in uproar. On 11 January, Pym, Holles and the rest emerged to a delirious celebration, in which they appeared to the cheering crowds on a festive Thames barge. Court and government swiftly self-liquidated. Catcalls of 'privilege' hounded anyone recognized as having a court connection. Charles skulked around the periphery of London – at Hampton Court, Windsor, Greenwich – trying to find some way back to the moderate position he had already thrown away. But there was no way back. Contingency plans for outright conflict were now, in effect, operational. The queen was sent off to The Hague to pawn the crown jewels so as to fund an army. Prince Rupert of the Rhine, the king's twenty-two-year-old nephew, the laughing Cavalier himself, complete with a toy poodle called Boy, suddenly materialized at court. Preparations were made to try to secure key arsenals and ports. The king turned north, where he believed his best chance of rallying his forces lay. At Newmarket he was asked if he would agree to the militia being transferred to parliament's control for a limited time. 'By God, not for an hour,' was the answer. 'You have asked that of me in this which was never asked of a King and with which I will not trust my wife and children.'

What followed accelerated the likelihood, if not the certainty, of armed conflict. Since the king continued to refuse to sign the Militia Bill, its provisions were enacted unilaterally as an ordinance, transferring to parliament the right to commandeer men and munitions, and enabling it to appoint lord-lieutenants and deputy lieutenants in the counties to see to the execution of the orders. From his transplanted court at York the king countered by declaring anyone obeying those illegitimate officers to be guilty of treason. Invoking an ancient Lancastrian form of feudal mobilization, he then appointed his own 'Commissions of Array' in each shire to supply men to defend the Crown.

In its declaration to the king parliament had, for the first time, formally accused him of conspiring to wage 'civil war' against his own subjects, The words were out. They could not be unsaid. But even Puritan parliamentarians, like Bulstrode Whitelocke, were momentarily unnerved that actual bloodshed now seemed so near. The country, he told parliament, had 'insensibly slid into this beginning of a Civil War by one unexpected Accident after another, as Waves of the Sea, which have brought us thus far: And we scarce know how, but from Paper Combats, by Declarations, Remonstrances, Protestations, Votes, Messages, Answers and Replies: We are now come to the question of raising of Forces.' There was one last chance at settlement, when parliament delivered its 'Nineteen Propositions' to the king at York. But they were more a clarification of its own ideas on the future of England's government than any kind of negotiating position, since they included things they knew the king could not possibly concede, like parliamentary control over the education and marriage of his children, the vigorous prosecution of all Catholics (which would include his wife) and the transfer of all ports, forts and castles to their officers. The fact was that parliament, along with Pym, now simply believed that Charles, together with the Irish, was committed to an English Counter-Reformation. So until he was made harmless they would put the monarchy out of commission – forcing it to exercise its powers through committees – creating, in effect, a parliamentary regency, as if he had become insane.

With that last hope gone, the months ahead were dominated by a scramble to secure martial assets – plate, money, guns, powder, horses and hay – so as to be best placed when hostilities actually began. At the same time attempts were made to sway the undecided. The showers of propaganda sheets now became downpours. The royal printing press had been prudently taken to York so that the work of influencing the north could proceed apace. A battle of the Mercuries took place with the parliamentary newspaper, the *Mercurius Civicus,* answered and satirized by the royalist *Mercurius Aulicus*. And beneath the anathemas and the requisitioning something profoundly sad was happening: the Balkanization of England, not in the sense of its fracturing into coherent, warring regions (for there were virtually none), but in the collapse of communities and institutions – parishes and counties – which, despite differing sentiments and religious beliefs, had none the less managed to contain those conflicts in the interests of local peace and justice. Doubtless there must have been many places where the choice of allegiance was unthinking or even involuntary. Men and women followed habit, prejudice, their landlord, their preacher. And there were certainly those like Robert and Brilliana Harley on the one side and Viscount Scudamore on the other for whom the choice was pretty much a foregone conclusion. Just what they did about it, of course was another matter. (Surprisingly, Scudamore showed himself to be a rather tepid royalist when the time came for action.) And there must have been many more, like poor Thomas Knyvett, a Norfolk landowner, whose purposefulness was not at all equal to his predicament. 'O sweete hart,' he wrote to his wife, 'I am nowe in a greate strayght what to doe.' Walking in Westminster he had run into Sir John Potts, who had presented him with his commission from the Earl of Warwick to raise a company for parliament. 'I was surpris'd what to doe, whether to take or refuse. 'Twas no place to dispute, so I tooke it and desierd som'time to Advise upon it. I had not receiv'd this many howers, but I met with a declaration point Blanck against it by the King.' Richard Atkyns, then twenty-seven years old and living in strongly parliamentary Gloucester, believed that no one who had heard the trial of Strafford and 'weighed the concessions of the King' could be against him, but that 'fears, and jealousies, had so generally possessed the kingdom, that a man could hardly travel through any market town, but he should be asked whether he were for the King, or parliament'.

What is truly extraordinary about the spring and summer of 1642 is the wealth of evidence testifying to the agonies of allegiance, the painful rigour with which many thoughtful souls pondered the weightiest question of their lives and how earnestly and honestly they endeavoured to justify their decisions to their friends, their family and themselves. Different men and women reached their point of no return at different moments in the great crisis, which had been gathering head since the opening of the Long Parliament. Cornwall – which is often thought of, not altogether wrongly, as an especially cohesive community – was shattered right down the middle. For the two leading figures among the Cornish Members of Parliament, who had travelled to London optimistically expectant of peaceful reform, it had been their responses to Strafford's attainder that had separated them. Sir Bevil Grenville was the grandson of the pirate-patriot sea captain Richard Grenville, but after his education at Exeter College, Oxford, he became the very paragon of a learned, energetic country gentleman, devoted to his wife, children and land (in that order), an experimenter with new techniques for tin smelting, a breeder of Barbary stallions and a life-long enthusiast of classical history, philosophy and poetry. In 1626 he had been among the fiercest Cornish critics of the forced loan, had turned out his freeholders on behalf of Sir John Eliot and William Coryton and had been devastated by Eliot's death in the Tower. But in 1641 he was appalled at the attainder of Strafford, seeing it as the kind of naked manipulation of justice he had attacked when it was practised by the court. Grenville was one of eight MPs from Cornwall (including Coryton) who voted 'nay' and who tried to persuade Sir Alexander Carew to follow their example. 'Pray, Sir,' wrote Grenville to Carew, 'let it not be said that any member of our county should have a hand in this ominous business and therefore pray give your vote against the Bill.' Carew's reply was unclouded by equivocation (and would come to haunt him in the years that followed before his execution in 1644): 'If I were sure to be the next man on the scaffold with the same axe, I would give my consent to the passing of it.' Others in Cornwall who had long been friends, and had lived in mutual amity and respect, now divided: Sir Francis Godolphin of Godolphin (and his son, the poet Sidney) for the king; Sir Francis Godolphin of Trevneague for parliament.

Although none of Lord Falkland's Great Tew friends had any trouble with the act of attainder (one suspects none of them much liked the bleak, brusque Wentworth), they parted company, first over the attack on the bishops and then again over parliament's Militia Ordinance. Hyde and Falkland saw the Ordinance as a demonstrably unlawful usurpation of the sovereign's legitimate prerogative; indeed, a test case of whether the king was to be granted any sort of prerogative at all. But their legalistic friend and MP John Selden truly believed that it had been the king who had acted illegitimately, not being entitled to impress any of his subjects except when the realm was plainly threatened by *foreign* invasion. Selden thus remained loyal to parliament. Conversely, there were those like Lord Montagu, who were at pains to be understood as supporting the most parliamentary monarchy there could possibly be, short of conferring on the institution some sort of exclusive and transcendent sovereignty. To his son William, Montagu wrote that:

> It is most sure he is not of a true English spirit that will not shed life and all that he hath for the maintenance and preservation of parliaments consisting of the King, Lords and Commons. But to have the ordinance bind all the subjects to England without the consent of the King is of most dangerous consequence and a violation of all the privileges of parliament and the common liberty of the subject; therefore I would to God that the Lords and Commons would be pleased not to stand upon that. My heart, hand and life shall stand for parliaments but for no ordinance only by Lords and Commons.

For Sir Edmund Verney the choice was simpler, yet so very much harder. For he found himself governed by an unforgiving and unequivocal obligation of duty, even while his moral sense and his intellect told him the cause was worthless. Edward Hyde discovered his friend Verney's melancholy predicament at York, when he asked him to put

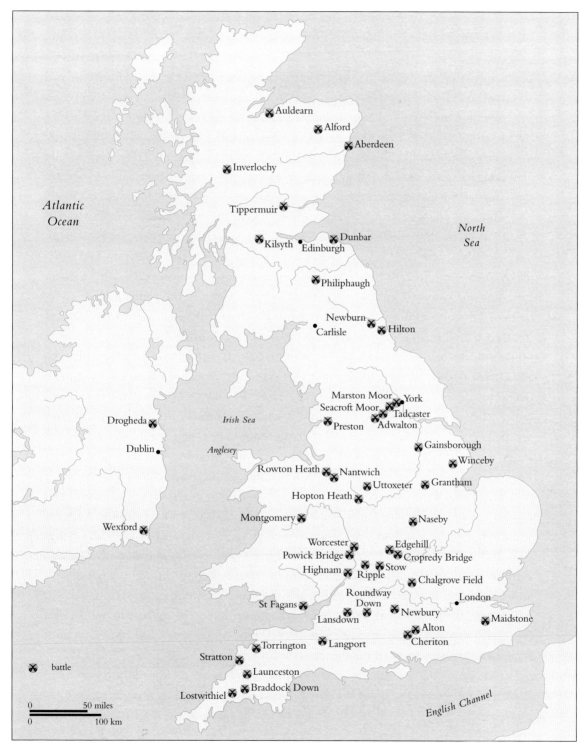

The civil wars, 1640–51.

on a face of public cheerfulness, the better to raise the spirits of the fearful royalist soldiers. Verney replied smilingly to Hyde that:

> I will willingly join with you the best I can but I shall act it very scurvily … you have satisfaction in your conscience that you are in the right; that the King ought not to grant what is required of him and so you do your duty and your business together. But for my part, I do not like the quarrel, and do heartily wish that the King would yield and consent to what they desire; so that my conscience is only concerned in honour and gratitude to follow my master. I have eaten his bread, and served him near thirty years, and will not do so base a thing as to forsake him; and choose rather to lose my life (which I am sure I shall do) to preserve and defend those things which are against my conscience to preserve and defend.

The Verneys, who had been the model of a companionable, loving gentry household, were now torn apart. Ralph, who had sat next to his father in the parliaments of 1640, had not just expressed his support for their cause but had taken the solemn oath of loyalty required of all members after the passing of the Militia Ordinance. Oaths were no light matter in the seventeenth century, especially to a Puritan. The act sharply separated him not just from his father but also from his younger brother, Edmund, who could not understand Ralph's failure to perceive his duty to his king as well as to his father. They were still, somehow, a family. In the early summer the steward at Claydon was getting letters from Sir Edmund at York asking him to prepare the defence of the house with carbines, powder and shot, 'for I feare a time maye come when Roags maye looke for booty in such houses; therefore bee not unprovided; but saye noething of it, for that maye invite more to mischeefe that thinek not of it yet … gett in all such monnys as are owing you with all speede, for wee shall certainly have a great warr. Have a care of harvest, and God send uss well to receave the blessing of and returne thancks for it. I can saye no more — Your loving master.' But the steward was also getting letters from Ralph in London asking him to search for his father's best pistols and carbines to be sent on to his father at York! For a time in the late spring of 1642, when tentative feelers were being put out between king and parliment, the Verneys and their friends clung to the hope that there might yet be peace. But on 1 June both houses of parliament passed the Nineteen Propositions for the future of England.

Not surprisingly, hopes of accommodation dwindled away to nothing. By late August it seemed certain that the Verneys, father and eldest son, would end up as enemies. Eleanor, Lady Sussex, an old friend of the family, parliamentarian by sympathy and conviction, but socially very much in both worlds, wrote to Ralph on

9 September that she had had a letter from his father. 'It was a very sade one and his worde was this of you: "Madam he hath ever lane near my hart and truly he is ther still", that he hade many afflictyon uppon him, and that you hade usede him unkandly.' Sir Edmund had, she said, become 'passynate, and much trublede I belive that you declarede yourselfe for the parlyment: a littil time will digest all I am confident'. And she asked Ralph in return to humour his father as much as he could: 'lett me intrete you as a frende that loves you most hartily, not to right passynatly to your father, but ovour com him with kandnes; good man I see he is infinitely malincoly, for many other thinges I belive besides the difference betwixt you.'

All over England, in the summer of 1642, disengagements and separations, often described as 'unnatural', like the prospect of civil war itself, were taking place in communities that for so long had shared customs, territory and beliefs. Very few counties or even towns were so politically homogeneous as to make the decision of allegiance a matter of course or obvious self-interest. Essex was overwhelmingly parliamentarian and much of Wales deeply royalist, but even in shires such as Warwickshire, where there were strong partisan presences – like the Grevilles – parts of those counties, in this instance in the north, were far more mixed in their loyalties. And there were a few regions – Cumberland and Westmorland – that tried to be studiously neutral and avoided organizing either parliamentary or royalist musters. The actual event of the musters – and the response they received in county and market towns – was a warning to those on the wrong side of the fence that they should either move to safer territory or prepare to defend their houses and farms as best they could.

Lady Brilliana Harley was one of those who decided against moving, being unafraid, as she later said, to die in defence of the family estates and godly religion. Her husband, Sir Robert, away in Westminster, very much a moving spirit in the committees of parliament, advised her to stay put: he could not quite believe that much harm could come to her in remote northwest Herefordshire, especially since there were friendly ties between the Harleys and fellow-gentry in the county, even when they parted company on religious beliefs. But in the summer and autumn of 1642 it quickly became plain to Brilliana that her household was an island of parliamentary puritanism in an ocean of royalism and that the old, dependable bonds of gentility might not survive the coming conflict. She was already the butt of popular abuse, some of it genuinely menacing. At Ludlow, she wrote to their son Edward, she had heard that a maypole had been set up 'and a thinge like a head upon it ... and gathered a greate many about it, and shot at it in derision of roundheads'. And their old friend Sir William Croft had made it no secret that, while in private he still respected Lady Brilliana, this could have no effect whatsoever on his public conduct as a loyal servant

of the king. Before long Brilliana and her household were enduring abuse while in the grounds of Brampton Bryan, from 'exceeding rude' country people on their way to market at Ludlow who shouted from the roadway that they wished 'all the Puritans and roundheads at Brampton hanged'. When, later that year, royalist soldiers took two of her servants away to prison, she asked Viscount Scudamore to intercede, appealing, anachronistically, to 'the many bonds by which most of the gentlemen in this country are tied to Sir Robert Harley, that of blood and some with alliance and all with his long professed and real friendship and for myself that of common courtesy, as to a stranger brought into their country, I know not how all those I believed to be so good should break all these obligations'. But, little by little, Brampton Bryan was becoming a godly stockade, with frightened preachers and schoolmasters and Puritan friends coming to the house for shelter. How long it would remain safe was anyone's guess, but with royalism strong not only in Herefordshire but also in Shropshire to the north and in Wales to the south and west, Brilliana must have put in extra prayer-time for the help of the Almighty.

In the third week of August 1642 Charles I decided to raise his standard. He was, as yet, in no position to do more than wage the heraldic equivalent of war rather than the real thing. Far fewer counties had produced men, money and plate for him than for parliament. The navy had come out for parliament, and the king had suffered the indignity of being locked out of Hull by its governor, Sir John Hotham. An attempt by Lord Strange to seize an arms depot in the little Lancashire town of Manchester had ended with his troop of horse being chased out of the town by indignant, armed fustian weavers. But the king had been promised troops and horse in thousands from Wales and Shrewsbury, and he evidently felt confident that the quality of his officers and the rapid training that his professional soldiers, not least the young Prince Rupert, were giving the cavalry would prevail over the superior numbers of the parliamentary army, commanded by the dour veteran of the Dutch wars, the Earl of Essex – the first husband of the notorious Frances Howard. So the standard was to go up, the Rubicon to be crossed, and the man to whom this honour fell was the Knight Marshal, newly appointed standard-bearer, the fifty-two-year-old Sir Edmund Verney. It was a heavy duty, literally, for the thing needed twenty men to get it upright in the field just outside Nottingham castle. 'Much of the fashion of the City Streamers used at the Lord Mayor's Show,' one antiquarian remembered, several flags were mounted on a huge pole, the top one being the king's personal arms, with a hand pointing towards the crown and beneath it the imperious, optimistic motto 'Give Caesar His Due'. The flag was paraded around by three troops of horse and 600 infantrymen. Just as the trumpets were about to sound and the herald to read the royal proclamation, Charles

Brampton Bryan, home of the Harleys, was besieged by royalists in 1643 and burnt to the ground in 1644.

suddenly asked for the paper, a quill and some ink and, still on horseback, started to make some last-minute revisions. When he was done and the herald nervously attempted to read the document, corrections and all, the flag went up, along with the army's hats, high in the air. The standard was carried back to the castle and hoisted to be seen for miles about. But that night a powerful storm got up and the flag was blown down. It was two days before the winds and rain abated enough for it to be raised once more. Those (and there were plenty) in the habit of searching for omens were not encouraged. For Sir Edmund Verney, though, the die was very definitely cast. His charge read 'that by the grace of God they that would wrest that standard from his hand must first wrest his soul from his body'.

By the time the royalist army assembled at Edgehill in Warwickshire, its prospects had been transformed. Charles's forces were now more than 20,000 strong, of whom about 14,000 mustered on the ridge in the early morning of 23 October. At the top of the hill, with his sons, Charles, the Prince of Wales, and James, the nine-year-old Duke of York (under the watchful eye of Hyde), as well as Prince Rupert carrying his toy poodle Boy, the king took his 'prospective glass' and looked down at the parliamentary troops drawn up in the vale of the Red Horse below. Not only did the king have the immense advantage of the sharply sloping terrain, with no trees and only a few hedges offering cover, he also knew that the Earl of Essex's army was exhausted even before a shot had been fired. Moving quickly from Shrewsbury, Charles had managed to slip between the parliamentary strongholds of Warwick and Coventry. Essex had had to play belated catch-up, attempting unsuccessfully to place his army across the route to London before it was too late. The first contact between the two armies had not been encouraging for Essex. A skirmish at Powick Bridge near Worcester the previous month, on 23 September, had ended in an embarrassing rout when Essex's Life Guard had evidently been incapable of understanding, much less performing, a 'wheel about' in the face of Prince Rupert's cavalry charge and had given themselves their own orders to flee.

Close to the king, surrounded by the royal Life Guard in their red coats and holding the standard (much reduced in size to make it portable) was Sir Edmund Verney. His family would have been horrified if they had known he was wearing no armour other than a helmet, being convinced that a full cuirass was more likely to kill a man by impeding his movement than to protect him. Some of his closest friends were there, too; Hyde with the king, Falkland somewhere amid the cavalry. There were drums, the unfurling of regimental flags, coloured scarves tied like sashes over their armour to identify friends in the heat of battle. Already there had been serious trouble over the dispositions. The Earl of Forth and the commander of the infantry, the Earl of Lindsey, had got into an angry row over whether musketeers should be interspersed within the pikemen in the Swedish manner or whether, as Lindsey wished, in the older 'Dutch' style, in separate units – better fitted, he thought, for untried soldiers. Tactlessly, the king and Prince Rupert had voted Swedish, at which point the affronted Lindsey had thrown down his baton and marched off in a pout to head his own regiment. Cavaliers were like that. Still, there was much obvious affection for the king, who rode down the line dressed in a black velvet coat trimmed with ermine, the only flash of bright-ness the silvery starburst of his Garter badge. 'Your King is your cause, your quarrel and your captain,' he told the troops and promised them his grateful remembrance for their service. He spoke too quietly, as was his custom. But there were huzzahs anyway.

From his position in the valley, at the parliamentary centre, Denzil Holles, one of the five 'birds' of January, Dorchester's own MP in arms, would have had a good view of the formidable array of royal forces mustering on the ridge. From among the trained bands and apprentices in London he, like so many of his friends and colleagues, had raised his own troop of foot soldiers and had dressed them also in red coats, that being the cheapest of the available dyes. (One of the hoariest myths of the civil war is that there were no coloured uniforms. Lord Brooke's men were outfitted in bright purple!) John Hampden was supposed be en route, and Arthur Haselrig, he knew, had barely eluded capture by the king's army in the east Midlands. Of what lay in store for him should the parliamentary cause collapse on the battlefield, Holles could have no doubt. On their marches back and forth through the West Country these soldiers had already established a kind of brutal routine: taking what they could get when and as they needed it, abusing any church or priest or village they decided was 'papist', smashing and burning communion table rails, occasionally saying their prayers. Fortunately, it was harvest time and they were marching through the prolific west Midlands. 'Our food was fruit for those that could get it,' wrote one apprentice turned soldier, Nehemiah Wharton, in Worcestershire. 'Our drink was water; our beds the earth; our canopy the clouds, but we pulled up hedges, pales and gates and made good fires; his Excellency [Essex] promising us that, if the country relieved us not the day following, he would fire their towns.'

Their panicky encounters with Prince Rupert's cavalry along the way could not have done much for the morale of the foot soldiers, and there they were again on the brow of the hill. At least, now there were some guns. Scattered amid the lines of cum-bersome 16-foot pikes were musketeers, busy now checking the tarred rope that would act as a fuse for their weapons, knocking firmly into place the forked and grooved supports on which the muskets and arquebuses had to rest before they had

Above: *Sir Edmund Verney*, by Anthony Van Dyck, *c.* 1640.
Opposite, top: Edgehill, the battlefield today. The distant tower marks the spot where Charles I raised his standard.
Opposite, below: *Prince Rupert, Count Palatine*, attributed to Gerard Honthorst, *c.* 1641–2.

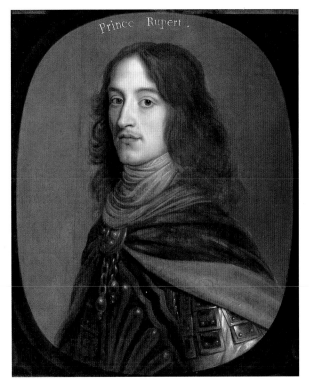

any chance at all of hitting their target. Some field guns were deployed in front of the centre, but firing upwards, against the bias of the hill, was not exactly going to be easy.

So indeed it proved. Around three o'clock Essex thought to compensate for his topographical disadvantage by cannonading the royalist infantry centre. Most of the replying cannonade came from guns positioned too far down the slope to get much ricochet effect, and it may have been the disappointing performance of the king's artillery, together with the sudden appearance of a parliamentary officer, Sir Faithful Fortescue, tearing off his orange scarf in a dramatic gesture of defection, that persuaded Rupert to begin his cavalry attack. For the parliamentary forces, sitting on their horses or standing with their long pikes in front of them, watching a trot become a canter and seeing the fire of their own muskets and carbines apparently having no effect on the advancing horsemen, the moment of truth had arrived and the reality of war slammed into them. Waves of horsemen came at the terrified parliamentary troops, cutting in at a sweeping angle, which ensured that they were completely unchecked by musket fire. Panic hit the parliamentary right. Their cavalry and some of the infantry broke and fled. Rupert's horsemen slashed a path right through and charged off in pursuit of the fleeing parliamentary troopers like so many huntsmen after the fox. Their chase was 3 miles all the way to the village of Kineton, where the parliamentary army had kept its baggage, now taken in a riotous triumph by Rupert's cavalry. A mile further on John Hampden, marching to the field with his own troops, collided with the runaways, heading for cover like rabbits.

Rupert and his horsemen supposed the battle already won. Prepare the libations. At some point the prince decided he had better return to Edgehill, if only to help with the mopping up. What he found was carnage. The royalist army had been left completely unprotected when, against orders, the cavalry reserve stationed behind Rupert, its blood maddened by contempt for the runaway enemy, had joined the pursuit. Tally-ho!

It was a catastrophic mistake. By no means all the infantry in the parliamentary centre had disintegrated, although it was a close thing. Again it was the Scots or at least one old Covenanter, Sir William Balfour, who made the difference to the destiny of England. While Colonel Thomas Ballard plugged the infantry gap, Balfour rallied his cavalry reserve amid the flying mêlée. They charged the royalist foot soldiers, whom Sir Jacob Astley had led into the fight prefaced by a prayer: 'O Lord! Thou knowest how busy I must be this day. If I forget Thee, do not thou forget me.' A stand was made long enough and firmly enough for the shaken troops, including Holles' London apprentices, to begin to close and mount a gradual, slogging advance up the hill towards the unprotected royalist left flank. Further royalist charges impaled themselves on masses of pikemen. The two forces of pikemen and musketeers met, hand-to-hand, like two lumbering, predatory monsters caught in each other's bristling spikes. And they went at it, hour after hour. The little Duke of York, who had been moved further back for safety by his father, could still see the terrible slaughter below, and all his life he marvelled at the memory, neither side giving ground except to exhaustion. 'The foot being thus ingaged in such warm and close service,' he wrote later, 'it were reasonable to imagine that one side should run and be disorder'd; but it happen'd otherwise, for each as if by mutuall consent retired some few paces, and they stuck down their coulours, continuing to fire at one another even till night; a thing so very extraordinary that nothing less than so many witnesses as there were present, could make it credible.'

In the midst of all this push of pike, smoke and fire and banging of metal was Sir Edmund Verney. The flag gripped in his hand had, of course, made him the most obvious target of all. His eulogists would say that he cut down sixteen soldiers before seeing his own servant Jason die in front of him and then disappearing himself into a mass of oncoming troopers. The flag was carried off but then recaptured by a Life Guard, who disguised himself with the orange scarf of the parliamentarians and brought it back to the king.

Only the October nightfall and sheer dead-dog exhaustion ended the battle. The royalist army held the field. Essex, who thought he should keep together what remained of his force for a possible second engagement should the king decide to move on towards London, fell back on the security of Lord Brooke's Warwick Castle. But the royalist army, although attempting to celebrate a technical victory, was, in fact, torn to pieces. If it wasn't exactly a retreat neither was it a gesture of self-confidence. About 3000 lay dead in the Warwickshire valley, countless more were grievously wounded. The cold was bitter, so sharp that the few who were discovered alive the next morning owed their survival to the freezing temperatures, which had cold-staunched their wounds. The commanders of both armies, especially those who had not seen the bloodshed in Europe, were in shock. The tally-ho war was over.

Little help could be expected for the royalists from a countryside filled with the tenant farmers of Lord Brooke and Viscount Saye and Sele. Although Charles might have seized the moment and attempted a quick march to London, his depleted and mutilated army needed recuperation and reinforcement. So the king made for Banbury, whose garrison surrendered without a fight, then staunchly royalist Oxford, which was to be his capital for the duration of the war, and finally Reading.

In the House of Commons Ralph Verney had to sit through a reading of Lord General Essex's dispatch, which claimed optimistically that Edgehill (then known as the Kineton fight) had been a 'blessed Victory which God hath given us upon the Army of the Cavaliers, and of those Evil Persons, who upon Sunday the 23rd of this Instant, engaged his Majesty in a dangerous and bloody Fight against his faithful Subjects'. But Ralph was lost in a maelstrom of sorrow. His father, the enemy, had fallen holding the king's flag. No one seemed to know exactly what had happened to him or where his body could be found. Lady Sussex wrote to Ralph in condolence: 'I have the saddest heart and deepest wounded soul that ever creature had, he being, I confess to you, the greatest comfort of my life.' Ralph replied:

> Madam, Last night I had a servant from my Lord of Essex's Army, that tells mee there is noe possibility of finding my Deare father's Body, for my Lord Generall, my Lord Brooke … and twenty others of my acquaintance assured him hee was never taken prisiner, neither were any of them ever possessed of his Body; but that hee was slaine by an ordinary trooper. Upon this my man went to all the ministers of severall parishes, that buried the dead that were slaine in the battle, and none of them can give him any information of the body. One of them told him my Lord Aubigney was like to have been buried in the fields, but that one came by chance that knew him and tooke him into a church, and there laid him in the ground without soe much as a sheete about him, and soe divers others of good quallity were buried: the ministers kept Tallies of all that were buried, and they amount to neare 4000. Madam, you see I am every way unhappy. I beseech you afford me your prayers.

Sir Edmund Verney did appear again – but only to the villagers (including a minister and a justice of the peace) who some months later swore they beheld a vision of a terrible engagement of phantom armies contending in the night sky, and there in the middle was the standard-bearer, holding fast to his king's flag. Others claimed that someone, somewhere had found Sir Edmund's severed hand, with the portrait ring of the king on his finger, still clutching a piece of the pole.

None of this was any consolation to Ralph Verney. His father's death shook his faith in the war. In the following year, 1643, he was among many (including Denzil Holles) who tried to find some way out of it, if necessary by putting out feelers to the king. After the collapse of tentative negotiation with the court at Oxford, signatures were demanded for the Solemn League and Covenant with the Scots, an alliance committed to pursuing the war to total victory. Ralph Verney could not bring himself to sign. Instead he disappeared and took his family with him into exile in France.

That the war was to be a long, grim, grinding business had already been

apparent when the king's attempt to smash parliament by taking London stalled at
Turnham Green, on the western outskirts of the capital, in November 1642. A week
before the royalist army, now somewhat depleted by leaving garrisons at Reading and
Oxford, had been confronted with trained bands at Brentford, including Denzil
Holles' redcoats. Another of Rupert's cavalry charges had cut through their lines, however, and pushed the troopers stumbling back into the Thames, where many of them
floundered and drowned, weighed down by their armour. But the fear that gripped
London also produced an immense outpouring of volunteers, determined to stand in
the way of the Cavaliers' retribution. On Sunday, 12 November, 24,000 of them, plus
hordes of women and civilians supplying them with food and encouragement, faced
12,000 soldiers of the royalist army. Many of the defenders were armed with nothing
better than cudgels or pitchforks, but there were a lot of them. And after a day-long,
nervous stand-off at Turnham Green Charles decided against risking his army and
took it back to Oxford.

Edgehill had taught Charles that the conflict would not be settled by a single, epic
battle. Turnham Green taught him that, however disorganized and amateurish, parliament was capable of mobilizing resources that could equal or outgun his own. It was
crucial, then, to husband and strengthen his own assets in regions of the country where
he could depend on a solid base of gentry support and where the population might be
more receptive to the heavy taxation needed to fund the war effort. This boiled down,
essentially, to the west and northeast and Wales. Once his military power base was solid,
he could move from the periphery of the country towards the strategic centre, gradually drawing a noose around the neck of London. Parliament, on the other hand, knew
that as its core supply areas in eastern and southeastern England were held secure, the
capital would be fed and armed. Preventing the royalist army from making inroads into
East Anglia and the east Midlands, lying as they did between the king's northern and
western power bases, became crucial for parliament. In 1643 the establishment of an
Eastern Association, linking the county defence committees under the unified command of Lord Mandeville, now the Earl of Manchester and one of the few peers to
remain with parliament, was meant to make the rapid deployment of Cromwell's foot
soldiers, guns and horse, when and where they were needed, more efficient.

The war that year broke down into regional theatres of conflict, especially in
Yorkshire and the West Country. They were no less nasty or bloody, and no less ruinous
to the towns and country that felt their shock, for being such local events. And they
were both very unpredictable. The size of the forces waxed and waned with the enthusiasm and loyalty of the gentry who brought them into the war, and they were constantly plagued by defections of common foot soldiers and troopers who deserted in

large numbers after battles, whether victorious or defeated. ('Home, home' was the repeated cry of London apprentices in Devon and Cornwall, who knew they were very far away from Cheapside and Southwark.) But then, after all, their gentlemen officers seemed to change sides with dismaying regularity, at least during 1643, and mostly in one direction – towards the king, whose fortunes were certainly in the ascendant that year. In Yorkshire Sir John Hotham, who had turned the king away from Hull, and Sir Hugh Cholmley, a ship-money resister, both switched sides. In Cornwall Sir Alexander Carew, who had been so implacably determined to see Strafford beheaded, plotted to hand over Plymouth to the royalists, was exposed by one of his servants, arrested, taken to London and summarily tried and executed. With things definitely not going according to plan in the western campaign, Sir Richard Grenville, the brother of Sir Bevil, suddenly discovered that, after all, religion had been 'a cloke for rebellion' and changed his allegiance, becoming one of the most ruthlessly cold-blooded of all the royalist generals.

The fact that, especially in the early years of the war, many of the generals on either side were so alike in their social and cultural personality, indeed had often known each other well, either in parliament or in the country, and spoke the same kind of language of patriotic disinterest, must also have weakened, or at least constantly tested, their allegiance. The two generals who faced each other in the murderous little war in the West Country, Sir William Waller and Sir Ralph Hopton, respectively from Gloucestershire and Somerset, and both professional soldiers, were virtually inter-changeable types, even in religion, where Hopton the royalist was as much of a sober Puritan as Waller and had voted not only for Strafford's attainder but even for that bug-bear of the royalist cause, the Grand Remonstrance. It had only been when parliament arrogated to itself power over the militia that Hopton had changed allegiance. He was, then, as close as possible to the mind-set of his adversaries. During a brief lull in their campaign, Hopton wrote to Waller asking for a meeting. Waller had to turn him down but in terms that suggest just how deeply the distress of their broken friendship went.

> To my noble frend, Sr Ralphe Hopton at Wells
>   Sr
> The experience I have had of your worth, and the happiness I have enjoyed in your freindshipp, are wounding considerations to me when I looke upon this present distance between us. Certainly my affections to you are so unchangeable, that hostility itself cannot violate my freindshipp to your person, but I must be true to the cause wherein I serve. The ould limitation usque ad aras holds still, and where my conscience is interested all other obligations are swallowed upp.

I should most gladly waite upon you, according to your desire, but that I looke upon you as you are ingaged in that party, beyond the possibility of a retreat and consequently uncapable of being wrought upon by any persuasions. And I know the conference could never be so close between us, but that it would take winde and receive a construction to my dishonour. That great God, who is the searcher of my heart, knowes with what a sad sence I go on upon this service, and with what a perfect hatred I detest this warr without an ennemy. But I looke upon it as Opus Domini, and that is enough to silence all passion in mee. The God of Peace in his good time send us the blessing of peace and in the meane time fitt us to receive itt. Wee are both upon the stage, and must act those parts that are assigned us in this Tragedy. Lett us do itt in a way of honour, and without personall animosities. Whatsoever the issue be, I shall never relinquish the dear title of

> Your most affectionated friend
> and faithfull servant
> Wm Waller

Three weeks later at Lansdown, near Bath, Hopton's army charged Waller's hilltop position and captured it, along with guns and prisoners but at savage cost to himself. Of the 2000 who had ridden up the hill, only 600 were left alive in the pyrrhic victory. Among the 200 infantry who had died in the same attack was Sir Bevil Grenville, another friend of Waller's, pole-axed at the summit. Hopton himself had been badly slashed in the arm. Inspecting prisoners the next day an ammunition wagon exploded, burning and temporarily blinding him, so that he needed to be carried in a litter, knowing that at any time Waller's troops, defeated but rested at Bath, might swoop down on his battered and bedraggled army. On Roundway Down outside Devizes a week later, Hopton's army, despite its general being more or less unable to see or ride, again triumphed, this time overwhelmingly. Two weeks later, on 26 July, the walls of Bristol, thought to be impregnable, were stormed by Hopton's Cornish army and the city, under the command of Saye and Sele's son Nathaniel, surrendered to Prince Rupert.

The fall of Bristol sent shock waves through all the godly hold-outs in the southwest. To the godliest of them all, Dorchester, William Strode brought disturbing news of Cavalier besiegers who had thought nothing of climbing up 20-foot walls. In his view Dorchester's defences would keep the town safe for about half an hour. Those who had vowed to live and die with their Covenant now had a sudden change of heart. John White fled to London; William Whiteway tried to take ship out of Weymouth and was intercepted by a royalist patrol. On 2 August, having been assured

Sir William Waller, by Cornelius Jonson, 1643. Popularly known as 'William the Conqueror' for his early successes in the civil war, Waller was later defeated by his friend Sir Ralph Hopton at Lansdown in 1643.

that a quick surrender would guarantee them against plunder, the citizens of Dorchester opened the town to Cavalier troops. They were plundered anyway.

With the royalists now in command of most of the strongholds and towns of the west, Lady Brilliana Harley, locked up in Brampton Bryan, braced herself for the worst. She was in dire peril. Sir Robert (who belatedly had reconsidered his advice that she should remain in Herefordshire) was still in London without any way to reach home. Her sons Ned and Robert were in Waller's army and, she hoped, safe. Most of the godly clergy and families had long since fled, many to Gloucester, which was holding out against a royalist siege. Her friends' abandoned houses had been gutted and vandalized, their livestock taken and slaughtered, the tenant farmers and labourers terrorized, and the lands themselves forfeit to the king. Defending Brampton behind its fourteenth-century gatehouse were fifty musketeers, attempting to protect another fifty civilians, including her family physician, a few of her godly lady friends and her three youngest children, Thomas, Dorothy and Margaret. By late July, 700 foot soldiers and horse troopers were camped around Brampton, building breastworks close to her garden from which they could fire cannonballs and musket shot at the house. There was nothing much that Brilliana could do except pray, wait and inspect her own defensive works. The siege, when it began in earnest, went on for six and a half weeks. There were daily bombardments, the defenders reduced to using hand-mills to grind their grain into flour for bread. The roof of the hall was smashed in, but despite the relentless regularity of the fire surprisingly few were killed, except Brilliana's cook, another servant and one of her woman friends. Priam Davies, a parliamentarian captain present throughout the siege, claimed, not implausibly, that Brilliana was most upset by the perpetual and noisy enemy cursing coming from the 'breast works in our gardens and walks, where their rotten and poisoned language annoyed us more than their poisoned bullets'.

Throughout the siege Brilliana remained in regular contact with the besiegers, who themselves hoped for a negotiated end rather than having to storm the house, and kept them talking as a ploy, while hoping for some relief from parliamentary troops. Eventually, in September, the royalists were called away to reinforce the siege of Gloucester and left her still the mistress of Brampton Bryan. She set about levelling the earthworks and replanting her garden and orchards. She also badly needed to restock the estate with cattle and took them from neighbours who had become enemies. Brilliana the pious had become Brilliana the plunderer, but God, she knew, understood the compulsion of her plight.

God, in fact, had other plans for Brilliana Harley. In October, apparently quite suddenly she fell into a 'defluxion' of the lungs, convulsed with terrible bloody coughing and on Sunday 31 October 1643, to general shock and grief, she died. When Sir Robert got the news, like the Calvinist he was, he bent before the inscrutable design of the Almighty: 'having received the sad news that the Lord has taken from me my dear wife, to whose wise hand of providence I desire with a heart of resignation humbly to submit'. Stirred by Brilliana's example, the defenders of Brampton Bryan continued to hold out against further attacks until April 1644, when they finally gave up the house to troops acting in the name of the governor of Hereford, Barnabas Scudamore, the viscount's brother.

The autumn of 1643 was perhaps the time of greatest gloom for the parliamentary cause. The 'birds' of 1642 had been plucked by defections and death. In June 1643 Hampden had been mortally wounded at the battle of Chalgrove Field. Denzil Holles had been so shaken by the adversities of the year that he was among the most conspicuous of those who were trying to reach a negotiated peace with the king. Haselrig's troop of cuirassiers, known from their armour and red coats as the 'lobsterbacks', were among those destroyed in Hopton's great victory at Roundway Down in July, although Haselrig himself lived to fight many more political battles. John Pym was dying, horribly, of intestinal cancer, but not before he had put together the alliance that, more than any other single event, would rescue the parliamentary position and determine the eventual outcome of the war: the Solemn League and Covenant with the Scots.

In 1637 Scotland had begun the resistance to the absolutism of Charles I, and seven years later the Covenant would all but finish him off. Only the obstinately anglocentric need for home-grown heroes can explain the general impression that Oliver Cromwell was somehow single-handedly responsible for defeating Charles I in the first civil war, when his role was late and limited (although often decisive and invariably successful). Without the intervention of the great Covenanter general, Alexander Leslie (at the Scottish parliament's request elevated by Charles to be Earl of Leven in 1641), Cromwell might never have had a chance to celebrate those victories. Ironically, the League between the Covenanters and the English parliament, which delivered a huge army to the critical campaign in Yorkshire, was the first concerted attempt to make a British union since the abortive efforts of James VI and I. To seal the alliance, Pym and the godly party in the Lords and Commons had, in effect, to promise that there would be a Presbyterian concordance among the Churches of England, Scotland and Wales. Since there was a Scots army under Monro vigorously (not to say brutally) campaigning there, it seemed only a matter of time before Ireland, too, was brought into the fold. So when the Lords and Commons gathered on 25 September 1643 to take the oath of loyalty to the Solemn League and Covenant in St Margaret's Chapel, Westminster, an astoundingly inverted version of the Stuart dream of union – a godly Great Britain – seemed wondrously within reach.

On 19 January Leven crossed the Tweed with 18,000 foot soldiers, 3000 horse, 500 dragoons and 16 cannon. For the second time in five years Northumberland was under Scottish occupation. To defend the Tyne, Newcastle had 500 foot and 300 horse. A royalist disaster was obviously looming. Troops were hastily rushed from wherever Charles could get them, especially from the south and west, but Waller's victory in the next round of his wargames with Hopton, at Cheriton in March 1644, took one of those resources away.

York, which for so long had seemed impregnable as the king's capital of the north, found itself the target of a huge eleven-week siege, the city surrounded on all sides by parliamentary and Scottish troops. Its outlying villages were laid to waste, and everything in the farms was taken and used by the besiegers. An observer of the destruction inside the city, Simeon Ashe, wrote: 'Had thine eyes yesternight with me seen York burning thy heart would have been heavye. The Lord affect us with the sad fruits of wasting warres and speedily and mercifully end our combustions which are carried on with high sinnes and heavy desolations. Truly my heart sometimes is ready to breake with what I see here.'

Gradually, the fate of York and with it the north of England came to be seen, by both sides, as the fulcrum on which the fate of the entire war would turn. The king kept just enough of his army in the southwest to keep the Earl of Essex and Waller detained, while, with an immense effort, the Duke of Newcastle and Prince Rupert assembled an army large enough to break the siege and compete on equal terms with the combined forces of the Covenant and parliament. Early on a sultry 2 July, 40,000 men faced each other on Marston Moor, a few miles from the city. It was neither a good place nor a good time for a battle. There had been a violent rainstorm, making the Yorkshire heath boggy, and there was a wide ditch separating the two armies, which stood a half mile from each other, sweating into their armour. For once Rupert was not especially anxious to begin the proceedings – not even, for that matter, to give battle. The afternoon wore on, a long cat-and-mouse game, with Rupert waiting for a premature cavalry attack to stumble over the ditch and be ready to be picked off. But before he knew it, Cromwell's horse, on the parliamentary left, was charging over the ditch and on to his soldiers, slashing its way through to the rear. In the furiousness of the charge Cromwell took a wound to the neck and head and had to leave the field, which, since the royalist left had badly beaten Sir Thomas Fairfax's troops, should have given them their opportunity, with the pikemen and musketeers as usual pushing and firing at the centre. But, at the defining moment of his career, Cromwell came back into the fray, along with the Covenanter general David Leslie. Cromwell had become justly famous for the battlefield discipline of his horse, and instead of letting them waste precious time and energy rampaging through the enemy's baggage train, he wheeled his troopers round to the now unprotected rear of the royalist right flank. It was this fast-moving parliamentary cavalry that had the advantage of the lie of the land and rode down on the virtually surrounded royalist centre, folding in on itself.

After three hours, there were 6000 dead on Marston Moor. The cream of the king's infantry had been wiped out. The Duke of Newcastle, who had emptied his own coffers to supply Charles with an army, had witnessed its complete destruction and had nothing left to finance another. He would not, he said, remain to hear the laughter of the court, preferring instead to go into exile with just £90 to his name. For Oliver Cromwell, though, the victory was an unmistakable sign that the Lord of Hosts was fighting alongside his godly soldiers. Writing to his brother-in-law, Colonel Valentine Walton, he declared that 'God made them as stubble to our swords', before going on to darken the rejoicing by telling Walton: 'Sir, God hath taken away your eldest son by a cannon-shot. It brake his leg. We were necessitated to have it cut off, whereof he died. Sir, you know my trials this way [Cromwell had lost his own son, Oliver junior, to sickness while he was serving in the army]; but the Lord supported me with this: that the Lord took him into the happiness we all pant after and live for. There is your precious child full of glory, not to know sin nor sorrow any more.'

By the end of the month York had capitulated. The only bright spot for the king was Cornwall, where the Earl of Essex (who had insisted on taking command over Waller) had managed to get an army of 10,000 hopelessly trapped within a 5-mile strip of land between Lostwithiel and Fowey. Charles, who was personally commanding the campaign (and enjoying it), asked the earl if he would now consider joining him in a united campaign to clear the Scots from the north, but Essex declined, preferring to depart from his army by boat once he had seen the cavalry break through and escape. Philip Skippon (another who was offered a place in the royalist army by Charles and who rejected it) was left to deal with the débâcle at Fowey, negotiating for his foot soldiers an honourable retreat that turned into a logistical and human nightmare. One of the royalist soldiers who was watching the retreat saw a 'rout of soldiers prest all of a heap like sheep … so dirty and dejected as was rare to see'. Stripped of food, clothes, boots and shelter, attacked by the country people (especially the women), Skippon's men slept in soaking fields and drank from puddles and ditches. One of them remembered being 'inhumanly dealt with, abused, reviled, scorned, torn, kicked, pillaged and many stript of all they had, quite contrary to the articles of war'. Disease, starvation and untended wounds made short shrift of the army, so that just 1000 of the 6000 who had left Fowey dragged themselves into Poole.

By the end of the year parliament was in control of thirty-seven of the fifty-seven counties of England and Wales and the majority of the most populous and strategically important towns, with the exception of Bristol, Exeter and Chester. But the king was not yet defeated. At the second battle of Newbury in October he had managed to avoid a potentially lethal pincer movement by the armies of Waller and Essex and slugged out the day to an exhausted tie. The wear and tear of Newbury was enough to prevent Charles from breaking through, but not enough to finish him off. And Charles was aware, as much as parliament, of the increasingly acrimonious relations between Waller and Essex on the one hand and Manchester and Cromwell on the other, all of whom were barely on speaking terms, so much did they suspect and despise each other. Attempting to flatten the king was like trying to swat a particularly annoying and nimble housefly. And, although by all measure of the military arithmetic, Charles was losing ground, there was an ominous sense among the military commanders on the parliamentary side that he was prevailing – at least politically – just by avoiding obliteration. As the Earl of Manchester put it: 'If we beat the king ninety and nine times yet he is a king still and so will his posterity be after him. But if the king beat us once we shall all be hanged and our posterity be made slaves.' To which Oliver Cromwell, who was rapidly coming to despise what he thought was Manchester's inertia and pusillanimity, retorted, pithily: 'If this be so, why did we take up arms at first?'

Manchester and Cromwell's arguments over how best to use the now formidable army of the Eastern Association were much more than a tactical squabble. Cromwell suspected that what he said – in public – was Manchester's reluctance to prosecute the war with all possible energy and severity resulted from a misguided anxiety not to destroy the king too completely lest a great void in the polity be opened up. For his part, Manchester accused Cromwell of filling his regiments with social inferiors of dangerously unorthodox religious opinions, who would be unlikely to subscribe to the Presbyterian rule they were all supposed to be fighting for, north and south of the Scottish border. Oliver Cromwell was, as time would show, no social leveller, nor did he see the army as a school of political radicalism. But he was a recognizably modern soldier in his belief that men fought better when officers and men had a common moral purpose, a bonding ideology. The old knightly ideal by which gentlemen would lead and their loyal men would follow was, he thought, no longer adequate for the times nor for their cause. It was necessarily the Cavalier ethos, not their own. This is what Cromwell meant after Edgehill when he had told Hampden,

'Your troopers ... are most of them old decayed serving men and tapsters, and such kind of fellows, and ... their troopers are gentlemen's sons ... You must get men of a spirit ... that is like to go as far as a gentleman will go, or else I am sure you will be beaten still.' And when he told the Suffolk committee that 'I had rather have a plain russet-coated captain that knows what he fights for, and loves what he knows, than that which you call a gentleman and is nothing else,' he was not so much asking for a democratized army as for a morally and ideologically motivated godly army. In the bitter debate with Manchester, which lasted into the winter of 1645 and was aired in the House of Commons, Cromwell made it clear that a godly army need not (as the Covenanters assumed) be a rigidly Presbyterian one. More than once he came to the defence of a junior officer accused of being a Baptist or some other kind of unofficial Protestant, on the grounds that those who were prepared to die for the righteous cause should not be slighted to appease the Scots. Whatever Britain Cromwell thought he was fighting for, it was not a Presbyterian united kingdom.

Presbyterians, like Manchester, Essex and Harley, and 'Independents', as those who took the more inclusive and tolerant line on worship called themselves, could at least agree that the war needed to be brought to the king with maximum force in 1645. To that end, parliament attempted to separate politics from the military command by enacting a Self-Denying Ordinance, which required all members of the Lords and Commons to resign their military posts, or vice versa. This effectively removed most of the principal protagonists – Essex, Manchester and Waller – while creating a unified New Model Army under the command of Sir Thomas Fairfax, the only senior general for whom no one (yet) had a bad word and who made a point of being politically neutral. Apolitical though he was, Fairfax did share with Cromwell a sense of how this core parliamentary army ought to be run. It was to be zealous and godly (a lot more psalm-singing), and it was to be exemplary in its discipline. The standard unwinding techniques for soldiers – drink, cursing and whoring – were to be replaced by quiet sessions with *The Souldiers Catechisme*. Plunder would be savagely punished. (That, at any rate, was the idea: all very nice and Christian in principle but suicidal to enforce in the aftermath of a particularly hideous and prolonged siege.) In return for their sobriety and enthusiastic self-sacrifice, the soldiers were to be made to feel that their generals – all their officers, in fact – genuinely cared for their welfare, that they would be provided with boots, food and shelter, and that when they were lying screaming as their arm was being sawn off they would know there had been a point to it all. Cromwell and Fairfax were in absolutely no doubt of the point to it all.

Translating that certainty into total victory was another matter. Although by the spring of 1645 it looked unlikely (if not impossible) that Charles could win in

England, he was now fighting for, and in, Britain. A setback in one of his kingdoms might always be compensated by success in another, and to the wearied and vexed parliamentary generals it seemed that he could go on playing this military shell game indefinitely, until his enemies were all at each other's throats. For there were now internal civil wars in all four of the British nations. They were not taking place in discrete theatres of conflict but were all tangled up in each other's fate. Because Charles could thank his remote Plantagenet ancestors for the most indestructible of his fortresses in Wales, what happened there, especially in the Marches, at castles like Chepstow and Monmouth, would ultimately affect the course of the war in England. Welsh soldiers were already making up a significant part of the royalist armies fighting in the west. Scottish Covenanter troops were stuck in Ireland protecting Presbyterian Ulster against the Gaelic Confederacy, which, given the central importance of the papacy and Owen Roe O'Neill, they believed was the same thing as protecting Scotland and England from impending invasion by the Antichrist. That eventuality seemed much closer in June 1646 when Monro lost a crucial battle at Benburb in County Tyrone against Owen Roe O'Neill.

And in the autumn of 1644, the Covenanter-Catholic, Scots-Irish war came back to Scotland itself, when Alasdair MacColla landed in the western Highlands with a force of 2000 Irish, supplied by his Clan Donald kinsman, the Earl of Antrim, and drawn almost exclusively from Catholic Ulster. It linked up with the even smaller army of James Graham, Marquis of Montrose, whose ambition was to open a second front for Charles in northern and western Scotland. With the bulk of the Covenanter army still in England (from which the English parliamentary command could certainly not afford to release it), Montrose was gambling that he could open a back door to power, rally the Highlands and islands, cut through the weakened Lowlands and go all the way to Edinburgh, where he would overthrow the Covenant and establish a Scottish royalist regime. With that army, he would then invade England and turn the tide there as well.

That was the plan, at any rate − a pan-British, anti-Covenanter solution for the whole country − and it was blessed initially with a spectacular series of military successes against the weakened Covenanter-Lowland armies. But the reason Montrose and MacColla were winning in the autumn and winter of 1644–5 had almost nothing to do with the Marquis' British strategy or his personal alienation from the Covenanters and everything to do with two ancient Scottish feuds. The first was the relentless war between the Calvinist Lowlands and the largely Catholic northwestern Highlands. But even within the Highlands, the obscene slaughters of the Scottish wars were powered by the visceral, unforgiving hatred between Clan Donald (both its Irish and Scots branches) and the Campbells of Argyll. The further away from the killing hills the campaign went, the harder it was for Montrose to keep his army together, although the lure of sacking cities like Perth and Aberdeen helped. The butchery at Aberdeen was especially sadistic, lasting over three days and involving the cold-blooded murder of anyone thought to exercise any sort of public office or authority – advocates, merchants, the masters of the hospitals and almshouses, and scores of other civilians – and leaving a deep legacy of enmity between Irish and Scots. There was, said a contemporary Aberdonian: 'killing, robbing and plunder of this town at their pleasure. And nothing hard bot pitiful howling, crying, weeping, mourning through all the streets. Som women they preseet to defloir and uther sum they took perforce to serve them in the camp.'

Even the tactical style of the Irish–Highland army defied expectations of modern warfare. Like its English counterpart, the Covenanter infantry had at its heart six-deep platoons of musketeers who, to be effective, were supposed to execute a 'counter-march'. This involved the first line filing to the back of the six once its weapons had been fired, with the next line replacing them. By the time the original row returned to the front they were supposed to have completed a flawless and extremely rapid reloading. But without intensive drill practice the movement was, in fact, seldom either flawless or swift, and it was precisely at that moment that the Highland and Irish soldiers dropped their own muskets and charged with sword and shield, cutting a bloody route through the floundering musketeers and pikemen. The 'Highland' charge (already much used in the Irish war by the Gaelic-Catholic soldiers) was primitive but astonishingly effective. And there were other ways in which the armies of Montrose and MacColla inconveniently refused to abide by the rules, continuing their campaign into the deep Highland winter, especially in the Campbell lands, where villages were devastated, and (as would remain the practice all through 1645 and into 1646) indiscriminately killing any men or boys who might one day serve as soldiers. After a while, strategy simply dissolved into clan cleansing. For MacColla killing as many Campbells as possible became the main point of the campaign, while for Archibald Campbell, Earl of Argyll, counter-killing as many of the Clan Donald and their allies, the MacLean, was equally satisfying. And so the carnage went on and on and on, indifferent to seasons or landscape: blood in the snow, blood in the heather, blood in the pinewoods. In one particularly gruesome atrocity, some hundreds of Campbell men, women and children were herded into a barn, which was then burned to the ground.

Montrose did, in the end, succeed in reaching deep into the Covenanter Lowlands, establishing himself not at Edinburgh, then in the grip of a terrible wave of the plague, but at Glasgow. At Philiphaugh in 1645 his army suffered its first serious defeat, but by early 1646 he was still in a position to do great damage in Scotland on behalf of the royalist cause. So it must have been a shock when, at the beginning of May 1646, Charles himself went to the Covenanter army then besieging the town of Newark and put himself in the hands of the Scots.

But then Montrose's campaign (and the battle of Benburb in Ireland) had been the *only* thing that had gone right for the king in 1645 and early 1646. By the time the New Model Army was deployed in April 1645, parliament, together with its Scots allies, could put 50,000 men in the field and had perhaps the same number in garrisons – much the biggest military force ever to be seen in Britain. The king could field half that number at most. Penned up in Oxford, he had few choices. The first was to cut his losses and respond positively to peace terms set at Uxbridge earlier in the year. But the Solemn League and Covenant had required the king to accept a bishopless Presbyterian regime along with the new Directory of Worship, already distributed in place of the Book of Common Prayer, and this Charles found just as repugnant as he always had. Fighting on, unless he just sat in Oxford waiting for the inevitable siege, meant choosing between moving west or north.

A second option for Charles, recommended by Prince Rupert, was to play to his strengths by moving west and maintaining his military power base along a line of strongholds from Exeter through Bristol and Cardiff to Carlisle, to join with the still undefeated army of General Goring, drawing the parliamentary army into deeply hostile territory and keeping the crucial seaways open to Ireland from whence cometh, it was hoped, some help. Alternatively, a third choice would be to move north towards Montrose, hoping his victories would prove contagious and uniting their armies. After a good deal of dithering, mesmerized by Montrose's success and by an understandable feeling that everything decisive that happened in his reign happened in Scotland, Charles chose the northern option. At the end of May 1645 his army took and sacked Leicester and was moving northeast. Its break-out had the effect, as intended, of drawing Fairfax away from the siege of Oxford and hastening Cromwell eastwards to protect East Anglia. But it also had the undesired effect of bringing those two armies together to face the king in what was obviously going to be a decisive battle, near the Northamptonshire village of Naseby.

Even without the New Model Army forces, Charles was outnumbered by Fairfax. But again over-ruling Rupert's caution, he decided to give battle anyway. By the time they deployed on two facing hilltops with a marshy little vale between them, the two forces were massively disproportionate. Cromwell and Fairfax had about 14,000 men, the king only half that number. And numbers counted. Remembering his mistake in waiting at Marston Moor, Rupert took the initiative, charged right away

down his hill and, carried by the momentum up the facing slope, sliced through the
cavalry on the left flank, commanded by Cromwell's future son-in-law, Henry Ireton,
who was wounded in the onslaught. But only about half of Ireton's cavalry strength
broke from this initial hit. Yet again, Rupert's horse was soon off plundering the baggage train, leaving the royalist infantry in the centre to push pikes with Fairfax's foot
soldiers and the Scots. At just the moment when it looked as though Fairfax's numbers would inevitably take their toll, Cromwell charged, his tight lines of horses crashing into the royalist cavalry that remained on the left flank. At the critical moment
Charles, dressed in a gilt suit of armour, tried to charge Cromwell's victorious troopers with his Life Guard. Horrified aides took the reins of his Flemish horse and led it
away, a move that was misread in the field as a command for tactical withdrawal. The
crumbling became a collapse. In two hours it was all over. Seeing his men exposed
to a slaughter, Astley surrendered 4000 foot and 500 officers, as well as the complete
royalist artillery train and thousands of muskets and arquebuses. Virtually nothing was
left of the royalist army except its dead on the field of Naseby. In the captured baggage train were the king's correspondence, personal and military, as well as £100,000
worth of jewels, coaches and plate. A troop of Welsh women, called 'Irish whores' by
the victorious troopers, were, needless to say, mercilessly butchered or mutilated.

Within a month or two there was almost nothing left of the royalist war machine
in England. Another decisive victory by Fairfax over Lord Goring at Langport in
Somerset destroyed its surviving western command. One by one the major centres –
Bristol, Cardiff, Carlisle – fell. Garrisons that held out were besieged with the utmost
ferocity. When, after a massive siege in October, Cromwell's army finally took the
heavily fortified Basing House built by the Catholic Marquis of Winchester (Mary
Tudor's Lord Treasurer) and still owned by his heir, they were convinced they were
rooting out a nest of filthy idolatry and put to the sword everyone they could find in
the burning ruins, civilians as well as soldiers, women as well if they offered any resistance. The great architect and orchestrator of the court masques, Inigo Jones, fled with
only a rough blanket to protect him from naked indignity. Paintings and books were
taken to London to be burned in a great public bonfire, and whatever was left of the
furniture or jewels found there was the soldiers' to sell.

On 26 April 1646 Charles left Oxford. He had cut his hair; wore a false beard
and was dressed without any of the trappings of a gentleman, much less those of a
king. Only his chaplain and a single manservant went with him. For a while he hid in
disguise in Norfolk, hoping he might yet escape by sea and perhaps join the queen in
France. But this was the heart of Cromwell country, and the ports were being watched.
His better chance lay with the Scots, even the Covenanter Scots, for he knew that,

Presbyterian though they were, their vision of the future assumed the continuing presence of a king. Exactly what sort of king, however, was evidently open to dispute.

And dispute the nations of Britain did, in words and fire for another three years, which were almost as ruinous and certainly as divisive as the previous three. For if peace had broken out in 1646, it was only in the sense that sieges and battles had, for the time being, ended.

Just what the new England, what the new Britain, was supposed to be, what the prize was for which so many had laid down their life, was unresolved. So many of the principles for which parliament had gone to war in the first place in 1642 had been made redundant by the transforming brutality of the conflict. The one thing that had not changed was the conviction, shared by a majority of parliament, that they needed some sort of king, chastened, emasculated, restrained and reformed, but a king none the less, as an indispensable element in the constitution. So the traditional political fiction that the king had been 'led astray' into the war by wicked and malignant 'men of blood' was maintained, the better to cleanse the Crown of permanent, institutional guilt. By the same token, those held responsible for the crime of civil war and who were exempt from any kind of pardon and indemnity – and who therefore might well be brought to trial – were no fewer than seventy-three, starting with Prince Rupert. Equally, anyone who had fought for the royalist side or aided or abetted them in any identifiable way was to be excluded forever from holding any kind of local office or trust. This, in effect, was to perpetuate the painful division of the governing and law community that had opened up in 1642. And since the king had shown such contempt for what, in retrospect, seemed like the modest proposals for his restraint set out by parliament five years before, he now had to be fettered with bands of steel. Control of the militia and armed forces was to be transferred to parliament for twenty years, and it went without saying that neither high officers of state nor his council could be appointed without parliament's consent, nor foreign policy action taken without its approval. While Presbyterianism was the order of the day, the eventual fate of England's Church was left, for good political reasons, to future settlement.

What kind of Britain did this augur? The Marquis of Argyll, for one, believed that at last a 'true union' of Scotland and England – unforced, sympathetic in godly amity, the opposite of James VI and I's marriage of high Churches, and certainly the opposite of Charles's Arminian coercion – was now at hand. But then, of course, with the Clan Donald still torching his villages and murdering his clansmen, and with the Catholic-Irish Confederacy unsubdued and capable of supplying new armies to make his people wretched, Argyll had very practical reasons to sound so fraternal. The war that at the beginning had been fought to keep the several nations of the British

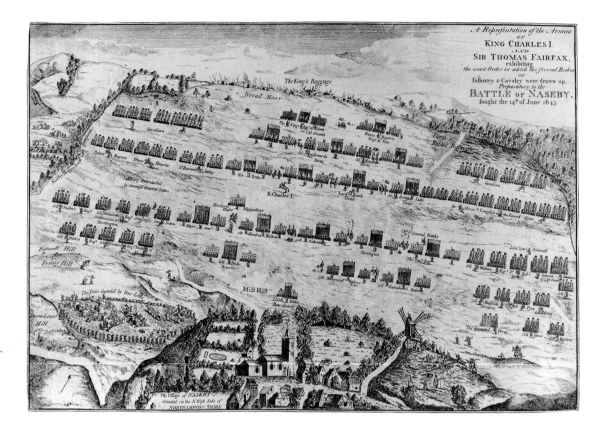

Top: Plan of the battle of Naseby, 1645.
Above: *Sir Thomas Fairfax, General of the Forces*, by an unknown
artist, *c*. 1650. Fairfax led parliament to victory at Naseby.

archipelago apart was now pulling them together, although on terms that were often mutually at odds. Driven by the imperatives of the Catholic Counter-Reformation, the Irish revolt had now accepted a view of itself that had once been only the fantasy of its enemies: that the restoration of the old Church was the prelude to the destruction of heresy in England and Scotland. Conversely, the Presbyterians in Ulster now thought there would never be any peace or safety for themselves in Ireland without the active military involvement of the rest of Protestant Britain. We are still living with the consequences of that assumption.

Oddly enough, in 1646–7 it was England that rather wanted to be left alone and paid the Scots army £400,000 to go away, leaving the king behind. (The Scots, Charles remarked with grim irony, had bartered him away rather cheaply.) To be left alone, though, was not the same as to be left in peace. Militarily pacified, politically England was a vacuum filled by an uproar. The old polite community of law and government that had ruled since the Reformation had been shattered, some thought (wrongly, as it would turn out) beyond repair. In counties ravaged by war, justices of the peace were partially replaced by county committees empowered to mobilize money and arms, while JPs survived to look after traditional administration and crime. The county committees were hated by civilians for billeting soldiers and levying taxes, and they were hated by the army for failing to pay them adequately and reducing them to either beggary or theft. By 1646–47, however, as parliamentarian control was established throughout England, JPs everywhere started making a comeback. The wielder of power in England now was not, as everyone had imagined when the war began, parliament, but the army: a massive military machine the likes of which had never before been seen in Britain. And when the fighting was more or less done, the men of this hungry, angry and poorly paid army were perfectly prepared to mutiny, seize their officers, march to new quarters without permission or refuse to decamp. In the last years of the war, the New Model Army at least had also been socially transformed, with the officer corps drawn from sections of society that were much broader and lower down in the pecking order than anything thought possible before 1645. This did not necessarily mean that its opinions were more radical – the startlingly proto-democratic Levellers, such as John Lilburne, were still an influential minority. But it did mean that something new had been unloosed on the English polity: a reading, debating soldiery with a burning desire to settle accounts with its parliamentary paymasters. And while they were at it, an extremely important element in the army, beginning with Cromwell and Ireton, was becoming increasingly hostile to the 'Scottish' Presbyterianism that had been imposed on England by the Solemn League and Covenant. Let the Scots have a Kirk, said the Independents, and let godly English congregations elect ministers according to their own understanding of faith and desired forms of worship.

In the summer of 1647 this perilously volatile mixture of religious hostility and economic anger brought England very close to another civil war, this time between parliament and the army. But it was a contest in which only one side had the guns. Parliament's idea of neutralizing its problems with the army had been to demobilize it, even before it had come to terms with the king. For its part, the army was hardly likely to agree to its disbandment before its grievances had been properly addressed. Indignant that their orders were not being obeyed, parliamentary leaders, especially Denzil Holles, began to wax constitutional. They claimed (with some reason) that the protection of parliament's authority was the reason for which the war had been fought in the first place and that threats against the integrity and independence of the 'representatives of the people' were a kind of tyranny no less mischievous than that of the king. But in 1647 the army not only had the guns they also had ideologues – although they did not always share the same ideology – such as Ireton or Colonel Rainborough, who ventured to argue that parliament was in fact a 'decayed' body and that the army was a great deal more representative of the people than was the genteel body at Westminster.

On 3 June the quarrel over sovereignty turned literal when a detachment of Fairfax's soldiers, led by Cornet George Joyce, seized the king himself from Holmby House in Northamptonshire. Two days earlier they had hijacked the bullion intended for their disbandment. In the same week Fairfax agreed to the establishment of an unprecedented institution, a General Council of the New Model Army to consist of both officers and elected men from each regiment. With money, force and the king in hand, the army could now literally call the shots. It began to demand the impeachment of Holles and ten other members of the Commons, including Sir Robert's son, Edward Harley, who resisted the redress of their grievances, in particular their arrears of pay, indemnity for conduct during the war and adequate pensions, all genuinely matters of life and death for the battle-hardened soldiers. The army also wanted the kind of religious regime dear to Cromwell, one that respected the independence of congregational preference rather than one that surrendered to Presbyterian enforcement.

There were no heroes (and perhaps no villains) in this sorry showdown. The summer of 1647 witnessed the peculiar spectacle of a professedly apolitical commander, Fairfax, leading (out of conscience for the welfare of his men) a highly politicized army prepared to impose religious liberty at the point of the sword. If that were not paradoxical enough, the men they hated, the parliamentary Presbyterians, were defending the right of the elected representatives of the nation to impose a Calvinist

Church on England by virtue of their votes! Holles and his friends, including Edward Harley, the champions of parliamentary sovereignty against the army (as they had been against the king five years before), were prepared, if necessary, once more to use the pressure of the crowd (another tactic revived from 1642) to get *their* own way. Mobs were excited, 'monster petitions' drawn up. The London apprentices and soldiers who had already disbanded from armies other than the New Model mobilized for their protection. When, at the end of July, a vast and heavily armed demonstration forced both houses of parliament to support the Holles Presbyterian line, bloodshed seemed inevitable. MPs and peers on the losing side, including Manchester, escaped from London to Fairfax's camp and the Lord General began a march on London, making it clear that if the city did not open its gates he would blow them open. On 2 August the New Model Army was peacefully admitted. London – and by extension England – was now under the gun.

In its turn, the army now set out terms for settlement with the king in its Heads of the Proposals. Needless to say, Charles was delighted to be able to play one lot off against the other, especially as the army's conditions turned out to be a good deal more lenient than those currently on the table from parliament. Only four, not seventy-three, royalists were to be exempt from a general pardon. Parliament, called biennially, would exercise control over the armed forces for just ten, not twenty, years, and royalists could be elegible to return to local office after five years. Charles was now in the agreeable and unlooked for position of watching a Dutch auction for his signature. He waited for the bids to go ever lower.

Amid the debris of the English state were survivors who were desperately trying to put the pieces of their lives back together and attempt to make some sense of what had happened to them, their beliefs and their country. For some, this was close to impossible. In 1647 Nehemiah Wallington's sister-in-law, Dorothy Rampaigne, the widow of Zachariah, came back to England to see what she could recover of her deceased husband's estate. But the Wallingtons were horrified to learn that since Zachariah's death Dorothy had taken an Irish Catholic as her lover and protector. This turned upside down everything the Wallingtons had ever believed. 'Oh, my sister,' moaned Nehemiah, 'my heart aches and trembles to consider of yoiur sad and miserable condition … in regard to your poor soul.' Dorothy had not only lain 'with that Irish rebel' and hidden her pregnancy but had carried on with her 'sins and wicked ways' with such shamelessness as to guarantee a terrible judgement from heaven. Nehemiah's wife, Grace, implored her sister to send her only remaining child by Zachariah, a boy called Charles, to London to be protected from the infections of the

Above: *Charles I and James, Duke of York*, by Sir Peter Lely, *c.* 1647.
Opposite: The Verney family monument in the church at Middle Claydon, Buckinghamshire. At top left, Sir Edmund Verney with his wife, Dame Margaret; beneath them, their eldest son, Ralph (also called Raphe), with his wife, Dame Mary, who died in exile in 1650.

SACRED.
To the Memory of the
Euer Honored
S.r EDMVND VERNEY who was
K.t Marshall 16 yeares.
And Standard Bearer to Charles y.e King
In that memorable Battayle
of Edge Hill.
where he was slayne.
on the 23 of October
1642.
Beinge then in the two and
Fiftith yeare of his Age.
AND
in Honour of
Dame MARGARET his wife
Eldest Daughter of S.r Thomas
Denton of Hellesdon K.t
by whome Hee had
Six Sonnes and Six Daughters.
She Dyed at London
on y.e 5.th and was buried here on y.7.
of Aprill 1641.
In the 47 yeare of
Her Age.

ALSO TO THE PERPETVALL HONOVR AND
MEMORY OF THAT MOST EXCELLENT AND
INCOMPARABLE PERSON DAME MARY SOLE
DAVGHTER & HEIRE OF IOHN BLACKNALL OF
ABINGDON IN Y.e COVNTY OF BERKES ESQ.r AND
WIFE OF S.r RAPHE VERNEY (ELDEST SONN OF
THE SAID S.r EDMVND AND DAME MARGARETT)
BY WHOME SHE HAD THREE SONNES AND
THREE DAVGHTERS WHEROF ONLY EDMVND
AND IOHN ARE LIVEING. SHE DECEASED
AT BLOIS IN FRANCE, ON THE 10.TH DAY OF
MAY 1650 BEING ABOVT THE AGE OF 34 YEARES
AND WAS HERE INTERRED ON THE 19.TH OF NOVEM.BER
FOLLOWING. WHERE HER SAID HVSBAND (AT WHOS.e
CHARGE AND BY WHOSE APPOINTMENT THIS MONV-
MENT WAS ERECTED) INTENDS TO BEE BVRIED:

Antichrist and to be brought up in a proper godly household. For whatever reasons, Dorothy did, indeed, send Charles to the Wallingtons, where he was trained as an apprentice turner by Nehemiah, becoming a master himself in 1655.

Ralph Verney's life also changed in 1647–8 as dramatically and as painfully as the condition of England. Although he had never been a royalist, his flight and continued absence in Blois had made him officially a 'delinquent', subject to the sequestration of his estates. In 1647, after much deliberation, he sent his capable wife Mary back to England to see if something could be done to recover them. He had hoped to use his connection with Lady Sussex, who had waxed so considerate at the time of his father's death, to advance his cause but she was now on her next aged husband, who turned out to be none other than the Puritan Earl of Warwick. Faced with the embarrassing reminder of her past in the shape of Mary Verney, Lady Warwick became suddenly hard of hearing to her propositions. Mary none the less persevered with the county committee and eventually 'Old Men's Wife', as Ralph and Mary called her in their private code, did her bit. In January 1648 the sequestration was lifted. But Mary paid a terrible price for her tireless efforts. Claydon itself, when she finally got to it, was miraculously still standing, though it had been used as a barracks for soldiers, and the rats and moths had munched their way through much of the furniture and hangings, especially, to Ralph's distress, the 'Turkie Worke' rugs. But their house's dilapidation was nothing compared to the personal tragedy that followed. Pregnant throughout her lobbying campaigns, Mary was finally delivered of a boy, whom she christened Ralph, only for him to die while still an infant. The same week she heard from her husband that their little daughter Peg had died as well. Ralph, though full of grief, wrote to his distraught wife bravely, in the stoical Christian manner: 'Tis true they are taken from us, (and thats theire happinesse); but wee shall goe to them, (and that should bee our comfort). And is it not much the better both for us and them, that wee should rather assend to heaven to partake of theire perpetuall blisse, than they descend to Earth to share with us our misfortunes?' But he was, in fact, unhinged by sorrow and told his nephew Dr Denton that he would leave France and travel somewhere – Italy or the 'barbary desert' where he could seek out his death. Once gone, he thought his widow and their remaining children would be free to start a new life unencumbered by the taint of his political past. The rescue of his estate, though, thanks to Mary, lifted his spirits out of the slough of despond, and after all their troubles the couple were reunited in Paris in the spring of 1648. They had two more years together in France before Mary's death from a lung disease. It was still not safe for Ralph to return, and he was obliged to ship her body back to Buckinghamshire in its coffin where it was buried before a little company of friends in Middle Claydon church.

The World Turn'd Upside Down: or A briefe description of the ridiculous Fashions of these distracted Times ... 1647.

An endgame began. In November 1647 Charles had escaped the custody of the New Model Army, but only as far as the Isle of Wight, where he was swiftly shut up in Carisbrooke Castle. It was, none the less, a kind of political liberty, since he was still allowed to entertain offers for his endorsement from the lowest bidder. They now included the Scots – not, of course, the purest of the Covenanters (who were appalled by the overture) but a critical element of the less zealous nobles, fearful that the formidable English army, which had neutered parliament, would target them next. A Scotland subjected to the New Model Army would be a Scotland in which a bedlam of sects would be unloosed. It was not to be thought of. The Scots also knew that in his troubles Charles was more popular than he had ever been at the height of his powers. So they came to the Isle of Wight and made him the best offer yet: a Presbyterian settlement for just three years in the first instance and a voluntary acknowledgement of the Covenant. Under the terms of this 'Engagement' (seen also as a way to end the Scottish civil war), the Scots army, together with a newly raised royalist army from northern England, would, if necessary, impose the settlement by force.

Charles, the Duke of Hamilton and royalist stalwarts like Sir Marmaduke Langdale, who had somehow survived Marston Moor and Naseby, could only imagine that they might well reverse the outcome of the first civil war, because since December 1647 whole regions of southern England and Wales had risen in revolt. Unfortunately, for those who wanted to turn a rebellion into a cohesive army, the cause for which they were in insurrection was not Charles (though he was extremely popular) but Father Christmas. Maypoles and the celebration of St George's Day and, of course, Charles's accession day, along with other heathen and seditious revels, had already been outlawed by the Presbyterian parliament. But Christmas – the longest festive celebration and the one arguably that everyone needed at the darkest time of year – was the major target for those bent on cleaning up the calendar and making the Lord's Sabbath on Sunday the only day of rest, and 5 November, the festival of redemption from papist despotism, the only permissible celebration. But to force shopkeepers to keep their businesses open on Christmas Day was hard work for the constabulary, who were already busy ripping down the holly and ivy in towns like Bury St Edmunds and Ipswich, where the citizens festooned the streets in deliberate defiance. The greatest Christmas riots occurred in Kent and rapidly swelled into an all-out armed rebellion. The insurrection was bloodily put down, but 3000 of the rebels escaped over the Thames to Essex, where they held out against Fairfax for months on end behind the great Roman walls of Colchester.

The only real chance of a serious royalist revival, though, depended on the rest of Britain. And in the summer of 1648, the rest of Britain failed Charles. A rebellion in south and central Wales was smashed, leaving Cromwell to besiege Chepstow and Pembroke and mop up the resistance. While relatively charitable terms had previously been offered to those surrendering to besiegers, this second round of war had made iron enter Cromwell's soul, and he often let his soldiers do their worst. Having cleaned up Wales like some latter-day Edward I, he turned to the Scots and between 17 and 19 August 1648 annihilated them first at Preston and then at Winwick.

Although parliament in the spring of 1648 had passed a resolution continuing to declare that the government of England should still consist of king, lords and commons, Cromwell, and more particularly his increasingly militant son-in-law Henry Ireton, no longer really thought so. After the first civil war they had been prepared to buy into the fiction that Charles had been misled by 'men of blood'. And many of those surviving culprits were summarily tried and executed. But now there was nowhere else for blame to go. The chief sanguinary was Charles Stuart himself. In the previous year, the Leveller *Agreement of the People* had already spelled out the unmentionable: a kingless, bishopless Britain. As a demand from the army's rank and file it was not to be tolerated by such as Ireton, but now in the bitter aftermath of the second civil war they sought to make it their own. They had not come to this conclusion in any delirium of constitutional experiment, but rather with the intense pessimism with which parliament itself had concluded that Strafford had to go for 'reasons of the security of state'. If anything, Strafford had been much more blameless than Charles I. Ireton reasoned now that Charles's escape and the second civil war, not to mention the still unsubdued Irish Confederacy, ruled out ever considering another negotiated treaty with the king. He would never abide in good faith by its terms, nor fail to be a magnet for the disaffected, especially in such difficult times of soaring prices and plague. And perhaps more decisive than all of this, at least for Oliver Cromwell, was his infuriated conviction that Charles had defied the judgement of Providence, so clearly declared at Marston Moor and Naseby. Perhaps then (Cromwell still could not quite bring himself to this) the monarchy had to go. Whether Charles had to die was quite another matter. What, after all, was the point, when a whole club of healthy little Stuarts were standing in line in France and Holland as potential successors?

It was when the parliamentary Presbyterians realized that the trial of the king was now a distinct possibility that they hastened to pre-empt it. In September 1648 a deputation went to Newport on the Isle of Wight to talk to the king one last time. But Charles was himself now lost to a peculiar euphoria, both wily and holy. One day he would imagine that he could continue to exploit the deep differences between parliament and army, that one or the other would *need* him to prevail. And on the next day he would meditate on his coming martyrdom. His grandmother had felt and behaved in precisely the same way at Fotheringhay. But if Mary had been certain of her martyrdom, she died not quite knowing where the allegiance of her son James stood. Charles, on the other hand, had no such anxiety about the Prince of Wales. All those Van Dyck family portraits, it turned out, were in their way no more than the truth. The Stuarts were, whatever their many other character failings, a loving and loyal family. So Charles was increasingly prepared, even eager, to deliver himself to his fate, convinced that his death would wipe clean his trangressions and follies, excite popular revulsion and guarantee the throne for his son. 'The English nation are a sober people,' he wrote to the Prince of Wales, 'however at present under some infatuation.' He was sure that sooner or later they would recover from this unfortunate delirium. So why should he have any interest in baling out the Presbyterians by agreeing to terms that he had already turned down? He might even have privately enjoyed their transparent desperation.

On 16 November 1648 Fairfax, who had failed to persuade the king to sign a version of the army's 'Heads of the Proposals', was now more or less compelled to agree to a ferocious 'Remonstrance', largely written by Henry Ireton. It demanded the trial of the king and the abolition of the monarchy. But none of this, by now, could have been much of a shock to Charles. At his most apparently impotent, there was a weird sense in which Charles was at last in control, if not of his immediate destiny, then of his posterity. His worst moment became his best moment, his execution his vindication. He must have taken satisfaction from the knowledge that everything that would be done to him could only be done by making a nonsense of the principles for which parliament had claimed to go to war: the protection of the liberties of the subject. It was but a small step now for Charles Stuart to claim that, all along, *he* and not they had been the shield of his subjects, the defender of the people.

And so it fell out. When Colonel Thomas Pride stood at the door of the Commons on 6 December with his sword-carrying heavies, stopping members who had voted for the Newport Treaty from entering and arresting others, he was violating precisely the parliamentary independence that the war had been fought to preserve. The truncated 'Rump' Parliament that resulted was more a mockery of the institution than anything the Stuarts had ever convened or dissolved. Of the original stalwart tribunes of the Long parliament, only Oliver St John and Henry Vane the younger embraced the military *coup d'État* with any enthusiasm. The 'high court', packed and processed into compliance by manager Ireton, was more farcically arbitrary than any of the prerogative courts that the Long Parliament had abolished as the tools of despotism. It seems that Cromwell was, for a long time, painfully aware of these transparent manipulations of legality and deeply troubled by the prospect of a trial. As late as December 1648 he still referred to those who had 'carried on a design' to depose Charles as traitors. But at some point over the next few weeks he had decided that Providence was, after all, unmistakably demanding the punishment of the 'man of blood', the 'author' of the civil woes. A special high court of 135 commissioners was hand-picked, with a great deal of trouble taken to include a cross-section of the English notability – landowners, army officers and MPs. One commissioner who absented himself from the proceedings was Fairfax. When his name was called at the very beginning of the roll, it was answered by Lady Fairfax, sitting veiled in the public gallery: 'No, nor will he be here; he has more wit than to be here.' Oliver St John likewise decided against making an appearance. Certain precautions had to be taken. The presiding judge, John Bradshaw, wore a hat with a special metal lining 'to ward off blows', and the prisoner was kept well away from the public galleries.

Anyone with even a passing acquaintance with the history of the previous century might have known that it was a bad idea to put members of the house of Stuart on trial. Exacting and nimble displays of legal punctiliousness, followed by a dignified preparation for martyrdom, were their forte. Charles had been brought from Windsor to Westminster, where he dined and lodged as 'Charles Stuart', without any of the service and courtesies due to a sovereign. It was as though legally he were dead already. But there were formalities to go through. On 20 January, beneath Richard II's great hammerbeam roof in Westminster Hall, the short figure in the black hat and grey beard, his face drawn and haggard, was told by the lawyer John Cook that he was being arraigned for his chief and prime responsibility for 'all the treasons, murders, ravages, burnings, spoils, desolations, damages and mischiefs to this nation'. Asked to plead, he refused, demanding instead to know by 'what power I am called hither … I would know by what Authority, I mean, lawful; [for] there are many unlawful Authorities in the world, Theeves and Robbers by the high ways … Remember I am your King, your lawful King, and what sins you bring on your heads, and the Judgement of God upon this Land, think well upon it … before you go further from one sin to a greater.'

Denying the court its show trial, complete with witnesses, Charles, without his habitual stammer, reiterated his refusal to acknowledge the competence of its jurisdiction. When he reappeared on 22 January he was hoping to read the text of a written explanation of his reasons for refusing to plead, insisting that as king he could not be held accountable to any earthly judges and that nothing lawful could possibly be derived from a body that had removed one part of its indivisible law-making sovereignty. The only possible claim to such jurisdiction was through the revolutionary utterance, already made by the Rump Parliament when it asserted on 4 January that 'the people are, under God, the source of all just power'. Charles, not hesitating to expose the coercion behind the fig leaf, protested that it was common knowledge that this parliament's claim to represent the people was belied by the detention and exclusion of many of its representatives. Here was Charles Stuart in effect making the claim that he, and not the army or a fraudulent parliament, was the true guardian of the welfare and freedom of the people. That, of course, was what his most articulate and disinterested champions, like Edward Hyde, had wanted him to say all along. Needless to say, the impresarios of the trial were not going to allow Charles to say these things out loud. He was silenced before getting very far with his statement and after much protest taken away from the court. The following day the same exchange ended when Bradshaw admonished Charles that he was 'notwithstanding you will not understand it … before a Court of Justice'.

'I see I am before a power,' was Charles's accurately laconic response. For the remainder of the proceedings the court merely sat as a committee eventually passing judgement on 27 January and sentencing him to be 'put to death, by the severing his Head from his Body'. The following day Charles was brought back to hear his fate.

Opposite: *Charles I at his Trial*, by Edward Bower, 1649. Charles, clad in gold and black, wears the 'uniform of melancholy'.
Top: Death warrant of Charles I, 1649, which called for the king to be 'put to death by the severing of his head from his body'.
Above: *An Eyewitness Representation of the Execution of King Charles I*, by Dirk Weesop, *c.* 1649. An imaginary reconstruction of the execution, highlighting the mixed reactions of the crowd.

When he asked to be heard again, he was about to be denied when one of the commissioners, John Downes, protested that Charles ought to be allowed to speak, drawing from Cromwell an intimidating rebuke – 'What ails thee?' When he heard himself condemned as a 'tyrant, traitor and murderer, a public and implacable enemy to the Commonwealth of England', Charles allowed himself a last, droll chuckle. Once again he asked to speak and once again was denied on the not unreasonable grounds that he 'had not owned us as a court'. He was taken away protesting, 'I am not suffered to speak. Expect what Justice other people will have.' A bare fifty-nine members of the court signed the death warrant, Cromwell and Ireton prominent among them.

Elizabeth I had wanted Mary Stuart's execution to be carried out in the utmost secrecy, away from the public gaze. Cromwell and Ireton were convinced that as many people as possible should see Charles beheaded, both to dissuade any attempts at rescue and to do God's work without the slightest tremor of shame or hesitation. So a scaffold was erected in Whitehall and a huge throng gathered on the cold morning of 30 January. Charles was walked up the back stairs of Inigo Jones's Banqueting House through the great hall where he and Henrietta Maria had danced in royal masques celebrating their loving communion with Britannia and with each other. The Palladian windows of the palace had long been boarded up, so that Rubens' great paintings in the ceiling overhead could hardly have been visible to the little king as he stepped through the room and out through an opened window on to the platform, where death awaited. But up there none the less were the great painted jubilations of Stuart power and wisdom: Peace clasping Prosperity; the protection of Mercury and Minerva; the enraptured union of the crowns embodied in embracing putti. This insistent, unreal vision of a happy, united Britain, this compulsion to bring together those ill-matched partners, Scotland and England, was what had sustained the Stuarts and what (not for the last time) had ruined them.

Perfectly composed and dressed in two shirts, lest shivering be mistaken for fear, Charles noticed that the block was extremely low to the wooden platform and asked if it might not be raised a little. Apparently it could not, no reason being given. And at last he was allowed to give his speech, written out on a paper that he opened on the scaffold. 'I never did begin a War with the two Houses of Parliament, and I call God to witness, to whom I must shortly make an account, That I never did intend for to incroach upon their Privileges, they began upon me.' Then followed an instant history lecture, his much delayed, personal response to the Grand Remonstrance of 1642. But it was not Edward Hyde's thought-out political theory of a constitutional monarchy so much as an expression of personal sorrow and anger. Charles remained indignant that the power of the militia had been taken from him and deeply remorseful for his collusion in the unjust death of Strafford for which God was now properly punishing him. He ended by declaring that 'For the People … truly I desire their Liberty and Freedom as much as any body whomsoever; but I must tell you, That their Liberty and Freedom consist in having of Government, those Laws, by which their Life and their Goods may be most their own. It is not for having share in Government (Sir) that is nothing pertaining to them. A Subject and a Soveraign are clean different things.'

No one had ever accused Charles I of pandering to the public. From beginning to end, through all the tactical twists and turns of his short-sighted but not ignoble career, he had remained utterly constant in his belief in the divinity of his appointment. The celestial hosannas of Rubens' pictures were for the likes of him and him alone. 'I go from a corruptible to an incorruptible Crown; where no disturbance can be, no disturbance in the world,' he said, in that deep, quiet voice. Stray hairs tucked back into his white cap, he lay down before the low block, and the executioner, Richard Brandon, cut through his neck with a single blow.

Cromwell had given notice that he would 'cut his head off with the Crown on it'. But the famous 'groan by the thousands then present' that greeted the king's head as it dropped into the bloody basket and was then held aloft by Brandon could not have been very reassuring. For the person of the monarchy had already proved to be separable from the institution. In his last days, while yielding nothing of the highness of his sovereignty, Charles had managed, despite all the attempts to gag him, to assert a teaching that he would have done better to have learned seven years before: that armed power could not remake the broken legitimacy of the English, much less the Scottish, state. The point was well taken. But if anything had been learned from the tragic experience of the reign of Charles I, it was that henceforth the mere assertion of a divinely appointed right to rule would not suffice for political peace. It would only be when a monarch of both England and Scotland would manage to square the circle, and see that the authority of the Crown might actually be strengthened not compromised by parliamentary partnership, that the violent pendulum swings of the English and Scots polities would find their equipoise. That is what the notoriously anachronistic, Whiggish and self-congratulatory Victorians believed, at any rate. And, as a matter of fact, they were right.

CHAPTER
3

For the forthright and the adamant, it was time to begin again; to bleach the country of the stains of the past. 'Whatever our Fore-fathers were,' declared Henry Marten in parliament, 'or whatever they did or suffered or were enforced to yeeld unto, we are the men of the present age and ought to be absolutely free from all kinds of exorbitancie, molestation or Arbitrary Power.' All over the country in the early months of 1649, acts of obliteration, big and little, got under way. Young Isaac Archer, living near Colchester, had been spending time innocently gluing pieces of decorative silk to prints, when his father, William, 'with a knife, I know not why, cutt out the picture'. The picture was of Charles I. In the weeks after the king's execution, the remnant of the purged parliament lopped off its own head by abolishing the House of Lords as 'useless and dangerous'. The monarchy itself followed the peerage into the trash, denounced as 'unnecessary, burdensome, and dangerous to the liberty, safety and publick interest of the people'. The Great Seal, which gave acts of parliament the force of law and which bore the likeness of the monarch, was defaced and replaced by the stamp of the House of Commons, bearing the optimistic inscription 'In the First Year of Freedom by God's blessing restored 1648'. Writs, which had formerly required acts to be carried out in the name of the king, were now issued in 'the name of the Keepers of the Liberty of England'.

So there was a 'Commonwealth'. But what was that – an absence or a presence? Official bravura papered over popular uncertainty and confusion as to where, exactly, sovereignty now lay. There was no shortage of suggestions, of course. 'At that time,' wrote Lucy Hutchinson, the wife of a staunchly Puritan soldier, 'every man allmost was fancying forms of government.' The problem was who was to judge between them. To look for arbitration was to stare at a void.

As it happens, voids were a topic of compulsive fascination among philosophers, both natural and political. Learned disputes raged over whether vacuums could occur at all in nature; and if they did, whether they indicated utter vacancy, or the presence

LOOKING FOR LEVIATHAN

Oliver Cromwell (detail), by Erasmus Earle, *c.* 1655.

of a mysteriously 'subtle matter', albeit invisible and indeterminate. In 1644 the Italian physicist Evangelista Torricelli had performed the famous experiment which set off the debate. Torricelli took a glass tube, sealed at one end, filled it with mercury and then put it upside down into a basin, also filled with mercury. He had made, in effect, a primitive barometer. Atmospheric pressure pushed the mercury up the tube, but not all the way. Between the top of the mercury level and the sealed end of the tube was a space. But what was inside that space: a something or a nothing? This was what divided 'vacuists' from 'plenists', those for whom a vacuum was a possibility in nature and those for whom the *horror vacui* was a paramount truth.

The philosopher Thomas Hobbes was a plenist, someone for whom a vacuum was as abhorrent in the government of the state as in the operations of nature. When Charles I was executed in January 1649, Hobbes was living in Paris, debating the mystery of the Torricellian gap with French philosophers like Marin Mersenne, and writing, among other works, his answer to the dilemma posed by the vacuum of sovereignty. Published two years later, in 1651, his *Leviathan* would be profoundly shocking to the royalists who had confidently assumed Hobbes to be one of their own, for it seemed to counsel submission, indeed *unconditional* submission, to the self-appointed powers which had rushed into the space left by the dead king. Worse, in that same year, Hobbes acted on his convictions by returning to England, now governed by parliament and Council of State, both filled with unrepentant regicides. For someone thought to have owed everything he had – station, employment, security – to royalist families like the Cavendishes, this was unforgivable apostasy.

Hobbes, the son of a Wiltshire parson and the nephew of a prosperous glover who had given him the means to be educated at Oxford, had subsequently been tutor to the future second Earl of Devonshire, William Cavendish. No sooner had he come into his own than he proceeded to squander it, to the detriment of his old tutor who, according to his friend John Aubrey (the nonpareil of seventeenth-century gossips), wore out his shoes and caught colds from wet feet going 'up and downe to borrow money'. But after the second earl died in 1628, Hobbes continued to collect monies for the Devonshires, extracting the forced loan of 1628 and billeting soldiers in the homes of loan refusers. In 1640 he had stood, unsuccessfully, for parliament from Derby, as a loyal champion of royal prerogative and the personal rule. Perhaps, though, his defeat in the polls made Hobbes (who prided himself on the clarity of his prescience) see the writing on the wall. For he took himself off to exile in Paris well before the war began. His patrons the Cavendishes duly lost battles and fortunes and then trooped to Paris themselves to join the court in exile. Still in favour, Hobbes became mathematics tutor to the Prince of Wales and to his prematurely dissipated companion, the second Duke of Buckingham. Geometry, which for Hobbes was one of the few uncontestable realities in the universe, bored both his charges. According to Aubrey, Buckingham relieved the tedium of his instruction by languidly masturbating, while Charles thought his tutor 'the oddest fellow he ever met with'.

The publication of *Leviathan* would certainly not have made the prince any less bemused. Apart from supplying arguments for accepting the outcome of the civil war, it also seemed to attack institutional Christianity with such withering scepticism that in court circles Hobbes was deemed little better than an atheist. 'It was below the education of Mr. Hobbes,' complained Edward Hyde, who had enjoyed his company in the circle of Viscount Falkland at Great Tew, '& a very ungenerous and vile thing to publish his *Leviathan* with so much malice and acrimony against the Church of England when it was scarce struggling in its own ruins.'

Hobbes was a materialist, a rationalist, and not really a Christian in the sense of subscribing to gospels full of miracles and sacred apparitions. But he certainly believed in some sort of deity to whom alone otherwise absolute sovereigns had to render account. If for nothing else, Hobbes's God was needed to keep Leviathan honest. And he was certainly unequivocal in his condemnation of the rebellion against the king. His later history of the civil war, *Behemoth* (1679), begins with an imaginary view from the Devil's mountain, of 'all kind of Injustice, and of all kinds of Folly that the world could afford'. But in 1650 he believed that moral anathema was no help at all in answering the paramount questions for everyone caught in the sovereignty vacuum. It was all very well to follow the lament 'the king is dead' with the shout 'long live the king' if you happened to be in Paris, since that was indeed where the new king could be found. But suppose you were stuck in Wiltshire? Then the questions that preyed on you were not about propriety but self-preservation. To pretend otherwise was self-deluding humbug. Simple but inescapable anxieties forced themselves on any rational person. What will become of me and mine? Who should be obeyed? On whom can we depend for our elementary needs of safety? Who will stop differences of opinion and differences of religion – for, argued Hobbes, there will always be such differences, incapable of adjudication – from becoming causes for endless, murderous war? Who will stop soldiers from burning dwellings, stealing animals and assaulting the defenceless? Who will enforce contracts – the very touchstone of justice? Who would allow us to sleep quietly in our beds? And how may such a protector be known: by faith or by reason?

They are the terrors of orphaned children who had seen their father-ruler killed in front of them; who, in counties ravaged by war, had seen familiar adjudicators – bishops and priests – effaced from the landscape of authority. Those anxieties would

Top: The Great Seal of the Commonwealth, 1651, with the House of
Commons on one side, was distinctly Republican in design.
Above: *Thomas Hobbes*, studio of Isaac Fuller, *c.* 1660.

Frontispiece to *Leviathan* (1651) by Thomas Hobbes.

not be put to rest with the return of the bishops and the judges when Charles II was restored to his throne in 1660 and received his old maths tutor once more at court. For the Restoration closed, but it did not heal, the puncture wounds with which the civil war had pierced the body politic. Beneath the skin there was still traumatized tissue, which could be made raw and bloody again by collisions with misfortune. Plague, fire, defeat and paranoia would shake the confidence of the English in the protective authority of the throne and would make allegiance once more arguable, contingent. Forty years after the Great Seal of the beheaded king was defaced, his son James would drop it into the Thames in an act of perverse self-destruction. The political barometer would feel the pressure of altered atmosphere. The mercury of liberty would rise. A vacancy at the top would be declared.

The cure for fearfulness, Hobbes thought, was the frank acknowledgement that it was the natural and universal condition of man. Hobbes knew all about fear. According to John Aubrey, the philosopher claimed that he had been born prematurely in 1588 as the result of his mother taking fright at the prospect of the Spanish Armada. Terror of the unknown, 'feare of power invisible … imagined from tales publiquely allowed', Hobbes daringly claimed, was the source of most if not all religious experience. Pious fictions – like miracles, revelations or the existence of the soul itself – which could neither be proved nor disproved, might be a consolation for the anxious, but they were of no use in helping men escape the pitiless war of all against all, which was their lot in a state of nature. The only true asylum from anarchy lay in the surrender of liberty to an omnipotent sovereign – the Leviathan – in whom all individuals would be subsumed. What, after all, was the point of clinging to the freedom of mutual self-destruction? Neither sanctity, nor tradition, nor moral pedigree could confer on a government the authority to claim obedience. If Leviathan offered safety and justice, if Leviathan could keep disputes over beliefs from becoming acts of violence, then Leviathan was legitimate.

If this was not an atheistic answer, it was a shockingly amoral and impious one. And it was an affront to royalists because, in the aftermath of the death of Charles I, all they had was piety. Hobbes mocked 'immaterial' things. But for the devoutly loyal, the immaterial presence of the king was their solace and their hope, and they clung with desperate consolation to any and every purported relic that came their way: to little pieces of brown cloth said to be stained with the blood of the royal martyr; to the ribbon-bound locks of hair sworn to have come from the decapitated head. Above all they hung on the every last word of Charles, collected in the *Eikon Basilike*, the book of his meditations. Despite the attempts of the Commonwealth to suppress it, 'The King's Book' was an immediate publishing sensation. No fewer than thirty-five editions (plus an extra twenty-five for unvanquished Ireland) appeared in 1649 alone, the first just a week after the beheading. In March 1649 an especially popular expanded edition, complete with the king's prayers and his speech on the scaffold, was made available. Charles's posthumous campaign of persuasion was perhaps the most successful he ever waged. Dead, he seemed more ubiquitous and materially present in England, Scotland and Ireland than he had ever been when he was alive. And this was exactly what Charles had intended. For although the editorial genius behind his book was the clergyman Dr John Gauden, Charles had taken enormous pains to present himself (like his grandmother Mary) as a martyr for the Church (in this case the Church of England).

The *Eikon Basilike* was designed as the king's spiritual legacy, the gospel according to St Charles, in sure and pious hope of the resurrection of the monarchy. Complicated (but to contemporaries intelligible) Christian symbolism dominated the frontispiece designed by William Marshall, engraved by Wenceslaus Hollar and obviously in tune with the king's presentation of his posterity. Its themes were consolatory: comfort for the bereft, steadfastness in turmoil, light in the darkness. Palm trees – the trees thought never to die and thus the ancient emblems of the resurrection – continue to grow, even under the weight of royal virtue, while the rock of faith (also an emblem of the true Church) remains immovable in the storm-tossed sea. The grace bestowed on the king-martyr was represented as an illumination, the reception of light. Out of the murky skies a shaft of sublime light strikes the head of the kneeling king and imbues him with vision. Blessed with celestial sight he is able, as his parting words promise, to leave his corruptible, earthly crown at his feet and behold his reward, the heavenly crown of glory, radiant with stars.

By the end of the first year of the Commonwealth, 'The King's Book' was everywhere, showing up like an irrepressible phantom, even in miniature editions designed for concealment. Its undeniable popularity disconcerted the stewards of the new state whose own sense of legitimacy depended on their conviction that it was they who represented the 'honest' and 'godly' kind of people. Apparently there were more of their countrymen enslaved to the old despotism than they had anticipated. Royalist newspapers like John Crouch's scabrous weekly *The Man in the Moon* 'shone its light' on the devilish Commonwealth, while the Man's dog, Towzer, shamelessly lifted his leg on proclamations of the Rump Parliament. Something had to be done to counter these scandalous influences. So John Milton, already established as a dedicated propagandist for parliament, was mobilized to enlighten the deluded. Milton was fast losing his own sight. His greatest works – *Paradise Lost* and *Samson Agonistes* – would be the masterpieces of his long years of blindness and defeat. He had

Top: Frontispiece to the *Eikon Basilike* (1649) by Charles I.
Above: *John Milton*, engraved after William Faithhorne, 1670.

published a volume of poetry in 1645 and thought of prose writing as merely 'the work of my left hand'. But he also thought of himself in the classical tradition of virtuous republicans such as Cicero who had laid aside 'idle' pursuits to place their eloquence at the service of the state. With his own vision dimming, Milton would none the less be the physician of the 'blind afflictions' of the common people, the kind of myopia that made them hanker, sentimentally, for the late, unregretted tyrant.

So in February 1649, in the midst of the royalist hagiography, Milton published the essay that brought him to the attention of the beleaguered leaders of the Commonwealth, not least Oliver Cromwell, for whom Milton made no secret of his ardent admiration. *The Tenure of Kings and Magistrates* went unerringly to the vacuum-anxiety, attacking the parliamentarians who had become queasy or even indignant at the king's trial and punishment, beginning to 'swerve and almost shiver ... as if they were newly enter'd into a great sin ... when the Commonwealth nigh perishes for want of deeds in substance, don with just and faithfull expedition'. Why, if they now flinched from its proper and legal outcome, had they embarked on the resistance against the king in the first place? Could they not see that by resorting to arms, the king had unilaterally torn up the contract with his subjects: the bedrock on which his authority rested. When he had raised his standard at Nottingham he had dethroned himself. God and parliament had merely affirmed that fall from grace by his defeat. For Milton there *was* no vacuum of authority to lose sleep over. It had always been lodged in the sovereign people whose conditionally appointed executive the king had been. Once stripped of that shared and limited power, Charles Stuart had to be judged for his crimes like any other felon. To accept his assertion that only God could judge him was a dangerous absurdity, since it put in question his earthly accountability for *any* laws or treaties he signed or promises he forswore (including his coronation oaths).

Historically, this was entirely back to front. The war had begun in 1642 not to remove Charles but to constrain him. The 'people' had not existed as a party to the conflict except through their representatives in parliament. But everything had changed in the brutal second civil war, the war of 1648, which had indeed turned into a life-or-death struggle, at least to Cromwell, who treated Milton's publication like the job application it more or less was. The poet duly became secretary of foreign tongues to the Council, responsible for translating Latin and European documents into English and vice versa. So it was as a dependable attack propagandist that, in October 1649, Milton took his polemical sledgehammer to the *Eikon Basilike*. His *Eikonoklastes*, 'The Image Breaker' (1649), took the carefully manufactured image of sanctity apart, extracting from the book the passages he thought most fraudulently self-serving. But chopping up 'The King's Book' proved untidier work than chopping up the king, and not much more popular. Milton later confessed that this was a job he had been told to do, which may account for the hectoring manner of its tone and style, alternating between needling, posthumous interrogations (as if Milton regretted not having sat himself on the court which had judged Charles) and bursts of epic denunciation. To Charles's famous comments in the House of Commons that 'the birds have flown', Milton added images which turned the king into a carrion carnivore feeding off the carcasses of the free: 'If some Vultur in the Mountains could have open'd his beak intelligibly and spoke, what fitter words could he have utter'd at the loss of his prey?'

Milton's invective may have been more persuasive than his political theory. For his daringly advanced argument, that the authority of governments was based on popular consent and that they were at all times beholden to, and limited by, the will of the sovereign people, left wide open the problem of how the people were supposed to exercise their rediscovered majesty and in whom they could safely put their trust? Parliament, of course, ought to have been the answer. But to many among the traditional governing class – even those who had fought under its flag – the purged, single-chamber assembly of 1649, that came to be known derisively as 'The Rump', bore no resemblance at all to the representative institution that had taken to the field in defence of the nation's liberties in 1642. Those who had been 'excluded' in 1648 for their known opposition to the trial of the king never regarded the Rump and its executive Council of State as anything more than an illegitimate usurping power.

Attacks on the presumption of the Rump Parliament and its councillors to fill the void left by the defunct monarchy came from those who thought it was not nearly bold enough, as well as from those who questioned its audacity. For the hottest Protestants, free to speak their minds in the void left by bishopless England, the only proper successor to King Charles was King Jesus. Prophecies abounded that a new millennium was at hand, and that the destruction of Antichrist and the coming of the Last Days were imminent. Combing through the books of Daniel and Revelations, the most fervent declared that the Four Monarchies – of Egypt, Persia, Greece and Rome – would now be succeeded by a Fifth: the reign of the godly, the visible saints. To those gripped by this ecstatic fervour, the execution of the king had not just been a political act but a sign from God that he had indeed chosen England as his appointed instrument for a universal redemption. And the freshly sanctified country would look like no other realm, for its mighty would be laid low and its humble raised up. Under the rule of the saints 'no creature comfort, no outward blessing' would be denied.

For the Fifth Monarchists and a multitude of other equally fervent sects, the emptiness left by the dethroned king was not a void at all but the antechamber to glory. Their preachers and prophets said so in the streets and to rapt congregations of apprentices and artisans. But the message resonated with special force in the army where sabres had been honed by the fire of sermons. The army remained, as it had been since 1647, the dominant institution in the country, for although royalism had been defeated in England, it was very much alive elsewhere in the islands. On learning the news of Charles's execution, the Presbyterian regime in Scotland had immediately declared his son King Charles II of England and Scotland. In Ireland, not only had the Catholic confederacy not been defeated, it was now reinforced by the explicitly royalist army of the Duke of Ormonde. And since over the past decade the outcome of power struggles in England had been determined by events in Scotland and Ireland, it was impossible for the military to let its guard down and be lulled into a fool's peace.

So England remained an armed camp, a place of troopers and horses and armourers and arsenals; an occupied country in all but name, where law might as easily be delivered on the point of a sword as in the magistrates' court. It was an army, moreover, which had changed almost out of all recognition in the course of a decade. The officer corps, especially at the junior level, was younger, less traditionally educated, drawn from lower down the social scale and passionately religious. Since something like 70 per cent of artisans – shoemakers, weavers, coopers, tanners and so on – could read, the rank and file had a political awareness of its destiny and that of the country, and of their own part in shaping it, that was absolutely new in England. In the autumn of 1647, each regiment had elected two Agitators to represent it at the army Council and they had the audacity to debate with Cromwell and Ireton at Putney on the future of the country's political and social institutions. Their grievances with parliament over arrears of pay and pensions had likely been in part inspired by Leveller writers and orators like John Lilburne, Richard Overton and William Walwyn into a crusade to transform England into something which, if not quite a representative democracy, was none the less shockingly radical by seventeenth-century standards. Under the Leveller proposals, the franchise would go to all male householders over the age of twenty-one. Parliaments would be annual and members debarred from sitting consecutive terms. Tithes supporting the clergy and excise taxes on food would be abolished, and the law would be simplified and made accessible to the whole people.

As far as Lilburne and his fellow-Levellers were concerned, they were not asking for the moon, just the 'free-born' natural rights which Anglo-Saxons had apparently enjoyed before being crushed beneath the Norman yoke, rights which had only been partly restored by Magna Carta. Twenty to thirty per cent of adult males in England in fact *already* had the vote, and once the categories that the Levellers continued to exclude (servants, apprentices and paupers) were subtracted they could reasonably argue that they were merely extending to the rest of the country what was already *de facto* household suffrage in towns like Cambridge and Exeter. For the most part, Walwyn, Overton and Lilburne were at pains to distance themselves from any imputation of social egalitarianism. The label of 'Leveller' had originally been a hostile accusation. When they called their newspaper *The Moderate* there was no irony intended. They believed in rank, they insisted. They believed in orderly government.

All the same, they could hardly avoid the impression that they were radicals since it was unquestionably true. If they did not want to see a great social levelling, they did want some sort of attention to the just complaints of the poor. The Levellers were trying to make more fortunate citizens see that these starvelings were not the armies of travelling beggars that haunted the imaginations of constables and magistrates, and which could be whipped out of sight and out of mind. The new poor were often settled folk – agricultural labourers and artisans, or even tenant farmers – who had been distressed or made destitute by the disruptions of the war, their fields burned and their carts and animals requisitioned (in other words stolen) for the troops. The abolition of the tithe was meant to help the tenant farmers, but the Levellers also wanted the Commonwealth government to initiate some sort of sustained programme of relief for the needy rather than abandon them to the Elizabethan poor laws. Even more daringly, they argued that those immediately above pauperdom should be considered active members of political society. At the Putney Debates the naval officer and MP Colonel Thomas Rainborough declared that 'The poorest he that is in England hath a life to live as the greatest he,' and insisted that no man should have to live under laws to which he had not personally given his own express consent.

This was an argument of genuinely revolutionary boldness and it appalled the officers whom Lilburne assailed as the 'grandees' of the army – Ireton, Fairfax and Cromwell. They came to believe that the Levellers and their allies in the army were hell-bent on subverting both the godly discipline of the troops and, for that matter, the entire social and political order. Against Rainborough's literal interpretation of the sovereignty of the people, Ireton argued the sovereignty of property: 'no person hath a right to an interest or share in the disposing of the affairs of the kingdom … that hath not a permanent fixed interest … and those persons together are properly the represented of this kingdom.' In other words, a man's estate counted when it came to the vote. A parliament stuffed with lawyers, moreover, was unlikely to feel warmly about the Levellers' proposals to democratize the law. Oliver Cromwell's own attitude to the importance of social rank was best summed up in his later dictum: 'A noble-man, a gentleman, a yeoman. That is a good interest of the nation and a great one.'

Bitter enemies though they became, Oliver Cromwell and John Lilburne none the less shared a history. Lilburne, who like Cromwell came from a family of county gentry, was always one of those restless souls, easier to recognize in the nineteenth than the seventeenth century, who seem destined to be outsiders. In his twenties he had been arrested for circulating pamphlets attacking Laud and the bishops, and his savage sentence in 1637 had been one of the *causes célèbres* which helped make the Star Chamber notorious. Lilburne had been flogged through the streets of London from the Fleet to Palace Yard, then set in the pillory (from which he continued to harangue the crowds) and finally incarcerated in the Tower of London for more than two years in conditions of brutal deprivation and restraint. It had been Cromwell, in fact, who had brought Lilburne's plight to the attention of the Long Parliament and got his release. Commissioned as a captain in the regiment of Lord Brooke, Lilburne was captured by Prince Rupert's soldiers in the rout at Brentford and was subjected to an exemplary trial for high treason at Oxford. Had not parliament made it clear it would exact retribution on its own royalist prisoners, he would have been executed then and there. For the bravery of his demeanour during the trial the Earl of Essex offered Lilburne £300, a sum his chronically indebted family could hardly afford to turn down. But, of course, Lilburne did just that, announcing he would 'rather fight for eightpence a day until the liberties and peace of England was settled'. As an officer in the Eastern Association he would certainly have encountered Cromwell, and he made no secret of sharing Oliver's dim view of the Earl of Manchester's capacity for command. Shot through the arm at Wakefield, repeatedly robbed and plundered and seldom paid, Lilburne was in a sorry enough plight in 1645 for Cromwell to write to the Commons recommending he receive the special pension he had been voted on account of his treatment by the Star Chamber, but which had failed to materialize.

This, however, was as far as their comradeship went. Cromwell raised no objec-tion to Lilburne's imprisonment twice in 1646, first in Newgate, then in the Tower where he was committed by the House of Lords for accusing the peers of, among other things, 'Tyranny, Usurpation, Perjury, Injustice and Breach of Trust in them reposed'. It didn't help that when Lilburne appeared before the Lords, he refused to take off his hat, which was taken (as intended) as a refusal to acknowledge their right to try a 'freeborn Englishman'. In Newgate he barricaded himself in his cell and stuck his fingers in his ears to avoid hearing the charges against him. It was two more years before Lilburne was finally released. But nothing, not even being deprived of writing materials, seemed to be able to gag him as pamphlet after pamphlet somehow issued from the Tower and into the streets, apprentice shops, garrisons and Baptist churches. During 1647 the Levellers began to mobilize mass petitions, often delivered by noisy crowds wearing the Leveller token of a sea-green ribbon in their hats. Cromwell was in no doubt at all that Leveller agitations, with their demands for direct political representation, were undermining military discipline. After the high command had forbidden a 'general rendezvous' of the army, two regiments none the less showed up at Corkbush Fields near Ware in Hertfordshire to hear the Leveller Agitators, carrying their literature. The papers and green ribbons were ripped from their hats, the meeting broken up at sword point, and one mutineer shot.

The Levellers were not yet finished as a threat to the 'grandees'. Through the second civil war *The Moderate* continued to voice the programme set out the year before in their 'Agreement of the People', as well as to point fingers at backsliders and adventurers in parliament. (Astonishingly, some of the Leveller chiefs even began to make contact with the king in hopes of persuading him to become a patron of their household democracy.) After Charles's defeat Ireton grafted some of their principal demands – the abolition of the House of Lords and the monarchy, and annual parliaments – on to his own official proposals for republican government. But by the beginning of 1649 Overton, Lilburne and Walwyn were convinced that the Commonwealth had been delivered into the hands of an oligarchy every bit as rapacious, self-serving and heedless of the needs of the masses as the one it had replaced. Lilburne's snarling rebuke to the House of Lords in 1646 held just as well for the Rump Commons three years later: 'All you intended when you set us a-fighting was merely to unhorse and dismount our old riders and tyrants, that so you might get up and ride in their stead.'

Lilburne detested everything about the new regime. He had been against the execution of the king and had refused to support his trial on the grounds that it violated all the principles of equity encoded in the common law. Even Charles Stuart he believed was entitled to the same benefits of Magna Carta as Freeborn John, including the right to trial by jury. When three of the captured royalist commanders – the Scots Duke of Hamilton, Lord Holland and Lord Arthur Capel – were awaiting trial in the Tower (they would be beheaded shortly after the king in front of the parliament house), Lilburne sent them law books for their own defence. The response of the Leveller leaders to a formal ban on political discussions in the army was a two-part pamphlet called *England's New Chains,* which at the very least put in question any kind of obedience to a regime they condemned as illegitimate. On 28 March 1649 Lilburne, Overton and Walwyn, together with a fourth colleague Thomas Prince, were arrested and dragged before the Council of State. There (according to Lilburne), both they and the councillors were treated to a fist-pounding eruption of rage by Oliver Cromwell:

> I tell you … you have no other way to deal with these men but to break them or they will break you; yea, and bring all the guilt of the blood and treasure shed and spent in this kingdom upon your heads and shoulders, and frustrate and make void all that work that, with so many years' industry, toil and pains, you have done, and so render you to all rational men in the world as the most contemptible generation of silly, low-spirited men in the earth … I tell you again, you are necessitated to break them.

Not surprisingly, then, the Levellers who refused to acknowledge the authority of the Council were packed off to the Tower. But then something quite astonishing – and to the hardened grandees of the army incomprehensible – happened. A petitioning campaign for their release immediately broke out in London, mobilized by Leveller women. In 1646 Lilburne had already gone against the grain of virtually every household manual (a Puritan speciality) by insisting, and in print, that women 'were by nature all equall and alike in power, dignity, authority and majesty [to men]'. Leveller women had always been directly involved in the movement's campaigns. Elizabeth Lilburne had been politicized through her early efforts to spring her reckless spouse from one prison or another, moving from the expected tear-stained pleas to unexpected assertions of the rights of man and woman. Mary Overton seems to have been, from the beginning, a radical at heart. For printing and distributing her husband's tracts, she had been brutally punished, dragged through the London streets by a cart, as she was holding her six-month-old infant, while being pelted and abused like a common whore. But the most articulate and impassioned of the sisters was the charismatic preacher-turned-Leveller Katherine Chidley, who tried to make the Commonwealth understand the particular sufferings of their sex and to institute poor relief for their assistance:

> Considering that we have an equal share and interest with men in the Commonwealth and it cannot be laid waste (as it now is) and not we be the greatest and most helpless sufferers therein; and considering that poverty, misery and famine, like a mighty torrent is breaking in upon us … and we are not able

to see our children hang upon us, and cry out for bread, and not have where-
withal to feed them, we had rather die than see that day.

The outrageous temerity of women giving voice to these grievances was profoundly
shocking to mainstream Puritan culture, devoted as it was to an especially draconian
hierarchy of the sexes in which the woman's role was that of obedient, quietly
devoted helpmate. When Elizabeth Lilburne and Katherine Chidley, at the head of a
mass demonstration of women, presumed to petition parliament for the release of the
Leveller leaders, they met with a predictably dusty response: 'The matter you petition
about is of a higher concernment than you understand, the House have an answer to
your Husbands and therefore you are desired to go home and looke after your own
businesse, and meddle with your huswifery.'
    But the Leveller women did not go home. Instead they made sure that the
Manifestation, published from the Tower under the names of all the imprisoned
Levellers, was widely distributed in London. Its quasi-theological touches − comparisons between the sufferings endured by the Levellers and those inflicted on Christ
and his disciples − suggest the authorship of William Walwyn, the grandson of a
bishop. But the *Manifestation* was less of a treatise and more an explanation to the
obtuse of why, after so much persecution, deprivation and frustration, they had no
choice but to persevere, whatever further ordeals might come their way. In its
determination and bleak pathos, the *Manifestation* is a vocational manifesto of an
unmistakably modern profession: the revolutionary calling.

> 'Tis a very great unhappinesse we well know, to be always strugling and striv-
> ing in the world, and does wholly keep us from the enjoyment of those con-
> tentments our severall Conditions reach unto: So that if we should consult only
> with our selves, and regard only our own ease, Wee should never enterpose as
> we have done, in behalfe of the Common-wealth: But when so much has been
> done for recovery of our Liberties, and seeing God hath so blest that which …
> has been desired, but could never be atained, of making this a truly happy and
> wholly Free Nation; We think our selves bound by the greatest obligations that
> may be, to prevent the neglect of this opportunity, and to hinder as much as lyes
> in us, that the bloud which has been shed be not spilt like water upon the
> ground, nor that after the abundant Calamities, which have overspread all quar-
> ters of the Land, the change be onely Notionall, Nominall, Circumstantiall,
> whilst the reall Burdens, Grievances, and Bondages, be continued, even when
> the Monarchy is changed into a Republike.

John Lilburne, c. 1640, one of the foremost Levellers, who fought for freedom and reform, loudly championing the rights of the individual.

All the same, the four denied that they were 'impatient and over-violent in our motions for the Publick Good', hoping to achieve their ends through another 'Agreement of the Free People', which they proceeded to publish from their 'causelesse captivity' on 1 May 1649. The document was serious and not impractical: a legislature of 400 chosen 'according to naturall right' by all males over twenty-one years old, other than paupers, royalists and servants. Neither military forces nor taxes could be raised without its consent, but the limits of that parliament's power were spelled out as forcefully as its jurisdiction. It was not to infringe freedom of conscience; it was not to coerce anyone into the military, nor to create any kind of legal procedures not provided for in the common law. It was neither to limit trade, nor to impose capital punishments or mutilations for anything other than murder and certainly not for 'trivial offences'. No one, except Catholics who insisted on papal supremacy, was to be disqualified from office on account of their religion. Judged by what was thought politically acceptable, in the Commonwealth, this *'(third and final) Agreement of the [Free] People'* was a non-starter. But this did not mean that the kind of assumptions and arguments made by the Levellers should be thought of as utopian (hence their desperation to mark out clear differences from Gerrard Winstanley's 'Diggers', who preached community of land and goods). Leveller principles would have a future, in fact, and not just in America.

But the soldiers who continued to read Lilburne, Overton and Walwyn (and who knows, perhaps Katherine Chidley too) could not wait around for the future. In April a mutiny over pay in London turned into a mass demonstration at the funeral of one of the executed mutineers. In mid-May, another mutiny broke out among some troops passing through the garrison stationed in the staunchly Puritan town of Banbury in Oxfordshire. Two more regiments mutinied near Salisbury and attempted (but failed) to join the Oxfordshire rebels. On 13 May, Cromwell and Fairfax marched a pursuit force 50 miles in a single day, catching the mutineers in the middle of the night at Burford on the edge of the Cotswolds. Seven or eight hundred fled, but 400 were captured of whom four were sentenced to be shot and three were. The next day, Cromwell went off to receive an honourary degree in law from Oxford University. Ringing Leveller statements continued to be published from Bristol before the heavy hand of the army came crashing down again. There was nothing to connect Lilburne directly with the mutiny, but he did his best to remedy that by publishing *An Impeachment of High Treason against Oliver Cromwell and Henry Ireton* in August. In October, though, it was Lilburne who was tried for treason at the Guildhall in the city of London, where he played brilliantly to the gallery by insisting that the jury alone was empowered to issue a verdict and the judges merely 'cyphers' of the people's will. It duly acquitted him and Lilburne was freed without conditions, the other three in the Tower following, provided they subscribed to the oath of engagement which the Commonwealth now required of all its citizens. Walwyn, Overton and Prince agreed, but everyone from Cromwell down knew better than to ask John Lilburne.

By the autumn of 1649 it was clear that, whatever else was going to fill the space left by the monarchy, it was not going to be the visionary Commonwealth of the Levellers. Bought off, intimidated or imprisoned, their officers dispersed; the rank and file of regiments thought unreliable were shipped off to Ireland where they could vent their fervour and frustration on the benighted rebels. Their leaders eventually went their separate ways. The philosophical Walwyn became an amateur authority on matters medical, John Wildman made a packet from speculating in confiscated royalist property, Overton went to France, while Lilburne took up sundry social causes and grievances before being banished for life in 1651. In exile in the Netherlands, he attempted to make sense of what had happened by reading deeply in the classical literature of Roman republicanism: Livy and Sallust. But the texts only seemed to confirm for him the gloomy likelihood of oligarchy or tyranny. Returning to England in 1653 he published again, was imprisoned again and eventually ended up a Quaker.

Leveller fire transmuted into Quaker light is less startling than it might seem, for any number of former political zealots faced with the ferocity of the republic's repression turned to religion in their search for truth and deliverance. And this spiritual migration was not just a matter of consolation for thwarted populists. If Levelling had failed, it had to be because God had willed it so, wanting the brethren to turn aside from the 'carnal' world and look elsewhere for salvation. Elsewhere meant, first and foremost, within themselves, in the recesses of their being, which had been overlaid by carnal things: appetites, words, ambitions. Buried beneath all that worldly muck were the spotless hearts and souls of the children they remained in their innermost spirit and which, once released from the bondage of the carnal world, could be opened to receive the light of God's grace.

The first apostles of this personal redemption were utterly convinced, even when locked up in the stinking darkness of a dungeon, that they were walking in the time of light. God had willed the terrible wars, not for carnal alterations – a parliament, a republic – but so that the institutions of false authority should fall away. Away had gone bishops. Away had gone presbyteries. What was left was freedom – the precious freedom for them to find their way. In Rome 1650 may have been the Jubilee year, and Pope Innocent X was erecting his own column of light, the obelisk, in the Piazza Navona. But it was an age of miracles for the seekers after grace. For while the

Commonwealth and the generals were adamant about the monopoly of armed force and the control of expressly political opinions, they were (especially Cromwell) equally insistent on freedom of conscience for any sect or confession (other than Catholics, naturally) who caused no threat to the public peace. Just what constituted such a threat, of course, was often left to the judgement of local magistrates whose threshold of outrage was often much lower than Cromwell's, as the Quakers in particular were to discover. But this brief period of benign neglect produced the most fertile proliferation of spiritual enthusiasms since (or for that matter before) the Reformation. Some were organized, like the Baptists, into Churches, but others were frequently no more than cult followings gathered around the personality of charismatic preachers like Abiezer Coppe or the Ranter Laurence Clarkson.

From group to group they differed wildly on, for example, the status of Scripture (some of the Ranters and Quakers thought it no more than an historical document) or the importance of baptism and church marriage (which the Quakers rejected along with any other outward sign of communion). But what they all had in common was an intense aversion to any kind of formal ecclesiastical authority or institutional discipline. Calvinism's dogma of predestination, with its irreversible separation of the elect and the damned, they rejected out of hand as utterly inconsistent with God's love, which could be received by any who opened themselves truly to his grace. The most extreme of their number, such as Laurence Clarkson, taught that, since God was perfect, the idea of sin, and the shame which went with it, must have been a human invention, and to the scandal of other Christians went about conspicuously testing their theory by living openly with a series of concubines. The disregard for formal authority, pushed to its logical extreme and professed by Quakers as well as Ranters, was that God lived in each and every one, and was simply waiting to take possession of the transformed believer.

Separated from the fraudulent and redundant authority of the clergy, salvation could now be a free, voluntary act by anyone old enough to know what she or he was doing (hence the Baptists' refusal to countenance infant baptism). The mere idea of a parish was an arbitrary geographical absurdity, a jurisdictional convenience masquerading as a Church. Why should all the people who happened to live within the same bounded area be supposed, by that fact alone, to be brethren or sisters in Christ? Church buildings themselves the Quakers ridiculed as 'steeple houses', mere piles of stones built for carnal admiration and which had to be broken up, in spirit if not in fact, before the enslaved flocks could be converted into Children of Light.

The sects satisfied two quite different visions of the imperfect alteration of the state from kingdom to Commonwealth and pointed a way ahead in two quite

Top: *The Quakers' Meeting,* by Isaac Beckett, after Egbert van Heemskerck, *c.* 1680.
Above: *The Ranters Ranting,* a satirical woodcut, *c.* 1650.

separate directions. For Fifth Monarchists like John Rogers, Vavasor Powell and Major-General Thomas Harrison, their noses buried in scriptural prophecy, the new, last age had dawned with the beheading of the king. So they were under an obligation not to turn their back on the state but to convert it to the rule of the Saints, and so be in a position to prepare the Commonwealth for the consummation of prophecy. Their soldiers, magistrates and preachers had to infiltrate, not abandon, the public world, the better to bend it to God's command.

For the Quakers and those who thought like them, this obstinate attachment to carnal affairs was only compounding the problem. Polities were, by their very nature, incapable of spiritual transformation, and hence should simply be shunned, the better to concentrate on what counted – the alteration of individual personalities to fit them for the admission of light. Self-assertion, the quality that made men leaders, had to give way to self-nullification.

Their lives, then, became journeys towards sweet nothingness, which began, necessarily, with an uprooting from familiar habits. When he was barely nineteen, George Fox, a Puritan weaver's son, began his wanderings away from his home in Drayton-in-the-Clay in Leicestershire (much to his father's displeasure). It was 1643 and Fox walked through a landscape torn apart by the war, plodding patiently in his grey leather coat along roads travelled by troopers and munitions wagons. In the garrison town of Newport Pagnell on the Bedfordshire/Buckinghamshire border, he watched Sir Samuel Luke's soldiers rip out statues from the churches and smash them in the streets. And he listened to the ex-tailor and army captain Paul Hobson sermonize the troops, denouncing the vanity of 'steeple houses' and insisting that a church was but a gathered body of believers. Two years later, while Fox was roaming the orchards in Leicestershire, he began to experience the 'openings' which exposed him to illumination. By 1649 he was now ready to begin his wanderings in earnest. It helped that he had a modest inheritance from which he could supply his even more modest wants on the road. In Derbyshire villages populated by hungry lead miners, for whom neither king nor parliament had done much, he preached against tithes and approached potential converts, unbidden, to attempt a 'convincement'. More perilously, he began to disrupt Presbyterian lectures, shouting of the woe to come and the awaiting light.

Soon, Fox was planning his interventions to provoke the maximum attention and became, to the Presbyterians especially, first a nuisance and then an intolerable menace. For his fearless temerity Fox spent months at a time in prison, in the filthiest of conditions. But (just as with Lilburne) his confinement only enhanced his reputation and did nothing at all to quiet him. In fact he began to get attentive visitors. In Derby, where he was sentenced to a six-month spell in 1650, a jailor asked if he might share his cell for a night to listen to Fox's instruction. Irrepressible, Fox moved north to Lancashire and Yorkshire, gathering converts not just from the poor but also from the propertied classes – the wonderfully named high sheriff of Nottingham, John Reckless, and Margaret Fell, the pious wife of a Lancashire JP, both of whom opened their houses to Fox to use as an asylum and recruiting headquarters. At Wakefield he brought in the ex-weaver and New Model Army quartermaster James Nayler, who was already a gifted preacher and would be for Fox both a blessing and a curse.

The quaking began. Although he used them freely enough to attack 'sprinkling' and 'steeple houses', Fox taught his flock to despise and mistrust words; reason was the enemy of the light. When suffused by it, the 'Children of the Light', as they called themselves, felt a great trembling of the earth as if it was opening like their own souls, and they themselves began to shake and sway and sometimes sing for joy. The community they felt in this state of grace was important, for it insulated them, up to a point, from the very real perils and penalties they faced from the carnal world. For without question the Commonwealth, and the Protectorate after it, felt threatened by the Quakers, notwithstanding their continual protestations of indifference to politics and loyalty to the powers that be. They were somehow deeply offensive. They refused to doff their hats or to be quiet in church. Indeed, they came to church specifically to make an ungodly noise. Fox was punched in York Minster, and in Tickhill, Yorkshire, he was smacked in the face with a Bible, dragged from the church and tossed over a hedge. He was sat in stocks, pilloried, repeatedly arrested and jailed, despite a modicum of protection from John Bradshaw, president of the court that had tried Charles, a Councillor of State and a friend of Margaret's husband Thomas Fell.

Yet he remained indomitable. In the spring of 1652 Fox climbed to the top of Pendle Hill, on the border between west Yorkshire and Lancashire, and beheld, if not the Promised Land, then the green Ribble valley stretching west to the Irish Sea, a whole country waiting to be gathered. 'I was moved', he wrote, 'to sound the day of the Lord.' He bathed in the Light.

As far as Thomas Hobbes was concerned light was just a 'fancy of the mind caused by motion in the brain'. Like everything else in the human world, it was not mystery but matter and capable of explanation by sound reasoning. At the same time that Fox was in the throes of his illuminations, *Leviathan* appeared, its premise being that matters of religion ought to be shunted off into the realm of metaphysical speculation where they belonged. Politics and government could only be decided by hard-headed, unflinching logic. Moral distaste was neither here nor there. Reason demanded submission to whatever sovereign had the capacity of providing peace and law.

When he got back to England in the spring of 1651, Hobbes discovered that, for all the shouting and prating, there were others who thought very much like himself when it came to the criteria of allegiance. One of them was Marchamont Nedham, the most prolific and ingenious of the parliamentary journalists, whose *Mercurius Britannicus* jousted with its royalist rival *Mercurius Aulicus*. For a brief spell in the late 1640s, Nedham had switched sides. But once the war was over, he reverted to the Commonwealth and was its leading propagandist. Not only did Nedham now subscribe readily to the official 'Engagement' that the Commonwealth required of all its citizens, he was prepared to develop a public position which might be used to reconcile the countless thousands of royalists in England to accepting the *de facto* power of the Rump Parliament and its government. Nedham started from the same premise as Hobbes: that the paramount reason to institute any government and to accept subjection to it was its power to offer protection to subjects, otherwise prey to anarchy. Nedham's argument, reinforced by Hobbes, replaced the question 'Is it proper?' with the question 'Does it work?' And with that apparently simple change in perspective, for better or worse, modern political science was born.

So was Oliver Cromwell Leviathan, the 'artificial man' in whom all men were combined in one indisputable, unarguable sovereign? Later, when he was Lord Protector, his steward John Maidstone described his appearance as though it was indeed a one-man national monument: 'his head so shaped, as you might see it a storehouse and shop … a vast treasury of natural parts'. But however slavish the sycophancy, it's to Cromwell's credit that he never quite seemed to fall for it. Nor is there any serious evidence that, from the beginning of the Commonwealth, Cromwell aimed at any sort of personal supremacy, regal or otherwise. Though those who came to hate him, like Edmund Ludlow, believed that his repeated declarations of aversion to high office were hypocritical, masking a monomaniacal ambition, there is good reason to believe them sincere. Cromwell certainly showed some of the symptoms of absolutism – colossal self-righteousness, haughty intolerance, a frighteningly low threshold of rage, a coarse instinct for bullying his way past any opposition. But he also lacked the one essential characteristic for true dictatorship: a hunger to accumulate power for its own sake. For Cromwell, the exercise of power was a necessary chore, not a pleasure. And it was not undertaken for personal gratification. Whatever his many failings, vanity was not one of them. He saw the warts clearly and without extenuation, and they were not merely on his face. Throughout his life as a public figure, Cromwell

(209)

Numb. 14.

Mercurius Politicus.

Comprifing the Summe of all Intelligence, with the Affairs, and Defigns now on foot, in the three Nations of *England*, *Ireland*, and *Scotland*.

In defence of the Common-wealth, and for Information of the People.

——————*Itáverrere Seria Ludo.* {Hor. de Ar.Poet.

From *Thurfday*, Septemb. 5. to *Thurfday*, Septemb. 12. 1650.

LAS, poore Tarquin, *whither wilt thou go!* you know, in *Numb.* 5. I told you, all my Feare was, that He and His *Jockies* would never ftand to it, and that one *Rout* or *Retreat* would make Them not worth a *Pamphlet*; and then I and my man *Mercury* fhould be out of employment. I told you likewife, that the late rumor of a *Rout* which came by the way of *Carlifle*, was as it were *the foreftalling of a Victory*, and that it would prove *a Propheticke piece of Intelligence*; which being now fulfilled to the purpofe, wee muft convert our *Satyrs* into *Praifes*, our *Boaftings* into *Humility*, our *wits* into *Admiration*, and imploy all our Faculties to magnifie the good hand of God toward us; for *This is his doing, and it is marvellous in our eyes*, and in the eyes of our *Enemies*, Themfelves being Judges.

E e And

Front page of the popular parliamentary broadsheet *Mercurius Politicus*, 1650, edited by the Commonwealth's leading propagandist, Marchamont Nedham.

believed himself to be no more than the weak and imperfect instrument through which an almighty Providence worked its will on the history of Britain. Often he sounded like the stammering Moses, drafted by an insistent Almighty into business he would rather leave to someone else.

But there was, as he wrote to Oliver St John in 1648, no shirking the call: 'The Lord spake thus unto me with a strong hand and instructed me.' Cromwell, then, believed he worked for God. Real dictators believe they are God. It was those who fancied themselves little gods, from Charles I to the republican oligarchs of the Rump like Henry Marten and Sir Arthur Haselrig, who most aroused Cromwell's contempt. He mistrusted power-seekers and personal empire-builders and constantly questioned their motives, including his own. 'Simplicity' was a word he used repeatedly of himself and his conduct, and it was the highest of moral compliments. Better, always, to be thought naïve than wickedly sophisticated. If he was no manipulator, then nor was Cromwell (unlike Ireton) much of an ideologist of the new Britain. Arguably, the survival of the republic was jeopardized by his complete indifference to creating anything like a true commonwealth culture to replace that of the defunct royal regime. In the last analysis Cromwell was not that far from Fox (whom he found both fascinating and repellent) in believing in the ultimate triviality of 'carnal' forms of government. They were all, he said, following St Paul, 'dross and dung in comparison of Christ'. This spiritual loftiness was personally admirable, but it was also politically fatal to the perpetuation of the Republic. To prolong itself, the Protectorate needed Cromwell to be more of a Leviathan, more of a ruthless sovereign, than he could ever manage to stomach. This is both his exoneration and his failure.

Though he is an obligatory fixture in the pantheon of heroes, along with Caesar, Napoleon and all the usual darlings of destiny, the wonder of Oliver Cromwell is that for so much of his life he showed absolutely no inkling of what awaited him, nor any precocious impatience to be recognized as exceptional. For the greater part of his fifty-nine years he toiled away in dim mid-Anglian obscurity, amid the cabbage fields, very much the provincial country gentleman-farmer. For most of his career the man who was to become the arbiter of power in Britain was breathtakingly innocent of it. Likewise, the greatest general of his age was completely unschooled and unpractised in the arts of war. Cromwell was not, then, someone who instinctively knew that he was fated to ascend. On the contrary, he thought of himself as a casualty of a triple fall – social, political and spiritual. His rise was the ungainly clambering of a man making his way up the forbidding stone face of Purgatory.

Socially, Cromwell spent most of his early life on the narrow edge of respectability rather than embedded comfortably within it, for he was the son of a second son.

He was tantalisingly close to real fortune. His grandfather, Sir Henry, had been sheriff of both Huntingdonshire and Cambridgeshire, a member of the Elizabethan parliament and opulent enough in his entertainments at least to be called 'the Golden Knight' by the Queen. His oldest son (also called Oliver) also managed to cut a stylish figure both at court and in East Anglia: a herald at the funeral of James I; married into Dutch and Genoese banking money. All of which made the much more modest circumstances of Oliver's father, Robert, glaringly uncomfortable. Uncle Oliver's money was needed to keep the modest estate afloat and to send young Oliver (the only surviving boy in a family of seven children) to the Inns of Court in London. There, however, he made what seemed to be his saving fortune by marrying Elizabeth Bourchier, a wealthy London fur-trader's daughter. He seemed very much on his way up. With a legal education and some funds in hand he was elected to the parliament of 1628 which saw the dramatic struggle over the Petition of Right. But there was no sign, in that momentous year, that Oliver Cromwell was anything but a silent back-bencher while the debates over prerogative and the common law were thundering around him. All that is known of his presence amid the political furore was that the royal physician, Sir Theodore Mayerne, treated Cromwell for severe depression – *valde melancholicus* – a condition that would often revisit him. (In fact, his wild mood swings – from bursts of disconcerting laughter while praising the Lord for a particularly comprehensive annihilation of the enemy, to his descents into scowling gloom – suggest the classic symptoms of clinical depression.)

Whatever the cause, around 1629–30 Cromwell's fortunes seem to have collapsed. By 1631 his circumstances had become so parlous that he was forced to sell almost all of his land and transplant himself to St Ives in Huntingdonshire. There he farmed about 17 acres, not as the squire of the manor but as a yeoman tenant, leasing holdings from Cambridge colleges and working the land alongside his hired hands. Cromwell's social descent and his experience of rural toil in these years gave him a closeness to the speech and habits of ordinary people which became a priceless asset when he translated it into the charisma of military command. He never lost the soft East Anglian burr in his voice, and when he spoke about the 'plain russet-coated captains', the 'honest' men he wanted at the core of his army, Cromwell knew exactly what and whom he was talking about. Before his fall from genteel ease, he had also been on the losing end of a bitter local political dispute in Huntingdon when the royal government had changed the borough charter. Cromwell was among the local gentry discomfited by the changes and, for the first but not the last time, let the vainglorious winners feel the rough edge of his tongue. One of his adversaries complained about the 'disgraceful and unseemly speeches' he made against the mayor and

Above: *Henry Ireton,* attributed to Robert Walker, *c.* 1655.
Opposite: *Oliver Cromwell,* by Robert Walker, *c.* 1649.

recorder of Huntingdon, which were aggressive enough to get him reported to the Privy Council.

De profundis, politically marginalized, socially demoted, submerged below sea-level in the sodden Fens, Cromwell was suddenly reborn. It was this conversion experience, so he believed (rather than a timely inheritance from a bachelor uncle), which started him on the road to redemption. A justly famous letter to his cousin, the wife of Oliver St John, written later in 1638, but recalling his redemption, is a classic of Pauline-Calvinist reawakening: 'Oh, I lived in and loved darkness, and hated the light. I was a chief, the chief of sinners. This is true; I hated godliness, yet God had mercy on me. O the riches of His mercy!'

His political election – to the Short and then the Long Parliament in 1640 as member for Cambridge – was less important than his spiritual election to stand forth and do God's bidding. Or rather, political life for Oliver Cromwell *was* a spiritual office. Whatever accountability he might nominally have to his electors or to the king was as nothing compared to his accountability before God. Although he had become a man of some substance again, living in Ely, Cromwell still thought of himself as a marginal man in the world of the grandees. His distance from and deep scepticism of oligarchs and aristocrats, even those who professed proper parliamentary opinions, gave him the unwavering resolution they often lacked. While he was deeply committed (and would always be) to the prevailing social order, he did not believe it would be subverted by a forthright challenge to the king's presumptions. On the contrary, only by resisting those presumptions, the corrupt arrogance of a court, could this ancient and essentially benevolent English hierarchy be securely preserved. Unlike many, in and out of the parliaments of 1640–2, Cromwell was not afraid of a fight, always provided that it was for a godly cause. He was convinced, much earlier than most, that a great struggle between the forces of righteousness and unrighteousness was inevitable and that to pretend otherwise was false comfort. By knowing that it would be so Cromwell made it so, becoming the most vocal member of the Commons to demand that the authority to appoint Lords-Lieutenant and to muster militia be transferred from the king to parliament. As far as Cromwell was concerned, the war did not begin with the raising of the royal standard in Nottingham but much earlier, in the Irish rebellion behind which he saw the bloody hand of Stuart machination. Putting the country 'into a posture of defence', he urged, with a clarity which Hobbes would have grudgingly admired, was no more than an act of timely self-preservation.

So where others dithered and hesitated, Oliver Cromwell acted. Having raised a troop of sixty horse in Cambridgeshire, he used it to seize Cambridge Castle for the parliament and to stop the removal of college and university plate to the king's war chest. Dead straight-ahead decisiveness was to be the hallmark of Cromwell's spectacular career during the war itself (in such contrast to his later indecisiveness in the world of pure politics). He had no time for those whom he suspected – first Denzil Holles, then the Earl of Manchester – who fought, always with an eye to negotiation rather than to total victory, or for those like Essex who he thought shrank from engagement. Equivocation was unworthy of the helmeted Jehovah who he knew fought on his side. Inside the hymn-singing, pocket Bible-carrying New Model Army, Cromwell turned Gideon: the leader of a godly troop. He played it for all it was worth, helping John Dillingham, editor of *The Parliament Scout,* to drum up the Cromwellian reputation as a general in his newsbook, because he undoubtedly believed that he had been designated by the Lord of Hosts to lead his captains and corporals. And Cromwell also understood that the rank-and-file soldiers would respond better to an officer who never betrayed any doubts about the rightness of the cause or the certainty of eventual victory. This spiritual armour-plating did not make Cromwell any less of an intelligent tactician, for all his lack of military experience or training. What he brought to Marston Moor and Naseby (and learned from the failure at Edgehill) was a cavalry strong enough to take the impact of an enemy charge and flexible enough to regroup for a counter-offensive to which an undeployed reserve could be added for additional force. He was also blessed with the one quality without which all paper planning would be useless: an infallible sense of timing. Cromwell could 'read' a battle, right through the din and the choking smoke and the chaos, and have an uncanny sense of how to react to its ebb and flow. This did not mean, however, that he sat at a distance surveying the carnage with his perspective glass. On the contrary, he was usually to be found in the thick of it, leading charges, urging on pikemen and dragoons, risking (and sometimes taking) a wound but always surviving. His personal bravery and steely composure in the heat of battle won the trust of men who were being asked to put themselves in harm's way. How could they not believe in a general who never lost? (Even the indecisive second battle of Newbury was at worst an unsatisfying draw.) With every fresh victory, Cromwell's soldiers had proof that they were themselves protected by the general's close relations with Providence. Faith that his soldiers were truly doing God's work was not the same, though, as assuming that the army rather than parliament should dictate the political fate of the nation.

The two Cromwells – the socially conservative believer in the ancient constitution and the zealous evangelical reformer – were still at odds within his own personality. Despite the presence of true Puritans like Sir Robert Harley in the

parliament, Cromwell, like Ireton, was unsure of its commitment to godly reformation. But the thought of imposing a settlement at sword point on parliament still
made him uneasy, right through the crisis of the summer and autumn of 1647. A
regime of generals, however pious, was not what he had fought for. A year later,
though, many of these reservations had fallen away in the ferocity of the second civil
war. Presbyterianism no longer seemed the vanguard, but the rearguard, of the pure.
Its parliamentary champions such as Holles seemed frightened by true liberty of
conscience and even prepared, like the Scots, to make a cheap bargain with the king
to secure the interests of their own narrow Church. They had 'withdrawn their shoulder from the Lord's work through fleshly reasonings', he wrote. So even though he
let Ireton do the hatchet work and disingenuously remained at a distance from
Colonel Pride's Purge, Cromwell was no longer a devout believer in the sacrosanct
untouchability of the Long Parliament. He was already the sceptic of the mask of
legalism. 'If nothing should be done but what is according to the law,' he would
say before yet another of the purges he sponsored (that of the second Protectorate
parliament), 'the throat of the nation may be cut while we send for some to make a
law.' This is the rationalization of all *coups d'état*.

When Cromwell joined the republic's Council of State in 1649, however, he
never imagined he was presiding over the conversion of a parliamentary state into a
military-theocratic dictatorship. It was merely the old parliament, riddled with equivocation and bad faith, that had needed to be got rid of. And when on 15 March he
accepted the command of the expedition to suppress the Irish revolt Cromwell did
so, in his own mind, as the servant rather than the master of the 'Keepers of the
Nation's Liberties', as the Rump styled itself. Even as 'Lord-Lieutenant' Cromwell
was still, in theory at least, subordinate to the commander-in-chief of the Commonwealth armies, Fairfax. All the issues of titles and authority, which seemed to exercise
many people, were for Cromwell beside the point. 'I would not have the army now
so much look at considerations that are personal,' he told the Council of State,
'whether or no we shall go if such a Commander or such a Commander go and
make that any part of our measure or foundation: but let us go if God go.' He was
clear in his own mind that, unless Ireland was subjugated, it would always remain the
springboard of an invasion of England: perhaps even half of a pincer movement, with
the other thrust coming from Scotland where Charles II had been declared king. So
while the innocent might think 1649 a time to sit back and settle the Commonwealth, for Cromwell it was still very much a pressing wartime emergency.

But emergency or not, what Oliver Cromwell then perpetrated in Ireland in the
autumn of 1649 has been remembered as one of the most infamous atrocities in the

entirety of British history, an enormity so monstrous that it has shadowed the possibility of Anglo-Irish co-existence ever since. Unquestionably, events of appalling cruelty took place at Drogheda and Wexford. But exactly what happened, and to whom, has for centuries been clouded with misunderstanding. Only recently have Irish historians like Tom Reilly, a native son of Drogheda, had the courage and scholarly integrity to get the story right. Getting it right, moreover, is not in any sense exoneration or extenuation. It is explanation.

The first thing to get right is just who the victims at Drogheda were. The vast majority were neither Catholic nor Gaelic Irish, nor were any of them unarmed civilians, the women and children of Father Murphy's largely mythical history published in 1883. For in the first instance Cromwell was being sent by the Council of State and the Rump Parliament to confront not the Catholic Confederates who had risen in 1641, but a royalist, largely Protestant army led by the Duke of Ormonde, which for many years, until the execution of the king, had been fighting against, not alongside, the rebels led by Owen Roe O'Neill. Drogheda, from the beginning a staunchly loyalist Old English town, had in fact defied the siege of Phelim O'Neill's insurgent army in 1641. At the time, then, when Cromwell and thirty-five of his fleet of 130 ships, carrying 12,000 troops, set sail from Milford Haven, there were no fewer than four distinct armies in Ireland: the Gaelic-Irish forces of the Confederacy, dominated by Owen Roe O'Neill and Cardinal Rinuccini; the royalist army of Ormonde; the Scots-Presbyterian army in Ulster of General Monroe, which had been pro-parliament but since the proclamation of Charles II in Scotland was now potentially another enemy of the English; and finally the English parliamentary forces commanded by Lieutenant-Colonel Michael Jones. It's quite true that a negotiated truce between the royalist army and the Irish-Catholic Confederation had simplified this military quadrille for Cromwell, but as much as he heartily detested Roman Catholicism and believed that the Irish rebellion was a Trojan Horse, not just for the Stuarts but for Rome and even Spain (he was to his marrow an Elizabethan in this respect), he also identified the immediate and most formidable enemy in Ireland not as Irish Catholic but as royalist. If he was about to be merciless in his onslaught it was because he had been equally implacable in his prosecution of the evidently unfinished second civil war.

Cromwell made no secret of his contempt for the native Irish population. In common with many of his Puritan contemporaries, he believed the pornographic exaggerations of the atrocity propaganda by which most Englishmen got news of the rebellion of 1641: all those impaled Presbyterian babies and mutilated patriarchs in Ulster and Leinster. 'You, unprovoked,' he wrote to the Irish bishops in 1650, 'put the

English to the most unheard-of and most barbarous massacre (without respect of sex and age) that ever the sun beheld.' There's also no doubt that his credulous belief in the bestiality of the Irish hardened him against any suffering that might be inflicted on the native population as a result of the campaign. But this did not turn him to genocide. Soldiers, not civilians, were the targets of his fury. In fact, and in keeping with his practice in past campaigns in England, Cromwell went out of his way, publicly, to threaten retribution against any of his troops found assaulting the unarmed and unresisting population. Before the siege of Drogheda ever got under way, two of his men were hanged expressly for violating that prohibition. Nor did Cromwell have any particular relish for the inevitable bloodshed. It was precisely because he might have anticipated General Sherman's dictum that 'war is hell' that he resolved to wage it with maximum ferocity, the better to shorten its duration.

Whenever there was a chance of intimidating a defending stronghold into capitulation without loss of life, Cromwell did whatever he could to make that happen. At Drogheda, commanding the main road between Dublin and Ulster, he believed there was just such a chance, since the commander, the royalist veteran (and one of its few Catholics) Sir Arthur Aston, was hopelessly outnumbered, not least in the heavy artillery department where Cromwell could bring massive siege mortars to bear on any attack. In an attempt to obtain Aston's peaceful surrender on the morning of 10 September Cromwell delivered a chilling ultimatum to him:

> Sir, having brought the army belonging to the parliament of England before this place, to reduce it to obedience, to the end the effusion of blood may be prevented, I thought fit to summon you to deliver the same into my hands to their use. If this be refused you will have no cause to blame me. I expect your answer and rest, your servant, O. Cromwell.

Aston, of course, summarily rejected the ultimatum. The experience of the long-drawn-out siege of 1641–2 and the apparently imposing walls of Drogheda made him believe that the town could hold out against the first shock of Cromwell's assault, at least long enough for him to be relieved by troops supplied by Ormonde. As it turned out, he was tragically deluded twice over. Drogheda's walls did not hold, and on the day of the attack Ormonde's troops were nowhere in sight, though he had sent a small number of reinforcements to the garrison the day before. It took Cromwell's guns no more than a few hours to blast breaches in the outer walls, but longer for his infantry to penetrate those breaches, furiously defended by royalist soldiers among whom was young Edmund Verney, Ralph's brother. The gaps choked with wounded and dying,

Cromwell himself led a third and decisive charge into the breach. The defenders fell back into a flimsily defended stockade area on Mill Mount, while some of them retreated to the tower and steeple of the Protestant Church of St Peter.

What then happened was not unprecedented in the appalling history of seventeenth-century warfare, and especially not in the Irish wars. The Scottish-Presbyterian General Monroe massacred 3000 at Island Magee. After the battle of Knockanauss in 1647 Colonel Michael Jones had 600 prisoners killed in cold blood and deserters from his own side (including his own nephew) hanged. But it was, all the same, an obscenity. Cromwell's own account of what he did is startlingly unapologetic and without any kind of procrastination or euphemism: 'our men getting up to them (Aston and his men on Mill Mount), were ordered by me to put them all to the sword. And indeed, being in the heat of action, I forbade them to spare any that were in arms in the town, and, I think, that night they put to the sword about 2000 men.' At least 3000 royalist soldiers were massacred in Drogheda, the vast majority not as they were frantically fighting the parliamentary troops, but when they had all but given up and were either surrendered or disarmed. The refusal of quarter to unresisting, defeated men was a calculated slaughter. At St Peter's Church, Cromwell had his soldiers burn the pews beneath the steeple to smoke out the defenders who had taken refuge in the tower, with the result that many fell to their deaths in flames along with the bells and masonry which came crashing down. The murders were so inhuman that it seems certain that not all of Cromwell's officers could bring themselves to obey his orders and that some actually went out of their way to save their enemies.

This atrocity inflicted on soldiers, few of whom were either Irish or Catholic, is surely sufficiently unforgivable to indict Cromwell, without any additional need to subscribe to the fiction that he deliberately or even passively extended the massacre to civilians. As Reilly correctly points out, the stories of women and children raped and mutilated, derive in their entirety from non eye-witnesses, virtually all of them either passionate royalists (like the antiquarian Anthony Wood), who published the stories during the Restoration witch-hunts against republicans, or compilers of accounts at least one or two centuries after the fact. Wood's brother Thomas, who had fought for the royalists in England, then switched sides to parliament, then reversed his allegiance again in the Restoration, was notorious for his buffooning and indulgence in tall tales, and, obviously anxious to exonerate himself, was the source of many of the juiciest stories. His version of Drogheda, repeated by Anthony, supplied the story of Aston being beaten to death with his own wooden leg (though he was certainly robbed by his killers of gold worn on a belt around his body), and that of the mysterious martyred 'virgin' (how would they know in the heat of battle?) arrayed

Ireland, by Gio Giacomo Rossi, 1689.

James Butler, First Duke of Ormonde, by Sir Peter Lely, *c.* 1660. Popularly known as 'James the White', for his mane of fair hair.

in her finest jewels and finery, who was stabbed in the 'belly or fundament' by marauding troopers. None of this apocrypha is needed to make the case for the prosecution. The most damning witness against Cromwell is Cromwell, who makes no bones about his deliberate intention to perpetrate a slaughter so ghastly that it would dissuade other strongholds from making Drogheda's mistake and refusing peaceful capitulation.

The strategy of terror worked. In many other places along his march – New Ross, for example – the fate of Drogheda did indeed guarantee a bloodless surrender. Even at Wexford, where the defending troops and civilian inhabitants, unlike those at Drogheda, were Catholic and holding the town for the Irish Confederacy, and where there was another terrible slaughter, the military governor had not in fact refused to capitulate before the violence began on 11 October. Although he had, as usual, made it unequivocally clear what would happen were his ultimatum refused, Cromwell promised the governor, Colonel Sinnott, that should there be a surrender he would let the soldiers and non-commissioned officers depart peacefully, once they had undertaken not to take up arms again, and make the officers prisoners. 'And as for the inhabitants, I shall engage myself that no violence shall be offered to their goods, and that I shall protect the town from plunder.' Sinnott never got this note. While negotiations were still under way firing broke out, and in no time at all the parliamentary troops were inside the city killing as many of the other side as they possibly could. Once again it's no mitigation of the horror to realize that civilians were not among the masses of dead at Wexford. The most tragic and numerous civilian deaths occurred when there was a panicky rush for the boats moored at the quayside. Overloaded, they inevitably capsized, drowning. At least 2000 perished – 300 by drowning – at Wexford that day, including priests (some of whom, understandably, may have been armed) as well as soldiers.

Cromwell is unlikely to have shed tears for the fate of the Fathers. He made no secret of the fact that he did not regard the priesthood as innocent bystanders to the conflict, but as conspiring agents of the forces of Antichrist. When the Catholic prelates of Ireland accused him, at the end of 1649, of deliberately aiming to 'extirpate' their religion from the country, Cromwell responded, in January 1650, with a lengthy, thunderous denunciation which exposed in the most extraordinary way the intensity of his passions and prejudices and his selective, Protestant version of Anglo-Irish history:

You say your union is against a common enemy ... I will give you some wormwood to bite on, by which it will appear God is not with you. Who is it that created this common enemy? I suppose you mean Englishmen. The English! Remember ye Hypocrites, Ireland was once united to England; Englishmen had good Inheritances, which many of them purchased with their money; they or their Ancestors from many of you and your Ancestors … They lived Peaceably honestly amongst you. … You broke this union!

It was the clergy, he asserted, who were responsible for deluding the poor common people in the snares of their theological fraud, while reaping the benefits of wealth and rank. Cromwell bluntly owned up to his refusal neither to tolerate the saying of the Mass 'nor suffer you that are Papists: where I can find you seducing the People, or by any overt act violating the Lawes established'. Catholics in Ireland, in other words, were to be treated just as harshly as, but no worse than, Catholics in England. As far as private practice was concerned, they were to be left alone: 'As for the People, what thoughts they have in matters of Religion in their owne breasts I cannot reach; but thinke it my duty, if they walk honestly and peaceably, not to cause them in the least to suffer for the same, but shall endeavour to walke patiently and in love towards them: to see if at any time it shall please God to give them another or a better minde.' As for the charges of 'extirpation' through 'Massacring, destroying or banishing the Catholique Inhabitants … good now, give us an instance of one man since my coming into Ireland, not in armse, massacred, destroyed or banished; concerning the two first of which, justice hath not been done or endeavoured to be done.' As the evidence shows, he had a point. But Cromwell's passions, rather than his reason, rose like a tidal wave at the end of his tirade. Scornfully rejecting the notion that the English army had come expressly to rob the Irish of lands, he readily conceded that the soldiers had been, as usual, promised recompense from the confiscated lands of proven rebels, but:

> I can give you a better reason for the Armies comming over then this; *England* hath had experience of the blessing of God in prosecuting just and righteous causes, what ever the cost and hazard be. And if ever men were engaged in a righteous cause in the World, this wil be scarce a second to it … We come to breake the power of a company of lawlesse Rebels, who having cast off the authority of *England*, live as enemies to humane society, whose Principles (the world hath experience of) are to destroy and subjugate all men not complying with them. We come (by the assistance of God) to hold forth and maintaine the lustre and glory of English liberty in a Nation where we have an undoubted right to doe it.

Top: *Charles II when Prince of Wales* (detail), studio of Adriaen
Hanneman, *c.* 1648–9. A rare portrait of the young prince during
his exile in the Low Countries.
Above: *James Graham, First Marquis of Montrose*, attributed to
William Dobson, *c.* 1640.

This is, to the core, absolutely authentic Cromwell and today it makes unbearable reading. It is not the same as the unwitting confession of a genocidal lunatic, but it is the unwitting confession of a pig-headed, narrow-minded, Protestant bigot and English imperialist. And that is quite bad enough.

Even for his most devoted warrior, however, God could occasionally drop his guard. Except at Clonmel in County Tipperary, where Cromwell botched an attack, there was not a lot the remaining royalist and Irish armies could do to stop the relentless campaign of subjugation. Most of the strongholds in Munster in the south fell to his army. But his own troops were not immune to Major Hunger and Colonel Sickness, which launched a pitiless offensive in the awful winter of 1649–50. Cromwell himself became seriously ill as the attrition rate in his army rose to devastating levels. Even though he issued draconian prohibitions forbidding his soldiers from wantonly stealing and looting from the native population, the orders were unenforceable. In all likelihood, several hundred thousand more died from those kinds of depredations, as well as from the epidemics of plague and dysenteric fevers which swept through war-ravaged Ireland, than from the direct assault of English soldiers. It was, all the same, a horror, and it went on and on and on.

Cromwell was recalled by the Council of State in April 1650 and appointed Ireton as his deputy, but the country was still by no means pacified. Ireton would die on campaign the following year, and Ludlow, with good reason for trepidation, became temporary commander-in-chief, until July 1652, when he was replaced by Charles Fleetwood. Forcibly reunited with England, Ireland went through another huge transfer of land: the gentry and nobility associated with the revolt were stripped of their estates in the east, centre and south, and transplanted to much smaller and much less fertile lands in stony Connacht in the west. Some of the officers and men taken prisoner on the campaign – at Wexford, for example – were treated as chattel prizes and sold as indentured quasi-slaves for transport to Barbados.

Cromwell returned to England the Puritan Caesar. More than Marston Moor, Naseby or Preston, it was the Irish campaign in all its gruesome ugliness which had made him an English hero. He had revenged 1641. He had laid the lash on the barbarians. He was covered in laurels and greeted by shouts of acclamation. Thousands cheered him on Hounslow Heath. The young Andrew Marvell addressed a Horatian ode to the victor, confident that he remained unspoiled by triumph:

How good he is, how *just*,
And fit for highest Trust:
Nor yet grown stiffer with Command,

But still in the *Republik's* hand:
How fit he is to sway
That can so well obey.

Whether or not Cromwell's head was beginning to be turned by all this noisy
adulation, he continued to insist that he was still the servant of God and the
Commonwealth. And, debilitated as he was by whatever sickness he had contracted
in Ireland, Cromwell also knew there was at least one more decisive campaign to
fight in the interminable British wars before the task of 'healing and settling', as he
often referred to it, could be undertaken. Marvell agreed:

But thou the Wars and Fortunes son
March indefatigably on.

This next war would be in the north. For in the summer of 1650, the twenty-year-
old Charles II had arrived to assume his throne in Scotland. It had not been his first
choice for a theatre of counterattack. In every way, not least the presence of
Ormonde's army, Ireland would have been (as Cromwell had guessed) a much more
desirable operational base, but the events of late 1649 had put paid to that hope. So,
more in desperation than jubilation, Charles had met with Scots negotiators in
Holland and had agreed to their dismayingly severe condition that he sign the
National Covenant which had first seen the light of day as a battle-cry against his
father. Much had happened since 1637, of course, and *in extremis* even Charles I had
been prepared to accept it as the price for Scottish support. All the same, Charles II
was, as the Scots themselves knew, an even more unlikely Presbyterian, being not
much given to professions of Calvinist repentance. He was, even at twenty, working
hard on accumulating sins to repent of, beginning with the first of a long string of
mistresses, Lucy Walter, who bore him the bastard Duke of Monmouth. As a young
man Charles was already what he would be all his life: effortlessly charming, affable,
intelligent, languid and hungrily addicted to sex, in every respect the polar opposite
of his chaste, austere, publicly conscientious but neurotically reserved father. When
Charles II was introduced to Lady Anne Murray, who had helped his younger brother
James escape from England disguised as a girl, he promised that, if ever it was in his
power to reward her as she should deserve, he would do so. 'And with that,' she
wrote, 'the King laid his hand upon mine as they lay upon my breast.' This was the
sort of gesture that came naturally – for better or worse – to Charles. It was almost
impossible not to like him and almost as impossible to take him seriously. But once

in Scotland, he chafed against the vigilance imposed on him by the Covenanter leaders like the Marquis of Argyll, hoping somehow to be liberated by a genuinely royalist Scottish army led by Montrose – until that is, the hitherto indestructible and elusive Montrose was betrayed by the Scottish parliament, seized, taken to Edinburgh and hanged and quartered, his several parts distributed throughout Scotland.

The Covenanter suspicion of royalist contamination of their army led them to purge it of any officers and troops whom they believed to be potentially disloyal. The result was a large but unwieldy and amateurish force, led by General David Leslie. It was this army that Cromwell smashed at the battle of Dunbar in September 1650. He had come to the command only after Fairfax (whose wife was a Presbyterian Scot and who had fought alongside the Covenanters) had refused to lead the northern expedition. The numerical odds were against Cromwell, but he offset them with one of his headlong cavalry-led onslaughts right at the thick of the Scottish force an hour before dawn when they were not yet properly mustered. Thousands were killed in the brief mêlée, thousands more taken prisoner.

The Scots retreated, as so often before, out of Midlothian and Fife across the Forth to Stirling, and Charles was duly inaugurated at Scone on 1 January 1651. But despite appalling weather and over-extended supply-lines, Cromwell took the war to them, crossing the Firth of Forth. In the summer of 1651, Charles and Leslie took what they thought was the audacious step of leaving Cromwell's army floundering in the rain and mud while they marched west and south into England itself. The hope was (as it would be for Charles's great-nephew Bonnie Prince Charlie in 1745) that, once inside England, a nation of burning Stuart royalists would flock to his standard. And, as in 1745, it never happened. It was not that the entire country was so devoted to the new Commonwealth that rallying to Charles was under any circumstances unthinkable. It was rather that the armies of the republic were so obviously still formidable that it made absolutely no sense to anyone but the most blindly devoted royalist to hazard their safety by supporting so reckless a gamble. So the march down western England to Worcester – where, as Cromwell noted, the civil wars had begun – was a lonely and exclusively Scottish business. Cromwell had let them go deep into the heart of England from which there could be no way back. What had begun as a daring venture had become a steel trap closing fast on Charles II. Another substantial army moved north and west to join Cromwell. Together, outside Worcester, some 28,000 Commonwealth troops faced a royalist-Scottish army of hardly more than half that number. The result was a bloody catastrophe, which ended at twilight with men still hacking at each other in the streets of the city.

Oliver Cromwell returned to an even noisier triumph in London than had

Top: A plan of the battle of Dunbar, 1650, showing on the right Cromwell's camp by the town of Dunbar; in the centre lies Broxburn House where Cromwell planned his surprise night attack.
Above: Scene of the battlefield today, with Bass Rock and the Firth of Forth in the distance.

King Charles II on Humphrey Penderel's Mill Horse, by Isaac Fuller, *c.* 1665. At one stage during his flight from England, Charles rode an old cart-horse lent by the Penderel brothers. When the prince quipped about his slow-moving mount, Humphrey Penderel retorted that the poor creature was carrying the weight of three kingdoms on his back.

greeted his Irish victory. Charles embarked on the extraordinary six-week flight from captivity, which was the coolest and bravest thing he would ever do. Although once he got back to Paris and the exiled court he invented a great number of details – to avoid incriminating his helpers, it was said, but also because he evidently enjoyed telling the stories – the truth of his adventure was astonishing enough. Disguised as a country yeoman, with his mane of black curls cropped short, his face darkened with nut juice to look more weather-beaten and wearing a rough leather doublet, Charles outsmarted and outran his pursuers. Relying on a network of royalists in the West Country, many of them Catholics and thus expert at improvised concealment, Charles hid first in the Staffordshire woods around Boscobel House, the home of the Penderel brothers. Then, having failed to cross the Severn in an attempt to get to Wales, Charles was first hidden in a hayloft and then walked in the rain back to Boscobel, where he slept exhausted in one of the great oaks in the park while troopers searched the estate for him. For royalist legend-makers it was a perfectly emblematic moment: the young hope of the future safely cradled in the fatherly embrace of the ancient English tree. There followed a ride across country disguised as 'William Jackson', the manservant of Jane Lane; failure to find a safe passage either from Bristol or from Bridport in Dorset, where the quays and taverns were crawling with Commonwealth soldiers about to be shipped to the Channel Islands; and then abortive wanderings along the south coast before finally finding a reliable ship, the *Surprise,* at Shoreham in Sussex. Given the £1000 price on his head, and his willingness to test the limits of his disguise by engaging in reckless banter about the rogue Charles Stuart (the sort of game that amused the king), it was astonishing that he was not, in fact, betrayed or discovered. To royalists who had reconciled themselves to submitting for the time being to Leviathan, his near miraculous survival gave them a consoling legend to develop in competition with Cromwell's depressing record of invincibility.

Charles II's escape, dependent as it was on so many helping hands, says something important about this very English revolution: that it was (for its own good) deficient in those elements which make for the survival of republics – police and paranoia. Whether you were a gung-ho republican like Edmund Ludlow, a visionary like John Lilburne or a wistful royalist like John Evelyn, it was glaringly obvious that the Commonwealth had signally failed to develop an independent republican culture to replace the banished monarchy. No revolution, especially not those in eighteenth-century France or twentieth-century Russia or China, could hope to survive for even as long as they did without a conscious cultural programme for the redirection of allegiance. Those programmes were aggressively, even brutally, executed to orchestrate loyalty in the interests of the new state. (Hobbes would have understood this very well.) In their requirements of public demonstrations of allegiance – sung, sworn, chanted, enthusiasm reinforced by fear – they would make political neutrality either an impossibility or a crime. There could be no going back.

Nothing of the sort happened in the Britain of the 1650s. And in this sense the shocking drama of the beheading of Charles I is a misleading guide to the true nature of the Commonwealth and Cromwell's Protectorate. For the men who ran the country were not Jacobins, much less Bolsheviks, in stove-pipe hats and fallen collars. They were clear-eyed pragmatists who were prepared to mouth the necessary shibboleths about 'Liberty', always provided these were vague enough to avoid a commitment to anything like a systematic programme of radical change in, for example, the procedures of the law (as the Levellers had wanted). There had been a lopping all right, a lopping such as has never happened before or since. The king, court, house of peers and bishops had all gone. But this still left a lot of England undisturbed – the England that most of the bigwigs who now ran it, like Henry Marten and Arthur Haselrig, had grown up with, and were partial to and, for all the sound and fury of 1649, had never dreamed of doing away with in the name of some imagined new Jerusalem. Their Zion was still comfortably seated, thank you very much, in the magistrate's chair, in the county hunts and in city counting houses, and in the 1650s it was doing very nicely. So it was possible for unrepentant royalists like John Evelyn (again in startling contrast to the fate of émigrés in the French Revolution) to travel back and forth between London and the Stuart court in Paris, armed with a passport issued to him personally by John Bradshaw, the judge who had presided over the court which had tried the king and who had sentenced him to death! In that same year, 1649, Evelyn bought himself another country estate, and in February 1652 he came back for good, in effect taking the Leviathan option offered by another of the returnees, his friend Hobbes, 'no more intending to go out of England, but endeavor a settled life, either in this place [Deptford], or some other, there being now so little appearance of any change for the better, all being intirely in the rebells hands'.

But no prospect, either, for Evelyn of some nightmarish descent into revolutionary terror. In fact he saw, at first hand, an impressive demonstration of the republic's commitment to upholding the traditional regime of law and order after he had been relieved by a pair of robbers at knife point, while riding through Bromley forest, of two rings (one emerald, one onyx) and a pair of buckles 'set with rubies and diamonds'. The mere fact that Evelyn wore all this glittering hardware at all while out for a ride scarcely suggests he thought of the Commonwealth to which he had returned as an inferno of social chaos and disorder. And he was right. After two hours tied up against an oak 'tormented with the flies, the ants, the sunn', he managed to get loose, find his horse and ride to 'Colonel Blount's, a greate justiciarie of the times, who sent out a hugh & crie immediately'. In London Evelyn had notices of the mugging printed and distributed, and within a mere two days knew exactly what had become of his valuables, which were duly restored to him. A month later he was summoned to appear at the trial of one of the thieves, but not being 'willing to hang the fellow ... I did not appeare'. For the swift return of his jewellery and the exemplary apprehension of the malefactors Evelyn was 'eternaly obliged to give thanks to God my Savior'. But he might also have given some credit to the smooth operation of the law in regicide England. For the next eight years of the interregnum he spent his days much as he would had there been a king on the throne, the significant exception being the difficulty of finding acceptable sermons to hear and the prohibition on celebrating Christmas, which upset him greatly (especially when one clandestine service was raided). But he went about his business, attending to his own estates and advising acquaintances and learned colleagues and gentry on the landscaping and arboriculture of their properties.

In the summer of 1654 Evelyn was able to stay for an extended time in Oxford, now transformed from the Laudian capital of the king and governed by heads of colleges like his host Dr Wilkins of Wadham, approved of by the Protector. Obedient or not, Oxford was none the less a congenial place of science and learning where Evelyn made the acquaintance of many of the prodigies who would be his colleagues in the Royal Society, including 'that prodigious young Scholar Mr. Christopher Wren, who presented me with a piece of White Marble he had stained with a lively red [presumably in imitation of porphyry], very deepe, as beautifull as if it had ben naturall'. In fact Evelyn's entire journey through England – through the West Country and back to East Anglia and Cromwell's Cambridge – is a record of a country conspicuously going about its business, war damage being repaired, farms flourishing (even in a decade of some economic dislocation), gentlemen planning 'beautifications' to their houses and gardens. It was certainly not a country in shock.

And it was still being run largely by men of a practical, rather than a messianic, temper. To read the journal of a man like Bulstrode Whitelocke, the Middle Temple lawyer turned Buckinghamshire gentleman and MP, Commissioner of the Great Seal and a friend of Cromwell's, is to be struck once more by the relentless normality of his life, by the imperturbable continuity before and after the killing of the monarch. What electrified Whitelocke in 1649 was not Charles I's death. A staunch parliamentarian and moderate Puritan inclining towards the Independent view of liberty of conscience, he had none the less been against the trial and had declined to serve as one of the commissioners of the court (a gesture which in Jacobin Paris would have booked him a certain date with the guillotine). But Whitelocke had more important things to think about – above all the death of his second wife, Frances, a trauma which almost unhinged him. With all his misgivings about what the Commonwealth was supposed to be, and his sense that any English state ought to have 'something of a monarchy' about it (he suggested the youngest Stuart, Prince Henry of Gloucester, as a potential replacement, being of an age to be re-educated in political virtue and moderation), Whitelocke sailed on serenely in public life.

Men like Whitelocke, as well as the other dominant figures of the Council of State and the Rump Parliament, invested far more time and energy in preventing any sort of radical change than in promoting it. Their tenure in power suggests perhaps what a pragmatic government might have looked like had Charles I actually succeeded in winning over men like John Pym, rather than just appointing a few token opposition figures to his Privy Council in 1641. Instead of the firebrands he feared, Charles might have had what men like Henry Marten, Henry Vane and Arthur Haselrig had become – businessmen of state, mercantilists, money-managers. And, in their swaggering, beady-eyed way, fierce patriots. For if there *was* some sort of republican ideology that had replaced the inadequate and suspect policy of the Stuarts and around which the English (rather than the British) could indeed rally, it was that of the aggressive prosecution of the national interest. It's all too easy to think of the Commonwealth after the battle of Worcester as living in a kind of pious peace. In fact, it lived in profane war with first the Dutch, then the Portuguese and then the Spanish. It was, as behooved a set of rulers who were excessively misty-eyed about the memory of the sainted Virgin Queen, the most successful warrior state, especially on the high seas, since the death of Elizabeth, in glaring contrast to the string of military fiascoes perpetrated by the hapless Stuarts. Admiral Blake succeeded where Buckingham had failed. Cromwell at his most merciless triumphed where Essex had failed. The republic hammered out an empire not only in Britain (where both James I and Charles I had most pathetically failed) but overseas too, in the North Sea and the Baltic and beyond in the Atlantic, both sides of the equator. It was commercially rapacious and militarily brutal, beery chauvinism erected into a guiding principle of state. So a better guide to this kind of Britain than the execution of its king would be the Navigation Act of 1651, which prohibited any ships other than British or those of the country of origin from bringing cargoes to Britain, thus taking deadly aim at the shipping supremacy of the Dutch. It was a policy to maximize business which (another first) the state was prepared to back up with war if that's what it took. Often it did.

Was this it, then? Was this the reason nearly 200,000 had lost their lives in battle, and far more than that number through disease and misery, just so that Britain could be run by a corporate alliance of county gentry and city merchants? Henry Vane and Arthur Haselrig, and the Rumpers might have said, yes. For it may not be the new Jerusalem but it is no small thing, this liberty of self-interest and of religious conscience. It's a big thing. (And it would seem unquestionably big when making a return appearance at Philadelphia in 1776.) But for Oliver Cromwell, the godly Caesar, it was never, somehow, quite big enough. He was haunted by the thought that this do-as-you-like Britain was too paltry a dividend for all the blood sacrifices that had been made. His long, rambling speeches to the parliaments of the interregnum, which must have been almost as much torture to listen to as they were to give, combed relentlessly through the history of the civil wars in a hopeless effort to define the essential, redeeming meaning of the conflict.

Cromwell could never establish, to his own satisfaction, that clear and unarguable rationale because, just as he was hoping to 'heal and settle' the nation, the civil war was being fought all over again within his own personality. It was the same struggle that continued to frustrate the search for political peace in England: the war between godliness and good order. And the outcome for Cromwell, as for the Commonwealth, was far from clear.

Enough of him belonged to the party of order to respect its strong sense that the Stuarts had been fought so as to keep England the way it was imagined to have been until they came along. That was an England in which monarchs had been bound by the common law and in which there had been no way to tax the people but through parliamentary consent. The country gentleman in Cromwell respected and subscribed to this social conservatism. But anyone who endured his speeches to parliament would have known that there was also a godly zealot inside Cromwell, for whom moral reformation was paramount. For this zealous Cromwell, it made no difference how the war had begun. What mattered was how it must end. 'Religion was not at first the thing contended for but God brought it to that issue at last and at last it proved to be what was most dear to us.' He had worked by indirection, making the Stuart Pharaoh stiff-necked so that his Chosen People might rise and depart. But the vision of the Promised Land was a revelation that no one could have imagined at that setting forth, and it was the task of Cromwell to bring the people to it.

So he was Gideon no more. He was Moses. And the Rumpers seemed to him, more and more, like the worshippers before the Golden Calf. Cromwell looked coldly at the unscrupulous trade in confiscated properties, at the vulgar swagger of republicans such as Henry Marten whom he despised as a drunken libertine, and he was scandalized by the profanation of God's bounteous grace. Cromwell's view of government was essentially pastoral, or, as he would say later, constabular. It was the obligation of men to whom God had given authority and good fortune to provide disinterested justice for their charges. What he saw in the Rump was good law denied to the people so that lawyers might line their pockets. He saw fortunes being amassed in land and trade, and men being sent to fight against the Dutch so that merchants could fill their warehouses and fatten their moneybags. Was it to satisfy such carnal appetites that his troopers had left their limbs behind on the fields of Marston Moor and Dunbar? 'The people were dissatisfied in every corner of the nation,' he would say in a speech in July 1653, justifying the action he took against the Rump, 'at the non-performance of things that had been promised and were of duty to be performed.'

What galled him most was the Rump politicians' air of self-evident indispens-ability. He, on the other hand, had always considered the regime of 1649 to be provisional, pending the settlement of a proper constitution for the Commonwealth. The time-serving and procrastination, he concluded, had gone on long enough. The Rump needed to expedite plans for its own liquidation. But for a year, at least, Cromwell, who genuinely hated the idea of forcing the issue at sword point, tried, together with colleagues in the army council, to get the Rump leaders themselves to concentrate on the transformation of the Commonwealth into a properly 'settled' form. Much energy and time was spent attempting to reconcile the parties of order and zeal. In early December 1651 Cromwell called a meeting of prominent members of parliament, including Whitelocke, Oliver St John and Speaker William Lenthall, together with senior generals, some of them, like Thomas Harrison, who were becoming impatient to transform the prosaic Commonwealth into something more closely resembling a new Jerusalem. Together they discussed what form the new state should take. Most of the generals said they wanted an 'absolute republic', the MPs a 'mixed monarchy'. But one of the generals – Oliver Cromwell – allowed that some sort of monarchy might suit England best.

A little less than a year later, Bulstrode Whitelocke, the Commissioner of the Great Seal, found out why. As he strolled through St James's Park with Cromwell, the general suddenly asked, 'What if a man should take upon him to be King?' Whitelocke (by his own account) replied with disarming candour, 'I think that remedy would be worse than the disease.' He went on to explain that, since Cromwell already had the 'full Kingly power' without incurring the envy and pomp of the office, why should he do something so impolitic? This dousing of cold water was not what Cromwell wanted to hear. Even less welcome was the home truth that 'most of our Friends have engaged with us upon the hopes of having the Government settled in a Free-State, and to effect that have undergone all their hazards.' While Whitelocke hurried to assure Cromwell that he personally thought them mistaken in their conviction that they would necessarily enjoy more liberty in a Commonwealth than in a properly restrained monarchy, he warned him that the risk of any kind of quasi-monarchy would be to destroy his own power base. 'I thank you that you so *fully* consider my Condition, it is a Testimony of your love to me,' Cromwell replied. But Whitelocke knew that the general was not ready to hear home truths.

> With this the General brake off, and went to other Company, and so into *Whitehall*, seeming by his Countenance and Carriage displeased with what hath been said [especially Whitelocke's advice to make contact with Charles II!]; yet he never objected it against [me] in any publick meeting afterwards.
>
> Only his Carriage towards [me] from that time was altered, and his advising with [me] not so frequent and intimate as before; and it was not long after that he found an Occasion by honourable Imployment [an embassy to Sweden] to send [me] out of the way … that [I] might be no obstacle or impediment to his ambitious designs.

Even if he was not (yet) to be a king, Oliver Cromwell was moving towards an unembarrassed sense of himself as the man chosen by God to settle the political fate of the British nations, to end the 'confusions' of the time. The messiah was coming to dominate the manager. Psalm 110 was much on his mind and his lips: 'The Lord shall send the rod of thy strength out of Zion: rule thou in the midst of thine enemies.' After the deed was done, Cromwell and his officers liked to pretend that the country was desperate to be shot of the Rump. Probably, because of the taxes they had levied to finance the war against the Dutch and the armies in Scotland and Ireland, the parliament and Council of State were indeed unpopular. But that only added to the Rump's own conviction that, once it had got the army off its back, properly reduced and obedient to the civil power, it could lighten the tax load and be seen as the nation's saviour. To the senior army officers, of course, this diagnosis of the Commonwealth's ills was exactly back to front. They and not the Rump were the true guardians of the people's interests. If not the army, then who else could call the oligarchs to account for not properly attending to the plight of the common people, their denial of simple justice, the provision for a sound ministry? In other words, both sides suspected each other of scheming their self-perpetuation on the backs of the

Top: *Oliver Cromwell*, by Samuel Cooper, *c.* 1650–3. On sitting for his portrait, Cromwell asked for a picture that would be 'truly like me and not flatter me at all but remark all these ruffnesses, pimples, warts ... otherwise I will never pay a farthing for it'.
Above: *Cromwell's Dissolution of the Rump of the Long Parliament*, 1653.

citizenry. Both sides saw the precondition for 'settling' the Commonwealth as being rid of the other.

Oliver Cromwell, as usual, would decide the matter, though not exactly in a temper of calm deliberation. He was both soldier and politician, and for some time could see the truth in both sides' assertion that they were the authentic representatives of the people. But by early 1653 he was coming off the fence and down on the side of the troops whose welfare he had so often vowed to defend. In particular he was offended by the Rump's presumption that it could dismiss the soldiers who had given so much to the nation, without adequately attending to their claims of arrears of pay and pensions. He still felt that the parliament could be induced by persuasion, or, if that's what it took, by other means, to go quietly, consenting to its dissolution and making proper arrangements for its elected replacement. But his threshold of suspicion was low. When the Rump leaders such as Thomas Scot, Vane and Haselrig produced a plan for the piecemeal reconstitution of parliament, as and when individual members retired rather than at one fell swoop, Cromwell assumed this was a strategy of shameless self-perpetuation. Worse, he believed the gradual elections would be likely to guarantee an assembly packed with Presbyterians or 'Neuters' hostile to the work of godly reformation that he now thought was the Commonwealth's true justification. Out there in the country, he felt sure, there were pure-hearted Christians who might yet be brought to Westminster to fulfil God's purpose for England. But since the unclean and the powerful stood in their way, they needed help in getting over the stile placed in the way of realizing the republic of the saints. So, at the discussions he convened between parliamentary and army leaders, Cromwell proposed the creation of some sort of executive council to act as steward during the gap between dissolution and new elections – a body which might scrutinize the credentials of those putting themselves forward for the House. Though the Rump, in fact, owed its own preservation to Colonel Pride's Purge in 1648, five years later it was unembarrassed about presenting itself as the guardian of parliamentary freedom against military intimidation.

Still, swords were swords. And the bullies were starting to finger the scabbards. Veiled threats of military intervention were hinted at. It seemed to work. By the evening of 19 April Cromwell evidently believed he was very close to an agreement on a plan for the dissolution and replacement of the Rump. The parliamentary leaders said they would sleep on his proposals and halt discussion on their own plan until they had given them proper consideration.

But on the following morning Cromwell learned that, instead of abandoning their own plan, the Rump leaders were hastily reading it to the House. Always on a short fuse, he now exploded. Reneging on an agreed course of action was final proof, if ever he needed it, that there was no disgraceful subterfuge to which the politicians of the Rump would not stoop if it served their own selfish interests. 'We *did* not believe persons of such quality could do it,' he said in his July 1653 speech narrating the event.

Cromwell stormed down Whitehall escorted by a company of musketeers. Leaving them outside the doors of the parliament house, he took his usual place in the chamber and for a while appeared to respect its conventions, asking the Speaker's permission to speak, doffing his hat and commending the Rump for its 'care of the public good'. But this was meant as an obituary, not a vote of congratulation, and as Cromwell warmed to his work niceties were thrown aside. Speaking 'with so much passion and discomposure of mind as if he had been distracted', he now turned on the dumbstruck members, barking at them for their indifference to justice and piety; their corrupt machinations on behalf of lawyers (an obsession of Cromwell's); and their wicked flirtation with the Presbyterian friends of tyranny. 'Perhaps you think this is not parliamentary language,' one account has him saying forthrightly. 'I confess it is not, neither are you to expect any such from me.' The hat went back on (always a bad sign), as Cromwell left his seat and marched up and down the centre of the chamber, shouting, according to Ludlow (who was not there but heard the details from Harrison), that 'the Lord had done with them and had chosen other instruments for the carrying on with his work that were more worthy'. Foolhardy attempts were made to stop him in full spate. Sir Peter Wentworth from Warwickshire was brave enough to get to his feet and tell Cromwell that his language was 'unbecoming' and 'the more horrid in that it came from their servant and their servant whom they had so highly trusted and obliged'.

But Cromwell was now in full exterminating angel mode, glaring witheringly at the special objects of his scorn and fury: not just the presumptuous Wentworth, but Henry Vane and Henry Marten, accusing them (though unnamed) of being drunkards and whoremasters. Finally he shouted (again according to Ludlow), 'You are no parliament. I say you are no parliament' and called the musketeers into the chamber. The boots entered noisily, heavily.

The symbols of parliamentary sovereignty were now treated like trash. The Speaker was 'helped' down from his chair by Major-General Thomas Harrison; the mace, carried before him, was called 'the fool's bauble' and taken away by the soldiers on Cromwell's orders. The immunity of members was exposed as a joke. When Alderman Allen tried to persuade Cromwell to clear the chamber of soldiers, he himself, as treasurer of the army, was accused of embezzling funds and put in armed custody. The records of the house were seized, the room emptied, the doors locked.

It was what, in the depressing lexicon of modern politics, we would recognize as a text-book *coup d'état*: the bludgeoning of a representative assembly by armed coercion. In fact it was at this precise moment on the morning of 20 April 1653, when the argument of words gave way to the argument of weapons, that Cromwell himself crossed the line from bullying to despotism. In so doing he undid, at a stroke, the entire legitimacy of the war which he himself had fought against the king's own unparliamentary principles and conduct. When he sent the Rump packing, Cromwell liked to think that he was striking a blow at 'ambition and avarice'. But what he really wounded, and fatally, was the Commonwealth itself, whose authority (if it was not to be grounded on pure Hobbesian force) had to be based on the integrity of parliament. It's true, of course, that the Rump had lost its own virginity five years before when its members allowed themselves to be ushered through Colonel Pride's file of soldiers while their colleagues were barred from the chamber. And Cromwell was certainly right to believe that, if upstanding godliness was the proper qualification for serving in parliament, Marten and his ilk were unworthy of their charge.

But none of this matters a jot besides the indisputable butchery of parliamentary independence that Cromwell perpetrated that April morning, a killing that makes the presence of his statue outside the House of Commons a joke in questionable taste. Was it not to *resist* precisely such assaults on the liberty of the House that in the spring of 1642 parliament had determined to fight King Charles, with Cromwell himself among the most militant in asserting the House's control over its own defences? How was this any different? Had England beheaded one king only to get itself another more ruthless in his indifference to parliament than the Stuarts?

Oh, but this *was* quite different, Cromwell would insist in his speech of 4 July 1653 to the first sitting of the new assembly. His purpose in dismissing the Rump had been not to deliver the *coup de grâce* to parliamentary government, but to give it a new lease of life. His dearest wish was to save the Commonwealth, not kill it. Leaving the Rump to its own devices, he argued, would have done just that, by hastening a parliament full of men fundamentally hostile to the essential causes for which the Republic stood – liberty of conscience and justice for the people. Instead of these saboteurs who would have killed liberty by stealth, there would now sit a gathering of dependably righteous men, appointed rather than elected, who would act as godly stewards for sixteen months while the proper institutions of government were finally 'settled'.

The truth was that, as usual, Cromwell was learning on the job. He really had no clear idea at all what kind of assembly, if any, could or should eventually replace the remnant of the Long Parliament. God for him certainly didn't lie in the details, always too petty to merit his concentrated attention. Instead he spoke in cryptic pieties – 'have a care of the whole flock' (this to the new nominated assembly) … 'Love all the sheep, love the lambs, love all, and tender all' … 'Jesus Christ is owned this day by your call and you own him by your willingness in appearing here' – none of which was especially helpful when deliberating on the fine print of constitutional arrangements. On the other hand, this kind of parsonical hot air did encourage the most optimistic of the saints, such as the Fifth Monarchist Major-General Harrison along with militant preachers like Christopher Feake, John Rogers and Vavasor Powell, to believe that the long-heralded day of the 'saints' appointment was finally at hand. So they pushed for a 'Sanhedrin' of seventy (all of their godly persuasion) to be summoned to save Britain-Israel. Harrison in particular became very excited by the coming rapture and stalked about in a scarlet coat, his red face coloured by 'such vivacity and alacrity as a man hath when he hath drunk a cup too much'. For a brief, thrilling few weeks it seemed that Cromwell shared their high-temperature elation. Did he not address them as being on 'the edge of … promises and prophecies'? Psalm 110 was invoked yet again, as if Cromwell himself was already in the throes of the anticipated rapture: 'Thy people shall be willing in the day of thy power, in the beauties of holiness from the womb of the morning: thou hast the dew of thy youth.'

But this was not Jerusalem. It was England, where rapture and politics seldom cohabit, at least not easily. And when the fervour had abated and Cromwell had calmed down a bit, his political id, the Huntingdonshire country gentleman, leery of disorderly enthusiasm, predictably reasserted itself. And from a glance at the men of the new assembly it was obvious that the Council of Officers had chosen men as impervious to the ecstasies of revelation as any of their parliamentary predecessors; men in fact who resembled squire, rather than preacher, Cromwell. Two-thirds of the 140 were landowners, 115 of them justices of the peace. They included four baronets, four knights of the shire, an aristocrat – Lord Lisle and the elderly Provost of Eton, Francis Rous, who had been an MP. Most of them bore names like Gilbert, William and Charles, not Adonijah or Hezekiah. So although the assembly became known after its London representative Praisegod Barbon, leather merchant and Separatist, as the 'Barebone's', this was not, for the most part, a gathering of wild-eyed millenarians. What other choice was there? Once the army grandees had turned their back, on both the Leveller programme of expanding the franchise and the hotter Christian sects, the only social group from which the new assembly could be chosen was the same ride-to-hounds class (with perhaps a tad more conspicuous piety) that had always populated the benches at Westminster. Not surprisingly, then, men who would become hardy perennials of the Restoration parliaments – men such as Edward Montagu,

Samuel Pepys's patron and later the Earl of Sandwich, and Anthony Ashley Cooper, (like Hobbes and Aubrey a Malmesburyite) erstwhile royalist commander in Dorset and later the Earl of Shaftesbury – first made their entry into politics in the assembly which we imagine, wrongly, to have been a temple of Puritanism.

When it became apparent that the vast majority of the Barebone's Parliament were just the usual squires from the shires and would resist the zealots' deeply cherished goals such as the abolition of the tithe, the most fervent of the saints, like Thomas Harrison, departed in high dudgeon. The militant preachers Feake and Powell, who had initially hailed the assembly as the coming reign of Christ, were now left crying in the wilderness, their messianic ambitions reduced to campaigning for the propagation of the gospel in Wales. When the members of Barebone's did manage to agree on dramatic changes, it was in the direction of less religion rather than more, nowhere so dramatically as in the abolition of marriages in church. For three years after 1653, only marriages solemnized before a justice of the peace were considered legal. But this certification by magistrates was not exactly the reborn evangelized Commonwealth that the Fifth Monarchists had anticipated. Unaccountably, too, Cromwell appeared reluctant to prosecute the war against the Dutch with all the ardour they wanted, but seemed to be conniving at a peace. Their dreams frustrated, they took to name-calling, denouncing Cromwell as 'a man of sin' and 'the old dragon' and damning the moderates as the 'unsainted'. Tiring of the rant, and thwarted from the kind of practical government they looked for from the Commonwealth, the leaders of the moderates, including William Sydenham and Anthony Ashley Cooper, came to Cromwell on 12 December 1653 and, in a reversal of what had happened the previous April, voluntarily committed institutional suicide. Resigning their commission on their knees before him, they implored Cromwell to put the miserably captious assembly out of its misery. He was only too happy to oblige.

Barebone's was the closest that Britain (for there were representatives from Ireland, Wales and Scotland in the nominated assembly) ever came to a theocracy: a legislature of Christian mullahs, and it was not very close at all. For all Cromwell's holy thunder about the imminent reign of the righteous, the crackpot frenzy of their matter and manner put him off the saints in a hurry. He seems to have been genuinely horrified by the licence which summoning the godly assembly seemed to have given to every hedgerow messiah to declare his hobbledehoy flock a 'gathered' Church. And he couldn't help noticing that, while the sects were only too happy to avail themselves of the liberty of conscience guaranteed to them by the Commonwealth, they were not inclined to extend that toleration to any of their competitors in the battle for souls. Predictably, then, he became increasingly intolerant of their intolerance. When Christopher Feake and John Rogers made scandalous comparisons between the General and Charles I he had them locked up in the same filthy airless holes in Lambeth Palace where a century before his namesake Thomas Cromwell had incarcerated those who didn't agree with *him*. When Rogers was later dragged out for a show debate with Cromwell, he demanded to know whether he appeared as prisoner or freeman, to which Cromwell responded, with a peculiar mixture of sarcasm and sanctimoniousness, that, since Christ had made us all free, it must be as a freeman. After the charade, the free Christian was dumped back in his cell.

On 16 December 1653, just four days after the gathering of the saints had been dispatched into limbo, Oliver Cromwell was sworn in, at a pompous ceremony in the Court of Chancery, as Lord Protector. The title had last been used by Edward Seymour, Duke of Somerset, during the minority of Edward VI. Given the fact that Somerset ended up on the block, this was not an auspicious precedent. But for the compulsive history-readers of the seventeenth century, the late 1540s meant the hallelujah years of Thomas Cranmer's evangelism, when that first Lord Protector had presided over England's Protestant conversion from Roman error. And Cromwell knew better (at this stage) than to give himself aristocratic airs. On his way to a reception in the Grocers' Hall given by the Lord Mayor he made sure to be seen riding humbly bare-headed through the streets.

There was no need to bother Cromwell with the institutional minutiae of the new regime. Anticipating (not to say expediting) the débâcle of the nominated assembly, the more down-to-earth members of the Council of Officers had a prefabricated 'Instrument of Government' ready and waiting to be put to work. Its principal author was the intelligent and extremely ambitious General John Lambert, who seems to have understood his Cromwell better than anyone since Henry Ireton and to have known when to move him away from prophecy and back to power. Concentrated power and authority were, so Lambert persuaded Cromwell, the best hope of the 'healing and settlement' he was always going on about, and the Instrument of Government would deliver them, he promised, without sacrificing liberty. For the country was to be governed now by 'a single person and parliament' – the formula which became the Protectorate's constitutional mantra for the remainder of Cromwell's life. In fact it was the Lord Protector's Council of State that exercised the day-to-day functions of government. The Council of State was an embryonic cabinet of fifteen to twenty men, many of them drawn from the most managerial figures in the Barebone's assembly including his old comrade and cousin-in-law Oliver St John, Edward Montagu and Anthony Ashley Cooper (until he left the Council in December 1654), along with its secretary and *de facto* chief of security, John Thurloe.

Above, left: *Charles I on Horseback*, engraving by Peter Lombart after Anthony Van Dyck, *c.* 1655.
Above, right: *Oliver Cromwell on Horseback*, engraving by Peter Lombart after Anthony Van Dyck, *c.* 1655.
Opposite: *The Embleme of England's Distractions, As also of her attained, and further expected Freedome, & Happiness*, 1658.

But, on paper at any rate, the Protectorate parliaments were not just window-dressing. They were to be elected every three years, to have representatives from all four nations of Britain and to sit for at least five months of each year. In other words they corresponded to the proposals set out by the most advanced parliamentarians of the 1640s, and for that matter to what would actually come to pass after the next round of revolution in 1688–90.

The constitutional blueprint was the easy part. The real problem for the future of the remade kingless state was not its formal design but its political workability. Realistically, as old Hobbes knew, for all the completeness of the apparent victory over the king this new Britain still had trouble in converting passive consent into active allegiance. The problem was compounded by the fact that the closer the Protectorate came to effective and acceptable (if not popular) government, the less distinguishable it became from a monarchy: not perhaps the old Stuart monarchy, but some sort of monarchy none the less, embodied in a virtuous, responsible prince, respectful of the common law and a dependable guarantor of limited religious liberty. This was, in fact, exactly how Cromwell saw himself, and why he had so much trouble thinking up reasons why he should *not* become king – the kind of king parliament had wanted in 1642 and 1647 and which the obtuse, self-destructive Charles Stuart had spurned. This was just the latest of Oliver's convictions about God's intentions for him and for his country. (After all, not all the kings of Israel had descended from the same house. David had not been the son of Saul.) With this conviction lodged in his mind, Cromwell inched towards majesty. His likeness appeared on the Great Seal of the Protectorate. In 1655 his head was superimposed on Van Dyck's equestrian portrait of Charles I. In another engraving he appeared as the armoured Peacemaker in the classic imperial pose between two pillars, decorated with the kingdoms of England, Scotland and Ireland kneeling in grateful supplication while a dove of peace (or the Holy Spirit depending on your theological position) fluttered above his laurel-clad brow.

In that same print Cromwell also features as the modern Ulysses, the Great Navigator who had steered the ship of state safely between the hazards of Scylla and Charybdis. The fact of the matter, though, was that Scylla and Charybdis in the shape of the only two groups on which the Protectorate could base its government – republican zealots and managerial pragmatists (old Cromwellians and new Cromwellians) – still represented opposite and mutually threatening poles of power. If Cromwell steered too close to the pragmatists he risked dangerously alienating the army officers and even the republican politicians of the ousted Rump who had never forgiven him for their expulsion. If he moved more dogmatically towards the zealots, he invited anarchy and the erosion of his own authority as the great, inclusionary Peacemaker.

Ironically, if Cromwell had had a *more* arrogant and dictatorial confidence in his own authority he might have responded to the repeated requests to become king by doing so, thus creating a third way which he could then have presented to the nation as the best way to ensure stability. But the fact was that, for better or worse, Oliver Cromwell was not really cut out to be Leviathan. For almost three years he took a back seat to Lambert and Thurloe in the practical administration of the government, and the political course he steered between the zealots and pragmatists consisted mostly of reactions to whatever had happened to be the most recent threat. In war a famous strategist, in peace Cromwell seldom escaped the trap of tactics. So when the elections to the first Protectorate parliament, which met in September 1654, produced a crop of survivors from the Rump (like Thomas Scot and Arthur Haselrig) who had no intention of accepting the Instrument of Government, Cromwell's reaction was to authorize yet another purge, evicting anyone not prepared to sign an oath of 'Recognition'. So much for the zealots.

There was one occasion, though, when – providentially, Cromwell might have said – religious conviction and patriotic pragmatism perfectly dovetailed and that was the re-establishment of the community of English Jews. It's not a moment that can be glossed over lightly in the checkered history of Cromwellian England because, however mixed or even confused his motives, Oliver's actions did for once have a measurable and completely benevolent result. For the Jews and their descendants the Protector's title was something more than a formality.

This is not to say that Cromwell's inclination to bring the Jews back to England proceeded from the 'tender-heartedness' optimistically ascribed to him by the chief promoter of the immigration, the scholar and rabbi Menasseh ben Israel, then living in Amsterdam. Like so many of his evangelical contemporaries, Cromwell was responding in the first instance to the messianic timetable which decreed that, only when the Jews had been converted could the decisive destruction of Antichrist get under way. Conversely, Menasseh's cabalistic programme required that only when the Jews had been dispersed among *all* the nations of the earth, would the Messiah appear, his people restored to Zion and the Temple rebuilt. Which was all well and good, but had more pragmatic motives not also nudged Cromwell in that direction the readmission would never have got as far as it did. And those concerns were not about redemption but about money and power.

There had, in fact, been a small community of Marrano (Spanish and Portuguese Jews, supposedly converted to Christianity) living and trading illicitly in the City of

London, enough to have founded a secret synagogue in Creechurch Lane. City merchants divided between those who believed the Sephardi Jews, with their network of co-religionists scattered throughout the Hispanic and Netherlandish trading world, were a priceless source of commercial and military intelligence, and those who feared that, if given a foothold, the Jews would drive out the competition. John Thurloe, though, was someone who believed they could only further the ambitious plans to build an English mercantile empire in the Atlantic at the expense of the Spanish, Portuguese and the Dutch. And it was he who encouraged the Jews to take steps to seek readmission. At the beginning of 1655 the proposal was put before the Council of State, where it got a distinctly cool reception. Rumours circulated that Cromwell was about to sell St Paul's to the Jews to be turned into a synagogue, that good English merchants would be driven into poverty by the notoriously rapacious Israelites.

But Cromwell went ahead none the less. In October 1655 he had a personal meeting with Menasseh who was lodged in the Strand near the Protector's house. The encounter was the stuff of the Apocrypha if not the Scriptures. Menasseh thought of Cromwell as a second Cyrus who would further the holy aim of the return to and rebuilding of Jerusalem, and was said, in some of the more self-serving Christian accounts, to have pressed his hands against Cromwell's body to make sure he was, after all, made of mortal stuff. But there were few men of any learning and religious passion in Amsterdam who could withstand the spellbinding mixture of sanctity and intelligence combined in Menasseh's person. It's easy to imagine the two of them exchanging educated opinions on scripture, ancient history, prophecy and science. A momentous sympathy was established. So, although a majority of the Council were against the measure, making it impossible for Cromwell to move to a formal readmission, Oliver used his personal authority both to protect those who were already in London as well as others who might discreetly arrive. It was not what Menasseh had hoped for. Anything short of a public readmission and the prophecy of the full dispersion would fail. Despondent and impoverished, he had to appeal to Cromwell for funds to get himself and the body of his son, who had died in London, back to Amsterdam. He died himself not long after.

But a community had been reborn. In 1656 the outbreak of war with Spain made assets belonging to subjects of the Spanish Crown residing in England subject to forfeiture. One of the affected merchants was Antonio Rodrigues Robles, who petitioned the government to have the seizure annulled on the grounds that he was not a Spaniard but a Jew. When his case was tacitly upheld, it became possible, for the first time for three and a half centuries, for Jews to live, trade and worship openly and, for the most part, untroubled in the City of London. The oak benches on which those Jews first parked their behinds in the little synagogue of Creechurch Lane still exist, moved to the later and much grander temple of Bevis Marks. They are narrow, backless and unforgiving, indistinguishable from the benches of any Puritan chapel – hosts and guests sharing common furniture.

The pragmatic managers of state who, whatever their personal feelings about the readmission of the Jews, understood that it was, after all, in the state's interest, were men whose vision of the world (and of Britain's place in it) was essentially mechanical and commercial rather than evangelical: technicians of power; data-gatherers; calculators of profit, not Christian visionaries. If the goal of the Protectorate was to build the new Jerusalem, then the first thing these men wanted to know was the price of its bricks. We think of these few years as anomalous in British history, but, in this respect at least, king or no king, for good or ill, they mark the true beginning of modern government in these islands. It was at this time that a commercial empire was being created, often by means of unscrupulous military aggression and brutal inhumanity, in the slaving islands of the Atlantic. On the New England seaboard a Commonwealth, at once godly and lucrative, was beginning its spectacular history at Massachusetts Bay. But another empire was being founded too: an empire of knowledge – scientific knowledge that was acquired not just for its own sake but as the raw material of power.

The men who saw a natural continuity between scientifically acquired information and the effective mastery of government would later describe themselves as 'political arithmeticians'. William Petty, who coined the phrase, was himself an astonishing example of the type. The son of a clothier, Petty went to sea only (it was said) to be abandoned by his shipmates with a broken leg on the French coast. Educated first by Jesuits in Caen, subsequently in the rough school of the Royal Navy, Petty revealed himself to be a prodigy at mathematics and natural science – enough of one anyway to be employed in Paris by Thomas Hobbes. Perhaps he was also enough of a Hobbesian to return at the end of the civil war to England, where, still in his twenties, he fell in with the group of scientists who included Robert Boyle, adamant royalist but still more committed 'natural philosopher'. Every such man of science needed a marvel which would command public attention, and Petty, now a qualified physician, got his in 1650 in the shape of Ann Greene, who had been hanged for the murder of her illegitimate child. Rescued in the nick of time from anatomical dissection, Greene, who had been pronounced definitively dead and packed into a coffin, was resuscitated by Petty, who bled her, looked after her and in the end raised a dowry for her marriage. It was the kind of tale that the anecdotalists of the press loved, a relief from the bitter passions of politics. It made Petty famous and it got him elected as a fellow of Brasenose College, Oxford.

It was in Oxford that Petty would first have encountered the nucleus of the company of scientists who, with the Restoration, would be the founders of the Royal Society: Warden John Wilkins of Wadham College, young Christopher Wren and Robert Boyle. They were looked on benevolently by Oliver Cromwell. Boyle may have been a royalist but his brother was Lord Broghill, one of Cromwell's closest friends and advisers. Cromwell himself paid a visit to Wilkins' lodgings where his daughter Elizabeth and her husband, the MP and member of the Committee on Trade, John Claypole, were staying, and took an obviously keen interest in the optical and mechanical devices displayed there. William Petty, though, had ambitions that went beyond the circles of the learned. In 1652 he moved to Ireland as Physician-General to the army (which badly needed medical help), and in the years which followed, applied his acumen for statistics to the business of mapping much of the forfeited land previously identified by the Civil Survey, 1654-6. This was not a matter of disinterested cartography. Petty's land survey was meant to provide Oliver's son Henry, the adversary of the zealot officers, with what, in both senses, was a measured design for the transfer of land from the defeated Irish landowners to the conquering army. He was now the anatomist of the mutilated body of Ireland, working day and night, dictating to short-hand clerks, to complete his assignment. Petty had turned himself, in effect, into the chief scientist of dispossession, but he persuaded himself that his precision was infinitely preferable to the still rougher justice of a chaotic and greedy land grab by the army. He was, after all, not just in the business of eviction but also in that of transplantation, finding land in Connacht on which the displaced Irish could be resettled. When after a year he delivered his immense work to Henry Cromwell, it was a map of population, ownership, land and beasts such as had never been seen before in British history. By mastering the data Petty had become, much to the disgust and dismay of ideological republicans like Ludlow who thought him the Protector's bootblack, the proconsul of Irish colonization. And he was not yet thirty.

For better or worse, men like William Petty were the prototype of the English bureaucrat: as polished in Latin poetry as they were proficient in higher statistics. They gorged on memoranda and got tipsy on the power machine that was the new English state. This was just as well since the scale of business tackled by the Protectorate's Council of State was positively gargantuan. On one, not atypical, day, for instance, the agenda ran to sixty-two items.

But energetic and competent as they might have been in their government offices, the administrators, the 'Yes, Protector' men, knew that all their efforts would come to nought unless they managed to rebuild the old alliance between Whitehall and the counties which had broken down so completely in the 1640s. That meant taking political, as much as administrative, decisions – to restore as justices of the peace the traditional landed gentry who had been roughly supplanted by the county committees appointed during the civil war. So, along with some of the trappings of the monarchy at Whitehall, innumerable, tentative little restorations took place in the counties. Men who had steered clear of, or who had been kept from, the magistracy now came back to pass judgement on drunks and thieves. The calendar of county society began to recover something like its ancient routines. Gentlemen (including the Protector's oldest surviving son Richard, who made no secret of his enjoyment) galloped after stags again. Houses that had been wrecked, plundered or had fallen into neglect during the war were repaired and restored, their parks and farms restocked. Neighbouring landowners could entertain each other again over supper, a pipe and (thanks to the peace with Portugal) a glass of port. Although dancing and theatre were still officially frowned on, music and poetry were again encouraged (not least at Cromwell's own court) as edifying entertainments. The stirrings of pleasure were obscurely sensed. And they were not a good sign for the godly state.

The more republican and zealous members of the Council of State – Lambert himself and his fellow army officers Disbrowe and Charles Fleetwood – looked on the reawakening of the old county communities with misgivings. By encouraging them to come out from beneath the ruins and reseating them in their old places of authority, might not the Protectorate be sowing the seeds of its own undoing? From his perch in Ireland, Lieutenant-General Ludlow was even more incensed at what he took to be craven abdication of republican power to 'time-serving Cavaliers', lawyers and 'corrupt parsons', 'and in the meanwhile such men as are most faithfull to the publique interest for which so much blood hath been spilt … such as have been valiant in the field and ventured their lives … for the liberties of the people, such as have all along in the greatest revolutions and dangers … appeared in their purses and persons for the true interest of the Nation, that these honest men should be thus slighted and undermined' he thought a cause for scandal, contempt and alarm. For such men to come into parliament was to invite back royalism in a Trojan Horse.

In the spring of 1655 their suspicions seemed to have been confirmed when a royalist rising, incompetently led by John Penruddock, broke out in Wiltshire. It was quickly smashed, and was followed by the usual parade of hangings and beheadings, Penruddock's taking place in May. But the sudden threat, together with well-founded fears of assassination, was enough to jolt Cromwell out of complacency. He was also

Sir Ralph Verney, by Sir Peter Lely, *c.* 1680.

badly shaken by the disastrous outcome of an expedition against the Spanish in the Caribbean, an unaccustomed military fiasco which he took as God's verdict on the sinfulness of the nation. Statistics weren't everything, it seemed.

Time, then, for contrition. Time for repentance. Time for a heavy dose of zeal. For about a year and a half from July 1655 Cromwell let the outriders of righteousness, the major-generals, have their head, inflicting on England a coercive military regime the like of which had not been seen since the security states of Walsingham and Thomas Cromwell. Over the reassuring map of the counties were laid twelve military cantons, each governed by a major-general. Their mission was, in the first instance, a police action, dismantling the embryonic county militias and replacing them by rock-solid loyal cavalry financed by a 'decimation' – collecting a tenth of the value of royalist or suspected royalist estates. Security and pre-emptive deterrence were thus economically combined. But Cromwell, and to an even greater degree his generals, were also convinced that a true pacification meant tackling the task which so often had been shirked or postponed in the name of reconciliation: the rigorous conversion of profane, carnal England to a state of godly submission. In the name of the decimation, gentry like Sir Ralph Verney, who had returned to England but whose record as a supporter of parliament in 1642 was not enough to clear him of suspicion, were summoned to appear before the generals and their assessors and give security for their levies. Failure to pay meant confiscation or imprisonment.

Very quickly the major-generals became a flying squad for righteousness. Quixotic though it was, this was a crusade that the Puritan zealots had been fighting since the beginning of the civil war, when James I's permissive *Book of Sports* had been burned by the Common Hangman and edicts published to make sure pleasure never happened on a Sunday; now once more 'no persons shall hereafter exercise or keep maintain or be present at any wrestling, shooting, Bowling, ringing of bells … masque, Wake, otherwise called feasts, church-ales, dancing and games'. Away too with cock-fights, cock-running, horse-races and bear-baiting. Woe betide anyone caught putting up a maypole, working on the Sabbath or furtively celebrating Christmas. Alehouses were to come under vigilant licensing and inspection and were to be purged of fiddlers and gamblers. The Swearing and Cursing Act punished anyone caught uttering a profanity with a fine according to their status (more for gents than commoners). Children under twelve heard saying something filthy were to be whipped. Convicted fornicators were to spend three months in prison, adulterers to suffer the death penalty.

This is the stereotypical image we have of Cromwell's England: a dour Puritan Sparta where the military was mobilized to wipe out fun. And as far as the ambitions of the major-generals go, it's not altogether wide of the mark. But, needless to say, the experiment in enforced virtue was a dismal flop, not least because of the impossibility of supplying the manpower to police it. Lacking their own Enforcers for Christ, the major-generals had no option but to fall back on the constables and justices who were already in place. And they were very unlikely to be sympathetic to the great work. On the contrary, the records of local magistrates are full of malefactors who paid no attention whatsoever to the morals police. Punishment, when it was meted out, was often an elaborate joke. When John Witcombe of Barton St David in Somerset was put in the stocks for swearing, his own minister, protesting the illegality of the law, brought him ale to keep his spirits up. In Cheshire, a servant girl who had been denounced as flagrantly violating the Sabbath by working on a Sunday was (incorrectly) judged a minor so that, instead of being fined, she could be 'corrected' by her master. In the presence of the local constable her punishment was 'turned all into a jest. The master plucked off a small branch of heath from a turf and therewith gave her two or three such gentle touches on her cloathes as would have not hurt an infant two days old.'

In many places this must have been as deep as the bite of 'Cromwell's mastiffs' reached. Secretary Thurloe's papers are full of their bitter complaints at the hopelessness of their task. 'I am much troubled with these market towns,' Major-General Berry wrote from Monmouth, 'everywhere vice abounding and the magistrates fast asleep.' But if their attempt to impose godliness on horseback was a failure, they did alienate enough of the people whom the Protectorate needed to survive – the county gentry – to give Cromwell serious pause. Although the military regime did its best to intimidate during the elections of 1656, the results produced a majority which swept parliament clean of their supporters and dismantled their entire structure of power. Prodded by the pragmatists on the Council, Cromwell now swung back – permanently this time – to a conservative regime of 'settling'.

In the summer of 1657 he accepted the 'Humble Petition and Advice' and a government that was virtually the same as the reformed monarchy envisioned by the Long Parliament, the one critical difference being the commitment to protect liberty of conscience. But even this commitment was beginning to wobble, as the threshold of censure on Christian sects deemed scandalous became much lower. Despite assuring Cromwell (he could not take an oath) in a face-to-face interview that he submitted to the powers that be, the Quaker leader George Fox was still repeatedly locked up in conditions of nightmarish filth and squalor as a menace to the public peace. When he attempted to warm himself by lighting straw in one of his cells, his gaolor pissed on the fire to put it out and threw shit on the prisoner from a gallery above. Horrible though these trials were, they were nothing compared to the fate of Fox's maverick protégé James Nayler, tried for blasphemy by parliament and the Council of State in the late autumn of 1656. Nayler's crime had been to ride through Bristol in imitation of the Saviour (pretending that he *was* Christ, said his prosecutors), his few disciples crying hosanna as he trotted through the rain-soaked streets. For his deranged temerity Nayler was pilloried for two hours, his forehead branded with a 'B' for blasphemer, his tongue bored through with a hot iron, and flogged through the streets of London – and then taken to Bristol to be flogged all over again before being incarcerated. He endured the excruciating torment with astonishing fortitude, but died four years later still suffering from its after-effects.

To his credit, Cromwell seemed as disturbed as anyone by the punitive overkill of the House and actually questioned the legitimacy of the trial. Afterwards he seemed to want to moderate the power of a single House and so became open to the restoration of a second, upper chamber, designated unimaginatively as 'the Other House'. Bulstrode Whitelocke was installed there as Viscount Henley, alongside Cromwell's two new sons-in-law, Viscount Fauconberg and Robert Rich, the Earl of Warwick. History seemed to be on fast rewind to 1642, with Cromwell playing the part of the king-who-might-have been. As John Pym had wanted, parliament now had the authority to approve or veto appointments to the high offices of state. No taxes could be raised or declarations of war or peace made without its consent. In fact, the constitution of 1657 was so close to being the responsible monarchy, constrained by the common law, which the civil war had been fought for that it seemed only logical to cap it with a responsible king. Whitelocke, who had been against the idea five years earlier, had now evidently changed his mind, personally urging it on Cromwell as the best way to stabilize the future of the reformed state of Britain.

But though he was tempted, in the end Cromwell could not manage to turn himself into King Oliver I. Political reasons certainly weighed in his decision to reject the offer (provided he could none the less name his successor as Protector), for generals Lambert and Fleetwood all but threatened a major mutiny in the army should he dare to mount the throne. But Cromwell showed he could handle the army by abruptly cashiering Lambert and purging the officer corps of any he thought disloyal to his regime. The most serious restraint came, rather, from his own exacting conscience: his deeply felt certainty that, since God had decreed the 'extirpation' of the monarchy in England, it was not for him to overturn that decision. If a new sign came from Providence that he should indeed be a king unto Israel that would be different. But the Almighty fought shy of direct communication in 1657 and the brow of the Protector remained unanointed.

Oliver Cromwell would, in fact, get to wear the crown, but only once he was dead. On 3 September 1658, the anniversary of the battles of both Dunbar and Worcester, he passed away. While he was breathing his last a tornado-like tempest bore down on England, ripping out trees and sending church steeples (with their unused belfries) crashing to the ground. To the omen-conscious (which meant virtually everyone), this was no coincidence. It was the Devil coming to get his due, for an old story had circulated that after the battle of hair Worcester Oliver had sold his soul for supreme power. There were other dire portents. Although 1658 was a rare year free of battles, won or lost, the shadow of mortality still seemed to fall heavily over the nation. The winter had been brutal. Crows were found with their feet frozen to branches. Trade stopped. Grain prices went through the roof. An epidemic of the 'quartan' fever (probably some form of influenza) held in its deadly grip a country already weakened by plague. Poor John Evelyn had his darling five-year-old prodigy son die in late January, and a second child perish barely two weeks later. 'Here ends the joy of my life,' he wrote later, 'for which I go even mourning to my grave.' Terrified survivors in the cities abstained from fish and flesh and ate nothing 'but sage posset and pancake or eggs or now and then a turnip or carrot'. Whatever she ate, fever and cancer carried off Cromwell's favourite daughter in August. The Protector fell into a distraction of sorrow and then seemed to go under with the sickness himself. At Greenwich John Evelyn joined the crowds watching a beached whale thrash its flukes hopelessly on the mudflats, blood pouring from its wounded spout. Even reasonable men were mindful of the portent. *Leviathan* was in its death throes.

By the time the leaves were on the turn Oliver was dead, though not quite gone. There had been a botched embalming. The regime, which wanted to preserve the Protectorate, had started by failing to preserve the Protector. But before the inevitable atrophy, an effigy had been cast from the body. It was then exposed for a lying-in-state at Somerset House, in the manner of the medieval kings, robed in imperial purple, the shrine lit by a great incandescence of candles. But then it was decided that he should be winched upright, and there he stood for another two months, stiffly erect like a mannikin, crown on head, sceptre and orb in his hand, king at last. On 23 November there was a massive state funeral which ended in ignominious fiasco. According to the French ambassador (who was not exactly innocent in the débâcle), altercations about diplomatic precedent and protocol delayed the beginning of the enormous procession, which took seven hours to file through London. By the time it finally got to Westminster Abbey it was nearly pitch dark, and the inadequate supply of candles inside the church made it impossible for the ceremonies to be prolonged. So for the ruler who, above all others, had most loved

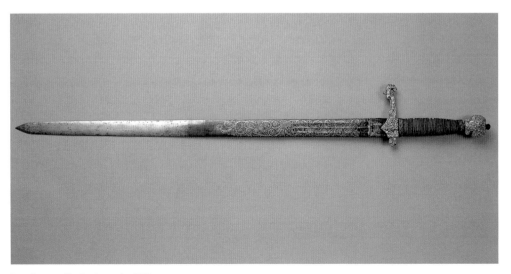

Top: Cromwell's death mask, 1658.
Above: Cromwell's ceremonial robe sword, with which he was buried.

sermons, and who relentlessly meditated out loud on God's purpose in history, there were no funeral orations, no prayers, no preaching. Just a few short sharp blasts on the trumpets before the effigy was bundled into a waiting tomb. But not before little Robert Uvedale, one of the Westminster school boys summoned to attend, had made his way through the chaotically exiting crowd and stolen away with a souvenir, the 'Majesty Scutcheon' on which the arms of the British nations were figured on a flag of white satin.

Had Cromwell been able to write his own funeral eulogy, what would he have wanted to say about his extraordinary career? Certainly not its trajectory from obscurity to supreme power, because, avidly as he embraced it, there was always a side of Cromwell which was deeply disgusted by it. When, not long before he died, he protested that he 'would have been glad to have been living under a woodside, to have kept a flock of sheep rather than to have undertaken such a place as this was', the confession seemed, and was, perfectly genuine. His was, in fact, the classic case of great power falling to the very person who least wanted it, and precisely for that reason. The only hero of the civil wars who wanted it even less was Thomas Fairfax, who never quite recovered from the trauma of the trial and execution of the king – and who would re-emerge from his Yorkshire obscurity to help put Charles I's son back on the throne. Cromwell could never be that self-effacing because he had, like Moses, gone through an experience of the Call, just as surely as if he had heard a voice coming from the Burning Bush, and believed that his life thereafter was devoted to the execution of God's design for the nation.

Ironically, it was just because that design seemed to be a work-in-progress for Jehovah who only vouchsafed glimpses of it now and then, even to a servant as doggedly devoted as Cromwell, that he never much felt the need to work out a consistent strategy for the republic, nor a policy which might have been able to reconcile the self-evidently conflicting claims of parliamentary liberty and Christian godliness. Nor did he even bother to arbitrate in any consistent way between zeal and freedom. Rather he let God show him the way. And if God changed his mind every so often, well that was His privilege.

Buried amid the immense screed of Cromwell's pious circumlocutions to parliament was, however, a genuine statement of what he wanted for England, if circumstances would ever permit. (That he could *make* the circumstances permit, nudge God along a bit, was a thought he dismissed as sacrilegious.) It turns out that the vision of this angry, ruthless, overbearing, self-torturing man was a thing of consummate sweetness, humanity and intelligence. More astonishingly still, the most deeply felt principle of the man who created the matrix of the modern English state was, in its essence, liberal. For at the heart of that conviction lay tolerance: the unforced hope that men (provided they were not Catholic) might be allowed to be left alone to receive Christ in any way they wished; to hoe their few acres and keep their pigs, untroubled by the rude intrusions of the state – always provided they did not conspire against the freedom of others. After all his slaughters, his marches and his red-faced fits of shouting, what Oliver Cromwell really wanted, for everyone, was a quiet life: 'a free and uninterrupted Passage of the Gospel running through the midst of us and Liberty for all to hold forth and profess with sobriety their Light and Knowledge therein, according as the Lord in his rich Grace and Wisdom hath dispensed to every man and with the same freedom to practice and exercise the Faith of the Gospel and lead quiet and peaceable lives in all Godliness and Honesty without any Interruption from the Powers God hath set over this Commonwealth.'

It would be perhaps another two and half centuries before anything like this dream could be realized. And by then, really, no one much cared.

CHAPTER 4

Not long after Cromwell died, John Dryden wrote, with premature optimism, 'No Civill broyles have since his death arose / But Faction now by Habit does obey'. The question on everyone's mind – could the Protectorate survive the loss of Oliver – was about to be answered resoundingly in the negative. At first it seemed as though Oliver's named successor, his eldest surviving son, Richard, might make a go of it. Loyal addresses poured in, and the thirty-one year old was recognized as decent, honest, well meaning and quite without his father's alarming irascibility. His greatest asset was that no one could think of any reason to dislike him. But this was also a liability. Richard's conspicuous inability to command Oliver's selectively deployed menace made him politically defenceless as well as clueless. His father had known all along that Richard was too amiable for his calling, too softly seated upon the cushions of life's many pleasures. He made no one break out in a sweat, either of exertion or of fear. This became a problem when Richard, faced with the usual choice of depending on the army or the pragmatists, opted heavily for men like Ashley Cooper and Montagu. However conservative Oliver might have seemed, the generals, beginning with Fleetwood, felt that through the brotherhood of arms they could always recall him to the colours of the 'Good Old Cause'. Richard, on the other hand, seemed more the plaything than the master of his civil servants. So out of a sense of self-preservation – for themselves and for the republic – the generals made common cause with the same Rump politicians they had ousted in 1653. It may be that by the spring of 1659 they felt they had no choice, for the generals were themselves being hard pressed by junior officers, angry about forty-month arrears of pay; about the political purges that had taken place in the last years of Oliver's Protectorate and about the systematic policy of replacing them with the old county militias under the control of the gentry.

In April that year, after a petition bearing 20,000 signatures calling for the return of the Rump Parliament was presented to the Protector, and after he had been given to understand that if he failed to heed it a military insurrection was in the offing,

UNFINISHED BUSINESS

Coronation Procession of Charles II to Westminster from the Tower of London (detail), by Dirck Stoop, 1661.

Richard abdicated. He was summarily ordered to depart from Whitehall with his family (including his younger brother Henry, who might have made a much more formidable successor). The Rump Parliament (all forty-two members of it who showed up) was recalled. The Protectorate, which hard-core republicans like Ludlow had never ceased to regard as a defiled thing, was abolished and the Commonwealth restored. But what was immediately restored with it, of course, was the ferocious mutual hostility of the republican politicians and zealot soldiers, which had caused its disappearance in the first place. Without Oliver Cromwell to hold the ring they proceeded to tear each other, and what remained of the kingless state, to pieces, spinning into an anarchy from which the only possible escape was the return of the monarch. The extraordinary irony about the restoration of Charles II is not that he became king because the country desperately needed a successor to Charles I. He became king because it desperately needed a successor to Oliver Cromwell.

As late as August 1659, when an attempted royalist rising led by Colonel George Booth was easily suppressed, it seemed that the odds against the imminent return of Charles II were still prohibitively steep. But the fratricidal self-destruction of all the alternative contenders for power – not just Rump against army, but even Rumper against Rumper (Vane and Haselrig were at each other's throats and Ludlow hated both of them) – precluded any kind of republican stability. Opposing factions argued furiously about whether there should be one house of parliament or two, whether an upper house should be elected or appointed, while the real house, the house of the republic, was burning down around them. Crazily short-sighted though it seems in retrospect (no crazier in truth than many other revolutionary situations), the parties concerned were much more interested in destroying their immediate enemies than in agreeing on a secure republican regime that might have locked out a monarchy for the foreseeable future. It was, indeed, the republicans who killed the republic.

Somehow, England in 1659 got sucked into a temporal worm-hole to emerge ten years earlier, in 1649, when everything – government, religion, social order – had been fluid, and no one quite knew how any of those matters might be resolved. Suddenly, in 1659, the pamphlet market was once again flooded with experimental proposals, tracts and broadsides. The country was back in its Torricellian gap, the void-in-a-void. Leveller tracts reappeared and with them a surge of apprehension among the horsey classes that democracy was about to strike down the counties. Fifth Monarchists like Christopher Feake belatedly declared that the real kingdom of Christ had not after all been frustrated, only postponed by Cromwell, the Antichrist. George Fox, in one of his brief vacations from prison, published *Fifty-Nine Particulars* 'to bring the nation into a Garden, a free nation, a free people', to abolish the fee-gouging of lawyers, to take care of the blind and lame; to ban the carrying of swords, daggers and guns for all those who did not require them in their office; and, not least, a reform dear to his heart, to improve the conditions of gaols so that 'prisoners might not lie in their own dung and piss'.

The pragmatic survivors from the government of the Protectorate stood back from all this ferment in horrified disbelief. At the Rota Club in London, William Petty could sit down with James Harrington to discuss the latter's *Oceana*, in which, for the first time, the necessary connection between property and political power was exposed. But not for a minute could they countenance his 'agrarian law' limiting the size of landed estates. Experiments were not good for business, and they could see that the economy was suffering from the breakdown of orderly government. Shops were closed, trade stopped and tax strikes were threatened. Customs and excise dues went uncollected. Goldsmiths moved their stock out of London for safe-keeping. And it was more than ever obvious that a choice between inflexible republican zealots, who represented only themselves, and military dictatorship was no choice at all. They had built a formidable state – commercially dynamic, fearsome on the high seas, dependable in its revenues, scientific in its administration, a state built in partnership with, not against, the gentry of the counties. Before it was irreparably lost they needed to do their utmost to restore the stability enjoyed under the Protectorate. And since neither the republicans nor the generals would provide it, where else was there to go except to Charles Stuart? With any luck he would be the next Protector.

Like many sea-changes in British history, this was not a gradual but a sudden decision, made by men such as Montagu, Lord Broghill and William Petty, who all voted with their feet at some point between the summer of 1659 and the end of the year. When John Evelyn decided to publish his royalist *Apology* late that year he made much of the fact that he was committing a capital offence. But he went ahead all the same and was gratified, though not perhaps surprised, that it was 'universally taken up'. It was a sign of things to come that the man he approached to get a copy to Charles II was the Commonwealth's own Lieutenant of the Tower, Herbert Morley. Evelyn believed this man would not betray him, since they were old schoolfellows. But he would still never have dared entrust him with the mission had he not also believed the Lieutenant was acting from prescient self-interest. Countless others did the same. Thomas Hobbes's axiom that allegiance ended when the state's capacity to protect had irreversibly broken down could never have seemed more glaringly self-evident.

The man who finally pushed Britain over the edge to Restoration, 'Black George' Monck, was Hobbes's kind of general, someone for whom the tactics of self-preservation had been learned the hard way. He had been born into an old gentry family in Devon, and his strongest links were to the Grenville family, who themselves produced royalist heroes and parliamentary turncoats during the civil war. Monck, who early on was a one-man weathervane, had his doubts about the prospects as well as the rightness of the royal cause but was personally converted by a meeting with Charles I. He should have stayed doubtful. Captured at the battle of Nantwich in 1644, he spent the next two years in the Tower, where at least he met the Presbyterian seamstress Anne who later became his wife. In 1646 Monck took the Covenant oath and went to Ireland as a colonel for parliament. He became close to Cromwell, whom he first met in August 1649 and evidently came to trust and revere. He fought along-side Cromwell at the battle of Dunbar in 1650 and, although without any naval experience, was made a commander of the fleet during the war with the Dutch, in which he proved himself indisputably clever, tough and brave.

While the republic was disintegrating in England during 1659 Monck was in secure command of the army of Scotland. Although his old royalist allegiance made him a natural target for those who wanted him to come out early for Charles, Monck stayed aloof, not at all sure, for once, which way the wind was blowing, nor what would be the right, as well as the smart, thing to do. What *was* apparent to those who still hoped for a republican military regime – Lambert and Fleetwood – was that they could not expect any support from Monck, whose army was the most coherent and concentrated in Britain. And although he attempted to muster what forces he could, even Lambert knew that without Monck they were finished. At the point when he realized his game was up Fleetwood commented bitterly that 'the Lord had blasted their Counsels and spat in their faces'. When Monck began his self-authorized march south from Coldstream near Berwick on 2 January 1660, with 7000 troops, it was as a soldier against rule by soldiers. But if it was clear what he was against – army interfer-ence in parliament – it was much less clear what he was for. The rump of the Rump, which had been restored at the mere prospect of his coming to London, hoped and assumed he was marching to protect *them*. But Monck kept his cards close to his chest and his powder dry, and at some point en route he was obviously impressed by the wild enthusiasm, not for preserving the Rump but for getting rid of it. The cry, nearly universal, was for a 'free' parliament, which meant the return of all the members of the Long Parliament who had been shut out by Pride's Purge.

By the time Monck got to London at the beginning of February, the call for a 'free parliament' had developed from a campaign for constitutional amendment to something more like a desperate cry to get the country out of the chaotic hell that the Commonwealth had become. It was also, increasingly, the royalism that dared not (yet) quite speak its name. If appeals for liberty had once meant the end of kingship, now they very definitely meant its reinstatement. Even blind John Milton, standing by in impotent dismay as the republic unravelled, conceded its unpopularity in his last published attempt to reverse the rush back to monarchy. In his *Readie and Easie Way to Establish a Free Commonwealth* he argued that a minority had the right to force the majority to accept freedom, while the majority could not coerce the minority into sharing their subjection as fellow-slaves. But the crowds of apprentices in London (as in Bristol and Exeter) who mounted demonstrations for the 'free parliament' that everyone knew would open the door for the king did not want to be forced to be free. They wanted to be subjects. Women offered their own verdict on the Rump by lifting their skirts, bending over and shouting: 'Kiss my parliament!'

On 11 February Samuel Pepys, who for five years had been a clerk in the Exchequer (the protégé of his powerful kinsman Edward Montagu), stood at the end of Strand Bridge and counted bonfires. There were thirty-one on the bridge alone. 'At one end of the street, you would think there was a whole lane of fire, and so hot that we were fain to keep still on the further side,' he wrote in his diary. The entire city seemed to have been turned into one great open-air spit, on which rumps – some fowl, some beef – were being roasted. The streets were greasy with celebration. It was not just meat that was being cooked, but the Commonwealth. Earlier that day it had been decided to readmit the members of parliament who had been shut out by Pride's Purge over eleven years before. Pending a new 'free' parliament, Londoners were voting, as usual, with their bellies. There were carillons of carving knives on the city streets. 'The butchers at the Maypole in the Strand', wrote Pepys, 'rang a peal with their knifes when they were going to sacrifice their rump.'

History was now respooling fast. Men who had not shown themselves in politics for many years, like Sir Thomas Fairfax, reappeared along with their colleagues from the Long Parliament who had never forgotten the humiliation of their 'seclusion' in 1648. Two of the 'birds' of 1642, Denzil Holles and Arthur Haselrig, now faced each other, doubtless in mutual mortification – one of them about to be a republican on the run, the other headed for a Stuart peerage. But the pragmatists, not least Montagu, passed smoothly from one regime to the other. The parliament, which had first assembled twenty years before, now – heavily nudged by Monck's soldiers and an armed royalist militia – killed itself off, ordering its own dissolution and the 'free election' that all concerned knew would produce a parliament for Restoration.

Although, in a last gesture of piety towards the civil-war parliamentarians, royalists who had actually fought for Charles I were excluded, a hundred of them were none the less elected and duly took their seats in the 'Convention' Parliament of

March 1660. Another fifty-eight members were unequivocal royalist supporters. Virtually the same number – close to 150 – were parliamentarians, although that did not make them republicans. Most of them belonged to the gentry, who had all along wanted a reformed monarchy. And now, so they hoped, they would at last get one. The terms that they sent with Monck and their commissioners to Charles II at Breda in the Netherlands were calculated to test his willingness for a reconciliation: an amnesty for those on the parliamentary side in the civil war (the regicide signers of Charles I's death warrant excepted), a degree of liberty for 'tender consciences' and guarantees against reversing the changes in property that had taken place during the interregnum. But the Convention Parliament did not insist, as a precondition, on the king committing himself to executing these policies. For his part, Charles's response from Breda on 4 April was shrewdly handled, offering a forty-day period of 'grace' for amnesties but leaving any exceptions to the discretion of later parliaments, the same going for matters of religion and property. To make parliament, rather than himself, the arbiter of these matters already seemed to advertise that the son would not go the way of the father.

On 23 May 1660, Samuel Pepys watched Charles, along with his younger brothers and his cousin the boy Prince of Orange (later to be King William III) come on board the flagship of the Commonwealth, the *Naseby*, at Scheveningen near The Hague. Pepys kissed their royal hands to the sound of 'infinite shooting of guns' and took dinner 'in a great deal of state'. After dinner the *Naseby*'s name was repainted as the *Royal Charles*. For Pepys and his patron Montagu, as well as for Monck and Thurloe – all Cromwellians – it was as painless as that. In the afternoon they set sail for England and the king

> walking here and there, up and down (quite contrary to what I thought him to have been), very active and stirring. Upon the Quarterdeck he fell in discourse of his escape from Worcester. Where it made me ready to weep to hear the stories that he told of his difficulties that he had passed through. As his travelling four days and three nights on foot, every step up to the knees in dirt, with nothing but a green coat and a pair of country breeches on and a pair of country shoes, that made him so sore all over his feet that he could scarce stir.

Pepys listened and listened, obviously agog. This was not what he had anticipated. The tall man with his mother's black curly hair, dark eyes and thick lips was a spell-binder – someone who could, when he chose, scatter magic. Literally days after disembarking, Charles had touched 600 sufferers from scrofula in one emphatic demonstration of the healing power of the king. Thirteen years before parliament had appointed a commission to draft a declaration denouncing the practice of touching for the 'king's evil' as an absurd superstition. But here were the hordes of ordinary people, some with swollen or tumorous lymph glands, others with styes or mouth blisters, all convinced that royal magic had returned. In twenty years, 90,000 of the scrofulous would receive the royal touch and a gold chain to hang around their necks.

John Evelyn, who had endured the kingless decade with unrepentant royalism burning in his breast, could hardly credit what was happening: 'The greedinesse of all sorts, men, women & children, to see his Majesty & kisse his hands, in so much as he had scarce leasure to Eate for some dayes.' Even as hard-bitten an old Presbyterian as Denzil Holles of Dorchester, who had fought Charles I at Edgehill, now addressed his son with slavish adulation as 'the light of their [the people's] eyes, the breath of their nostrils, their delight and all their hope'. On 29 May, Charles II's birthday, not far from where Pepys had counted bonfires, Evelyn watched the cavalcade of 20,000 horse and foot escorting the king through London,

> brandishing their swords and shouting with unexpressable joy; The wayes straw'd with flowers, the bells ringing ... I stood in the strand, & beheld it, & blessed God. And all this without one drop of bloud, & by that very army, which rebell'd against him: but it was the Lord's doing ... for such a Restauration was never seene in the mention of any history, antient or modern, since the returne of the [Jews from their] Babylonan Captivity, nor so joyfull a day, & so bright, ever seene in this nation: this hapning when to expect or effect it, was past all humane policy.

Not everyone was celebrating in the heady days of May 1660. Edmund Ludlow, fortieth on the list of fifty-nine signatories of the death warrant of the king, watched the same revels with mounting disgust and disbelief. Jerusalem had suddenly become Sodom. What could you expect? 'The Dissolution and Drunkenness of that Night,' he hurrumphed, 'was so great and scandalous, in a Nation which had not been acquainted with such Disorders for many Years past, that the King ... caused a Proclamation to be publish'd, forbidding the drinking of Healths. But resolving, for his own part, to be oblig'd to no Rule of any Kind, he publickly violated his own Order in a few days, at a Debauch in the Mulberry Garden.' Above all, Ludlow was horrified to see 'the Horse that had formerly belonged to our army, now put upon an Employment so different from that which they had first undertaken; especially ... that for the most part ... they consisted of such as had engaged themselves from a Spirit of Liberty.'

Top: *The Embarkation of Charles II at Scheveningen* (detail), by Johannes
Lingelbach, 1660.
Above: *Charles II*, by Pieter van der Banck, *c.* 1660.

On 30 January 1661 – the anniversary of Charles I's execution – the remains of Oliver Cromwell, his son-in-law, Ireton, and John Bradshaw, who had presided over the court that had judged the king, were 'dragged', as Evelyn gleefully wrote, 'out of their superbe Tombs [in Westminster among the Kings], to Tyburne, & hanged on the Gallows there from 9 in the morning 'til 6 at night, & then buried under that fatal & ignominious Monument, in a deepe pitt.' Evelyn thought back to the chaotic magnificence of Cromwell's funeral in 1658. It had been just two and a half years between embalming and dismemberment. 'Oh,' he exclaimed 'the stupendious, & inscrutable Judgements of God.'

As far as Ludlow was concerned, Cromwell got what he deserved. For it had been his betrayal of the nation's liberties and his greed for power that had killed the republic. But now the unswerving friends of liberty were paying the price. Dismay was followed by consternation and fear as army 'grandees' were abruptly turned into fugitives or supplicants desperately working the good offices of men who had been timely turncoats. The republicans looked on in horror as old friends and comrades associated with the death of Charles were brought before punitive tribunals, swiftly condemned and subjected to hanging and live quartering. Two of the regicides were dragged on a sled to Tyburn while facing the decapitated head of a third, the Fifth Monarchist 'Saint' Major-General Thomas Harrison. Ludlow made contingency plans for a rapid escape. Milton, now quite blind, reflected on the iniquities that must have deserved this rod across their backs.

What of those who *had* jumped in time, who had been instrumental in bringing about the Restoration? Did these rituals of revenge make them just a little nervous? In May 1661 Samuel Pepys stood in the immense, glimmering cave of Westminster Abbey on the coronation day of Charles II and watched while fistfuls of silver and gold were flung high in the air, the coins and medals ringing as they hit the stone slabs. But the shower of treasure did not fall on his shoulders, positioned as he was at a properly respectful distance from the throne. The tailor's son may have come a long way from Fleet Street, but he was still just clerk to the Navy Board. So he was obliged to observe while his betters scrambled for the royal bounty, like so many bridesmaids scuffling for the nosegay. 'I could not come of any,' he complained ruefully to his diary.

What could he 'come of'? What could men like Pepys expect from the new reign? It was one thing to purr contentedly as he was massaged by the famous royal affability; another to be completely confident that men who had served what was now euphemistically referred to as 'The Old State' would find the same favour in the kingdom. The presence, both political and physical, of the portly Lord Chancellor

Clarendon – who had inflated alarmingly along with his new peerage – helped calm some of these anxieties. Clarendon was, without question, the ballast of the Restoration, the man who could bring a dose of political sobriety to the understandable inebriation of the vindicated Cavaliers. In the Long Parliament, as Edward Hyde, he had been a reformer. But so much had since happened to make those mild changes pale into insignificance that Clarendon's moderation could now pass as the staunchest royalist conservatism. Without surrendering the legitimate prerogative of the Crown, Clarendon was anxious to reanchor it in a stable constitution: parliament and king engaged in trusting, mutual dependence. While Pepys, along with many of the younger servants of the Restoration, was as apt as any courtier to snigger and cavil at Clarendon's weighty self-importance, he was actually very grateful for his settling authority. Clarendon, he knew, was unlikely to spurn the talents of ex-officers of the Protectorate – especially in so critical an area of expertise as the Navy – merely to keep the kingdom pure. Purity did not seem to be much on Charles II's mind. So Pepys would have been gratified, but not perhaps surprised, to see his patron Edward Montagu promoted to the earldom of Sandwich. Pepys was also enough of a realist to appreciate that, if some carcasses had to be thrown to the baying hounds of the Cavaliers, he had better make sure his was not one of them. No one with so well-developed a sense of irony would have missed the fact that those who were now most incriminated by the posthumous notoriety of Cromwell were – like Vane, Bradshaw, Ludlow and Harrison – precisely the republicans who had most hated him! So, with his wife Elizabeth, Pepys could move into his new lodgings at the Navy Board secure in the knowledge that this new state, like the old state, needed capable, industrious men like him; men who knew where to find things like guns, ships, men and money. Especially money.

All the same, though, he was bound to have felt just a little uncomfortable amid the obscure gorgeousness of the coronation. The serried ranks of bishops and barons were men who seemed to know by instinct, as well as by education, how to play their parts in this ponderously antique performance. What would Cromwell have made of the apparition of the 'King's Champion' riding, in full coat of mail, into Westminster Hall during the banquet and flinging down his gage to challenge anyone who might impugn his royal master?

Well, perhaps King Oliver might even have suffered this nonsense as a necessary mummery, a plaything for the landed and the hare-brained. But he would certainly not, like Charles, have rounded up the scrofulous to be touched 'for the king's evil'. Could the ironic, urbanely quizzical Charles really believe in all this foolishness? It was the same Charles, after all, who patronized the natural philosophers of Gresham

College, and who endorsed a 'Royal Society' as a fellowship of the learned who might converse and even dispute without destructive acrimony. To some, in fact, the king himself seemed to be of this inquisitive mind, poring as he did over the latest time-pieces and telescopes, scrutinizing the universe as an ingeniously constructed apparatus put together by the Celestial Mechanic.

So, when all was said and done, could Charles be expected to preside over a realm of even-tempered reason? The Declaration of Breda, issued in April 1660, had promised 'Liberty to tender Consciences' precisely as an antidote to 'the Passion and the uncharitablenesse of the times [which] have produced severall Opinions in Religion, by which men are engaged in parties and animosities against each other'. But what transpired in the first years of his reign hardly fulfilled the promised hopes of 'freedom of conversation'. Charles may have wished to be sweetly reasonable, but the 'Cavalier' Parliament, elected in March and April 1661 – and not replaced until 1679 – was much more interested in vindication than moderation. The old soldiers who had bled for the king (either in their persons or in their purses) doubtless felt the savage punishments meted out to the republicans were merited by the enormity of their crimes. But the real thirsters after satisfaction were the clergy, especially the bishops, who, after the downfall of Laud had suffered humiliations inconceivable in the history of the English Church: the imprisonment and execution of the Arch-bishop, expulsion from the House of Lords and extirpation from their own dioceses, the very name and office of bishop made shameful. Now the mitres and monstrances were back, nowhere more triumphantly than at Ely, where Christopher Wren's formi-dable uncle Matthew was restored after years of unrepentant incarceration in the Tower of London where he had shared a cell with Laud. Matthew was Zadok glori-fied, Oded set up on high, and he let it be known in no uncertain terms that the pernicious pack of 'fanatics and sectaries' who had desecrated the sanctity of the Church of England would never again be allowed to delude the credulous and make trouble in the house of the Lord.

A pathetic Fifth Monarchist riot in London in January 1661, which mobilized all of fifty supporters to its cause, gave the militant bishops and their allies in the sub-sequent Cavalier Parliament all the pretext they needed to reject the efforts of both Clarendon and the king to loosen the severity of the restored Church of England. For all the grandeur of his demeanour, Clarendon was a pragmatist and had no interest in provoking and perpetuating disaffection. Better the Puritans should scowl from within than from without the Church. So he had hoped that either the Church of England's dogma could be broadened enough to allow some of the Nonconformists to be reconciled, or else that the penalties for active conformity might be unenforced.

The king wanted the same leniency for Catholics. But prelates like Wren and Gilbert Sheldon were having none of this. So notwithstanding the fact that it represented everything the Lord Chancellor opposed, parliament enacted a series of punitive acts known collectively as the 'Clarendon Code' and expressly designed to strangle the life out of non-Anglican Christian worship. Knowing that the sects had drawn their strength from urban artisans and merchants, dissenting ministers were banished to a distance at least 5 miles outside town limits. Strict examination of the orthodoxy of professing clergy was to be enforced, and those tainted with the least signs of Nonconformity weeded out. And of course it was not just the wilder fringe cults – the Muggletonians and the Seekers – that were the target of all this draconian scrutiny. The acts were intended to marginalize, and then uproot, the entirety of English Presbyterian Calvinism. Presbyterian opposition to the republic in the 1650s and support for the Restoration was as of no consequence now. The bishops were adamant in their belief (not unfounded) that Puritan heterodoxy had been the great engine of disaffection against Church and king. If those institutions were to be made secure against a repetition of rebellion, the opposite conclusion from Clarendon's middle way had to be embraced. English Calvinism needed to be wiped out.

So – astonishingly – a whole culture of teaching, preaching, praying and singing, a culture that had so deeply coloured faith and politics for at least two generations, was made to go away. If it survived at all it did so with permission, not as of right but furtively and apologetically. In 1662 on the anniversary of the St Barthlomew's Eve massacre, hundreds of Nonconformist (overwhelmingly Puritan-Presbyterian) ministers were evicted from their livings. In December of the same year the king issued a Declaration of Indulgence, expressing his intent to ask the Cavalier Parliament to grant him power to dispense with the Act of Uniformity, but he was defeated in March 1663 by his own, much more intransigent parliament! In November 1663, Pepys heard his clerk Will Hewer's 'Uncle Blackborne' speak with quiet but deep resentment of the 'many pious Ministers of God – some thousands of them [who] do now, beg their bread' and of 'how highly the present Clergy carry themselfs everywhere, so as that they are hated and laughed at by everybody'.

This transformation of a highly visible and even more highly audible culture into a closeted, family Church was one of the great disappearing acts in English history. It was neither permanent nor universal. Dissenting Christianity would survive and revive (especially in the next century). And the enforced collapse of Calvinism encouraged recruits to Nonconforming Churches like the Quakers, which were free from political suspicion. But the future of British history was profoundly affected in ways as yet undiscernible to the confident bishops and the Cavaliers who made the

Top: *Edward Hyde, First Earl of Clarendon, Lord High Chancellor*, by
Sir Peter Lely, *c.* 1662.
Above: *John Evelyn*, engraved after Robert Nanteuil, *c.* 1650.

Clarendon Code. What they did was not so much eliminate Puritanism as displace it, sending it into exile from where, in the future, it would cause at least as much trouble to the British monarchy as it had in the past: places like Belfast and Boston.

The shutting of mouths was completed by the closing of presses. The repeal of the act requiring triennial elections brutally pruned back the young growth of competitive politics. A licensing act now effectively gagged the free press of the Commonwealth by giving a publishing monopoly over works of history and politics to the orthodox university presses or the officially regulated Stationers Company. The unrepentant old Laudian journalist Roger l'Estrange was given effective censorship authority over London's master-printers, whose numbers, he proposed, should be cut from sixty to twenty. Bad things could happen to those who flouted that authority, however idiosyncratic their publications. John Heydon, for example, was thrown into prison merely for casting the king's horoscope – deemed a seditious act – and publishers like Giles Calvert, who had specialized in treatises of political theory, ended up in Newgate. Clubs, such as The Rota, where competing arguments about the constitution and government had been freely debated in 1659, were shut down; coffee-houses, where the agitators had met, were patrolled and spied on.

For the prophets and preachers, the printers and journalists cast out into the wilderness, their dispersal handed the realm to Pharisees, harlots and parasitical courtiers. But it was not necessary to be a Puritan 'fanatic' to be scandalized by the profligacy and promiscuousness of Charles II's court. Even to staunch Anglican Royalists like John Evelyn, the addiction of the king and his brother to debauchery was an affront to the Almighty by whose benevolent grace the king had been restored to his throne. But the king, now in the narcissistic prime of his mid-thirties, was impervious to criticism. He lolled on downy pillows of flattery, assiduously fluffed up by a succession of fawning poets (many of whom, like John Dryden and Edmund Waller, had once fawned on Cromwell), and would dandle his bastards on the royal couch along with his glossy spaniels and mistresses. There was an instinctive graciousness about the king (unlike his cynosure Louis XIV, which made it physically painful, if not outright impossible, for him to refuse favours to those women who had so unhesitatingly received him into their bed. The brightest and most ambitious of them made the most of the moment. Barbara Palmer, Lady Castlemaine, for example, insisted on being treated as a true consort, accumulating not just wealth but power, and at times dictating who might and who might not be received by the king. As a helpless bystander to Charles's captivity between the sheets, Clarendon was in a state of infuriated torment. Under Cromwell, the aggressive (if intermittent) pursuit of virtue had threatened to undo the stability of government. Now, the equally aggressive pursuit of vice promised to have the same effect. For if sophisticated Londoners were unshocked by the fashion parade of over-frizzed curls and over-exposed bosoms, the same, so Clarendon feared, was not true of opinion in the shires. When the secret marriage of his own (pregnant) daughter, Anne Hyde, to Charles's brother, James, Duke of York, was announced, Clarendon was so aghast that he recommended the king behead her for her temerity. His horror was occasioned not just by James's reputation for lechery, which surpassed even that of the king, but by the inevitable whispering campaign that he had contrived the marriage to create a royal dynasty of Stuart-Hydes (something that duly came to pass but, not exactly in the way Clarendon imagined or feared).

He was not alone in these anxieties. When things went very badly wrong with the government of the realm a few years later, in 1667, Sir George Carteret, Pepys' colleague at the Navy Board, reminded him that the want of 'at least a show of religion in the government, and sobriety' had been the cause which

> did set up and keep Oliver, though he was the greatest rogue in the world. And that it [decency] is so fixed in the nature of the common Englishman, that it will not out of him … while all should be labouring to settle the Kingdom, they are at Court all in factions … and the King adheres to no man, but this day delivers himself up to this and the next to that, to the ruin of himself and business. That he is at the command of any woman like a slave [and] … cannot command himself in the presence of a woman he likes.

That the affairs of the flesh and the affairs of state need not necessarily be mutually exclusive is documented – exhaustively – by the diaries of Samuel Pepys. His hands were seldom still, whether they were busily penning memoranda on the state of the timber supply, or travelling through the underthings of the latest woman to take his fancy. But for Pepys these dalliances were not distraction so much as invigoration: the grope that refreshes.

> 3 October 1664 Talk also of great haste in the getting out another fleet and building some ships. Thence, with our heads full of business, we broke up, and I to my barbers and there only saw Jane and stroked her under the chin; and away to the Exchange and there long about several businesses, hoping to get money by them. And thence home to dinner … But meeting Bagwell's wife at the office before I went home, I took her into the office and there kissed her only. She rebuked me for doing it; saying, that did I do so much to many bodies else,

it would be a stain to me. But I do not see but she takes it well enough; though in the main, I believe she is very honest.

To say his days were full would be an understatement. Apart from his business at the offices of the Navy Board, Pepys managed to take in several plays a week, meetings of the Royal Society, bibulous assemblies in tavern, and musical recitals. Hungry for news, gossip or flirtation Pepys roamed the capital by boat, by carriage or on his own two feet, searching for whatever he needed that particular hour, that particular day: information from the arsenal at Woolwich, or the dockyard managers at Deptford; girls who made themselves available in the alleys off Fleet Street; a shipyard carpenter's wife; the latest telescope from Richard Reeve's shop; the sleekest black-silk camelot suit coat from his tailor.

Pepys was one of the great inspectors, whether of the inviting curve of a woman's breast or the supplies of cordage available to the fleet. He was compulsive about tallies, not least of his own assets as well as the kingdom's, and was distressed whenever he detected shortfall. When he thought his long-suffering wife Elizabeth was frittering the substance of their fortune on dress he subjected her to bullying accusations, and when she presumed to argue back slapped her about the face (as he often did) for her temerity. This ugly side of his character, however, was seldom on show to his large circle of friends and colleagues, who took him to be the most companionable and learned of men. And Pepys was easiest amid like-minded fellows who shared his view that the accumulation of knowledge was the pillar, not just of understanding but of power. So he could be counted on as a booster of experimental and scientific projects designed for the benefit of the kingdom, like John Evelyn's proposals, set out in his *Fumifugium,* to make the verminous, insanitary, smoke-choked city safer and healthier, or William Petty's invention of the double-keeled boat – even when the king politely ignored the one and saw the other founder in its first sailing trial, drowning those on board.

It became apparent, in fact, that for Charles science was an amusement, an indulgence of toys like time-pieces and eye-pieces rather than a meticulously sustained inquiry. The king (like the rest of polite society) was charmed by Robert Hooke's engravings of the magnified louse in the *Micrographia,* and he was content to have his patronage attached to the deliberations of the Royal Society. But he also made sure to broadcast his bewilderment at the goings-on at Gresham College whereby grave men busied themselves 'spending time in weighing of ayre'. But it never occurred to Charles to see the proceedings of the Royal Society as more than the eccentric diversions of a gentlemen's club, certainly not as a model of inquiry and debate settled by

Samuel Pepys, by John Hayls, 1666. Pepys recorded sitting for his portrait in his diary, complaining, 'I ... do almost break my neck looking over my shoulders to make the posture for him [Hayls] to work by'.

Above: *The Greenwich Observatory: Interior of the Camera Stellata*, after Robert Thacker, 1676. One of a set of prints commissioned to commemorate the opening of the Royal Observatory in 1676.
Opposite: *Bring out your Dead* was the mournful cry heard at night as carts coursed their way through the city's streets collecting corpses. As coffins could not be built fast enough, bodies were tossed into grisly pits on the outskirts.

experimental observation, favoured by the likes of Petty and Boyle. When calamity struck the kingdom, as it did in a succession of stunning hammer-blows between 1665 and 1667, the instinctive response of the king, as well as of his subjects, was to invoke not the illuminations of science and the arguments of reason but divine intercession through penance, fasting and prayer.

So the appearance of a comet in the summer of 1664 struck observers, not with astronomical wonder (though those in possession of Richard Reeve's telescope could observe its blazing tail with unparalleled clarity), but with the same dismay that this phenomenon had always inspired as a presage of disaster. Those like Clarendon who had bitterly opposed the war against the Dutch, into which the king had entered with such bellicose optimism, felt even queasier when they saw the dusty pallor trembling in the night sky, notwithstanding an early naval victory at Lowestoft. By the following summer, when the Dutch showed no sign of surrender and plague carts were carrying thousands to the burial pits every week, the Jeremiahs seemed vindicated in their prophecies that God's hand would be laid across the back of the sin-steeped kingdom.

And there was not much that science could do about it, other than count London's dead with modern devotion to the seriousness of statistics and the mapping of the epidemic (8252 deaths in the first week of September, 6978 from the plague).

Understanding of the generation and transmission of the sickness was scarcely any more advanced than when it had first struck in 1348. Because it was thought that cats and dogs spread the plague, the Lord Mayor of London ordered a general slaughter: 40,000 dogs and perhaps (by Pepys's reckoning) 200,000 cats were duly massacred. That they were so swiftly rounded up and dispatched testified to the fact that what *had* modernized since the medieval epidemics was the policing of mortality. Daniel Defoe's heart-rending account of the harvest of bodies in 1665, *A Journal of the Plague Year*, was written more than half a century after the event, but was based on reliable memories of contemporaries, including one of Samuel Pepys's amanuenses, Paul Lorrain. What Defoe describes is a culture divided into the mad and the methodical. Unhinged prophets walked naked in the streets roaring for repentance before the race was consumed altogether, while platoons of watchmen patrolled the streets enforcing the requirement that households become hermetically sealed at the first sign of infection. While the court, the aristocracy and the professions (including, of course, physicians) fled London just as fast as they could, common citizens were locked up by the watch in their own houses, prisoners of the contagion, left to succumb, starve or survive. The regulations may have been designed to seal off the country from the plague, but inevitably the infection always outran the ability to contain it, and in the meantime they condemned Londoners to be deprived of any hope of work or sustenance except what came their way by charity. The desperate who attempted to escape the net risked arrest and prosecution. From Alderman Hooker, Pepys heard of a saddler 'who had buried all the rest of his children of the plague; and himself and wife now being shut up, and in despair of escaping, did desire only to save the life of this [their surviving] little child; and so prevailed to have it received stark-naked into the arms of a friend, who brought it (having put it into new fresh clothes) to Greenwich'. And for once Pepys and his colleagues were moved enough to allow the child to stay there in safety.

One-sixth of London's population died in the plague of 1665. The misery ebbed with the onset of cool weather, but the trepidation hung around. Pepys was inhibited from wearing his fine new periwig for fear that it was made of hair cut from infected bodies. Following astrology, as the almanacs reminded their preternaturally anxious readers, was numerology; the tail of the comet heralded the sign of the Beast, his number being, as everyone knew: 666. Sure enough, in the first week of September 1666, up from the bituminous regions of hell, came the diabolical fire. Prophets like Walter Gostelo and Daniel Baker had long been warning that the new Sodom, steeped in lechery and luxury, would be consumed by the fiery wrath of an indignant Jehovah. But the more sober John Evelyn, watching thousands upon thousands arrive each day from the country, blocking the alleys with their carts, cramming the stinking, congested, drought-stricken city, also believed that, should a dry wind catch a casually released flame, a general ignition would occur.

Still, the violence of the conflagration caught almost everyone else unawares. The warm southeasterly, which blew in with the last dog days of August and the first of September, was feared as the carrier of contagion, rather than as a fire-lighter. So when, in the early hours of Sunday morning, 2 September, Sir Thomas Bludworth, the Lord Mayor of London, was woken from his sleep and told that the fire that had begun in the bakery of Thomas Farinor in Pudding Lane had already consumed much of Fish Street Hill and was advancing towards Thames Street, his response was: 'Pish! A woman might piss it out', before going back to sleep, irritated by the disturbance. As he snored on, the flames found their way into the warehouses flanking the Thames between London Bridge and the Tower, brim full of tallow, pitch, tar and brandy wines. A rolling fireball came roaring and sucking out of the narrow streets, feeding on the overhanging timbered bays and gables. In an hour or two another 300 houses had been swallowed up by the fire. Panic took hold. People came flying out of their homes, pushing carts full of their possessions, making for the river where they dumped their wooden boxes in the grimy water to float and bob along in the spark-flecked darkness. The lanes became choked with traffic; faces were choked with scorching smoke. The elderly were carried through the streets in their beds or in improvised wheelbarrows. Told how serious the situation had become, Pepys got up before dawn, walked to the Tower and climbed to one of the high storeys from where he saw the fire working its way along London Bridge, devouring the piled-up houses and shops as it ate its way hungrily across the span. Only the pigeons stayed put in their windows and eaves until their feathers caught fire, leaving them to flutter pathetically, their wings alight.

Pepys made his way up-river, his boat navigating between the crates of household possessions as he kept his face away from the 'showers of firedrops' that flew with the wind. At Whitehall he told the king that only the immediate demolition of houses in the path of the fire, depriving it of kindling and creating fire-breaks, could contain the conflagration. For once Charles was not about to make light of the situation and gave orders that this should be done right away. A system of couriers between the City and the palace was established to keep the king informed of the progress of the fire. When Pepys got to the Lord Mayor, very much awake now 'like a man spent, with a hankercher about his neck', he found that Bludworth had gone from complacency to distraction: 'Lord what can I do? People will not obey me.' The Lord Mayor protested that he was pulling down houses as fast as he could but – not surprisingly – he was encountering resistance from those whose property (but not their persons) happened to be in the demolition zone. The truth was that Bludworth himself was still deeply reluctant to take action, worrying about the cost to house- and store-owners.

By the end of Sunday the fire, stoked by the wind, had destroyed the most densely populated core of the old city between the Tower and the Bridge. The thick pall of smoke, still lit here and there by bursts of flame, hung over London so thickly that it turned the September sun blood-red. John Evelyn, for whom the city's health and welfare had become a personal passion, was distraught.

O the miserable & calamitous speectacle, such as happly the whole world had not seene the like since the foundation of it, nor to be out don, 'til the universal Conflagration of it, all the skie were of a fiery aspect, like the top of a burning Oven, & the light seene above 40 miles round about for many nights. God grant

mine eyes may never behold the like, who now saw above ten thousand houses
all in one flame, the noise & crackling & thunder of the impetuous flames, the
shreeking of Women & children, the hurry of people, the fall of towers, houses &
churches was like an hideous storme ... Thus I left it this afternoone burning, a
resemblance of Sodome, or the last day ... It call'd to mind that passage of 4 *Heb:*
non enim hic habemus stabilem Civitatem: the ruines resembling the picture of *Troy.*
London was, but is no more!

On Monday, 3 September, the fire travelled beyond the huddle of houses, shops, taverns and warehouses, jumping the narrow Fleet river that bisected the old city, to
reach the Royal Exchange and Lombard Street. 'Rattle, rattle, rattle was the noise
which the fire struck upon the ear as if there had been a thousand iron chariots beating down upon the stones,' wrote Thomas Vincent of the experience of being trapped
in the burning near the Exchange, 'whole streets at once in flames that issued forth as
if they had been so many great forges.' Pepys now began to fear for his own property
and possessions. While there was still time he sent his valuables off to a friend at
Bethnal Green and, together with Sir William Penn, buried their official papers in a
pit dug in Tower Street by the Navy Office. Then the two men, their shirts filthy with
soot and smoke stains, dug their own deep hole. Into it went precious things: bottles
of wine and Pepys's Parmesan cheese. At the end of the day he wanted to let his father
know the terrible news that St Paul's and all Cheapside were on fire, 'but the post-
house being burned, the letter could not go'. The next day, Tuesday, 4 September, was
even worse, with the gusty breeze blowing the flames still further, north and west. On
that terrifying Tuesday, the fire showed itself no respecter of the great public institutions of the city. Over forty of the livery company halls went up in flames, and the
Guildhall itself burned for twenty-four hours. By some miracle the city archives,
which had been hastily stored in the crypt, survived. Not so the enormous stock of
books kept by the sellers in the churchyard precincts of St Paul's. Seeing the fire
coming straight towards the cathedral, they had made a panicky rush to store them in
the booksellers' favoured chapel of St Faith's in the great church. Some managed to
get their barrow-loads there; others, caught in the mass of human traffic and desperate
not to be trapped, ended up dumping the books in the open yard. When the fire
caught up with them it ignited the paper and parchment in a huge bonfire, the blackened pages flaking and flapping around amid the roaring air. But the books in St
Faith's ended up no better off. For at the critical moment of the blaze most of the
superstructure of the choir crashed into the chapel below, completing the incineration of the books. Then the lead on the roof liquefied: 'The stones of Pauless, flew like

granados,' wrote Evelyn, who had been on a tour of inspection of the cathedral just a week before on 27 August; 'the Lead mealting downe the streetes in a streame, & the very pavements glowing with fiery rednesse, so as nor horse nor man was able to tread on them.'

The immensity of the disaster seemed to mock the pretensions of king and government to be a protector to the people. But unlike during the plague epidemic, when they had got themselves out of the capital as quickly as possible, Charles and his brother were very much in the thick of the efforts to contain and fight the fire. James was put in charge of containment and demolition. There was not much that could be done with water. The summer's drought had reduced the levels of the city cisterns, and in any case most of the wooden pipes carrying water to the pumps and squirts had themselves been destroyed by the heat. But it was possible to fight fire with fire, and once the opposition to the demolition programme was finally over-ruled, and whole streets of houses blown up using military mines and tunnels, it began to have some noticeable effect. On Wednesday, 5 September, the wind started to drop. The conflagration began, at last, to be held in check.

The king himself was seen in the streets attended by just a few guards, doing what he did best – giving away gold (for once, to the deserving). But even his genuinely kindly presence could do little to abate the trauma experienced by the multitudes – now at least 100,000 – who had been made homeless by the fire and who wandered about the smouldering ruins of the city. Tents had been set up at St George's Fields and Moorfields where the refugees camped in a state of shock. Evelyn saw many 'without a rag, or any necessary utinsils, bed or board, who from delicatnesse, riches & easy accomodations … were now reduc'd to extreamest misery & poverty'. By the end of the week, the tent cities of the homeless stretched all the way north through Islington and Primrose Hill to Highgate. If many were disconsolate at the catastrophe, just as many were in the grip of anger, looking for someone to blame for their predicament. So Charles went to the camp at Moorfields to quell the ugly rumours that the fire had been set by either the Papists or the Dutch – or, in some improbably unholy alliance, by both. James intervened to stop a Dutch baker being lynched, but the French were still conspicuous targets. A Westminster School boy, William Taswell, saw one of them floored by a blacksmith with an iron bar. It had not been foreigners who had caused the disaster, Charles told the destitute and the homeless; it was, rather, the hand of God. And for whose transgressions, exactly, they might have asked, looking the king in the eye, had London been turned into a second Sodom?

When the rain started on 9 September, a week after the outbreak of the fire, allowing some early stocktaking, the scale of the devastation appalled even the pessimists. London, blackened and shattered, looked as though it had been broken by a cruel siege. Some 13,200 houses had been destroyed in 400 streets and courts. Eighty-seven churches, six chapels, much of St Paul's Cathedral and forty-four halls of the livery companies, as well as the Guildhall, the Exchange, the Custom House, Bridewell Prison, the great law courts, four bridges and three city gates, were gone. The damage was estimated at almost £10 million.

Of course, when Evelyn lamented 'London is no more', he was technically rather than demographically accurate. Three-quarters of the old City of London, the most densely populated core of shops, warehouses and small dwellings, had indeed been burned, but the metropolis now consisted of two cities (London and the rapidly expanding Westminster), or perhaps even three, with Southwark, Rotherhithe and Lambeth making another conurbation on the south bank. The fire had been contained before it could get through to the newer sprawling areas to the west and north, which housed both the very rich and the very poor. But it was precisely because the palace at Whitehall and the fashionable new streets, like Piccadilly where Clarendon had had his outrageously palatial town house built by Sir Roger Pratt, had been unscathed by the destruction that it was especially incumbent on the rich and powerful to show themselves solicitous about rebuilding the dwellings and public meeting-places of the less well-to-do. 'Restoration' might finally mean something other than so much poetic rhetoric. Now there was something solid, something serious to restore.

On 11 September, just two days after the rain had started, dousing any more fears of minor reignitions, the Savilian Professor of Astronomy at Oxford asked for an urgent audience with the king. Christopher Wren was then in his early thirties, a little younger than Charles. He could expect a cordial reception because his father, also Christopher, had been Dean of Windsor and had put his own life on the line during the civil war to preserve some of the treasures of the chapel, not least the archives of the Order of the Garter that Charles I had so passionately and so hopelessly cherished. Dean Wren had died before the Restoration, but his more famous and much more intransigent brother Matthew, the Bishop of Ely, had emerged from captivity determined to perpetuate Laud's programme for authority and beauteous decorum in the Church. The erstwhile Bishop of London, Gilbert Sheldon, now Archbishop of Canterbury, was one of young Christopher's patrons and had commended him to the king not just as someone capable of abstruse mathematical demonstrations, but as a prodigy who could turn his nimbly versatile intellect to practical and architectural matters. Although Wren chose not to go, he had been asked, as early as 1661, if he could advise the king on the fortifications of Tangier, which were about to be passed

Top: *The Great Fire of London*, Dutch School, *c.* 1666.
Above: *The Dutch in the Medway*, by Willem Schellinks, 1667.

to the Crown as a result of Charles's marriage to the Portuguese princess, Catherine of Braganza.

The flames had barely died away when Wren drafted for the king's inspection a plan for the rebuilding of the City of London. He must have worked on the project at startling speed, day and night, since he managed to anticipate by some days the more considered plans of two of his close friends among the Royal Society circle of scientists, John Evelyn and Robert Hooke. Wren's determination to get his ideas before the king's eyes in advance of any rival plans stemmed not so much from egotistical ambition (though Wren was no shrinking violet) as from his certainty that the breathtaking radicalism of the plan would shock conventional expectations of how the destroyed city should be rebuilt. Most of those expectations – including the king's – assumed that the buildings and streets of London would be reconstructed as and where they had stood before the fire. The immensely important exceptions to this assumption, embodied in the Rebuilding Act of February 1667, were the requirement to build in brick and stone, the ban on overhanging storeys and the broadening of selected streets so that an accidental fire on one side would not automatically catch on the other. Noxious industries that used combustible materials, like dyeing, tanning and brewing, were also to be moved out from the centre of town, preferably across the river.

Most of these prophylactic measures had been proposed by Evelyn's *Fumifugium* five years before. But Wren had his eye on something far more daring than fire precautions. He wanted an utter transformation of the old city: nothing short of the creation of a new Rome on the banks of the Thames, with a great domed basilica replacing the burnt-out Gothic hulk of old St Paul's. The vision, laid out so audaciously before Charles, was something Wren believed most perfectly expressed the spirit of a new Londinium: a marriage of antiquity and modernity, the colossal and the commercial, the sacred and the entrepreneurial. At its heart was a great oval piazza, but it was to be dominated by a Pantheon of business – a new, colonnaded Royal Exchange. Radiating out from its hub would be broad streets, optically calculated to afford sweeping, geometrically satisfying vistas of the public edifices and monuments (not least one to the fire itself). Studded throughout the new metropolis would be fifty-odd rebuilt churches, situated without any regard to the old boundaries of parishes, which Wren believed had been made redundant by the fire. New parishes could surely be redesigned about these architectural imperatives, not the other way round. Surely, as a man of science and high taste, the king could see the logic of this argument? Did he not want a capital worthy of all those odes eulogizing him as the new Augustus?

Charles, who had spent years in Paris watching that city transformed by architects such as François Mansart, Le Mercier and Louis Le Vau, was flattered by Wren's disarming instinct for grandeur. And his initial reaction was to congratulate and encourage the young man on his visionary optimism. But – advised by harder heads on the Privy Council – he also knew that he was no Pharaoh (or Bourbon) who could simply order it into existence. The merchants, brokers and tradesmen wanted the life of the city to resume just as quickly as possible, and just where it had been interrupted by the fire. The thousands whose bread depended on their work for those enterprises could not afford to wait around until some gleaming vision of the phoenix-metropolis had been realized. Even the very limited scale of alteration (the broader streets) required compensation to be paid to those displaced by the building, derived from a tax (on shipped 'sea coal') that needed authorizing by parliament. And parliament, even a Cavalier parliament, was not in the utopia business. Those country gentlemen may have had the great text-books of architectural and city design, antique and neo-classical – Vitruvius, Palladio and Serlio – in their libraries, but, with rare exceptions, the vellum gathered dust and the folios stayed uncut.

So Wren's marvellous vision was doomed to be unrealized. He would, though – over three decades – get to build a fair number of his churches, themselves wonders of the new architecture, which thoughtfully combined Protestant concern for the centrality of preaching (through his acoustically calibrated interiors) with steeples, tiered with tempietti and balustrades, pilasters and columns, translated from baroque Rome and Paris to London. And Wren would, of course, give the country the greatest of all its sacred buildings: not just a new cathedral, but a national basilica.

Even had he wanted to, Wren would never have escaped St Paul's, the rebuilding of which gave him such grief and such glory. His uncle Matthew's cell-mate Laud, at the height of his power, had imposed a massive fund-raiser on the country for the renovation of the dangerously unsound ancient structure (whose spire had fallen from the tower in an earlier fire in 1561). And before his execution, Laud had set aside £800 in his will to further the work of renovation. For Matthew the task of bringing St Paul's back, not just from architectural peril but from desecration, was the true meaning of the Restoration: a cleansing of profanity. When the parliamentarian army had come to London in 1647 and 1648, cavalry troopers had stalled their horses there; and after the king's execution the statues of Charles and James that had surmounted Inigo Jones's west portico had been pulled down and smashed. The cathedral plate had been melted down for the army, the stained glass shattered, pews and choir stalls chopped up for firewood. The royalist antiquarian William Dugdale's instinct that a terrible iconoclasm was at hand had been proved only too accurate, but

Top: *South-west View of Old St Paul's*, engraved by Wenceslaus Hollar, *c.* 1660.
Above: *Ruins of St Paul's Cathedral*, by Thomas Wyck, *c.* 1673.

happily he had completed his detailed description of the fabric and interior of the cathedral before the worst could happen. So, armed with this inventory (beautifully illustrated by Wenceslaus Hollar), Bishop Wren, along with the then Bishop of London, Gilbert Sheldon, and the Dean, William Sancroft, appointed themselves the Nehemiahs of the purified temple.

Christopher's piety was of an altogether quieter kind than that of his uncle. But he was, in his way, a deeply pious Christian, and he was not going to shirk the challenge. Saturated in the literature of Roman and Renaissance architectural theory, he had a lifelong ambition to transplant classical architecture into England in such a way as would be consistent with the Protestantism to which he was devoutly committed. Laud had offended, because his 'innovations' had come to be seen as somehow an alien, even sinister, presence. Christopher Wren wanted to make spiritually beautiful and architecturally grand building seem *at home* in England. The fact that we now think of Wren as a quintessentially English architect suggests how completely successful he was in achieving this ambition. But the truism blinds us to the immense and painfully protracted difficulty he had in squaring the circle of a classical, colossal style for a Protestant, parliamentary nation. Somehow Wren managed his life's work — although with innumerable compromises that embittered and saddened him – but the Stuart monarchy, which he believed would anchor itself through his public achievement, failed. His work at St Paul's began as the showpiece of the Restoration, but it would only be accomplished after a revolution. And these two events were, in fact, crucially and meaningfully connected. What tied them together was the old lethal dance between Romanophilia and Romanophobia.

Wren's connection with St Paul's began in 1663, when a Royal Commission was set up to examine the soundness or unsoundness of the structure after the ordeal of the Commonwealth. The Surveyor-General of the Royal Works was the poet Sir John Denham, and it was decided to take advice from architects who included the fashionable house-builder Roger Pratt and the unknown Oxford mathematician and astronomer Christopher Wren. Wren had had no formal architectural training and had been foisted on the commissioners by Sheldon, who had daringly commissioned him to build the ceremonial theatre in Oxford that bore his name. Wren had borrowed from the precedent of the ancient theatre of Marcellus in Rome to create an arena, and since, unlike its Italian counterpart, the building could not be open to the skies, he had enclosed it with a roof, supported by disguised buttresses and painted on the inside with a dazzling *trompe l'oeil* classical allegory. With this commission under way, Wren had no hesitation in disregarding the much more provisional recommendations of Pratt to repair and restore St Paul's, especially its great tower. Instead, he proposed the demolition of the tower altogether and the removal of its columns. Surmounting the crossing in its place would be a great ribbed dome, carried on a drum and supported from within by eight massive piers. More eccentrically, it was to be surmounted, not by a conventional lantern but by a pineapple spire – the fruit of choice for architectural ornament, it is true, and possibly a compliment to the king, whose garden at Kew had just presented him with the first home-grown specimen.

Roger Pratt was not amused. In fact he was incensed at the temerity of this unknown and inveighed to the bishop, his patron Clarendon and the king against the extravagance and impracticality of the scheme. But Charles, guided by Sheldon, was in fact enough taken with the suggestion to refrain from any sort of veto. And in the summer of 1665, while London was in the grip of the plague, Wren took a journey that, if anything, made him even more resolved to pursue his vision of a Romanized basilica. His sojourn was not in Rome but in Paris. But architecturally speaking, Rome was *in* Paris in the person of its great genius Gian Lorenzo Bernini, whom Wren duly visited at his house where he saw the drawings of his stupendously audacious (and unrealized) plans for the east front of the Louvre. The contrapuntal rhythms of Bernini's rendering of the façade, swelling and receding, convex and concave, obviously made an impact on the impressionable Wren, since he too aimed for that kind of music in stone in the most ambitious of his own plans for St Paul's. But the rebuilding of Louis XIV's Paris and the great classical houses of the Ile de France, like Vaux-le-Vicomte, while more formally austere than Bernini's building language, gave Wren an opportunity to see at first hand how domed churches and colleges could be successfully transplanted into settings very different from Rome. French architects had felt free to play with the possibilities offered by different kinds of cupola: Bramante's hemispherical plan for St Peter's or Michelangelo's loftier, more tapered version. And Wren must also have admired the energy and clarity with which the royal architects carved their way through the clutter of medieval streets parallel to the Seine to create great axial thoroughfares converging on spacious squares, the house façades harmonized by classical pilasters.

When Wren arrived back in London his head was buzzing with creative ingenuity, and he was impatient to press on with his ideas for the all-out, rather than makeshift, reconstruction of St Paul's. On 27 August 1666, in the company of John Evelyn as well as the still intensely antagonistic Pratt, a tour of inspection of the cathedral was made. Plumb lines dropped from the top of the columns supporting the tower found that they leaned, in some cases as much as 6 inches or a foot away from true perpendicular – a variation that Pratt had a hard time accounting for as the prescient intention of the original Gothic architects, concerned to allow for settling.

But it was, of course, the great fire, which broke out six days later, rather than any invincibility of Wren's arguments, which settled the matter. Even *after* the fire, though, it was by no means a foregone conclusion that Wren would be allowed to implement his Romanizing dream. For much as Charles might have *liked* to have been Louis XIV and to be able to order grandeur into existence with a wave of his cane, he was not and he could not. Parliament had to be consulted when money needed to be spent, and the Cathedral Chapter's concerns, which were often practical rather than aesthetic, had to be listened to.

Wren, however, was only intermittently paying attention. The summer of 1667 had added yet another body blow to the credibility of the restored monarchy to be the divinely appointed protector of the nation. Charles and his governments had been unable to protect the country from plague and fire. And now they had shown themselves incapable of fulfilling the elementary obligation of defending the country against foreign invasion. Astoundingly in June, a Dutch fleet commanded by the great admiral Michiel de Ruyter had sailed up the river Medway with impunity, landed soldiers at Sheerness, stormed the river forts at Upnor and Chatham, broken the barrier chain and destroyed or captured the better part of the English fleet. The king's flagship, the *Royal Charles* (which as the *Naseby* had been the terror of the North Sea), was taken back to Amsterdam in triumph.

Panic was followed by a bitter sense of humiliation, which in turn was followed by fury. As an official of the Navy Board, Pepys was lucky to escape with his position more or less intact; his senior, Peter Pett, was hounded from his place and sent to the tower. Predictably, the hue and cry turned on the most conspicuous scapegoat, Lord Chancellor Clarendon – even though he had been vocal in criticizing the decision to go to war as recklessly ill-advised. His grandiose house was attacked, and Clarendon became genuinely frightened that, with talk of impeachment in the air, he might suffer the same fate as Strafford. Before that could happen he took himself back into the exile from which the Restoration had rescued him. Always hag-ridden by the ghosts of history, he would now try to exorcise them by writing it. And the partisan masterpiece that is his *History of the Rebellion and Civil Wars in England* was the result.

The shock of 1667 only made the need for some sort of triumphalist statement, testifying to the undimmed grandeur of Crown, Church and country, more urgent. Perhaps the Almighty might smile a little more generously on his afflicted kingdom if a great Solomonic temple could be built to extol him. And Clarendon's fall had also removed as an obstruction his pet architect, Pratt, who prudently chose to occupy himself henceforth with gentlemen's estates, including his own. In due course Wren

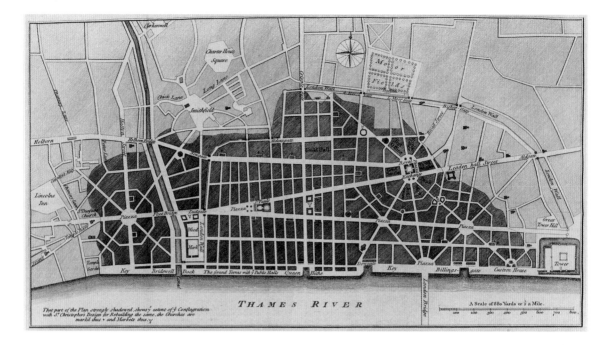

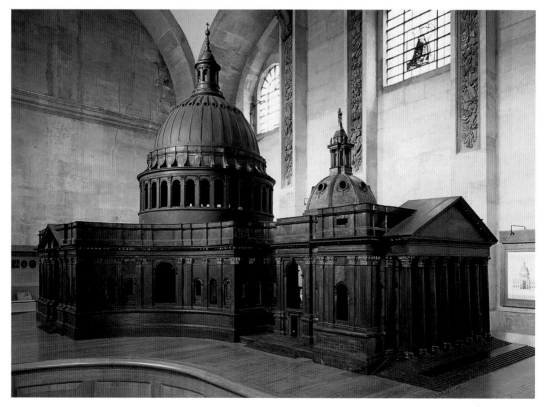

Top: *Sir Christopher Wren's Plan for Rebuilding the City of London after the Great Fire in 1666*, from *Noorthouck's History of London*, 1660s.
Above: Wren's Great Model for St Paul's Cathedral, 1672–3, showing the Greek cross design.

Top: Wren's plan of the Greek cross for the Great Model, 1672–73.
Above: A view of the interior of the Great Model, 1672–3.

became the new Surveyor-General. But the relatively modest scale of his first design for a new St Paul's suggested that he was still conscious that funds were tight. Following the practice of the great Italian masters he admired so much, Sebastiano Serlio and Andrea Palladio, in 1669 Wren had the carver Richard Clear and the master-joiner William Clear build a scale model, which was put on display at Whitehall for the king's delectation. From the surviving fragments and drawings, it is apparent that Wren had not yet taken the great leap of imagination that would produce a truly stunning design. The cupola from his 1663 plan remained, but it was oddly attached (over a square base) to a conventionally rectangular nave, made somewhat grander by the colonnade, which was to be built along its exterior length. Most controversially, the dome dominated the east end of the church – the end that had been most badly damaged by the fire. The immediate concern of the chapter was to have a new choir built as quickly as possible so that some semblance of church worship could be restored, before the rest of the rebuilding was tackled. But since that choir was now housed within the domed structure, acceptance of the plan was to become committed to its most ambitious, time-consuming and expensive feature.

The king liked Wren's first plan enough to allow his new Surveyor-General (who at last felt secure enough to resign his chair of astronomy at Oxford) to go ahead with the enormous project of demolition that had to precede any construction. Since the ruined and burnt-out walls of old St Paul's had, paradoxically, been strengthened by all the molten lead that had poured down them from the roof, the demolition took on the aspect of a military siege. An army of labourers, miners and excavators was drafted to the site, with Wren himself and his assistants directing the campaign from their custom-built office opposite the north side of the churchyard. While the work was under way Wren and his friends from the Royal Society, Evelyn and Hooke, took advantage of the excavations, dug deep enough to assure the architect that he was not imposing his monumental structure on sand, to see what remains of previous antiquity might surface. From the account given by his son in his biographical *Parentalia*, the finds were more extraordinary than anything that could have been anticipated, and they made a profound, even emotional impression on the always historically minded Christopher. The story of a labourer bringing Wren a stone to mark some spot in the works, and discovering that it bore the prophetic lapidary inscription *Resurgam* ('I will arise') is well known. But this is the least of it. For as the excavators dug they travelled back down through London's history, through the medieval and Norman foundations, discovering an ancient burial site. Saxon pins and jewellery were uncovered and then, deeper down, the remains of a Roman mortuary: urns that had contained the ashes of the dead, fragments of vividly decorated pottery.

Wren and his friends and colleagues busied themselves in their shirtsleeves in the trenches of the dig, sorting, dating, arranging and classifying. Even deeper still they found, to their amazement, sea-shells buried in the sandy rock, so that in his mind's eye the architect saw the archaic geology of the place, Ludgate Hill, no hill at all but a low strand washed by the ocean and the primitive Thames a 'sinus of the sea'.

With antiquity made immediate, and Roman London, especially, staring him in the face, Wren's architectural imagination suddenly took wing. His second design, again translated by the Clears into an exquisite model 18 feet long, spoke of a pure revelation, an act of inspired courage that produced from Wren the most beautiful building never to be built in Britain.

Wren's design of 1673–4 confronted the awkwardness of attaching a domed crossing and choir to a traditional nave (like setting a new head on an old body) by doing away with the nave altogether, in fact, by creating the kind of church that had never been seen in Britain before. Instead of a long corridor opening up at the crossing into a tall lantern (like his uncle's church at Ely), Wren envisioned a vast scooped out central basilica, full of light and air and sound: a Greek cross, three of the arms being equilateral, the fourth slightly elongated to provide an entrance vestibule. The vestibule, fronted by a flight of noble steps, would itself be surmounted by a smaller rotunda, serving as a kind of architectural overture to the immense cupola that lay beyond. The exterior walls of the Greek cross would be convex, setting up an exhilarating counterpoint with the concave circularity of the drum on which the great dome rested.

Wren had evidently not forgotten Bernini. But to the stunned *cognoscenti* who examined the model in the Convocation House, this was evidently just the problem. They had asked for a new St Paul's. And what Wren had given them was a new St Peter's. Had he fronted it with a set of enfolding colonnaded *braccia,* as in Bernini's new piazza, he could not possibly have done anything more aggressively Roman. The immediate and overpowering sense that they had been given something disturbingly alien, something that, as was pointed out, looked nothing like any known English cathedral, was especially ironic since Wren prided himself on having created an expressly Protestant house of worship. By abolishing a conventional nave-and-choir design and the screen barriers that separated them, he thought to bring the congregation closer to the essential experience of Anglican-Protestant worship, which, after all, was the sermon. His, he was convinced, was a church built for the auditory reception of Christ's word, not for the glimpsed exposure of visual mystery down a darkened tunnel, as in Catholic sacred spectacle. He may even (with some justification) have felt that, just as the teachers of the Reformation justified their emphasis on word over

Above: *Sir Christopher Wren, Kt, President of the Royal Society*, by an unknown artist, *c.* 1675, celebrating his completion of St Paul's.
Opposite: St Paul's Cathedral.

image from what they took to be the aural evangelism of the early Christian fathers, so he was returning to those days of conversion when the great pagan temples had been made over into basilicas for the true faith.

At the outset it was not clear that the king was among those who were shocked into opposition. But the chapter, in particular the vocal and formidable Dr Edward Stillingfleet, was appalled and confounded by the Great Model. However impeccably Protestant Wren might have thought it, they could not help but read it as a Catholic structure, something that belonged to the Rome of Pope Alexander VII rather than to the Anglican capital of King Charles II. The chapter was anxious not to repeat the mistakes of the Laudian campaign for sacred beautification, which had been attacked as popery by the back door. They insisted on a design that reverted to the traditional Latin cross with its long nave and separated choir, not least because they knew that the whole cathedral was very seldom used, and that, other than on holy days, they needed only the smaller space of the choir for daily services. Before long these many arguments began to make a decisive impression on the king. Around 1672 his brother James had been received back into the Roman Church, and Charles himself, as Pepys later discovered, had been privately and secretly moving in that direction himself. That only increased the necessity of *not* building something that looked to most people like the temple of the Pope.

Crestfallen at the reception of the Great Model, Wren mounted a campaign to try to have the king over-rule the objections of the Cathedral Chapter. But persuade, argue, even implore as Wren tried, Charles had made up his mind. While no objection was raised to some sort of domed crossing, Wren was ordered to meet the chapter's complaints by reverting to a traditional Latin cross. Almost as if in a sulky demonstration of the impossibility of squaring (or rectangularizing) the circle, that first 'Warrant' design was the most absurdly incongruous of all Wren's plans, obediently attaching a long nave to a bizarre double-tiered dome consisting of a Bramante-like squat circular base with a peculiar Michelangelesque onion dome on top: an Anglican pagoda. After the inevitable failure of this monstrosity, it would take Wren years to come up with a more acceptable compromise, largely by surreptitiously ignoring some of the restraints and reverting to his original vision of 1663, in which there would be two grandiose statements on the cathedral – the mighty dome at the east end and a great portico at the west, the two connected by a spacious nave.

That is the cathedral as it stands today, more or less. But it's impossible to sit in the nave, with its echoes bouncing off the columns, and not dream of Wren's banished basilica, where perfect sound would have been bathed in limpid pools of light. Although he carried on with his work at St Paul's, Wren was devastated by the rejection. It was said that, as he heard the king's final decision, tears stood in his eyes. And although he was supposed to have been consoled by the grant of his knighthood, Wren's cup of sorrow overflowed during 1674. He was defeated in an attempt to win election to the House of Commons for Oxford and endured the death of first a child, and then of his wife, in 1675. His ambition to convert London into a new Rome had been a victim of terrible timing. For between the inception of the idea and Wren's attempt to persuade the earthly powers of its 'beauty and convenience', something ugly had happened to English politics. That something was the return of the prime patriotic neurosis: anti-Catholicism.

It had never really gone away, of course. Between the Gunpowder and the Popish plots the equation of Catholicism with 'enslavement' to the demonic power of tyrannical, Jesuitical Rome shrank to the margins of the great events of the mid-century wars and revolution. And understandably so, since by the Restoration probably not much more than 1 per cent of the population of England (probably rather more in Scotland) remained actively practising Catholics. But the power of anti-Catholicism as a polarizing force in politics, and the ease by which it could be exploited to unleash uncontainable forces of hysteria, fury and panic, were out of all proportion to the reality of the threat. In 1641 it had been the perception that Charles I was secretly behind the Irish insurrection and that he would use Catholic soldiers against both the Scots and English that had convinced men like Pym and Cromwell that the king could no longer be safely entrusted with control of the militia. In that sense at least, anti-Catholicism had been the proximate cause of the civil war. In 1649 Cromwell's conviction that a royalist army in Ireland might still be used to reverse the victory of parliament made him determined to annihilate resistance in that country and created in the wake of his conquests the first kingless Britain. Running through two centuries of British history like a scarlet thread – from Walsingham's security state in the 1570s to the Gordon Riots in the 1780s – was the adamant conviction that Rome's war on heresy had ruled out the possibility of being loyal to both Church and king (or Commonwealth). Even those, like Cromwell, who had passionately believed in religious liberty, axiomatically denied that liberty to Catholics. Milton, the great guardian of the free conscience, refused to allow that Catholics were, in fact, Christians at all. For at least a century – ever since the publication of Foxe's *Actes and Monuments* (the 'Book of Martyrs') – national identity had been hammered out against the anvil of a perennially threatening, fiendishly devious, politically tyrannical and spiritually demonic Rome. The only question had been which power had been better able to protect the heart of the nation from the dagger of the Antichrist pointed at it – king or Commonwealth, parliament or Protector?

The credentials of the Protectorate as an Anglo-Protestant warrior-state, much vaunted by Cromwell in a rabidly anti-Spanish oration to parliament, had taken a fatal blow when the 'Western Enterprise' in the Caribbean came to ignominious grief on Hispaniola. And the religious and political anarchy of 1659 had provided a perfect opening for the Restoration monarchy to advertise itself as ensuring strength through a return to order and conformity. This is, indeed, what Clarendon and Archbishop Sheldon genuinely believed: that a return to the unquestioned authority of the Church of England, not some deluded and divisive liberty of conscience, was the best bulwark against the subversion of 'fanatics' – whether Calvinist, Quaker or Catholic. And through the honeymoon years of Charles II's reign, notwithstanding his attempt to pass a Declaration of Indulgence in 1662, the assumption among the vast majority of the county gentry was that this was the staunch opinion of the king as well. Whatever his shortcomings as a model of upstanding Christian propriety, Charles at least went through the motions of Anglican observance, and when taxed with the consequences of his relentless lechery responded disarmingly that he did not believe 'God would damn a man for a little irregular pleasure'.

But elegant flippancy only took you so far. In good times it advanced general merriment, a quality the Restoration consciously promoted against the public grimness of the Protectorate. In bad times, though, the banter could suddenly seem wan and facetious. (Evelyn, the devoted monarchist, quickly sickened of it as so much political confectionery.) The avalanche of misfortune that crashed down on England after 1665 raised questions among the more pious gentry in the shires, who were by no means all unreconstructed Presbyterians, about the seriousness with which Charles took his coronation vow to be the Defender of the Faith. The shamelessness of his debauchery, the squalid promiscuousness with which he took both mistresses and spaniels into his bed (sometimes, it was said not inaccurately, at the same time), undoubtedly had a cumulative effect on men who identified with the supposedly independent, old-fashioned virtues of 'country' as against the licentious sink and rapacious self-promotion of the 'court'. It was an article of country-Cavalier faith that their displeasure with court and courtiers would never affect their allegiance to the king himself. But over the long stretch of bad years, country suspicion and hostility towards those around the king deepened, and with it came anxiety that the king's proverbial laziness, self-indulgence and irresolution (so unlike his sainted father) might yet lead the country into crisis, even before Charles had deigned to notice it. John Evelyn, who always had his ear to the ground when it came to the prejudices of the gentry, echoed them by judging that Charles, who 'would doubtless have been an excellent prince, had he been less addicted to women, who made him uneasy and

Two of the king's favourite mistresses: (above) the French Catholic beauty *Louise de Kéroualle, Duchess of Portsmouth*, by Pierre Mignard, *c.* 1682; (top) her popular Protestant rival, *Nell Gwyn*, by Simon Verelst, *c.* 1680.

always in want to supply their unmeasurable profusion', was sovereign of everything except himself.

Towards the end of the decade, these fears, for a while amorphous and unarticulated, began to take on much crisper definition. There was, to begin with, the disturbing fact of royal childlessness. The barrenness of the Portuguese Catholic queen, Catherine of Braganza – in unhappy contrast to the fecundity of Charles's many mistresses – was surely some sort of punishment laid on the kingdom. If you looked at the world through the correct – which was to say the most conspiratorially acute – lenses, you saw right away something so rotten that it could only have originated in the filthy stews of the Whore of Babylon (aka the Jesuit-ridden Papacy). Fatal sterility and spendthrift concupiscence were part of the same plan – to sap the vitals of sturdy Protestant England.

Fruitlessness led to fretfulness. Without a direct heir, the next in line to the throne was the king's brother, James, Duke of York, whose own confessional allegiances seemed much closer to those of the Queen Mother, Henrietta Maria, still very much alive and very much the unrepentant Catholic, utterly convinced that the downfall of her husband had been his wishful thinking that a strong monarchy could be created in an Anglican, parliamentary country. James, described as 'the most unguarded ogler in England', was every bit as much of an unappetizing lecher as his older brother, but, unlike Charles, managed to alternate hearty bouts of lust with equally fierce orgies of sanctimoniousness. James's first marriage, to Clarendon's daughter Anne Hyde, had shown that he could indeed produce children, at least daughters. Demoted by James's mistresses to an object of ridicule, Anne sought consolation in the Hyde family weakness, the table, and like her father expanded in girth as she declined in dignity. When she died in 1671, leaving the two girls, Mary and Anne, who would both become queen and who resisted their father's efforts to make them follow him back into the arms of the Roman Church, James lost no time in taking a second wife in 1673: the unquestionably Catholic (and strikingly beautiful) Mary of Modena.

With that marriage, and the prospect of a Catholic heir, the threshold of anti-Catholic hysteria dramatically lowered. A year or so earlier, James had gone public for the first time, declaring his return to the Roman Church by conspicuously failing to attend Anglican communion at Easter. This calculated advertisement of his confessional allegiance put the Anglican hierarchy and the gentry in the shires on notice that, unless something changed, they could expect a Papist king and perhaps a Papist dynasty to follow. Hackles rose in Hampshire. Paranoid though the reaction was, had the guardians of the Anglican settlement known the whole truth their suspicions would have turned to apoplexy. For on 25 January 1669 (significantly, the feast of the conversion of St Paul) Charles II had expressed his regrets to his brother that he was not able to profess openly the faith to which he too was genuinely drawn. No one (other than the Pope himself) could have been gladder to hear of this than Louis XIV, who had been targeting his own secret weapon – the glamorous Louise de Kéroualle – directly at the place he knew it was bound to score a direct hit: Charles II's bed. It certainly did no harm to the French king's strategy. For Louise cantered between the royal sheets, routing her rivals, as brilliantly as Louis triumphed on the battlefield, and Charles was helplessly seduced by both of them. Louise bore Charles a son in 1672 and in 1673 was made Duchess of Portsmouth. And in 1670, Charles was grateful enough to sign a clandestine treaty with Louis. Although he was encouraged in this direction by some of his inner circle of ministers – particularly Lord Ashley, Henry Bennet, Lord Arlington, and Thomas Clifford – the terms of the treaty were shocking enough to be kept from the majority of the Privy Council and especially the dourly suspicious Scot, John Maitland, Earl of Lauderdale. This was just as well, since any objective observer would have to conclude that what Charles had done, in his obtuse recklessness, was to mortgage his sovereignty to the king of France, or rather replace dependence on an English parliament by dependence on the bounty of the French purse. In return for a Versailles hand-out, handsome enough to free Charles from the inconvenience of having to go cap in hand every few years to parliament, the English king had committed himself to easing the conditions of English Catholics and perhaps, when a suitable occasion arose, even declaring his own true confessional allegiance. And there was more. Charles had committed himself to joining Louis's surprise attack on the Protestant Dutch Republic, a policy much easier to justify in England as payback for the humiliation of 1667.

To suggestions that some sort of deal had been made with France, Charles II simply lied, flatly denying there had been any under-the-table treaty. In fact, the provisions of the secret Treaty of Dover exceeded the most feverish nightmares of anti-Catholic conspiracy theorists. The birthright that Charles had casually bartered away   was, after all, not his to give away but parliament's. And there was still worse. Had the king bothered to reflect in any detail on the issues that had caused so much grief for his father in 1641, he might have recalled that the suspicion that Charles I was about to call in a foreign, Catholic (Irish) army had been top of the list. That had been the red rag waved at the parliamentary bull, which more than anything else had provoked them to strip the king of his control of the militia. It had, in fact, triggered the civil war. So what did his son do in 1670 but agree to the importation of *French* troops in the event of facing his own domestic rebellion?

Some of Charles's ministers who led him into this suicidally reckless stratagem

THE STUART, ORANGE AND HANOVERIAN DYNASTIES

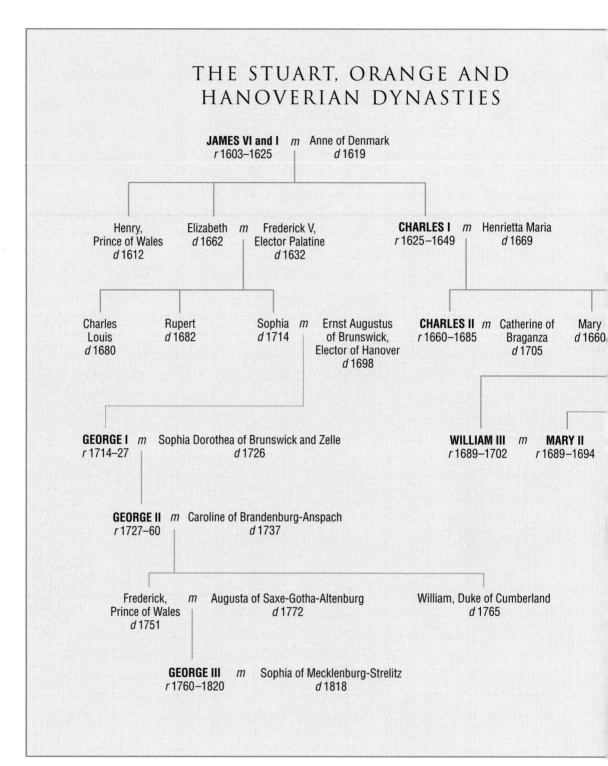

JAMES VI and I   *m*   Anne of Denmark
r 1603–1625   *d* 1619

Henry,   Elizabeth   *m*   Frederick V,   **CHARLES I**   *m*   Henrietta Maria
Prince of Wales   *d* 1662   Elector Palatine   *r* 1625–1649   *d* 1669
d 1612   *d* 1632

Charles   Rupert   Sophia   *m*   Ernst Augustus   **CHARLES II**   *m*   Catherine of   Mary
Louis   *d* 1682   *d* 1714   of Brunswick,   *r* 1660–1685   Braganza   *d* 1660
d 1680   Elector of Hanover   *d* 1705
                                                   d 1698

GEORGE I   *m*   Sophia Dorothea of Brunswick and Zelle   **WILLIAM III**   *m*   **MARY II**
r 1714–27   *d* 1726   *r* 1689–1702   *r* 1689–1694

GEORGE II   *m*   Caroline of Brandenburg-Anspach
r 1727–60   *d* 1737

Frederick,   *m*   Augusta of Saxe-Gotha-Altenburg   William, Duke of Cumberland
Prince of Wales   *d* 1772   *d* 1765
d 1751

GEORGE III   *m*   Sophia of Mecklenburg-Strelitz
r 1760–1820   *d* 1818

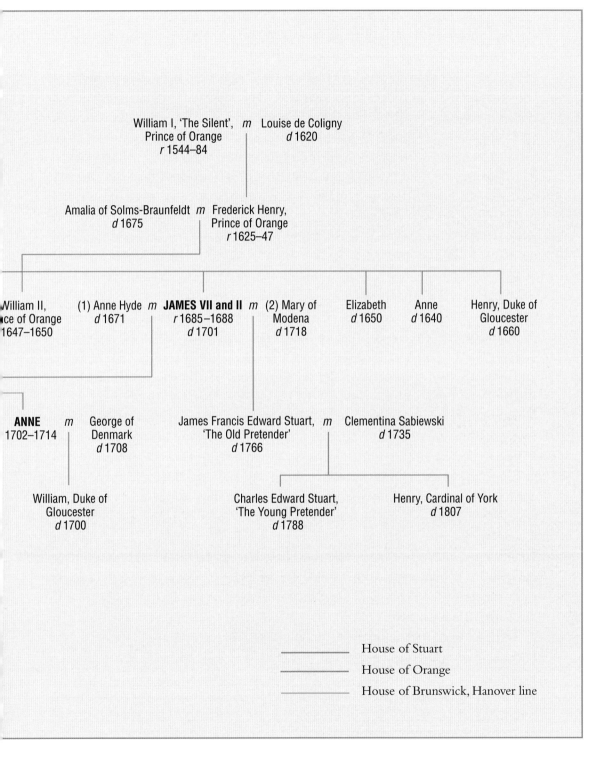

William I, 'The Silent', *m* Louise de Coligny
Prince of Orange   *d* 1620
r 1544–84

Amalia of Solms-Braunfeldt *m* Frederick Henry,
d 1675   Prince of Orange
r 1625–47

William II,   (1) Anne Hyde *m* **JAMES VII and II** *m* (2) Mary of   Elizabeth   Anne   Henry, Duke of
nce of Orange   *d* 1671   *r* 1685–1688   Modena   *d* 1650   *d* 1640   Gloucester
1647–1650   *d* 1701   *d* 1718   *d* 1660

ANNE   *m*   George of   James Francis Edward Stuart, *m* Clementina Sabiewski
1702–1714   Denmark   'The Old Pretender'   *d* 1735
            d 1708   *d* 1766

William, Duke of   Charles Edward Stuart,   Henry, Cardinal of York
Gloucester   'The Young Pretender'   *d* 1807
d 1700   *d* 1788

House of Stuart
House of Orange
House of Brunswick, Hanover line

had their own reasons. Clifford, as it would be discovered before he committed suicide, was a secret Catholic. Lord Arlington probably was, too, although he justified the
Declaration of Indulgence of March 1672 essentially as a measure designed to
strengthen, not weaken, the security of the state, especially against Nonconformists
notorious for their unreconciled republicanism. For while the Declaration meant that
Catholics were now allowed to worship in *private* houses (a detail that did nothing to
allay suspicions), Dissenters, ostensibly receiving even-handed treatment, were
required to apply for the official licensing of their places of gathering and worship.

The dramatic, undeclared opening of Charles's second war against the Dutch in
May 1672 and the success of both English warships and Louis XIV's armies, who
occupied two-thirds of the country, reducing the most powerful state in the world to
chaos, was such an unalloyed source of gloating to patriotic opinion, still smarting
from the débâcle of 1667, that for a while it silenced questions about the king's
motives for issuing the Declaration of Indulgence. But quite quickly the war deterio-
rated and with it any kind of consensus. The young Prince of Orange, William III,
took over as the Captain and Admiral-General of the panic-stricken Dutch Republic,
on the brink, so it seemed, of annihilation. The scapegoats of the nightmare, the
brothers De Witt, who had led the Republic to the great victory of 1667 and then
into this catastrophe, were physically torn to pieces on the streets of The Hague.
William, who had been kept powerless by Jan De Witt, shed no tears. But nor did he
capitulate to the aggression. Instead of coming to terms, as expected, with the kings of
France and England (both of whom were his relatives), William became an overnight
Protestant hero by rallying his Fatherland to all-out defiant resistance. Flattering comparisons were made with his great-grandfather, William the Silent. The dykes were
once again cut, as they had been almost exactly a century before, and Louis XIV's
army, like Philip II's, became literally bogged down. Instead of mopping up resistance,
it sank into the peaty mire. Dutch fleets began to inflict brutal attacks on English and
French ships, and very quickly the war consensus inside the English government
unravelled as defeats presented irresistible opportunities for critics among the country
party to present the botched war and the Declaration of Indulgence as a sell-out to
the Gallo-Catholic menace.

The incoming administration, committed to making a separate peace with the
Dutch and reversing the Declaration of Indulgence, was led by Thomas Osborne,
shortly to be Lord Danby. Although every bit as ambitious and self-seeking as the
men he replaced, Danby was the very first English politician to present himself to the
nation, quite self-consciously, as the Voice of the Shires: the country gentleman's
friend and mouthpiece, fiercely Anglican, staunchly conservative, unquestionably

royalist, but in an English, not a Frenchified, way. His government set its seal on power by forcing (on pain of denying the king revenues) the rescinding of the Declaration of Indulgence. In its place was put an anti-Catholic Test Act, which required all holders of any public office – including magistrates, members of parliament and officers of state, or of the army and navy – to deny the Catholic doctrine of transubstantiation and to conform in every way with the Anglican settlement. Thus the two pillars of Charles's rapprochement with Louis – toleration for Catholics and the anti-Dutch war – were simultaneously shattered. Privately, Charles let his regrets be known but complained that his hands were tied by parliament. Privately, Louis thought any king who would permit such contemptible insolence was hardly worthy of the office. Most incomprehensible of all to him was Charles's willingness to see his own brother, the next in line to the throne, deprived of his high office as Lord High Admiral for refusing to take a 'Test' imposed on royal blood by a noisy rabble of presumptuous commoners.

After the upheaval of 1672–3, the five years of the Danby regime that followed are often presented as some sort of placid recuperation, in which the potentially explosive nature of anti-Catholicism had been neutralized by heavy doses of Anglican rectitude and all around happiness with the status quo. By this account the even more tumultuous, near-revolutionary crisis that followed the 'revelation' of the fake Popish Plot came out of a clear blue sky as well as out of the criminally paranoid brains of Titus Oates and Israel Tonge. But their bizarre allegations of Catholic plots to assassi-nate the king and replace him with the Duke of York could not possibly have sent the country into the most extreme political convulsion it had experienced since the civil war unless the ground had been very well prepared in the preceding years. For if Danby's original claim to power had rested on his promise to purge the body politic of anything resembling pro-French Catholicism, many of his critics came to the conclusion that the remedy seemed worse than the disease. Danby's management of members of parliament as something like a 'Crown' party; his manipulation of patron-age conditional on political obedience; his attempt to make office-holders sign a formal renunciation of any resistance to the monarch on any grounds; and his will-ingness to perpetuate, indefinitely, the life of the already long-lived Cavalier Parliament of 1661, all seemed evidence that he was actually making English govern-ment over in the image of the absolutism he professed to abhor.

These critics were not altogether wrong. Before the 1670s, opposition to gov-ernments had been moved by, and expressed in, dislike of particular men (Strafford or Clarendon) and particular measures (ship money). Not since 1640–42 had politics been articulated in such sharply ideological terms. And it was the adversaries of the power of the Crown, so apparently entrenched by Danby, who made the going. Lord Shaftesbury, who as Anthony Ashley Cooper had been successively a Barebone's MP, a Cromwellian Councillor of State and a Restoration Chancellor of the Exchequer, has been seen as the epitome of the scoundrelly opportunist, reaching for whatever politics was most likely to propel him into power and keep him there. And Shaftesbury was certainly not free of opportunism. He had, after all, been evicted from office by Danby and was impatient for revenge. But without perverting the truth too indecently, Shaftesbury could, as he began to don the mantle of the Guardian of the Ancient Constitution, plausibly claim to be revolving back to the principles that had begun his political career: the Cromwellian polity sketched out in the Humble Petition and Advice of 1657 of a 'government of a single person and [a bicameral] parliament'. There was, after all, a rich historical tradition to draw on, stretching back even beyond the Provisions of Oxford and Magna Carta to the purported Saxon *witangemot*, which insisted that royal power had always rested on conciliar consent. What made the royal polity of England English, and especially un-French, was that it had always been a contract. This is what the Stuarts, misled by councillors like Danby who hoped to swell their own fortunes on the back of an over-mighty sovereignty, failed to understand. Any subject expecting to be protected from the ever present Catholic-tyrannical menace across the Channel by Crown-engrossers such as Danby was deceived. For only under an authentically English mixed monarchy, one prepared to concede that sovereignty was shared among king, Lords and Commons, could the liberties of the people and the Protestant Church be truly safeguarded.

During the 1670s, precisely because Danby's domination of parliament was so successful and the royalist ideology of divine right and non-resistance so entrenched, those who begged to differ had to look elsewhere to broadcast their competing view of the constitution. So it was in the streets, coffee-houses, clubs, taverns and printing shops rather than at Westminster that in the 1670s the rough prototype of party politics was born. Clubs like Shaftesbury's Green Ribbon, meeting at the King's Head tavern in Chancery Lane, where like-minded members could convince themselves of the wickedness of the Crown party and the existence of a Catholic conspiracy, multiplied, so that by the time the Popish Plot broke there were no fewer than twenty-nine such clubs in London alone and the most successful produced provincial affiliates in towns like Taunton, Bristol and Oxford. London's rapidly multiplying coffee-houses offered, as one astonished visitor from Florence testified, snug alcoves where news could be thirstily digested, along with one's coffee or chocolate, quite free of official censure or intimidation. Some were famous hotbeds of gossip, among them Hooke's and Wren's favourite, Garway's in Change Alley, London (where tea was introduced to

England along with constitutional radicalism), and Aubrey's Rainbow in Fleet Street. The clash of polemics during the 1670s had fuelled a phenomenal resurgence in the business of multiple-copied 'separates' and intelligences on politics that streamed out into the provinces from London, and that made exhilarating reading compared to the drearily official *Gazette*. Between 1679 and 1682 no less than seventeen new newspapers would be founded, most of them expressly to promote a party view. Other spectres of political life of the 1640s and 1650s returned to harass Charles II as they had Charles I and Cromwell. Petitioning movements, which had not been seen since the Commonwealth, began to be mobilized again, especially when some sort of Catholic bogey was the motivator. Apprentice gangs – the sons of men who had taken to the streets in the 1640s – now reappeared with all their old, violent energy. Satirical poems, squibs and broadsides, which had long been available to high-placed patrons, now put on their street dress: ballads and bawdy verse hawked in the taverns. The theatrical innuendo became an art form. The galleries waited for it, then lapped it up, hooted and brayed with pleasure. And none of the scribblers could complain that Charles II had failed to provide them with rich material.

None of this, it has been well said (though perhaps too often), yet amounted to anything like a world divided by recognizably *modern* party politics. Loyalties were still notoriously fickle, their protagonists quite capable of switching sides at the drop of a hat. None the less, the embattled ideologies – divine right kingship and the 'mixed' monarchy – did represent two genuinely and mutually incompatible visions of what the authentic political constitution of England had been and ought to be. Whigs, in particular, liked to reach back to medieval statutes to emphasize the continuity of a peculiar English tradition, Shaftesbury insisting that 'the parliament of England is that Supreme and absolute power which gives life and Motion to the English government', the patriotic mantra drummed home over and over. Conversely, each of them identified their opponents as embodying politics that were, literally as well as metaphorically, foreign to England. Which is why the aggressively and self-consciously English antagonists in this war of ideas reached for the most unsavoury foreign labels they could think of by which to demonize their opponents, namely something associated with either the Scots or the Irish. Thus (a few years later during the Exclusion crisis surrounding James's succession), the defenders of Crown supremacy took to name-calling those whom they accused of dragging the country back to a civil war as Scots-Presbyterian outlaws or 'Whiggamores', and the Whigs returned the compliment by claiming that behind the disingenuous arguments to stand by Church and throne, their adversaries were nothing more than Irish-Catholic rebels or 'Tories', from the Gaelic *toraighe*, meaning a bog-trotter or bandit.

During the 1670s something much more serious than traded abuse was going on in English politics. Positions were hardening and polemics flying. No one in 1678 was ready to predict, much less desire, a new civil war. But equally no one thought that some sort of fundamental crisis about the government of England, some sort of 'revolution' in fact (in the contemporary sense of the term), was likely to be averted, so long as the heir apparent remained the avowedly Catholic, suspiciously quasi-absolutist James, Duke of York. In 1677, before Titus Oates ever opened his mouth, the MP for Hull, the poet Andrew Marvell, neither the most credulous nor the most opportunist of Englishmen, who had come of age, politically, in the Protectorate, let it be known in print that 'There has now for divers Years, a Design been carried on, to change the Lawful Government of England into an Absolute Tyranny, and to Convert the Established Protestant Religion into down-right Popery.'

The fact that the kind of convictions expressed in Marvell's *Account of the Growth of Popery and Arbitrary Government in England* were so commonplace helps to explain the otherwise astoundingly hysterical response to Oates's 'revelations' of a plot, master-minded by the Jesuits, to murder the king (some of his 'informants' believed by the knife, others by poison), to replace him with the Duke of York and to institute a French-Catholic absolutist state supported by French troops. The allegations were, of course, a pack of ugly lies, but they were artfully concocted ugly lies. Titus Oates was a monster of malignant ingenuity, but he was no fool. His active homosexuality had ensured that in his twenty-nine years there was virtually no major English institution from which he had not been ejected: his Cambridge college (Gonville and Caius); his Church of England ministry in Kent; the navy, where he had signed on as chaplain to avoid perjury charges incurred while a curate; and finally he had been thrown out of the Jesuit colleges Colegio de los Inglese Valladolid, in Spain, and St Omer, in France, where he had gone as a purported convert. All of these places, of course, had offered Oates both irresistible opportunities and draconian penalties. But in his relatively short scapegrace life Oates had already shown himself to be an accomplished predator who, even when found out, managed somehow to avoid the worst consequences of his malice.

He was clever enough, in fact, to turn the latest notoriety, expulsion by the Jesuits, into something like evidence of both knowledge and integrity! As Oates rolled off his fantastic whoppers, it does not seem to have occurred to anyone to wonder whether or not his rough treatment at the hands of the Jesuits (though not as rough as the navy) might not have been a motive for a campaign of personal revenge. Shamelessly, Oates claimed that he had only gone over to St Omer as a kind of spiritual double-agent, the better to plumb their nefarious designs on the liberties and

Church of England. And to give this outlandish claim more credibility, Oates acted as though he was indeed some sort of self-appointed spy, keeping as many careful notes and records of conversations with the Jesuits and their hireling assassins, both at home and abroad, as Robert Hooke or John Evelyn made of their experiments and their gardens. Oates was, in his own repulsive way, a *virtuoso,* lavishing as much attention and care on the fabrication of truth as the natural philosophers paid to the acquiring of it. In fact, the first person to whom Oates confided his knowledge of the Plot, the London clergyman Israel Tonge, flattered himself with the reputation of a scholar (he did in fact have an authentic doctorate) and kept company with some of the most eminent of the Fellows of the Royal Society. This did not, however, make Tonge rational, since he subscribed to the popular fantasy that the Great Fire of London had been started by Catholic arsonists. And it was that conflagration that had destroyed Tonge's vicarage along with his library of natural philosophy – had, in fact, ruined his life.

It was because Tonge had such powerful connections that he managed to get Oates an audience with the king himself to hear the shocking substance of the forty-three articles of the conspiracy. Charles was, understandably, incredulous; but his initial amusement at the improbability of the whole story, not least the incrimination of the queen's doctor, gradually gave way to enough anxiety to send the matter on to Danby. In the last week of September 1678 Oates appeared before the full Privy Council, and his apparent mastery of minutiae convinced some of them at least that there might be something to the story, however fantastic it seemed at first.

Oates knew his public. He had mixed into his story exactly the kind of sensationalism the suggestibly anti-Catholic public loved to hear: arson, poison, criminal doctors, wicked queens, malevolent monks. And as details leaked out, the story took fire like lightning striking dry leaves. The high-ups fanned the flames. Whether he believed it or not (and there is no reason to suppose he did not believe it) Shaftesbury saw it as Danby's come-uppance and railed against the first minister, who, while pretending to keep the country safe from Catholic intrigue, had actually invited it. At this stage, sceptics were still attempting to keep the thin walls of common sense from collapsing altogether. But two pieces of unexpected good luck for Oates ensured the rout of reason. First, one of the innumerable figures named in his list of the wicked, the Duchess of York's secretary, Edward Coleman, had actually corresponded with Louis XIV's confessor about the chances of a Catholic restoration in England – not in itself an act of criminal treason, rather an act of criminal stupidity, since Coleman had failed to destroy the letters and left them to be easily decoded. Even better, on 17 October, the body of Sir Edmund Berry Godfrey was found on the grassy slopes of Primrose Hill. Godfrey just happened to be the magistrate who had first taken Oates's sworn deposition about the plot. Speculation that he might have committed suicide rapidly gave way to a verdict that Godfrey had been murdered. Only the most ingenious and desperate thought that the culprits had actually belonged to the *anti-Catholic* hue and cry, trying to provoke a violent reaction.

If that were in fact the case they had done their work very well, since Godfrey's body was publicly exhibited surrounded by candles, as if he had been martyred in the cause of saving Protestant England. Mania now took possession of the country. Conveniently, November was, thanks to Guy Fawkes, the month for anti-Catholic bonfires. Now the 5 November celebrations turned into massive 'Pope Burnings', some attended by thousands of people. More Pope Burnings took place on 17 November, the anniversary of the accession of Good Queen Bess who had stood strong and steadfast against the Romish threat. The public imagination was gripped by the vision of imaginary Catholic 'night riders' roaming the countryside, looking for Anglican clergymen or justices of the peace to murder. To guard against the threat, apprentice gangs armed themselves, some of them with the 'Edmund Berry Godfrey' daggers that were so popular that 3000 of them had been sold in a day. By the time that Oates appeared before the full House of Commons he was able to state quite categorically and without fear of contradiction that 'there has been and still is a damnable and hellish plot, contrived and carried on by Popish recusants for the assassinating and murdering of the King and for subverting the government and rooting out and destroying the Protestant religion.'

Seeing a genuinely popular movement boiling up from below like some volcanic discharge, Shaftesbury, who had his own paid agents, made sure to channel the energy to his own and his party's advantage. Enthusiastically and inventively perjured 'informants' and 'witnesses' were paraded before parliament, beginning with the swindler and thief, William Bedloe, who claimed to have direct knowledge that Jesuits had killed Godfrey and to have seen his body at the queen's palace at Somerset House. Accusations of treason and murder now moved from known Catholics and priests to alleged 'sympathizers', among them Samuel Pepys. A former servant testified that Pepys had all along been a secret Catholic; and, much more damagingly, another long-time crook, John Scott, swore that he personally knew Pepys to have favoured and advanced Catholic officers in the navy and to have given the French plans of fortifications and ships in preparation for their planned invasion. It was enough to send Pepys to the Tower of London, where John Evelyn dined with him and sympathized with his plight. But it was a back-handed tribute to the plausibility of Oates's conspiracy story that even Fellows of the Royal Society, who were supposed to have no difficulty in recognizing the truth when they saw it, differed among themselves.

A True Narrative of the Horrid Hellish Popish-Plot, the first part ... (detail), 1682. A burlesque on the Popish Plot illustrating 'How Sir Godfrey Berry is Kill'd, his Body they hide ... how Jesuits disguis'd, our Houses do fire; How subtly they Plot, and King's Death Conspire; Of divers Great Lords drawn in ... An Army of Irish, and Pilgrims from Spain'.

For poor Pepys, the whole thing was a tissue of villainy. Evelyn hated Oates no less, but found him regrettably credible. To his credit, Pepys was not prepared to let the infamy roll over him. He fought back by hiring his own investigator, one John Joyne, to ingratiate himself with Scott, follow his movements and produce evidence of his disreputable life – not, as it turned out, a hard task. Pepys survived, unlike the twenty-four innocents who lost their lives to the witch-hunt.

By the end of 1679, after a Pope Burning attended, it was said, by a crowd of 200,000, the ugly energy unleashed by the Plot was converted by Shaftesbury into a specific political programme. Danby's intimidated government had crumbled and he himself faced impeachment unless, Shaftesbury made it clear, a new election was called. Monster petitions were mobilized (again recalling the 1640s); one from London, Southwark and Westminster was 300 feet long and bore 16,000 names. The king conceded. The election – contested in an unprecedented number of boroughs – was fought, sometimes bitterly and violently, and duly produced exactly the over-whelming Whig majority in the Commons that Shaftesbury needed. It came to Westminster, moreover, hot for a specific political goal, Exclusion: the elimination of the Catholic Duke of York (and any heirs he might have with Mary of Modena) from the line of succession. On Charles's death, the crown was to pass instead to his eldest illegitimate son, the Duke of Monmouth. For that matter, so Shaftesbury's propaganda claimed, the Duke was actually no bastard at all but the legitimate heir, since Charles, unbeknownst to everyone at the time and since, had actually married his mistress Lucy Walter during their relationship in Paris.

It was an extraordinary crisis in the life of the British monarchy. At stake were not only the lives of countless hundreds victimized by the lies and hysteria but also the fate of the polity itself. To concede the Exclusion was to accept that parliament had the constitutional authority to judge the fitness or unfitness of a prince to suc-ceed to or occupy the throne. And neither Charles II nor the Tories were about to make that concession. *Patriarcha,* a treatise actually written fifty years before by the Kentish gentleman philosopher Sir Robert Filmer, was now published. It argued that God had directly given earthly authority to Adam, from whom all kings were lineally descended – a direct line of succession that could never be broken by any kind of inferior intervention. Shaftesbury and the Whigs in their turn revived some of the most radical thought surviving from the Commonwealth that insisted on the contrac-tual nature of the monarchy – not least, of course, the first of John Locke's *Two Treatises on Government.* Much of this was too heady for most of the Whig rank and file in the Commons, who were easier with the familiar platitude (recycled, for example, by Denzil Holles, still very much in action) that in England monarchy had always been

Two popular playing cards commemorating the Rye House Plot, 1685, which tried in vain to put Charles II's eldest son on the throne: (left) the loyal people of Taunton pay homage to the Duke of Monmouth; (right) after his capture in the New Forest, Monmouth was beheaded at Tower Hill.

bound by the law, not least its obligation to uphold the coronation oaths, and that parliament most certainly did have a right, not only to judge the degree to which those obligations had been kept but also to 'bind, govern, limit, restrain and govern the descent and inheritance of the Crown'.

Shaftesbury, though, had left his days with Oliver Cromwell far behind. He was no Ireton, not even a Pym. Ultimately he shrank from pushing Exclusion to the point where he might be forced to mobilize a new civil war over it. And the more his side was actually accused by the Crown and the Tories of wanting exactly that outcome, the more Shaftesbury recoiled from it. It was prudence rather than political queasiness that brought him up short before committing the country to a conflict he was doubtful he could ever win.

He was right. But where did that fatal pessimism leave him? Since he was not prepared to contemplate another revolution for a kingless England, Shaftesbury was fatally dependent on the force of public opinion and intimidation persuading Charles II to capitulate voluntarily to Exclusion. But there was something about the extremity to which he had been put that drew from the languid old lecher a demonstration of such political toughness and finesse that it ran rings round Shaftesbury, supposedly the great master of strategy. First, Charles sent his deeply unpopular brother and his wife out of the country, thereby removing from the scene the person who provoked most hatred and fury. But having made a concession, Charles then proceeded to stamp his high heels on the principles that mattered. On the issue of the exclusively royal pre-rogative to rule in matters of succession, Charles was as adamant as Elizabeth had been a century before. If, as seemed all but certain, he died childless, James, Catholic or not, *would* succeed. But – and this was the critical manoeuvre – as long as James insisted on remaining a Catholic, his would have to be a reign with a difference. Whatever his private beliefs, they could not affect the solemn obligation embodied in the coronation oaths to defend and protect the established Protestant Church of England. And to allay the suspicions that had got his father into such irreversible trouble, the Catholic king would have to agree to abstain from making his own appointments to high ecclesiastical office and transfer control of military appoint-ments to parliament.

It was an inspired circumnavigation of the conflict. The Church had surely been saved, without compromising the authority of the Crown in matters regarding suc-cession. And Charles's 'expedient' seemed reasonable enough to begin turning public opinion back towards the king. But when a second Whig-dominated House of Commons was elected (after Charles had dissolved the first), Shaftesbury was too confident in his apparent triumph to notice the slight tremor in the ground under him until it became the gaping fault that swallowed him up. The Commons passed an Exclusion Bill by a two-to-one majority, while the Lords defeated it by the same majority. The deadlock meant that Charles was in a position to call Shaftesbury's bluff, and he coolly proceeded to do so (after having taken the precautionary measure of pocketing another massive hand-out from Louis XIV). In 1681 a third parliament was summoned to Oxford, where the Crown and its enemies had tested their wills in 1258. All sweet reason, Charles tabled his 'expedient' once more, only to have it brushed aside, as he had calculated, by Shaftesbury's insistence on Exclusion. The only way forward now was a resolution by force. Indeed, some of the Whigs showed up at Oxford in arms, while others talked openly of a return to the Commonwealth – exactly the ammunition Charles needed to make his case that it was the Exclusionists, not the loyalists, who were pushing the country towards civil war. In the end, he knew that Shaftesbury just did not have the stomach for a true battle; and just in case he did, with Louis XIV's gold jingling in the royal treasure chest, Charles knew that this time, unlike in 1642, the Crown had the funds to mobilize in a hurry.

So what followed Oxford, as far as the Exclusionists were concerned, was – nothing. With nowhere to go, they divided into those who sharpened their sabres and those who shuffled back in anti climactic gloom to their horses and houses. With the wind shifting smartly, the villains of the piece – the fantastic cast of con-men, cut-throats and repeat-perjurors who comprised the case for the Popish Plot – were the first to smell trouble and promptly turned king's evidence, confessing one by one to the pack of lies. During the trial of George Wakeman, the queen's doctor, Chief Justice Scroggs launched the first attack on Titus Oates's veracity. What might have been a revolution now collapsed. Acquitted of high treason, Shaftesbury fled to Holland where he died in 1683. Oates was arrested in 1684 – for cruising, of course – but the next year was tried for and convicted of perjury, for which he was savagely flogged, set in the pillory and then sent to prison. Never pinned down for long, though, he re-emerged in 1688 and died (what else?) a Baptist preacher.

Buried beneath the débâcle, Shaftesbury left something behind other than a reputation for breathtaking political cynicism, and characteristically the pieces of his legacy were at complete odds with each other. On the one hand, his willingness to patronize and make credible the political theory of John Locke and other exponents of a contract theory of government had given a new lease of life to genuinely radical ideas, which, it had been assumed, had perished for good in 1659. The notion that the government derived its legitimacy not just from its capacity to protect (as Hobbes had argued), nor simply from scriptural authority (as Filmer had insisted) but from the consent of the governed as well, who, when they entrusted it with power, had *not* thereby surrendered their natural rights of liberty and property, would have an extraordinary future ahead of it. The proposition that 'Every form of Government is of our Creation,' wrote Locke, 'and not God's and must comply with the safety of the people in all that it can' was still radical and even shocking. But it was no longer unusual or outlandish to read or hear it uttered. Nor was the allied axiom that in entrusting a government (or a monarch) with authority, those from whom it ultimately derived ought not to be assumed to be alienating their rights to call it to account, should it grossly exceed its lawful authority; should it, in fact, pass from authority to tyranny, or even flout the liberties it was appointed to protect. Perhaps these arguments may have stayed marginal to English politics for the best part of another century. But across the Atlantic, the refusal of southern New Englanders to truckle to what they saw as the 'arbitrary' power of the royal governor of all New England, Sir Edmund Andros, and instead to set out on a self-authorized exodus to

Connecticut, already showed that the seeds sown in the rich but unsavoury soil of the Exclusion crisis could bear fruit.

Ironically, though, what the founding fathers of Connecticut were objecting to was precisely the aggressive manipulation of official authority that was *also* Shaftesbury's legacy. For during his brief period in power, he had out-Danbyed Danby by using every conceivable political lever – patronage, bribery, judicial intimidation and a massive print propaganda campaign in the now uncensored press – to build what he and the Whigs hoped would be an invincible political machine. And this was the machine that was conveniently handed over to Charles II and his new ministers – in particular Laurence Hyde, Earl of Rochester (Clarendon's son), and Robert Spencer, Earl of Sunderland – who used it to build massive ramparts around the restored authority of the monarchy. The years from 1683 to 1688 were years of packings and purges. Town corporations suspected of being unfriendly to the succession were required to turn over their charters, which were duly amended to produce more obliging local governments. Unhelpful judges were weeded out, zealous Tories rewarded with place and favour. It was all very carefully engineered, and with a veneer of legality; but between them Charles II and his last government managed to build a machine of state power the likes of which his father and grandfather (or for that matter Protector Cromwell) could scarcely have dreamed. But then they had lived in what now seemed an incomprehensibly remote age, driven by passions and clouded by pious prejudices. Men like Sunderland, though, were modern political animals, whose understanding of humanity presupposed the usefulness of the baser, regrettably universal instincts of greed, ambition and egotism. Shaftesbury, when all was said and done, had come from a generation of men who fancied themselves technicians of administration. Sunderland and his kind, on the other hand, were the first modern political managers for whom money was the lubricant of power.

They knew, moreover, all about the tactical deployment of half-truths and bogeymen. If there were any murmuring of protest from the shires about the high-handed and arbitrary interference in local affairs, all they had to do was to invoke the dreadful spectre of Cromwellian revolution and they could expect the gentry to shut up and pass the port. In 1683 a group of republicans – among them two aristocrats, Algernon Sidney and Lord William Russell, as well as the ex-Leveller John Wildman – frustrated and embittered by Shaftesbury's betrayal, turned to conspiracy instead in an attempt to put Monmouth on the throne. As soon as this Rye House Plot was discovered, the government realized that it was a gift, not a threat. The principals were beheaded for treason, Sidney heroically insisting, in a letter to the Sheriff of London written on the eve of his execution, that 'God had left Nations to the Liberty of setting up such

Governments as best pleas'd themselves' and that 'Magistrates were set up for the good of Nations, not Nations for the honour of Magistrates'. Armed with such incendiary confessions, the government could defend its aggressive policy of interference in town charters, its packings and purgings, as a matter of state security.

But for the misfortune of having to leave the earthly world he had enjoyed only too visibly and too much, Charles II could die in February 1685 in the satisfying knowledge that he had made the realm safe for the monarchy. Evelyn's last sight of the king was, for him, a depressing spectacle, 'unexpressable luxury, & prophaneners gaming & all dissolution, and as it were total forgetfullnesse of God (it being Sunday Evening) ... the King, sitting & toying with his Concubines Portsmouth [and] Cleveland ... A French boy singing love songs, in that glorious Gallery, whilst about 20 of the greate Courtiers & other dissolute persons were at Basset round a large table, a bank of at least 2000 in Gold before them ... a sense of utmost vanity.' There was always time, though, Charles must have reckoned, for repentance. At the last he accepted his brother's offer to be received back into the arms of the Mother Church, confessed his sins (or a necessarily abbreviated digest of them) and was duly granted the Catholic rite of absolution. And Charles might have taken even the privacy of this last little ceremony as a happy instance of how the Stuart monarchy might survive within an Anglican kingdom. How wrong his mother had been and how well this boded for the prospects of his brother! All James had to do was to abide by the intelligently laid-out limits within which he was free to practise his confession; accept the fact of parliamentary elections without having to surrender his prerogative (in, for example, a choice of ministers) to them; defer to parliament in military and ecclesiastical appointments; and then sit back on a throne cushioned by common sense.

At first, it seemed that this was precisely what would happen. Although it suited later Whig history to argue that, from the very beginning, James II was an alien, un-English presence in the body politic, bound to end in expulsion, there was, in fact, nothing inevitable at all about what finally unfolded. (Indeed, even *after* William of Orange's landing at Torbay on 5 November 1688, James, had he behaved intelligently, might easily have kept his throne.) One of the new king's first acts was to promise to William Sancroft, Archbishop of Canterbury, that he would 'undertake nothing against the religion which is established by law', but adding, rather ominously 'unless you first break your word to me'. And it was evident, moreover, from the largely uncontested elections of 1685 and the favourable Tory-monarchist majority returned that James had inherited the continuing groundswell of public loyalty left by his brother. When the Duke of Monmouth attempted an insurrection in the West

Country (at the same time as a rising led by the Duke of Argyll in Scotland) to make Exclusion a fact by force of arms, he was defeated as much by the massive indifference of the vast majority of the population as by his own military and political ineptness. Even the brutal 'Bloody Assizes', presided over by the enthusiastic hanging Judge George Jeffreys, remains more notorious in subsequent Whig history than at the time, when rows of gibbets were nothing special in the political culture.

Unreconciled Whigs could reassure themselves that in the end, Death, the Great Excluder, would win the battle for them. For James was fifty-two when he became king, middle-aged, if not actually rather elderly by the standards of the seventeenth century, and still without a son. His heirs were his two daughters by Anne Hyde, Mary and Anne, both of whom had ignored their father and remained Protestant. In 1677, Mary had been married off by Danby to none other than the Prince of Orange, soon to be William III, now cast (and for good reason) as the international hero of Protestant resistance to the aggressive Catholic expansionism of Louis XIV. William's story, moreover, was known in England through the brilliantly produced propaganda histories of the war of 1672, complete with graphic illustrations by the geniuses of Dutch history prints, Romeyn de Hooghe and Abraham de Wicquevoort. In these unforgettable images the French-Catholic troops of Louis XIV are depicted, much like the Spanish a century before, as subhuman marauders, revelling in rape and mutilation (impaled babies, eviscerated pregnant mothers, roughed-up grandpas – the usual thing), while the invariably fat, gloating friars sing masses in Protestant churches reconsecrated to Rome.

It was exactly this ominous sense of the resurrection of an international war of religion, and the unsettling sense that he had got himself marooned on the wrong side that were to be James's undoing. His brother had bequeathed him a state constructed from pragmatic ingenuity. But surely God had anointed him with the holy oil for purposes other than just lubricating the wheels and cogs of power? If, after all his family's troubles and travels, the Almighty had seen fit to set him on the throne, how could he turn aside from doing His will? And doing it urgently.

It was hard, at first, to take this intensity of mission seriously. For all his dark solemnity James seemed to behave, in crucially telling respects, precisely like his brother, sleeping with his mistress Catherine Sedley even while making a parade of openly going to Mass. Surely, then, this was a man, whatever his coarse humourlessness, who understood the arts of convenience, political as well as sexual. Why ruin a good thing? What was *wrong* with the 'arrangement' made by Charles II – that James would not be expected to enforce the penalties against Catholics so long as he made no attempt to repeal them?

James II, after Sir Godfrey Kneller, *c.* 1688.

But the temperamental difference between the two sons of Charles I *was* genuine and did have serious implications for the political fate of Britain. Hard-boiled though he could be, Charles II was by nature a pluralist, someone who was quite prepared to listen to people with whom he did not necessarily agree (other than Shaftesbury, that is). But if Charles accepted, to some extent, variety, James was relentlessly single-minded. Not surprisingly, he was proud of inventing a 'Universal Sauce' made from parsley, dry toast and vinegar, and beaten in a mortar, which he thought equally suitable for dishes of fish, flesh and fowl. If they were ground fine enough, and with enough perseverance, he may have supposed he could make his own views of Church and state palatable to his people. He could not, in all conscience, remain content with the bounds set by his brother. From the beginning of his reign he chafed at them. James's goal was not, of course, to force England back to Rome overnight. The slightest historical acquaintance with the ill-starred reign of Mary Tudor made that course of action obviously undesirable. But he certainly meant to go beyond the timid attempt of his brother in 1672 to allow Catholics some relief from the penal laws and the practice of their religion within their own four walls. He made it clear to Sancroft and the bishops, as well as to his Tory ministers, that he would be satisfied with nothing less than free and open public worship. And he was not going to forget the humiliation of his own ejection from office as a result of the Test Act. It should either be repealed, or what he claimed to be the 'dispensing power' of his royal prerogative could be used to publish a Declaration in effect suspending it, along with the other penalties for Catholic and Nonconformist practice.

But that 'dispensing' power had already been judged illegal in both 1662 and 1672 when Charles II had advanced his much more cautious measures. So why James should have imagined that the High Church and Tory country gentlemen who had flocked to the Stuart cause against Shaftesbury and Monmouth should now change their minds was a mystery. Equally, James over-rated the ease with which he could persuade his natural constituency that there was nothing untoward in reopening the formal relations with Rome, sundered since the 1530s, nor in re-establishing four Apostolic vicars-general for England, nor in appointing Catholic officers in the army and navy. And why did he imagine that he could make the English people, whose anti-Catholic prejudices had certainly not been leavened by the exposure of Oates's fraud, accept the overnight visibility of Catholic practice – monks and nuns in their habits, public processions on feast days, churches echoing again with the sounds of the Mass? But by 1687 James was no longer listening – at least with any degree of attentiveness – to the voices of reason. He was issuing warnings and veiled threats to the bishops that they had better not think about opposing his will, or 'I shall find a way to do my business without you.' James was listening to the voices in his head. And they were singing Hosannas.

At which point a word of warning is in order. What then unfolded was not a simple struggle between the forces of reaction and progress, between benighted absolutism and constitutional liberalism. That was certainly the history of the 'Glorious Revolution' that the Whigs liked to tell. But the Whigs were only the principal and not the exclusive beneficiaries of that revolution (there was a large bloc of Tories in the post-revolution parliament), and they certainly did not bring it about. What made the difference between the fiasco of the Exclusion crisis and the victory of 1688 was the fact that *Tory* England – the bishops, the peers and the country gentry – was driven, despite its adherence to the doctrines of non-resistance, to resist. Among the famous 'Seven' who issued an invitation to William to come to England to secure a 'free parliament' and the Church of England was none other than that ultimate anti-Whig, Danby. For the Tory commitment to obey had never been unconditional. Obedience to *lawful* commands was their watchword. And by January 1688 they had become convinced that it was James who was the real revolutionary, who sought to overturn everything the Restoration had stood for, and who now had at all costs to be stopped. Even the staunchest Tory allowed that it might be possible for a king to unking *himself* (as Edward II had done), so sundering the bonds of loyalty tying subject to monarch.

Well, *was* James a revolutionary? To consider calmly and dispassionately what the two sides in the confrontation of 1687–8 actually stood for is to scramble all our conventional clichés about the good, the bad and the constitutional. Whatever else 1688–90 may have been it was certainly not, as Macaulay thought, a Manichaean struggle between the forces of light and darkness. Many of the things that are said about James are extrapolations from the received wisdom that he got what he deserved; that the long-nosed face (which actually was no more or less 'haughty' than any other portrait type of that period) betrays a man of incurably despotic temper. Not all of this image is wrong. James had obviously not graduated from the same charm school as his brother. But he was at least as intelligent as Charles, had shown himself more competent in naval battle and was, without question, a lot more conscientious in his attention to government. Much of the stereotype of the brutal autocrat is a projection backwards from the story written by the winners. There is no question whatsoever, of course, that James was indeed a divine-right absolutist who believed that parliament had the right to offer advice and criticism and even propose legislation, but that he had the right if he so chose to reject all of it and to have that be the end of the matter. But the *cause* for which James was apt to get stirred up was, after all, toleration, that 'liberty of conscience' that Cromwell had so often warbled about, only extended, unlike the Cromwellian state, to Catholics. No wonder, then, that some of James's warmest allies were not just Catholics, but dissenters like the Quaker William Penn the younger. And by no means all the men of science and reason were to be found in the camp of his enemies. Pepys, for one, James's Secretary of the Navy and the epitome of humane reasonableness, remained loyal to the bitter end. It is odd, in fact, that while in conventional histories the European 'enlightened despots' of the *eighteenth* century, like Frederick the Great and the Emperor Joseph II, get credit for *imposing* toleration on their subjects, the same benefit is not extended to James II. In Ireland, James was the first English king who actually made a strenuous and politically dangerous effort to reverse the brutal wars of colonization that had disfigured the country and dispossessed its native landowners since at least the reign of Elizabeth I. His cardinal sin, to Macaulay, was that he unaccountably appeared to favour the people whom the Victorian historian called the 'aboriginals'. Conversely, those who opposed James were essentially held together in a classically Cromwellian alliance of bigotry, as the war of 1689–90 would make unequivocally clear.

But – as so often before in this story of the British wars of religion – having registered all these caveats, it is equally important to understand what the Whigs got *right*. Their suspicion that James's benevolence in extending toleration beyond Catholics to the 'fanatick' Nonconformist sects was a tactical rather than a whole-hearted gesture was not unfounded. Suppose, those sceptics might have argued, the king's dispensation of the Test Act allowed full and open Catholic practice and teaching, so that the Roman Church would (as James made no secret of hoping) be in a position to reconvert England by persuasion; what would such an England actually look like? Was Louis XIV's France, for God's sake, internationally famous for its tolerant atmosphere? Was France a kingdom where all manner of Christians could peaceably profess their confession? All the sceptics had to do was to point to the most infamous act of Louis's reign, which took place in the same year as James's accession (and together with the usual French hand-out to the Stuarts): the uprooting and expulsion of the entire Huguenot community of France. This was not something that was seen in England as a remote and unimportant act. The saga of the cruelly treated Huguenots, together with their exodus to Protestant lands – especially the Netherlands – was an event which actually *defined* allegiances in the mid-1680s and that seemed to point towards the inevitability of another pan-European war. Among the places in which the Huguenot diaspora settled with its immense treasury of wealth, skill and talent was, of course, London. It was not just fellow Dissenters who made them welcome. Henry Compton, the Bishop of London –

who incurred so much of James's displeasure that he had him removed from his diocese – was the foremost organizer of relief for the stricken refugees. And, of course, their story was told and retold over and over again in the pathetic images produced by the Dutch engravers and writers.

Not surprisingly, then, Nonconformists were not at all united in gratitude to James for his efforts on their behalf. Presbyterians in particular warned against accepting favours from the king who, in the end, was committed to a Church and an absolutist style of monarchy that was to its very marrow deeply intolerant. In Ireland, where he had a free hand politically, toleration of Protestant dissent was actually banned. And James's virtual declaration of war on the traditional English institutions that presumed to oppose his will – the universities, the bishops and the judiciary – and the ferocity with which he fulminated against them did not suggest a prince who was truly interested in a tolerant, spiritually pluralist commonwealth. 'Get you gone!' he told the Fellows of Magdalen College, when he expelled them from their fellowships after they had opposed his nomination of a Catholic to be their President. 'Know I am your King. I will be obeyed, and I command you to be gone. Go and admit the Bishop of Oxford, Head, Principal, what do you call it, of the College … I mean President of the College. Let them that refuse it look to it. They shall feel the weight of their sovereign's displeasure.'

There was a middle way open to James (as there had been for Charles I), and it was urged on him by William Penn. Settle for *de facto* toleration without insisting on the formal repeal of the Test Act, he pleaded, and all those whom you have dangerously alienated in Church and shires will return to their natural loyalty. But James II had, in effect, decided to ditch them in the belief that somehow a coalition of opposites – Catholics, ultra-monarchists and Dissenters – could see him through the crisis. He doubtless imagined that he was imitating his brother's firmness in 1680-81. In that instance, however, Charles had drawn to him the majority of the political country, while James was in the process of alienating it. It had been Shaftesbury who had boxed himself into an untenable corner through his inflexibility. Now it was James's turn to do the same, with equally calamitous results. In hindsight it seems incredible that the king could have seriously hoped to offset the enormous power of both the Whig and Tory gentry and aristocracy by so improbable an alliance of Catholics and Dissenters. But his trump card, he must have believed, was the potency of the royal mystique. By invoking the supreme authority of the Crown, which the Tories had for so long themselves trumpeted, James hoped at the very least to divide them and to take enough of them along with him to dispense with the Test Act, pass his new Declaration of Indulgence, without parliamentary approval if necessary, and agree to accept Catholic officers in the army. And, in fact, the idea was not so fabulously far-fetched. The Marquis of Halifax had been dismissed in October 1685 for refusing to go along with the pro-Catholic plans, but Sunderland stayed. The tug of loyalty to the Stuarts for which so many old Cavalier families had fought and suffered was very strong, and had James exploited it with more cool intelligence and a modicum of flexibility he might yet have prevailed. But something told him, disastrously, that for all their belly-aching the Tories would in the end come round to his way of things. Where, after all, could they go?

The answer was, of course, to the Dutch Republic and to William. This was the critical difference between the failed revolt of 1680-85 and the success of 1688-9. All the Whigs had in play in the earlier crisis, as an alternative to the legitimate heir, was the conspicuously illegitimate Duke of Monmouth. But James's own daughter, Princess Mary, was another matter entirely. And her husband the Prince of Orange was by now legitimate in an entirely different sense: the symbolic figurehead of the European resistance to French domination. Not that it was in the mind of the 'Seven' who turned to William in 1688 to have Mary replace James on the throne. Had that been mooted, Tories like Danby would never have dreamed of going along with the plan, nor could they have carried the gentry with them. Rather, they wanted to bring William and his troops in to make James cease his unlawful behaviour. On just what constituted unlawful the Whigs and Tories had some measure of, but not complete, agreement. They could agree, for example, on the illegality of the dispensing power, on the need to force James to liquidate his standing army and its Catholic officers. But while that, together with the retention of the Test Act, was good enough for the Tories, the Whigs wanted to have him accept the 'fundamental law' of parliamentary government: that parliament was an equal partner in government, not merely a disposable source of advice.

And what about William himself? What did he want? First and foremost, what-ever was good for the Dutch Republic. Seen from the perspective of purely British history, the revolution of 1688 seems something spontaneously and indigenously gen-erated. The Victorians, especially Macaulay, saw the event as one of those moments that expressed the glorious peculiarity of the English tradition of liberal parliamentar-ianism, as if somehow the island itself had choked on Catholic despotism, coughed it up and been returned to health, to normality, courtesy of William and Mary. But the truth is different and altogether more European. As so often in the past – in 1066 for example – a turning point in English history was decided by the forces of interna-tional, not national, history. It took an immense foreign armada of possibly 600 vessels, carrying perhaps 15,000 Dutch and German troops, to bring about the fall of

James. And even this would not have been decisive without the victory at the battle of the Boyne in Ireland two years later. What happened there was essentially the Irish theatre of a huge international conflict. It was fought mainly between non-English Europeans – the French under the Duc de Lauzun on one side, and on the other a force of 36,000, two-thirds of whom were Dutch, German and Danes, and were commanded successively by Field Marshal Schömburg and, when he fell, by King William. The only actor in this military drama who had any decisive effect and who was indisputably English was John Churchill, whose defection in November 1688 from King James to Prince William was crucial, and whose violent destruction of Irish resistance two years later was even more decisive. So it was not surprising that, ennobled as the Duke of Marlborough, he would succeed William as the great commander of the European war against Louis XIV.

The critical event of 1688 is better described as the invasion it undoubtedly was, rather than as a 'revolution'. It had been contemplated by William in the Netherlands long before he had an official invitation. William was shrewd enough to know that it would be a gamble. But by the spring of 1688 he had come to believe that it would be worse *not* to embark on it. The controlling imperatives were all Dutch. The *rampjaar* or year of disaster in 1672 had been the unforgettable moment that defined William's identity as it had scarred for ever the memory of Dutch history. The republic had come close to being wiped off the face of Europe as an independent power through an encircling alliance of France and England, and whatever it took to prevent that from recurring William would do. His marriage to Princess Mary had seemed to militate against a repetition of the Treaty of Dover. But although her father was now on the English throne, William was not so sure. James was, of course, on the take from Louis XIV just as his brother had been. And if he were unable to get his way with the relief of Catholics, it was all but certain that he would look to French military as well as financial aid. Moreover, William was well aware that, as far as ruining the Dutch Republic was concerned, Louis XIV knew that there was more than one way to skin a cat. The Dutch could be struck at through economic and systematic (though undeclared) naval actions, preying on their colonial trade. Massively dependent on imports of grain and timber from the Baltic, they were critically vulnerable to a concerted attack from both French and English ships. So during the mid-1680s Louis XIV and his more bellicose ministers repudiated their agreements signed at the Treaty of Nijmegen in 1679 and began to let privateers loose. Either way, Louis must have reckoned, he couldn't lose. Either the arrogant Dutch commercial empire would piece by piece fall apart, or else the republic would be forced back into a war that once again it would have to fight on two fronts.

William was perfectly aware of this and, resigned to the coming conflict, set about putting the republic in the best possible position to fight it. The campaign in the field had to be preceded by a campaign of persuasion, and that too had to be fought on two fronts. At home he needed to convince the previously peace-inclined commercial cities, especially Amsterdam, that unless they accepted his war policy they would suffer irreversible harm from French economic and maritime aggression. Then William went on a diplomatic offensive among the German princes, and especially with the Holy Roman Emperor in Vienna, emphasizing that the incorrigible expansionism of Louis XIV represented so paramount a threat to the stability of Europe that it cut across old lines of confessional allegiance.

There was, of course, yet a third front for William in the public-relations war that had to be won before his military plans could be made operational, and that was the domestic crisis in England itself. Here, his best ally was James II. For by the beginning of 1688 James had committed himself to a collision course with all the good and great who had stood by his brother and himself a decade before. Brushing aside any moderate advice, and dismissing any ministers who had the temerity to offer it, James was reinforced in his own myopic obstinacy by men like Sunderland, who saw in grovelling loyalty a way to make themselves arbiters of power and were prepared, if necessary, to publicize their own conversion to the Catholic Church. Persuasion was abandoned for intimidation. The size of the standing army available to James was almost doubled, much of it drawn from Irish troops commanded by Catholic officers. In April, the king ordered his Declaration of Indulgence to be read on successive Sundays from the pulpit. When a group of bishops, including Sancroft, attempted to explain their refusal to authorize the readings, James exploded in a storm of rage, declaring their objections to be 'a standard of rebellion'. All those who were not now unreservedly for him were, in effect, to be considered and treated like traitors. The most prominent of the objecting bishops were arrested and tried in what turned into a public-relations disaster for the beleaguered king. They were acquitted, but not before one of the justices had delivered his own stinging verdict on the manifest illegality of the dispensing power. The liberated bishops emerged from confinement to find themselves celebrated up and down the country as the champions of the country's liberties and the guardians of the Reformation. Bonfires were lit, and effigies of the Pope, and of James's confessor, Father Petre, fed to the flames.

None of this affront caused James to hesitate for a moment in his headlong sprint off the cliff. Let the bishops have their day, for he had something incomparably more powerful going for him: a Prince of Wales. For, after years of disappointments, Mary of Modena had actually been delivered on 10 June of a healthy baby boy, baptized with Roman rites as James Francis Edward Stuart. Predictably, and notwithstanding the queen's visible pregnancy over the previous months, the infant was immediately denounced by James's now innumerable enemies as a fraud: some other baby, perhaps produced by one of the royal mistresses, and now deposited in the royal crib to thwart the succession of Mary and her husband, Prince William. At any rate, the shock of the news immediately accelerated the timetable of the Dutch military operation. Just a week after the announcement of the royal birth, and doubtless prompted by the Dutch ambassador Dijkvelt, the 'Seven' sent their formal invitation to the Prince to come to England, not as conqueror but as the protector of Protestantism and liberty. It was exactly a century since the launching of the Spanish attack on Elizabeth's kingdom, a fact not lost on the defenders of the queen's legacy. But this would be the Good Armada, and the Protestant wind, this time, would be kind to its ships.

Looking on with increasing dismay and disbelief at what was happening in England, Louis XIV had in fact already offered James military help, but had been brushed off by the Stuart king's unfaltering sense of righteous invincibility. Now, when James could have used it, it was too late, for Louis had committed a sizeable army to the Rhineland where William had made sure the troops would be tied down. But, even at this critical juncture, James was held back from switching his own military resources from domestic intimidation to a posture of national defence. He could still not bring himself to believe that his daughter Mary would allow her husband to launch a full-scale invasion against her own father. And though this seems, in hindsight, a pathetically naïve delusion, the family ties winding about the two chief protagonists of this great drama did, in fact, bind them closely together. James was not just William's father-in-law, he was also his uncle. His sister (also called Mary) had been married to William's father (also called William). And despite the historical divide, which would, after 1688, always separate them, they had much in common beside shared blood. Both were orphans of political upheavals. A year after Charles I had been executed, William's father, the Stadholder William II, had marched on Amsterdam to bend the city to his will – a tactic right out of the Stuart manual on political persuasion. Not long after this *coup* William II died, just before the birth of his son. His political enemies seized the opportunity to revenge themselves and, to preclude any further attempt at Orangist aggrandizement, made William III a ward of state and proceeded to abolish the Stadholderate. The prince had grown up as both pupil and captive of his political enemy Jan de Witt who attempted to turn him into a good republican, in much the same way that there had been talk during the Protectorate of making the youngest Stuart, the Duke of Gloucester, a 'safe' king.

Both James and William, then, had gone through the experience of loss and humiliation. Both had leaned on surrogate fathers – de Witt and Clarendon – about whom they felt at best ambivalent. Both ended up leading guarded, somewhat secretive lives, hardening themselves against adversity. As Duke of York, of course, James had had an incomparably easier time of it than William III in the Stadholder-less republic. But his position was not so strong that it could protect him against ejection from office as a result of the Test Act or from being sent out of England during the Exclusion crisis (to Scotland, where he inflicted as much as damage as possible on the Presbyterians). The two of them ended up as taciturn, habitually suspicious personalities, despising courtly banter and putting little faith in political negotiation unless backed up by the hard facts of military force.

In one respect, which would in the end prove critical in 1688, James and William differed radically: the value they placed on printed propaganda. Here, their backgrounds told. Although he had come to power over the bodies of the de Witts and was restored as Captain and Admiral General, William still had to contend, over sixteen years, with the complicated, interlocking, highly decentralized institutions of the Dutch Republic. It was no good simply blustering and bullying his way to leadership, because in the last resort money, not princely mystique, spoke loudest in a country that was the prototype of a modern polity, a place where decentralization rather than the concentration of power worked best, where the marketplace of ideas as well as commodities required religious pluralism. Knowing the Dutch Republic's reputation for toleration, James actually tried to trade on it. When, during their many exchanges of correspondence, James tried to represent his own Declaration of Indulgence as a commitment to toleration, he was shocked to find William actually defending the Test Act as a regrettable necessity for Anglican peace of mind about the future of their Church establishment.

William's response suggests that in the summer of 1688 he and his Chief Minister, Grand Pensionary Gaspar Fagel, were paying as much attention to the public-relations end of their enterprise as to military planning. The manifesto, of which a massive 60,000 copies were printed both to herald the arrival of the Dutch army and to justify its presence, carefully avoided the slightest suggestion that William and Mary were coming as conquerors to set themselves up in James's place. The aim, repeated over and again, was a restoration, not a revolution: the restoration of Church, of orderly parliamentary government, of the rule of law, in fact the restoration of a true English monarchy instead of the Catholic 'tyranny', ruled by Jesuits, arbitrary courts and Irish troops that James was in process of instituting.

As in 1066 and 1588, though, strategy was the prisoner of providence, otherwise known as the weather. It was three months before the enormous armada and its huge cargo of troops, many of them the cream of the Dutch army, were able to sail from Scheveningen. The chosen landing place, perhaps influenced by the most influential of the English sponsors, Danby, was the northeast coast (where Henry Bolingbroke had begun his campaign against Richard II), far enough from James's concentration of troops in the southeast to be able to establish some momentum before meeting the king's army. Danby had promised that a supportive rising would begin in his own county of Yorkshire. But while the Protestant winds of late October were kind enough to William's fleet, they blew him the wrong way, from the straits of Dover towards western rather than northeastern England. Eventually God stopped being coy and revealed himself to be a Protestant gentleman, for it was on the anniversary of the deliverance from the Gunpowder Treason, 5 November, that William made landfall near Torbay in Devon.

When he had taken in the full seriousness of his position, James II went from disbelief to consternation. In panic, he threw into reverse almost everything that had given offence. The Declaration of Indulgence was withdrawn; a new election was called, for which Roman Catholics were not to be eligible; the most senior officers of Church and state who had been dismissed were reinstated. But it was much, much too late. As far as the huge coalition of the disaffected was concerned – and especially the Tory gentry and the Church – only the presence of William's army and the prince himself could possibly guarantee that James would keep his word and neutralize his pet standing army. In fact, had he shown some presence of mind, James might still have been able to control the situation or at least contain the damage, for on paper at least his troop strength was easily twice that of the Prince of Orange. But those 40,000 men were dispersed around the country, and James had collapsed back into a realm of ancient nightmares in which nothing, especially not the physical safety of a royal family, could be taken for granted. So he kept at least half his available troops in the south back in London. It was far from certain, moreover, whether the rest of the army sent southwest towards Salisbury would fight when it came to it. Mutinies against Catholic officers were reported as commonplace. And then came another massive blow, which seemed to shock the king more than anything since hearing of the Dutch fleet passing the straits of Dover: his younger daughter, the Lady Anne, had disappeared, re-emerging as a defector in the camp of her brother-in-law.

James now led what was left of his army into Wiltshire. His own condition did not inspire confidence. Insomniac and suffering from chronic nose-bleeds, he seemed as disoriented by his predicament as his army, which lacked any kind of maps. Supposing he decided to tackle William head-on, no one had much idea of how to find him. And James was so nervous of having left the queen and the Prince of Wales behind in a capital depleted of troops that in the end he gave up looking for William and retreated from Salisbury back to London. Before he got there he learned of the defection of the general in whom he had placed most confidence, John Churchill. It was a betrayal he never forgave or forgot.

Free to advance, his army swelling daily, William played his hand with great care and subtlety. He would advance his army to no more than 40 miles west of London, he let it be known, it being understood that James would withdraw his troops a like distance east. In between, the parliament could deliberate on the fate of the kingdom, free of any kind of intimidation. The moderation of these demands was, in fact, deceptive. As the royal position disintegrated, the Whigs could hardly refrain from the opportunity, not just to disadvantage James but be rid of him altogether. And it was equally impossible for William not to be tempted by his amazing run of luck into seeing himself as something more than an arbitrator. But to keep the Tories in the camp meant making at least a show of sweet reason and hoping that James, true to form, would spurn it. James's only ploy at this point was to call William's bluff and accept the terms. But in the first week of December he was haunted by memories of his father falling into the hands of the enemy, losing all freedom of action and, inevitably, his life. James was, if anything, even more anxious about the Prince of Wales's safety, for in the person of the baby boy lay the eventual redemption of his cause. So he prevaricated just long enough to see the queen and the Prince of Wales safely off to France. A few hours after he had told a meeting of lords that he would remain and continue negotiations with William, James himself made his escape. It was 3 a.m. on 11 December 1688. Burning with furious chagrin at his plight, driven by absurd passions, he enacted one last childish gesture of malice. The writs for the new free parliament were brought to him along with the Great Seal. The writs were promptly burned, the Great Seal dropped into the Thames as he crossed to the south bank. He might just as well have lowered his throne into the muddy water.

For the Whigs, of course, this completely unanticipated turn of events was better than anything they could have imagined in their wildest dreams. Initially, the Tories were appalled, for throughout the campaign they had been in denial that they were in the business of dislodging James from his throne; rather, merely making him heed the law. Before long, however, the most thoughtful Tories realized that the abrupt exit of the king had actually let them off the hook of their own conscience. It remained abhorrent to think of themselves as in insurrection against their anointed monarch. But what if the throne could be said to have been vacated – opening a void that nature and the state abhorred? The argument had been used before, speciously, in

William III Landing at Torbay, by Jan Wyck, *c.* 1688. Behind him, on the shores of Torbay, William's Protestant forces land safely, blown by a fair east wind.

1399 when Richard II's vacation had been spent mostly in the Tower. But this time James had indeed gone on his travels. If they did not want – heaven forbid – England to relapse into a Commonwealth, a royal solution had better be found, and quickly.

For a moment, all these calculations were thrown into disarray by the improbable return of James to London. When he was almost on board ship, he had been recognized (though as a fleeing priest, not as a king), searched and physically harassed. In fact, such was his pathetic condition that it actually inspired sympathy from the London populace for the first time in years. Fortunately for William and the Whigs, James was not listening to the cheers. His only thought was to get out of the country again as quickly as possible, and in this, of course, his captors were only too delighted to assist. This time he did not come back.

With the throne now well and truly vacant, the second Convention Parliament in thirty years debated the future of the realm. Despite the fact that both Whigs and Tories (the latter returned as a minority but a substantial one) and the country thought of the assembly as a free parliament, it actually met under the conditions of a foreign occupation, with Dutch troops patrolling Westminster, Whitehall and most of the City of London. And, needless to say, William's ambitions had grown and hardened as his military position in England had become unchallengeable. James's presence in France had altered the dynamic of their conflict in ways that no longer allowed for sentimental niceties. For James was there, not just as a guest, but as an ally in an international war that had already ignited across Europe. So some sort of half-baked provisional arrangement – of the kind that parliament presented to him – might not be enough security for the kind of test he would imminently face. In fact, the Convention had divided. The Whig majority in the Commons was all for William and Mary becoming monarchs right away, and doing so on the grounds that James had demonstrably violated his coronation oath and had dethroned himself by breaking his contract with the people. The Tory majority in the House of Lords, however, refused to acknowledge any such contract and instead took refuge in the 'vacancy' argument, by which the throne must needs be filled without altering its divine-right sovereignty. The compromise was that William and Mary would be made regents until the death of James, at which point they could ascend the throne as his already designated lawful heirs. No mention was made by either side, of course, of the inconvenient existence of the Prince of Wales.

But it was precisely the fact of the Prince of Wales – and the possibility that as time went on his legitimacy would seem more, not less, credible – that made William realize, with his peerless sense of timing, that if he failed to seize the moment, he would squander an advantage that might never return. So, with the Dutch Blues on the streets, he simply rejected every overture short of the crown itself. He knew, of course, that in the last resort the Tories had no alternative. Veiled threats that if the matter were not settled he would depart forthwith sent them into a tizzy of anxiety. On 6 February, the House of Lords capitulated.

A week later, on 13 February 1689, William and Mary were declared king and queen. At their coronation on 11 April, before the crowns were set on their heads a reading took place of the Declaration of Rights, passed by the Convention. The moment was not just ceremonial, but profoundly significant for the future of the monarchy in Britain. For it solemnized the Crown's commitment to the reforms of the Long Parliament and the Protectorate as a condition of its authority. No more standing armies; no dispensing power; no resort to extra-parliamentary taxation; no resurrection of special courts and tribunals, ecclesiastical or civil; freedom to petition guaranteed; free elections; annual parliaments. Later in the spring an Act of Toleration was passed. It fell a long way short of the promise of its billing, not extending to all Christian sects (those, for example, who denied the Trinity). But, as John Locke wrote to a friend in the Dutch Republic, 'Toleration has now at last been established by law in our country. Not perhaps so wide in scope as might be wished for by you and those like you who are true Christians and free from ambition or envy. Still, it is something to have progressed so far. I hope that, with these beginnings, the foundations have been laid of that liberty and peace, in which the Church of Christ is one day to be established.'

Whatever else it was, the English state of 1700 was unquestionably not the Stuart monarchy of 1603 or 1660. But William's government did have a true predecessor – and that was the Protectorate of Oliver Cromwell. For the regime that had been all too briefly established in 1657 – of a 'single person and [a bicameral] parliament' guaranteeing regular elections and limited toleration – looks like the authentic blueprint of what actually came to pass after 1688. In this sense, at least, the real 'Interregnum' might be seen as 1659–87! Just as the government sketched out in the Humble Petition and Advice had corresponded to what a majority of the country's ruling landed elites wanted then, so the Williamite government corresponded to it a generation later.

This was not what old Edmund Ludlow, the last of the regicide republicans, had foreseen when, at the age of seventy-one, he left his Swiss exile on Lac Leman for England to see first-hand if William was indeed, as he hoped, the new 'Gideon'. Ludlow took with him bitter memories of comrades assassinated in Lausanne, or dying sad and poor in exile, or of soldiers of the 'Good Old Cause', such as Algernon Sidney in England, betrayed and hanged. But Ludlow fondly imagined that the issue in 1689 was the same as it had been forty years before, namely 'whether the king should govern as a god by his will and the nation be governed by beasts, or whether the people should be governed by themselves, by their own consent'. Once in London, though, aside from congenial evenings spent with the survivors of countless republican débâcles, such as John Wildman, Ludlow was doomed to disenchantment. William had no interest whatsoever in encouraging a government based on popular consent. He was neither a crowned republican nor Gideon. He was, for Ludlow, the worst of all reincarnations: a second Cromwell. It was not long before indignant noises were made in the Commons about the presence of so notorious a regicide as Edmund Ludlow – indignation endorsed by the new king. Before worse could happen, Ludlow returned his old bones to the limbo from whence they came.

Future Ludlows would have to travel a little further in search of their elusive Promised Land: across the Atlantic, in fact, where many of those seeking a truly new world, such as William Penn the younger, could find space to make it. The 'Revolutionary Settlement' turned out to be neither. But that, paradoxically, was its greatest strength and accomplishment. The unsettlement of 1689 – and with it the creation of a polity within which mutually conflicting views on what had happened and why could be sustained – was a measure not of failure but success. For a kingdom of debate had been created, in which it was possible for fierce arguments about the constitution and government of the state to be conducted without necessitating outright civil war.

Thomas Hobbes – who had survived to see the Popish Plot – had insisted that the containment of argument was impossible short of the surrender of liberties to an omnipotent adjudicator, the Leviathan. But if William were indeed powerful, he was certainly not omnipotent. It was a back-handed compliment to the rough-house ebullience of party politics that the king was so shocked and vexed by it. He had imagined he would lead a grateful and united nation into the European war, which he assumed to be as much in English as Dutch interests. Instead, he discovered that what he had effected had developed a political momentum that refused to march in lock-step with military obedience. The more he pressured, the more trouble he got. In the 1690s, with the country at war, the first parliamentary Committee of Account, to which government officials were obliged to report, was established. And the Triennial Act (another revival of 1657) ensured that parliamentary oversight would be a permanent, not an intermittent, feature of the English political system. However irksome for the king, William would learn to live with these inconveniences. For it turned out that what the country needed was not, after all, a Leviathan, but a Chairman of the Board.

Nothing like this peculiar regime, in which viable government co-existed with party polemics, existed anywhere else in Europe. However puffed up with self-congratulation, Macaulay was justified at the end of volume III of his great *History of England* in seeing the implanting of a genuine parliamentary system as the precondition for avoiding the later fates of absolute monarchies, destroyed by much fiercer revolutions: 'For the authority of law, for the security of property, for the peace of our streets, for the happiness of our homes, our gratitude is due, under him who pulls down nations at his pleasure, to the Long Parliament, to the Convention and to William of Orange.'

But who, exactly, were laying flowers on the bier of William of Orange? The English, naturally. For Macaulay neglected to add in this anthem that English liberty was won over Irish and Highland-Scottish corpses. That if 1689 were a triumph for England, it was a tragedy for Britain. And that outside England, lawlessness, insecurity of property, war in the streets and bitter domestic sorrow were as much the enduring legacy of what Cromwell and his reincarnation, William, wrought as any of the glories of the Glorious Revolution.

For although Ireland may be at the western edge of Europe geographically, it can never escape the inexorable effects of the Continent's wars. Not for the first or last time, it found itself fighting a European war by proxy and paying, as a result, a terrible price. When William set out on the enterprise of England he knew very well that his campaigns were unlikely to stop at the Tweed or the Irish Sea. His pessimism served him well. In March 1689, a month before William and Mary were crowned, James arrived in Ireland, supported by 20,000 French troops under the command of the Duc de Lauzun. Tens of thousands of Irish Catholics streamed to volunteer for his army. In May in Dublin, James and the 'Patriot Parliament' rescinded Cromwell's Land Settlement (perpetuated by his brother Charles), restored confiscated lands to their original owners and brought Catholics back into every branch of government. For the first time since the wars against Elizabeth, Ireland was in the hands of native Irish (Macaulay's 'aboriginals'). Unfortunately it was also in the hands of James II and the French, neither of whom were especially interested in what the Irish wanted except as a stepping stone to the reconquest of England and the re-establishment of an authoritarian Stuart monarchy there. James formally anathematized the constitutional settlement in England as 'contrary to the law of God, nature and the nation'. In return, the Irish parliament produced a reassertion of divine-right kingship categorical enough even for James, who in 1692 would candidly instruct his son that his only proper recourse was to a Catholic court, guarded by a Catholic army. 'Your Majesty's right to your Imperial Crown is, originally, by nature and descent of blood, from God

The Royall Orange Tree … engraved by R. Taylor, 1691, a popular print illustrating William's victories, from his landing at Brixham in 1688 to the bombardment and surrender of Limerick in 1691.

alone by whom kings reign and not from your people, not by virtue of any contract made with them or any act of your estates on their behalf … neither the peers nor the people, collective or representatively have or ought to have any coercive power over the persons of the kings of this realm.'

The armies that faced each other twenty miles north of Dublin on the last day of June 1690 were divided, then, by more than the river Boyne. They also stood for utterly different historical destinies for Britain. Neither offered a particularly happy outcome. But perhaps the measurement of felicity is beside the point. The point is that they represented contrasting visions of power. In James's tents between the walls of Dublin and the river were encamped the servants of a cult: the mystery of the godlike king, the obedience of the Christian flock, the unquestioning service of the faithful. William, on the other hand, was the chief engineer of a war machine. His grandfather Maurice had led the first armies to use printed drill manuals. When William looked out across the river at the French–Irish lines he did so through the most accurately lensed telescope that Dutch instrument-makers could devise (though he was looking the wrong way when an opportunistically fired cannon-ball nearly took his head off on the eve of battle). His army was truly international, containing Danes and Germans as well as Dutch, Huguenots and English, as befitted the king of a multinational corporate state. And it was funded, of course, by international finance – Portuguese Jews and Huguenots, precisely the kind of people for whom the absolutist monarchies found no place.

In the end, it's true, machinery was not what decided the battle but, rather, intelligent and daring strategy, accomplished by horses, riders and shooters. William sent a division of his army down river to ford it and outflank the defenders while his own troops rode straight across in a headlong attack. Surrounded as the French and Irish were on three sides, panic inevitably ensued, with James himself not especially keen to fight to the bitter end. After a night spent in Dublin, he made one of the hasty departures, at which by now he was well practised, and settled down to end his political career, as he had begun it, as a guest of the king of France.

To many, then and since, it looked like the end of a chapter. And so it was, if the book is a history of England. But if the book is a history of Britain, the Boyne was just the turning of another bloody page.

CHAPTER

5

In Williamite Britain, showing up late could get you killed. William III came from a culture that set great store by good timing. In 1688, his own carefully maintained and calibrated political clock (as well as the luck of the Protestant winds) had made the difference between a throne and a débâcle. The Dutch king expected men, money, armies to move like clockwork, with reassuring predictability. Although the kingdom he now governed fell far short of those ideals of regular movement, the winding of a spring, the greasing of a wheel might yet make the machine keep proper time and motion.

There were some places within his new realms, though, that seemed regrettably indifferent to punctiliousness, nowhere more than the Scottish Highlands. There, where a third of Scotland's population lived, loyalty seemed still to be governed by codes of honour and bonds of kinship that appeared timeless, impervious to the quickening of modernity. Although from Edinburgh or London such places, with their predilection for cattle stealing, evidently seemed backward, they could still muster crude force enough to do damage to the fragile machinery of power that William and his Scottish allies were putting in place. At the river gorge of Killiecrankie, in the southeast Grampians, on 27 July 1689, John Graham, first Viscount Dundee, obstinately and sentimentally loyal to King James, threw 2000 Highland warriors, some of them barefoot, down the hillside against 4000 musketeers and dragoons. In ten minutes 600 Highlanders, including Dundee, died under a hail of well-drilled fire. But in the same ten minutes they had sliced to pieces as many of the enemy, caught fumbling with the muzzles of their muskets as the claymores came brightly at their heads.

Ultimately, it would not matter. In the spring of 1689 James VII (James II of England), the last in the line of Stuart kings who had been on the throne of Scotland since 1371, was formally deposed. But William ruled securely only south of the Forth. The shock of Killiecrankie, and continuing resistance in the ungovernable Highlands, made William's allies in Scotland, especially the Campbells, determined to bring the

BRITANNIA
INCORPORATED

Glencoe pass in winter.

clans to heel. The means would be moderation where that worked, coercion and slaughter where that seemed to be needed. In the summer of 1690 a warship sent from Ulster sailed through the Hebrides, burning down Jacobite villages and killing those unlucky enough to be found there. On the island of Eigg, all the adult men were away fighting on the mainland, so the women were raped before being put to the sword.

In August 1691 the principal leader of the campaign, the Earl of Breadalbane, published an order stipulating 1 January 1692 as the deadline for making a formal act of submission to King William. Perhaps this was too *much* time to get the intended result. For while there were some clan chiefs who did indeed make a pledge of allegiance, urged on by the Governor of Fort William, Colonel Sir John Hill, there were others who held out as long as they could, hoping for some military miracle from France or Ireland, or perhaps just wrestling with their consciences. One such clan was the MacIains of Glencoe, a branch of the fervently Jacobite Clanranalds. Their chief, the twelfth Chief of Glencoe, Alasdair Macdonald, who had fought at Killiecrankie, procrastinated – fatally, as it turned out, and long enough to get selected by Breadalbane for an exemplary killing. A glance at the map made it all seem foolproof. Eight hundred soldiers from the new, palisaded Fort William on Loch Linnhe would be sent to torch Glencoe, about 8 miles (13 km) south, where 600 mostly unarmed villagers lived in groups of crofts scattered through the valley. Blood would of course have to be shed if the exercise in terror were to have its proper effect. But no one would hear about it because the troops could block off the mountain passes leading into the steeply walled valley.

Things began to go wrong with these careful calculations when Alasdair Macdonald belatedly decided to make his submission. He had waited until the last possible moment in the hope of obtaining permission from the Jacobite court in France to relinquish his old oath of loyalty to James. When no word came, and the clock was ticking ominously down to the New Year, he finally made the journey over the old Highland Way to the west of Ben Nevis and down to Fort William on 31 December to make his pledge to the new King. But he was told by Colonel Hill that he was in the wrong place and was sent off again through the deep snows, south across the western Highlands of Argyll to Inveraray on Loch Fyne. Detained en route, Macdonald finally appeared at Inveraray on 2 January, one day late. Hill had given him a letter to take to the Sheriff of Argyll, Sir Colin of Ardkinglas, in the hope that the submission of 'the great lost sheep Glencoe' would be acceptable even if late. But the sheriff was away and heard Macdonald out only on 6 January, warning ominously that it would be for the Privy Council in Edinburgh to make a final determination on the lawfulness of the submission. A day later, John Dalrymple, the 'Master of Stair',

William's counsellor on Scotland, wrote to the commander-in-chief with orders confirming that the lands of the chiefs who had failed to submit would be ravaged: 'Glencoe hath not taken the oath at which I rejoice. It will be a proper vindication of the public justice to extirpate that den of thieves … It were a great advantage to the nation that thieving tribes were rooted out and cut off. It must be quietly done, otherwise they will make shift for both men and their cattle … Let it be secret and sudden.' On the 16th Breadalbane signed the order for a killing.

The soldiers arrived at Glencoe on the first day of February. Their officer, Captain Robert Glenlyon, was a Campbell, but distantly related to the MacIains, as were many of his men. Tradition required that hospitality be offered, and for ten days 120 officers and soldiers were lodged, warmed and fed against the bitter Highland winter. On the 12th an order arrived commanding Glenlyon 'to fall upon the rebels, the Macdonalds of Glencoe, and put all to the sword under seventy'. At five in the morning, in the icy darkness, the troops butchered at least thirty-five of their hosts. The elderly chief, Iain MacIain, was shot in the back while he was rising from his bed to dress, his widow robbed of her rings and stripped naked. Unlike many other women (also stripped) and children, who died of exposure, she was rescued by her sons. At Inverrigan, Glenlyon had nine men shot and reserved for himself the *coup de grâce* with a bayonet. Attacked by a sudden fit of conscience he attempted to prevent the killing of a small boy, but the soldier shot him anyway, commenting that to spare a nit was to ensure the growth of a louse. Corpses were defiled with dung, cattle driven into the hills. But far more villagers escaped than perished – enough, since the troops had failed to seal the passes at either end of the valley, to make sure the story got out.

There was an immediate outbreak of hand-fluttering and pious professions of regret in London and Edinburgh, especially by those who, directly or indirectly, had actually been responsible for what was now called 'slaughter under trust'. The obligatory inquiry was instituted at Holyroodhouse. The Scottish Parliament formally expressed its horror. Breadalbane and the Master of Stair became the scapegoats for what had been an entirely premeditated act of official murder.

For all the mistimed cues and fatal stumbles, the dawn massacre in the heather floor of Glencoe, the 'weeping valley', anticipated the standard operating practices of the British Empire, to be repeated countless times, over the next two centuries, in America, Asia and Africa. 'Backward peoples' were to be given the opportunity to collaborate and, if they accepted, would be welcomed to a proper share of the spoils and to a partnership in the modernizing enterprise. Rejection – invariably characterized as unreasonable – would invite annihilation. In the 1690s the two opposed worlds ought not to be thought of simply as English and Scots, with the anti-Jacobite Scots

cast as unscrupulous cronies of the colonial power to the south. For the crucial conflict was taking place *within* Scotland, between two cultures: one based on the ancient
obligations of honour and kinship, the other on the aggressive pursuit of interest and
profit. That some sort of climactic battle between those societies would take place in
the century about to dawn might have been predicted by the prescient. But what
could never have been anticipated was the transformation that actually followed, so
complete and so breathtaking that it turned Scotland from a victim of the English state
into the bulwark of the British Empire, from the hard-luck case of Britannia into its
most dynamic and aggressive working partner.

In 1700, that future was virtually unimaginable. The Highland clan was governed
by the regularity of tradition and an immemorial calendar of work and tribal play –
the seasonal obligations of pasture and hunting and the family rituals of celebration
and mourning. Clan loyalty was built on the assumption of a common tribal ancestor.
Even though this was, more often than not, a myth, it created a genuine bond, which
extended all the way from the chief through his bigger tenants, the tacksmen, to the
simple crofter. If the grandest lairds were beginning to develop a preference for
Bordeaux over ale and whisky and an ear for the viola da gamba as well as the pipes,
the Highland tacksman was still close to the crofters. Like them he still wore the plaid
and spoke Gaelic, ate herring and oatmeal and blood pudding, and kept his sword at the
ready to answer the call of honour. Like them he lived by contracts dictated by custom,
and sworn by word of mouth.

South of the Forth, in urban, commercial, Lowland-Protestant Scotland, as well
as in metropolitan England, contracts were made with money and law, written on
paper, signed in ink and sealed in hard wax. In that world the bonds of family were
more and more a matter of business and property: the maximization of estates; the capitalization of farms; production for urban markets on both sides of the border of the
Tweed. With more to sell, the appetite for buying grew. Silverware and pottery dishes
began to be common in Lowland farmhouses along with linen sheets and grand bed-
steads with turned posts. It was a society that had not yet turned the corner into
modernity, but it had craned its neck and seen what it was like.

In the years after Glencoe, both Scotlands (but especially the south) endured the
misery of what became known as the 'ill years'. For several summers in a row the sun
refused to appear. Torrential rain deluged the country and continued into the autumn,
turning the stunted crops of barley and wheat into sodden slurry and making any kind
of harvesting impossible. Occasional years of respite suffered from the seed deficits of
their predecessors. Cattle and sheep developed murrain and footrot. The first (and
mercifully last) great famine in living memory dug its talons into Scotland. At least

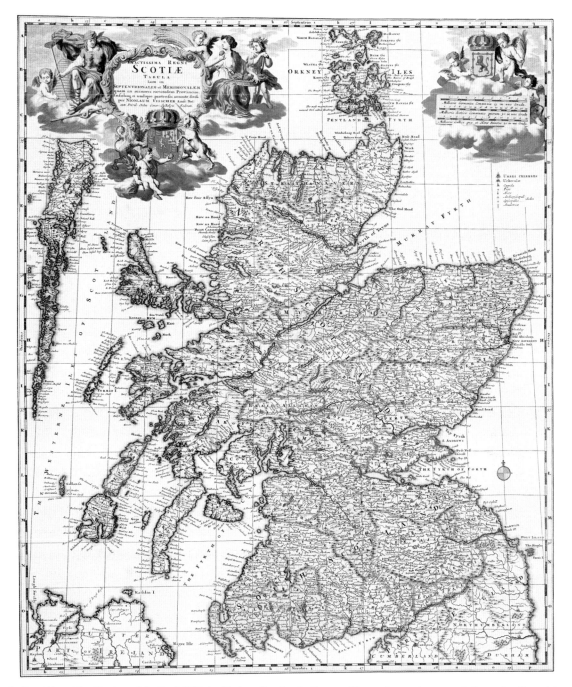

An Exact Map of the Kingdom of Scotland, 1690, by Nicolaus Visscher the Younger. The curving north coast and distorted outlines of the isles of Lewis and Skye were common misconceptions until about 1750.

5 per cent of Scotland's one and a quarter million population died of hunger. Patrick Walker, a pedlar in the Highlands, claimed to have seen women in distress after all the meal had been sold, 'clapping their hands and tearing the clothes off their heads crying, "How shall we go home and see our children die in hunger?"' Sir Robert Sibbald, the first Professor of Medicine at the University of Edinburgh and author of *Provision for the Poor in the Time of Dearth and Scarcity* (1699) catalogued the wild herbs and grasses that might be digestible and recommended that cats be eaten if there were no other kinds of meat. The highways were full of destitute, disbanded soldiers, vagrants of all kinds. Plainly, it was a time to steal or starve.

In all this darkness, though, there were some Scots who believed they could see the light. It shone from a plan that they were convinced, would raise Scotland virtually overnight from impotence and misery into a global power, rich beyond the dreams of any Glasgow counting-house. A New Caledonia was to be planted across the Atlantic athwart the trading routes of the world at the isthmus of Darien, just south of Panama. There amid the palms, fortunes would be made that would seed a Scottish prosperity the like of which had never been seen.

The scheme was not as lunatic as it might at first sound. The 'free port' was to be created about 150 miles (240 km) away from where the Panama Canal now cuts between the Pacific and Atlantic oceans, and with very much the same commercial logic behind it. Its most eloquent advocate, William Paterson, a Scot who had made money in the West Indies and had been a founder of the Bank of England, argued persuasively that what was holding back the expansion of Asian–European trade was the ruinously lengthy and dangerous choice of journeys, around either the African Cape of Good Hope or the South American Cape Horn. If the Company of Scotland could realize its dream, all this would change. Ships from China and Japan could sail east and at New Edinburgh exchange cargoes with ships sailing west from Europe. With freight costs slashed, the goods thus shipped would become more cheaply available in their respective domestic markets. Demand would soar correspondingly, and the volume of trade increase exponentially. And sitting on top of the world's newest and most prosperous exchange and mart would be the Scots, taking portage, marketing and banking charges off the top and waiting for the next great fleets to sail in from the Pacific and Atlantic.

The Darien projectors were not, in fact, proposing anything more outlandish than the kind of services that had been offered for centuries in Amsterdam. This may, indeed, have been the very reason why the circle of Dutch money men around William III felt so threatened by the scheme. But the project also struck at the reigning economic orthodoxy of the time, which conceived of international trade as a zero-sum game, playing for shares of a fixed amount of goods and gold. To maximize that share meant using the power of the state – militarily if necessary – to lock up exclusive sources of colonial supply, and to enforce a monopoly of shipment and marketing for the home country's vessels and ports. Pepper, tea, silk or sugar were to be carried *only* in the ships of officially licensed and chartered companies.

But Paterson's 'Company of Scotland Trading to Africa and the Indies' was something else again: a shameless commercial maverick disrupting orderly procedures of mercantilism. Its first – its only – great project would be the creation of a tropical free zone, where sellers and buyers from who knows where could come together on the little neck of land between the oceans to haggle and clinch deals at mutually agreed prices. No wonder everyone in London – other than Paterson's circles of Scots and well-wishers like Daniel Defoe – wanted it to fail. Lobbying hard against it in the English parliament, the Royal African Company predicted that if this unregulated monstrosity were allowed to establish itself, there would be a mass migration of England's merchants and seamen across the Tweed and 'our commerce will be utterly lost'. In one week the stock of the other pillar of English colonial trade, the East India Company, fell from 72 to 50 pence.

If the reaction in London to a Scottish American hypermart verged on the hysterical, the Scots themselves made no secret of the fact that they thought of the Darien venture as a break-out from the economic stranglehold of English power. One of the Company's most fervent supporters, Andrew Fletcher of Saltoun, wrote that all his countrymen's 'thoughts and inclinations as if united and directed by Higher Power seemed to have turned to trade … the only means to recover us from our present miserable and despicable condition'. No one in Edinburgh in the summer of 1695 could possibly have missed the significance of the moment. At one end of Holyroodhouse the Glencoe inquiry was under way, at the other end a debate on the new trading company – Scotland's past and Scotland's future weighed together.

So when the first fleet of three ships sailed out from the Firth of Forth in July 1698 flying the blue-and-white saltire, and the company flag of llamas, Indians and an optimistically rising sun, it was carrying more than the 1200 men, women and children selected to be the first colonists. It was carrying the hopes of the entire country. And much of its money. The response to an English prohibition on capital investment in existing enterprises had been an outpouring of investment in the Company of Scotland. Fourteen hundred subscribers had anted up £400,000 of working capital needed to float the first voyages to Panama, and since some of those subscribers were institutions, the actual number of individual investors was much bigger. The true believers went all the way through Scottish society and could be found in the north as well as the south of the country, from dukes and countesses to advocates, from surgeons and preachers to small shopkeepers, tanners and gunsmiths, from Glasgow and Edinburgh to Selkirk, Inverness and Aberdeen. To look at the Company's ledger book is to see entrepreneurial Scotland attempting to get under way, sailing for better times.

It was not a good sign that on the first days of the journey the fleet got separated in a dense fog off Orkney. But this would not be the worst or the last of its problems. In a much more serious sense, the Darien expedition had no idea where it was going. Its main source of intelligence, not only about the sea route but also about the conditions likely to face the fleet when and if it arrived, was a surgeon called Lionel Wafer who had served with the pirate Henry Morgan in the Caribbean. Wafer was impressively detailed with his information. Darien, he assured the projectors, was a paradise. The water was fresh; the game plentiful; the fish virtually jumped into the waiting pan. The climate was benign, the soil rich; corn grew thick and tall. The natives, governed by their grand 'Emperor', were friendly and peaceful and so vain that they spent much of their day combing their long dark hair. The Company swallowed the whole story. Together with the rest of their cargo, 10,000 combs were loaded on to the ships: wooden for the simple people, horn for the middling sort, pearl-inlaid for the Emperor and his courtiers. What else would be needed in New Caledonia? Some 2808 Presbyterian catechisms to convert the pagans and 380 Bibles for the settlers; 1440 good Scottish hats and a copious supply of wigs, without which no respectable Darienite could think of emigrating. They had, after all, been promised 50 cultivable acres (0.2 sq km) of paradise and inside three years a house built at the Company's expense. Gentility was waiting in the balmy tropics. In no time at all they would be the lairds of the lagoon.

Even before the expedition got anywhere near Darien the dream had turned into a nightmare. The ships were either becalmed or battered by violent storms on the eight-week journey across the Atlantic and south through the Caribbean. Crew and passengers died at the rate of five per week from the usual dysenteric diseases. When the settlers reached the 'Golden Island' pinpointed by Wafer as their ideal haven, their New Edinburgh, they discovered it was mostly a mosquito-infested swamp. And the natives apparently were not desperately awaiting their shipload of combs, or in fact anything else the Scots had to offer. There was no Emperor, no court, no realm: just feral pigs and spear fishermen. Aware they might be attacked at any minute by the Spanish, who evidently did not share the Scots' view that Darien was 'vacant' land, those who had survived dysenteric fevers and had not gone down with malaria spent their time and energy in the sweltering, rain-soaked forest hacking out a primitive palisaded stockade and lugging enormous cannon into their bravely christened Fort St Andrew.

By spring 1699, they were dying at the rate of ten a day. Though they had brought 14,000 needles, their clothes were hanging off them in stinking, mildewed rags. There was no ripe fruit hanging on the trees begging to be picked. The 'game' was elusive and the remains of their shipped supplies were alive with maggots. A handful of dried peas was shared out between five. The peas would then be skimmed for worms when boiled up. The beef, one of them wrote, 'was as black as the sole of my foot and as rotten as the stump of a rotten boot'.

Ten months after they had left Scotland, all they had to show for the great plan to build a New Caledonian free-trade fortune was a ditch 20 feet deep and 25 feet wide (6 x 8 m), still called by the Panamanians 'Punta des Escoces', Scotchmen's Point. But there was no bustling New Edinburgh, no colony of thrifty, self-supporting farms; no tidy little harbour ready to welcome the incoming fleets, no portage industry set to haul chests across the neck of the isthmus; nothing in fact except a miserable collection of sodden, rat-infested grass huts, a dilapidated fort and 400 graves.

Those who could summon the energy and the will left the hell-hole of Darien and limped home. A few weeks later a Spanish raiding party, thoughtfully encouraged by the English, burnt the huts and destroyed Fort St Andrew. So when a second expedition, oblivious of the fate of its predecessor, arrived in the winter of 1699 all it found were ruins, rapidly being repossessed by the rain forest. 'Expecting to meet with our friends and countrymen,' one of the new arrivals wrote, 'we found nothing but a howling wilderness, the Colony deserted and gone, their huts all burnt, their fort for most part ruined, the ground which they had cleared adjoining the fort all overgrown with weeds, and we looked for Peace but no good came, and for a time of health and comfort, but beheld Trouble.'

Back in Scotland, when the full extent of the disaster at Darien sank in, it assumed the magnitude of a national trauma. The futile venture had eaten up a full quarter of Scotland's liquid capital. But the most serious casualty of the fiasco was the last best hope of a national regeneration. That hope – of Scotland going it alone and outflanking the English trading empire – disappeared in the morass of Darien. Self-reproach for any naïveté about the expedition disappeared in an immediate wave of intense anger and hatred against the bullying English who had doomed it to disaster. The Governor of Jamaica, it was known, had issued a proclamation actually forbidding English colonists, merchants or seamen, from giving any assistance to the beleaguered Darienites, however desperate their plight. Direct collusion with the Spanish was suspected. In the inflamed atmosphere, counter-actions were taken in the economic war, allowing Scots to trade with an enemy of England in time of war. When the *Worcester*, a ship believed to have harassed the Darienites, was caught in port at Leith, its captain and two of its crew were summarily tried as 'pirates' and hanged, to rejoicing in the streets.

But revenge was not a viable strategy for the future. Scotland had come to an obvious fork in the road ahead, and the serious day when it had to choose could not be postponed much longer. It could slog on, becoming ever more impoverished and isolated, even perhaps defying England by calling back the Stuart child born in 1688 to reign as James VIII of Scotland. But this would be tantamount to a declaration of war, and there was no guarantee that the French would prove any more reliable or more powerful an ally than they had been in the past. The new war that had broken out in Europe suggested that the armies of Louis XIV were less invincible than the ceiling murals in the Hall of Mirrors at Versailles would suggest. The alternative, however bleak for those cherishing Scotland's independence, was union. By no means all of the governing class or even the people were uniformly hostile to it. A proposal had been tabled in 1689 but had been rejected by the English Convention Parliament. After the Darien fiasco, however, a large section of the nobility, especially those with cross-border economic interests and property, and many of the commercial and professional classes of the Lowlands, had come to accept that some sort of closer association was needed and even desirable. The best option would be a federation, the two kingdoms retaining their separate political identities. But by the middle of the first decade of the eighteenth century, the Scots were not going to be allowed the luxury of prolonged consideration.

For war and the succession had made Scotland's allegiance a critical issue for the English government. In 1702 William III had died after being thrown from his horse when it stumbled over a molehill. His sister-in-law, Anne, optimistically celebrated as 'the teeming princess of Denmark', had not, alas, made good on the promise. For Anne came to the throne after five infant deaths, at least thirteen miscarriages and two episodes of pseudocyesis. The chances of her producing a surviving heir were assessed pessimistically. Her last surviving son, Prince William Henry of Gloucester, had died in 1700 at the age of eleven. Threatened with the undoing of 1688 and the jeopardizing of a Protestant succession, with the Act of Settlement of 1701 the Whig defenders of the Revolution had gone as far afield as Sophia, Electress of Hanover, daughter of Charles I's sister, to pre-empt the much more obvious Catholic James Edward Stuart (not to mention 56 other Catholic heirs). A sign of their determination to avoid a Jacobite restoration was the passage in 1706 of the Regency Act, establishing an emergency Council of State following the Queen's death and pending the arrival of the Hanoverian successor. So with England at war with James's patron and protector, Louis XIV, it now became even more imperative for the security of the realm that

Scotland be made to sign on to the Hanoverian succession. Chivvied along, the Scottish parliament at first demurred, insisting on making its own separate arrangements for the throne of Scotland. An ugly economic war looked likely, perhaps a prelude to the real thing. In 1705, an Alien Act was passed in Westminster, shutting down most of the cross-border trade and deeming any Scots in England to be foreign subjects.

The blackmail worked. In 1706 commissioners from the two parliaments, not just the English but (in response to an astonishing proposal by the Duke of Hamilton) also the Scots chosen by Queen Anne's government, met in separate rooms to consider a union of realms. The two sides never confronted each other face to face, communicating only through messengers. In the streets of Edinburgh and Glasgow there were riots. Daniel Defoe, ex-bankrupt, who had got out of prison by volunteering his services to Robert Harley as a spy and (in various guises – a 'fish merchant' in Glasgow, a 'wool manufacturer' in Aberdeen) a propagandist for union, became alarmed in Edinburgh in October 1706. 'I had not been Long There,' he wrote back to Harley, 'but I heard a Great Noise and looking Out Saw a Terrible Multitude Come up the High Street with a Drum at the head of them shouting and swearing and Cryeing Out all Scotland would stand together. No Union. No Union. English Dogs … and the like. I Can not say to you I had no apprehensions.' The crowd broke down the doors of one of the treaty commissioners, Sir Patrick Johnson, with a sledgehammer, terrorizing him and his wife until 'the lady in despair and fright came to the window with two candles' calling for the Town Guard.

Defoe may have been a paid secret agent of the English government, but there is no doubt that he was sincerely committed to his mission of persuasion. His *Six Essays at Removing National Prejudices Against a Union with Scotland*, published in 1706–7, scornfully satirized those in both countries who liked to boast of the purity of their race, when in fact, Defoe argued, the history of Britain was a history of happy mongrelism and had been all the better for it. Paterson, the Scots founder of the Bank of England and the Darien projector, was one of his close friends, and Defoe's vision of a British future was of a free and natural movement of men, goods and ideas across the borders of the old enemy kingdoms. The new Great Britain was supposed to end, once and for all, the endless history of sorrow and bloodshed that had come between England and Scotland. These kinds of sentiments, however well meaning, probably converted very few. Palms needed to be greased before the deed could be done, though on what scale remains difficult to determine. Sums of money were certainly distributed to secure the necessary votes for passage of the Union Bill through the Scottish parliament, and promises of landed estates were certainly dangled before obliging Scottish peers. But in the currency of early eighteenth-century politics, no

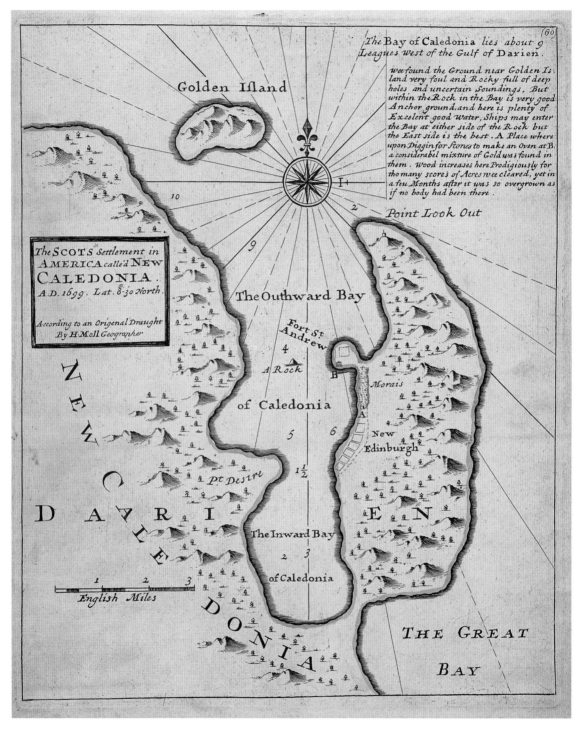

The Bay of Caledonia lies about 9 Leagues west of the Gulf of Darien.

(60)

wee found the Ground near Golden Island very foul and Rocky full of deep holes and uncertain Soundings, But within the Rock in the Bay is very good Anchor ground. and here is plenty of Excelent good Water, Ships may enter the Bay at either side of the Rock but the East side is the best. A Place where upon Diggin for Stones to make an Oven at B. a considerabel mixture of Gold was found in them. Wood increases here Prodigiously for tho many scores of Acres wee cleared, yet in a few Months after it was so overgrown as if no body had been there.

Golden Island

Point Look Out

The SCOTS Settlement in AMERICA call'd NEW CALEDONIA. A.D. 1699. Lat. 8-30 North.

According to an Origenal Draught By H. Moll Geographer

The Outward Bay

Fort St Andrew

A Rock

B

Morais

of Caledonia

A

New Edinburgh

N E W   C A L E D O N I A

D A R I E N

Pt Desire

The Inward Bay

of Caledonia

1   2   3
English Miles

THE GREAT BAY

Above: *The Scots Settlement in America called New Caledonia,* by H. Moll, 1729.
Opposite: The loading inventory from the Darien fleet, *c.* 1698.

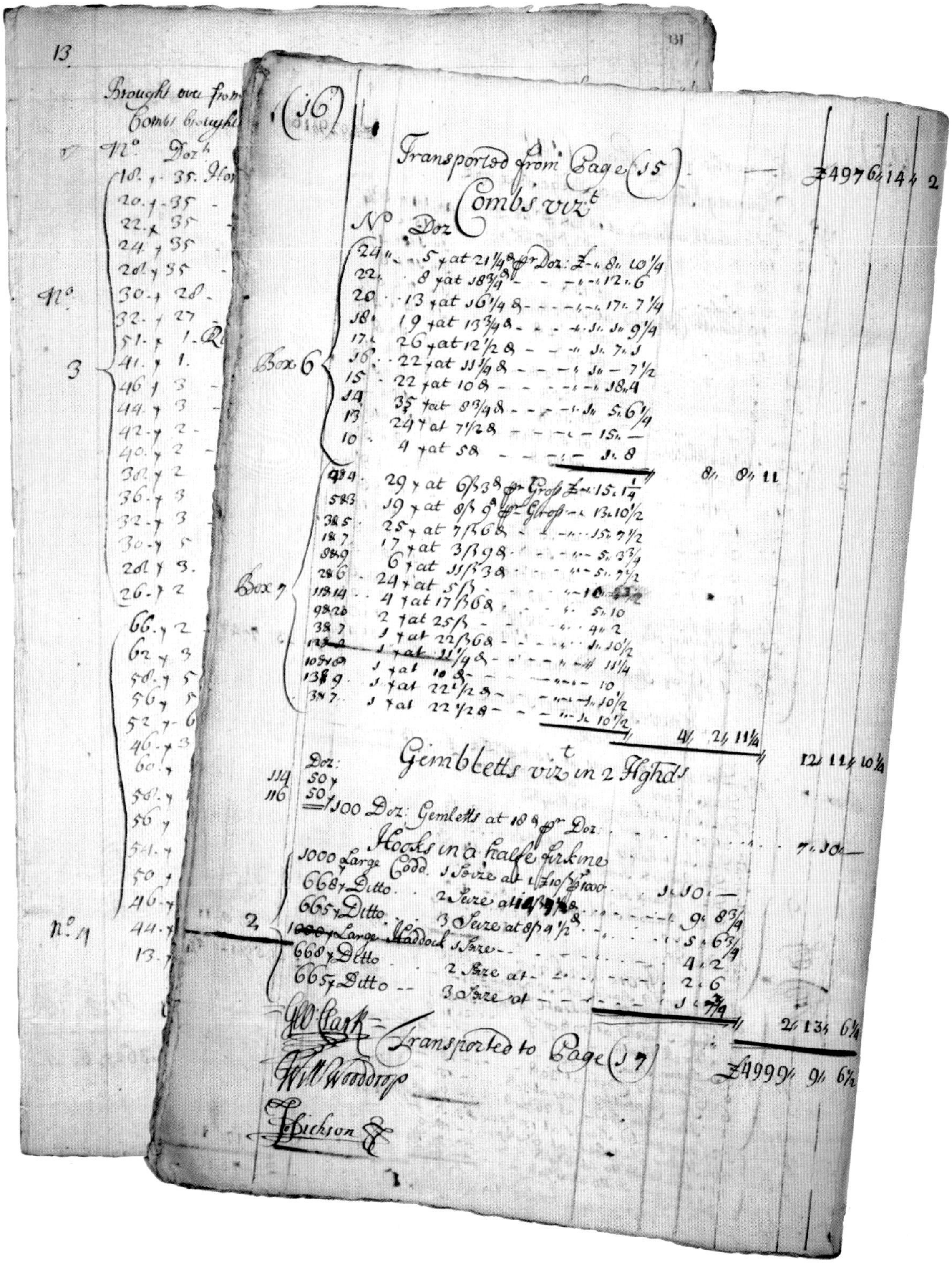

13

Brought over from
Combs brought

N°	Doz
18.	35
20.	35
22.	35
24.	35
28.	35
30.	28
32.	27
51.	1
41.	1
46	3
44	3
42	2
40	2
38	2
36	3
32	3
30	5
28	3
26	2
66	2
62	3
58	5
56	5
52	6
46	3
60	
58	
56	
54	
50	
46	
44	
13	

N°
3

N° 11

(16)

Transported from Page (15) — — £4976.14.4.2

Combs viz.t

N° Doz

Box 6
24	5 at 21¼ pr Doz	£.8..10¼
22	8 at 18¾	..12..6
20	13 at 16¼	..17..7¼
18	9 at 13¾	..9¼
17	26 at 12½	..7..
16	22 at 11½	..7½
15	22 at 10	..18..4
14	35 at 8¾	..5.6¼
13	24 at 7½	..15..
10	4 at 5	..8

8..0..11

Box 7
44	29 at 6/3 pr Gross	£.15.1¼
58	19 at 8/9 pr Gross	13.10½
38	25 at 7/6	..15..7½
18	17 at 3/9	..5..3¾
84	6 at 11/3	..5..7½
28	24 at 5/3	..10..4½
18	4 at 17/6	..5.10
98	2 at 25/3	..4½
38	1 at 12/6	..10½
108	1 at 11/4	..11¼
138	1 at 10	..10
38	1 at 22½	..10½
38	1 at 22¼	..10½

4..2..11½

12..11..10½

Gimbletts viz in 2 Hghds

	Doz:	
114	50	
116	50	

1500 Doz: Gimletts at 18 pr Doz — — — 7..10..

Hooks in a halfe firkine

1000 Large Codd	1 Seize at 4/10 pr 1000	9.10..
668 Ditto	2 Seize at	9..8¾
665 Ditto	3 Seize at 8/4½	5..6¾
1000 Large Haddock	1 Seize	4..2
668 Ditto	2 Seize at	2..6
665 Ditto	3 Seize at	1..7¾

2..13..6¼

Geo Clark   Transported to Page (17)   £4999..9..6½

Will Woodrop

Jo Dickson &

decisions got taken without these kinds of lures, and some of the cash clearly went to Scotsmen who continued to vote *against* the union. As far as enthusiasts like Defoe were concerned, the biggest sweetener of all was above board and public. To make the union of the two national debts more palatable, the English parliament had voted to offer £398,085. 10s. – the precise 'Equivalent' of all the losses incurred on the Darien expedition. For those still suffering the disastrous consequences of their unfortunate investment, this was not a trivial compensation.

In the winter of 1706 it needed just six weeks for the Act of Union to go through Westminster, ten for Holyrood. There were still hold-outs against it, unable to bear the loss of Scottish independence, however grim the alternatives and however improved the economic outlook. Andrew Fletcher of Saltoun, for one, bitterly opposed the union as a conspiracy to defraud Scotland of its liberty; and before the juggernaut rolled over him, John Hamilton, second Baron Belhaven, delivered in parliament on 2 November 1706 a Shakespearean lament for his country: 'Like Caesar sitting in the midst of our Senate attending the final blow ... looking about her covering herself with her royal garment and breathing her last'. Like other pro-unionists, Defoe mocked the melodrama uttered by the 'rough, fat, black, noisy man more like a butcher than a lord'. But he was honest enough to admit (in private) that 'a firmer union of policy with less union of affection has hardly been known in the whole world'. And he would eventually sympathize with Belhaven's sadness, visit him in prison, befriend and console him.

Brutal and peremptory though the process may have been, the union was not a crude annexation. The Scottish Kirk retained its own identity and governance, the two systems of law were largely kept separate, and no changes were made to Scotland's universities, burghs and hereditary criminal jurisdictions. The parliament at Holyrood was to be done away with, by voting for its own abolition, but Scotland was to have 45 members in the Commons and 16 elected, so-called representative peers. The first set of MPs was elected by the Scottish Parliament in 1707, but from 1708 general elections were held in the Scottish constituencies. To the dismay of some, the number of MPs had dropped dramatically from 157 to 45, but this might seem less of an outrage against a representative system when one considers that for much of the eighteenth century the entire Scottish electorate numbered only some 2600 in a population of one and a quarter of a million. What Scotland lost in 1707 was certainly not a democracy. But still it had been a true political nation, a place in the world. And now as the Chancellor of Scotland, James Ogilvy, Earl of Seafield, said as he signed the Act of Union, 'There's ane end of ane auld sang.'

If one of those new Scottish members of parliament wanted a heartening vision of the Britain to which he had become attached – with whatever measure of reluctance or enthusiasm – all he had to do was take himself down-river to Greenwich to the handsome new Royal Naval Hospital. Christopher Wren's twin, colonnaded pavilions could not help but put the traveller in mind of the Cour Royale, the grandiose approach to Versailles. But at Greenwich the approach was by way of the Thames, and the vista, as befitted an institution of charity, was public and not blocked off by grandiose screens and grilles. Inside the Great Hall facing the chapel, the invidious contrasts with French autocracy continued in the ceiling allegory painted by James Thornhill: the first great visual manifesto of the post-1688 monarchy. The allusions to the most famous allegories of the baroque monarchies – Rubens' apotheosis of James I at Whitehall and Le Brun's fawning celebration of the Sun King, Louis XIV, at Versailles – were glaring, the better to mark the differences between despots and constitutional monarchs. On Thornhill's ceiling, Apollo had changed sides from the vainglorious absolutist to William and Mary, the champions of Protestant freedom. Louis had taken things from the peoples of Europe: territories, cities, farms. But William was a giver, restoring to a duly grateful continent the cap of Liberty, while the arch-enemy (thinly disguised as Arbitrary Power) lies trampled beneath his feet. The invidious comparisons are trumpeted throughout the allegory. Over there, the curses of serfdom, popery and blind superstition. Over here, the wisdom of the arts and sciences to guide the omniscient, benevolent king. Over there, the Jesuits, over here, Newton. It would be these milder but sterling virtues that would make Britain great: Prudence, Temperance and Charity.

The blessings of charity are personified in the apparently venerable presence of the most senior pensioner in the Hospital, the reputedly ninety-seven-year-old John Wall (who in fact was constantly in trouble with the authorities for his filthy language and incorrigible drunkenness). But then it is vain to look to allegories to tell the truth. The image of the new Great Britain – peacefully devoted to toleration and freedom – was at odds with the historical reality of a state transformed by nearly three decades of war into an immense and formidable military machine. During the Restoration, the English army seldom consisted of more than 15,000 men. By the end of the War of the Spanish Succession in 1713, there were over 90,000 men in the army and more than 40,000 in the navy (although by 1715 this had dropped to a peace-time force of 32,000). Military spending – more than £5 million a year during the Nine Years' War, 1689–97 and over £7 million a year during the War of the Spanish Succession – had almost doubled, rising from £36 million to £65 million. By 1710, military spending had swallowed up almost 10 per cent of Britain's entire national income. To build a single first-rate ship would cost between £30,000 and £40,000. Keeping soldiers in the field and ships on the high seas, and supplying them with adequate victuals and munitions had added £40 million to the National Debt and created another kind of army – which would not be demobilized once the fighting had stopped: bond-holders, tax-assessors and accountants; customs-and-excise men, thousands upon thousands of them. By the end of the wars, Britons were being taxed twice as heavily, per capita, as their French counterparts, a burden that would only get heavier as the relentlessly martial eighteenth century rumbled on.

Bureaucratic, militarized and heavily taxed though post-revolution Britain was, there was one feature of the Greenwich myth that was true. While Louis XIV could simply decide how much money was needed for his campaigns and then decree the funds into the treasury, in Britain the monarch and his ministers had to ask for it. So whether he liked it or not – and assuredly William did not – he and his successors had no choice but to go to parliament to fund their wars.

Virtually everywhere else in Europe, if not the world – from Ming China to Mughal India to Romanov Russia to Hohenzollern Prussia – the more militarized the state, the stronger the king. But in Britain, the longer the wars went on, the stronger *parliament* became, as the purse whose strings it controlled so tightly became bigger and bigger. Apart from the States General and provincial estates of the Dutch Republic, Britain was the only major European power where senior military men – generals like Marlborough – also sat in parliament and assumed a role as power-brokers, not to subvert parliamentary government but to reinforce it.

In one of the greatest ironies of British history, positions traditionally taken by monarchists and parliamentarians were now reversed. The Whigs, who in the reigns of Charles II and James II had insisted on limited monarchy, now found themselves to be running the war, while the Tory champions of unlimited monarchy were mistrustful of it, not least because nearly a quarter of all money voted in 1702–13 for expenditure on the army was going to foreign (especially Dutch) subsidies! The Tories also began to present themselves to the electors of the counties as the champions of the over-taxed landed classes, held to ransom by men whose commitment to the war was driven as much by profit as principle. It was a turnaround worthy of Dean Swift's most biting satires on the squabbles of Big Enders and Little Enders, but it had an entirely serious effect on British politics. For as long as the little-king party ran the war government, and the big-king party was more often than not in opposition, the role reversal dictated a benevolent equilibrium and ruled out the possibility of military autocracy.

Better yet, the Tories – who in the reign of Charles II had been content to see a single parliament renewed for more than fifteen years – now wanted more, not fewer, elections. Their most articulate spokesman, Henry St John, Viscount Bolingbroke, who cast himself as the guardian of ancient English liberties, even went so far as insisting that frequent revolutions were a sign of political vigour. The Whigs, of course, felt that 1688 had been all the revolution the country needed, but since the revolutionary settlement had guaranteed triennial elections it was all but impossible for them to avoid regular political upheaval. And, for better or worse, the politics was the kind of combative partisanship that, without any anachronism, we can recognize as prototypically modern. The two parties were at each other's throats, not just on the specific policies of the day (the corruption of ministers, the propriety and expense of the war, the profiteering of contractors) but also in their reading of the Revolution of 1688 and the character of the political nation that had been created – or reaffirmed – as a result of it. Paradoxically, neither of the parties was especially eager to represent what had happened as a historical rupture with the past. As the principal beneficiaries of the change, the Whigs were not about to endorse a view of opposition that seemed to license resistance to the king's ministers. So they portrayed themselves as the real conservatives and James II as a renegade, like his father before him, bent on violating the fundamental tenets of the 'ancient constitution' – the rule of law, the Protestant settlement and the proper restraints imposed by parliamentary government. The 'revolution' that deposed him had been, then, an act of lawful resistance, the restoration of the authentic constitutional monarchy under which the nation now lived. 'The tyrant conspired to enslave free-born Englishmen into SLAVES,' a typical Whig polemic shouted, 'the CREATURES of Popery and Tyranny! He would have had Papist Irishmen in your houses … quartered on your wives and daughters; he would have made TORQUEMADAS of your judges. He had broken his sworn CONTRACT with his people and Resistance to his despotism was a sacred duty, the calling of patriots.'

The Tories remained adamant that the Whigs had usurped the title of defenders of the monarchy, while deforming its character. That monarchy remained what it had been before 1688: a divinely appointed office. Their own participation in 1688 had not in any way altered or compromised the sacrosanct nature of the institution, but had merely been an *ad hominem* act filling the vacancy that James had unfortunately created. There had been a change of personnel, not a change of constitution:

> RESISTANCE which is nothing but foul HYDRA-HEADED REBELLION is a very MON-
> STROSITY, an abomination unto God to whom alone it is reserved to decide the
> fate of His Anointed … King James was not cast out – Truly he resigned his throne
> and this being vacant Prince William was invited hither. But he has been captive
> to wicked counsellors, has dragged the country into wars so that his minions could
> line their pockets with our TAXES. Not content with plundering your purse they

conspire at the DESTRUCTION of the true Church of England by a most disingenuous allowance of OCCASIONAL CONFORMITY (which is nothing other than the
pernicious TOLERATION of Dissenters), his minions, the SEEDS OF CROMWELL, are
even now encompassing the MURDER OF TRUE, Divinely-Appointed MONARCHY.

The abuse could get ugly and personal. William III, his bitterest enemies put it about,
was not only foreign and corrupt but a homosexual eunuch too, which explained his
difficulty in begetting heirs. A typical serenade of the period went:

> He has gotten in PART the shape of a man
> But more of a monkey, deny it who can
> He's the tread of a goose, the legs of a swan
> A DAINTY FINE KING indeed!
> He is not qualified for his wife
> Because of the cruel midwife's knife
> Yet BUGGERING BENTINCK does please to the life
> A DAINTY FINE KING indeed!

The differences between Whigs and Tories, then, were not just the petty quibbles of
gentlemen who, once the political name-calling was done, could get together over a
glass of wine or a tankard of ale. These differences cut to the bone. They went to rival
coffee-houses (the Whigs to Old Slaughter's, the Tories to the Cocoa Tree) and
different clubs (the Whigs to the Kit Cat, the Tories to the Honourable Board of
Brotherhood from 1709, or Edward Harley's Board from 1720). They were two armed
camps, bent on mutual destruction, and contested elections were fought with everything the combatants could get their hands on: money, drink, entertainment, shameless promises of jobs, juicy libel and, in the last resort, either the threat or the reality
of a serious brawl.

From the poll-books kept by many constituencies we know that, even though
the electors were for the most part the social inferiors of the candidate, they were anything but docile or easily impressionable. The voters of the fiercely contested counties
were freeholders: literate, opinionated, informed by the newspapers and journals that
mushroomed after the abandonment of the Licensing Act, and predictably bloody-
minded about the hot-button issues of the day like toleration of Dissenters or
Catholics and the imposition of new excises. By the standards of the time, the size of
the electorate was surprisingly large: a quarter of a million adult males or 15 per cent
of that population. And it was divided right down the middle, county by county,

village by village. The poll-books of even the most modest hamlets show electors voting their party choice, irrespective of the opinion of the local squire – and switching that choice from election to election.

The battle for power was so intense and so vicious that politicians and their respective camp followers – placemen and pen-pushers, hacks and roughnecks – were not inclined to be magnanimous in victory. As Queen Anne got older, and the anxiety about the succession became more acute, the temptation to make a pre-emptive strike on the enemy was virtually irresistible. Politicians on the losing end of elections were now faced with losing, not only their jobs along with the little barony of dependent supporters they had accumulated but their liberty too. Being out of power and out of place could now also entail impeachment, imprisonment, total personal and political ruin. To allow a floored antagonist to get up off the mat was to court destruction. Equally, to fail to nip a potent, scurrilous campaign in the bud while it was still an irritation rather than a threat was to show fatal weakness.

So, with an eye to their future after the aged Queen Anne had gone, the Whigs decided to pluck out the most annoying thorn in their flesh: the ultra-Tory, High-Church preacher Dr Henry Sacheverell. In 1709, thirsty for confrontation, Sacheverell had, in his own words, 'hung out the bloody banner of defiance' and on 5 November had preached a violent sermon in St Paul's before the Corporation of London, condemning the Glorious Revolution of 1688 as a transgression against God's anointed and accusing the Whigs of putting the Church of England in danger by its *de facto* policy of tolerating Dissenters. For Sacheverell, both crimes were tantamount to bringing back the evil days of the Commonwealth, an overturning of everything that England truly was. To make sure that his alarm bell would be heard, he had 100,000 copies of the sermon printed and distributed. By 1710, the campaign to discredit the Whigs as the destroyers of the true Church had become ubiquitous and vocal. The government – unpopular through the prolongation of the war in Europe and the high costs in excises it placed on the people – either had to brazen out the shouting or stamp on Sacheverell before he became a real menace.

In 1710 Sacheverell was impeached in the House of Lords. The trial was a public-relations fiasco for the government. Henry Sacheverell became a hero of the streets of London, and Dissenter meeting-houses and chapels, including those of the Huguenot community who had settled around Spitalfields after their expulsion from France, were ransacked and burned to the ground. Sacheverell was escorted to his trial each day by a guard of myrmidon butchers and mobbed wherever he was sighted by delirious crowds yelling his name and issuing death threats against the Whig ministers. Inside parliament Sacheverell upended the onus of guilt, prosecuting not only

Above: *Greenwich Hospital from the River*, by Samuel Wale, *c.* 1748.
Opposite: *William and Mary Giving the Cap of Liberty to Europe*, by
James Thornhill, *c.* 1700–20, detail from the ceiling of the Painted Hall,
Greenwich Hospital. Flanked by the Virtues in heaven, William and Mary
represent Peace and Liberty vanquishing Tyranny, symbolised by Louis
XIV's broken sword.

the government but also the entire Whig version of the history of 1688 and especially their claim to lawful resistance, which he dismissed as a wicked oxymoron. Pro-Sacheverell riots broke out in virtually every major town in the southwest and Midlands and, faced with a breakdown of order and insufficient troops to repress it, the government decided to cut its losses, whatever the embarrassment. Sacheverell was given a transparently trivial sentence – suspended from preaching for three years and the offending sermon to be burned by the public hangman. The news was greeted with bonfires and bells around the country, reminiscent of scenes at the Restoration of 1660, as well as another round of chapel-breaking. In the next election, the Tories swept to power.

When the Queen died in August 1714, the political nation held its breath. Anything and everything was on the cards, including another round of civil war. Street violence between party gangs became commonplace, the 'Mughouse' vigilantes paid by the Whig John Holles, first Duke of Newcastle, taking it to the High Tory and Jacobite mobs that had ruled the alleys since the Sacheverell riots. Rumours took wing. Before she died, it was said, Queen Anne had let it be known that she wished her Catholic half-brother James Edward Stuart to succeed her, not the Elector of Hanover, and had even signed a will to make her intentions clear. But however hard they searched, no one could come up with the document that would get in the way of the succession of the uncharismatic middle-aged Elector George. The Jacobite press ridiculed him mercilessly as a lecherous dolt, with not a word of English at his command, sporting two mistresses, one fat, one thin, both ugly, who had not scrupled to have one of his own wife's former lovers murdered. His coronation was greeted with another wave of rioting in at least twenty English towns. Predictably enough, it was even worse in Scotland. At Inverness the proclamation of George's accession was interrupted by the town magistrates and 'God save the King' shouted down by cries of 'God damn them and their king'.

Not surprisingly, George took it personally and blamed the Tories for encouraging if not actually engineering the hostile demonstrations. As much of a soldier-king as William III, George also disapproved of the unseemly hastiness with which they had sought peace with France and the poor terms on which the Treaty of Utrecht had been settled in 1713. He wanted them out of power. Purges were conducted on office-holders and money taken from the civil list for the 1715 election, which duly produced the enormous Whig majority the king desired. Faced with the prospect of years in the wilderness and a permanently unsympathetic king, the Tory leaders, the Duke of Ormonde, and Bolingbroke, panicked and took a flyer on the alternative – James Edward Stuart. In hindsight it seems like an unbelievably foolhardy, if not insane, gamble. But after Sacheverell, Jacobitism had got into the blood-stream of English politics to a degree that would have been unthinkable ten years before. Even so, the problem – and it was a huge one – was that a King James III/VIII was only going to be a possibility courtesy of a French invasion. And after decades of interminable war, an emptied treasury, desperate impoverishment, near famine conditions and partial occupation, France, if not Louis XIV, was utterly exhausted. Besides, an attempt had been made to land James Edward in Scotland seven years before, in 1708, which, although triggering a panic at Westminster and the passage of the Treason Act, ended in an ignominious débâcle. The ostensible leader of the rebellion, the Duke of Hamilton, had swiftly disappeared to Lancashire at the critical moment. A flotilla of English warships had barred the entrance to the Firth of Forth, while James's face erupted in an unkingly flowering of measles. The would-be James VIII never landed.

Without a better planned and better executed French military action in 1715, the only hope that the Tories and Jacobites had was for an uprising to begin in Britain itself – starting, of course, in Scotland. And this was very much on the cards. The glowing vision of mutual prosperity and pan-Britannic harmony sketched by boosters of the union like Daniel Defoe had, of course, failed to materialize. Arguably Scotland, even Highland Scotland, was no worse off than it had been before 1707, but new taxes on linen, malt and salt had been introduced, and no bonanza in Scottish exports to England had opened up. After the failure of the 1708 Jacobite plan the English law of treason was put into effect along the border, with fresh hardship for all those living in that region. The most obvious beneficiaries of the union had been those who were already among the richest and most powerful Scots, like the Duke of Argyll. There were other nobles, in particular the Earl of Mar, Secretary of Scotland from 1713 to 1714, who had served in the Tory governments of Anne, who saw 1715 as the coming of a long Whig winter – and then acted to guarantee it.

On the assumption that James would arrive with the French in force, and that there would also be an English uprising in the old Catholic region of Northumbria, Mar raised his standard at the ancestral stag-hunt at Braemar in September. In the northeast Lowlands other disaffected nobles rallied to him, and in the west some (though not all) of the clans began to rally their Highland followers. Throughout Scotland, in fact, not just in the Highlands, support for the Hanoverian regime melted away alarmingly. Defensive trenches were dug in front of Edinburgh Castle. Perspiration flowed freely in London. Already in July, plans had been made for a hasty exit to Holland for George I.

But even though it may have had more going for it in 1715 than 1745, the

Jacobite rebellion never came close to overthrowing the union and its German king. At Sherriffmuir, on 13 November, Mar's 4000 Jacobites fought a much smaller force of around 1000 under Argyll to a draw but still failed to take either Glasgow or Edinburgh. Reduced to futile marches and counter-marches, while waiting for a French invasion that seemed mysteriously postponed, the rebels found the momentum draining away from the rising. The English and Scottish components of a joint army had no sooner come together than they fell out and became reduced (as so many times before) to a raiding and wrecking force until finally cornered in Lancashire.

The *coup de grâce* actually took place a long way from the Tweed and the Tay at Versailles. Just a few days before Mar came out for the Stuarts, their greatest patron, Louis XIV, had died, leaving an infant great-grandson as his successor. Any chance that the Regent, Orléans, had of stabilizing his country and relieving it of the crushing burden of taxation depended on a peace policy. There would be no invasion. Just over six weeks after he had arrived in Scotland on 22 December 1714, James was back on board returning to France. Not long afterwards, the whole Jacobite menage – 3000 Irish, Scots and English – which for years had camped at St Germain on Louis XIV's long-suffering generosity, was removed to the less grandiose milieu of Bar-le-Duc in Lorraine. Their cause was still gallantly flattered. But the truth was that they had become an expensive nuisance.

In England the Whig government and the king could breathe just a little more easily. The northern earls were, in the ancient style, beheaded for their treason (as their predecessors had been in 1569), allowing the Earl of Derwentwater to make a magnificently histrionic speech, on 24 February 1716 from the scaffold at Tower Hill, custom-ordered for Jacobite hagiographers. But even if, in hindsight, the rising of 1715 might look like a storm in a teacup, and even though successive Whig governments cynically conjured up the Jacobite bogey whenever they wanted an excuse to intimidate or incarcerate their political opponents, the threat had in fact been serious. And it didn't go away. In March 1719 a mini-armada of 29 Spanish ships and 5000 troops, with arms for another 30,000, set sail from Cadiz for Scotland, although the Protestant wind intervened as close as Coruña, dispersing it and stranding the Pretender.

Britain, though, was not yet becalmed. If anyone in 1715, or even 1720, had predicted that the next two decades would see an astonishing drop in the wind-speed of politics in Britain, they would have been written off as hopelessly deluded. But from being a political nation notorious for its feverish hyperactivity and infuriated partisanship, early Hanoverian Britain became – almost – sedate. And the man who administered the sedative was Sir Robert Walpole.

It was Walpole's intuition (as much as his calculation) to present himself as the soul of common sense. But much as he cultivated the impression that his bottom-heavy 'soundness' and common-sense pragmatism rose naturally from his roots among the Norfolk gentry, 'Squire Walpole' resembled the typical country gentleman about as closely as King George III would approximate to the average farmer. And although he would never have made a profession of it, Walpole's approach to politics arguably owed much to John Locke – not the Locke of the two *Treatises on Government* but the Locke of the *Essay concerning Human Understanding*, first published in 1690 and already run through several editions by the time Walpole was in his political apprenticeship. Of course Walpole was uninterested in the finer points of Locke's epistemology – the science of how we acquire dependable knowledge. But in common with many of his contemporaries he surely took on board Locke's flat denial of truths grounded in revelation rather than experience. If attachment to mutually intolerant beliefs, of the kind that had so bitterly divided the political nation, had not been brought about by some irrefutable epiphany but rather had been the product of particular historical happenstance, then perhaps another kind of historical happenstance could make them go away.

So Walpole set out to preside over a politics of reasonableness rather than righteousness. His management style was meant to make room for the realization of the non-political life, a principle abhorrent to the classical tradition that had dominated the seventeenth century, in which life was political or nothing. Walpole had the modern instinct that the pursuit of material satisfactions could take the edge off mutually destructive ideologies, so he did his best to massage the inflamed body politic with the ointment of epicureanism. Property, tranquillity and pleasure were to replace intransigence, intolerance and anathema as the sovereign instincts of public as well as private life. For the gentleman, the panelled library and the well-stocked deer park would do better than the venomous libel and the reckless conspiracy. For the common sort, honest toil and the satisfaction of simple wants would do better than drunken uproar and riot. Of course there was a huge element of self-interest in the propagation of this pastoral view of political quiet. Walpole wanted to de-fang English politics principally to ensure that his enemies remained toothless. But there is also no doubt that he tapped into a genuine sense of exhaustion at the factional bitterness that had disfigured public life since the death of Charles II. Richard Addison, the editor of the *Spectator*, spoke for many when he wrote that 'there cannot a greater judgement befall a country than such a dreadful spirit of division that rends a government into two distinct people and makes them greater strangers to one another than if they were different nations … a furious party spirit which rages in its full violence … fills a nation with spleen and rancour and extinguishes all the seeds of good nature, compassion and humanity.'

The antidote, administered by Walpole, was what his generation called 'politeness' – not just in the modern sense of good manners (although that was not unimportant), but rather a civilized self-restraint. The polite man, unlike the passionate man, wanted to strengthen the social bonds between men rather than sunder them; to give society an appreciation of the interdependence of its parts rather than the inevitability of its conflicts and incompatibilities. So the great project of Walpolean pragmatism was an attempt to change the subject of British politics – away from conviction and towards the practical business of making a fortune. The pursuit of self-interest, he might have said, ought not to be confused with aggressive selfishness; for instead of dividing the nation into so many discrete individuals, it actually tied them together in mutually compatible and fruitful enterprises. From such pursuits would come the greater good of the country. Which would *you* prefer, he might have asked, the unsparing attack of principles that led to incessant war and chaos, or what he had to offer: peace, which in turn would relieve the landed interest of the grievous burden of land taxes they were always complaining about, and political stability, all the desirable ingredients of what today might be classified as a healthy business environment?

From the beginning, Walpole had bet that the politics of the future would be more concerned with portfolio management than religious passion or legal debates. In 1712, at the height of the Tory ascendancy, he had been sent to prison for embezzlement, and the painful experience had taught him a lesson about the tight interconnection between political and financial fortunes. In 1720 he was able to put that precocious understanding to good use. He had been a minister in the Whig administrations of George I off and on for five years. Though there were still well over 200 Tories in the House of Commons by 1720, their Jacobite flirtation had, for the time being, broken them as a serious threat. But no sooner had the Whigs established their dominance than they themselves fractured into competing baronies and factions based on interest groups rather than ideologies. Driven by a ferocious ambition, Walpole was just one of a number of equally unscrupulous and intelligent sharks circling governments in Westminster, their nostrils sensitive for the slightest whiff of blood. It was only when the South Sea Bubble burst in 1720 that his reputation changed from one of shrewdness to indispensability, and this was a reputation largely of his own careful manufacture.

The plan, dreamed up by the South Sea Company, was going to make everyone happy, except perhaps the directors of the Bank of England. Its pet project was an idea that was simplicity itself: essentially the privatization of a large portion of the National Debt. As the government's wartime demands had become more urgent, so the interest rates payable on long-term obligations like annuities had become steeper – around 6 per cent. The Company, founded in 1711 and always more of a financial management organization than a commercial enterprise, offered to buy out that burden. Holders of long-term irredeemable bonds like annuities (on which interest was payable every year until the holder died) would be persuaded to trade them for company stock. The Company, now capitalized to the tune of some £40 million, would be given the monopoly to trade in 'The South Seas and West Indies'. A similar scheme, cooked up in France by the Scottish financier John Law, who had invented a 'Mississippi Company', seemed, for the moment, to have worked like a dream. But despite the vision of exotic riches, everyone understood that the South Sea Company was a ship-less wonder, essentially a fund-management company. The only reason why a holder should want to make the trade of annuities against stock was a belief that the swift appreciation of South Sea stock would make him more money than he could ever dream of in a lifetime's receipt of annual interest payments.

The prophecy was self-fulfilling. Between January and June 1720, South Sea stock rose from 128 to 950 and peaked at 1050 on 24 June. Annuity holders climbed over each other in the crush to get their hands on certificates, sending the price through the roof. Rents soared. New shell companies sprang up overnight with equally spurious commercial rationales: companies formed to trade in human hair or woad or coral fishing. On 23 May the government auditor, Harley, wrote to his brother Sir Robert, now Earl of Oxford, 'The madness of stockjobbing is inconceivable.' It must have seemed, as booms always do, that it must go on for ever; a perfect instance of the fit between public interest and private profit. Until, that is, some prominent stockholders decided enough was enough, took their profit and departed. Isaac Newton made £7000; Thomas Guy, founder of the London hospital of that name, £180,000. The rhythm of selling began to accelerate, and the stock suddenly started to dip, then tumble, and finally, as panic took hold, it went into free-fall: between 1 September and 1 October, its value collapsed from 725 to 290. Countless investors who had dreamed of making overnight fortunes were now left with neither their old dependable annuities nor stock of any serious value. Lord Londonderry lost £50,000; many less exalted were wiped out. The country was left drowning in worthless paper, thrashing about looking for someone to blame.

There were plenty of choice targets: John Aislabie, Chancellor of the Exchequer from 1718 to 1728, and Walpole's principal rival, who had himself held £77,000 worth of South Sea Stock at almost 100 per cent profit; Charles Spencer, the third Earl of Sunderland, who had been one of the project's principal promoters. But Robert Walpole was certain it was not going to be him. He had muttered some lukewarm reservations about the Company that he now suggested had been deep and solemn second thoughts. But in fact Walpole had been lucky, not prescient. He had invested

George I, studio of Godfrey Kneller, *c.* 1730.

heavily himself, had sold some stock too early (unlike the canny Guy) and then, repenting, had tried to buy in again at the precise moment when it was poised to depreciate. Luckily for him, the bid had been held up by a delay in the mail. But Walpole did nothing to allay a wholly undeserved impression of clairvoyance. His real art, at this moment, was less financial wizardry than crisis management. He knew very well that the government itself was on a sound footing. Whatever the cost to individual stockholders, the Treasury had relieved itself of nearly 80 per cent of all its previous annuity holders. Fortunes had been lost. But others had been won. So the crisis was more psychological than fiscal. Like FDR in 1932 he understood that the first priority was to stop the self-seeding fear. Noises needed to be made about a rescue scheme for the Company, however vaguely defined and ambiguously guaranteed. Happily his own shrewd investment manager and banker, Robert Jacombe, came up with one, largely based on the reconsolidation of Company stock into solid Bank of England obligations.

It was not so much what he said as the way he said it. When Walpole spoke to the House of Commons with his effortless geniality and evenness of temper, the stricken calmed down and began to feel unaccountably better as though they had all had a glass or two of his best port. Better yet, when he read them balance sheets that would normally have had them perspiring with bewildered anxiety, they discovered – miracle of miracles – that they could actually understand what he was talking about. And it didn't seem, after all, the end of the world. The carriages and the hunting hounds could stay.

In short order Walpole became the rock to which apparently foundering fortunes, financial and political, anchored themselves. And for his ability to shield the culpable from the consequences of the disaster he also became known as the Skreen Master – the master, we would say, of spin. Everyone was in his debt, not least because he had his hands on explosive information as to who exactly had bribed whom to get the Company deal done. Aislabie would have to be sacrificed but Sunderland was spared. King George, whose own hands were not clean (nor were those of his mistresses), was agog with admiration and gratitude. Walpole's ministerial colleagues, especially Sunderland, who had sniped at his presumptuous ambition, grovelled before his apparently arcane mastery of the spreadsheets, not to mention the discreet success with which he kept them out of prison. The serried ranks of the Whigs on the benches of the Commons loved him for deflecting popular anger. Even the more independently minded country gentry at least appreciated him making good his promise to keep the country out of the foreign wars that would raise their tax rates.

Walpole repaid their appreciation by departing from tradition and remaining in the Commons on becoming 'First Lord of the Treasury', not so much Prime Minister as Prime Manager. Part of the decision was a matter of prudence. Apart from the solid core of Tories there was also a sizeable group of independent members, and those two non-government factions needed to be kept apart for his own ministry to maintain its domination. So no pains were too great in his careful cultivation of loyalty in the House. 'So great was Walpole's love of the Commons,' wrote the Earl of Chesterfield, 'that when going to face the House he dressed as carefully as a lover going to see a mistress.' In keeping with Walpole's belief in the bonds of mutual interest over the alignments of ideology, he built a barony of connections and obligations. And they began with small, telling gestures. Rival politicians like the Whig specialists in firebrand 'patriot' oratory, William Pulteney and John Carteret, could always outshine him. But they could never outdine him. Walpole made a point of ensuring that every new Whig member of the Commons dined with him *tête-à-tête*. With a glass of his best claret in your hand, a juicy haunch of mutton oozing on the trencher and Cock Robin's glittering eyes twinkling benevolently in your direction as if the life of the party, the state of the nation depended on *you*, how could you possibly not swear undying devotion and loyalty to his interest?

And then, to be sure, there was the matter of jobs. Walpole sat at the heart of a vast empire of patronage. There had, of course, been first ministers before him who had made it their business to dispense offices to their followers or to strip them from the unobliging. But the expansion of the British state during the long decades of war had resulted in a massive multiplication of posts, especially in the strategically lucrative departments of revenue enhancement – customs, excise, land-tax assessment – and this gave Walpole an unprecedented bonanza of jobs to distribute. Some of them might be pure sinecures requiring nothing more of the holder than to sit back and collect, and these were especially useful assets in securing votes in the Commons. Many others were appointments that required real effort and even a modicum of integrity. But they conferred status as well as cash on the holder and could make a somebody out of a nobody especially in their native county or town.

In retrospect it is possible to see that what Walpole built was Britain's (in fact the world's) first party-political machine. He owned the placemen in parliament primed to vote as directed. And since the passage of the Septennial Act in 1716 (the pretext of which was to keep dangerous Jacobitism at bay) elections now came just once every seven years, extending the life of members' offices that much longer. Walpole had the hacks scribbling away to persuade the country that he was working assiduously in its best interests (as he quite sincerely believed he was). He had George I eating out of the palm of his hand, especially when his managerial skills produced the civil-list money needed to keep the king and queen in decent style. And lest anyone imagine they could break ranks from his parliamentary coalition of office-holders, placemen and Whig loyalists, he had the necessary information to make them think twice about such rashness.

Perhaps the most breathtaking evidence of Walpole's sense of invulnerability was the house he built for himself in Norfolk, the most incautiously palatial building made for a non-aristocrat since Cardinal Wolsey made the mistake of creating Hampton Court. Houghton Hall was the Whig Xanadu: the last word in opulence. Anything that riches could buy Walpole bought – marble in cartloads, figured damasks and watered silks, furniture designed by the painter and architect William Kent and made from exceptionally expensive mahogany, antique busts, extraordinary masterpieces of Renaissance and baroque art – Titian, Rubens, Poussin, Holbein, Murillo – all shipped to the East-Anglian pleasure dome, some of them by strategically placed ambassadors and consuls in Rome or Madrid. Walpole's son, Horace, who was to become a compulsive connoisseur of painting and an acute critic, undoubtedly had his eye educated by his father's collection and grew up there, dressed in clothes made of French silk, attended on by his own retinue of footmen. But Houghton was not just an eye-popping demonstration of the good life that Walpole promised to the landed classes. It was also a statement of grandeur meant to stun the sceptics into acknowledging that only someone securely in command of the destinies (and money) of the nation could possibly afford something on that scale of conspicuous waste.

His entertainment was Lucullan. In one year alone, and to one of his six wine merchants alone, Walpole returned some 500 dozen empty bottles. To those who had sampled the Haut Brion and the Lafite at one of the 'Norfolk Congresses', as the parties were called, it went without saying that, if King George had the throne, it was Cock Robin who had the palace.

Walpole's critics, like Edward Harley, may have sneered at the vulgarity of Houghton, exhibiting 'very great expense without either judgement or taste'. But there is no doubt that its owner's shameless appeal to enlightened self-interest was infectious. With the glittering prizes dangled before their noses, the governing caste of the country – some 180 peers and 1500 country gentry – lined up to trade party passion for Palladian architecture. They stopped shouting and started building. And what they built were sanctuaries from social unsightliness. Just as Walpole's political management was designed to choke off the din of political belligerence, so the building style recommended to the Whig oligarchs was meant to insulate them from any contact with the grubby irregularity of the material world. The managed state would be complemented by the edited landscape, both in the interests of the most advertised

Above: *Sir Robert Walpole as Master of the King's Staghounds in Windsor Forest*, by John Wootton, *c.* 1730.
Opposite: Houghton Hall, Norfolk: (top) the Grand Salon, filled with designs by William Kent, such as the painted, ornamental ceiling and gilt furniture; (below) the Stone Hall, a 40–foot cube, walled with classical stone sculpture and relief.

virtue of Walpolean England: harmony. In the treatises of architectural virtuosi like Richard Boyle, third Earl of Burlington (who seems to have been a covert Jacobite), the agreement of parts was a matter of geometry, as it had been for the ancients. But the cohesion and grace of the Hanoverian country house was a contrivance: the appearance of harmony through the manipulation of reality; continuous spaces and sight lines achieved through acts of separation and obliteration.

Earlier generations of country houses had most often been fronted by a road connecting them with a neighbouring village and parish. Now, however, status was measured by the distance separating the rustics from the lord, so the grander the house, the more deeply enclosed it was within its encircling park. At Houghton, a stone column marks the place where the local village once stood. Its proximity to Walpole's great house became an inconvenience, so he had it demolished and moved farther away, beyond the gates. Once through those grandiose iron-grille barriers, bearing (as at Versailles or Blenheim) the coat of arms or monogram of the owner, the visitor would approach the house via a long avenue of elms or plane trees, which also served to demarcate a barrier between the managed property and the wild wood. The breadth of the avenue would be optically calculated to frame vistas of the great house, standing on its raised platform of grass like a throne upon a dais. Instead of rustics straying about the environs of the house, there would be choice domestic animals: a carefully selected herd of ornamental sheep or cattle. But this too was an illusion. It was, in fact, especially inappropriate to invoke the Palladian aesthetic since a prime principle of Andrea Palladio's revival of the Roman villa in the Veneto was to re-create the closeness between landowner and his working farm. At the Villa Barbaro in Maser, Italy, for example, farm buildings, with room for animals, are linked to the main house by an arcaded loggia. At Houghton and houses like it, any whiff of the barnyard was banished well beyond the precincts, and the old clutter of stables, kitchen gardens or duckpond removed from the close vicinity of the house. Although, from the windows of the house, terrace, gardens and manicured pasture on which the glossy beasts grazed would appear to be a single unbroken space, it was in fact cut in two by the intervention of the ha-ha, a deep but narrow trench effectively preventing the animals from wandering towards the house.

The inventor of the ha-ha was Walpole's landscape designer at Houghton, Charles Bridgeman, and the conceit was also pure Walpole in that it converted a military trench into an ornamental effect. Discreetly defended pleasure, the appearance of inclusiveness through the policing of exclusion might have been the watchword of the regime. The grazing animals – especially deer and their woodland habitat – were protected by the most ferocious anti-poaching laws enacted in England since the

Angevins. In 1723 Walpole's parliament put no fewer than fifty capital offences on the statute book, most of them dealing with poaching, the cutting of trees (or even tree limbs) and the robbing of fishponds. In enacting the savage code of penalties, the government was responding to a sudden crime wave in Waltham Forest in Essex, committed by gangs with blackened faces. For those who have argued that Walpole was merely using a disingenuously concocted Jacobite scare to impose a judicial terror on the countryside on behalf of the landed oligarchy, the Waltham Blacks have been described as heroes of the poor: Hanoverian Robin Hoods liberating the rich man's venison, or men on the margin of subsistence just attempting to keep body and soul together. In this particular case, though, there seems little doubt that for once Walpole's low threshold of paranoia was perfectly justified since the most recent research makes it incontrovertibly clear that the Waltham Blacks were, in fact, part of a well-organized Jacobite underground.

Justified or not, however, when the Whig government made it possible for a man to be hanged for taking a sheep, it was completing the security arrangements deemed necessary to protect the investment that the oligarchs had made in their property. Walpole made good his promises to use the institutions of government to look after the interests of the landed classes. Land taxes were kept low, and enclosure acts got rid of the scattered strips that had supported families for centuries, replacing them with consolidated, rationally planned, profit-yielding farms. Smallholders who had kept the odd pig or goose and grown a few crops on their strips now had their land taken away for paltry compensation or sometimes none at all. Reduced to living entirely off wage labour, they could hang on in their village or trudge off to somewhere else in hopes of better prospects. The stewards who had seen them off remained quite dry-eyed. It was a shame, no doubt, but agriculture was no longer a matter of sentiment, much less a charity. Like virtually everything else in Hanoverian England, it was strictly business.

If landowners needed to treat their country property as a money-pump it was because, increasingly, they also needed to keep up appearances in town. And while it was possible to cut something of a figure in a provincial town, especially those like Bristol or Glasgow where money came pouring in from the colonial trade, anyone of real ambition had to be seen in London. Walpole may have liked to play the country magnate at Houghton, but his house in Chelsea was just as important as a headquarters for political strategy.

For London, arguably, was the one empire of men and money that escaped from Walpole's managerial control. No one political boss, not even someone of Walpole's inexhaustible, omniscient talents, could manage a city of some 700,000 souls – easily the biggest urban concentration in all of Europe. One in ten of the population of

England lived there and one in six had spent some time working there, and every day the country wagons and carriages would disgorge yet more hundreds looking to cash in on the dazzling fortune they imagined the city to promise. As a headache for political management London was a special source of aggravation, since it acted as a magnet for some of the most creative and independent men of talent, and had generated a market for their ideas independent of anything the Crown could adequately control. As a centre of patronage the court had already begun to atrophy somewhat under the later Stuarts, and the much more parsimonious and philistine Hanoverians completed the process of shifting the centre of attraction from court to city. By the 1730s there were in London some 550 coffee-houses and scores of clubs, all with ardent, literate clienteles for whom irreverence, often of a brutally malicious tenor, was as much a necessary daily diet as mutton pies and ale. And the likes of Steele and Addison, Swift and Pope, whose *Dunciad* (1728) railed against the scandalous scoundrel time of the pax Walpoleana, were more than ready to supply them.

And London was also a great, and potentially subversive, dissolvent of rank. Foreigners, accustomed to more rigorously policed separation of the social orders, were horrified by the promiscuous jostle of the city as well as its gut-packing greediness and roistering, drunken violence, and especially by the indiscriminate mingling of classes in the pleasure gardens. Paris could not yet boast anything like Ranelagh or Vauxhall where, since all the men carried swords and all the ladies arrived in painted finery, many of both in masquerade, it was quite impossible to distinguish between the genteel and the common.

The same was true of the great pleasure hubs of the city. The only marker of esteem, the only necessity for gratification in a place like Covent Garden, was money (or at least credit). And there was so very much to buy. Every kind of prostitute for a start, from fake-virginal to fake French to 'singers and dancers'. If you were after something more specialized, then Harris' *New Atlantis* or *The Whoremongers' Guide to London* could help find cross-dressers, flagellants, gay 'molly-houses' or posture girls who would dance naked over a silver reflecting dish. And if all this parade of vice sickened, more innocent pastimes were also available – like the hunchback Robert Powell's puppet show in Covent Garden, or the coffee-house of the retired actor and murderer Charles Macklin who had stabbed a colleague in a fit of rage and who kept his own private theatre of oratory where he gave voice on issues of the day. As the morning dawned, Covent Garden would fill with other kinds of vendors: pie-men and sellers of dried and fresh fruit and vegetables, dolls and toys, hats and canes.

It became a commonplace of moralists to deplore the seductions of display, the knowing arrangement, designed to prick the appetite. But there was no stopping it

Morning, by William Hogarth, *c.* 1738.

Gin Lane, engraved by William Hogarth, 1751. The panorama of urban death, right to the hanging man in the background garret.

with clucking against iniquity. Shops – and there were, it was estimated, 20,000 of them in London – were increasingly fitted with glass windows, bowed in front to expand the area of effective display. Streets were better lit, so that the rituals of inspection became part of the experience of what, for the first time, can be described without anachronism as shopping. The mistress and master of the household as well as their servants might now take themselves to ogle exotica newly arrived on the market, like oriental goldfish, blue macaws or warbling finches. Previously inaccessible luxuries were now manufactured and priced to find a market among the middling sort of people: Delft blue-and-white pottery somewhat resembling Ming china, from which to sip your tea or chocolate; glass stemware in the shape of bells or bugles for cordials and wines; pewter or silver tankards for ale. And if drink led to the indulgence of other vices you could arm yourself (as contemporaries put it) against sexual diseases with the first commercially produced condoms: lambskins in packets of eight tied with silk for the well-to-do, linen soaked in brine for the not so well-off.

The city as a great Bartholomew's Fair – a gorgeous, chaotic theatre of eye-popping spectacle and greedy consumption – helped the oligarchs as much as it threatened them, since from Walpole's view it all acted as a political opiate, or at least a distraction. Better that energy be driven by the gratification of the senses than committed to the revival of partisan and religious wars. But for precisely that same reason, the increasing number of Walpole's critics in the late 1720s and 1730s saw the gilded web inducing a vicious stupor: robbing the deluded of the innocence of their bodies, the soundness of their minds and the integrity of their souls. London, they said, took free men and women and made them slaves.

The works of William Hogarth and Henry Fielding are full of victims of the Mephistophelian city, arriving dewy-fresh from the country, falling for scoundrelly promises of easily gotten fortune and descending swiftly into a bottomless pit of iniquity, disease, madness and death. But the credit trap could make short work of even the most urbane and socially sophisticated, and the drop from fashion to incarceration (for a debt as small as £2) was a descent into hell. Robert Castell, whose beautiful folio on Roman villas, *The Villas of the Ancients: Illustrated* (1728), was on the shelves of every country gentleman who fancied himself a new Pliny or Horace, found himself in the Fleet in 1728 at the mercy of his gaoler, Thomas Bambridge. Unable to pay the costs of his imprisonment Castell was thrown into a local spongeing house full of smallpox victims, effectively a sentence of death that duly overtook the unfortunate author.

Prison was one of the most robust growth sectors of Britannia Inc. Accordingly, the going rate for a wardenship rose steadily in the Macheath years of Walpole's prime. The sum of £5000 was what John Huggins paid for the wardenship of the Fleet, and he scaled his tariff of residential charges to the inmates to ensure that he got a decent return on his investment. Just £5 would get you your very own cell, a few shillings more something approximating food and (a hot-ticket item for purveyor and customer alike) regular rounds of beer or prison-distilled gin. If these rates were beyond your reach, you took your chances in the packed common prisons, sleeping on the filthy straw with no air, light or sanitation.

And that was the *basic* service, before Huggins began a programme of cost-cutting to minimize his outgoings: ignoring clogged drains; shoving ever more bodies into ever smaller spaces; raising the fee prisoners were charged for their own shackles. As for the utterly destitute, they were using up valuable customer space, so Huggins did whatever it took to move them along to a Better Place. Sometimes they were inconsiderate enough to refuse to go. One morning a group of visitors to the prison chapel were surprised to see a completely naked, breathtakingly filthy man, covered only with a half-shredded mattress, burst in upon their meditations, feathers stuck to him with his own excrement, looking, one of them thought, like a demented chicken. As soon as the visitors had made a hasty exit, Huggins had the pathetic figure thrown right back into the freezing shed from which he had somehow escaped. He died soon afterwards.

Word of such horrors got out – especially when they involved gentlemen like Sir William Rich, put in a room full of unburied corpses for daring to strike the warden. A parliamentary committee was established to investigate the state of prisons and published a report documenting conditions of unimaginable degradation. Hogarth, whose own father had done time for debt, painted the committee – for some reason in their own chamber rather than in the prison offices where they actually conducted their interviews. In one crucial respect, though, Hogarth's vision is accurate. The manacled, trussed-up prisoner – actually a Portuguese Jew – has become a martyr, almost Michelangelesque in his torment, while the gaoler, shifty and sinister, is made to appear the real malefactor.

In the late 1720s, the cry of 'Who are the *real* criminals?' became common in the news-sheets and coffee-houses of London. Everywhere the line between the law-breakers and the law-enforcers seemed arbitrary. In 1725 the Lord Chancellor, the Earl of Macclesfield, was himself convicted of embezzling £80,000 during the South Sea Bubble. Conversely, when he was executed at Tyburn the same year, the most famous of all England's criminals, Jonathan Wild, was recognized by observers like Lord Chesterfield as having the distinctive quality of a 'man of parts' who, had circumstances been different, might have been 'rather born for a ribbon round his shoulders than a rope about his neck'.

Wild's career had begun, like that of so many others, as a pimp running a 'buttock and file' racket, stealing from the clients of whores while they were busy in bed. But like the upwardly mobile apprentices of the legitimate trades, Wild aspired to a better kind of business and found his true vocation as a master-receiver. Presiding over an enormous emporium of stolen goods, Wild made himself indispensable to both the robbers and the robbed. The thieves needed him to fence their loot and keep quiet about where he had got it; the householders needed him as the only sure way to get it back, there being no police force to do it for them. It was a perfect entrepreneurial loop. Making sure there was no evidence to connect him to the crimes, Wild made no secret that he was actually running the gangs of highwaymen, housebreakers and cutpurses whom he was purporting to nail. Occasionally, for the sake of keeping up appearances as the 'Thieftaker General', he would in fact give one up to the magistrates — a regrettable sacrifice for the sake of business credibility. And he was not above complaining that the sums offered for the retrieval of stolen goods hardly compensated for all the onerous expenses incurred in organizing highway robbery. There were the horses to stable, the feed, the lanterns.

Twelve days before Wild was hanged the shrewdest and most honest of all writers on the freebooting English economy, Bernard de Mandeville (who scandalized moralists by acknowledging the correlation between consumer extravagance and the general accumulation of wealth), saw this master-criminal's true significance as having transformed petty larceny into a genuine industry, complete with regulated hours and places of work, and strict books kept on turnover and profits. He expressed his amazement at the hypocrisy of magistrates who 'not only know and see this but … continue to make use of such a person for … evidence and in manner own that they are beholden to him in the administration of justice'. Wild's authentic impersonation of the entrepreneur was capped, posthumously, by having Daniel Defoe ghost his gallows confession — which, needless to say, became an immediate best-seller.

It was the genius of John Gay to take the coffee-house truism that the lawbreakers and the law-makers were interchangeable and turn it into the greatest hit of the eighteenth century: his 'Newgate Pastoral', *The Beggar's Opera* (1728). The audiences who roared abuse at Peachum the Thieftaker of course recognized him as Jonathan Wild, just as they cheered Macheath the highwayman as a stand-in for Jack Sheppard the housebreaker, who had gone to the gallows a year before Wild and had become a street hero for escaping from prison no fewer than four times. But although there was a minor figure in Gay's show called 'Bob Booty', it was just as obvious that Peachum, the extortionist and swaggering man of parts, the man who pretended to civic virtue while bleeding everyone white, was also a thinly veiled caricature of Walpole himself.

So when *The Beggar's Opera* took London and then the provinces by storm it took anti-Walpole satire out of the pages of opposition journals and into the taverns, coffee-houses and theatres. Perhaps it stung to be depicted as the Gangster-in-Office, but Walpole had a hide like an elephant and was certainly not about to fold his tent and depart at the behest of John Gay. He also comforted himself with the knowledge that much of the wave of opposition fury stemmed from their consternation that the new king, George II, whose hatred of his father had led them to believe he would inaugurate his reign by disposing of his prime minister, had instead succumbed to Walpole's inexplicable spell. But although the newly aggressive tide of criticism did not for the moment do much to disturb his stranglehold on power, it did bear witness to a rising tide of revulsion at the world of which Walpole complacently boasted: a sense that beneath the platitudes about peace and stability lay brutality, corruption and misery. Dig beneath the dross, the moralists said, and you will find disease and death.

A walk through the seamier areas of London, through the rookeries and alleys, was a walk over bodies. The supply of very potent, very cheap gin had created an entire sub-culture of dependency and violence in the city comparable only to the crack-houses of the 1980s. Hogarth's famous graphic nightmare of a world in deathly auto-destruction was, of course, a polemical exaggeration. But not altogether, since we know of at least one mother, Judith Dufour, who became notorious for strangling her own baby daughter and selling every stitch of her own clothing to satisfy her craving for a dram. There came a point, though, when someone got tired of stepping over half-dead babies in the gutter or infant corpses thrown into the Fleet Ditch along with the 'blood, guts and dung' that, according to Pope, one expected to find there.

Thomas Coram had made his fortune in Massachusetts from the Atlantic timber trade. All that he wanted was to settle down to a quiet life in Rotherhithe where he could see the Thames and the tides. But the sight of the tiny abandoned corpses in the streets would not let him alone, and he also knew that the mortality rate for infants born in the poor house and sent out to wet nurse was close to a 100 per cent. Opulent London was a hecatomb for babies. So Coram determined to tap some of the city's fortune to establish a foundling hospital, a place where infants, legitimate or illegitimate, could be deposited, no questions asked, and would be given a decent chance of survival. For almost twenty years he made himself a nuisance to his friends, lobbying the great and the good and going so far as to petition the king, until the necessary funds were raised.

He also had to beat back accusations that a place to deposit bastards would reward depravity with impunity and thus further encourage it. Working with Hogarth, Coram had a fund-raising letterhead shamelessly designed to milk every kind of sympathy.

In the drawing on the letterhead, Coram himself appears as a saintly patriarch leading his happy and smiling charges towards a better future. The campaign worked. George II – seldom a pushover for hard-luck stories – melted, along with the queen, and after that the Quality lined up to donate.

The hospital opened its doors in 1741 to its first children. The governors trooped into their council room where they looked at art that had a bearing on their newly discovered mission – Francis Hayman's *The Finding of the Infant Moses in the Bullrushes* (1746), for instance. But the most arresting sight would have been the enormous, full-length portrait of old Captain Coram himself, set against the kind of classical column usually reserved for princes, aristocrats or military heroes. The portrait was as close as Hogarth ever got to a revolutionary act, for it audaciously transferred to this bluff old fellow the customary attributes of royalty; the royal charter, for example, with its seal lay in his hands. The world and its oceans – the orb made literal – was seen as the source of Coram's virtuous fortune. Even the hat by his right foot was significant, for it was meant to remind spectators of another of the tireless Coram's campaigns – to protect British hatters from foreign competition. Needless to say, he had requested that his only remuneration for that advocacy be one of their hats. In other words Coram, in Hogarth's grand depiction (as well as in reality), was everything Walpole and his cronies were not: selfless, philanthropic, modest in his appearance and imbued with civic religion. He was a free man. He was a patriot.

Virtue and good intentions, though, would not alone guarantee the realization of Coram's vision. The hospital was so overwhelmed with demand when it opened that it needed a lottery to decide admission. Anxious mothers lined up to draw coloured balls from a bag. Draw a white ball and your baby was in; draw a red ball for the waiting list; a black ball would send mother and baby back to the streets.

But acceptance brought with it its own kind of poignancy. Inside a cabinet, still kept at the Foundling Hospital, are preserved some of the saddest things left to us from the eighteenth century: the keepsake tokens given to babies by their mothers on the point of abandoning them to the hospital. Although some social historians assume that the appallingly high rates of infant mortality would have inured these mothers to loss, the whole history of response to the Foundling Hospital, not to mention the care and affection given to ensuring that some sort of memento would survive, says otherwise. Though all the objects record a kind of emotional desperation, not all of them speak of destitution. A mother-of-pearl heart with the initials of the infant engraved on it was expensive enough to have been made for a mother from a relatively well-off family, doubtless being protected from disgrace. In many other cases, however, the extreme simplicity of the pieces does suggest hardship. Often they were nothing more

Opposite, top: *The Committee of the House of Commons (the Gaols Committee)*, by William Hogarth, 1729, possibly painted in Fleet Prison, London. The prisoner in full irons might have been the Portuguese, Jacob Medez Solas, one of the first debtors to be gaoled in Fleet Prison.
Opposite, below: *The Foundling Hospital*, by Richard Wilson, *c.* 1741, founded by Thomas Coram.
Top: *Captain Thomas Coram*, by William Hogarth, 1740, shown with the Foundling Hospital's Royal Charter in his hand.
Above: A foundling keepsake, *c.* 1740, one of many left by mothers entrusting their babies to the care of the hospital.

than objects that the mothers happened to have in their possession at the moment of parting: a hazelnut drilled through for a string, to be worn as a pendant or amulet against misfortune; a thimble; a homely sewn heart; or just a flimsy piece of ribbon to be transferred from a mother's hair to a baby's wrist.

History can be a heart-breaker. For the reason we know about these objects, the reason we still have them, is that they never reached their intended recipients. Those responsible for the children's welfare, for better or worse, had decided it would not be in their best interests to give them a reminder of the shame of their origins. Yet, somehow, neither could they bring themselves to destroy them. Instead they went to that most eighteenth-century of limbos: a cabinet of curiosities.

The Foundling Hospital could not create an asylum of health and good cheer overnight. Close to 40 per cent of the first generation of infants died within its walls, although even that was an enormous improvement over the rate of the orphaned or abandoned. And the cause of Coram's Hospital had another kind of effect too: the creation of a new kind of culture, self-consciously apart from the country of aristocratic estates and county hunts – the middle-class parish at work, well-off but busily charitable, interested in virtue rather than fashion, redemption rather than wit. There had been public philanthropy before, of course – organized by the trade guilds as well as Crown, nobility and the established Church. But this was the first time that men and women who belonged to the world of the commercial economy – tradesmen, merchants and bankers – came together with well-known writers, artists and sculptors in a campaign of conscience to attack a notorious social evil.

They were also committed, not just to correcting ills but to a constructive vocation too – and what they wanted to construct were patriots. If the children deposited in the Foundling Hospital survived they were to be turned into model Britons of the future: not the gin-soaked delinquents of the alleys or little criminals on their way to a date with Tyburn's tree, but hard-working, God-fearing, industrious and enterprising model citizens. 'Patriotism' was on the lips of the men and women who launched these little crusades of moral and civic reform in the commercial and port towns of Britain, and increasingly it meant not just a sense of native pride but a commitment to social and political virtue as well. Patriotism, in fact, described itself as everything the Walpole political machine was not: modest in display; disinterested in conviction; impervious to corruption; jealous in the defence of the 'liberties of free-born Britons'; hostile to arbitrary power. Though the anti-'Robinocracy' opposition was made up of very different political types – Tories and Jacobites, independent Whigs, lobbyists for colonial trade and the aggressive expansion of maritime power – they all felt that if there were indeed a new Great Britain, it was they, not Walpole and his creatures, who embodied it. They attacked his devotion to the excise as a way of keeping the land taxes low, and especially the powers given to the collectors who could search warehouses and shops, locking up alleged malefactors without showing due cause. In 1733, when Walpole attempted to expand the powers of search and seizure still further, he was met with a coalition of resistance, not least from meetings of merchants and tradesmen throughout the country who demanded that their MPs vote against the bill as a violation of Magna Carta. When Walpole was heard to refer to a group of them lobbying against the bill at the door of the House of Commons as 'sturdy beggars', the news, relayed quickly through the press, triggered a storm of public indignation: 'Would not every FREE BRITON think the promoter of it [the Excise Bill] An ENEMY to his country? Would he not justly incur the Censure of the Roman Senate and deserve to have that sentence denounced against him "Curse on the Man who owes his greatness to his COUNTRY'S RUIN."'

When the offending bill was withdrawn, the cities, towns and boroughs of England were jubilant. Effigies of Walpole were burned; parades and processions marched through the streets trumpeting the imminent end of the Great Corrupter and the Robinocrats. As it turned out, the celebrations were premature. But the writing was on the wall, not least because, over the years that followed, the opposition press succeeded in painting a picture of Walpole's government as more committed to its own selfish interest than to the interest of the country, especially when it came to standing up for the rights of merchants on the high seas. In 1737 a print called 'The British Hercules' depicted a bare-footed jack-tar, modelled heroically in the manner of the Farnese Hercules in Rome, holding a paper inscribed 'I wait for orders' in front of a prostrate lion and an idle fleet at Spithead. Xenophobic propaganda drummed up the cause of captains whose ships had been boarded by Spanish coastguards. When one of Captain Jenkins' ears had been sliced off, it was claimed, by a Spanish cutlass, and introduced to the House of Commons by 'Patriot' opposition leaders, like William Beckford, as a victim of dastardly papist brutality on the high seas, prints were published showing captured British seamen starving in Spanish dungeons. More than forty addresses and petitions were sent to parliament from the port cities – Bristol and Liverpool – as well as London and Edinburgh. Walpole's way, as ever, was management: a negotiated 'Convention' with Spain, which, because it kept the right of Spanish coastguards to search for contraband, triggered another outpouring of bellicose idignation. A young MP, William Pitt, aired his precocious oratory by attacking the Convention as 'nothing but a stipulation for national ignominy ... the complaints of your despairing merchants, the voice of England, has condemned it'. The pressure for war, both inside and outside parliament, was becoming irresistible. It would happen

The British Hercules, engraved by William Hogarth, 1727.

with or without Walpole. The Spanish saved him by obtusely refusing to ratify the Convention, thus giving Walpole a belated *casus belli*.

In 1739, the new maritime patriotism got its first *bona fide* popular celebrity: Vice Admiral Edward Vernon. With just six ships Vernon had managed to capture the Spanish Caribbean depot of Porto Bello in the isthmus of Panama, the principal base for coastguards, in November 1739, and overnight he became the toast of the taverns, the clubs and the streets. Inns were renamed for him, and Porto Bello roads and streets sprang up not just in London but all over the country. Villages were renamed Porto Bello in Staffordshire, Sussex and Durham. In Fleet Street, a pageant featured a painted pasteboard showing Porto Bello, in front of which a kneeling Spaniard surrendered to a triumphant Vernon. Silver tankards, Staffordshire stoneware mugs, engraved glass goblets, snuff boxes and teapots bore Vernon's likeness, the icon of his little fleet and the universally echoed slogan 'six ships'. In the spring of 1741, the Vernon bandwagon took to the hustings at Westminster and five other constituencies in an organized campaign to throw out Walpole's placemen and elect the naval hero as a public thorn in his side. At Westminister, on the very doorstep of parliament, and where the public street campaign was especially rowdy, troops were used to close the polls early to avoid humiliation.

The Vernon clamour could embarrass the Walpolean regime, but it could not win the war. After Porto Bello came the anti-climax of a botched attack on Cuba. Armed with accusations that he had, once again, betrayed the true cause of the nation, Walpole's opponents combined in a concerted attack, and this time had the parliamentary numbers to make it count. Before he could be pushed, Walpole chose to walk in February 1742. With him went peace. In decade after decade following Walpole's fall Britain would be at war, and whatever the coalition of enemies the country faced, at the heart of them would be the arch-competitor on land and sea, France. Just as in the sixteenth century England's national identity had been beaten out on the anvil of fear and hatred of Catholic Rome and Habsburg Spain, so British identity was forged in the fires of fear and hatred against Catholic, absolutist France. In 1744 an invasion panic struck southern England. George II was off in Germany leading his troops (as he had insisted) beneath the standard of the Electorate of Hanover. Garrisons had been emptied to supply the war on the continent. Britannia had to fend for itself. Only the Channel separated Britain from the frightening spectre of Jesuit inquisitions, wooden shoes, slavish prostration before the Bourbon despot, the end of good ale and the beginning of barbarous food. The ever dependable Protestant wind came between the French fleet and a landing. But both government and people knew that this was only a respite and not a victory. It did not take a strategic genius to predict that, sooner or later, the government of Louis XV would play the Jacobite card, in either Ireland or Scotland, or both.

The failure of the rising of 1715 had set back the Jacobite cause, but it had done nothing to rob it of its burning sense of righteousness and of the inevitable triumph of Stuart legitimacy over the usurping Hanoverians and their lackeys in parliament. The Jacobites still had their court-in-exile in France and a network of agents and diplomats throughout Europe that promised a rising, not only in Scotland but in England too. A war fought against the British, not only in Europe but in America, the Caribbean and southern India, would, at the very least, put an enormous strain on its military manpower, giving the Jacobites their best chance of success in many years.

All the same, when on 19 August 1745 Prince Charles Edward Louis John Cazymyr Sylvester Severino Maria Stuart, the son of the elderly James VIII and III and the grandson of James II, stood in his plaid at the head of the loch in Glenfinnan, watched his standard being raised and told the assembled clansmen that he had come to make Scotland happy, he was putting a brave, bold face on what was already proving to be an unlikely gamble. He had arrived at Glenfinnan from the Hebridean island of Eriskay with the 'seven men' of folklore, as well as a chaplain, valet, pilot and clerk. And he had nearly not made it at all. The two French vessels carrying the Prince and his party across the Irish Sea had run into a British warship, the *Lion,* 100 miles west of the Lizard. Although the Prince's ship, the *Doutelle,* lay safely out of range of British fire, the *Elizabeth* was badly damaged. In a long and murderous exchange of broadsides with the *Lion,* the two ships smashed each other to pieces so comprehensively that it was no longer possible for the *Elizabeth* to heave to and offload some 1500 muskets and 1800 broadswords intended for the Jacobite campaign. So Charles Edward had little to give the 200-odd clansmen other than hope and the undoubtedly glamorous charisma of his personality. What turned the day from quixotic adventurism into something more serious was the arrival, later that afternoon, of another 800 men led by Cameron of Lochiel.

It says something about the complicated allegiances in what was, in effect, another round of a Scottish civil war that had been going on for nearly two centuries that Cameron of Lochiel was not the epitome of the stag-chasing backwoods primitive clan chief. If anything, he was like an increasing number of Highlanders, more obviously part of the new than the old Scotland: a hard-headed businessman who capitalized on harvesting timber from his estates. As someone with a foot in the new economy as well as his heart in the old cult of honour, Cameron had mixed feelings about the arrival of the Prince. Before he would entertain the idea of committing his followers he asked the Prince for an insurance policy – not the sign of reckless patriotism. Should the entire enterprise come to grief, could the Prince promise that he would be reimbursed for all the sacrifices that would undoubtedly be asked of him? By the end of the afternoon, though, romance had defeated prudence; the tug of loyalty had triumphed over business acumen. Cameron pledged himself and his men to the Prince, and the Rubicon was crossed.

A thousand men did not a Restoration make. For although Scotland was the entry-way, the prize for the Stuarts was always meant to be Britain. And for there to be any chance of success, three interlocking strategies had to click together at exactly the right time. It went without saying that most of Scotland needed to come out in open revolt. But as the unhappy precedent of 1715 had shown, that would be of no avail unless Jacobites in England rose in the numbers their spies had promised. And, not least, a French invasion force of not fewer than 10,000 men had to be landed somewhere to complete the pincer effect and disperse Hanoverian attempts at repression. To the pessimists who observed that such invasions had a long history of failure, the Stuarts might well have ground their teeth a little and invoked one wholly successful invasion: from the Netherlands in 1688!

For some weeks the government in Westminster was unsure whom or what to believe about the rumours that the Prince had landed and begun a march south through Scotland. It divided between complacency and panic. The complacent view was that Charles Edward would waste his minuscule force attempting to besiege the impregnable Highland forts William and Augustus, by which time his untrained Highlanders could be picked off by the regular soldiers of Lieutenant-General Sir John Cope. But there were some in the government who had a much gloomier diagnosis of what was in store, believing it to be inconceivable that a landing of any kind would have been made without the assurance of a prompt French or Spanish invasion to follow soon afterwards. 'The undertaking,' one of these pessimists wrote, 'in its present appearance seems (as it is the fashion to call it) rash and desperate. But I cannot think it is altogether to be despised. We are so naked of troops that if a body of men was to be flung over no-one can say what may be the consequences.' The gloomy truth, Henry Pelham wrote, was that in England there were hardly enough soldiers to stand guard at the royal palaces or put down a smugglers' riot, much less resist an invasion of any strength.

The collapse was much faster and much more shocking than anyone in London could possibly have imagined in their worst nightmares. Charles Edward had sensibly bypassed the fool's target at Fort William and moved directly to take towns like Perth, where he knew he had the edge in numbers over local defences. Nervous that all he could put in the field was 1500 troops against the (wrongly) reported Jacobite army of 5000, General Cope made a tactical retreat all the way north to Inverness, leaving the Scottish Lowlands virtually undefended. On 17 September the Prince took Edinburgh. Dazzling though the prize seemed to be, it was a long way from being a complete triumph. The Provost and his council had decided against resistance. But their prudent decision was not at all the same as enthusiastic endorsement of the Prince's cause. Should the military balance of power change, they could as easily revert to Hanoverian loyalism. There were, in fact, still two well-supplied regiments of dragoons holed up in Edinburgh Castle, defying all attempts to winkle or starve them out. Most of these soldiers were Scots, and their continued loyalism was not atypical of many of the Lowland population. Even in the Highlands only about half the clans rallied to the Prince, so that through most of the '45 there were probably more Scotsmen fighting against Bonnie Prince Charlie than for him.

Increasingly, business got in the way of sentimental allegiance. Running short of money to pay their troops, the Jacobite officers were informed that the necessary funds were locked up in the castle along with the dragoons. None the less, they thought it worthwhile inquiring whether – at reasonable rates of interest – some of the cash might be made available to stop their men taking their desperation out on the city. It must have seemed like a reasonable proposition, since it met with a favourable response. Money was delivered from the castle to the Jacobites so that the two camps could carry on pretending to fire at each other.

Freshly supplied and financed, morale high and bellies full, on 21 September 1745, the Jacobite army marched out to meet General Cope's troops at Prestonpans, 8 miles east of Edinburgh, each army some 2500 strong. What ensued was one of the most notorious fiascoes in British military history. Cope had managed to station his soldiers between the river and a bog, but, informed by a deserter about the Hanoverian positions, the Jacobites used a track through the mire to march to their rear and caught them literally napping before dawn. In the rout 300 British soldiers were quickly killed. The only professional loyalist army in Scotland had been destroyed. Needless to say, in London the disaster was blamed not on the incompetence of the officers but on the cowardice of the rank and file.

The almost unexpected completeness of their success forced the Jacobite army to consider what it was they were truly supposed to be: the liberators of Scotland or the restorers of the Stuart dynasty to all of Britain? The issue was thrashed out on 30 October at Holyroodhouse, where the Prince had taken up residence in the palace of his royal ancestors. Charles Edward argued that, even tactically, the right decision was to take the campaign into England. He and his followers had enjoyed extraordinary success only because of the temporary absence of concentrations of Hanoverian

A drawing of highland warriors, attributed to John Clerk of Penicuik, *c.* 1746. The 'Penicuik' sketchbook is a unique and masterly document of the human face of the Jacobite war, at times mordantly satirical, at other times full of pathos and disgust. At his best the artist rises to the heights of a Scottish Goya.

troops in continental Europe, but the day could not be far off when numbers of those soldiers would return. A far more formidable threat would face them than the soldiers they had surprised at Prestonpans. The question was: where would be the best place to confront it? The Prince insisted that the other two pieces of Jacobite strategy all pointed to the necessity of a march through England. Without a campaign there, catching the enemy while he was still weak, the English uprising was unlikely to be at all successful – and without that rising the French invasion might not happen at all. It was imperative to be able to demonstrate to Versailles that this was not to be a repetition of 1715, that they were in earnest.

Lord George Murray, the ablest of the Jacobite generals, was much more cautious; still nervous about their position in Scotland, much less in Britain overall, wanting to consolidate a position in the Highlands where the war could be fought on their own terms, systematically breaking down the pro-Hanoverian clans, making the Stuarts the impregnable masters of the north and daring the English to come after them and risk more defeats like Prestonpans.

The differences aired at the council of war at Holyroodhouse were not just about military strategy. They went to the heart of why everyone in the Jacobite war was risking their neck. Was it, as Murray and the Highland soldiers believed, for Scotland, to restore the old world before the union and to recover a free and independent Scotland? Or was it, as the Prince imagined, a crusade to undo 1688: to throw the Hanoverians off the throne of Britain, to restore not just James VIII but James III?

After intense debate, the Prince won the argument – at least about strategy – by a single vote. The Jacobites marched south, moving at such a brisk pace that General Wade, based at Newcastle, who had expected to bar their way, instead found himself constantly outpaced. In rapid succession Carlisle, Lancaster, Preston and Manchester all fell to the Prince's army, virtually without a shot being fired in their defence. Each time Wade's troops attempted an interception by crossing the Pennines terrible weather held them up, and by the time they reached their destination on the western side of the mountains the Jacobites had moved on. It was the British, not the Jacobite, soldiers who were suffering the worst privations. On 19 November James Cholmondeley, the colonel of the 34th Foot, wrote to his brother, the earl, about one of the worst of those marches across the Dales. They had, he said, endured 'miserable roads, terrible frost and snow. We did not get to our grounds till eight and as my quarters were five miles off I did not get there till eleven, almost starved to death with cold and hunger but revived by a pipe and little good wine. Next morning we found some poor fellows frozen to death for they could get nothing to eat after marching thirteen miles.'

By the beginning of December the Jacobites were closing in on Derby. The predicted mass uprisings in the English cities had not yet materialized, but nor could it be said that northern populations in the path of the march had risen as a man to defend the house of Hanover. Instead there were reports of merchants, landowners and bankers in Northumberland, Yorkshire and Lancashire taking to the highways along with their movable wealth and families. As the sense of an unstoppable momentum became more ominous, London caught a violent attack of the jitters. There was the usual run on the Bank of England, and the usual atrocity stories to feed the hysteria, featuring children tied to the walls of Carlisle Castle so that, if royal troops attempted to take it, they would be obliged first to massacre the lambs. But there were also the first stirrings of some patriotic resistance and Scottophobia. 'God Save the King', which in an earlier form had actually been a Stuart song, was now sung for the first time as a national anthem in the theatres of Covent Garden and Drury Lane. Volunteer associations in some sixty counties had produced men willing to serve in the militia.

On 10 December, three regiments of infantry and one of horse guards were ordered out to a camp at Finchley, which the commander of the army, George II's son, the Duke of Cumberland, had established 'just in case', he said, the Jacobites whom he meant to engage at Northampton should give him the slip, as they had done so many times to Wade. Four years later Hogarth painted the scene along the Tottenham Court Road, and although he had the luxury of hindsight, his teeming, riotous picture – a huge and profitable success when it sold as a print from 1751 – does say something about England at its chaotic moment of truth. No wonder, when George II saw the painting, he erupted in fury: 'What, does the fellow mean to make fun of my guards?' For the soldiers in the picture (and everyone else for that matter) are not exactly paragons of martial discipline. This England is less parade ground than fairground (Hogarth's preferred metaphor over and over again for its sprawling, unruly energy). Bare-knuckled prize-fighters go at it under the sign of the Garden of Eden like Cain and Abel. On the right hand the realm of vice assembles by the King's Head, featuring the likeness of Charles II and one of the late monarch's favourite pastimes, the whorehouse. A falling soldier spurns his Good Samaritan's water for what he really wants: a tipple of gin; a groper makes the milkmaid spill her milk while a crazed hag, probably meant to be Irish, with a cross on her cape, brandishes a Jacobite broadside. Opposite them are the *relatively* virtuous. The trees are in leaf. The courtyard in which the pugilists battle is the Nursery of 'Giles Gardiner'; a mother suckles her baby. And the forlorn mother-to-be clinging to the departing soldier's arm carries 'God Save the King' and a portrait of the Duke of Cumberland in her basket.

As a portrait of group energy this is distinctly a back-handed kind of flattery. Somehow, Hogarth asks us to believe that this disorderly rabble will compose itself into the disciplined troop seen in the background marching off towards Highgate Hill. But this is the miracle of England, patriot-style, strength from liberty. To spite the king, when he heard about his well-publicized objections Hogarth dedicated the engraved version to Frederick the Great, the King of Prussia, 'Encourager of Arts and Sciences' (in invidious contrast to the philistine Hanoverians). But perhaps there was a shade of irony there too, for his vision of bloody, bruising, riotous England was precisely the opposite of machine-tooled Prussia, the barrack-house kingdom.

Whether Hogarth's scratch army could pass the test of combat, few (other than Cumberland) were at all sure. Until Culloden in April 1746, the Hanoverian armies did not defeat the Jacobites in anything like a serious battle. At Falkirk, in January 1746, where 8000 soldiers had been committed on each side, much the biggest engagement of the war, the Jacobites had won the day but failed to press home their temporary advantage, wasting time, men and money until all three ran out in a futile siege of Stirling Castle at the end of the month. In the end, as in 1715, the Jacobites defeated themselves, and less on the battlefield than in the council room. At Exeter House in Derby, on 5 December 1745, five days before the march out to the Finchley camp, another critical debate had taken place on the future strategy of the campaign.

Overleaf: *The March to Finchley*, by William Hogarth, 1750.

Much the same arguments that had divided the Prince from Lord George Murray continued to exercise them. London is just 130 miles (200 km) off, said Charles Edward; a handful of militiamen and Finchley stands between us and a glorious Restoration. Move on the capital and the French will undoubtedly come. Our friends in England will declare themselves, and 1688 will seem a bad memory.

Murray was not to be moved. For months the Prince had been promising the imminent appearance of the French and they were still nowhere to be seen. The 3000 English Jacobites who were supposed to be rallying to the cause had proved equally elusive. All he could see was a pyrrhic victory: the Jacobite army trapped in London, its rear cut off by Cumberland, the reinforcements arriving daily from the Continent. It was time, he insisted, to cut their losses, to make a stand in the heartland of their cause: in Scotland. The very force of his argument betrayed a fundamental insecurity about the viability of the whole enterprise. For in the last resort, successful as he had been, Murray was uncertain whether armed Jacobitism could survive anywhere other than Scotland, north of the Firth of Forth; or at least he wanted to pitch his tents as close as possible to a safe refuge should the balance of military power turn ugly. Perhaps folk memories of his ancestor Andrew Murray and of Robert the Bruce may yet have played over in his mind? Whether the cult of honour could survive in the new Britain of cash contracts and the drilled bayonet was increasingly moot. At any rate, this time he had the better of the debate. The Jacobite army, with the Prince sulking on his horse, turned about and retreated north. Needless to say, they had barely begun their long tramp home when Louis XV and his ministers were finally impressed enough by the progress of the Jacobites into England to send the long-awaited invasion fleet!

It was much too late. Battered by heavy winds and by the hero of Porto Bello, Admiral Vernon, the French probably would have been of little help. As it was, the Jacobite march north turned into a prolonged nightmare. Slowed by snowstorms and harried by Cumberland's pursuing army, now much reinforced, the retreat became ever more ragged and desperate. Garrisons manned by their troops on the advance into England were now left to treat with Cumberland as best they could. At Carlisle the Duke refused to accept the surrender of the Scots garrison in the castle, freeing him from treating the prisoners according to the conventions governing prisoners of war. This was a rebellion, not a war between gentlemen. Any Englishmen believed to have cooperated with the Jacobites were summarily hanged, and hundreds of their soldiers were crammed into a tiny, suffocating space, without air, light or water. Subjected to inhuman suffering, they were reduced to licking the slimy cavities of the interior rock wall for drops of moisture.

By the time that winter turned to spring in the Highlands it was clear to the Jacobites that whatever its temporary successes – as at Falkirk – their campaign was lost. With every week that passed, the Hanoverian advantage in men and guns told. By the time the two armies faced each other at Culloden, some 6 miles east of Inverness, on 16 April, Cumberland's force, about 9000 strong, was almost twice the size of the Prince's army of some 5000. And, more important, it was armed with heavy cannon and the new, lethal combination of stabbing and firing machines – the bayonet. On a sodden piece of land his generals had begged the Prince not to make his battlefield, the Highlanders charged uphill, a northeaster blowing hard in their faces, and straight into the Hanoverian guns that tore holes through their ranks. The charge that had been so terrible at Killiecrankie turned into a stumble of survivors, carried along by their own fatal momentum and some desperate instinct of clan solidarity. An hour after the firing had started there were between 1000 and 1500 Jacobite Highlanders dead on the field and 700 more taken prisoner.

All things considered, it was better to be one of the dead and be spared the sight of the Hanoverian soldiers coming at the wounded to break their bones and further mutilate their bodies before finishing them off. As many as 1000 of the helplessly wounded may have perished in this gruesome manner. The cold-blooded slaughter of the wounded and the methodical hunt for those in flight was justified in England by orders, purportedly given by the Prince before Culloden, to give no quarter. But those orders were a pure invention of Hanoverian propaganda. In fact the march through England had been fastidiously careful to avoid alienating local populations and captured troops who it was hoped, might yet be recruited to the cause of King James III. But Cumberland relied on the paranoid caricatures of the Highlanders as half-evolved primitives, the better to justify his own pitiless repression. And the bloodier he got, the better England liked it. Handel wrote *See the Conquering Hero Comes*, first performed in 1746, to celebrate his triumph. Medals and gifts poured in to express the gratitude of the boroughs and towns. In Newcastle, the Trinity House society of mariners and merchants presented him with an ornate gold box in appreciation for delivering them from the Scottish plague.

After Culloden it might still have been possible – as some of their leaders had always thought – for Jacobite resistance to continue in the fastness of the Highlands and islands, until they could at least extract some sort of amnesty out of the government. Only three-fifths of the Prince's army, after all, had been present at Culloden. But Charles Edward Stuart broke his cause with the same kind of carelessness with which he had made it, summarily declaring it irretrievably lost and ordering an every-man-for-themselves, going on the run himself until he could ship back to France.

Behind him he left a population prostrated before a systematic exercise in state terror inflicted by one part of Britain against the other. Some of it was accomplished by physical force – whole villages burned to the ground without much close inquiry as to the sympathies of the local population. Cattle were stolen; thousands of crofters were turned off their land. What violence began, legal coercion completed. Hereditary jurisdictions were abolished, thus destroying at a blow the patriarchal authority of the clan chiefs and the entire chain of loyalty that depended on them. Speaking Gaelic was forbidden, as was wearing the plaid *unless* serving with the royal army (in which case, in a stroke of psychological cunning, it was positively encouraged). Everything about the ancient Highland culture of tribal honour was uprooted and the broken remnants flattened into submission.

In London the trial and execution of Jacobite lords became public entertainment, just another of the shows for the diversion-hungry city. The drama, after all, beat anything to be seen at Drury Lane. King George reprieved George Mackenzie, third Earl of Cromarty, when his wife went sobbing before the king, falling to her knees and then fainting away in a pathetic swoon of grief and terror. Even a sovereign notorious for his indifference to the stage was shaken by the performance. William Boyd, fourth Earl of Kilmarnock, and Arthur Elfinstone, sixth Baron Balmerino, on the other hand, exited with heroic obstinacy, proclaiming their devotion to the divinely anointed Stuarts. The most colourful of the lot, Simon Fraser, twelfth Baron Lovat, had been found hiding in a hollowed-out tree-trunk in western Scotland. He had been a wicked opportunist, swinging between the two allegiances, remaining faithful to the king in 1745 but sending his son off to fight with the Prince. Now that the Jacobites had lost he blamed his predicament on the boy. Hogarth went to see Lovat and made an unforgettable print of the cackling old monster counting the clans on his fingers. En route to his trial, according to Horace Walpole, a woman stared into his coach and shouted, 'You ugly old dog, don't you think you will have that frightful head cut off?' To which Lovat replied without missing a beat, 'You damned ugly old bitch, I believe I shall.' He was right. So many people packed the site of his execution at Tower Hill, on 9 April 1747, that a specially built viewing stand collapsed (in yet another Hogarthian scene of downfall), killing seven, rather more than Lovat had ever dispatched in his life.

The London Scots looked on these terrible spectacles of retribution and humiliation (as well as what they heard of the miseries in the north) with a mixture of horror, pathos and rage. Tobias Smollett heard news of Culloden while drinking in a tavern and was so mortified by the raucous celebrations it set off among the English drinkers that, though no Jacobite, he felt impelled to write a dirge for the catastrophe that had overwhelmed his country, 'The Tears of Scotland'.

Top: *Prince Charles Edward Stuart*, by Antonio David, *c.* 1732. Bonnie Prince Charlie, the Young Pretender, led the highlanders in the Jacobite rising of 1745.
Above: *Combat at Culloden, 16 April 1746*, by David Morier, *c.* 1750, commissioned by the Duke of Cumberland.

Mourn, hapless Caledonia, mourn
Thy banished peace, thy laurel torn
Thy sons, for valour long renowned
Lie slaughtered on their native ground;
Thy hospitable roofs no more
Invite the stranger to the door;
In smoky ruins sunk they lie
The monuments of cruelty

With this wave of sorrow and self-pity washing over him Smollett must have asked himself, like so many of his compatriots in the aftermath of the '45, how it was possible, now, to be British. Some of them – a shrinking minority – would have answered flatly that it was not; that now they lived in a colony beneath the heel of the conqueror, with language, dress and customs outlawed. Henceforth, unrepentant Jacobites, the survivors of the cult of honour, had to live an occult life of relics and fetishes that could be hidden away and taken out for moments of furtive veneration: locks of Bonnie Prince Charlie's hair; torn fragments of his plaid; goblets painted with an indecipherable smudge of paint that only the initiated, equipped with the right reflecting base, could see the colours resolve themselves into an icon of the lost loved one, the boy born to be king, the saviour across the water. The memorabilia remained hallowed while the real Charlie went horribly profane in Rome. Too many mistresses, far too much drink, years of tedious, sentimental prattle over the port about what-might-have-been made him bloated, prematurely decrepit and squalid, living off the charity of the gullible. Staring at the cracked masonry of the Forum he became himself a ruin, draped in the mossy weeds of his own bathos.

But except as romantic entertainment the Prince had become irrelevant to the real future of Scotland, which in the decades after Culloden did not surrender to sentimental grief but turned itself instead into the most dynamically modernizing society in Europe. In 1749, four years after the battle, Dr John Roebuck and Samuel Garbett accomplished a different kind of victory at Prestonpans, opening their plant making sulphuric acid. Even before the '45, the old Highland way of life was being altered by the capitalization of land, the change from customary communities to productive investments. Villagers were cleared off smallholdings they had occupied and farmed for centuries to make way for blackface and Cheviot sheep or Highland cattle, both supplying the burgeoning markets of the Lowland and English towns. And the aggressive engineers of the clearances, both Highland and Lowland, like the Camerons of Lochiel, could just as easily be Jacobite as loyalist. What was left of the old way when

clan chiefs violated what had been the first obligation to their tenants: guaranteeing them the security of their tenure?

At least there was somewhere for the displaced to go. The clansmen who had been unable to break Britannia were now given the option of joining it, and many took it. In the second half of the eighteenth century tens of thousands of Highlanders were recruited into the British army and saw action in its many theatres of war around the world from India to Canada. Some 70,000 were said to have served in British regiments during the revolutionary and Napoleonic wars. And the annals of imperial government, as well as the barracks and the battlefield, are dominated to an extraordinary degree by famous Scottish names: Munros and Elfinstones, Murrays, Gordons and Grants. Even when some of the most obstinate Jacobites – like Flora MacDonald and her husband, who had famously helped the Prince make his escape – emigrated to America, they declared themselves (in North Carolina) as resolutely patriotic British loyalists during the revolutionary wars.

Instead of being colonized by the British Empire, then, the Scots colonized it themselves. Nearly half of those leaving fortunes worth more than £1000 in Jamaica in the second half of the eighteenth century were Scots. Glasgow grew rich off the transatlantic tobacco trade, and the great merchant capitalists like John Glassford and Alexander Speirs became some of the most economically powerful men in Britain. Speirs is a perfect example of the new kind of 'North Briton' whom Defoe had in mind when he attempted to imagine a happier and more prosperous Scotland within the union. Speirs had been a merchant of modest means until he married into one of the older tobacco families, the Buchanans. After that there was no stopping him, and Speirs, Bowman and Co. became one of the meteors of the transatlantic trade, sending their own Clydeside-built ships (using a dry dock constructed in 1762) on sixteen voyages to Virginia and the Carolinas between 1757 and 1765. In America, Scottish agents had established company warehouses that dealt directly with the growers, cutting out middlemen. Cheaper costs of handling and shipping the crop and a booming market throughout Britain meant a doubled turnover between the middle and the end of the century, and higher profits. Those profits (interrupted for a while by the depression of the early 1770s and the War of American Independence) in turn capitalized other sectors of the economy in which Speirs and his fellow Glaswegian tobacco lairds made investments: glassmaking, sugar refining, linen weaving.

It was the vindication of Darien, and it was an improvement on Darien. Separate from England, the Scots who imagined a new kind of future for their country had been helpless to withstand the kind of political and military muscle that the English could bring to their economic intimidation. As an integral part of a united kingdom,

they had been pulled into an increasingly indivisible economy that had transformed the entire country. The roads and bridges that had been built by General Wade and his teams of surveyors and engineers (including the artist Paul Sandby, who made a superlative record of the landscape), primarily for strategic purposes, now provided incomparably improved routes for the shippers of goods and the drovers of cattle and sheep. Highland products like kelp, slate, wool, whisky and even smoked fish (for there were hundreds of herring boats plying the waters of Loch Fyne alone) now found their way south to an English market. And the movement of men, merchandise and technology was genuinely two-way. James Watt, the Scot who provided a steam pump for the Greenock dry dock, teamed up with an Englishman, Matthew Boulton, to found Boulton & Watt, the Soho Engineering works near Birmingham; Coalbrookdale in the English Midlands sent its smelting technology north for the foundation of the Carron ironworks in Stirlingshire.

In the circumstances it cannot possibly be fortuitous that it was in Scotland, in the 'hotbeds of genius' that flowered in Edinburgh, Glasgow and Aberdeen, that the first theory of progress was systematically articulated. It was built, in the first place, on the denial of, or at the very least the sceptical indifference to, knowledge allegedly based on revelation, such as miracles. The kinds of miracles that the Scots were interested in were happening on Clydeside. Scotland, which had for so long been torn apart by confessional wars, was being healed by the cult of reason that flowered in the academies and reading clubs of these three cities. The culture that had been captive to nostalgia was rapidly turning into the empire of hard facts, the temple of the gospel of modernity. Both could be found housed in the extraordinary three-volume *Encyclopedia Britannica*, first printed and published in Edinburgh in 1768–71. Originally conceived by the Scottish printers Andrew Bull and Colin Macfarquar, it was edited chiefly by another Scot, the printer and antiquary William Smellie. The first revised and enlarged, ten-volume edition, 1776–84, was the brain-child of James Tytler, poet, printer, surgeon, chemist and hot-air balloonist, the very prototype of the new Scot. Just as English tourists were beginning to come north and ruminate soulfully on the Scottish tragedy on windswept moors and misty-shrouded lochs, Scottish writers and philosophers were brushing away the cobwebs of sentiment. First see with absolute clarity, argued David Hume, how it is we can know things for sure; and once sure of the solidity of our knowledge, make it work to make a society in which happiness might prosper. Happiness was what Bonnie Prince Charlie had promised his followers at Glenfinnan. But the chances of its realization, thought Hume and his fellow philosophers, depended exactly on the degree to which Britons liberated themselves from the old siren songs.

Top: The south front of Kedleston Hall, Derbyshire, 1758–65, the grand Georgian house designed by Robert Adam for Sir Nathaniel Curzon.
Above: Aerial view of Edinburgh New Town, designed by James Craig in 1767.

'This is the historical age and we are the historical people,' Hume announced. But for once he did not mean that Scotland, or for that matter the Britain for which he was an unapologetic champion, was history's fall-guy, doomed to the kind of repetitive cycles inscribed in the chronicles of antiquity. On the contrary, Hume, Adam Ferguson and Adam Smith looked at the epic of their own country and saw in one place the entire arc of human social development from hunting-gathering societies to nomadic herders, settled farmers and finally to true civilization: the beckoning world of commerce, science and industry, the world of the town. By the end of the century, no country in the world was urbanizing or industrializing more swiftly than Scotland.

The true Scotland was now to be discovered in the handsome squares and streets of the new Edinburgh and Glasgow. In 1767 James Craig, the nephew of the arch drum-beater for a united Britain and the lyricist of 'Rule Britannia', James Thomson, laid out the design for the New Town of Edinburgh. He inscribed on the plans some characteristic lines from his uncle's verse, comparing the edifices of the new Britain to a new Rome – in fact an improved Rome. Unlike Charles Edward Stuart, who was trapped in one kind of Roman reverie, the new Scots would return from the Grand Tour perhaps bringing with them plaster casts or antique medals supplied by the entrepreneur Gavin Hamilton, full of plans to make classicism commercial. And none brought off this apparently oxymoronic feat more triumphantly than 'Roman Bob', Robert Adam.

Thirteen years after Bonnie Prince Charlie brought the Jacobite army to its endgame at Derby, Robert Adam, the son of a successful Edinburgh architect, William Adam, came back to Derbyshire as a very different kind of invader, Britain's first invincible king of style. And in that capacity he took the country by storm. At Kedleston Adam was not shy about showing off his learning. The south front of the house is modelled on the Arch of Constantine and the domed salon on the Pantheon. But Kedleston was emphatically not a museum disguised as a country house. It was a brand-new style for a new kind of aristocrat. Its owner, Nathaniel Curzon, first Baron Scarsdale, had made his money and political power not just from land and political connections, the Walpolean way, but from the Derbyshire coal mines as well. And what he evidently wanted was a house in which wealth would not overpower the visitor with swaggering ostentation, but speak instead of noble, Ciceronian austerity, a temple of virtue and contemplation, cool, pure and benevolent.

Adam's triumph at Kedleston made him the most sought-after architect of his generation, an authentically British designer with offices in both London and Edinburgh, building in both countries. And part of the secret of his success was his ability to translate into building style the principle, articulated by Adam Smith, that what his generation called 'opulence' was not merely (as had been displayed at Houghton) a phenomenon of purely private accumulation; it was also a force for general happiness.

In 1746, while the last unfortunate survivors of Cumberland's terror were being tracked down, Adam Smith, the son of a customs officer on the north bank of the Firth of Forth, returned to his native country. He had turned his back on Oxford where, he wrote, the university had given up 'even the faintest pretence of learning'. But he also turned his back on the Scottish past for an exhilarating vision of what might be to come. The vision was based on Smith's rejection of guilt and sin, both the Catholic and Calvinist varieties. Instead, in *The Wealth of Nations*, written from 1766 to 1776, he laid out as a matter of historical fact man's instinctive and wholly natural drive towards self-betterment. That such an instinct was driven by motives of vanity and acquisitiveness was neither here nor there. Allowed to follow their natural urges, men would create, without even consciously willing it, a better world: a richer, more educated and freer society. And here Smith also turned away from the immense apparatus of Hanoverian state power. In the new world he was imagining it was no longer the enemy. It was simply an irrelevance. For no government was needed to legislate wealth; indeed, any that imagined it could was simply the victim of self-delusion. The best government was that which got out of the way and permitted the invisible hand of the market to do its work. The economic world, he wrote, was like a watch, the springs and wheels 'all admirably adjusted to the ends for which it was made'; so too the countless movements of industrious men would perfectly interconnect for the purposes for which God had made them.

That purpose was progress, material, moral and intellectual. And it was one of history's sweetest ironies that it fell to Scotland, bloodied, mutilated Scotland, to show Britannia the way ahead. If you want to see the future, the Scottish philosophers said, forget the vainglorious monuments of England's past, the dusty tombs and forbidding cathedrals. Come north, instead, to the new 'hotbeds of genius', to Glasgow and Edinburgh, and see what lies in store for Britain, perhaps for the world.

6

The Scene: Represents a plain surrounded by woods. On one side a cottage, on the other flocks and herds – distant prospect. A hermit's cave in full view over-hung with wild trees; wild and grotesque.

Enter: ALFRED with the Earl of Devon.

How long, O, ever gracious heavens, how long
Shall war thus desolate this prostrate land?

As our Anglo-Saxon hero, on the run from the Danes and flagging badly in energy and morale, was revealed by the candle-lights (in the usual tragick-antique costume of cuirass above, skirts below) bewailing his country's fate, the audience, we must assume, was putting on its own show of rapt attention. Anything less would have been not just impolite but imprudent too. For *Alfred. A Masque*, written in tandem by the Scottish poets James Thomson and David Mallett (*né* Malloch, but anglicized to improve his chances among the Sassenachs), with music by Thomas Arne, had been commissioned by the grandest of patrons, the hope of Free Britons: Frederick Louis, Prince of Wales. The performance at the Prince's house, Cliveden in Buckinghamshire, was ostensibly private. But in every way that really mattered it was an occasion designed to advertise publicly, especially in the gossip-greedy press, the credentials of the Prince and his supporters as True Patriots. The day, 1 August 1740, had been carefully chosen. It was the anniversary of the accession of his grandfather, George I, whom Frederick affected to respect in proportion to his public loathing for his own parents. It was also the day after the third birthday of his daughter, Princess Augusta, whose arrival had been made memorable by Frederick snatching away his wife, on the very point of delivery, from the King and Queen and insisting she give birth instead in his house at St James's Palace. If Queen Caroline's verdict on her son, 'the greatest ass … the greatest liar … and the greatest beast in the world' might seem a little strong,

THE WRONG EMPIRE

Signing the Declaration of Independence of the United States of North America on 4 July 1776, by John Trumbull, *c.* 1786–87.

especially when she made it no secret that to have him disappear from the world would not occasion waterfalls of grief, it was none the less understandable. But Frederick thought he had time on his side. His father, George II, was fifty-six; his unlamented mother had already departed three years before. He, on the other hand, was thirty-three and coming into his own.

Frederick would disappoint his followers by dying of a brain abscess in 1751. But on this summer night at Cliveden, with the Thames flowing sweetly by, it was possible to overlook his gambling and his women and his temper and see him instead as the cello-playing virtuous virtuoso, the epitome of the patriot prince, the guardian of liberty. Around him were gathered his political enthusiasts, erstwhile Walpole allies, but many of them had been turned out of office in 1737 when the tug-of-war over the Prince's revenues was at its fiercest. Now they were bitter enemies of the government. In all likelihood there would have been George Bubb Dodington, the most recent reconversion to the Prince's interest, swathed in brocaded silk beneath which his considerable bulk struggled, as Horace Walpole noted, to break free of its moorings. There too would have been Sir Richard Temple, Viscount Cobham (whom Walpole had not merely peremptorily dismissed but, unforgivably as far as Cobham was concerned, stripped of his command of the King's Own Horse regiment), with some of his own protégés, the 'Cobham cubs', his nephews the Grenville brothers, and William Pitt. There might also have been dissident Whigs like John Carteret. It is tempting, too, to include in the audience a particular ex-Tory politician for whom an Anglo-Saxon allegory would have had special significance: Henry St John, Viscount Bolingbroke.

Though Bolingbroke's disastrous flirtation with Jacobitism in 1714 was enough to bar him from the House of Lords, he was still an immensely influential figure. In 1738 he had published his *Patriot King* expressly as vocational guidance for the Prince of Wales. For Frederick, Bolingbroke had designed an improbably disinterested identity that would transcend selfish factionalism. As king, Frederick would ascend the throne sworn to purge the country of venality and oppression. But since Bolingbroke had also produced a history of medieval Britain purporting to see, from the very beginning, the forces of liberty and despotism locked in combat, Frederick's role would be to *restore* the ancient Anglo-Saxon spirit of freedom, which had its crowning glory in the reign of Alfred. It was Alfred, it was said (wrongly), who had originated trial by jury and who was habitually referred to as the 'Guardian of Liberty'. The Prince's own ambition to be considered the Hanoverian Alfred had already been signalled in 1735 when he had commissioned a statue of the Anglo-Saxon hero king from the fashionable sculptor John Michael Rysbrack for the garden of his town house on Pall Mall.

Mallett and Thomson, the anti-Jacobite Scots, were nothing if not obliging, and what they produced for the Prince and his circle that evening in 1740 was, in effect, Bolingbroke set to verse and music. Given the importance of the occasion, there could be no stinting on the performers. From Drury Lane, William Milward played Alfred while the great Kitty Clive took the part of the sympathetic shepherdess Emma. The musical attraction was the famous Covent Garden tenor Thomas Salway, who doubled as both the shepherd Corin and a bard whose solo rendition of a new song by Arne at the end of the masque was to be critical to the success of the entire evening. Before that cheering finale, though, the up-against-it king was roused to a fresh resolve to do battle with the alien forces of oppression by the spirits of three of his most glorious descendants, conjured up from the future by the clairvoyant hermit. The three royal phantoms – the Black Prince, Elizabeth I and William III – offer Alfred an inspirational glimpse of the imperial destiny awaiting his sea-girt realm (and unburden themselves of long, pull-yourself-together-for-Britannia homilies). But for the war-fevered audience of 1740 the last two would have had particular resonance, cast as they were as royal warriors for an expressly Protestant, anti-Spanish, Gallophobic nation. At that very moment the heir to the naval tradition, the universally acclaimed 'Free Briton', Vice-Admiral Edward Vernon, was busy fitting out a new fleet intended to attack the eastern end of Cuba.

His martial ardour duly rekindled, Alfred swears to rid the country of the foreign brutes: the cue for Salway to step out and celebrate the moment of patriotic reconsecration:

> The Muses, still with freedom found
> Shall to thy happy coast repair
> Blest isle! With matchless beauty crownd
> And manly hearts to guard thee.

At which point Arne's band would have struck up their fiddles, kettle-drums, oboes and brass, and taking centre stage, Salway (knowing a hit when he sang one) would have given the moment its all, his tenor lustily mounting the scale of the first verse like a sailor climbing to the crow's nest:

> When Britain fir- ir- ir- irst at HEAVEN's command
> A -ro- oh oh ohse from out the a-ay- zure main
> A -roh-oh -ohse from out the azure main
> THIS was the charter, the charter of the land

And guardian ay-ay-ay-ay-ANGELS sung this … strain.
[pause, drum roll]

Chorus: RULE, BRITANNIA … Britannia rules the waves.

Whether the applause was polite or deafening, the performance was not quite over. Back came the hermit (not to be confused with the bard) for a final oracle, prophesying British dominion of the seas. This, too, had already become a standard fixture of Alfredomania since on a reading of the *Anglo-Saxon Chronicle* he was credited (not completely without foundation) as the first native king to have built a formidable warfleet. If *Alfred* kept to the tradition of the masque this would have been the moment for an allegorical dumb show with personifications of the oceans (the 'golden South', the 'Soft East', the 'stormy North' and the 'vast Atlantic surge'), each accompanied by appropriate music from Arne, entering to unload their respective tributes to Britannia.

Hermit: Alfred! Go forth! Lead on the radiant years …
I see thy commerce, BRITAIN grasp the world
All nations serve thee, every foreign flood pays its tribute to the Thames
… Britons proceed, the subject deep command
Awe with your navies every hostile land
Vain are their threats, their armies all in vain
They rule the world who rule the main.

And then (surely) yet another chorus with more trumpets and drums:

Rule, Britannia, Britannia rules the waves.

Richard Temple, Viscount Cobham, at any rate was nobody's slave. Nor did he need tutorials from Bolingbroke on the antiquity or the posterity of British liberty. His entire career, he supposed, had been selflessly devoted to its preservation. A veteran of the wars against Louis XIV, he had fought for William and then for Queen Anne and Marlborough as colonel of a regiment of foot and had come to be known, for his passionate defence of the Glorious Revolution, as 'the greatest Whig in the army'. Cobham and his wife Anne, the daughter of a wealthy brewer, had no surviving children and instead had poured their affections into their nephews and nieces, the Grenvilles, and their money into one of the most beautiful if grandiose Palladian country houses in England: Stowe. It was, though, always meant to be more than a pleasure-palace, Cobham's Buckinghamshire retort to Walpole's Houghton. Stowe was

Top: *Alfred the Great*, by Michael Rysbrack, *c.* 1735, one of the heroes featured in *The Temple of British Worthies* (above) by William Kent, *c.* 1731–35, Stowe Landscape Gardens, Buckinghamshire.

supposed to stand for something: for the perpetuity of British freedom. James Thomson had written his ode 'Liberty' while staying there and probably read Bolingbroke's *Patriot King* in Cobham's library. The 'cubs' who congregated at the house – George Lyttelton, William Pitt and the Grenvilles – all saw themselves as very British lions, ready to roar.

It was in the park behind the house, though, that Cobham made his political sentiments unmistakably visible. Ironically, it was from the translated work of a French landscape architect, Dézalliers d'Argenville, that the designers of the inspirational garden had taken their cue. The lessons were all classical. The park was studded with little pavilions, domed and colonnaded like miniature versions of the Pantheon, and artfully sited atop knolls or at the end of pools of water which allowed the walker, following a carefully prescribed route, to pause, literally, for reflection. The fashion was self-consciously painterly, owing much to the enormous popularity of landscapes by Nicolas Poussin and Claude Lorrain among the English aristocracy. But in Cobham's case, the intended effect was deliberately historical and political. Between 1731 and 1735, he brought the architect William Kent to Stowe to design for the park a new set of structures, each of which was a piece of his own public philosophy. Opposite the Temple of Ancient Virtue (modelled loosely on the Temple of Vesta at Tivoli near Rome), Kent built a Temple of British Worthies. Though later also called a 'temple', the structure is not a solid pavilion at all, but an unroofed enclosure and terrace based on the classical exedra. Beneath a pyramid surmounted by Mercury (not just the usher to Elysium but the god of commerce), a sweeping, semicircular wall enclosed a row of niches, each with its own pediment, in which were placed the 'bustoes' (as the printed guides called them) of the worthies.

They were divided, right and left, into heroes of contemplation and heroes (and one heroine) of action. Both groups included inevitable and uncontroversially admirable figures – Shakespeare and Bacon among the thinkers (as well as Richard Gresham, the founder of the New Exchange); the Black Prince and Elizabeth I among the doers. But there were other personalities who were much more assertive embodiments of Cobham's conviction that patriotism was ever the enemy of 'slavishness': John Milton among the thinkers and John Hampden among the doers. It may be that, as a fellow Buckinghamshire gentleman of the opposition, Cobham flattered himself as a latter-day Hampden, a century on. For it was in the 1730s that not only Milton but Oliver Cromwell too was experiencing a revival of sympathy. Cromwell was being taken not just as another epitome of a Free Briton but as one of the founders of the modern British Empire as well. And the 'bustoes' of the doers did, in fact, make up a procession of the creators of Anglo-British maritime and imperial power: Alfred, the 'creator' of the navy (sculpted again by Rysbrack, who must have been knocking them off on an Anglo-Saxon production line); Elizabeth; but also Sir Walter Raleigh and Sir Francis Drake who, the inscription read, 'through many perils was the First Briton that adventured to sail round the Globe and carried into ... the Seas and Nations the knowledge and glory of the English Name'.

The connection between the championship of liberty at home and the creation of a maritime, commercial empire overseas was at the heart of the new, the first truly British, patriotism. Bolingbroke spoke for all the Patriots when he insisted that 'the Empire of the Seas is ours; we have been many Ages in Possession of it; we have had many Sea-Fights, at a vast effusion of Blood and Expense of Treasure to preserve it and preserve it we still must, at all Risks and Events if we have a Mind to preserve ourselves.' As the heirs to their heroes Drake and Raleigh, Cobham and his protégés believed that this empire would be something new in the world precisely because it would not suffer from Rome's fatal addiction to territorial conquest, a vice that had led to despotism at the heart of the empire and auto-destruction on its over-extended frontiers. The aristocratic 'boy Patriots' had seen for themselves on the Grand Tour (on which Thomson, for example, had travelled as a tutor) the eloquent ruins of that imperial hubris in Rome. Pompeo Batoni's paintings of themselves posed against the melancholy debris of the Palatine Hill, as well as Giovanni Battista Piranesi's extraordinary engravings, first published in the 1750s, acted as a salutory reminder of the history to be avoided. Four years later, during the wars against the French, Cobham had Kent build him a Gothic Temple of Liberty in tawny ironstone (a more ruggedly earthy material than the creamy oolitic limestone of the classical buildings), decorated inside with the imaginary heraldry of the Saxon kings. Over the door, an inscription from Pierre Corneille's *Horace* (1639) left no one in doubt: 'Je rends grâces aux dieux n'estre pas Romain' – 'I thank the Gods that I am not a Roman'.

As the years went by and the history of the British Empire turned from fantasy to military reality, Stowe turned into a theme park of the Empire of Liberty. One of the Grenville boys, Thomas, killed in the naval battle off Cape Finisterre in May 1747, was memorialized by his own column. Another obelisk went up in 1759 to mourn (along with the rest of the nation) the most celebrated of all imperial martyrs, James Wolfe; yet another monument towards the end of the century commemorated James Cook. Significantly, Stowe became the first country house in Britain to open its park and gardens to the public, and to print inexpensive guides to go with the visit. By the early 1750s, prospective patriotic tourists had a choice of at least three (some as cheap as sixpence; others, with engraved views, two shillings and six pence) to lead them round the patriotic landscape. At the Palladian Bridge they could ponder the bas-relief depicting 'The History of Commerce and the Four Quarters of the World bringing their Productions to Britannia'. Inside the Temple of Friendship, in a gallery filled with the heads of Pitt, Cobham (passed on to his British elysium in 1749), Lyttelton and the rest, they could crane their necks at a painting of Britannia yet again enthroned in her glory and congratulate themselves on their good fortune to live in a country in which liberty and empire, usually mutually exclusive, were so harmoniously and so miraculously conjoined.

When they ritually invoked 'liberty', though, what did its champions actually mean? In the first instance, freedom from the 'slavery' of Roman Catholicism (which perhaps pained the Catholic composer of 'Rule, Britannia', Arne). But they were recalling a very specific historical tradition of seventeenth-century resistance to the efforts of 'despots' either to smuggle it in surreptitiously (in the case of Archbishop Laud and Charles I) or to impose it through a standing army (like James II). Liberty meant parliamentary consent to taxation; regular elections; and habeas corpus – all the virtues assumed to be absent from the slave states of Catholic Europe and that had been immemorially rooted in English (even Anglo-Saxon) nationhood. Liberty meant the constant reiteration of its historical epics – Magna Carta, the Petition of Right, and, most recently and therefore most hallowed, the Bill of Rights of 1689 – and its heroes and martyrs: John Hampden, John Milton and Algernon Sydney. In the 1730s, the attacks on Walpole had added a modern inventory of despots: the Robinocrats, perhaps even worse than the Stuarts because of their hypocritical pretence to be defending the principles of 1688 that, by means of the Septennial Act of 1716 (elections every seven, rather than every three, years), parliamentary placemen and sinister armies of excise-men, they were in fact bent on corrupting and annihilating. In contrast to the grovelling hacks and the epicene toadies who lived off the leavings of the oligarchs were the honest sort of the country, men who sweated for a living: ordinatry country gentlemen, merchants, decent artisans, men of commerce – the 'Heart Blood' of the nation. It was these men who believed themselves tyrannized by the arbitrary powers of Walpole's excise-men, and who looked to the promotion of blue-water empire to fulfil their partnership between trade and freedom. So when they spoke of liberty they meant, among other enterprises, the liberty to buy and sell slaves.

For one thing is certain about this generation: the kind of liberty they mouthed so freely was not for black Africans, whose welfare had definitely not been uppermost in the minds of those who had written Magna Carta or the Petition of Right. It seldom occurred to those who parroted nostrums about the empire of liberty that its prosperity depended on the enslavement of hundreds of thousands of Africans, since it would take another generation before 'natural' equality would join liberty in the

George II, by John Shackleton, *c.* 1755.

radical canon. For an African to invoke the precepts of a Free Briton, these patriots supposed, was to make a mockery of their meaning. So while William Kent was erecting his memorial to the founding fathers of the empire of the free seventy-seven Akan-speaking Antiguan slaves, the leaders of an aborted rising intended to seize the island on the anniversary of George II's coronation in October 1736, were being publicly burned alive. If the authorities on the island followed the Procedures described by Hans Sloane, later physician to George II, the slaves would have been nailed 'on the ground with crooked sticks on every Limb, and then applying the Fire by degrees from the Feet and Hands, burning them gradually up to the Head, whereby their pains are extravagant'. According to official records, five slaves were broken on the wheel, six gibbeted alive and seventy-seven burned – a total of eighty-eight executions in less than four months. Those less directly implicated in the plot might have got away with a castration, a mutilated hand or foot or a flogging 'till they are Raw, some put on their skins Pepper and salt to make them smart'.

The irony that an empire so noisily advertised as an empire of free Britons should depend on the most brutal coercion of enslaved Africans is not just an academic paradox. It was the *condition* of the empire's success, its original sin: a stain that no amount of righteous self-congratulation at its eventual abolition can altogether wash away.

And there were other twists of historical fate waiting just round the corner for the empire-builders – outcomes that they could never have foreseen in the bright prospectus of the foundation years. The blue-water character of the British Empire, the preference of its promoters for business opportunities over territorial conquest; and their instinct that military and commercial ventures should be mutually exclusive were supposed to immunize it from the evils notorious, not just in the empires of antiquit, but also in the imperial autocracies of the recent past – Ottoman and Catholic-Spanish. The British Empire was supposed to satisfy itself with just enough power, and just enough central regulation, to make the interlocking parts of its economic machinery work with well-oiled smoothness. Properly 'planted' and protected from foreign despoilers and interlopers, the colonies would furnish raw materials to the motherland, which in turn would send its manufactures and finished goods back. With a buoyant home market, the suppliers across the sea would make enough money to afford their imports and would plough some of the proceeds into making their plantations even more productive; this would lower costs, which in turn would make the goods more widely available to a bigger proportion of the population back in Britain. The rising tide of reciprocal good fortune would lift all boats, and, without the expense and distraction of vain conquests to protect, the empire of freedom and enterprise would knit the world together in an endlessly benevolent cycle of mutual improvement.

By the end of the eighteenth century it was apparent that this was not how things had worked out. Instead of an empire of farmers and traders the British Empire was, overwhelmingly, an empire of soldiers and slaves. The Americans who had taken the professions of liberty most seriously had flung them back in the teeth of Britain and gone their own way. And instead of an empire based on lightly garrisoned commercial stations around the world, Britain had somehow found itself responsible for nearly a million Caribbean slaves and at least 50 million inhabitants of the Indian subcontinent. The British had gone east to make a little money on the side and ended up, somehow, as the Raj. The footnote had become the main story. Look around the streets of urban Britain today, and you see that it still is.

So just how had Britain ended up with the wrong empire?

From the beginning the British Empire was habit-forming. The genial encouragement of addiction was its speciality: a quiet smoke, a nice cup of tea, a sweet tooth (and, a bit later, a pipe of opium) – exotic rarities converted into consumer cravings, exceptional wants turned into daily needs. Where profit beckoned, distaste could be overcome. King James I may have published tracts against the filthy weed *Nicotiana tabacum* ('good Countrey-men let us (I pray you) consider what honour or policy can move us to imitate the barbarous and beastly manners of the wild, godles and slavish Indians … in so vile and stinking a custom?'), but the first settlement the Virginia Company established to grow it still bore his name. Given the chance, the Jamestown settlers would have preferred to discover the gold and silver that seemed to have fallen into the lap of the Spanish empire of the south. But there was no gold in the Chesapeake Bay and the settlers had to make do with their dependably prolific flop-leaved plant. Many times, during the first half of the seventeenth century, the English tobacco colonies seemed close to obliteration: victims of disease, vicious wars with the Native Americans (in which the English, as well as the natives, slaughtered men, women and children) and their own profligate, unrealistic expectations. The climate, the insects and the unwelcome gifts they carried devoured men. Though 6000 immigrants had come between 1607 and 1625, in the latter year a census found the population of Virginia to be just 1200. Yet, as the tobacco habit became ingrained in European culture and Virginia leaf was established as the marker of quality, demand boomed, prices rose and the settlements in Lord Baltimore's Maryland and in Virginia hung on, consolidated and pushed inland. Attracted by the possibility of owning 'manors' of hundreds of acres, the younger sons of gentry and tradesmen arrived to become tobacco barons. Supplying the labour, alongside a limited number of African slaves, were boys – median age sixteen, seldom over nineteen; boys in their tens of thousands, out from the rookeries and tenements of London and Bristol, about 70 to 80 per cent 'indentured' (contractually committed) to

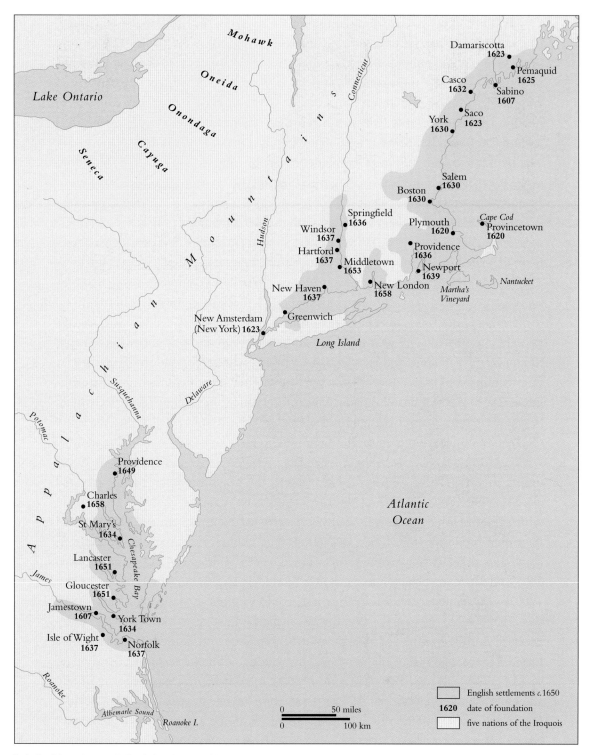

Early English settlements in North America, *c.* 1600–1700.

A reconstruction of an early settler's house, Jamestown, Virginia, *c.* 1700.

work for three to five years for room and board before being freed to claim a small plot of promised land, to hire out their labour or set up shop.

This was how the colonial 'planting' was supposed to work: an anti-social no-hope population drained from the mother country and set to work with every prospect of 'improvement'; the land itself likewise kissed by amelioration; the mother country on the (carefully controlled) receiving end of a valuable raw commodity, busy turning out goods that it could ship back to the growing colony. And, unlike in Ireland where the obstreperous natives happened to be Christians (of a deluded, papistical sort) and could attract the support of mischievous foreign powers to make a nuisance of themselves, the American natives, who were evidently resistant to the Gospel, could now be shoved further and further up-river and into the trees and hills. Sir Francis Wyatt had spoken for the whole Anglo-American project in 1622 when he unblushingly declared that 'our first worke is expulsion of the Savages to gaine the free range of the countrey … for it is infinitely better to have no heathen among us, who at best were but thornes in our sides, than to be at peace and at league with them'.

But then it all went badly wrong. Beginning in the 1680s, tobacco prices began to decline and then went into free-fall, bankrupting the smaller planters, brokers and processors. The shock was not enough to abort the Chesapeake experiment altogether. There were upwards of 50,000 settlers in Maryland and Virginia, and they managed to find a more diversified range of crops to farm – indigo and wheat in particular. The colony would survive, and the tobacco market revive in the next century, but the bonanza was, for the time being, over.

Or, rather, it was elsewhere. For another kind of craving was sweeping through Europe in the second half of the seventeenth century, one that would transform the British Empire from a niche in the world economy to its star performer. The craze for hot, powerfully caffeinated beverages began with coffee, brought from the Islamic world via the janissaries of the Ottoman Empire as they moved further west into central Europe. Vienna would resist the Turkish siege, but it was defenceless against the coffee bean. The American cocoa bean, consumed as drinking chocolate, had been passed from Central American culture to their Spanish conquerors and refined and made marketable by the Dutch, always with their eye on the creation of new market openings. Both coffee and chocolate were widely available in the London coffee-houses by the third quarter of the seventeenth century.

But for some reason, which – as yet – no amount of anthropology, much less economic history, has managed to explain satisfactorily, it was the east Asian drink brewed from the leaves of *Camellia sinensis* that, right from the beginning, was the British favourite. When Thomas Garway sold 'China Tcha, Tay or Tee' in both leaf and brewed liquid from in his coffee-house in Exchange Alley in 1657, it was probably the choice green leaves of Hyson or Sing-lo grown in Anwei and Chekiang provinces. Anticipating some of the more miraculous claims made for green tea recently, Garway promoted it as a wonder drug: 'wholesome, preserving perfect health until extreme old age, good for clearing the sight'; it would pacify 'gripping of the guts, cold, dropsies and scurvies' and would 'make the body active and lusty'. But by the turn of the eighteenth century, when Tcha was being sold in at least 500 coffee-houses, black leaf, grown around the Bohea mountains of Fukien, on the southeastern coast, had conquered the market. The best of those teas, like Souchong, needed longer drying time, but enough of it could be processed and exported by the East India Company from Canton to lower the price and thus reach a wide market. Even more significantly, in the first decades of the eighteenth century Bohea made a crucial crossover from commercial drinking establishments into the domestic world, first in the houses of fashionable quality, but by the second decade among the trading and commercial classes and even artisans. It became, *par excellence*, the politely sociable drink, to be taken preferably at home and with its little rituals and ceremonies more often than not in the hands of women. By the 1730s close to a million pounds of tea a year were being imported from China to Britain by the East India Company, which could sell it on the London market for four times what it had paid in China.

And although the evidence for its timing is necessarily anecdotal, it seems likely that from the beginning tea, like the more aggressively bitter coffee and chocolate, was thought to need sugar to make it palatable. When the first porcelain tea sets were being made, it would have been unthinkable not to have included, along with the teapot and milk jug, a sugar bowl. In 1715 Dr Frederick Slare, admittedly so shameless a booster of the miraculous qualities of sugar that he could recommend it not only as a cure for eye ailments but also as an ideal dentifrice, announced, in effect, the arrival of the modern British breakfast. 'Morning repasts called Break-fasts,' he wrote authoritatively, 'consist of bread, butter, milk, water and sugar', adding that tea, coffee and chocolate as the beverages of choice all had 'uncommon virtues'. The old early-morning meal of home-brewed small beer, bread and perhaps cheese or smoked fish was on its way out, at least in urban Britain. By the time that Hannah Glasse's *The Art of Cookery Made Plain and Easy*, the first cookbook directed at the middle classes, was published in 1747, its recipes assumed the wide availability and inexpensiveness of sugar. 'To make a rich cake' called for 3 lb. of 'double-refined sugar' to 4 lb. of flour; 'Everlasting Syllabub' used a pound of double-refined sugar to 2.5 pints of cream, 'Syrup of peach blossoms' (a wonderful idea) 2 pounds; and both Mrs Glasse's 'cheap' rice-puddings (baked as well as boiled) also used sugar as a basic ingredient. The British sweet tooth, gratified by tarts and puddings, flavoured creams and cheesecakes, jams, marmalades and jellies, had arrived with a vengeance in the national diet. It was an alteration of appetite that revolutionized the history, not just of Britain but of the world.

Sugar had been widely known and consumed in medieval Europe, but its high price and exotic origin meant that it was considered as either a spice or a drug. The most common sweetener, conveniently and locally produced, was honey. So when sugar shows up in the account books of grand aristocratic households like that of Simon de Montfort, the Earl of Leicester, at Kenilworth, it is rarely in amounts of more than a pound or two. It had reached Christian Europe via the Islamic world, and it had been a crusader dynasty, the Lusignans, sometime kings of Jerusalem, who had made the first attempt to domesticate it for production on Cyprus. But sugar cane is native to the tropical monsoon regions of southeast Asia from New Guinea to the Bay of Bengal, and to reach its mature height of 8 feet (2 metres) it needs the combination of drenching, daily rainfall and hot temperatures. It was precisely the difficulty of establishing it in the drier Mediterranean region, under optimal growing conditions, that kept yields relatively low and prices comparatively high. So for centuries sugar remained a drug or a spice, in both cases an exotic luxury rather than a daily commodity. But its Portuguese shippers and growers, abetted by Dutch and Jewish traders and refiners, were constantly moving west, out into the warmer Tropic of Cancer latitudes of the Atlantic, to Madeira and São Tomé, for example, in search of the perfect combination of heat and rain. Famously (although almost by accident when ships were blown southwards off course), they found what they were looking for in the former Portuguese colony of Brazil.

But there was something else that sugar cane needed if its golden juice was going to pay off, and that was intensive, highly concentrated, task-specific applications of manpower. For the cane was an unforgiving and volatile crop. It could not be farmed and harvested in a single growing year since it took at least fourteen months to ripen. But once it had reached maturity, the cumbersome grass needed to be harvested quickly to prevent the sugar going starchy. Once stripped and cut, the cane in its turn had to be speedily taken to the ox-powered vertical crushing rollers before the sucrose concentration of the juice self-degraded. Every subsequent stage of production – the boiling of the juice, the arrest of the boiling process at the precise moment for optimum crystallization, the partial refining in clay-stopped inverted cone moulds, the lengthy drying process – demanded the kind of strength, speed and stamina in tropical conditions that indentured white Europeans or captive Native Americans were ill equipped to provide. Both populations proved themselves hard to discipline, prone to drink and rebelliousness. They ran away a lot, and they died like flies from the stew of insect- and water-borne diseases that simmered away in the humid sunlight. But the Portuguese sugar lords and, more specifically, their Dutch and Jewish brokers knew it was worth persevering. All that the merchants of Pernambuco needed to solve in order to make a packet was the labour problem.

So, where to turn for a labour supply that was strong, disease-resistant but obedient, like the cattle that turned the crushers? Where else, of course, but where the Portuguese were already making money from the commerce in ivory, gold and humans – West and Central Africa.

It was a truly Faustian moment. And there *were* those who recognized the Mephistophelean nature of the compact. The Jesuits in Brazil condemned as the grossest blasphemy any equation between men and animals. Other, equally honourable Fathers of the Church and jurists in the Spanish empire wrote forthrightly to Philip II on the unspeakable, unchristian, evil of enslavement. But other councillors and clerics were prepared to justify enslavement on the pious pretext that it was a way to bring the heathen Africans to the Gospel. And, besides, were they not captives from their own tribal wars? The arguments were transparently defensive and sometimes disingenuous, but imperial Spain (which had incorporated Portugal in 1580) was desperately short of funds, and it was more expedient to listen to the permissive, than the prohibitive, arguments. By 1630 there were probably over 60,000 African slaves working in the sugar estates of Brazil, and the investment was paying off handsomely for all concerned except its traumatized, brutalized victims.

Since the reign of Elizabeth, English interlopers (competing with the Dutch) had been buying slaves on the coast of West Africa and selling them to Hispanic America. But by the middle of the seventeenth century envious glances were being cast in the direction of Brazil (where the Portuguese and Dutch were slugging it out for sovereignty), and where it was obvious immense fortunes were to be made. The Dutch – as any quick visit to an Amsterdam baker or confectioner would have made apparent – had already succeeded in introducing sugar as a staple of daily diet rather than a rare and expensive luxury. And the English were aware that, even if it were highly volatile in the early stages of production, sugar was extremely stable in shipping and warehousing. It was marvellously versatile and market-adaptable, yielding not just two qualities of sugar (refined and cruder 'muscovado') but also molasses, treacle and rum. As a commodity for long-distance trade it was impossible to beat.

But where could the English find a place to grow it, safe from the long arm and the heavy hand of the Spanish? Early attempts were made in Bermuda, but the tiny island off the coast of South Carolina was too dry, too cool and too remote. Barbados, on the other hand, seemed the answer to their prayers. Hanging out in the ocean, on the extreme windward edge of the Antilles, its annual rainfall averaged 60 inches (over 1500 mm) a year – all the moisture the sugar cane could possibly need; and its breezy exposure could be harnessed to turn the sails of windmills to crush the cane. It was as far as it could be from the Spanish centres of power in Cuba and Hispaniola while still being in the Caribbean, and it was the first port of call for ships coming across the Atlantic from either Africa or England. Even its topography seemed perfect, with low-lands sloping down to a coast with some hospitable natural harbours in the south and a wet, upland northern plateau quickly named 'Scotland'.

Perhaps sugar may have been on the mind of the mariner John Powell when he first made landfall on Barbados en route back from the Guianas in 1625. But the colo-nial product of choice at this time was tobacco, and for a generation or two efforts were made to grow a crop on Barbados. Competing with Virginia and Maryland, however, was hard work. The island was covered with a dense canopy of rainforest – mastic and ironwood, poisonwood, hoe-stick wood and locust – which took twenty years to clear for adequate growing space. Even then, the leaf never managed to achieve the vaunted quality of Virginia tobacco. And there were the same labour trou-bles that plagued the Chesapeake Bay plantations. The Irish indentured labourers were especially restive under their crippling regime of toil, and the teenage boys who came from England wilted and collapsed in the heat. In 1649 – the year of revolution in England – there was a slave plot on Barbados, suppressed with merciless, characteristi-cally Cromwellian brutality. Even before the rebellion some of the first-generation planters such as James Drax, a landowner of Anglo-Dutch background, had been experimenting with slave labour shipped on his own account from Africa. Now the slave-sugar nexus seemed a much better bet than the struggle with tobacco, especially when the Dutch were prepared to advance planters capital for milling equipment and even show them how to use it. The crop took off. As early as 1647 an owner of 50 acres reported that 'provisions for the belly … at present is very scarce [since] men are so intent upon planting sugar that they had rather buy foode at very dear, rather than produce it by labour, soe infinite is the profitt of sugar workes'.

As early as 1655, three years after that first coffee-house opened in London, Barbados was shipping 7787 tons of sugar back to England, and there were already 20,000 slaves on the island against 23,000 whites, well over half of whom were probably indentured servants. When Richard Ligon arrived two years later, the well-founded reputation of Barbados as a gold-mine had already been established. Drax had built himself a Jacobean manor house on the upland plateau and 'as we passed along the shoar', Ligon wrote, 'the Plantations appeared to us one above the other like several stories in stately buildings which afforded us a large proportion of delight'. It was common knowledge that an up-front outlay of £1000 (advanced from the Dutch) invested in 200 acres, a windmill (sometimes, along with the boiling house, shared with a neighbour), a distillery to make rum and a hundred odd slaves would yield, within a very few years, an annual income of £2000. No wonder, as Henry Whistler noted in 1655, 'the gentry here doth live far better than ours do in England.' They were, by far, the richest men in British America.

It was precisely between 1640 and 1660, when the rhetoric of liberty was being most noisily shouted at home, that the slave economy of the British Empire was being created in the Caribbean. (Cromwell's baffled disappointment that God had somehow decided that Hispaniola should not, after all, be British was partly consoled by the capture of Jamaica in 1655.) And this timing was not, alas, a coincidence. For if making an 'empire of liberty' meant keeping it clean of Catholics, no one wanted this more than the hard-nosed, coffer-counting men of the Protectorate (in many cases, of course, identical with the hard-nosed men of the Restoration). The impeccably Puritan Earl of Warwick had, after all, been among the most enthusiastic pioneers of settlement and slaving in the Caribbean two decades earlier. So Barbados filled up with shackled Africans while its white Assembly resounded with the pieties of self-government. The island became a little Commonwealth, but without the gloomy inconvenience of the morals police. Barbados was divided into parishes, each run by a vestry (as is still the case), and its manorial gentry, in their magisterial role, adjudicated the common law much as they did in Berkshire or Cheshire. But they also adjudicated the slave code, which declared the punishment for running away to be mutilation and the penalty for theft of any article worth more than a shilling death. Wilfully killing a negro might incur an inconvenient fine, but it was virtually impossible to prove it. And with Bridgetown and its other harbours made easily defensible, the island was safe from the Catholic scourge. It was a planting full of blessings, an Ulster in the sun.

The restoration of the monarchy only made things better. On vacation from losing battles, Prince Rupert of the Rhine went slaving up the Gambia in West Africa and made a tidy profit on it. Once his cousin Charles II was king he became instrumental in founding the Company of Royal Adventurers into Africa in 1660. Initially chartered with a 1000-year monopoly of trading rights in western Africa, it was re-chartered in 1663 as the Company of Royal Adventurers Trading into Africa, commonly known as the Royal African Company. By the time its ships deposited their first human cargoes at Bridgetown there were already well over 30,000 slaves on Barbados, twice as many blacks as whites on the island. By 1700 the number had risen to around 50,000. (A century later the slave population on Barbados would number some 70,000, with roughly another 400,000 on Jamaica.) Barbados had become the forcing house of

Above: *A Topographicall Description and Admeasurement of the Yland of Barbados ...* by Richard Ligon, 1657.
Opposite, top: *A View Taken Near Bain, on the West Coast of Guinea in Africa*, engraved after Richard Westhall, *c.* 1789. A contemporary print illustrating a native slave raid on an African village.
Opposite, below: *Description of a Slave Ship*, 1789, showing how slaves were packed into the ship's cramped and stifling hold.

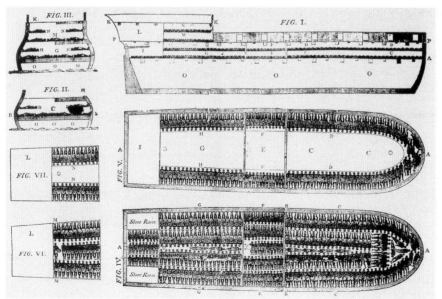

high-end, fast-profit, industrially organized slave capitalism. The patchwork landscape of relatively small farms – 10 acres or so on average – worked by racially mixed gangs of indentured servants and slaves had gone forever. In its place were 350 large estates of more than 200 acres and scores more of about 100 acres, all of them worked almost exclusively with African slave labour. Quakers like George Fox visited Barbados, preached that 'all blacks, whites and tawnies' were equally God's creatures and asked the planters to use the slaves gently and free them after a period – but stopped short of demanding abolition. The indefatigable old Puritan Richard Baxter, though, was more damning in 1673 when he asked, 'How cursed a crime is it to equal men to beasts. Is this not your practice? Do you not buy them and use them merely as you do horses to labour for your commodity … Do you not see how you reproach and condemn yourselves while you vilify them all as savages?' But even when they were occasionally embarrassed into conceding the human cost, the planters (and indeed the merchants at home) shrugged their shoulders and asked what a Negro would do with liberty. The bottom line, always, was money. Daniel Defoe, as usual, was shockingly blunt and absolutely truthful: 'No African Trade, no Negroes; no Negroes, no Sugars … no Sugars … no Islands, no Islands, no [American] Continent; no Continent, no Trade; that is say farewell to all your American Trade, your West Indian Trade.' The poet William Cowper was later to write a little comic verse on this predicament:

> I own I am shocked at the purchase of slaves
> And fear those who buy them and sell them are knaves
> What I hear of their hardships and tortures and groans
> Is almost enough to draw pity from stones
> I pity them greatly but I must be mum
> For how could we do without sugar and rum?

In the century and a half of the slave trade, from the 1650s to 1807, between three and four million Africans were transported out of their homelands to the New World in British ships. Between nine and twelve million were abducted and sold as chattel property by the traders of all the European nations involved: it was the single largest mass abduction in human history. A million and a half of those died en route during the hellish crossing known as the Middle Passage, the second leg of the Britain–Africa–West Indies–Britain route that gave rise to the term 'triangular trade'. Of course, it was not only white Europeans and Americans who were responsible for this enormity. It had been the Portuguese discovery of a thriving trans-Sahara slave trade, harvested and delivered by African warrior dealers, which had made the traffic possible in the first place. But the demand for slaves trans-shipped to the New World became so voracious in the late seventeenth and eighteenth centuries that it created incentives for the raiders – usually native or Portuguese – to reach far beyond their traditional catchment zones, to make opportunistic descents on stricken and defenceless villages. By the early eighteenth century, raiding parties were moving well north of the Niger and deep into western Sudan. And a region already suffering from repeated plagues of locusts and droughts was now made even more insecure. In some of the worst-hit areas it was not uncommon for desperate villagers to sell their children or even themselves.

There was another sense in which the transatlantic slave trade was qualitatively more inhuman than the norms of slavery prevailing in the Islamic and pagan African worlds. For slaves in these regions, while indisputably unfree, were made into status objects, attached to the households, court and military retinues or seraglios of their owners. They were, in every sense, prized. And this had also been true for slaves in urban Europe: blacks in Dutch or English households were shown off and cosseted as if they were exotic pets. Never before, though, had masses of one particular race – black Africans – been treated as mere units of production in the calculus of profit. By definition, slaves had always been property. But now they were inventory: priced, sold, packaged, freighted, resold, amortized, depreciated, written off and replaced. They were, as Baxter had said, nothing more than beasts of burden. Perhaps the most shaming aspect of that dehumanization was the retrospective adoption of a set of racist commonplaces in the apologetic literature claiming that Africans were animal-like in their incapacity to feel pain or even emotion in the same manner experienced by the white races.

Who knows when the awareness of their bestialization made itself inescapably clear to the terrified Africans themselves? By the time they reached their first selling point – from the holding pens at places like Cape Coast Castle – they had already endured a succession of traumas. Olaudah Equiano, the Ibo who wrote his memoirs in the mid-eighteenth century under his bizarre slave name of Gustavus Vasa, taken from the Swedish kings, had been well aware of the dangers of abduction as a child. When the adults of his village were away at work in the fields he would climb trees to sound the alarm when suspicious persons made an appearance. One day, none the less, he and his sister were taken. It was when they were separated that misery first took hold: 'I was left in a state of distraction not to be described. I cried and grieved continually and for several days did not eat anything but what they forced in my mouth.' Though he was to see his sister again, it was a moment of false hope, for Equiano, like countless others, was deliberately uprooted from any kind of familiarity – country, customs, language, kin. When he was taken on board the slave ship and 'tossed up to see if I was sound', the sense that he had been reduced to a work-horse must have been unmistakable. The master of the *Hannibal*, Thomas Phillips, who wrote an account of a typical voyage of the 1690s, described even more degrading procedures when inspecting the shipment supplied by the African dealers at Ouidah. Searching for signs of the yaws that 'discovers itself by almost the same symptoms ... as clap does for us ... our surgeon is forced to examine the privities of both men and women with the nicest scrutiny, which is a great slavery but what can't be omitted'. Once purchased, the slave was branded on the breast or shoulder with the letter of the ship's name, 'the place before being anointed with a little palm oil which caused but little pain, the mark being usually well in four or five days, appearing very plain and white'.

There were other regrettable inconveniences that marred the smoothness of the loading process: negroes who were 'so wilful and loth to leave their own country that they have often leapt out of the canoes, boat and ship into the sea and kept under water till they were drowned, to avoid being taken up and saved by our boats which pursued them, they having a more dreadful apprehension of Barbados than we can have of hell'. Once on board there were still possibilities for suicide, especially since the slavers usually prowled the coast to take on extra cargo: the Africans would jump overboard, shackled or not. 'We have ... seen divers of them eaten by the sharks,' wrote Phillips, 'of which a prodigious number kept about the ships in this place [Ouidah] and I have been told will follow her to Barbadoes for the dead negroes that are thrown overboard in the passage ... I am certain in our voyage there we did not want the sight of some every day ... we had about twelve negroes did wilfully drown themselves and others starvd themselves to death for 'tis their belief that when they die they return home to their own country and friends.'

Other accounts register the inconsiderateness of negroes who went 'raving mad', or mutilated themselves during the passage, or who had the audacity to refuse to eat, thereby jeopardizing the value of the cargo. When the young Equiano declined his gruel of horse beans and vegetables, he was flogged until he changed his mind. But what the slavers and their surgeons described as 'melancholy' was almost certainly the semi-catatonic state characterized by sunken eyes, swollen tongue and extreme torpor that is induced by extreme, potentially fatal, dehydration. The average adult male weighing around 150 pounds needs under normal circumstances about 4 pints (2.3 litres) of fluid a day to recover losses from urine and sweat. The standard ration for slaves on the Middle Passage – a journey lasting anything from thirty to seventy days in anything but 'normal circumstances' – was a pint of water and 2 pints of soup. That ration was seldom if ever given in full, but even if it were the slave would still be in fluid deficit. If, over a long journey, he or she lost just 10 per cent of their body's

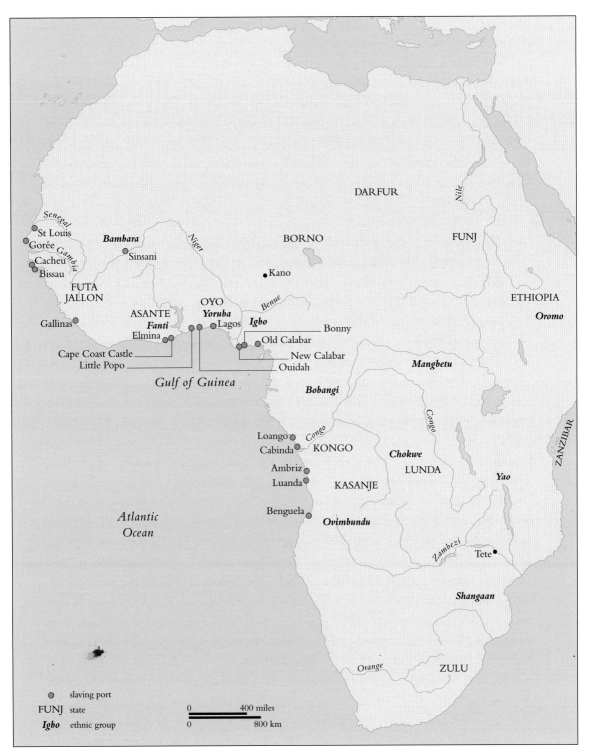

Major slaving zones and ports in Africa, *c.* 1700–1800.

80 pints (just under 50 litres) water content, they would certainly die. Between 10 and 20 per cent of slaves on board died this way.

Fluid loss from extreme perspiration was the first cause. When the ships were out in the open ocean, the slaves were taken up on deck twice a day for air, water and soup. If the sea were too rough, however, they would be kept in the stifling heat of the cramped holds, shackled in pairs and given less space (according to the Royal Africa Company specifications) than for a European pauper's coffin. If the ship was still sailing the West African coast (one of the hottest and dampest regions of the world) picking up more cargo, the climate below decks was even more dangerous. Olaudah Equiano recalled:

> The closeness of the place and the heat of the climate, added to the number in the ship, being so crowded that each had scarcely room to turn himself, almost suffocated us. This produced copious perspiration so that the air soon became unfit for respiration from a variety of loathsome smells and brought on a sickness among the slaves, of which many died, thus falling victims to the improvident avarice, as I may call it, of their purchasers. This deplorable situation was again aggravated by the galling [chafing] of the chains, now become insupportable; and the filth of necessary tubs into which the children often fell, and were almost suffocated. The shrieks of the women and the groans of the dying rendered it a scene of horror almost inconceivable.

Equiano is describing a perfect environment for faecal contamination, in which both shigellosis or bacillary dysentery, the 'red flux', and, more ominously, amoebic dysentery, the 'white flux', could rage. Commonly chronicled by surgeons aboard the slavers, both triggered violent spasms of vomiting and diarrhoea, which would induce further fluid loss. No wonder that when he was taken below decks for the first time Equiano 'received such a salutation in my nostrils as I had never experienced in my life'. Amoebic dysentery, which had a longer incubation period, attacked the victim in mid-voyage and was the more serious of the two infections since it lasted for weeks rather than days, with its victims suffering around twenty evacuations a day. Fluid losses would have been massive, triggering rapid sodium depletion and the excretion of potassium. Potassium loss in its turn would affect brain function, leading to the strange twilight dreaminess in which sufferers entered before their cardiac function was finally traumatized. Under the circumstances it is surely amazing that the mortality rate on slave ships was only around 12–15 per cent, though it could be as high as 20 per cent for children, who were naturally more vulnerable to acute dehydration than the adults.

What happened to them next, if they did survive to landfall, may have made the young slaves wish they had perished on board. Naked except for loincloths, they were paraded, poked and inspected all over again like livestock, their jaws clamped open for the inspection of teeth. A few were sold directly to planters. But many more were taken by wholesale merchants who confined them once more in a holding yard or pen. There they had to endure another extraordinary ordeal known to the planters as 'the scramble'. At Bridgetown in Barbados, Equiano described the prospective buyers 'on a signal given, such as the beat of a drum', rushing into the yard like bargain-hunters at a sale, sprinting towards the chained slaves and laying hands on them to secure their purchase. The most desirable job lots were young boys, just like Olaudah, between twelve and fifteen, for as David Stalker, a planter's buyer on the island of Nevis, explained, 'they are fully seasoned by eighteen and is [sic] full as handy as them that is born in the country, but them full grown fellers think it hard work never being brought up to it and take it to heart and dye or are never good for anything.' If they were too 'meagre', though, Equiano wrote, they would be put in scales, weighed and sold at threepence or sixpence the pound like cabbages. Bought again, they were branded again. Some of those branding irons survive in the museum at Bridgetown: made of fine silver, delicately fashioned in the form of a monogram, and indecently untarnished.

Now they truly belonged to King Sugar and toiled to make him rich. He was no sparer of age or sex. At least 80 per cent of the slave population worked, in some form or other, on the plantation for seventy to eighty hours a week. Some 20 per cent of those born there failed to survive beyond their second birthday, but if they did they had four or five years before they joined the 'third' work gang of the child labourers, gleaning, weeding, cutting grass and taking care of domestic animals. The 'second gang' comprised adolescents from twelve to nineteen, already out in the fields as well as tending to the animal population. The work on the second gang – around eleven hours of toil from before dawn to night – was so hard that many of the girls, in particular, died before they could graduate to the even more relentlessly back-breaking routine of the 'great gang' of adults. About 60 per cent of the total slave force in Barbados, Jamaica and Antigua worked in the 'great' or 'first' gang drilling holes for the new canes; cutting and stripping the harvest during the frantic 'crop time' between January and May; bundling and hauling the cumbersome canes at a smart-enough pace not to compromise the sugar quality. Looking on to see that the work was going quickly was the overseer, as often black as white, quick to use the whip should he see any laggards. Assignment in the mill or the boiling house was hardly an improvement. The vertical rollers that crushed the cane were notorious for taking hands with them since the cane had to be fed in manually, and hatchets were kept beside the mill to sever an arm before the entire body was pulled in. Slaves in the boiler houses worked in conditions of intense heat, dirt and exhaustion and were in constant danger of being scalded by the boiling syrup as it was poured from larger to smaller copper vats.

One would suppose that economic rationality might mitigate the severity of labour at least to the point where the planters could get full value from their investment, especially since deaths were never made up by births. Reproduction rates on the plantations were notoriously low – possibly 10–15 per 1000 compared with perhaps 20–30 per 1000 in Britain. But neither the balance of the sexes nor the way women were treated was likely to favour a home-grown slave population. Women were outnumbered by men almost two to one, and those who did become pregnant were not spared from work in the fields until they were virtually on the point of delivery. Those women were no more immune than anyone else from floggings administered by overseers if they lagged in the pace of their work. Poor nutrition, damp and vermin-infested huts, exposure to smallpox and yellow fever as well as diseases brought from Africa like elephantiasis and yaws, further added to the toll of miscarriages and low fertility. But it seems unlikely that the managers of the plantations were unduly troubled about wastage, at least until the third quarter of the eighteenth century when prices rose. For while it took at least £40 to raise a slave child to the point when child and mother could become productive, a new slave could be bought from the traders for between £15 and £30. No wonder, then, that, although 1.5 million slaves were imported into the British Caribbean during the eighteenth century, the population never rose above 800,000.

Violence – threatened or delivered – was what made the system work, and it fell with special savagery on African women. In one year, 1765, the estate manager of the Egypt plantation on Jamaica, Thomas Thistlewood, administered twenty-one floggings to thirteen women, each likely to have been no less than fifty lashes. (Equiano wrote that it was common to make the slaves kneel down after such a flogging and thank their masters for it.) Arguably, adult women endured the hardest lot of any section of the slave population, since so much was demanded of them – cooking, caring for infants, mending and washing clothes in addition to field work. And they also had to endure the habitual sexual aggression of masters and overseers who assumed they could copulate with any woman they chose whenever and wherever the mood took them: in the kitchen, pantry or laundry of the houses, or out in the yards and barns. Female field hands, like the men, worked naked but for a loincloth, and must therefore have been especially vulnerable. The fastidious data collector Thistlewood kept a regular slave mistress, Phibbah, with whom he carefully records having intercourse one hundred times during 1765. But in addition to Phibbah he had twenty-three other

Portrait of an African, once thought to be Olaudah Equiano, English School, *c.* 1780.

slave women on fifty-five separate occasions that year, most often out in the cane fields. Despite the resort to abortion by slave women who, forced to take more than one sexual partner, were terrified of alienating any one of them with a compromisingly coloured birth, 10 per cent of all births were in fact mulatto.

A small minority of the slaves of both sexes did manage to escape the punishing toil of the fields, either as domestic servants in the plantation house or as artisans who had brought with them from Africa specialized skills, which were much needed on the plantation. These coopers, masons, carpenters and blacksmiths, along with carters and wagoners as well as fishermen and even sailors, constituted a special class among the slaves, freer to move around and to buy and sell materials for their work. And there were times, too, when the slaves were not utterly dominated by the tyranny of the cane. The planters knew it was in their interest to give them some respite, and on Barbados there were some sixty free days and holidays a year. 'Free time' on Saturday afternoons and evenings was given over to the release of emotions and energies – often in music and dance, which the planters usually characterized as 'howling'. But in these brief moments of freedom business was at least as important as pleasure, for it offered a little taste of independence.

The Sunday market in towns like English Harbour on Antigua or Bridgetown on Barbados was where the African world remade itself. Beneath shady awnings, women and men sold vegetables or chickens that had been legally brought from villages, articles they had made themselves – baskets, pots, wooden stools, hammocks, ropes and gourd bowls, as well as objects they had managed to pilfer (often through relatives working as domestics) from the plantation house – nails and pieces of copper and lead. The 'hucksters', as the whites called them, sold their commodities sitting on the ground, or, if it were more obviously contraband (sugar, tobacco or rum), walking around the market waiting for selling opportunities. Money might change hands, but there were other objects that could be used as currency in the market: beads, copper wire or even cowrie shells, the exchange medium of West Africa.

The world of the market and the coopers' and carpenters' shops created a class of slaves who were more literate and assertive than the field hands, and whose social horizons were a lot broader than the cane fields. Because they depended on the artisans and carters in particular and got to know them well, some of the planters and their managers naïvely imagined that these more enterprising slaves might act as intermediaries between themselves and the mass of field hands. They were badly mistaken. The records of uncovering and suppressing rebellions almost invariably featured ringleaders from this 'slave elite'. Even though there was little chance of any of these revolts succeeding over the long term, especially in islands like Barbados where a potentially sheltering forest had been almost completely stripped to make way for cane, there was a steady drum-beat of rebellion, some of it, as in Antigua in the 1720s and 1730s and in Jamaica in mid-century, flaring into ferocious violence. 'Tacky's Rebellion' on Jamaica in 1760 took the lives of close to 100 whites and 400 blacks, as well as exiling 600 more, before it was finally put down with a great deal of difficulty.

Resistance to being reduced to a cipher in a manager's account-book (bought, worked, died) could also take forms other than violent insurrection. Among the socially traumatized slave community there were those who took it on themselves to preserve some sense of African tradition and cultural memory in a world that had been stripped of it. Different language groups, regions and tribes had been deliberately mixed to pre-empt any kind of potentially threatening solidarity. But the need for shared life, the need to make the scraps and shards of ancient, half-kept memory, was stronger even than slavery. African culture, though pulverized by terror and hardship, was reduced not to fine dust that could be blown away into the wind but to small, resistant grains that could be replanted, regrown, remade. And those new growths were tended by keepers of ancestral wisdom, keepers of the knowledge of religion, obeah healing and music. Because the tribal and language groups – Akan, Twi, Efik, Ewe – could not just be transposed to St Kitts, Antigua and Barbados, the healers, drummers, singers, weavers and carvers had to create unapologetically new forms from many strands of material, some inherited, others discovered, all shared. But it was, none the less, theirs – hard-earned, not the gift of their masters. In fact, the reluctance of the Caribbean masters in the early years to Christianize the slaves – lest literacy and religion produce a sense of presumptuous brotherhood in Christ, and lest the uses of literacy turn seditious – gave the Africans a generation or two to establish their own kind of syncretic culture, free from interference. When, finally, an effort was made to convert them, the missionary gospel was inevitably grafted on to cultural roots that had already sunk deep into the West Indian soil.

Rites of passage figure heavily in this new–old culture, none more important than funerals. From the beginning of the slave experience, cool observers like Thomas Phillips noticed that the Africans invariably treated death as freedom, and, *in extremis*, even shackled, did their utmost to swim to it (on the journey) or run away to it (on the islands). Was this not the ultimate irony of slave culture – that the masters would do what they could to keep their property alive, and the slaves would pay them back by seeking the liberation of death? To die in the Caribbean was to go home, and, to the bewilderment of clergymen like the Reverend Griffith Hughes, in Jamaica in the 1730s burials were occasions for outbursts of joy as well as solemnity. The bodies were laid out in fresh white cloths and were borne to the grave in a slow procession, the

Top: A sugar plantation, Barbados.
Above: Reconstruction of a sugar baron's house on Barbados, *c.* 1750.

women walking in pairs and dressed in white, the West African colour of mourning; 'both men and women which accompanying the corpse sing and howle in a sorrow- ful manner', as another observer, John Taylor, noted in Jamaica. Once the body was interred, along with it went provisions: cassava-bread loaves, roasted fowl, rum, tobacco 'with fier to light his pipe withal … and this they doe … in order to sustain him in his journey beyond those pleasant hills in their own country wither they say he is now going to live at rest'. Once the grave was filled up with dirt, the mood of the moment changed to singing, clapping and dancing, using gourd rattles, drums and baffalo, many of the mourners 'desiring the corpse [by kissing the grave] to acquaint their mother, father, husband and other relations of their present condition and slavery as he passeth through their country towards the pleasant mountains'. It was, in effect, a letter home, and the dead would be their courier.

Also deposited in the graves (and recovered now from excavations in slave ceme- teries on Barbados) were ornaments appropriate to a happy and ceremonious home- coming. From humble materials – dog teeth, copper wire and pieces of brass, as well as other objects familiar in African jewellery such as cowrie shells and glass beads – amulets and charms were lovingly fashioned. Slaves, who had been dispossessed of virtually everything, not least their humanity, managed somehow to create works of art and then gave them away to the dead so that they might arrive back home in dignity. It was the ultimate retort to the mindless cliché that they were no better than insen- tient beasts of burden.

By the middle of the eighteenth century, the mercantile 'empire of liberty' was critically dependent for its fortune on the economic universe made from slavery. The sugar produced by three-quarters of a million slaves in the Caribbean had become the single most valuable import to Great Britain, and it would not be displaced from that rank until the 1820s. Huge fortunes had been made, which translated themselves into grandiose country estates and houses in Britain, or the kind of institutional bequest that, from the money of the Codringtons in Barbados and Antigua, created the great library at All Souls College, Oxford, which bears their name. The profits from sugar may not have been a necessary condition of Britain's industrial revolution (as some historians of slavery have always maintained), since the amounts available for reinvest- ment probably did not exceed something like 2 per cent of the capital ploughed into purely industrial undertakings. But equally it's indisputable that the sugar–slave econ- omy had spun off enterprises of immense importance to Britain's dizzying growth. The elegance of eighteenth-century Bristol was paid for by the trade; and the port of Liverpool, which in the 1740s had sent three times as many triangular trade ships to Africa and the Caribbean as London, owed its expansion entirely to it. The great banking houses of Barclays and Lloyds were equally the creation of the Atlantic trade, but were afterwards able to provide capital to the manufacturers of England and Scotland. While Indian calicoes had once been among the exports shipped from Britain to Africa in exchange for slaves, the huge demand there for brilliant printed cottons was now supplied almost entirely by more cheaply produced British textiles. And the demand for the ancillary products of the sugar industry – molasses, rum and treacle – worked to tie together not just the West Indies and Britain but the continental American colonies and the Caribbean as well.

In the 1750s the swaggering plutocrats who embodied the West India fortunes – William Beckford and Christopher Codrington (the Governor of the Leeward Islands), the Pinneys and the Lascelles – began to throw their weight around back home at Westminster and in the corporation of the City of London. But although the older grandees of the counties may have looked down their noses at the pushy vulgarity of these nouveaux riches, they could not have denied their critical importance to the fate of the empire of the three oceans.

Yet despite what, to most jealous outsiders, seemed its outrageous share of good fortune, at that time the West India lobby did nothing but grumble about the difficulties it faced in preserving the sugar empire. The price of sugar was going down, it asserted, while the price of slaves was going up. Neither was precisely true. Sugar prices had indeed halved between 1713 and 1733 (the low point), but had recovered again by the end of the 1740s. If it was hard to work up sympathy for their purported plight as they bought yet another country house and raked in over 10 per cent annual profits on their investments, there was one item in their litany of complaints that did touch a raw nerve in Britain: fear of the French. For the British attitude towards the impertinence of French imperial competition managed to be arrogant and paranoid at the same time. For many of the apologists and tub-thumpers of Britannia's dominion of the seas, the mere idea of a French commercial empire was a comical oxymoron, for how could a nation so notoriously constituted from craven slaves of papist absolutism be taken seriously as entrepreneurial colonizers? (Never mind the fact that when Malachy Postlethwayt wanted to find a 'Dictionary of Commerce' to plagiarize for his own English version, *The Universal Dictionary of Trade and Commerce* (1751), he went to a French original.) Mysteriously, the evidence in the 1730s and 1740s pointed ominously to the rapid creation of a French empire in India and America but, especially in the Caribbean, that was becoming so successful so quickly that it seemed to the alarmists like a dagger pointed at the heart of the British imperial future.

They were right to worry. For although the French were late-comers at the colonial table, at least in the boom sector of the West Indies, they more than compensated

Statue of Christopher Codrington, by Sir Henry Cheere, 1734, Codrington Library, All Souls College, Oxford.

by the concentrated energy they brought to profit-making. As the British planters never failed to remind the home government, they had the advantage of being able, through the dynastic alliance of the Bourbon monarchs in France and Spain, to piggy-back their settlements in the Caribbean on older Spanish naval bases and colonies. No *guarda costas* were going to board French slavers or sugar ships to damage the property and persons of their cargo or crew.

By the 1740s, in fact, there were signs that the productivity of the French Caribbean sugar empire was beginning to outstrip that of the British. The French had their own slaver fleets built and fitted out at the dynamically growing port of Nantes at the mouth of the Loire; and they possessed their own locked-up sources of supply on the Gambia and in Senegal, pushing the British traders east into the Bight of Benin. In St Domingue, the western half of Spanish Hispaniola, they had a land area incomparably bigger than any of the British islands, even Jamaica; it was cut with rivers, which made the freight of goods easier and cheaper, and boasted both flat coastal plains and cooler uplands. The French plantations seem from the beginning to have been more productive than the British. At any rate they grew and shipped enough sugar to undercut prices in Europe, virtually taking that market away from Britain. And the French Caribbean was also more diversified, exporting coffee, cotton and indigo back home for profitable re-export.

As if this were not bad enough, there was also evidence that the French were being insolent enough to make inroads into the British colonial system of trade, encouraging British American ships to smuggle their own rum and molasses into British America and undercutting exports from Barbados and the Leeward Islands. So when the makers and keepers of British macro-economic policy looked at a map of the world, they could see only serious trouble coming from France. On the coast of southeast India, it's true, the erstwhile juvenile delinquent and disgruntled clerk turned military adventurer Robert Clive, together with Stringer Lawrence commanding the tiny army of the East India Company, had managed to thwart a French attempt to lock up the Carnatic as their own exclusive commercial satellite state. But the lesson in that vicious little war had been that a commercial edge was not protected by trade alone. The French were prepared, indeed they shrewdly assumed, the need to play politics with Indians (whether they were the Native Americans in North America or the Nawabs in the Carnatic), to offer their 'protection' in return for the ejection of the British. If that cost money and lives, so be it. What, then, were the British to do? Flinch from the challenge on grounds of expense and dangerous entanglements and concede the territory to the ambitious French? Or respond, as the gung-ho commanders of the East India Company had done, in kind, give the enemy a bloody nose and post the Keep Out sign on the

Indian Ocean? Needless to say, the government at home, presided over by the judicious Pelhams – Henry in the Commons, the Duke of Newcastle in the Lords – were more mindful of oceans of red ink than of blue-water imperialism. What they wanted was damage limitation. The treaty of Aix-la-Chapelle in 1748, which returned Madras to the British and the fort of Louisbourg, commanding the mouth of the St Lawrence north of Nova Scotia, to the French, seemed like just such a rational accommodation – a sensible division of spheres of influence. But no one who was thinking with any honesty or seriousness about global economic strategy could have been fooled. This was a breathing space, not a peace.

No one recognized with more pessimistic clarity that this was a moment of truth in the history of British power than William Pitt. It's easy enough to suppose that he had been born to imperial vision, being the grandson of Thomas 'Diamond' Pitt, the commercial interloper turned Governor of Madras who had become famous for hawking his 410-carat uncut rock for a mere £20,400, a price he described as 'cheap as neck beef'. (By a sublime irony it wound up at Versailles.) But the Pitts were not, despite the give-'em-hell career of the magpie governor, classic imperialist adventurers. They were, rather, country gentry from Dorset and Hampshire who numbered Elizabethan and Jacobean exchequer officials in their lineage. And they played politics by the rules. The rotten borough of Old Sarum, once the site of the Norman palace where William the Conqueror had been presented with the Domesday Book, but now just so much rubble in a field, was their very own pocket constituency. And though 'Diamond' Pitt had been a furious Whig, his son Robert, to his blustering father's outrage, turned Tory. Young William, by contrast, became a Whig and was to prove himself in politics by being a noisy nuisance to the Walpole interest.

William Pitt was not made for a quiet life. Even during his political apprenticeship friends and adversaries alike noticed that his moods alternated between elated bursts of hyperactive, hyper-articulate energy and deep troughs of paralysing gloom and despair. Contemporaries put this emotional oscillation down to the early signs of gout. And Pitt was certainly a sufferer from a disease that caused him a lot of joint pain. But the description of his switchback alterations of temper also corresponds very closely to the classic symptoms of manic depression, a behavioural disorder that seems to have afflicted an extraordinary number of those pantheonized as the builders of the British Empire, among them James Wolfe and Richard Wellesley.

Pitt's chosen form of neurotic release was the spoken word, delivered in the 'torrents' that so unnerved those who got in its way. It so happened that Pitt's fame as an orator occurred precisely at a time when an interest in Latin rhetoric, in particular in Longinus' treatise *On the Sublime*, with its self-conscious manipulation of the effects of terror and rapture, was much in vogue. No one was more conscious than Pitt that rhetoric was not just an academic art but a potent weapon too in contemporary politics. 'Arm yourself,' he wrote to his undergraduate nephew, Thomas, 'with all the variety of manner, copiousness and beauty of diction, nobleness and magnificence of ideas of the great Roman consuls; and render the powers of eloquence complete by the irresistible torrent of vehement argumentation, the close and forcible reasoning and the depth and fortitude of mind of the Grecian statesman.' Though no one disputed Pitt's often frightening vehemence, he was at his strongest when dropping into an otherwise orotund turn of phrase a pearl or two of perfectly calculated malice. Carteret, once his ally in the anti-Walpole coalition, was now the Hanoverian troop minister 'who had renounced the British nation and seemed to have drunk of the potion described in poetic fictions which made men forget their country'. Listening to him, the Commons became the Colosseum as much as the Forum, and the benches full of overgrown schoolboys watched gleefully as Pitt, tall and statuesque in posture (despite the gout), pointed his beaky nose at some unfortunate time-server, trapped him in the net of his irony and then jabbed away with Britannia's trident.

Even Seneca took a job, though. Conscious of this reputation for Roman uprightness, but hungry for advancement, in 1746 Pitt did something guaranteed to put him in a league of his own. He accepted a government office from the Pelhams, but refused its most lucrative perks. It was not just any office, but the Paymaster-Generalship of the army, one of the juiciest jobs that could possibly have come his way. Through the Paymaster's office went payments for military contracts. Into the Paymaster's pocket went the odd percentage or two for favouring this or that supplier. So turning his nose up at the customary rewards was a flamboyant way to disarm accusations that the patriot had sold out to the hacks. Drawing on the Bolingbroke playbook, Pitt ostentatiously deposited the Pay Office balance (from which Paymasters had been known to siphon the occasional thousand or two) in the Bank of England and declined the usual commission owed to him on arranging a military subsidy for the duchy of Savoy.

Pitt's cultivated pose as the lonely patriot may actually have been more solitary than he would have ideally liked. If he had been betting that he could forgo the windfalls of office because, with George II in his seventies, the bountiful reign of Frederick and his trusted ministers was about to dawn, Pitt was in for a brutal disappointment. His patrons were vanishing. Cobham died in 1749 and Frederick two years later, while the king, who made no secret of his dislike for Pitt, dismayingly soldiered on. In the end it didn't matter. For Pitt's sense of himself as a man meant to steer the course of British history was not, in fact, a sham. He was not a fake Cicero in a bad perruque but, for better or worse, a genuine visionary. And what he saw in his visions – obsessively – was America. Though his grandfather evidently had seen something irresistible (all those glinting carats) about Asia, and though Pitt himself was close to West-Indian sugar plutocrats like Beckford, he was convinced that it was America that would be the proving-ground of the empire of liberty. What happened in America would demonstrate whether the British Empire were to be not much more than an amusement for the tourists at Stowe or a dominion that would change the world.

Like everyone else who cared about naval power, Pitt subscribed to the conventional wisdom that, unless Britain controlled its home waters, its 'liberties' and security would never be truly assured. But unlike more conservative strategists, he also believed that the battle for commercial supremacy (which in the end would determine whether Catholic absolutism or parliamentary government would dominate the world) had to be taken to the French in America if it were to be decisively won. And like the West-Indian planters and the American colonists, Pitt did not think that time was on Britain's side. St Domingue, Martinique and Guadeloupe had already robbed Britain of its European re-export market, and now the massive fortress on Cape Breton Island at the mouth of the St Lawrence threatened the security of the priceless New England fishing industry. (Salt cod, sent to the West Indies, was about the only protein, other than beans, in the slave diet, and in return New England imported rum and molasses.) Pitt entirely subscribed to the view, coming out of America itself, that the French were engaged in a slow but systematic strangulation of British economic and political power in the New World. Native Americans were being suborned to deny New England trappers their share of the fur trade. Today it was beaver, tomorrow America.

So he was happy when a largely volunteer army under Governor William Shirley of Massachusetts, together with a small naval squadron, actually succeeded in taking the major fort of Louisbourg in 1745 – one of the few undisputed successes of 'King George's War'. A year later he supported the Duke of Bedford's memorandum urging a more general attack on Canada, to destroy the French fur trade with the Indians and rob it of mast timber for its navy. But not only was the attack shelved – too fraught with danger, too expensive; in the peace negotiations in 1748 Louisbourg was returned to France.

The problem of French America, as Pitt would come to recognize, was in fact much more serious than the battle over the St Lawrence and the eastern seaboard. It was, in essence, the battle for living space. The man who saw most clearly how high the stakes were was the scientist and practical man of letters Benjamin Franklin. His *Observations Concerning the Increase of Mankind* were written in 1751 (though not published until 1755) and went to the heart of what British America was to be. There were already upwards of 1.2 million people living in its several colonies, and that number, through natural increase, could be expected to double within a generation; so British America had to be expansive or it would atrophy in self-destructive claustrophobia. In other words, Franklin shared with the boosters of empire in Britain a conviction that it was an empire of liberty. But Franklin's American liberty was not just so much Whig hot air; it was material and territorial. He could see with a precision rivalled only by the French philosopher de Montesquieu the relationship between geography, demography and freedom; that in America (unlike crowded England) the availability of land gave material meaning to the ideal of self-sufficiency. And in his Britophil innocence Franklin, at least the Franklin of 1751, assumed that these sunny horizons would be shared by the guardians of the imperial future at home. When, in a century, the population of America actually surpassed that of the metropolis, a population dispersed over who knew how much of the continental land mass, such a moment, he supposed, could only be an occasion for shared celebration: 'What an accession of power to the British Empire by sea as well as land! What increase of trade and navigation! What numbers of ships and seamen.'

There was, however, something other than British obtuseness and self-interest in the way of realizing Franklin's dream of a westward-ho empire of freedom, and that was French strategy. French settlement in America consisted of three regions: 'New France' (Canada), from the St Lawrence to the Great Lakes; the mid-Mississippi 'Illinois country' (claimed as a result of a French expedition, by Sieur de la Salle, to the Mississippi delta in 1682); and Louisiana at its delta. They were all, of course, separated from each other by vast distances, and it was the determination of the ministers of Louis XV and especially his governors in Quebec to connect them with a chain of roads, navigated rivers, portage trails and forts. Critical to making the first connection between Canada and the Mississippi was the broad stretch of territory between the Alleghenies and Lake Erie known as the 'Ohio Country'. And it was in this densely forested land, crossed by rivers and peopled by Native American tribes, such as the Shawnees, Delawares and Mingos – roughly the region of modern eastern Ohio and western Pennsylvania – that the fate of America would be decided.

The Virginians – who claimed that the hinterland of America, all the way to the Pacific, including 'the island of California', had been included in their original charter of 1609 – had formed the Virginian Ohio Company in 1747, to survey and lay claim to trans-Appalachian lands. And the mid-Atlantic colonies – New York, New Jersey, Pennsylvania, Delaware and Maryland, whose own populations had boomed in the first half of the eighteenth century were themselves acutely interested in preventing the French and their Native American allies moving south from Canada, robbing them

William Pitt the Elder, First Earl of Chatham, by William Hoare, *c.* 1754.

of the fur trade there and pre-empting territory for westward expansion. The word most commonly used of French designs (and there were few more damning in the lexicon of colonial competition) was 'artful': the artful extension of 'lines within our colonies'; the artful seduction of the Native Americans to deny the British their proper share of fish and furs. But behind all that art was brute force, the application of a deadly choke-hold, crushing the life out of British America. The time had come to resist or expire.

In 1744 the Treaty of Lancaster was signed at Newtown in Lancaster County, Pennsylvania, and solemnized by the presentation of belts of wampum (freshwater shells used as currency) between commissioners of the British colonies and the Six Iroquois Nations. The Native Americans were given free passage across the British territories to hunt down their tribal enemies like the Cherokee and in return appeared to cede sovereignty over virtually the entire Ohio country. Trying to remain neutral in the Anglo–French wars, the Iroquois soon indignantly repudiated any suggestion that they had permanently alienated their rights over this enormous area; but it was enough to send a wave of trappers and mappers into the Ohio country to stake claims for King George, the Ohio Company and not least themselves. The French responded in the ways they knew best, sending out pre-emptive expeditions to lay down little lead plaques on a 3000-mile arc of territory; and followed that in the summer and autumn of 1752 with an intensive campaign of fort building, done on a Roman scale that cost 400 lives and 400 million livres. The French forts may have been built of logs, but, like Fort Duquesne, named for the strategically minded new governor in Quebec, they were serious structures with walls 10–12 feet-thick, the corners shaped in the arrowhead projections stipulated in European military text-books, and capable of garrisoning hundreds of men.

By early 1753 the battle of the hatchets and the surveying rods had become official. Even the Duke of Newcastle had become persuaded that something important was at stake in the backwoods of the colonies. The Scottish merchant turned American surveyor Robert Dinwiddie, who was to become Lieutenant-Governor of Virginia in 1754, dispatched a six-foot-two, twenty-one-year-old major with absolutely no command of French to carry a letter to the commandant of Fort Le Boeuf, demanding that the French cease and desist from garrisoning territories self-evidently belonging to King George.

George Washington may have had no French, but he understood the compelling interests of the British Empire very well. His half-brother Lawrence, after all, had named their property in Virginia 'Mount Vernon', after the hero of Porto Bello, and he first practised his profession as a land surveyor on behalf of the English aristocrat Lord

Fairfax, who was the dominant magnate in the northern neck of Virginia. But his early experience of defending those interests was unhappy. At a Native American village on the fork of the Ohio he met up with a French platoon that invited Washington to sup. 'The Wine, as they dos'd themselves pretty plentifully with it, soon banish'd the restraint which at first appeared in their Conversation … They told me it was their absolute Design to take Possession of the Ohio & by G— they would do it, for tho they were sensible that the English could raise two men for their one; yet they knew their Motions were too slow and dilatory to prevent any Undertaking of theirs.' At Fort Le Boeuf, Washington had much the same dusty reply, phrased with exquisite courtesy. The following year, 1754, he prepared and led an expedition. An early success (followed by a scalping and general massacre of French prisoners) turned into a much bigger disaster on 4 July, when Washington's soldiers, trapped inside their 'Fort Necessity', found their muskets unusable in a July rainstorm. Leaving wounded and dead behind, they ignominiously marched out from the fort and limped back to Virginia, leaving the French in jubilant command of the Ohio country.

For those in America and London who were not prepared to accept the French stranglehold on the western frontier, two options were left. Either a counterattack should be mounted by a force raised from all the colonies, in alliance with Indian warriors in substantial numbers. Or a true army, dominated by British regular troops and commanded by a British general, should do the job for them. Franklin, of course, was in favour of the first, more authentically American way and was one of Pennsylvania's representatives at a pan-American congress at Albany in the Hudson Valley, just a week after Washington's débâcle at Fort Necessity. For the first time a working military and political confederation of the British-American colonies was discussed in some detail. But the fires lit by the Albany meeting were immediately doused by the rejection of its agenda by all the separate colonial assemblies, who were too preoccupied with their own sectional interests. (The New Englanders wanted fishery protection; the New Yorkers wanted everyone else to pay for forts guarding their northern frontier.) But the ideals of a federation remained warm inside Franklin's head and heart. Some time during the latter part of 1754 he wrote to Governor Shirley outlining what he hoped for the future of British America. First, the western frontier had to be uncompromisingly defended against the French. But that defence had to be undertaken in a true spirit of the indivisibility of the empire: American citizen-soldiers and British regular soldiers in concord. And if the British government were truly prescient it would understand that its own best interests would be served not by subjecting America but by co-opting it; that it should make good the understanding that Americans were responsible for their own internal government; and that if money were needed for a

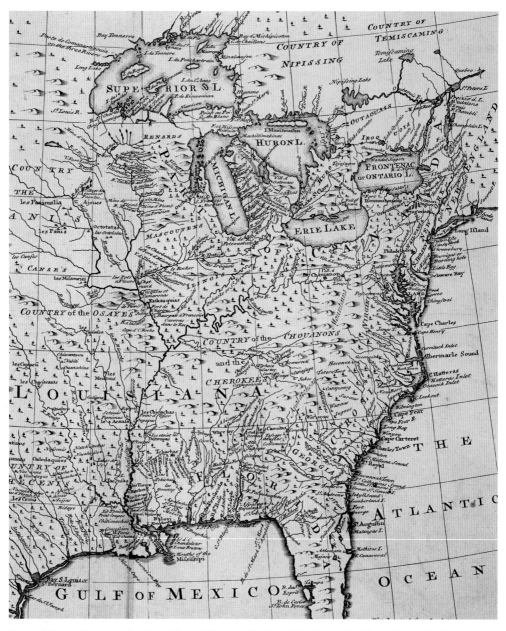

Above: *A New and Accurate Map of Louisiana, with part of Florida and Canada and the Adjacent Countries drawn from Surveys* ... 1752.

Opposite: *Benjamin Franklin*, by Charles Willson Peale, 1772, after David Martin.

common defence it ought to come from the consent of their own institutions. Economically, too, the interests of the mother and the children should be seen not as competitive but as complementary, so that the industries of America ought not to be penalized for narrow interests at home but should be regarded as the strength of the common empire.

Franklin's rational and benevolent vision of the British Empire paid its ideological inventors the compliment of taking their rhetoric about liberty at face value. But he presupposed a breadth of understanding, an appreciation of the strengths of American culture and society that had barely impinged on the conscience of the empire-builders at home. Their policies were designed not to respect distance but to abolish it, not to make room for diversity but to impose 'order' and uniformity. By the 1750s, the politicians at Westminster believed they already had a model of orderly, industrious integration, and it was called Scotland.

So naturally it fell to the Duke of Cumberland, the 'Butcher of Culloden', to nominate the general who would take the Ohio country campaign to the French and sort out, once and for all, who was sovereign. Edward Braddock was the ideal Cumberland protégé: a thorough-going, unsentimental administrator and a stickler for discipline. To show he meant business Braddock would take with him two regiments, the 41st and the 48th. Even the announcement had the British press relishing the assured victory and sketching an early self-portrait of the character of the British Empire: averse to conquest, slow to provoke, but, when roused, frightening in its might. 'We have now shown the world that the Dominion of the Sea is not an empty boast,' trumpeted *Jackson's Oxford Journal*, 'but such a one as we can and dare assert whenever it becomes absolutely necessary. We never disturb our Neighbour with our Intrigues, we never encroach on their Territories. … But when we are threatened, deceived and encroached upon ourselves … then … it [military action] appears to us as Justice.'

The French, it was confidently felt, must be shaking in their shoes. One British force was to retake Louisbourg, denying reinforcements; a second was to capture the forts at Niagara, travelling up the rivers from the Hudson; while Braddock himself would march on Fort Duquesne, where Washington had come to grief. Once that had been dealt with Braddock would advance north, rolling up resistance, and join the Niagara battalions at the lake: simple, decisive, swift. Washington and Franklin met the general at Frederickstown in Maryland just before the march of his two regiments. Washington went as aide-de-camp on the strength of his knowledge of the country, and Franklin had provided a spectacular token of Pennsylvania's appreciation of British protection by supplying each officer with the equivalent of the imperial pantry: 6 pounds of rice, raisins, chocolate, coffee and sugar; a pound each of green and Bohea black tea; half a pound of pepper; a whole Gloucester cheese; 20 pounds of best butter; two hams; 2 gallons of Jamaica rum and two dozen bottles of Madeira. This was what made it worth being British.

Unfortunately it was also what doomed Braddock to bloody fiasco on 9 July 1755. It was not just the 150 wagons and 500 pack horses bearing all these supplies that slowed him to a plod en route to the Monongahela forks. It was the necessity of cutting a laborious way through deep forest, widening tracks to make a road wide enough and level enough to get his supply train through without getting into potentially dangerous difficulties. His Mingo Native American guides had doubtless alerted Braddock to these obvious logistical realities, but as a Mingo chief, Scarouady, noted, he treated them barely better than 'dogs'. The dogs could bite. The 'contemptible savages' fighting for the French did not form up in the open like sporting Jacobites to take on Braddock's light infantry, but raked them with fire from invisible positions deep inside the forest. Weakened by dysentery and suffering acutely from haemorrhoids, Braddock let his training as an officer and a gentleman take over. As his boxed-in infantry attempted to return fire into the piny nowhere he remained imperturbable in the saddle, riding the line, encouraging the soldiers even as they fell in hundreds: a deliberately perfect target for the inevitable musket ball in the chest. Down went the redcoats like lead soldiers in text-book platoon formation, their fellows taking their place in the firing line, staying put as they dropped. By the time a modicum of self-preservation took over, and men actually began running for their lives, two-thirds of Braddock's force was dead or critically wounded. The French and their Native American allies had lost just twenty-three dead and sixteen wounded. Braddock died on the retreat and was buried along the road his sappers had cut. George Washington, who took the general's blood-soaked cloak back to Mount Vernon, did not in fact conclude that Braddock had been woefully mistaken in his tactics, only that his men had been inadequate to the task.

If one kind of Cumberland war guaranteed defeat, another, just as depressing, guaranteed a kind of 'success'. In Nova Scotia the Governor, Charles Lawrence, was engaged not just in pacification but in something more ominously modern: mass deportation. By the terms of the Treaty of Utrecht in 1713 the French-Catholic Acadians had been allowed to live peacefully in southern Nova Scotia, on the wrong side of the Anglo-French divide, provided they refrained from actively assisting the enemy. But as the Franco-British conflict in America heated up, their refusal to take a formal oath of loyalty to King George made them seem like a permanent fifth column, egging on the Native Americans to attack the outnumbered British. Lawrence was determined to get to them before they got to him, and set in motion

Defeat and Death of General Braddock in North America, engraved by E. Scott, *c.* 1755.

the appalling policy known to the Acadians euphemistically as '*le grand dérangement*'. At least 6000 of them who had been living on the shores of the Bay of Fundy were forcibly uprooted from farms, homes and land, and assembled for trans-shipment to Massachusetts, South Carolina and Virginia. The move was so sudden and so brutal that, even as the boats were being prepared to take them away, they could not quite believe they were 'actually to be removed'. On 8 October the first group was loaded. The British officer in charge wrote: 'Began to embarke the Inhabitants who went of very Solentarily and unwillingly, the women in Great Distress Carrying Off their Children in their Arms, Others Carrying their Decrepit Parents in their carts and all their Goods moving in Great Confusion and appeared a scene of Woe and Distress'. Colonists from New York and Massachusetts took their place in northern Maine and Nova Scotia. Half of the passengers on the first ship to the Carolinas died on board in conditions of extreme filth and hardship. Some thousands managed to escape to Canada, only to find the country changing hands with the imminent Seven Years' War. Another group made a great odyssey down Duquesne's strategic trail on the Mississippi all the way to Louisiana where they finally resettled, exchanging a diet of lobster and cod for crayfish and catfish as Acadian culture metamorphosed into Cajun.

The dogs of war had been unloosed (even if the American tails had wagged them). And from the beginning it was thought of as a world war, even by the habitually cost-conscious Duke of Newcastle. The strategy, though, was not in fact any different from the way in which the war of the 1740s had been fought. There would be a heavily subsidized European ally, Prussia, whose armies would pin the French down in Europe and divert both men and resources away from the imperial theatres in India, West Africa, the Caribbean and America. The bulk of the Royal Navy would, as always, be assigned to guard the home waters and raid and blockade French ports from the Mediterranean up the Atlantic coast, stopping reinforcements from reaching Canada. In America itself, 'long-injured, long-neglected, long-forgotten,' as Pitt said (exaggerating as usual), the old Braddock plan of simultaneously attacking Canada, the upper New York lake fort at Ticonderoga and Fort Duquesne in the heart of the Ohio country was revived. But along with it came many of the old mistakes. Braddock's replacement as coordinator of these campaigns was yet another Cumberland stop-gap, the Ayrshire aristocrat John Campbell, fourth Earl of Loudoun, whose enthusiasm for the military life had led him to plant a wood resembling a regiment of the line and who came with a retinue of seventeen servants, travelling mistress and mistress's maid. If anything, Loudoun's contempt for the colonials and their savage allies was even more patrician than Braddock's. Convinced that the whole bloody shower needed smartening up, he courted the hatred of American officers by insisting on the War Office policy of ranking Americans far below their counterparts in the regular British regiments and alienated the men by demanding that the British whip-happy code of military discipline (500 lashes for insubordination, 1000 for stealing a shirt) be imposed on the colonial troops who had never seen it, much less endured it. Exasperated by contraband trade between the French-Caribbean and British colonies, Loudoun's answer was to shut down trade altogether.

Loudoun's way of running the war represented a clear choice and the Americans knew it. An alternative would have been to co-opt the colonial troops and the Native Americans in a genuinely imperial coalition. This would mean entrusting the colonial assemblies and their governors with the power to raise men and money in the ways they best saw fit, and the ways best suited to part-time bachelor soldiers who would want to feel assured that when the worst was over they could get back to their farms and forges. Raising funds for these troops, as the governors knew, was better done through consent than by imperious demand. But men like Braddock and Loudoun saw the assemblies and even the governors as mere subalterns to be told what was needed and when and where to deliver it. To allow them any sort of latitude in military affairs, they believed, was to indulge their natural tendency to insubordination, to compromise discipline and to court defeat. Loudoun continually expressed his horrified astonishment that the colonials, especially the 'leading people', presumed to venture criticism or even opinion on imperial strategy. And the raw material of American troops he believed to be unfit for serious combat. Only integrating them into regular regiments and teaching them, fiercely if need be, how real soldiers conducted themselves would create a viable army.

Even though Loudoun had much of his way, defeat came all the same. In India the irrepressible and brutally efficient Robert Clive destroyed Siraj-ud-Daulah, the Nawab of Bengal, handing (whether it wanted them or not) the revenues of the richest province in Mughal India to the East India Company so that it could balance its books. But elsewhere the first two years of the war against France were a procession of disasters. In the Mediterranean Admiral Byng lost the island of Minorca, thought strategically vital for controlling the routes east to Italy and the Levant. Amid an ugly eruption of patriotic fury, Byng was sacrificed by court-martial to spare the government the odium. Worse, Admiral Boscawen's fleet failed to blockade the mouth of the St Lawrence effectively, so that reinforcements and supplies managed to get through to the armies of New France at Quebec and Montreal. On the New York lakes, it was the French and not the British who were on the offensive, capturing Fort William Henry in 1757.

It was the end of Newcastle. Pitt, who had raised a hue and cry for massive mobilization, had been brought into the administration, but kept (not least by the king's mistrust) from real power. At the end of 1757, though, with the prospects looking grim, Pitt was finally given his moment, and he leapt at it with the full conviction of someone who never for a second doubted that God had personally appointed him for the job. Among his first priorities was to make it clear that he would fight an American war the American way and to repair some of the damage done by the likes of Braddock and Loudoun. The latter was ignominiously recalled, and Pitt won friends in the American assemblies by committing the British government to reimburse the colonials for any expenses laid out for equipment and pay. Over £1 million would be earmarked for this. Whole-hearted collaboration instantly replaced surly assent: Massachusetts, for instance, voted for the supply of 7000 volunteer troops. Likewise Pitt repealed Loudoun's invidious weighting of ranks between the regulars and the colonials. Then he threw good men and pots of money at the job in hand. Generals – some of them, like James Wolfe and William Howe, in their thirties – were suddenly promoted, leapfrogging over their seniors. Others, like Jeffrey Amherst in command of the frontal attack on Canada, were given unprecedented troop strength: some 14,000 alone for the attack on Louisbourg. The French in America could probably put together no more than some 16,000 of their own soldiers together with whatever Native Americans they could mobilize, but those would now be counterbalanced by Mohawks and other tribes among the Iroquois nation who, seeing the writing on the wall, had gravitated towards the British. By the end of 1757 there were nearly 50,000 British imperial troops committed to the war in Canada, almost two-thirds of the entire population of New France. Almost £5.5 million was spent on the American sector of the war alone, £1 million for the navy and another £1 million on fulfilling the promise to pay for colonial troops. Pitt had succeeded in persuading the country that this time the war had to be all or nothing.

And it was to be a British, not an English, war. The first Highland regiment in the British army to serve abroad had been raised and deployed in Europe in 1745 – the year of the Jacobite rising. But those soldiers were predominantly drawn from loyal clans like the Campbells. By the time that additional regiments were formed for the American campaign their recruiting zone was much broader. There were Munroes from Galloway and Murrays from Inverness. It has been estimated that by the time the American war began one in four officers in the imperial army were Scots. They were to undergo a murderous baptism of fire.

In early July 1758 the portly General Abercromby (known unpromisingly to his own soldiers as 'granny'), in command of the expedition to take Fort Carillon at

Ticonderoga, decided, while a mile distant from the battle site, to send his troops on a suicidal frontal assault without first setting his artillery up on a hill where it might at least have given them covering fire. The result was predictable. The Black Watch and the Inniskillings quick-marched to the sound of bagpipes right into the tangle of sharpened tree-stumps set in front of the breastworks and never exited. A terrified officer in a battalion of Massachusetts volunteers, Archelaus Fuller, flat on the ground behind a log while French musket shot whistled past his ears, described 'a sorful s[ight] to behold, the ded men and wounded lay on the ground having som of them Legs, their arms and other [sic] lims broken, others shot threw the body and very mortly wounded; to hear thar cris and se their bodis lay in blod and the earth trembel with the fier of smal arms was a mournfull [h]our ever I saw'. This carnage continued for eight hours. Nearly 2000 dead and grievously wounded lay around the timber palisades. At sunset, not having heard anything from their officers, the survivors who had had the sense to lie motionless between logs tentatively rose from their brushy cover and disappeared into the woods like raccoons on the run.

Ticonderoga was, though, the first and last real catastrophe of Pitt's war. Only glories followed: first, the fall of great Louisbourg to Amherst and his brigadier James Wolfe in a conventional siege that unloaded such devastating ordnance on the town that it capitulated before it melted. Among those who witnessed the triumph was the thirteen-year-old Olaudah Equiano, who some years before had been bought by a sea captain, Michael Henry Pascal, as his page and servant. When Pascal went to serve in the Royal Navy in 1756, Olaudah went with him and found himself aboard the same ship as Wolfe en route to Cape Breton. At the end of the siege he was flooded with a kind of terrible wonder at the strange terrors of war: 'A lieutenant of the *Princess Amelia* [one of the ships] was giving the word of command and while his mouth was open a musket ball went through it and passed out his cheek. I had that day in my hand the scalp of an Indian king, killed in the engagement: the scalp was taken off by a Highlander.' Holding the scalp of an Indian king who had been killed by a Highlander, Equiano was getting an accelerated education in the multi-national empire.

The Native Americans would remain adversaries. But the former physician Brigadier John Forbes, yet another Scot, who had been assigned to the Ohio country campaign, assembled representatives of the Cherokees and Delawares, as well as other tribes, and brought enough of them over in a treaty agreement to make the capture of Fort Duquesne merely a matter of time. The French removed what they could of its munitions and blew it up. The fort settlement built in its place was called Pittsburgh.

In Europe Frederick the Great was more than holding his own against the French and their allies, which was just as well since £200,000 had been allotted annually for

Top: *General Amherst*, by Sir Joshua Reynolds, *c*. 1760.
Above: *A View of the Landing of the New England Forces in ye Expedition against Cape Breton, Louisbourg*, 1745.

his subsidy! But what was a mere £200,000 when everything suddenly seemed to be going Britain's way? Towards the end of 1758, parliament enacted a military budget for the coming year of £12.5 million – a sum that had never before been conceivable, much less granted. Half-borrowed, half-taxed, it sustained an army of 90,000, a navy of over 70,000, a territorial militia of between 30,000 and 40,000. It bought victory.

Sitting on top of all this bounty, Pitt could play around with the world. A raid on West Africa took French slave stations at Gorée and the Gambia; an expedition to the Caribbean, after some real difficulty, ended up taking Guadeloupe with its 40,000 slaves and 350 plantations. Within a year (to the consternation of British planters in Jamaica and Barbados, who were not at all sure they wanted this particular conquest) Guadeloupe sugar was flooding into the London market. In Bengal, Clive (if not the East India Company) was drowning in 'presents' offered by rival Indian nawabs. And in south India, an opportunistic attempt by the Comte de Lally to re-establish a strong military presence on the Coromandel coast was undermined by the inability of the French marine to break a British blockade.

All this, however, was but a sideshow to the main event, which, for Pitt after 1761, became the definitive conquest of Canada. Once this was accomplished, he believed there would be no stopping the future of British America, and by extension British power, which was to say, as he and the graduates of Stowe understood it, British liberty. The elements seemed to be helping, for Canada had suffered almost famine conditions in 1758, and the winter of 1758–9 was the most brutally cold in memory. With Louisbourg and Cape Breton Island fallen to the British, its plight would be desperate unless it was somehow resupplied. In the early spring of 1759 a few ships did manage to cut a path through the ice at the mouth of the St Lawrence, sneak past the British blockade and land some reinforcements and food at Quebec. This breath of life convinced the Governor, the Marquis de Montcalm, to entrench himself on the easily defensible Heights of Abraham at Quebec along with all the manpower he could muster – perhaps 16,000, including Canadian militia – and defy the British, also suffering from shortage of supplies, to come and get him. An alternative strategy would have been to evacuate the city, disperse troops to several different centres and settle down for a partisan war in a country whose natives and settlers could be relied on to be bitterly hostile to the British. But Montcalm's view carried the day at Versailles.

Amherst's was always the main army. But back in London James Wolfe succeeded in persuading Pitt to let him attempt an assault from the St Lawrence. Giving Wolfe 20,000 troops, Pitt perhaps felt he had nothing to lose. But for Wolfe destiny was calling. Sick with consumption, he was already seeing himself carved in marble on a patriot's tomb. But en route to passion play on the Plains of Abraham he very nearly failed in his plan for immortality. Hungry or not, Montcalm refused to be drawn from his massive defences around Quebec, his own bastions reinforced by the precipitous 200-foot bluffs on one side to the river and an equally sheer rock face on the inland side. Thwarted, Wolfe let his soldiers and Native Americans loose on a campaign of ferocious 'cruelty and devastation' on the surrounding countryside. If this were meant to goad Montcalm into emerging, out of concern or anger, it was an abysmal failure. All the French commander had to do was sit tight through the autumn and wait for the ice to close in on the river, trapping Wolfe or forcing him to retreat.

Something desperate was called for, so desperate that no one, not even Wolfe, seriously imagined it could work: a night-time ascent straight up the cliffs along a ravine trail identified by one Robert Stobo, who had been captured during Washington's failed attack on Fort Necessity and had lived in Quebec under easy half-imprisonment for some years before escaping to the British lines. It was only on the eve of the attack that Wolfe deigned to let his brigadiers, with whom he was barely on speaking terms, know what he had in mind. The idea was to feint downstream east of the city but sail in the opposite direction west, then allow the tide to drift thirty flat-bottom landing boats back down to the landing point. At five in the morning, the first hundreds of men scrambled up the slopes. There was a skirmish at the top, but not the all-out battle Wolfe had been assuming. The French soldier who brought news to the garrison at Quebec was unsure whether the British had stayed or gone back the way they came – the venture seemed so bizarre. Wolfe himself was astonished at getting 4800 troops and two cannon atop the Plains, where he lined them up, a scarlet ribbon extending half a mile across the plateau from one cliff to the other. He was set right between Montcalm and his supply lines and reinforcements, all now west of Wolfe. With food and munitions running out, and absolutely no room to manoeuvre around the rear of the British without dropping off the edge, Montcalm was dumbfounded by what had happened. Listening to the British drums and fifes, he realized he had no choice but to engage in something seldom seen in America: a formal battle. But if the troops he had sent west could be recalled in time, the advantage would suddenly be reversed. Wolfe's line would be trapped between two French forces with no route for retreat except back over the cliff.

By nine o'clock there was no sign of French troops from the west, and the cannon Wolfe had brought were doing damage to the French line. Highland pipes were skirling in the rain. Montcalm could wait no longer. His own numbers matched Wolfe's, but half of them were Canadian militia. They were supposed to advance in drill-order at a steady pace towards the British, halt at about 150 yards and then fire; but when given the order, the militia ran virtually at will towards the thin lines of

Opposite, top: *James Wolfe*, by George Townshend, *c.* 1760.
Opposite, below: *Death of the Marquis de Montcalm*, engraved by G. Chevillet, *c.* 1760.
Top: *A View of the Taking of Quebec*, English School, *c.* 1797.
Above: *Death of General Wolfe*, by Benjamin West, 1770.

immobile British troops, making any kind of coordinated advance, let alone reforming after the inevitable counter-volley, impossible. Wolfe, whose wrist had been
shattered by a musket ball, used his other arm to hold his soldiers back until the French
had reached as close as 40 yards. The British couldn't miss. An immense volley of fire,
'like cannon', both sides said, tore huge holes in both the white-coated French regulars and the militia. When the smoke cleared they were in full retreat. Wolfe took shot
in his guts and another in his chest, realizing the hero's consummation he had been so
determined to achieve. He would get his marble sepulchre in the Abbey. As soon as the
news reached England, wrote Horace Walpole, people 'despaired – they triumphed –
and they wept – for Wolfe had fallen in the hour of victory! Joy, grief, curiosity and
astonishment were painted in every countenance.' His cult was a gift to Pitt, who in
the House of Commons delivered an oration that was, in effect, an elegy over the bier
of a fallen hero from antiquity. Only – as the Stowe 'patriot boys' always wanted – this
was better than Rome.

There were other more prosaic, but more decisive, events to come, none more so
than Admiral Hawke's destruction in Quiberon Bay off Brittany of a French Brest fleet
still capable of threatening a Britain defended mostly by militiamen. The French held
out in Canada much longer than anyone supposed after the battle on the Heights of
Abraham. It was only the following year, in the summer of 1760, that, finally robbed of
any chance of reinforcement and supply, the French Governor, Vaudreuil, capitulated
to Amherst at Montreal. Part of his incentive to do so, rather than fight on, was the
fairly generous terms offered by Amherst. The 70,000-odd Canadians were required to
remain neutral in any future conflict between Britain and France, but in return were to
be allowed free practice of their Roman Catholic religion and even the guaranteed
appointment of a diocesan bishop for Quebec. As Vaudreuil must have correctly
calculated, French-Canadian culture and identity, if not its political existence, would be
preserved for generations to come.

Voltaire may have written Canada off as 'a few acres of snow'. But its conquest
utterly transformed the sense of the future for the British Empire. Franklin, for one,
who since 1757 had been living in London as the commissioner of the Pennsylvania
Assembly, was exhilarated and campaigned furiously against any thought of its return.
Taking in the storm of patriotic celebrations, the bonfires and the bell-ringing, the
feasts and the renderings of Garrick's 'Hearts of Oak' that erupted throughout the
country – especially in Scotland – Franklin was utterly convinced of the momentous
righteousness of the war. 'If ever there was a national war,' he wrote, 'this is truly such
a one, a war in which the interest of the whole nation is directly and fundamentally
concerned.' In the *annus mirabilis* of 1759, when triumph followed triumph, and, as

Horace Walpole boasted, 'our bells are worn threadbare with ringing of victories', Franklin travelled to Scotland where he made friends with the learned nobleman and writer on political economy and agriculture Henry Home, Lord Kames. To Kames Franklin must have confided his bursting pride on what had happened and the prospect it opened up of the realization of the indivisible empire of liberty. Had he not signed his petition to parliament 'A Briton'? To Kames, he wrote, 'I have long been of the opinion that the foundations of the future grandeur and stability of the British Empire lie in America; and though, like other foundations, they are low and little seen, they are nevertheless broad and strong enough to support the greatest political structure human wisdom ever yet erected.' Just seventeen years later he would put his signature to the Declaration of Independence. What happened?

Peace, in 1763, brought disenchantment. Olaudah Equiano had spent his adolescence on Royal Navy warships as one of the boys who ran for powder for the guns while colossal ships of the line burst into flames. He had watched boys and men torn apart by cannon-balls or pierced by splintering timbers 'and launched into eternity'. At the siege of Belleisle he saw 'above sixty shells and carcasses in the air at once'. Alternately terrified and elated, baptized a Christian, learning to read and write, acquiring books and a Bible, Olaudah had been led by his master, Pascal, to believe that when it all ended he was going to walk away from the terror and slaughter a free man. Instead he found Pascal first accusing him of attempting to run away and then, over his tears and angry grievance, reselling him to a captain who took him to the West Indies. 'Thus, at the moment I expected my toils to end, was I plunged … into a new slavery.' Pascal had robbed him of his books, his personal belongings, his only coat – and his hard-won dignity. In bitter distress – and knowing he was bound for the West Indies – Equiano wrote, 'I reproached my fate and wished I had never been born.'

William Pitt was in less extreme straits, but he too was angry, sick and miserable much of the time. On 25 October 1760, George II, who at the very end of his life had finally come to appreciate, rather than despise, Pitt, had finally died of a heart attack. Only good things were expected from his grandson and successor. He had been tutored by a friend of Pitt's, the Scot Lord Bute, in the precepts of Bolingbroke's *Patriot King*. The influence of his mother, the Dowager Princess Augusta, was equally obvious. Unlike his excessively Hanoverian predecessors, George III proudly and publicly 'gloried in the name of Briton'. His apparent artlessness seemed the very model of a Patriot. Doubtless his bust would shortly join the pantheon at Stowe. But in no time at all, Pitt was disabused of virtually all these assumptions. The friend Bute turned into an unfriendly rival, more sympathetic to those who wanted an exit from a war now thought cripplingly expensive. Pitt's obsessive determination to see the French not merely damaged and humiliated but annihilated as a potential imperial competitor, and his goal of destroying Spanish power in the Caribbean as well, looked increasingly irrational. The young king, it seemed, was listening to his tutor and shared his view of the 'mad' Pitt. Worse, the Stowe family was breaking up. When Pitt was forced out in 1761, the new Viscount Temple and one of his brothers-in-law, James Grenville, went with him, but George Grenville, who had become Bute's and Newcastle's poster boy in the Commons, did not. Pitt treated this as a betrayal, and for the next decade the two would be harsh political enemies. In 1763, when the Peace of Paris was signed, Pitt believed that Bute had sold out the interests of the Empire by returning Martinique, Guadeloupe and St Lucia to France, Havana and Manila to Spain, and by restoring the right of the French to fish the precious cod banks off Newfoundland, safeguarded by their possession of St Pierre and Miquelon in the St Lawrence.

But a glance at the map – and British statesmen did more than glance at it – must have confirmed their doubts about Pitt's sanity. The planters of Jamaica and Barbados were eager to restore, not retain, the sugar islands of Martinique and Guadeloupe before they outsold them in the vital American market as well as in domestic markets; and hanging on to a fishing monopoly was not going to alter the inescapable fact that, for all its recent disasters, France was still – demographically and militarily – the pre-eminent power in Europe. Inflicting a Carthaginian peace would only quicken the desire for revenge. When government ministers considered the immense extent of the newly enlarged Empire, from Bengal to Senegal, from Minorca to Montreal – elation at the fact that Britons, as Horace Walpole exulted, had been able to 'subdue the globe in three campaigns', whereas the Romans had taken three centuries, was necessarily tempered with a deep anxiety about how to pay for its defence. The enormous wartime army of over 90,000 had now been halved, but even at that strength was a crippling financial burden on a Treasury groggy with debt. Peacetime had also brought economic dislocation: there was a banking crash in Amsterdam whose effects rippled through the closely connected London money market, making credit suddenly tight; and the demobilization of vast numbers put pressure on employment at the same time that labour-intensive industries had to be cut back to pre-war levels. Harvests were poor, prices high; the populace in ports and towns more than usually riotous. A new round of excise duties on consumer goods would only make an already dangerous situation worse.

So it was inevitable that George Grenville, who succeeded the deeply unpopular Bute as First Lord of the Treasury in August 1763 (to the express disadvantage of Pitt, who had been approached for a return), should turn his tidy mind to the challenge of having the American empire – which he supposed could best afford it – pay for the

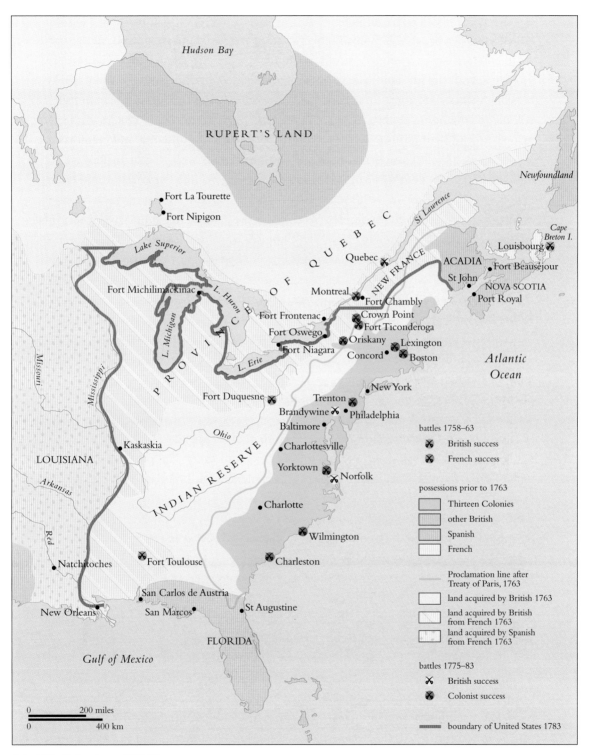

Colonial North America, *c.* 1758–83.

costs of its own defence. The logic of it must have seemed incontrovertible. Had not British America benefited immeasurably from the war? Had not money poured into its trade and industries from the mother country during the campaigns? Were not its prospects, with the immense territory of Canada added, bright? But now there had to be some sort of reckoning. First, the basic, self-evidently dependent relationship of the colonies to the home country, in which the former existed to supply Britain with raw materials while consuming its manufactures, needed to be restated and reinforced. Whatever Benjamin Franklin thought, no illusions should be held that Britain would tolerate, much less encourage, the growth of American manufactures that might compete with its own, nor would it look kindly on foreign countries that did so, least of all France and Spain, and their colonies. Secondly, if the costs of defending the American empire were not to become uncontrollable, the region of settlement had to be limited to lands east of the Appalachians; lands further to the west must henceforth be reserved to the Native Americans, without whose goodwill continuing and expensive trouble would be guaranteed. Thirdly, it seemed only equitable that the American colonies, for whose benefit it was constituted, should pay for their own defence through some form of additional revenue.

Just what those revenues should be deeply exercised the fastidious Grenville. On looking through the books of the American customs and excise he was appalled to discover that their operating costs were much heavier than their yield. The conclusion was certainly not to abolish them, but to impose a new substantial duty on the foreign commodity most in demand in America. And that, of course was French sugar, in particular the Caribbean molasses needed for distilling into the ubiquitous American food staple – rum. (British Caribbean molasses was inadequate in supply and high in price.) Grenville's proposed duty was sixpence a gallon. When protests – especially loud from the rum-happy New England colonies – were voiced, he cut it in half but backed it up by aggressive, quasi-military customs enforcement. In 1761, at the height of the Seven Years' War, when trading with the enemy was deemed a form of economic sabotage, 'writs of assistance' had been used to search and try smugglers in vice-admiralty courts (since colonial ones seemed reluctant to convict them). Now, to the anger and dismay of the commercial communities in Boston and New York – where smuggling was a way of life – those courts were to be continued in peacetime.

The trouble for Grenville – did he but know it – was that he was making trouble for the best-read smugglers in the world. And what they read was history: English history, the epic history of English liberty, the very same history that Grenville himself had so innocently admired in the park at Stowe. Inside the reading clubs of Boston and Philadelphia, and in the Societies for Encouraging Commerce, the crackdown on contraband, the heavy hand of the customs men and the special jurisdiction of the 'vice-admiralty' courts all triggered instant memories of Star Chamber. To resist them was to summon the noble shade of Hampden to defend the imperishable rights of free-born Britons. 'If our Trade may be taxed, why not our lands?' asked speakers at the Boston Town Meeting in the spring of 1764, scenting the whiff of tyranny. 'Why not the produce of our lands and everything we possess or make use of? This ... strikes at our British privileges which, as we have never forfeited them, we hold in common with our fellow subjects who are natives of Britain.'

And if the Sugar Act (1764) goaded them to complaint, Grenville's second really bright idea – a stamp tax to be imposed on paper used for all manner of articles from playing cards and newspapers to legal documents, broadsheets and advertisements – was the imperial equivalent of Charles I raising his standard at Nottingham. Grenville congratulated himself on the genius of the stamp tax because, unlike customs duties, it was, he thought, self-administering, free of onerous and abrasive searches. The duty would be paid on pre-stamped paper before it was used for whatever purpose. The bill had its first reading in the Commons (before a half-empty House) in early February 1765, and Grenville announced that it would not come into force until November to give time for representations from the colonies. Since, for all their grumbling, most of the colonies had in the end swallowed the Sugar Act, Grenville was still confident that the Stamp Act (1765) would be accepted as well. He had estimated it might bring in £100,000 in the first year, much more in later years. He certainly could have had no idea that he had just inaugurated the beginning of the end of British America.

But then Grenville, like most of his contemporaries in Britain, even those who imagined themselves well read, broad-minded and well travelled, really knew pitifully little about the reality of the American colonies. Those few Americans (like Franklin) with whom they had occasion to come into contact in London were, by definition, those who had the strongest affinity with Britain. Those with whom they had official business as governors in Boston or Williamsburg usually told them what they wanted to hear: indeed often encouraged them in taking a hard line with the colonists to discourage the signs of insubordination and presumptuous liberty they had noticed during the recent wars. When the politicians in London imagined America they imagined, largely, English men and women obediently transplanted. Sometimes they imagined Scots and Presbyterian Irish – but then those countrymen had served the Empire well in its army. Very seldom did they think of about 80,000 Pennsylvania Germans, 40,000 New York and Hudson valley Dutch, and many other populations – Quakers, Jews, African slaves – all of whom made America a much more heterogeneous, much less Anglo-pinko place than could be imagined at Westminster.

Nor from the fastness of Westminster could they imagine the electrifying intensity of local politics in towns like Philadelphia and Boston. In Boston, 2500 men out of a total population of some 16,000 were entitled to vote at the Town Meeting, whose sessions at Faneuil Hall were rowdily eloquent. Pitt and his generation liked to imagine themselves so many Ciceros. But Boston really was the size of the optimum face-to-face neo-Athenian democracy imagined by Rousseau in the 1760s; and its orators – James Otis, Sam Adams, Josiah Quincy and John Hancock – believed they were so many Demostheneses. Least of all did it really occur to the likes of Grenville and the Whig politicians that somehow the liberty-canon of British history might actually be turned against them – that they would now be cast as Laud and Judge Jeffreys – and that one day some young Virginian would be trawling through the Declaration of Rights of 1689 for a list of accusations to level at King George III.

And in truth that day was still far off. But the fact that Boston, especially, was a book-crazy, news-hungry, astonishingly literate (70 per cent for men, 45 per cent for women), habitually litigious place, with a strong religious disposition to see the world in terms of the embattled forces of good and evil, doomed the Stamp Act from the beginning. The city prided itself on its civic culture: its grammar schools and colleges, gazettes and libraries. And its educated leaders made conscious efforts to reach a popular audience. John Adams, for instance, wrote his articles on the errors and iniquities of British administration in the *Boston Gazette* under the pseudonym 'Humphrey Ploughjogger'. This was the kind of thing that would have been meat and drink to shopkeepers like Harbottle Dorr who read the *Gazette* avidly, scanned its woodcut illustrations and made copious commentaries about the stories that fed his indignation. With a population of 16,000 it was also a city small enough to place a high value on the transparency of politics. John Adams spoke for many in 1765 when he insisted that 'the people have a right, an indisputable, unalienable right, an indefatigable right to that most dreaded and envied kind of knowledge, I mean of the character and conduct of their rulers.' To such Bostonians, the Stamp Act seemed to announce not just an illegal tax but also a gag on the production and distribution of free political information. Yet for all these glaring sources of grievance, no one, least of all the Lieutenant-Governor and Chief Justice of Massachusetts, Thomas Hutchinson (who always had his doubts about the wisdom of the Stamp Act), had the slightest inkling of what was about to happen.

It is true that he ought to have been worried about being hanged in effigy at the 'Liberty Tree' on 14 August 1765. But Hutchinson was used to symbolic demonstrations of hatred. On the 26th the action became much more physically immediate. A riot of extraordinary savagery tore apart his elegant house in Boston, including its cupola, and threw his manuscript history in the dirt. Had he not fled on the desperate pleading of his daughter, the incensed crowd would probably have torn him apart too. There was a long tradition of rowdy, drunken street fighting in Boston, especially when rival gangs from the North and South End celebrated 'Pope's Day' (5 November) with their annual, violent football match. But on this occasion, and on Pope's Day 1765, crowds of tanners, dockers, seamen and carpenters who lived around the harbour combined forces, and with very specific targets in mind: Hutchinson and the distributor of the stamps, his brother-in-law Andrew Oliver. The mob had evidently been mobilized by men like the twenty-eight-year-old cobbler Ebenezer Mackintosh, but he in turn would have been listening to, if not actually taking instructions from, a secret group called the 'Loyal Nine' who had decided that only physical resistance would stop the introduction of the stamps.

The 'Loyal Nine' were in their turn taking their cue from men who were by no means roughneck mob-raisers, but articulate, resolute politicians who knew exactly what they were doing. In Boston they included the merchant James Otis and the ex-tax collector and brewer-maltster Samuel Adams. Their own instincts for dramatic resistance had been fired by the 'Virginia Resolves' moved by a young orator, Patrick Henry, who had compared the introduction of the stamps to the most iniquitous Roman tyranny; by blessings for their cause awarded from the pulpit by Jonathan Mayhew; and, from far off, by the report of an extraordinary speech given in the House of Commons on the day of the Stamp Act's first reading by Isaac Barré, half of whose face had been blown off on the Heights of Abraham. Fixing his one eye and mutilated cheek on Charles Townshend, who had just asserted the 'undoubted' right of parliament to tax the colonies on the grounds that they had been 'planted', 'nourished' and 'protected' by Britain, Barré opened up with a withering counter-attack, replacing the official version of selfless British paternalism churlishly repudiated with an altogether different history of the relationship between mother country and colonies. He thundered:

Planted by your care! No! Your oppressions planted them in America. They fled from your tyranny to a then uncultivated and inhospitable country … they nourished up by your indulgence? They grew by your neglect of them: as soon as you began to care about them that care was exercised in sending persons to rule over them … to spy out their liberty … They protected by your arms? They have nobly taken up arms in your defence, have exerted a valour amidst their constant and laborious defense of a country whose frontier, while drenched in blood, its interior parts have yielded all its little savings to your emolument.

Stirred by this conviction that the most hallowed principles of *British* liberty were at stake, the Stamp Act protests spread throughout almost all the colonies, forcing the distributors of the stamps to have serious second thoughts about the wisdom of their commission. Grenville had also succeeded in provoking a rare example of inter-colonial cooperation, at the Stamp Act Congress convened in October 1765 in New York to discuss measures to be taken. The delegates shied away from physical resistance but adopted a policy (already mooted in Boston) of boycotting imports of British luxury goods, on which so many incomes in the already disturbed home economy depended. In July Grenville's government fell – although for reasons unconnected with the American crisis. The Rockingham administration, which replaced him, was disposed, but not yet committed, to repeal (which even Thomas Hutchinson in Boston was urging). In the winter of 1765–6 debates of immense significance, attempting to grapple with the relationship between Britain and America, took place in parliament for the first time.

Centre stage were the hostile brothers-in-law Pitt and Grenville, both now out of power. Pitt made what for several years afterwards would be a crucial (though in reality arbitrary) distinction between 'external' taxation – the authority to regulate colonial trade – and 'internal' taxation (like the stamps), which trespassed on the right given to the colonial assemblies to raise taxes only with their consent. Grenville replied that if this distinction were to be taken seriously Britain would, in effect, have conceded a vital element of its sovereignty:

> The government over them being dissolved, a revolution will take place in America … Protection and obedience are reciprocal. Great Britain protects America; America is bound to yield obedience. If not tell me when were Americans emancipated? The nation has run itself into immense debt … and now they are called upon to contribute a small share toward the public expense … they renounce your authority, insult your officers and break out, I might almost say, into open rebellion.

Rising on his gout-crippled legs, Pitt then made the speech of his life:

> The gentleman tells us America is obstinate; America is almost in open rebellion. I rejoice that America has resisted. Three millions of people so dead to all the feelings of liberty, as voluntarily to submit to be slaves, would have been fit instruments to make slaves of the rest. I come not here armed at all points with law cases and acts of parliament with the statute book double down in dog's ears to

defend the cause of liberty; if I had … I would … have shown that even under former arbitrary reigns parliaments were ashamed of taxing a people without their consent. … The gentleman asks, when were the colonies emancipated? But I desire to know when they were made slaves.

Pitt asked that the Stamp Act be 'repealed, absolutely, totally and immediately'. And so it was. When the news was learned in Boston, John Hancock laid out a pipe of his best Madeira on the Common for citizens to help themselves. But the cause of repeal in London was perhaps best helped by a dazzling display of expertly informed advocacy from Benjamin Franklin, called before the bar of the House to answer questions from interested members including Grenville. To Grenville's claim that Britain had reimbursed the colonies already for their own outlay of expenses in the war, Franklin pointed out that in his state, Pennsylvania, alone the £313,000 laid out to equip and pay volunteer troops had been compensated by only £75,000 from the Treasury. To Grey Cooper's question on the 'temper' of America towards Britain before 1763 he replied, 'the Best in the World. They submitted willingly to the government of the Crown, and paid in all their courts, obedience to acts of parliament.'

'And to their temper now?'

'Oh,' replied Franklin, 'very much altered.'

Once they considered parliament the bulwark of their liberties; now, much less. When asked what would be the result if the Act were not repealed, Franklin answered candidly but devastatingly, 'The total loss of the respect and affection the people of America bear to this country and of all the commerce that depends on that respect and affection.'

These predictions gave Franklin no joy. As he wrote to his good friend, the Scottish luminary Lord Kames, 'I have had so great a part of my life in Britain and formed so many friendships in it that I love it and sincerely wish it prosperity and wish to see that union on which alone I think it can be secured and established. He added shockingly, 'As to America, the advantages of such a union to her are not so apparent.' For Franklin believed that time was emphatically not on Britain's side. His own vision of the future was uniquely informed by a sense that the destiny of nations was shaped, ultimately, less by inherited customs and traditions than by geography, population and social structure. Only the Scots, like Kames, David Hume, James Ferguson and John Millar, who themselves had thought about such things, de Montesquieu in France and some of his other, advanced friends at the 'Honest Whigs' Club, like Richard Price, could possibly comprehend this essentially sociological way of looking at the rise and fall of nations. The facts of the matter for Franklin were that, sooner or later, the immense expanse of America (whether or not officially bottled up by British regulations), the vitality of its natural population increase and the robustness of its immigration, together with the extraordinary possibilities offered by continental economic expansion, all virtually dictated that it would outstrip its parent country. And he probably subscribed, too, to the principle first articulated at the end of the Commonwealth in James Harrington's *Oceana* that, ultimately, the distribution of property determined the balance of political power. Before long the inventory, as it were, of American assets would of itself demand that the British adjust to reality. Even if, in the full flush of their imperial triumph over the French, the British could scarcely conceive of such an eventuality, it was going to happen. That was a certainty. It was up to the British, who chose for the moment to play the sovereign, whether they wanted this extraordinary American future to unfold as part of a genuine empire of the free, built on mutual respect and consent, or whether their short-term needs would blind them to their long-term interests.

To his regret, Franklin was not able to see William Pitt, increasingly infirm, pessimistic and evil-tempered. But even if that encounter had taken place it is extremely unlikely that he would have been able to persuade that 'friend' of the Americans to his view of the inevitable organic development of his country. For as much as Pitt was adamant in his opposition to the iniquitous stamp tax, he was equally adamant that parliament in principle was indisputably sovereign over the colonies. It was that unwavering assumption that led subsequent British administrations, even when making concessions to American grievances, to make categorical reiterations of that sovereignty. The stamps may have gone, but other commercial duties, the Townshend duties, were introduced in 1767, and the customs administration to enforce them became, especially in ports like Boston, notorious for the shamelessness of its smugglers, increasingly militarized. One of the most shameless of them all, the rich young merchant John Hancock, typically converted self-interest into ideology by calling one of his sloops *Liberty* and flaunting his intention of 'running' Madeira ashore. When a ship-of-the-line, the *Romney*, was summoned from Halifax, Nova Scotia, to assist the customs officers, riots in the docks made it impossible for it to do its assigned work.

It was the glaring fact that Boston and New York were not only uncowed by the threat of force but also rapidly becoming ungovernable that triggered the decision to use regular troops as police. The colonial ports had responded to the Townshend tariff of duties in 1767 by mobilizing a boycott of British imports; shippers and shopkeepers found to have violated it were denounced, intimidated, roughed up and sometimes tarred and feathered. Some 3500 redcoats under the command of General Gage were brought to the rowdiest of all the centres of protest, Boston. In a small, tight-packed city, they could hardly help being extremely visible – that indeed was the idea – and were habitually abused by jeering crowds (especially by young apprentices) as 'lobster sons of bitches'. The fact that the soldiers were allowed to moonlight in jobs like rope-making, which were usually held by the locals, did not help. By late 1769 brawls were common. And sometimes matters got completely out of control. On 23 February 1770 an eleven-year-old boy, Christopher Seider, joined a noisy protest of schoolboys and apprentices outside the shop of an importer, Theophilus Lilley, where he was shot dead by a customs officer. With feelings whipped up by a powerful woodcut of the shooting published in the *Boston Gazette*, his funeral turned into a mass demonstration, carefully orchestrated for maximum tear-jerking by Sam Adams. As many as 500 boys marched two by two behind the little bier, and behind them came at least 2000 adults.

On 5 March the inevitable disaster happened when a wigmaker's apprentice ragged a soldier all the way to the Custom House for an allegedly unpaid bill. When a guard struck the pursuing youth, a tocsin normally used as a fire alarm was sounded and mobilized a large and angry crowd. A small and frightened platoon of eight soldiers, sent to restore order, was surrounded by the crowd who pelted them with rock-solid snowballs. Terrified they were about to be manhandled or worse, they panicked and started shooting. Five were killed, including a black, Crispus Attucks, and an Irish leather breeches-maker, Patrick Carr. Several more were badly wounded. Only the appearance of Thomas Hutchinson, promising swift and proper legal action and evacuating the troops to Castle Island in the harbour, avoided much more serious bloodshed. Though it was recognized that the soldiers had acted out of fear rather than malice, and though they were defended by at least one well-known 'patriot', John Adams, their acquittal only contributed to the legend of a deliberate 'massacre' carefully cultivated by the widespread distribution of a print made by the engraver and silversmith Paul Revere, showing a line of British soldiers firing in unison at defenceless civilians. The print was also incorporated into an extraordinary front page of the *Boston Gazette*, its dense columns of print lined in funereal black and including images of five coffins, engraved with skulls in the manner of the tombs in the Granary and Copps Hill burial grounds. Though he knew better, Sam Adams (John's cousin) had no hesitation in publicizing the incident throughout the colonies as evidence of the murderous intent of the British to slaughter civilians who refused to truckle to parliamentary coercion.

Even at this point, however, there was nothing inevitable about the separation of America and Britain. Most Americans, even those deeply affronted by the economic and military policies of governments and parliament, still considered themselves in religion, language and historic culture ineradicably British. If anything, they felt passionately that *they* were the legatees of the 'true' British constitution, which had been abandoned in the mother country or somehow held hostage by a vicious and corrupt oligarchy. Some Americans who visited London and were shocked by the excesses of luxury and depravity they found there (while occasionally enjoying a sample of it) explained the lamentable abandonment of the old traditions of freedom by this sorry descent into voluptuary wickedness. But many still hoped the clock could yet be turned back to the days before 1763, a date that began to assume scriptural significance as the first year of iniquity. The virtuous king, evidently misled by wicked counsel, might yet be rescued from his misapprehensions. A changing of the guard at Westminster actually seemed to bode well. The author of the infamous customs duties, Charles Townshend, died. The non-importation campaign against British goods had begun to subside so gratifyingly that in 1770, when Lord North became First Lord of the Treasury, he could announce, without fear of being accused of surrendering to intimidation, that most of the objectionable duties would be repealed. In 1771 Franklin wrote optimistically to Samuel Cooper that there seemed to be a 'pause in Politics … should the [British] Government be so temperate and Just as to place us on the old ground where we stood before the Stamp Act, there is no danger of our rising in our demands'.

There was, however, one commodity on which Lord North, in his wisdom, decided to retain the duty: tea. And the storm that stirred this particular cup would overwhelm British America.

Few could have foreseen the repercussions in May 1773 when the Tea Act was passed through parliament. Looked at from London, it seemed merely a pragmatic expedient designed to get the financially beleaguered East India Company out of its difficulties. The Company had been chartered by Queen Elizabeth in 1600 and had established its first trading post on the west coast of India at Surat eight years later. As usual, the expectation had been that some exotic raw materials might be imported to England (and re-exported to Europe) in exchange for the sophisticated manufactured goods of the home country. But India, and especially its dazzling, printed cotton textiles, turned out to be a lot more sophisticated than anything produced in England. There was nothing that India wanted or needed in exchange for those 'calicoes' other than silver. So bullion poured out of England as the calicoes poured in, especially in the second half of the seventeenth century, generating a costume revolution as the light, brilliantly patterned fabrics gripped first the fashionable and then the middling classes. Only the panic-stricken representations of English linen manufacturers stemmed the flow of the imports. Happily, tea came along as a substitute and by the middle of the eighteenth century accounted for almost 40 per cent of its import business.

But – especially in America – heavily dutied British tea, although an obligatory item in the pantry, was expensive compared to virtually identical leaf smuggled by the Dutch. The non-importation campaign of 1768–9 had only made matters worse. By 1773 there was a tea mountain piled high in the Company warehouses in the City of London around Fenchurch and Leadenhall Streets, 18 million pounds of it. East India Company stock was in free-fall, and, as if this were not bad enough, the Company owed the government a substantial debt for unpaid customs duties, as well as the military protection of its trade. Lord North and the government were darkly considering its future. Then someone – a Scot, Robert Herries – had a bright idea. Why not abolish entirely the customs duties on tea imported into Britain, lowering the price to the point where it could undersell Dutch contraband leaf not only in Britain but even on the European and American markets? The answer was yes, but. Lord North had decided that he would repeal all the Townshend duties *except* for tea, if only to preserve the principle of parliament's right to impose tariffs on the colonies. Now, however, it was thought that the drastically lowered price of tea shipped into America through the East India Company would sweeten the modest payment of threepence a pound to the point where the Americans would hardly notice they were swallowing it.

They noticed. On 7 October 1773, when the first ships loaded with tea chests were already on the high seas, handbills signed 'Hampden' were posted and distributed in New York, warning that, under the diabolical guise of cheap tea, Americans were once again being lured to accept taxation without their own consent. The fact that the duty was to be used to pay for colonial administration and that many of the selected 'consignees' – the American merchants who would receive and sell it – were connected to the likes of the Governor of Boston, Thomas Hutchinson, only heightened the sense of a conspiracy. Two of the consignees were actually Hutchinson's sons, a third was his father-in-law. Hampdens suddenly were reborn everywhere. One of them, the Philadelphian Dr Benjamin Rush, his spirit possessed by the ghost of the foe of ship money, declared that 'the baneful chests contain in them a slow poison … something worse than death – the seeds of SLAVERY'. In Charleston, New York and Philadelphia the intended consignees were put under such pressure of intimidation as the instruments of reimposed taxation that nearly all backed off, promising not to accept the cargoes.

In Boston, the destination for four brigs, the sudden crisis was a godsend for Sam Adams, whose efforts to sustain the trade boycott against Britain had been meeting with increasing indifference – until the tea was on its way. At just the right time, private letters exchanged among Hutchinson, the Lieutenant-Governor Andrew Oliver and Thomas Whateley were discovered by Franklin and published. The letters

The Bloody Massacre Perpetrated in King Street, Boston, on March 5th, 1770 by a Party of the 29th Reg, front page of the *Boston Gazette*, engraved by Paul Revere, March, 1770.

The Boston Tea Party, 1773, engraved by an unknown artist, *c.* 1800.

sneered at the patriots, and expressed the hope that parliament and the British government would do its utmost to uphold the principle of their sovereign right to regulate trade and tax the colonies. The apparently devious way in which cheap tea was being used to seduce innocent and virtuous Americans to part with their liberty was evidence of the 'diabolical' nature of the design. On 29 November, the day after the first ship, the *Dartmouth*, carrying 114 chests of Bohea, had tied up at Griffin's Wharf, notices in town called on 'Friends! Brethren! Countrymen! The Hour of Destruction or Manly Opposition to the Machinations of Tyranny stares you in the Face!'

Boston instantly turned into a revolutionary hothouse with bells ringing to summon concerned citizens to public meetings. They came from the city, and they came from neighbouring towns and villages – Cambridge, Woburn, even Hutchinson's village of Milton. Thousands of them poured into Faneuil Hall – so many of them that the meeting had to be reconvened in Old South Meeting House, the fine Congregationalist Church, where light washed over the agitated speakers and their flock from high windows. The 'baneful weed' could not, would not be unloaded; nor would the iniquitous duty be paid. It would be sent back to London in proper disgrace. But, the poor merchants who had shipped it, all unsuspecting, pleaded, British law forbids, on pain of forfeiture, the return of any dutiable cargo once shipped out. To send it back would be to guarantee their ruin. Too bad was the majority opinion. In the meantime, Hutchinson and his family consignees had fled to the safety of Castle William, where they too refused to think about returning the cargo. So it stayed on board ships at the wharves, guarded, in effect, by the patriots while the stand-off continued and two more ships, the *Beaver* and the *Eleanor*, arrived.

By the third week in December a deadline loomed. If duty had not been paid by then, the customs officers would (doubtless with the help of troops) seize the tea as forfeit. Knowing that, faced with financial disaster, the consignees would capitulate, pay and unload, the Boston Committee of Correspondence, the organizing arm of the patriots, summoned further meetings. On the 16th Old Southie was again filled to capacity as orators denounced enslavement by the pot and Josiah Quincy attacked Boston's foes for their 'malice … and insatiable revenge'. An envoy, the ship's captain, had been sent to Hutchinson at Milton, demanding one last time that the *Dartmouth* be allowed to sail, if not for England, then at least out to the harbour castle so that it could be said to be on its way. Around quarter to six, with the light almost gone, Hutchinson would not be swayed. Sam Adams got to his feet to say that he could not see what more could be done to save the country. It was not so much an utterance as a signal. An Indian war-whoop sounded in the Church gallery; there were more at the door from a crowd of fifty or so, their faces crudely blackened with coal-dust, disguised as fancy-dress braves with blankets substituting for native dress. The 'Mohawks' whom handbills had warned might attack the cargoes of tea if a solution were not found were on the war-path, and it led right to the wharf. Most of them, like the shoemaker Robert Twelves Hewes, were working men who had been drawn into the world of direct political protests over the past four years, and they had been deliberately selected by the patriot leaders for their relative anonymity. But they had also been carefully instructed on what to do. The noise they made was enough to stop one merchant, John Andrews, from enjoying his evening cup of tea. Arriving at the door of the Meeting House he collided with a roaring crowd as it exited into the softly falling Boston rain, heading for the docks and the *Dartmouth* and the *Eleanor*.

By the light of lanterns the 'Mohawks' did their work, smashing their way with hatchets through 342 chests containing 45 tons of tea, value £9000: enough to make, it has been estimated, 24 million cups. Once split wide open to ensure maximum damage, the chests were heaved into the water where much of the loose tea escaped. A vigilant eye was kept on anyone who imagined that, for all their patriotic ardour, they might help themselves to a little by stuffing it down their coats or breeches. There was so much tea that before the job was done it began to back up against the sides of the ships as if the vessels were becalmed in some monstrous tide of Bohea slurry. The next morning, by the light of day, little boats went out into the water to make sure none of the cargo remained undamaged, using paddles to push the wooden chests and free-floating rafts of the stuff down into the muddy water. As they were drifting through the muck John Adams wrote in his diary, 'This is the most magnificent Movement of all … there is a dignity, a Majesty, a Sublimity in this last Effort of the Patriots that I greatly admire … the Destruction of the Tea is so bold, so daring, so firm, intrepid and inflexible, and it must have so important Consequences and so lasting, that I cannot but consider it as an Epocha [sic] in History.'

He was right. The Boston Tea Party was a classic instance of an issue and event, apparently trivial, even absurd, in itself, becoming floodlit into a great drama of national resistance. This was the way it was described in the instant accounts written in Boston for distribution throughout the colonies and carried there by a network of fast-riding couriers, not least the silversmith Paul Revere. Not everyone was impressed, of course. There were many, even on the patriot side, who were outraged by the wanton destruction of property and believed that those responsible ought to pay compensation. For a while at the end of 1773 and the beginning of 1774 it seemed possible that the action might isolate Boston rather than automatically win it sympathy in the other colonies. That, at any rate, was what Lord North's government was calculating when it decided to punish the city and colony in the most draconian manner possible. The port of Boston was to be closed until compensation was paid for the tea, guaranteeing financial ruin for its mercantile community and real hardship for its citizens. The 1691 charter of the Commonwealth of Massachusetts was to be called in and reissued so that a more orderly government would be established. A Quartering Act authorized the billeting of troops in unoccupied buildings and barns.

It was this act of coercion beyond anything that had happened before, which convinced waverers and sceptics who had doubted Sam Adams' insistence that they were facing not a reasonable and well-intentioned home government but a selfish and brutal tyranny that he was, in fact, right. George Washington, a stickler for the sanctity of property, wrote, 'The cause of Boston, the despotick Measures in respect of it, now is and ever will be the cause of America (not that we approve their conduct in destroying the Tea).' In the weeks and months that followed, as regiments landed and a naval blockade took up position outside the harbour, America was created. Planters as far away as South Carolina sent rice to Boston; farmers in Connecticut, New York and Rhode Island established wagon convoys to get food supplies to the inhabitants, represented as the innocent victims of British retribution. Most seriously, the first inter-colonial Continental Congress since the Stamp Act Congress convened in Philadelphia in September 1774 to consider a coordinated response. By the time the Congress opened in Carpenters' Hall in October, another action of the British government had added to its suspicions and fears. By the terms of the Quebec Act, passed in August, parliament had agreed to preserve the French system of civil law and to allow the 70,000 Francophone Catholics of Canada to practise their faith without penalities, their church to be supported by tithes. To the overwhelmingly Protestant Americans this heralded trials without juries, the effective end of habeas corpus and a government instituted in America without any kind of elected assembly, only a nominated council. It was 'slavery and wooden shoes' entering by the back door, or more precisely up the St Lawrence and down the Hudson. And it was the most obvious confirmation yet that George III was indeed a Stuart in all but blood. No wonder he displayed so many Van Dycks of Charles I at Windsor Castle.

What the king *ought* to be, wrote Thomas Jefferson in his *Summary View of the Rights of British America*, prepared for the Congress, was 'the chief officer of the people', who presumably could be dismissed and replaced if he failed to honour his contractual obligations to his subjects. But Jefferson was too ill to go to Philadelphia and those radicals who did – some of whom demanded that citizens begin military training – did not dominate the proceedings. Cooler heads argued for a breathing space in which parliament and the king might be petitioned to hear the justified grievances of America. It was, moreover, a long, deep breathing space. Only if redress of those

George III, studio of Allan Ramsay, *c.* 1767.

grievances had not been made by 10 September 1775 – a year hence – would the Americans begin a general cessation of all trade with Britain from 1 December.

It was a last, priceless opportunity for reconciliation, and it was not taken. Not, however, for want of statesmen on both sides recognizing that such a grace period might never come again. Even Lord North was attempting to hammer out some sort of middle way in which, if the colonies would agree to the sums needed for their own defence, they would be free to raise them in their own fashion and through their own assemblies. But could the British government, North asked an American representative, be assured that the several colonies would agree to their respective apportionments? No such assurance could be given. And, in any event, America had already gone past the point where it could be expected to accept even the *principle* of being taxed by the parliament at Westminster. For the king himself these last-minute efforts to cobble together some sort of agreement were so much sticking plaster over an open wound. Was it not evident, George asserted, that the colonists' pretence of disputing this or that imposition was so much disingenuous tomfoolery; that they had all along conspired to throw off the entire authority of parliament altogether? The only question now, as far as he was concerned, was whether the Americans were to be allowed to remove themselves from the allegiance they owed to their sovereign – king and parliament – without at least a fight.

Opinion inside Britain in the winter of 1774–5 was bitterly and frantically divided, especially in the mercantile cities whose trade faced catastrophe should war break out. Rival groups petitioning for reconciliation or military action contested for the same meeting halls in Manchester and Bristol and for the same signatures of mechanics and shopkeepers. Parliament was dominated by calls to inflict on the wicked and ungrateful children across the Atlantic a hiding they would never forget. On 20 January 1775 William Pitt, now Earl of Chatham, and tormented by sickness, arrived at the House of Lords in the company of his fifteen-year-old son William and Benjamin Franklin – with whom, at last, he had had earnest conversations about what, if anything, could be done to halt the march towards imperial self-destruction. Franklin was turned away from the door on the grounds that he was neither the eldest son nor the brother of a peer. Chatham entered, remarking as loudly as he could, 'This is Dr FRANKLIN whom I would have admitted.' He then put a motion to withdraw General Gage's troops from Boston, in other words to stop a war before it started. Though few of his peers believed it, he promised them it would be unwinnable. What he then went on to say proved just how carefully the old man had listened to Franklin. For the first time he was staring at the vast expanse of America, and he knew he was staring at defeat. 'What, though you march from town to town, and from province to province; though you should be able to enforce a temporary submission … how shall you be able to secure the obedience of the country you leave behind you? … to grasp the dominion of 1800 miles of continent, populous in numbers, possessing valour, liberty and resistance?'

And where did the peers who denounced the Americans for their temerity imagine their stubborn attachment to representation came from? Had they looked in the mirror lately? Had they read any good books about their own history lately?

This resistance to your arbitrary system of taxation might have been foreseen … it was obvious … from the Whiggish spirit flourishing in that country. … The spirit which now resists your taxation in America is the same spirit which formerly opposed … ship money in England; the same spirit which called all England on its legs and by the Bill of Rights vindicated the English constitution. … This glorious spirit animates three millions in America … who prefer poverty with liberty to gilded chains and sordid affluence; and who will die in defence of their rights as freemen.

To such united force, what force shall be opposed? – What, my Lords – a few regiments in America, and seventeen or eighteen thousand men at home! The idea is too ridiculous to take up a moment of your Lordships' time. … It is not repealing a piece of parchment that can restore America to our bosom; you must repeal her fears and her resentments and you may then hope for her love and gratitude … We shall be forced, ultimately, to retract: let us retract when we can, not when we must. … Avoid then this humiliating, disgraceful necessity. … Make the first advances to concord, to peace and happiness.

But the first advances were to Concord, Massachusetts, where, so General Gage had heard, the 'rebels' – for so they were already dubbed in the British garrison – had stored arms and ammunition. Throughout the late winter, not only in Massachusetts but in Virginia and Pennsylvania as well, the committees of correspondence had been taking steps to organize the defence of their own communities in citizen militias, hastened by rumours that not only British but foreign mercenary troops too (the armed lackeys of satanic despotism!) were on their way to America. On 18 April 1775 John Hancock and Samuel Adams were in Lexington where a company of 'minutemen' – a militia of farmers who could be instantly summoned in the event of an emergency – had been formed, guarding a cache of munitions. It was already known that Gage intended to march troops west to Lexington to arrest Adams and Hancock and seize the weapons. And the fact that for three days grenadiers and marines had been taken off duty and boats made ready was unlikely to keep the raid a secret. The only unknown was when this descent on the hamlets across the Charles river would take place; hence the famous arrangement by which a signal lantern would be set in the steeple of Old North Church to alert patriots in Charlestown to the departure of the soldiers – two for an approach by water, one by land. Three riders were to be dispatched to warn Hancock and Adams. One was arrested before he could depart; the other two, William Dawes and Paul Revere, got out of Boston, Revere rowing across the Charles beneath the guns of a British warship. Picking up a horse at Charlestown, he took the longer route but arrived first at the Reverend Jonas Clarke's vicarage just by Lexington Green. In the moonlight the green looked then (as it still does) the epitome of an English village, the kind of place that seems to describe the perpetuity of British America and not its imminent death-rattle.

Revere tried to carry his warning to Concord but was arrested by a British patrol before he reached there. But word was out. Hancock and Adams departed swiftly for Woburn and safety, the beginning of what would be a long journey through America, publicizing the events of the morning about to dawn. All around Boston, alarm bells and signal guns were sounding. When the six companies of British troops arrived at Lexington, just before light, they were confronted by about seventy minutemen drawn up on the green. One of the officers shouted, 'Disperse, ye rebels!', and the militia officer, Captain Parker, did apparently order a dismissal. While it was happening, a shot was let off, from which side, no one was sure. But the grenadiers let fly a musket volley. When the smoke cleared, eight men were dead and ten wounded.

At Concord the British cut down a Liberty tree and then faced a serious firefight, shot at from a hilltop by the Old North Bridge. Their retreat back through Menotomy to Charlestown turned into a nightmare as they were riddled with gunfire by more than a thousand militia often firing from behind walls and the cover of trees. This was not going to be an easy war.

News of the events of 18 and 19 April were carried 'on wings of wind' through the colonies, not least by Hancock and Adams who had been singled out by General Gage as the only rebels to be exempt from a pardon. By the time they reached Manhattan island, the streets were thick with impassioned crowds. In May the second Continental Congress, held in Philadelphia, appointed a Virginian, George Washington, to take command of their army of defence, signalling that Boston's war was now America's. Throughout the summer, the British found themselves effectively besieged by an American army whose size and strength they had never remotely anticipated from rude colonials. In June, Gage sent a formidable army up Breed's Hill to break the American position on Charlestown Heights, and in the process lost

Top: *George Washington at Princeton* (detail), by Charles Willson Peale, 1779.
Above: A contemporary view of Charlestown Heights, where General Thomas Gage sent an army to break the American position in June 1775.

92 officers and nearly 1000 men. They included Major Pitcairn, who had been at Lexington on 19 April and had sent a letter to London that had been shown to the king, who shared the major's opinion that 'once the rebels have felt a smart blow … they will submit'. By the time George III read it, Pitcairn was dead. Stunned by the casualties, Gage wrote to Viscount Barrington, Secretary-at-War, that the Americans were 'spirited up by a rage and enthusiasm as great as ever a people were possessed of … The loss we have sustained is greater than we can bear.' In response he was heavily reinforced, so that by July there were 13,500 British troops in Boston together with many thousands more loyalist refugees. But even with this enormous force it was not clear how long they could hold the city.

There was a war, but there was not yet anything like agreement among the Americans on its ultimate goal. The second Continental Congress remained divided. Could union with Britain be preserved if its government took America back to the halcyon days before 1763 and agreed to a broad degree of self-government including the right of self-taxation? Or was absolute independence now the only possible option? In early July 1775, Congress produced a declaration of 'the Causes and Necessity of Taking up Arms', which said that: 'We have not raised armies with ambitious designs of separating from Great Britain and establishing independent states. We fight not for glory or conquest. We exhibit to mankind the remarkable spectacle of a people attacked by unprovoked enemies.' Two days later an 'olive branch' petition from Congress, drafted by the Pennsylvanian John Dickinson, was sent to the king through the hands of the grandson of the colony's founder, William Penn. It began with a profuse statement of loyalty:

> Attached to your Majesty's person, family and government with all devotion that principle and affection can inspire, connected with Great Britain by the strongest ties that can unite societies … we solemnly assure Your Majesty, that we not only most ardently desire the former harmony between her and these Colonies may be restored, but that a concord may be established between them upon so firm a basis as to perpetuate its blessings, uninterrupted by any future dissensions to succeeding generations in both countries.

It was the last, best chance to save British America, and George III's ministers were having none of it. At such critical moments in the fate of nations and empires the historian wants to reach for some deep, sophisticated structural socio-political explanation. But what turned the corner, what made reunion out of the question, was, all too simply, the king and his government. They let it be known that the king was not interested in any communication from an assembly of rebels. On 23 August the Americans were formally proclaimed to be in a state of 'open and avowed rebellion'. On 26 October they insisted that the revolt was 'manifestly carried on for the purpose of establishing an independent empire'. It was George III and his advisors, then, who spelled it out, who in effect uttered a declaration of independence; and figures like Jefferson who, even as late as November 1775, were professing their deep reluctance to make a complete break, were also calling the king 'the sceptred tyrant' and 'the bitterest enemy we have'. The trouble was, this time no William III was at hand to appear as a constitutional king of America.

For Thomas Paine, whose *Common Sense* appeared in January 1776, no more kings need apply. Delude yourselves no further about the sainted British constitution, he argued. It is a sham and a ruin. Have no more to do with it: ''Tis time to part.' But though Paine's tract sold a staggering 150,000 copies, the founding fathers – John Adams and Jefferson in particular – were not so much men of a new democratic age as to be able, yet, to unhitch themselves from the great tradition of expressly *English* Liberty. If they were at war with the British Empire it was because it was the wrong empire: not the empire of liberty at all, but an unrecognizable perversion of the principles on which it had been founded. Even when they did take their pens in hand and finally draft declarations of independence in the late spring and early summer of 1776, after the British had evacuated Boston and the British government still refused to spell out the terms on which peace might be made, the nation builders instinctively reached back, not forward, to their pantheon of heroes. They were the same heroes who had appeared in Lord Cobham's monument at Stowe – Hampden, Milton and William III. In 1774, after hearing the news of Boston's coercion, and thinking about the future consitution of their state, Jefferson and some of his colleagues in the Virginia House of Burgesses trawled through John Rushworth's *Historical Collections* of documents from the epic of parliament's struggle with Charles I. And when he came, finally, to draft the Declaration of Independence, Jefferson's model for the long list of accusations against George III was the Bill of Rights of 1689 written to justify the removal of James II.

No one felt the irony more sharply than Chatham. He had repeatedly attempted to stop the war in its tracks, to no avail. Even in the unlikely circumstances that it would be won, it would, he told the Lords in January 1777, be a pyrrhic victory, for 'we are the aggressors. We have invaded them.' Everything he had made, even the triumph over France, was now unmade, for the old enemy was merely biding its time to profit from the débâcle. After the failure of the Saratoga campaign to isolate New England from the other colonies in October 1777, when North was desperate to resign and even George III was beginning to look for an exit from disaster, Chatham was spoken

of, crippled as he was, as the logical man to make a simultaneous peace with an independent America and war with a newly threatening France. On 7 April 1778, in
extreme pain, the famous vessel of his voice broken and halting, Chatham spoke in the
Lords, still hoping that some sort of connection might be preserved between America
and Britain, but ready to face, if necessary, a hostile alliance of France, Spain and
America. 'Any state is better than despair ... if we fall let us fall like men.' What use is
valour, said the Duke of Richmond, when we have no navy, no army, no money?
Chatham looked as though he would reply. He struggled heavily to his feet, swayed,
staggered a little, clutched his hand to his heart and fell into the arms of peers sitting
close by, one of them the master of Stowe, Lord Temple. When he died on 11 May the
empire of liberty, the right empire, died with him.

On 12 September 1786, Charles, second Earl Cornwallis, stepped from his pinnace on
to the Calcutta dockside. As befitted a new Governor-General of Bengal who was also,
for the first time in the history of British India, a peer of the realm and Commander-
in-Chief, his uniform was dress scarlet. Never mind that it was the same scarlet he had
worn five years earlier at Yorktown, Virginia, when his capitulation to Washington and
the French General Compte de Rochambeau had sealed the fate of the American war.
It was a new day for His Majesty's Empire in Hindustan, and Calcutta was sweatily
festive. Though the monsoon season was over, the town had not dried out. The cottony
mist clinging to the surface of the Hooghly river was already heavy with sopping
moisture and cadet regiments of mosquitoes, primed to puncture the rosy flesh of the
sahibs, were hatching from larvae on the brim-full tanks and ponds. The British
affected not to notice either the steamy heat or the buzzing pests. Cornwallis, forty-
eight years old, rotund and genial in a militarily correct way, was greeted by music,
cheering, bands, flags and boats draped with bunting; he cordially pumped handshakes
from senior officers, junior officers, Council Members, senior merchants, junior merchants, surgeons and chaplains; and heard whispered welcomes from ladies in broad-
brimmed, flower-bedecked hats. After breakfast at Fort William he was reverently
greeted, with stooping bows, by the native bankers, banians, kazis, judges and revenue
men without whom, he was given to understand, the government would be a nullity.
Everyone seemed so very obliging. Could these same persons, British and babu, truly
be the ravening 'birds of prey and passage' he had heard Edmund Burke denounce in
parliament in December 1783, the vultures whose wings he had come to clip?
    If Cornwallis were himself perspiring into his linen that morning in September,
it may not have been a mere effect of the climate. He had only agreed to accept the
king's commission after twice declining, in 1782 and 1785, and even now he was not

CHARLES EARL CORNWALLIS. 1783.

Charles, Earl Cornwallis, by Thomas Gainsborough, 1783.

without deep misgivings. He knew very well that he had been appointed by the young
Mr Pitt and his Foreign Secretary of State, the Marquis of Carmarthen, to redeem in
the east what had been lost in the west. Even before the Treaty of Versailles (1783) recognizing the independence of the American states had been signed, the French, whose
intervention in the war had made it inevitable, had seized the opportunity to pounce
on the wounded lion, returning to India to sponsor the Sultan of Mysore in his war
against the British. On Cornwallis' shoulders now fell the responsibility of staving off
further imperial collapse. It was a weighty thing.

Not that he felt he had anything with which to reproach himself, except for abandoning his Jemima who had implored him, tears in her eyes, not to go to America in
1778. When he had come back the following year, full of success and honour, she had
again begged him not to agree to another command. But his suspicions of the capacity
of the British generals in America, by turns reckless and timorous, would not let him
decline. When he received news that she was deadly ill he hurried to return. With every
dip of the ship into the resisting Atlantic trough, his anxiety and guilt grew more acute.
She had asked, ordered in fact, that a thorn bush be grown at her wordless tombstone,
and Cornwallis had honoured the mute reproach. He felt its pricks even now.

While Jemima was dying, so was British America. It was a cause of the deepest
anguish for Cornwallis, who had been one of the most determined critics of the foolishness of successive governments' policies that had led to the separation. In the House
of Lords he had been one of just four peers who had voted against parliament's assertion to tax its American colonies without their consent or representation. Throughout
the years of embittered intimidation Cornwallis had shared Chatham's despairing
sense of the futility of the government's coercive policy. But once the war had begun
and Cornwallis was asked to serve, his disagreement, however severe, immediately took
second place to his sense of duty. God knows he had tried to discharge it as well as he
could, even while chafing at the irresolution of his seniors – first General Sir William
Howe and then General Sir Henry Clinton. He had won the battles they had allowed
him to fight – at White Plains and Brandywine – but they had turned a deaf ear to his
wish that the northern and southern armies unite and strike, rather than disperse and
dig in. At the Delaware, had they done so, they might have finished off Washington
before the French had arrived. Once French ships had begun to command the
entrance to the Chesapeake and land thousands of troops and supplies, Cornwallis
understood that the British faced an entirely new war. Second in command to
Clinton, he had vainly attempted to persuade him that only a union of the armies in
Virginia – his marching north from the Carolinas and Clinton's south from New York
– could strike a decisive blow before it was too late. Clinton had sent but a feeble part

of his force under General William Philips, who had died shortly after their arrival, and with this inadequate army had ordered Cornwallis to an ultimately indefensible position at Yorktown. Surrounded, outnumbered, his men already exhausted from their pyrrhic victory at Guildford in March 1781, their supplies cut off by a French fleet sealing the Chesapeake, Cornwallis had held out for three weeks. When the outer redoubts of their fort were stormed, he had made the fateful decision to forgo the pointless sacrifice of his men's lives. Worn out and deeply depressed, his own health collapsed along with the fate of his army. On 19 October 1781, it was General O'Hara who made the formal surrender to Washington and led his troops away, their colours furled, drums beating, fifes playing (as well they might) 'The World Turned Upside Down', while the French lined the road out of Yorktown dressed in insultingly fresh white uniforms and black gaiters, the dandies of victory.

At home hardly anyone seemed to bear him ill will for the disaster, other than Clinton against whose public recriminations Cornwallis was painfully obliged to defend himself. But the king restored him to his office of Constable of the Tower. Barely a year later had come that first request to go to Bengal. Britain was smarting from the humiliation of what had happened in America; indeed, it was still actively embattled against an alliance of the French, Spanish and Dutch. Even from those who had opposed the war, there was no gloating over the outcome. Instead, public opinion had recoiled into a posture of wounded self-justification, professing astonishment that its purposes in America had been so badly misunderstood. It had not been a 'tyranny' that they had been defending, but the most liberal and enlightened constitution in the world: that of parliamentary sovereignty. The European monarchs in Madrid and Versailles who had colluded with rebellion would one day rue their reckless irresponsibility and cynical opportunism.

But although Cornwallis evidently shared the public need to reassert the disinterested nobility of the British Empire, he wondered whether India was truly an auspicious place to plant its flag. Was it, as the vituperative critics of the East India Company's rule claimed, so steeped in venal selfishness, a racket disguised as a business, as to be entirely beyond redemption? Could virtue, he wondered, survive the tropics? What was it the philosophers said about despotism thriving where the orange grew? He was unsure if oranges grew here, but it was obvious that in the Indies, East as well as West, liberty was insecurely planted. Stupendous fortunes had been made, not by making men free but by making them servile; not by probity but by corruption; not by a benign and responsible diffusion of that wealth to the natives but by the most shameless coercion and extortion. After Lord North's government had been sent packing, Charles James Fox had proposed legislation for the East India Company. His East India

Bill made provisions for a parliamentary commission. The reforming Act that resulted made a clean separation between commercial and governmental activities. Company administration was now accountable to a Board of Control in London that would include members of the Privy Council and a Secretary of State. The regulatory act was designed to contain and reverse the personal empires of power and fortune that, Edmund Burke (who had largely written it) claimed, had been created under the pretext of securing a fair field for trade. In the parliamentary debates on India on 1 December 1783 Burke had hurled one of his rhetorical thunderbolts against the infamies perpetrated, so he said, by the Company and its servants on the helpless and much abused body of long-suffering Hindustan.

The violence and rapacity of the Company's conduct could never, Burke asserted, be excused or explained by any savagery it claimed was threatening the peaceful prosecution of commerce, for the 'thirty millions' of British India, he said, were not

> an abject and barbarous populace … but a people for ages, civilized and cultivated – cultivated by all the arts of polished life while we were yet in the woods. There have been (and still the skeletons remain) princes once of great dignity, authority and opulence. … There is to be found an ancient and venerable priesthood, the depository of their laws and learning and history, the guides of the people while living and consolation in death; a nobility of great antiquity and renown, a multi-tude of cities not exceeded in population and trade by those of the first class in Europe; merchants and bankers, individual houses of whom have once vied in capital with the Bank of England.

What had happened to this magnificent civilization following the intrusion of the Company? If it had weakened, had the East India Company made it sturdier? If it were beset with strife, had the Company given it peace? If it were impoverished, had the Company brought the blessings of prosperity? Not a bit of it. India had been subjected to the squalid adventurism and wanton cruelty of arrested adolescents, banditti in tricorn hats.

> Our conquest there, after twenty years, is as crude as it was the first day. The natives scarcely know what it is to see the gray head of an Englishman. Young men (boys almost) govern there, without society and without sympathy with the natives. They have no more social habits with the people than if they still resided in England – nor, indeed, any species of intercourse, but that which is necessary

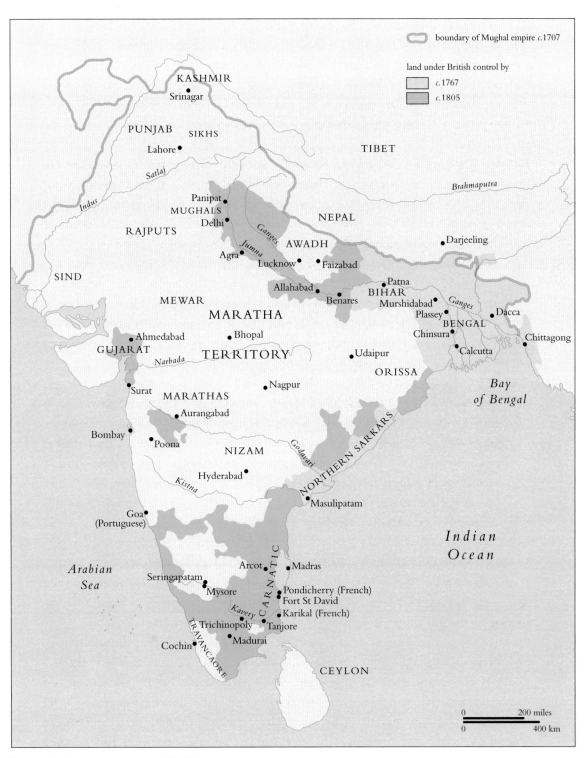

The rise of British power in India, *c.* 1750–1805.

to making a sudden fortune, with a view to a remote settlement. Animated with all the avarice of age and all the impetuosity of youth they roll in one after another, wave after wave; and there is nothing before the eyes of the natives but an endless, hopeless prospect of new flights of birds of prey and passage, with appetites continually renewing for a food that is continually wasting. Every rupee of profit made by an Englishman is lost forever to India.

Nor had the English compensated for power with the execution of good works. No bridges, highways or reservoirs had been built, Burke insisted (not altogether accurately): 'Were we to be driven out of India this day, nothing would remain to tell that it had been possessed, during the inglorious period of our dominion, by anything better than the ourang-utang or the tiger.'

And Cornwallis knew, with a sinking feeling, that he was supposed to make this right; that if the British Empire was to rise again, like the sun in the east, it would have to be through the imposition not of force but of justice and virtue. He would have to be the first of the true proconsuls of Bengal, not the convenient instrument of his countrymen's rapacity. He was under no illusions how difficult this would be. Perhaps the task would be impossible. In 1784 he had written:

> The more I turn it in my mind the less inclination I feel to undertake it. To abandon my children and every comfort this side of the grave; to quarrel with the Supreme Government in India, whatever it might be; to find that I have neither power to model the army or correct abuses; and, finally, to run the risk of being beat by some Nabob and being disgraced to all eternity, which from what I have read of these battles appears to be a very probable thing to happen – I cannot see in opposition to this, great renown and brilliant fortune.

In short, Cornwallis did not need another Yorktown, another America.

When William Pitt, the twenty-five-year-old son of Chatham, whom Cornwallis had so much admired, pressed, his resolution had wavered. 'Inclination cries out every moment, "Do not think of it; why should you volunteer plague and misery?" Duty then whispers, "You are not sent here merely to please yourself; the wisdom of Providence had thought fit to put an insuperable bar to any great degree of happiness; … Try to be of some use; serve your country and your friends.' In the end, once he had gained the government's agreement to place both civil and military supremacy in his hands (being only too aware that his predecessor, Warren Hastings, had faced personal enmity and political obstruction from the Calcutta Council), Cornwallis had accepted the commission. 'I have been obliged to say yes and exchange a life of ease and content, to encounter all the plagues and miseries of command and public station.' He would do his best to be a good Roman, an Aurelius beneath the banyan.

But when the English had first set their sights on India they had meant to be Carthaginians, not Romans; traders, not conquerors. No doubt the gentlemen relished the grandiose title bestowed on them by Queen Elizabeth's charter of 1600 as 'The Governor and Company of Merchants of London Trading into the East Indies'; but really they were commercial adventurers after a little something on the side to pay for the deer park or the fashionably gilt Thames barge. As a descriptive phrase, the 'East Indies' was deliberately indeterminate, for any fortune hunter with an eye to economic geography would not be looking to the subcontinent at all, but further east, to the Indonesian archipelago whence came the high-priced treasures of pepper, mace, nutmeg and cloves. But between them the Portuguese and the Dutch seemed to have locked up the spice islands. When the English struggled to establish toe-hold trading posts at Bantam in Java and on the South Moluccan island of Ambon, they had been outgunned by the hostile Dutch fleets. In 1622, they had decided to cut their losses and leave the Moluccas when a punitive Dutch expedition razed the factory and executed the ten English merchants in 1623 to make their point. It was to pre-empt being at the mercy of a Dutch spice monopoly that the English settled for an easier entry via the back door – India itself. There, they believed, they could negotiate with the representatives of the Mughal emperor on equal terms with the Portuguese and the Dutch, rather than deal with local sultans who had pre-emptively committed themselves to enforcing a commercial exclusion zone. From a trading base or 'factory' on the Indian coast the English would be able to import some spices directly, but also acquire silk and cotton textiles, which could be used to barter in Bantam. Surplus textiles could always be exported back to England and re-exported to Europe. It was not exactly the silver mines of Peru, but it was a start: worth, at any rate, the investment of the 200 or so stockholders who came together as the 'General Court' of the East India Company at Leadenhall Street and elected, every year, twenty-four directors to manage their common enterprise.

In 1608 the Company ship *Hector* anchored off the prosperous, busy port of Surat on the Gujarat coast of western India. Despite the truculent opposition of the Portuguese, whose 'factory' had been established not far away at Goa a half century before, the English managed to secure from the Mughal governor the licence they needed to trade in spices and cloth. But the grandiose aim of the Jacobean gentlemen-merchants was some sort of formally negotiated treaty with the Emperor Jahangir himself, and in 1615 Sir Thomas Roe was sent in the capacity of an ambassador

Above: *East India House, Leadenhall Street, London*, engraved by Thomas Shepherd, *c.* 1820.
Opposite, top: *Fort St George on the Coromandel Coast, India*, engraved by Jan van Ryne, 1794.
Opposite, below: *View of a House, Manufactory and Bazaar in Calcutta*, engraved by Francis Jukes, 1795.

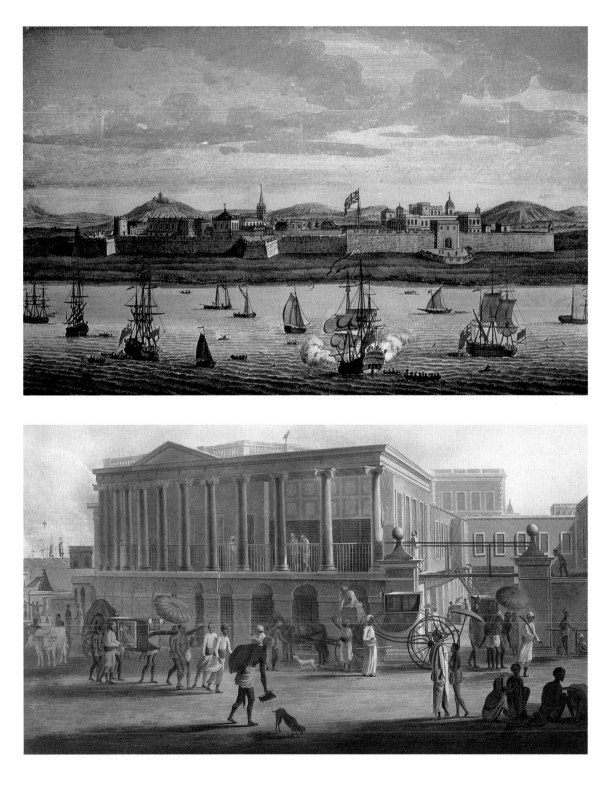

bearing letters from James I. The governor of Surat was unimpressed, and it was only a year later that Roe managed to obtain an audience with Jahangir, who was duly bemused both by Roe's refusal to prostrate himself in the accustomed way before the Peacock Throne (instead doffing his hat and bowing from the waist) and by the very idea of a far-off 'king' who would allow himself to be represented by common merchants. On the other hand, the emperor's councillors believed they had nothing to lose from the grant of a *firman* licence, allowing trade under immunity from imperial taxes. There was obviously nothing these *Feringhis* could bring that India might want except large quantities of silver, which the government was happy to have added to its coffers. Besides, cloth exports would provide work for the weavers, bleachers and dyers of the Mughal empire and spread the unquestionable splendours of their arts about the world. Might these new traders be an annoyance? No more, surely, than the buzz of a gnat around the hindquarters of a war elephant.

For two generations dividends were declared in the Company sales rooms at Leadenhall Street. As the seventeenth century wore on, however, they were shrinking, offset by heavy operational costs, not least those of defence against competitors and pirates. But although the outlook for the India trade was uncertain around 1660, its champions, like Josiah Child, who had made a fortune fitting out the fleets of the Commonwealth and Protectorate and who sailed on into the mercantile world of the Restoration, remained optimistic – always provided, he insisted, that the Company understand it would have to act with political and military boldness if its commercial operations were ever to be secure. By the 1680s there seemed to be something substantially worth defending. The Company had settled into a number of Indian commercial centres such as Masulipatnam in the southeast and Hooghly in west Bengal. In those cities it built warehouses and one-storey houses for its 'factors' and 'writers' (clerks), usually near the protecting shadow of the Mughal fort. But in the second half of the seventeenth century there were other sites – Bombay on the west, transferred to English control as part of the Portuguese Catherine of Braganza's dowry as queen of Charles II; Madras on the Coromandel coast; and, from 1690, Calcutta in west Bengal – where the Company custom-built its 'factories' inside a fortified bastion, facing the sea on one side and garrisoned with a handful of Company soldiers, Indian, Portuguese–Eurasian and other Europeans. Either within its walls or protected by them, clusters of one-storey houses were built from the mixture of matted hemp, brick-dust and lime called *pucca*. Facing them was a church in the reassuring English manner, complete with colonnaded porch, steeple and rows of boxed pews made of tropical hardwoods. Behind it lay a churchyard, its graves more populous than the pews. Beyond the walls of this 'White Town' a 'Black Town' of Indian merchants, clerks and money-lenders lived, while a third community of maritime workers – boatmen, stevedores, carters and fishermen – gathered closer to the harbour. Betwixt and between them all were small but extremely important communities of Armenians and Jews who acted as brokers and intermediary agents.

By 1700 the daily round of British life in India was already established: a hard ride before breakfast; morning prayers courtesy of the chaplain; business till the communal dinner (around two or three o'clock), with a tiffin of light curries staving off the pangs between; siesta after dinner; a little more business, then another ride, a fishing or fowling expedition, and cards and a light supper before bed. That was the official version, at any rate. But from less demure accounts, the colonies of bored, badly paid younger sons forced to come to India and brave the terrifying mortality (some 460 deaths in one hot season in Calcutta in a British population of 1200) behaved much as one would expect: gambling heavily; sinking vats of arrack while they did so; fighting and duelling among themselves; and either keeping Indian or Eurasian mistresses or visiting the Black Town brothels between doses of mercury to cure the maladies they acquired from over-indulgence there. Ostensibly in charge of all this was a president – not in any sense a true governor, but the senior merchant (in settlements where promotion came strictly by seniority), attempting to do the bidding of his masters in London while necessarily winking an eye at the extensive private business carried on by its servants in India to compensate for their niggardly salaries. At least the presidents knew how to put on a good show, never leaving the fort without an escort of armed Indian soldiers, two Union flags and the blare of 'country musick', loud enough, one commentator said, to make the natives believe we had gone mad.

It was not all bugles and bombast at Madras or Calcutta, however. For the prospects of British business in India had been transformed by the calico revolution in Europe. During the last third of the seventeenth century, virtually all social classes other than the rural poor discovered lightweight Indian fabrics – brilliantly dyed and figured silks for the well-to-do, and cottons, printed, painted or plain, for everyone. Calicoes and the more expensive silk-cotton mix chintzes changed lives. For the first time, materials other than heavy woollens and linens were available at prices to suit almost every income level. Calicoes, whether in bold prints or sheer gauzy muslins, were strong yet soft and, most important of all, were washable. No part of the male or female, adult or child's body, including the most private, was untouched by them. 'Few think themselves wel-dresst,' wrote one observer, 'till they are made up in calicoes, both men and women, in calico shirts, neckcloths, cuffs, aprons, nightroyls, gowns, petticoats, hoops, sleeves and india-stockings.' In London, as hundreds of thousands of pieces were sold every year, dividends at last became serious, and Company stock

Aurangzeb I at Prayer, Mughal, *c.* 1710.

soared. Predictably, success bred resentment. Silk weavers at home angrily petitioned the government, and 'calico-chasers' mobbed wagons full of the textiles. The government responded by banning imports other than goods for re-export and plain fabric, which could be patterned up at home. But despite the ban, unofficial calico trading went on, and there was certainly enough demand in continental Europe for the rosier forecasts of business to seem realistic.

The only problem was India. An onward and upward commercial trajectory – the realization of the blue-water empire of trade, unencumbered by costs of territorial conquest or government – presupposed the stable and hospitable business environment provided by the omniscient dominion of the Mughal empire. Although the emissaries of the Stuart monarchs and the first generations of merchants who came to the Mughal court resented the lordly superiority of their emperors and privately still believed their empire to be a peculiar mixture of barbarism and voluptuous decay, they needed its authority to hold the ring against their European competitors and maintain their protection against extortionate local potentates. But in the historical mind-set of men like Sir Josiah Child, putting the Company's trust, not to mention its inventory, into the safe-keeping of a permanent, stable Mughal government was a dangerous delusion. Either empires were on their way up (British) or they were on their way down (Mughal). The rebellion of the Hindu Maratha cavalry war-lords in central and western Bengal, led by their charismatic prince Shivaji, had persuaded Child that the decline of the Mughals was indeed going to be swift and irreversible. Their passing would leave great holes in the structure of their empire to be occupied by some potential adversary, either native or European, to British interests. Child's conclusion was for the Company to act before it was acted on, and believing the Mughals to be seriously weakened in the west he launched a disastrous military action in the 1680s. It succeeded only in ruining their establishment in Surat, provoking the blockade and virtual abandonment of Bombay and a grovelling submission to the Emperor Aurangzeb.

Child's understanding of the changes taking place in India was grotesquely mis-informed, save the one truism that there was indeed change. The Mughal empire was far from being on its last legs. Nor was the only alternative to its government some sort of howling barbarian anarchy: Huns in turbans about to plunge India into its Dark Ages. Ruled by the descendants of Tamerlane and Ginghiz Khan, it had evolved from a Turkic horseback warrior state into one of the great sedentary Muslim civilizations. At its height, under the Emperor Akbar I in the second half of the sixteenth century, it governed virtually all of north and central India through a unified system of law based on the Islamic Shari'a and on a centralized, Persian-language administration. Great palaces were built, none more extraordinary than Fatehpur Sikhri; and the Arabic and Persian court culture produced a great flowering of poetry and painting. But although the authority of the Mughals owed a great deal to the fearsomeness of their cavalry and artillery, to the lustre of their court and the energy and probity of their administration, they were governing an immense territory, major parts of which were not Muslim but Hindu. Their success at containing disaffection, then, rested on a careful balance between central authority – not least that of the omnipotent aura of the emperor himself, said to be infused directly with the light of God – and the co-opting of regional princes and peoples.

The key to that collaboration was the land tax, equal to as much as a third of the livelihood of India's many million farmers and peasants. In return for his obedience and military cooperation, the emperor would assign to a subordinate governor, or nawab, the land revenue of a particular province. After delivering to the imperial treasury the empire's portion (in silver, naturally), and after paying the costs of assessment and collection, the nawab would be free to enjoy what was left. Similarly the nawabs – of Bengal or Awadh, for example – contracted in advance with hereditary collectors, the *zemindars*, for the amounts due from their respective territories. They too made money from the difference between the sum due on their contract and what they could actually extract from the cultivators. In similar fashion, the empire actively encouraged the development of sophisticated and specialized commercial centres around its dominions, so that Bengal indigo or Gujarati cottons often travelled along the great trunk roads to far-distant urban markets.

For a century this seemed a magically self-sustaining system. But after the death of the combative Aurangzeb a decided shift occurred in the delicate equilibrium between central and local power. The drift towards greater regional autonomy was accelerated by the empire's evident inability to defend itself against the onslaught of brutal horseback invasions from both the Afghans and the charismatic Persian despot Nadir Shah, who in 1739 sacked Delhi in a storm of elaborately horrific cruelty: Nadir Shah watched enthroned before the city gates as throats were slit and bodies mutilated. Within central and western India itself the imperial armies were unable to prevent the Marathas from consolidating their power. And the various tribal raids on India were worse for being hit-and-run expeditions, their perpetrators uninterested (unlike the original Mughals) in settling amid the conquered and establishing something more than a cycle of extortion.

In the circumstances, it was inevitable that the Muslim officials and administrators to whom the empire had entrusted the government of whole regions should look out increasingly for themselves and their immediate subjects. Driven by both necessity and ambition, the nawabs of Bengal and Awadh, formidable men like Alivardi Khan and Shuja-ud-Daulah with their own provincial courts at Murshidabad and Faizabad, which disposed of revenue, law enforcement and soldiers, inevitably became more self-sufficient. Though they still thought of themselves as loyal to the emperor, they made their own offices hereditary and appointed their own men to their governments, irrespective of Delhi's wishes. Instead of responding to orders from the imperial treasury as to how much of the land revenue they were to keep and how much to pass on, they themselves increasingly decided on the shares.

As the struts and armature of the empire began to shake loose, it was these local potentates who became the focus of European attention in bids to outmanoeuvre or exclude their competition. In Bengal the late-comer but energetic French Compagnie des Indes had established a trading settlement at Chandernagor, and its ambitious governor, Joseph, Marquis de Dupleix, courted the nawab in Murshidabad to get an edge on his British rivals in Calcutta. Naval vessels from both countries – summoned, it was said defensively – began to manouevre for position and, once the War of the Austrian Succession (in which, in the line-up of European alliances, Britain and France were on opposing sides) began in earnest, to exchange fire. In 1746, in return for the capture of French ships, the French under Bertrand-Francis La Bourdonnais, operating out of their factory at Pondicherry, captured Madras, the jewel of the Company's possessions, and held it for two years. At the Treaty of Aix-la-Chapelle it was returned to the East India Company amid scenes of jubilation at Fort St George. But the initial skirmishing had escalated the struggle. For no one had taken Josiah Child's instruction that the achievement of profit was conditional on the exercise of power more seriously than Dupleix.

When Dupleix made his first intervention in the internal politics of southern India, he was in fact merely applying the kind of conventions used by the French with the native tribes of North America to sustain and reinforce their position. But in India they looked much more ominous. When the most powerful figure in the region, the Nizam of Hyderabad, died, a contest was triggered for control of the Carnatic. Dupleix backed Chanda Sahib, a veteran administrator, and was prepared to support him with regular French troops and Indian levies. Should he prevail, the British could look forward to the end of Madras and their calico fortunes. In competition they gave their support to Muhammad Ali Walahjah, the son of a mercenary soldier. Even more fateful for the future, Dupleix planned to finance his campaign with the proceeds from local land taxes. He insisted to his understandably anxious directors in Paris that the purpose of all this was ultimately commercial: that the creation of a fiscal–military power in south India was the last thing he intended. It would work out otherwise, though – and not for the French, but for their enemies.

The odds on the British prevailing in this struggle must have been steep. For a start, the credentials of their candidate to govern a predominantly Hindu, southern territory were not strong. Muhammad Ali was, as his name suggests, a Muslim, and his family came from northern India. But, famously, there appeared in Madras in the 1740s someone who, even as he built a personal empire that, by comparison, made Dupleix's strategy look timid, likewise protested that he was just the loyal servant of the East India Company. Robert Clive had never really been meant for trade. In Market Drayton in Shropshire he had been so ungovernable a child that his beleaguered parents, over-burdened with a swarm of offspring, had sent him away to relatives in Manchester. He liked it, but it didn't like him. Back in Market Drayton the adolescent Clive pelted passers-by from the church steeple and ran a minor extortion racket against local shopkeepers, who were obliged to fork over to Clive's gang in order to protect their stores from pillage and destruction. He was, obviously, good material for Company service in India and ended up, nineteen years old, in Diamond Pitt's Madras on the lowest rung of the hierarchy: the writer. For some years Robert Clive clerked away, bunking down in the sweaty collegiality of the bachelor boys, hating every minute ('I have not enjoyed one happy day since I left my native country'), pining for Manchester and relieving the tedium with the standard distractions of arrack, cock-fights, fistfights, gambling and (unless he was an unlikely exception) sex. The opium habit that, in all likelihood, ended up contributing to his death thirty years on, almost certainly began then and there. In the broiling heat his manic swings between elation and depression (virtually a job qualification for British empire-building) became wilder. Twice he tried to end it all with a pistol pressed to his temples. Twice – the story goes – the gun jammed.

In the war with the French, in which they and the British respectively acted, ostensibly, for Chanda Sahib and Muhammad Ali Walahjah, Clive's gangsterish intelligence and brutality found the perfect career opportunity. Careless of life, beginning with his own, he took chances that no one a little saner would ever have contemplated, gambling that if they came off he would be a god to his soldiers. When the French besieged the bastion of Trichinopoly rock, instead of marching directly on it Clive ordered a counter-march of his tiny troop of Indian and European soldiers to invest the fortress of Arcot and then dared the French to come and get it. They rose to the bait, drawing troops away from Trichinopoly and spending two months failing to take Arcot while Clive defended the stronghold to the last sepoy! It was not necessarily the turning point of the war, but it was a spectacularly tough feat of endurance, and it made him, at twenty-five, a Company hero. It also had the desired effect of allowing a British force to relieve the siege of Trichinopoly, capture Chanda Sahib and have him

Top: *A Nawab Holding Court*, probably Alivardi Khan, by an unknown artist,
Murshidabad, Bengal, *c.* 1760.
Above: *Shuja-ud-Daulah, Nawab of Awadh, Holding a Bow*, by Tilly Kettle, *c.* 1772.

beheaded in the shadow of the rock. Dupleix's credibility in France collapsed; the British installed Muhammad Ali Walahjah as the nawab of the Carnatic and were guaranteed the domination of southeast India.

But what for? For the dividend, of course; for the Company; what else? Clive and his fellow-soldiers always insisted that the force they were applying was just enough to pre-empt the Company from being locked out of whole commercial territories by the French. Even by the operational standards of the twentieth, never mind the eighteenth, century, a carefully measured degree of intervention could be justified as sound business practice in a part of the world where free trade and perfect competition were fantasies, and where abstaining from intervention was to cede the field to one's adversary. And there were, always, interested Indians – rival potentates, bankers and brokers, disaffected generals and revenue lords – ready to encourage the British, piggy-backing the redcoats to fortune and power. The danger, of course, for both the Company in London and the Indian opportunists, was that, once mobilized, military action and political involvement would come to be the master, not the servant, of business opportunity and would end up generating unanticipated problems that in turn would call for further and deeper military engagements until the point when a quick killing would no longer mean a trade opportunity. This is exactly what happened in Bengal, and what happened in Bengal landed Britain the wrong empire.

No one saw it coming, not even Robert Clive, back in England after the victory in the Carnatic, relishing his fame and fortune as the hard man of the East India Company, his pockets jingling with spare silver. Neither he, nor the court of directors, were under any illusion that the French would be content to cut their losses in the south of India without trying to compensate in the potentially much richer trading zone of the northeast. Their own factory at Chandernagor had the makings of a Gallic Calcutta, and their growing fleets could compete for control of the Bay of Bengal, sail by sail, with those of the East India Company. But the kind of spiralling competition that had caused so much damage in the south seemed to be contained by the much tougher and apparently more stable regime of Alivardi Khan, the nawab of Bengal. Taking advantage of the impotence of the Mughal court at Delhi to defend the empire, the nawab governed effectively from Murshidabad, 300 miles (400 km) up the Ganges from Calcutta, as a mini-Mughal, carving out a virtually autonomous kingdom that included not just Bengal itself, but also Orissa to the south and Bihar to the west. It was, in its own right, a huge, economically dynamic territory, and it was getting bigger by the year as estuary lands were reclaimed and put under rice, indigo or sugar. The European trading communities, which included the Dutch at Chinsura, were confined within their 'factories' and given limited licences to trade up-country (which meant, in effect, buying printed cottons and silks and handing over silver), and the idea that there might be some sort of break-out into an aggressive, free-wheeling armed state within a state seemed, even in the mid-1750s, inconceivable and, for everyone concerned, undesirable.

But the status quo was actually much shakier than would have been apparent to any visitor to Alivardi Khan's elegant court. He too was over-extended and had difficulty in preventing the Marathas from invading western Bihar and western Bengal. To generate the funds needed to shore up his army meant either becoming further indebted to bankers like the house of Jagat Seth, or putting heavy pressure on the *zemindars* with the predictable result of making enemies. The new defensiveness applied to the Europeans, too. With another round of Anglo-French hostilities coming, the two companies were determined to deprive each other of another Bengali speciality that had become strategic treasure: saltpetre. As they were manoeuvring for position in 1756, Alivardi Khan died and was succeeded by his twenty-year-old grandson, Siraj-ud-Daulah.

'Sir Roger Dowler' (as schoolboys of my generation still knew him) was the first official villain of imperialist history, the sadistic fiend who immured innocent Britons within the living tomb of the Black Hole of Calcutta. Pictures of the monster gloating over his victims, which illustrated Victorian and even twentieth-century 'empire stories', featured stereotypes of the oriental despot: curled mustachios as black as his heart. 'Early debauchery had unnerved his body and mind,' wrote Macaulay (which certainly could not be said of his own childhood) '… it had early been his amusement to torture beasts and birds and when he grew up he enjoyed with still keener relish the misery of his fellow creatures.' But Siraj-ud-Daulah was, of course, just your standard eighteenth-century Indian princely post-adolescent: impulsive, spoiled rotten, ill-informed and politically out of his depth. Given what had happened in the Carnatic, it was not, in fact, unreasonable for him to try to ensure that the ostensibly commercial companies stayed just that, by demanding that the European trading posts dismantle their fortifications at Chinsura, Chandernagor and Calcutta. The Dutch and the French obliged. The British did not, perhaps because Calcutta was now much more than a service extension of the trade depot. In the sixty years since Job Charnock had planted himself beneath his banyan tree by the Hooghly, in what was acknowledged then and ever since to be the unhealthiest climate in all India, it had grown into a sizeable city, in its own right with a population of at least 100,000. It was no longer just a strung-together agglomeration of weaving and fishing villages along the Hooghly but a tight little economic powerhouse.

Rightly or wrongly, the British felt that Calcutta was their creation and that it lived or died with the capacity to buy, up-country, the products that the Company needed to ship home (which its servants liked to trade, not always legally, to line their own pockets). The mere existence of the crudely built Fort William was the bargaining chip they needed to press claims for the protection and expansion of that trade, and they were not about to hand it over on a platter to the young nawab. The defiance was poorly timed since the ditch being dug to complete its defences had not been finished before Siraj-ud-Daulah marched on the city to enforce his will. He took it without much trouble, the president and most of the councilmen and inhabitants (about 450 of them) managing to flee before its capture. One of those who did not was Zephaniah Holwell, who along with a group of civilian and military prisoners was imprisoned on 20 June 1756 in a cell about 18 by 14 feet (6 by 3 metres), used for offenders in the Fort and long known by the British as 'the Black Hole'. It was Holwell's graphic account, *A Genuine Narrative of the Deplorable Deaths of the English Gentlemen and Others who were Suffocated in the Black Hole*, written on the journey home a year later that gave Britain its first imperial atrocity melodrama, perfectly tuned to the contemporary taste for the macabre and the sentimental, and complete with sons expiring as they held the hands of their fathers. Holwell claimed that 146 had been incarcerated and 43 survived. The best-researched modern evidence now suggests that he doubled the number of both prisoners and survivors. But this is still by any standards a grim reckoning, and the revisionist argument that some of the bodies were already dead, casualties of the fighting, does not make it any prettier. Some of Holwell's account must have been true: the stifling heat; and unhinged victims, their clothes torn off to give them a fraction more room, dying and making air available for others. But – as any survivors from among the Jacobites imprisoned in Carlisle Castle in 1746 would have confirmed – this kind of treatment was, unhappily, nothing unusual for the eighteenth century.

It was not, in any case, outraged humanity so much as strategic necessity that brought retribution down on the head of Siraj-ud-Daulah. Clive had been recalled to Madras to try to extend Company influence to another state, Hyderabad, but was now diverted north to Bengal in a combined operation with the ships of Charles Watson. Calcutta was taken from the sea in January 1757, and the nawab forced to reinstate all the Company's privileges and fortifications. At which point the gambit, which had been used successfully in the Carnatic, was reapplied in Bengal. A senior general in Siraj's army, Mir Jafar, angry at being passed over and alienated by the petulant antics of the nawab, let it be known that he would not be excessively grief-stricken were Clive to bring him down. The money-men, Jagat Seth above all, without whose resources any nawab was a broken reed, simultaneously gravitated to the power they instinctively thought to be a better long-term bet. At Plassey on 23 June 1757

Top: *Fort William in the Kingdom of Bengal*, engraved by Jan van Ryne, 1754.
Above: *Lord Clive Meeting Mir Jafar, Nawab of Murshidabad after the Battle of Plassey, 1757*, by Francis Hayman, *c.* 1761–2.

Clive's force of 2000 red-coated native sepoys and 1000 Europeans appeared to be massively outnumbered by an opposing army of 50,000, complete with elephant cavalry. But the disparity was a mirage, for only perhaps 10,000 of the nawab's troops were actually prepared to fight. Once it was obvious that Mir Jafar and his commanders would stand aloof from the combat, the entire army, critically dependent on command, collapsed. Siraj-ud-Daulah was swiftly murdered, and Mir Jafar was made nawab in his place.

There was, of course, a reckoning to be made for services rendered, and when Clive presented his bill (probably in advance of the battle) it was not for the faint of heart or shallow of pocket. The general was to be 'reimbursed' for his pains to the tune of a cool £234,000, a sum that instantly made the hooligan from Market Drayton one of the richest men in Britain, as well as 'Baron Clive of Plassey'. In addition he was assigned a revenue territory that would yield him an annual income of nearly £30,000. The fact that, of the £80 million purported to be in Siraj-ud-Daulah's treasury, no one could find more than £1.5 million had no effect at all on the scale of the confiscations.

Beyond the opportunism of personal plunder lay a much deeper question and one that the British Empire would face time and time again in its march across the globe. Was its military power to be used to strengthen or to weaken the native government they claimed to be 'assisting'? Which *truly* served the interests of a trading empire, the empire of liberty – a strong Indian regime or a weak one? The view in Leadenhall Street habitually voiced by the directors and their fiscally conservative chairmen like Laurence Sulivan was invariably one of damage limitation: stabilizing the situation to the point where Indian institutions could be depended on to provide the stability and peace needed for commerce to flourish. The immunity of Calcutta from Indian authority that was demanded after Plassey seemed to fit this bill. But, 15,000 miles and six months' sailing-time away, few of the Company men in India itself gave much time or credence to the practicality of self-containment. And some thought it the counsel of the weak. In a telling piece of advice, Clive told the directors in 1758 that 'such an opportunity can never again be expected for the *aggrandisement* of the Company'.

Specifically, did the Company want a pliable nawab (as in south India), or did it want to all intents and purposes to *be* the nawab? The Company men could tell themselves that, by stripping Murshidabad of an army and making it pay for British troops instead, they were only reacting defensively to the experience of 1756–7. But even the most ill-informed of them knew that the legitimacy of the nawab's government depended critically on shows of force – not just armoured elephants in battle array but also guards and police who could descend on a district or *zemindars* to pry loose the silver for the government treasury. Without that force, Indian administration was a hollow shell. Dictating to Mir Jafar that henceforth the Company would collect land revenue directly from the large district known as the 24 Parganas, and that *banians* (middlemen) trading under the Company flag should be allowed up-country to do business without the inconvenience of paying taxes – and doing all this on the grounds that the instability of the regime required this prudent measure of security – was, of course, to make a self-fulfilling prophecy. Predicting the collapse of viable Indian administration, the British did everything to ensure it happened. When, inevitably, Mir Jafar failed to meet his financial obligations and in desperation searched around for alternative allies, even the Marathas, he was replaced by his son-in-law Mir Qasim in 1760. When he in his turn presumed to lay down the law to British private traders, he was likewise disposed of and his aged father-in-law bounced back to Murshidabad.

Summoning or seeing off nawabs, manipulating the polity of Bengal until it frayed and tore and fell apart altogether may have suited the short-term interests of the British. Clive and his associates may even have imagined it gave the Company greater freedom of action. But in fact it locked Britain into a cycle of intervention, war and yet more intervention which it had expressly rejected, a syndrome that transformed an empire of business into an empire of military coercion. There was a particular kind of Indian soil on which soldiers did their very best to avoid pitching tents that was known to them as 'cotton ground'. For if it should rain at night while they were sleeping, what had in dry weather seemed to be a solid surface subsided first into dirty froth and then into a cavernous liquid sinkhole, swallowing tents, occupants and possessions. Though they imagined that what they were doing was 'laying the foundations' of something – and though their exploits have been treated by imperial historians as just that – Clive and his fellow-conquistadors in India were in fact setting those foundations on cotton ground. While they were airily hiring and firing nawabs, a much more decisive drama was unfolding to the northeast. On 14 January 1761, 60 miles (96 km) northwest of Delhi near the small town of Panipat, an immense battle took place between rival claimants to the legacy of the crumbling Mughal empire. On one side was the most formidable army the Brahmin Marathas had yet managed to assemble from their confederation of cavalry dynasts. On the other was an Afghan army under the command of Ahmed Shah Durrani. Like the Persian despot Nadir Shah in 1739, Ahmed Shah had invaded India essentially for the time-honoured purpose of ransacking the cities of the north. But he too had been drawn into a politically mobilized Muslim alliance – with the nawab of Awadh – to stop the Hindu Marathas from taking control of north and central India. The Muslims won the day as the Maratha horsemen were mown down by Afghan guns. But once victory was achieved the Afghans withdrew northwest along their looting route, ensuring that the result of Panipat was to open a great vacuum of power in the Mughal heartland that none of its potential successors – Bengal, Awadh or, further south, Hyderabad – was strong enough to fill.

Of course if the East India Company plan all along had been to move right into that space, then the decade after Panipat was too good to be true. By the time Company armies had defeated Nawab Mir Qasim and the nawab of Awadh at Baksar on the Awadh–Bihar border in 1764, it seemed to have become an unstoppable machine. By paying Indian soldiers higher wages than they were accustomed to receiving from the nawabs, and by paying them regularly, the Company was able to take on sepoys from the traditional pools of military recruitment in the villages around Banaras and southern Awadh, whose men now wore the red coats. After the nawab of Awadh's defeat, his own treasury was required to pay for those troops who obliged him with their 'protection'. It was the Market Drayton racket gone subcontinental. In Bengal, the army was able to be equipped with muskets, artillery, bullock trains and cavalry horses because from 1765 it became the direct recipient of the bonanza that was the land revenue. In an improvised ceremony at Allahabad that year, for which Clive provided a 'throne' in the form of one of his chairs set on top of his dining table, the Mughal Emperor Shah Alam had formally invested the Company with the power of the *Diwani*: the authority to collect taxes in his name. Though the nawab in Murshidabad still ostensibly retained powers of police and justice, the Company was now in effect the governing power, inserted into the moribund body of the Mughal empire from which it proceeded to gnaw its way out, parasitically and insatiably.

The paradox was that Clive had been sent back to India in 1764 by the Company not to expand its power and territories but as the agent of retrenchment. And to those in London who were painfully exercised by the costs – both financial and political – of William Pitt's empire, the experience in India was every bit as sobering as that in America. If you were the unfortunate person responsible for balancing the books in London, acquiring an empire could be every bit as disastrous as losing one. Needless to say, this is not how it seemed to the men on the spot, their brows garlanded with victory, their exploits celebrated in songs and paintings exhibited in Vauxhall Gardens, their coffers swollen to bursting with extorted Indian silver. With Clive himself setting the pace they began to spend freely in Britain itself, buying country houses and some-times, as at Sezincote in Gloucestershire, hiring architects to give them the air of an Indian palace. They began to throw their weight about in London and their money at parliamentary seats. As the 'nabobs', they displaced the West Indian planters as the most envied and detested plutocrats of the age.

Lord Clive Receiving from the Mogul the Grant of the Duanney (Diwani), by Benjamin West, *c.* 1774–95.

Acutely aware of the debate about the costs of empire in America, in the two years that Clive remained in India he continued to rationalize this metamorphosis from business to self-perpetuating military state as a golden fiscal opportunity. 'Bengal is in itself an inexhaustible fund of riches,' he wrote to the Directors, 'and you may depend on being supplied with money and provisions in abundance.' Specifically, the difference between what the Bengal land revenues would reliably yield, and what it cost to administer and police them, would be, he cheerfully predicted, pure profit, perhaps £1 million a year. And that profit would, in turn, provide all the capital needed to invest in the Company's cargoes, destined to be auctioned off at its London sales rooms. If you believed this then you believed in dreams come true, specifically the dream of equalizing the terms of trade rather than endlessly pouring silver down the great Indian drain. The self-sustaining neatness of the plan must have seemed even more irresistible when compared to the fiscal nightmare in America, where British troops and armed customs men had to wrest taxes from an infuriated population who accused the home government of instituting tyranny. In India, the Company reasoned, no one expected anything *but* tyranny, and under the auspices of the Union Jack they were likely to get less of it than under the nawabs. Better yet, they would do all the collecting themselves they had since the beginning of the Mughal empire. What could go wrong? The peasants would go on complaining. That's what peasants did. But they would cough up. The *zemindars* would hand over cash in advance to the Company and turn their men on any recalcitrant villages as they always had. Nothing was going to change except the ultimate ownership of the teak chests into which all this Bengal bounty would be spilled.

But everything did change. Seen from their palanquins borne along the trunk roads by a tottering quartet of bearers, or from the plush of their river barges, the countryside may have looked impervious to trauma, soaking up fiscal punishment along with the monsoon rains and still able to feed itself. But what would happen if the monsoons failed to deliver? This is exactly what happened in 1769 and 1770 when northeast India was plunged into desperate famine. Between a quarter and a third of the population of Bengal and Bihar died in those two years. Travellers remembered seeing saucer-eyed living ghosts, unfleshed ribcages sitting waiting to expire, massed flocks of kites descending on the carcasses – nothing quite fit for recording in Company school paintings. The famine was not the fault of the British regime. But the havoc and misery it had unleashed in Bengal during the 1760s had not helped the countryside to survive the blow.

It had been picked clean by the fortune-seekers, both native and British. In the face of the threats posed by the Marathas and the French, the pressure for land revenue had been fiercer than ever. The government in Calcutta had leaned on the *zemindars*, who had leaned on the villages. The proportion of their produce taken rose; their ability to save for the following year's seed dwindled. If they lost a cow to the collector, or because there was no straw to harvest, they lost milk, draft labour and dung bricks for fuel. Freed from all oversight, merchants with their own armed entourage flying the Company flag would invade the villages looking for cloth but imposing prices on the weavers and dyers – another species of legalized extortion. Burke's scalding polemic against 'the just and punctual hand that in India has torn the cloth from the loom, or wrested the scanty portion of rice and salt from the peasant, or wrung from him the very opium in which he forgot his oppression and his oppressor' was, to be sure, hyperbole. But it was not altogether misplaced. A much less partisan commentator who knew whereof he spoke, Richard Becher, confessed that 'the fact is undoubted … that since the accession to the dewanee, the condition of the people of this country has been worse than it was before.'

What Robert Clive had done in 1765 was to set a will o' the wisp scampering through Anglo-Indian history, the vain pursuit of which would decide the fate of its empire. For although at the very end of his career he insisted that the British should not recklessly extend their governmental supervision deep into the Mughal empire, he had held out the promise that grasping the nettle of Indian finances would sting only for a moment. Thereafter it was the answer to the Company's prayers – not just the harbinger, but the condition, of commercial profitability. By 1800 this principle had hardened into an unchallengeable truism, notwithstanding the fact that the Company's finances were turning an ever deeper shade of red and that it was the reverse of every principle that had been laid down by the founders of the empire of liberty and commerce. It was also, of course, the opposite of the precepts being codified in Scotland by the economist Adam Smith, that the less a government imposed itself the more easily the Invisible Hand could do its work (although Smith himself would make an express exception for military contingencies and for the 'special' circumstances of India). In a crude sense, of course, Clive was right, since no one coming from Devon or Dumfries who managed to survive their stay in Calcutta or Madras was likely to get poorer by the experience. Even as he pretended to have the interests of both colonizers and natives at heart, Clive himself stood out as the most outrageous profiteer of all. Reproved for his conduct in parliament, he typically brazened it out with a famous defence. After Plassey, 'a great prince was dependent on my pleasure, an opulent city lay at my mercy; its richest bankers bid against each other for my smiles; I walked through vaults which were thrown open to me alone, piled on either hand with gold and jewels! Mr Chairman, at this moment I stand astonished at my own moderation.'

Moderation, though, was not a word anyone else used of the Baron. In 1774, immoderately sunk in opium, Clive's life ended in an overdose.

Paradoxically, Clive's personal notoriety spared the logic of his interventionist imperialism from the scepticism it deserved. For if, somehow, with the best will in the world, British government in Bengal had failed to bring about general peace and prosperity, it could only be because wicked men, selfish men, perhaps led astray by greedy, opportunist natives, had abused their trust in order to line their pockets. The proper correction was not to examine the assumptions behind the proposition, but merely to find the right men and the right measures. The rest of British history in India was a search to do just that.

If the Company was looking for someone who represented the polar opposite of Robert Clive's brutal flamboyance, they could not have done any better than Warren Hastings. The son of an improvident clergyman who ended up in Barbados, he was from the beginning a solemn outsider. The clever but impoverished Westminster schoolboy, painfully shy, carried with him a tight-wound sense of dignified superiority that provoked, often on first encounter, either admiration or hatred. A writer with the company at seventeen, Hastings worked his way through the ranks, spending some time at Murshidabad. It was there, necessarily dealing with the nawab's administrators, judges and money-men, that Hastings realized, to a degree still unusual in the Company, that its fortunes would depend on plunging, not just into the politics of late Mughal India, but into its culture too. After learning Persian, Arabic, Hindustani and Bengali he became familiar with both the Hindu and Muslim codes of law and with the great works of their sacred and mythic literature. Whatever his other failings, it could not be said that Warren Hastings suffered from any of the cultural arrogance that became the hallmark of later generations of Britons in India.

For all the dourness of his demeanour and his bewildering habit of watering his wine (to Calcutta society yet another irritating sign of his moral loftiness), Warren Hastings was a man who fell in love easily and hopelessly. After his first wife died he fell for the blonde wife of a German artist calling himself 'Baron' Imhoff, and when the Baron returned to Europe Marian stayed behind and became the second Mrs Hastings in 1777. It was a love-match that endured as long as they did. But in a much more fatal way Hastings fell for India: its gorgeous clamour; the battered beauty of its shrines and temples; its heady, aromatic disorder. He wanted desperately to be a Mughal, or at the very least a nawab. He wanted to make the Company Indian. The East India Regulation Act (1773) steered through parliament by Lord North on the eve of the American Revolution seemed to give him the authority of his heart's desire, since it promoted him from governor of Bengal to the first holder of the new office of

Warren Hastings and his Wife, by Johann Zoffany, *c.* 1783.

'Governor-General', with seniority (much to their intense chagrin) over his fellow governors in Madras and Bombay. But what the Act gave it also took away. For the Governor-General was to rule in tandem with a council composed of four men appointed by the Crown and Company, his own vote counting no more in decisions than theirs.

This, on the face of it, contradictory decision, both to concentrate and to disperse the governing power, was in fact in keeping with shifting definitions (much tested by America) of the theory of constitutional checks and balances. To have even a faint chance of practical success presupposed an essential community of interests between the Governor-General and the council, with differences arising only on details. But from the very first day of their encounter relations between Hastings and the councillors thrust on him, three of whom had not the slightest working knowledge of India prior to arriving, were an unmitigated disaster. By giving them four salvoes short of a twenty-one-gun salute on their arrival in Calcutta, Hastings had given immediate offence to the likes of the spluttering Lieutenant–General John Clavering. In fact, their grasp of the meaning of protocol correctly divined that the mild humiliation was entirely intentional, for while Hastings, justifying his action to the directors at home, laughed it all off as absurdly 'frivolous', he made sure to say that he could not have done anything else without compromising the 'dignity' of his office.

In the tight little world of white Calcutta, such snubs and slights were the equivalent of undeclared war. (What a loss to English literature that Jane Austen never walked Tank Square or sat observantly beneath a banyan on Garden Reach!) And if the councillors took a dislike to Hastings personally, they were – with the exception of the amiably profligate Richard Barwell – no more enamoured of his policies. When he purged the revenue administration they believed he had done it to put in his own creatures in the place of those dismissed. When he launched a war against the Afghan Rohilla tribes on behalf of the Nawab of Awadh, they assumed he was doing it as a mercenary to take a cut of the proceeds. Company business became hostage to the playing out of personal vendettas, none more ferociously pursued than that between Hastings and another councillor, Philip Francis. When a Bengali–Hindu revenue administrator named Nandakumar testified (almost certainly falsely) in public that the Governor-General had taken bribes (although he might have taken unauthorized allowances), Hastings retaliated inciting a prosecution against Nandakumar for embezzling the estate of a deceased debtor. Nandakumar was arrested, indicted for forgery, tried by the new British Supreme Court in Calcutta and, after a mockery of an eight-day trial, sentenced to be hanged, on the authority of a British statute passed in the reign of George II that had little meaning in Hindu law or custom.

The travesty of justice was atypical of Hastings' governance, which was criticized for paying too much, not too little, attention to indigenous law and institutions. Part of the distaste felt by his enemies for Hastings was precisely that, in his eagerness to go native, he had forgotten himself, the Company and the commission he was supposed to discharge, which was to bring British government and justice to the Indians and not the other way about. It would be a sentimental exaggeration to say that the generals and the judges and the Francises barged in on an Anglo-Indian world that was genuinely pluralist. Like its sister cities Madras and Bombay, Calcutta was obviously and aggressively segregated between White and Black Towns. In so far as Indians filled the houses on Garden Reach and Chowringhee, they did so as servants: palanquin bearers, gardeners, cooks, watchmen, runners, sweepers, gatekeepers. But from the paintings of Tilly Kettle and Johann Zoffany (who came to India to repair his career after offending the royal family) it's apparent that for a brief ten or twenty years the boundaries between races and cultures were looser and more elastic, even mutually sympathetic, than at any time before or since. Sex is no sure guide to multicultural tolerance, but with European women still relatively scarce, and very prone to tropical infections, especially during pregnancy and childbirth, it was not uncommon for Company men to take long-term Indian mistresses or even in rare cases (like the Hyderabad resident James Achilles Kirkpatrick, who conducted a politically dangerous love affair with a young woman from the local Muslim aristocracy) to marry them. The lawyer William Hickey, who left a chatty diary of Calcutta in the 1780s and 1790s, wrote tenderly of his long-term lover Jemdani, for whom he bought a country house on the Hooghly where the two of them entertained their mutual friends. She was, he wrote, 'respected and admired by all my friends, by her extraordinary sprightliness and good humour … unlike the women in general in Asia she never secluded herself from the sight of strangers, on the contrary she delighted in joining my male parties, cordially joining in the mirth which prevailed'. What happened to the children of these unions suggests both the possibilities and the limits of relationships across the racial border, for, while the offspring were usually looked after very well and educated, whether that education took place in India or England depended very much on the darkness or fairness of their skin.

Though none of the Company men posed for their portraits along with their Asian mistresses, they did choose to have themselves depicted together with the *banians*, who managed private trade for them (circumventing official restrictions) and were a crucial source of both commercial and political intelligence. Many of them, like the *banian* shown with the trader John Mowbray, came from the culturally sophisticated gentry class of the *bhadralog* in Bengal, the dynasties that produced the Tagores.

In Britain there was a presumption that new money was philistine, but the commercial shrewdness of these men kept company with a devotion to poetry and to mythological and sacred texts. It was natural, then, for Warren Hastings to believe that effective Company government required more than information about the cultivation of indigo. It also needed a working familiarity with Indian languages, both classical and vernacular, with religion, law, history and politics. So, from the mid-1770s to his foundation of the Asiatic Society in Bengal in 1784, Warren Hastings became the first great patron of Indian scholarship for Europeans. A group of protégés, many of them very young, were commissioned to produce the works that he hoped would be the foundation of educated and disinterested government. Nathaniel Brassey Halhed's 'Gentoo Code', a digest of Sanskrit law-books, appeared in 1776. Some eleven years later, the first English–Hindustani dictionary, *A Dictionary, English and Hindoostannee,* was published in two parts from 1787 to 1790 by the Scottish physician John Gilchrist who had gone from Bombay to Faizabad, grown a long beard like a *sannyasi* (religious mendicant) and 'assumed for a time the dress of the natives'. Gilchrist spent years listening intently to his language teachers or *munshis*, working out the phonetics of the language, and went on to become the first Professor of Hindustani at the College of Fort William, founded by Governor-General Wellesley in 1800.

None of this is to say that Hastings or his oriental scholars – Halhed, Gilchrist, Colebrooke and Wilkins – seriously believed Indian languages, law and literature to be the 'equal' of the accumulated wisdoms of Europe. Part of their determination to educate their countrymen in Indian culture was to liberate them from excessive dependence on native informants who could use their monopoly of knowledge for untrustworthy ends. Ideally, Hastings would have liked European judges qualified to preside over, or at least perfectly able to understand the proceedings of, Hindu and Muslim courts, which under the regime of the 1770s were still the principal recourse of judgement for the vast majority of Indians. But neither is this to say that his 'orientalism' was simply another tool of domination. Hastings and his colleagues took their power as given. What they wanted to do was to exercise it with some sympathy for the place of their government. Was it, for example, the act of a crudely manipulative 'orientalist' to sponsor the first English translation of the *Bhagavadgita*, to make sure its translator got Company leave in Banaras to study Sanskrit and then to provide a preface? In a letter to the chairman of the court of directors, proudly introducing the work, Hastings made it clear that the value of such a translation was not just that it was 'useful' for 'social communication with people over whom we exercise a dominion founded on the right of conquest'. It was also, he wrote in a telling phrase, the gain of humanity … it attracts and conciliates distant affections; it lessens the

Top: *A View of The Tryall of Warren Hastings Esq before the Court of Peers in Westminster Hall ... 1788*, engraved after E. Day, *c.* 1790. Above: *Edmund Burke*, studio of Sir Joshua Reynolds, 1771.

weight of the chain by which the natives are held in subjection and it imprints on the hearts of our own countrymen the sense and obligation of benevolence. Even in England this effect of it is greatly wanting. It is not very long since the inhabitants of India were considered by many as creatures, scarcely elevated above the degree of savage life; nor I fear is that prejudice wholly eradicated, though surely abated. Every instance which brings their real character home to observation will impress us with a more generous sense of feeling for their natural rights and teach us to estimate them by the measure of our own. But such instances can only be obtained by their writings and these will survive when the British dominion in India shall have long ceased to exist, and when the sources which it once yielded of wealth and power are lost to remembrance.

Whether the recipient at Leadenhall Street, Nathaniel Smith, got the message, humane and optimistic as it was, is open to doubt. A few months later Hastings was in England – not as he expected, honoured, but violently and publicly vilified as a ruthless and corrupt martinet. If one were to believe the parliamentary indictment drawn up in the spring of 1786 by Francis' friend and ally Edmund Burke, so far from conducting his administration wisely and benevolently Hastings had acted with 'gross injustice, cruelty and treachery against the faith of nations' (the Afghan Rohillas, whom Burke fantasized as noble horsemen caught in the trap of Hastings' personal aggrandizement); had turned Awadh 'which was once a garden [into] an uninhabited desert'; and had indulged 'a wanton, and unjust and pernicious exercise of his powers and the great situation of trust which he occupied in India in overturning the ancient establishments of the country.' In Burke's fulmination, the wise owl had been turned into the vulture.

Though no one, least of all Burke, had the clarity or honesty to see what in fact was obvious, and though the purported charges were all about the Rohillas and Awadh, Warren Hastings was subconsciously being impeached for losing America. Who else was there, after all, to be used as scapegoat? Not King George, who somehow escaped from the ruin of his Atlantic empire with his popularity untarnished; not Cornwallis, who was on his way to succeed Hastings in Calcutta. Putting Hastings in the dock for all kinds of infamies purportedly inflicted on the Indians enabled Britain to exorcise its uneasy conscience about what it had *actually* done in America. What was said about Hastings would have been more accurately said about Gage's and Hutchinson's and Cornwallis' own ferociously terrorizing Lieutenant-Colonel in the Carolinas, Banastre Tarleton. Hastings was even reproached for having nearly lost British India, when in fact he had saved it. In 1780 he had been facing the triple threat of the Marathas; the aggressive Muslim Sultan of Mysore, Haidar Ali, who would come very close to taking Madras; and the French. At precisely the moment when the British Empire was going down to defeat in the west, it had been the urgency and intelligence of Hastings' strategy, buying off the Marathas from any temptation of an alliance with Mysore and then pouring troops into south India, that had prevented an 'American' disaster from occurring in the east. But since, in the stinging aftermath of Saratoga and Yorktown, it was impossible to criticize those actually responsible for the débâcle, the need to create a home-grown oriental despot – bungling and corrupt – became irresistible. This was the straw man whom Burke indicted as 'a Pacha with three tails'. 'Do you want a criminal, my lords?' he thundered at the impeachment.

> When was there ever so much iniquity ever laid to the charge of any one? … I impeach him in the name of all the Commons of Great Britain whose national character he has dishonoured. I impeach him in the name of the people of India whose laws, rights, and liberties he has destroyed, whose country he has laid waste and desolate … I impeach him in the name of human nature itself which he has cruelly outraged, injured, and oppressed, in both sexes, in every age, rank, situation and condition of life.

Anything else? No wonder poor Hastings was confused by his predicament. The man who had surrendered at Yorktown was on his way to the Governor's House at Calcutta while he himself was in the dock, pilloried as some sort of Ginghiz Khan in knee breeches, fighting for his reputation and his life. At least, unlike the situation with so many scapegoats before, there was no summary rush to judgement. When the ugly mood of post-American chauvinist breast-beating had passed and Britain was once more in a real shooting war with the French, Hastings, having served his turn as whip-ping boy for wounded national self-esteem, was duly acquitted. But it took ten years of his life, and he never really recovered from the shock and shame. For his part, the plumply well-meaning Cornwallis did what he was supposed to do in India, which was to fly the flag of the chastened but resurgent British Empire as breezily as he could.

The myth of his predecessor's infamy was, in fact, necessary to Cornwallis' pose, provided for him by Burke and by Pitt's Secretary of State, Henry Dundas, as the sweeper of the Augean stables. He would be the man come to bring True Britishness to India; to hear its groans; to repair the damage done by the occido-oriental despot Hastings. Away, then, with the parasites infesting the revenue department (and away they went). Also, no more of this nonsense about the government going native. Cornwallis' own view of the Indians' capacity for government was famously expressed by his statement that 'every native of India I verily believe is corrupt.' What the country needed was a good stiff dose of reform: not an orientalized Briton but a Britannicized orient; not an English nawab but a sensible JP in the Governor's house. And to keep his officials out of the way of temptation, they had to be decently paid and their sphere of action uncontaminated by low matters of trade. Henceforth those who did business and those who governed would be utterly different personnel. From the increasing indifference, even stigma, attached to Company business came a new sense of altered mission for British India. Whatever might be taken from India in the way of commerce would be repaid a thousandfold with something incomparably more precious than silver coin – the blessings of British institutions, the accumulated wisdom of its justice and the sound benevolence of its society. So when Cornwallis looked at the heart of the matter – the land revenues of Bengal – and saw (as there undoubtedly were) criminal abuses and a dismal panorama of dispossessions and famines, he concluded that what he had to do first was to forget all about pandering to native traditions. A new beginning had to be made, one based on sound first principles.

Those principles were those of the solid English landowner, which, beneath the epaulettes and the frogging, Charles Cornwallis undoubtedly was. To own land, he supposed, was not just proprietorship; it was trust. The progress that could be seen inscribed in every Norfolk village, in every rippling acre of wheat, was owed to the mutually beneficent relationship between the wise, ingenious gentleman–farmer (beginning with Farmer George) and the thrifty, enterprising tenant farmer. (Never mind, of course, that this happy tableau owed just as much to the brutal dispossessions of eighteenth-century enclosures.) In this smiling, rustic Britannia, the parties to this self-sustaining economic miracle could be assured of reaping the harvest of their efforts through knowledge of the fixity of both their tenure and their taxes. All that was needed to make rural India fortunate was for Cornwallis to provide the necessary measure of stability. Stability, it need hardly be said, was a product of settled social hier-archy. 'A regular graduation of ranks', wrote Cornwallis, 'is nowhere more necessary than in this country for promoting order in civil society.' It also went without saying that this solid social order would have to be anchored by the Bengali equivalent of the English gentry, who could be depended on to meet their obligations to the govern-ment without unduly burdening their tenants. The Governor-General imagined he found them in the *zemindars*. Historically, under the Mughals, the *zemindars* had been able to inherit and pass on their land allotments within their families. But this didn't mean they were true and outright owners of those lands, as in Britain. They had been assigned the income from them (after the emperor had had his due) as tax officials of the empire, not as aristocrats. But for Cornwallis, all these ambiguities were swept aside

Lord Cornwallis Receiving the Sons of Tipu Sultan as Hostages, Seringapatam, 25 February 1792 (detail), by Robert Home, *c.* 1792.

by his thirst for cleansing simplicity and his indomitably sunny view of the moral invigoration of ownership. So the *zemindars* were turned into the absolute proprietors of their estates, conditional only on them paying to the government the allotted sum on the appointed day. The assurance of passing on estates to the next generation in England was, after all, the incentive to improve them. Once these 'landlords' had some sense of the ceiling of their tax obligations, they could set about becoming model country gentlemen, collecting only so much from their 'tenants' (who were, in fact, innocent cultivators, some of whom had owned their own strips and fields) who would be left with a surplus to reinvest in next year's seed and stock. As the 'tenants' became more productive they could produce for the booming cash markets of the towns and an export market hungry for cotton, indigo, sugar and opium. All this would happen, moreover, beneath the mantle of peace and justice provided by an honest and impartial government. Courts based on English law as well as Indian courts would now hear grievances, and government-appointed district officials would protect the natives from extortion and see that the monies collected went where they were supposed to.

As everyone sheltered by this miraculously self-fertilizing system grew more prosperous, equally miraculous cultural changes would begin to take place. Simple peasants would become customers for British-manufactured goods and the new Bengali gentry would begin to assemble libraries, opening their eyes to the indisputable wisdoms of the European (which is to say British) enlightenment. The scales would fall from their eyes. They would abandon their disgusting idols and their devotion to gods with elephant heads, even perhaps receive the light of the Gospel. *Real* civilization was just around the corner. Cornwallis was sure of it.

That, at any rate, was the theory. If it worked in Scotland – and a disproportionate number of the young administrators and surveyors who were left to work out the practical details were, in fact, Scots – why should it not work in Bengal, Bihar and Orissa? But Cornwallis' system presupposed peace and stability. And instead of the promised peace there were almost continuous wars – with Mysore, with the Marathas and then with the French. Pressed hard for funds, many of the traditional *zemindars* themselves went into debt to meet their contracts with the government. Their armed men were sent to the villages to extract the last rupee. And when loans and extortion still failed to deliver what they needed to make good on their contract with Calcutta, they were dispossessed and sold up. The indebted country gentry of England had sympathetic bankers willing to perpetuate their credit, but there was no such facility in India. Not infrequently the *zemindars'* creditors simply moved into their debtors' properties, taking over their contract. So precisely the class whom the bluff

Cornwallis most mistrusted – the Calcutta money-men, like the Tagores – were the main beneficiaries of his system, becoming wealthy estate owners at exactly this time. Under their impatient stewardship the capitalization of the countryside accelerated as land, some of it reclaimed from the flood delta of the Ganges, was put under cash crops like opium, silk and cotton that could make money, pots of it, very fast.

In August 1789, when he had introduced his 'Permanent Settlement' of the land revenue, Cornwallis had promised the directors of the East India Company that his plan was 'well calculated to secure and even increase your revenues'. But if the Company and the government had hoped that the profits of the new regime would translate into balanced books, those hopes were buried under the dust-storms of war. Both the directors of the Company and Pitt's government had regarded Hastings military adventurism as not only immoral but also ruinously expensive, so Cornwallis' brief was to hold the line. But India would not let him. Hastings' prudent decision to make territorial concessions to the Marathas as the price of keeping them out of the arms of Haidar Ali had proved no more than a breathing-space. For in the twenty years after he had seized power from a Hindu dynasty the Sultan of Mysore had built the most powerful south Indian state since the demise of the empire of the Vijayanagars in the seventeenth century. Roads and bridges had been built, and the rural and market economy flourished. And though he remained a Muslim prince, Haidar Ali made sure to patronize Hindu temples and shrines. Even Cornwallis thought it a realm of gardens.

Until, that is, he went to war to uproot it. In 1782 Haidar Ali died and was succeeded by his charismatic son Tipu Sultan. During and after the wars that ended in the annihilation of his state Tipu was demonized by the British as another Siraj-ud-Daulah, an unhinged, bloodthirsty despot, and was habitually referred to as 'the usurper' who had supplanted the 'ancient Hindu constitution' – as if the British themselves were credible judges of legitimacy. But the pattern of rationalizing conquests in terms of saving the Indians from themselves was now well established both in India and especially at home. And what could be even worse than a fanatical Indo-Muslim warlord? A fanatical Indo-Muslim warlord who thinks he's a French republican! There's no doubt that Tipu welcomed overtures from the French, who clung to strategically significant Indian Ocean naval bases on Mauritius and Réunion, and that he was happy to use them to train some of his native and Arab-African troops in more aggressively European warfare. Since the American war it seemed to be a French, not British, empire that was in the ascendant, so why would he not at least flirt with the temptation? What was there about British policy that would lead him to believe that they, not he, were the aggressors?

So in May 1791, for the first time since Yorktown, Cornwallis went to war. In front of Tipu's great palace–citadel at Seringapatam his old nightmares caught up with him. His army floundered helplessly in the monsoon mud. Over-extended, lines of communication broke down. But somehow the army did manage to stay together, and in the cool weather of the following year it launched a new and ultimately successful offensive against the island fortress of Kavery. Tipu's defeat was serious enough to force him to surrender half his territories and his two sons as hostages for his good conduct. The avuncular Charles Cornwallis, taking the hands of the little chaps in turbans, became a standard feature of the iconography of imperial self-congratulation. This was an empire that would be firm but magnanimous.

The good Uncle Charlie Cornwallis left India in 1793. The home verdict was that he had done well by India and well by the Empire. At least he hadn't lost it. But it was a mark of the sea–change in the presumptions about what that empire was supposed to be that, instead of dismay about a cost-efficient trading concern turning into an open-ended territorial government, there was a sense of the historical rightness, the inevitability, of that outcome. The greasy-fingered writer of Clive's day, sweating it out in some inky hole in Madras between bouts of arrack-drenched stupor in the Black Town brothels, had turned into the lordly collector sahib doing the tour of the district in his palanquin, scrutinizing the welfare of the cultivators, consulting the collective wisdom of Edinburgh to see how that lot might be improved. Not so long before, freedom of movement and fairness of treatment for up-country traders meant knowing whom to bribe and whom to beat up. Now there were white men in wigs who would adjudicate such matters from a bench in Calcutta or Bombay. And where once fighting for the Company had rated a poor second to parading in arms on the battlefields of Germany, now it was the field for heroes, the theatre of celebrity.

So, at any rate, the three Wellesley brothers (born Wesley) from County Meath – Richard, the oldest and the political supremo; Henry, the man of business; and Arthur, the battlefield boy wonder – imagined when they arrived in India at the end of 1797. By the time they left, eight years later, India had made them and they, for better or worse, had made (in all but formal title) the Raj. Robert Clive had never commanded an army of more than 5000 men. By 1804 Governor-General Richard Wellesley, first Marquess Wellesley, was commander of an army of some 192,000, as large as that of many of the most powerful states of Europe. The Company – which was to say now, in all but name, the British government – was unchallenged in the subcontinent as the paramount power. Mysore was gone. The Mughal empire was a pathetic joke, its present head, Shah Alam, a blind and helpless dependant of his British keepers. Delhi had surrendered to Calcutta as the arbiter not just of power but of authority too. Awadh –

Top left: *Richard Wellesley, First Marquis Wellesley*, English School, *c*. 1785.
Top right: *Hyacinthe Gabrielle Roland, Lady Wellesley*, by Elizabeth Vigee-Lebrun, 1790.
Above: *A View of Government House, Calcutta*, engraved by Robert Havell the Younger, after James Baillie Fraser, 1826.

the mid-Ganges state studded with great cities like Lucknow and Faizabad – was a dependency. The Marathas had been divided and all but their last formidable fighting chief, Holkar, neutralized. A regional ruler who had kept his nose clean and made sure to jump on the rolling juggernaut of British military power, like the Nizam of Hyderabad, was preserved, but with a British Resident *in situ* to babysit his politics and a cantonment of redcoats (paid for by his own treasury) to make sure he wasn't naughty. And the debts of the East India Company had trebled, to the point at which they no longer bore any resemblance to commercial book-keeping and had become an institutionally funded obligation. From his palatial new Government House in Calcutta, a near copy of Robert Adam's neo-classical Kedleston in Derbyshire, Wellesley could deliver imperial utterances as if he were indeed the new Augustus: 'the foundation of our empire in Asia is now laid in the tranquillity of surrounding nations and in the happiness and welfare of the people of India.'

And this is always what Richard Wellesley of Castle Dangan, Eton, Oxford and a nice pocket borough thought he was *supposed* to do. At Eton, Caesar, Livy and Tacitus had been drummed into him. But walking around Rome on the inevitable Grand Tour, Wellesley kept company with the ghosts of Trajan and Hadrian. At Posilippo he made the pilgrimage to Virgil's tomb, the imminence of his own epic romantically flickering inside him. When he met the nawab of Arcot in May 1798 – a mere satrap of the Company, after all – Wellesley's head was turned by the sight of the escort of fifteen elephants, 'decorated with superb hammered cloth, embroidered in gold, silver and jewels and with golden turrets on their backs'. Established in Calcutta, the long-faced, charismatic Irishman moaned in letters to his voluptuous French wife Hyacinthe about how sexually aroused he became in the tropical heat. But he exercised his virility in other ways, demanding and acquiring the kind of political and military authority that neither Warren Hastings nor Cornwallis could have dreamed of. The pretext – or, as he would have insisted, the occasion – was the global war with the French that had the home government frantically on the defensive. Bonaparte, whose run of military victories in Italy had astonished and terrified the Coalition powers, had now sent an immense expedition to Egypt, which, if successful, could directly threaten the lines of communication and trade with India from the Red Sea. No one, least of all Wellesley, was underestimating the continuing French capacity to project their power all the way to Calcutta and to inflict serious damage through their proxies.

The most dangerous, or the most foolhardy, was Tipu Sultan, who, even as he pretended to abide by the terms of his treaty with the British, was plotting with the French to escape its stranglehold on his territories and power. As usual, Wellesley took the betrayal personally and represented Tipu's desperate attempt to cut loose from the shackles of British domination as the action of an unhinged aggressor bent on annihi-lating the Company: 'Professing the most amicable disposition ... he has manifested a design to effect our total destruction ... he has prepared the means and instruments for a war of extermination.' A huge army, with Arthur Wellesley one of the commanders, smashed its way into Seringapatam, where Tipu's body was found buried beneath a mound of the dead at the Water Gate. Among the cartloads of plunder taken by the British was the octagonal throne of the *padshah* – the Muslim emperor that Tipu had declared himself to be – with its canopy surmounted by a golden *homa* bird, the beak glittering with inlaid stones, the eyes and tail studded with pearls. The *homa* was said by some to resemble an eagle, by others a vulture. The same could be said of Wellesley's war machine.

Everything that could be removed from Tipu's palace – his sword, his battle helmet, the mechanical tiger that when wound up would devour a British soldier and produce satisfyingly plaintive cries – made its way back, first to Calcutta and then to England (where it all ended up at Windsor or at the Victoria and Albert Museum in London), but the real prize was a quarter of a million head of white bullocks and milch cattle. With this huge logistical asset, Arthur Wellesley could deploy a completely sup-plied mobile army wherever he needed, and, together with Lieutenant-General Gerard Lake, he took the war to the Marathas and the threat of war to Awadh.

Though many of the battles were still intensely fought, Richard Wellesley had brought a new generation of cavalry horses, mostly bred from Arab stock, to India and that, together with an edge in field artillery and supply wagons, told. In September 1800 the generalissimo wrote exultantly to his brother, 'We always kill the chief general and we always have the luck to be able to identify the body ... truly my star is in the ascendant in India. I ought to leave the country before my luck changes.' To Hyacinthe, whom he suspected of casual infidelity (the suspicion was mutual), Wellesley bragged like an adolescent, as if India had been mastered specifically to impress his wife and keep her out of anyone else's bed: 'Behold me covered with glory ... I have done in two months [at Mysore] what took three years in Cornwallis's time. Farewell dear soul, now all is quiet I am about to arrange the affairs of a conquered country.' He would disclaim most honours except the Garter, but if the king insisted – well, he might allow himself to be known as 'Viscount Wellesley of Mysore'.

This was a bit premature. Wellesley knew that, when the bills came in, the men whom he called 'the cheesemongers of Leadenhall Street' would have a fit. But the six months it took for news from India to arrive gave him all the time he needed to present the directors and the government with *faits accomplis*. He would make the rhetorical challenge over and over again: who knew better the true state of peril confronting

Top: *Storming of Seringapatam*, by T. Sutherland after W. Heath, 1815.
Above: Sultan Tipu's Tiger, *c.* 1790, a mechanical tiger devouring a British soldier, made for the sultan's amusement.

British power in India – the men who were there, or the men poring over maps in an office in Westminster? And once the deeds had been done and the body of yet another Maratha general slung on a cart, what was he supposed to do? Give back the territories? Restore the vanquished to their powers? Lay up trouble for the future? India, he said, did not set much store by magnanimity. India responded to unapologetic supremacy.

For all his instinctive Bonapartism Richard Wellesley was not, in fact, a pure military adventurer, still less someone tempted by visions of personal dictatorship – though some who watched the lantern-jawed magnifico process through Calcutta, led by an escort of sixteen horsemen, wondered (especially in contrast to bluff old Cornwallis, who preferred to drive his own little trap like a country squire off to the whipping fair). However misguided, Wellesley was quite sincere when he claimed that the full-tilt drive to paramountcy could be justified by the long-term economic blessings that would make, as he had predicted in one of his rare speeches in parliament, 'London, the throne of commerce of the world'. The short-term fiscal pain had to be absorbed in order to lay down what we would call the infrastructure necessary for a mutually benevolent economic relationship between Britain and India. If his predecessors thought this could be done by defensive half-measures, they had been deluding themselves. As long as there had been competitive Indian powers capable of causing trouble, neither peace nor profit could ever be expected. It never occurred to Wellesley that an India shared among smaller, internally coherent regional states – Bengal, Awadh, Mysore, Hyderabad – might be at least as viable as his paramount Raj, any more than it would have occurred to the boy from County Meath that a federal Britain of four nations made any sense. He was not interested in an empire run by accountants. Fatehpur Sikhri and the Taj Mahal told him that India had last been happy when ruled by one great authority, and he would see to it that the new Raj would be the proper heir of Akbar and Jahangir.

In 1800, Wellesley set the capstone on the arch of his triumphalism by opening the new College of Fort William. It was, he often boasted, the achievement he was proudest of: the nursery of a new generation of proconsuls educated in the laws, languages and religion of the races and nations to whose government they were now irreversibly committed. Along with *munshis* (teacher-secretaries), many of the young men initially patronized by Warren Hastings now took up posts at the college. After Wellesley had gone the college would be sacrificed to the needs of fiscal retrenchment and replaced by Haileybury College in England, but not before it had inculcated its official version of how what had begun as a commercial company, trading from modest posts on the sufferance of the Mughals, had ended up holding sway over a subcontinent. The chaotic and stumbling route to dominion, strewn with acts of self-deception and self-enrichment, was remade as a broad historical highway at the end of which was Wellesley's classical house of government. Instead of being part of India's problems (perhaps the main problem), Britain was the solution. It was meant to be. 'The position in which we are now placed', Wellesley declared in 1804, 'is suited to the character of the British nation, to the principles of our laws, to the spirit of our constitution, to the liberal and comprehensive policy which becomes the dignity of a great and powerful empire.' Britain would be the new Rome in a subcontinent that the Romans had never reached.

Was it really only seventy years since the inspirational inscription had been set in Stowe's Temple of Gothic Liberty, thanking the gods for not making the free British Romans? Was it only three generations since the founders of a maritime empire had insisted that theirs would be a dominion uniquely blessed by liberty, unencumbered by the pompous trappings of conquest? It was supposed to have been a minimalist empire: no big, expensive standing armies; no regiments of tax collectors; an enterprise built on mutual interest, not on military coercion. Hampden and Milton would bless it for minding its own business.

It had not worked out that way. There was business all right, along with the edicts and the elephants, but it was not exactly what the founders had had in mind when they had imagined a flow of raw materials coming into the metropolis and a flow of manufactures going out to the empire. India had never wanted what Britain produced, and it still didn't. Raw cotton was now being shipped from Bombay to England, but in the volumes and at the prices dictated by the likes of Henry Wellesley. Yet those who turned it into manufactured cloths in the spinning and weaving sheds of the industrial north needed something from Asia to reconcile them to their grinding labour and inadequate wages, and that something was hot and sweet: sugared tea. So East India Company ships sailed back from Canton loaded with black Bohea, and its profits would go some way to paying for 150,000 sepoys (for the fabled bounty from Indian land revenues seemed more than ever a mirage). But the profitability of the business depended on the Chinese being induced to take something other than silver in exchange.

And that something was Indian; that something was a narcotic. Despite a draconian ban on opium, the Ch'ing empire was incapable of preventing smuggling, and the number of chests of Bengal opium that found their way to China rose from hundreds to many thousands a year. The first famous victim of the opium habit had been Robert Clive. It had eaten into him so badly that it had overpowered even his other mainline addiction – for the rushing high of imperial supremacy. Most of those who came later to British India would resist the first craving. But as for the opiate of global mastery, nineteenth- and even twentieth-century Britain would remain helplessly hooked.

SELECT BIBLIOGRAPHY

Abbreviations BM Press – British Museum Press; CUP – Cambridge University Press;
OUP – Oxford University Press; UCL – University College, London; UP – University Press

PRINTED PRIMARY SOURCES

Abbott, W. C. (ed.), *Writings and Speeches of Oliver Cromwell*, 4 vols (Clarendon Press 1988)

Bowle, John (ed.), *The Diary of John Evelyn* (OUP 1983)

Bray, William (ed.), *The Diary of John Evelyn from 1641 to 1705–6* (Gibbings 1980)

Camden, William, *Remains Concerning Britain* (John Russell Smith 1974)

Carlyle, T., *The Letters and Speeches of Oliver Cromwell*, 3 vols, ed. S. C. Lomas (Methuen 1904)

Defoe, Daniel, *A Tour of the Whole Island of Great Britain* (1742)

Defoe, Daniel, *Union and No Union* (1713)

Edwards, Paul (ed.), *The Life of Olaudah Equiano, or Gustavus Vassa the African, Written by himself* (Longman 1988)

Firth, C.H., *The Memoirs of Edmund Ludlow, Lieutenant-general of the Horse in the Army in the Commonwealth of England, 1625–1672* (Clarendon Press 1894)

Gough, Richard, *The History of Myddle*, ed. David Hey (Penguin 1981)

Hobbes, Thomas, *Leviathan* (Everyman's Library 1914)

Holmes, G., and Speck, W. (eds.), *The Divided Society: Party Conflict in England, 1694–1716, Documents of Modern History* (Arnold 1967)

Hughes, Anne (ed.), *Seventeenth Century England. A Changing Culture: Primary Sources, Vol. 1* (OUP 1980)

Laslett, Peter (ed.), *Two Treatises of Government by John Locke* (CUP 1967)

Latham, Robert and Matthews, William (eds.), *The Diary of Samuel Pepys. A New and Complete Transcription* (Bell & Hyman 1985)

Nichols, John, *The Progresses, Processions and Magnificent Festivities of King James I* (1828)

Petty, William, *Political Anatomy of Ireland* (Irish UP 1970)

Sommerville, J. P. (ed.), *Patriarcha and Other Writings by Sir Robert Filmer* (CUP 1991)

Spalding, Ruth (ed.), *The Diary of Bulstrode Whitelocke* (OUP 1990, for the British Academy)

Taylor, William Stanthorpe, and Pringle, Captain John Henry (eds.), *Correspondence of William Pitt, Earl of Chatham,* 4 vols (John Murray 1838–40)

Verney, Lady Frances Parthenope, *Memoirs of the Verney Family during the Civil War,* compiled from the letters, and illustrated by the portraits, at Claydon House (Longman 1892–1899)

Walpole, Horace, *Memoirs of the Reign of George the Third*, ed. G. F. Russell-Barker (Lawrence and Bullen 1894)

OVERVIEW AND GENERAL SOURCES

Beier, A. L., and Finlay, Roger, *London 1500–1700: The Making of the Metropolis* (Longman 1986)

Black, J., *A History of the British Isles* (Macmillan 1997)

Bradshaw, B., and Morrill, J. (eds.), *The British Problem, c. 1534–1707* (Macmillan 1996)

Brewer, John, *The Sinews of Power: War, Money and the English State, 1688–1783* (Unwin and Hyman 1989)

Broun, D, *et al.* (eds.), *Image and Identity: The Making and Re-making of Scotland through the Ages* (John Donald 1998)

Cannon, J. (ed.), *The Oxford Companion to British History* (OUP 1997)

Clark, J. C. D., *Revolution and Rebellion* (CUP 1986)

Colley, Linda, *Britons: Forging the Nation, 1707–1837* (Yale UP 1992)

Connolly, S. J. (ed.), *The Oxford Companion to Irish History* (OUP 1998)

Coward, Barry, *The Stuart Age 1603–1714* (Longman 1994)

Davies, N., *The Isles* (Macmillan 1999)

Davis, J., *A History of Wales* (Penguin 1990)

Devine, T. M., *The Scottish Nation, 1700–2000* (Penguin 1999)

Ellis, S. G., and Barber, S. (eds.), *Conquest and Union: Fashioning a British State, 1485–1725* (Longman 1995)

Fletcher, Anthony, *Gender, Sex and Subordination in England 1500–1800* (Yale UP 1995)

Foster, R. F., *Modern Ireland, 1600–1972* (Penguin 1988)

Grant, A., and Stringer, K. J. (eds.), *Uniting the Kingdom? The Making of British History* (Routledge 1995)

Heal, Felicity, and Holmes, Clive, *The Gentry in England and Wales 1500–1700* (Macmillan, 1994)

Hutchinson, Lucy, *Memoirs of the Life of Colonel Hutchinson* (1973)

Hutton, Ronald, *The Rise and Fall of Merry England: The Ritual Year 1400–1700* (OUP 1996)

Kearney, H., *The British Isles: A History of Four Nations* (CUP 1989)

Kishlansky, Mark, *A Monarchy Transformed, Britain, 1603–1714* (Penguin 1996)

Kishlansky, Mark, *Parliamentary Selection: Social and Political Choice in Early Modern England* (CUP 1986)

Langford, Paul, *A Polite and Commercial People: England 1727–1783* (OUP 1992)

Lenman, Bruce, *An Economic History of Modern Scotland 1660–1976* (Batsford 1977)

Lynch, Michael, *Scotland: A New History* (Pimlico 1991)

Mitchison, Rosalind, *A History of Scotland* (Methuen 1982)

Patterson, Annabel, *Early Modern Liberalism* (CUP 1997)

Rosenheim, James, *The Emergence of a Ruling Order: English Landed Society 1650–1750* (Longman 1998)

Samuel, Raphael, *Theatres of Memory: Vol. 2: Island Stories. Unravelling Britain* (Verso 1998)

Scott, Jonathan, *England's Troubles: Seventeenth Century English Political Instability in European Context* (CUP 2000)

Skinner, Quentin, *Liberty Before Liberalism* (CUP 1998)

Smith, A. G. R., *The Emergence of a Nation State: The Commonwealth of England, 1529–1660* (Longman 1992)

Underdown, David, *A Freeborn People: Politics and the Nation in Seventeenth Century England* (Clarendon 1996)

Wrightson, Keith, *English Society 1580–1680* (Hutchinson 1982)

SECONDARY SOURCES
CHAPTER ONE

Amussen, S., and Kishlansky, M. (eds.), *Political Culture and Cultural Politics in Early Modern England* (Manchester UP 1995)

Anderson, M. D., *History and Imagery in British Churches* (John Murray 1971)

Ashton, R., *James I by his Contemporaries* (Hutchinson 1969)

Clarke, Aidan, *The Old English in Ireland 1625–1642* (Cornell UP and MacGibbon & Kee 1966)

Coward, Barry, *The Stuart Age: England, 1603–1714* (Longman 1994)

Burgess, Glenn, *Absolute Monarchy and the Stuart Constitution* (Yale UP 1996)

Cust, Richard, *The Forced Loan and English Politics 1626–8* (Clarendon 1987)

Cust, Richard, and Hughes, Anne (eds.), *Conflict in Early Stuart England: Studies in Religion and Politics, 1603–42* (Longman 1989)

Donaldson, G., *Scotland: James V–VII* (Edinburgh UP 1965)

Durston, C., *James I* (Routledge 1993)

Eales, Jacqueline, and Durston, Christopher (eds.), *The Culture of English Puritanism, 1560–1700* (Macmillan 1990)

Farrell, Lori Anne, *Government by Polemic: James I, The King's Preachers, and the Rhetoric of Conformity, 1603–1625* (Stanford UP 1998)

Fitzpatrick, Brendan, *Seventeenth Century Ireland* (Gill & Macmillan 1988)

Hill, Christopher, *A Nation of Change and Novelty: Radical Politics, Religion and Literature in Seventeenth-century England* (Routledge 1990)

Hirst, Derek, *Authority and Conflict, England, 1603–1658* (Arnold 1986)

Holstun, James, *Ehud's Dagger: Class Struggle in the English Revolution* (Verso 2000)

Howarth, David (ed.), *Art and Patronage in the Caroline Courts* (CUP 1993)

Jardine, L. and Stewart, A., *Hostage to Fortune: The Troubled Life of Francis Bacon* (Phoenix 2000)

Lee, Maurice (Jr.), *Great Britain's Solomon: James VI and I in his Three Kingdoms* (University of Illinois Press 1990)

Lockyer, Roger, *Buckingham: The Life and Political Career of George Villiers, First Duke of Buckingham* (Longman 1981)

McGrath, Alister, *In the Beginning, The Story of the King James Bible* (Hodder & Stoughton 2001)

Nenner, Howard, *The Right to be King: The Succession to the Crown of England, 1603–1714* (Macmillan 1995)

Parry, Graham, *The Golden Age Restored: The Culture of the Court, 1603–42* (Manchester UP 1981)

Peck, Linda Levy (ed.), *The Mental World of the Jacobean Court* (CUP 1991)

Pocock, J. G. A., *The Ancient Constitution and the Feudal Law: A Study of English Historical Thought in the Seventeenth Century* (CUP 1987)

Russell, Conrad, *The Crisis of Parliaments: English History, 1509–1660* (OUP 1971)

Sharpe, Kevin, and Lake, Peter (eds.), *Culture and Politics in Early Stuart England* (Macmillan 1994)

Smith, A. G. R. (ed.), *The Reign of James VI and I* (Macmillan 1973)

Sommerville, J. P., *Royalists and Patriots: Politics and Ideology in England, 1603–1640* (Longman 1999)

Strong, Roy, *Henry, Prince of Wales and England's Lost Renaissance* (Thames & Hudson, 1986)

Wendorf, Richard, *The Elements of Life: Biography and Portrait Painting in Stuart and Georgian England* (Clarendon 1990)

Willson, D. H., *King James VI and I* (Jonathan Cape 1963)

Wormald, Jenny, *Court, Kirk and Community: Scotland, 1470–1625* (Edinburgh UP 1981)

Zaret, Paul, *The Origins of Democratic Culture: Printing, Petitions and the Public Sphere in Early Modern England* (Princeton UP 2000)

CHAPTER TWO

Adair, John, *John Hampden: The Patriot* (MacDonald & Jane's 1976)

Adair, John, *Puritans* (Sutton 1998)

Adair, John, *Roundhead General: The Campaigns of Sir William Waller* (Sutton 1997)

Bennett, Martyn, *The Civil Wars Experienced: Britain and Ireland, 1638–61* (Routledge 2000)

Carlin, Nora, *The Causes of the English Civil War* (Blackwell 1999)

Carlton, C., *Going to the Wars: The Experience of the British Civil Wars, 1638–51* (Routledge 1992)

Cope, Esther, *Politics without Parliaments, 1629–1640* (Allen & Unwin 1987)

Cust, Richard, and Hughes, Anne (eds.), *Conflict in Early Stuart England: Studies in Religion and Politics, 1603–1642* (Longman 1989)

Eales, Jacqueline, *Puritans and Roundheads: The Harleys of Brampton Bryan and the Outbreak of the English Civil War* (CUP 1990)

Emberton, Wilfrid, *The English Civil War Day by Day* (Sutton 1995)

Fletcher, Anthony, *The Outbreak of the English Civil War* (Edward Arnold 1981)

Fraser, Antonia, *Cromwell: Our Chief of Men* (Weidenfeld & Nicolson 1973)

Gaunt, Peter, *Oliver Cromwell* (Blackwell, 1996)

Gough, Richard, *The History of Myddle* (Caliban Books 1979)

Hinds, Hilary, *God's Englishwomen* (Manchester UP 1996)

Hughes, Ann, *The Causes of the English Civil War* (Macmillan 1991)

Hutton, Ronald, *The Royalist War Effort 1642–1646* (Routledge 1999)

Kenyon, John, and Ohlmeyer, Jane (eds.), with Morrill, John (consultant ed.), *The Civil Wars: A Military History of England, Scotland, and Ireland, 1638–1660* (OUP 1998)

Kishlansky, Mark, *The Rise of the New Model Army* (CUP 1979)

Macinnes, Allan, *Charles I and the Making of the Covenanting Movement 1625–1641* (John Donald 1991)

Makey, W.H., *The Church of the Covenant 1637–1651* (John Donald 1979)

Morrill, John S., *The Nature of the English Revolution* (Longman 1993)

Morrill, John, S., *The Revolt of the Provinces: Conservatives and Radicals in the English Civil War, 1630–1650* (Longman 1980)

Morrill, John, S., *The Revolt in the Provinces: The People of England and the Tragedies of War, 1634–1648* (Longman 1999)

Pereceval-Maxwell, M., *The Outbreak of the Irish Rebellion of 1641* (McGill-Queen's UP 1994)

Porter, Stephen (ed.), *London and the Civil War* (Macmillan 1996)

Raymond, Joad, *Making the News: An Anthology of the Newsbooks of Revolutionary England* (Windrush Press 1993)

Richardson, R. C. (ed.), *The English Civil Wars: Local Aspects* (Sutton 1997)

Roberts, Jane, *The King's Head: Charles I, King and Martyr* (Royal Collection 1999)

Russell, Conrad, *The Causes of the English Civil War* (Clarendon Press 1990)

Russell, Conrad, *The Fall of the British Monarchies, 1637–1642* (Clarendon Press 1995)

Seaver, Paul, S., *Wallington's World* (Methuen 1985)

Sharpe, Kevin, *The Personal Rule of Charles I* (Yale UP 1992)

Stone, Lawrence, *The Causes of the English Revolution, 1529–1642* (Ark 1986)

Tyacke, Nicholas, *The Fortunes of English Puritanism* (Dr William's Trust 1990)

Underdown, David, *Fire from Heaven: The Life of an English Town in the Seventeenth Century* (HarperCollins 1992)

Underdown, David, *Revel, Riot and Rebellion: Popular Politics and Culture in England, 1603–1660* (Oxford Paperbacks 1987)

Wedgwood, C.V., *The King's War, 1641–1647* (Collins 1958)

Wedgewood, C.V., *The Trial of Charles I* (Collins 1964)

Young, John R. (ed.), *Celtic Dimensions of the British Civil Wars* (John Donald 1997)

CHAPTER THREE

Armitage, David, Himy, Armand, and Skinner, Quentin (eds.), *Milton and Republicanism* (CUP 1995)

Aylmer, G. E., *The Interregnum: The Quest for Settlement, 1646–1660* (Macmillan 1972)

Aylmer, G. E. (ed.), *The Levellers in the English Revolution* (Thames & Hudson 1975)

Barnard, T.C., *Cromwellian Ireland. English Government and Reform in Ireland 1649–1660* (OUP 1975)

Capp, B. S., *The Fifth Monarchy Men: A Study in Seventeenth-century English Millenarianism* (Faber 1972)

Danielson, Dennis (ed.), *The Cambridge Companion to Milton* (CUP 1999)

Fitzpatrick, Brendan, *Seventeenth-century Ireland* (Gill & Macmillan 1988)

Gardiner, S.R., *Oliver Cromwell* (Longmans Green & Co 1901)

Gaunt, Peter, *Oliver Cromwell* (Blackwell 1996)

Gaunt, Peter, *The Cromwellian Gazetteer* (Sutton 1994)

Hill, Christopher, *Milton and the English Revolution* (Faber 1979)

Hill, Christopher, *The Experience of Defeat: Milton and Some Contemporaries* (Faber 1984)

Hill, Christopher, *The World Turned Upside Down* (Penguin 1978)

Ingle, H. Larry, *First Among Friends, George Fox and the Creation of Quakerism* (OUP 1994)

Mack, Phyllis, *Visionary Women. Ecstatic Prophecy in Seventeenth Century England* (University of California Press 1992)

Morrill, John, *Oliver Cromwell and the English Revolution* (Longman 1990)

Ohlmeyer, Jane H., *Ireland from Independence to Occupation 1641–1660* (CUP 1995)

Reilly, Tom, *Cromwell: An Honourable Enemy* (Brandon 1999)

Richardson, R. C. (ed.), *Images of Oliver Cromwell* (Manchester UP 1993)

Rogers, G. A. J., and Ryan, A. (eds.), *Perspectives on Thomas Hobbes* (Clarendon Press 1988)

Roots, Ivan (ed.), *Oliver Cromwell: A Profile* (Macmillan 1973)

Schaffer, Brian, and Shapin, Steven, *Leviathan and the Air Pump: Hobbes, Boyle and the Experimental Life* (Princeton UP 1985)

Scott, Jonathan, *Algernon Sidney and the English Republic, 1623–1677* (CUP 1988)

Sharpe, Kevin, and Zwicker, Steven N., *Refiguring Revolutions: Aesthetics and Politics from the English Revolution to the Romantic Revolution* (University of California Press 1998)

Spalding, Ruth, *The Improbable Puritan: A Life of Bulstrode Whitelocke* (Faber 1975)

Stevenson, David, *King or Covenant?* (Tuckwell Press 1996)

Thomas, Keith, *Religion and the Decline of Magic: Studies in Popular Beliefs in Sixteenth- and Seventeenth-century England* (Penguin 1978)

Underdown, David, *Pride's Purge. Politics in the Puritan Revolution* (Allen and Unwin 1985)

Wheeler, J. S., *Cromwell in Ireland* (Palgrave 2000)

Woolrych, A., *Commonwealth to Protectorate* (OUP 1982; Clarendon 1982)

Worden, Blair, *The Rump Parliament, 1648–1653* (CUP 1974)

CHAPTER FOUR

Ashcraft, Richard, *Revolutionary Politics and Locke's Two Treatises of Government* (Princeton 1986)

Baxter, Stephen, *William III and the Defence of European Liberty* (Longman 1966)

Childs, J., *The Army, James II and the Glorious Revolution* (Manchester UP 1980)

Downes, Kerry, *Christopher Wren* (Allen Lane 1971)

Downes, Kerry, *The Architecture of Wren* (Redhedge 1982)

Drake, Ellen T., *Restless Genius. Robert Hooke and Earthly Thoughts,* (OUP 1996)

Furst, Viktor, *The Architecture of Sir Christopher Wren* (Somerset 1956)

Harris, Ian, *The Mind of John Locke, A Study of Political Theory in its Intellectual Setting* (CUP 1994)

Harris, Tim, *London Crowds in the Reign of Charles II: Propaganda and Politics from the Restoration to the Exclusion Crisis* (CUP 1987)

Harris, Tim, *Politics under the Later Stuarts: Party Conflict in a Divided Society, 1660–1715* (Longman 1993)

Hutton, R., *Charles II: King of England, Scotland and Ireland* (Clarendon Press 1989)

Hutton, R., *The Restoration* (OUP 1985)

Israel, Jonathan (ed.), *The Anglo-Dutch Moment: Essays on the Glorious Revolution and its World Impact* (CUP 1991)

Jardine, Lisa, *Ingenious Pursuits: Building the Scientific Revolution* (Little, Brown 1999)

Jones, James, Rees, *The First Whigs: The Politics of the Exclusion Crisis, 1678–1683* (OUP 1961)

Kenyon, John, Philipps, *The Popish Plot* (Heinemann 1972)

Lang, Jane, *Rebuilding St Paul's After the Great Fire of London* (OUP 1956)

Miller, John, *James II: A Study in Kingship* (Methuen 1989)

Ollard, Richard, *Clarendon and his Friends* (Hamilton 1987)

Picard, Lisa, *Restoration London* (Orion 1997)

Platt, Colin, *The Great Rebuilding of Tudor and Stuart England: Revolutions in Architectural Taste* (UCL Press 1994)

Porter, Roy, *London: A Social History* (Hamish Hamilton 1994)

Rosenheim, James, R., *The Emergence of a Ruling Order: English Landed Society, 1650–1750* (Longman 1998)

Speck, W. A., *Reluctant Revolutionaries* (OUP 1988)

Western, J. R., *Monarchy and Revolution: The English State in the 1680s* (Blandford 1972)

Whinney, Margaret, Dickens, *Wren* (Thames & Hudson 1971)

CHAPTER FIVE

Black, Jeremy, *Robert Walpole and the Nature of Politics in Early Eighteenth-century Britain* (Macmillan 1990)

Boulton, J. T., *Daniel Defoe* (Batsford 1965)

Brewer, John, *The Sinews of Power. War, Money and the English State 1688–1783* (Hutchinson 1988)

Brewer, John, and Styles, John, (eds.), *An Ungovernable People. The English and their Law in the Seventeenth and Eighteenth Centuries* (Hutchinson 1980)

Clark, J. C. D., *English Society, 1688–1832* (CUP 1985)

Cockburn J. S. (ed.), *Crime in England 1550–1800* (Methuen 1977; Princeton UP 1977)

Daiches, David, Jones, Peter, and Jones, Jean (eds.), *The Scottish Enlightenment 1730–1790. A Hotbed of Genius* (Saltire Society 1996)

Denvir, Bernard, *The Eighteenth Century: Art, Design and Society, 1689–1789* (Longman 1983)

Devine, T. M., *Clanship to Crofters' War: The Social Transformation of the Scottish Highlands* (Manchester UP 1994)

Devine, T. M. (ed.), *Conflict and Stability in Scottish Society, 1700–1850* (John Donald 1990)

Dickson, P.G., *The Financial Revolution in England* (Macmillan 1967)

Douglas, Hugh, *Jacobite Spy Wars* (Sutton 1999)

Gilmour, Ian, *Riots, Risings and Revolutions. Governance and Violence in Eighteenth Century England* (Hutchinson 1992 and Pimlico 1992)

Gregg, Edward, *Queen Anne* (Ark 1980)

Harvie, C., *Scotland and Nationalism: Scottish Society and Politics, 1707–1994* (Routledge 1994)

Holmes, G. (ed.), *Britain after the Glorious Revolution, 1689–1714* (Macmillan 1969)

Houston, R. A., and Whyte, I. D., (eds.), *Scottish Society, 1500–1800* (CUP 1989)

Jones, J. R., *Country and Court, England, 1658–1714* (Arnold 1978)

Lenman, B. P., *The Jacobite Clans of the Great Glen, 1650–1784* (Methuen 1984)

Lenman, B. P., *The Jacobite Risings in Britain, 1689–1746* (Eyre Methuen 1980)

Lynch, M. (ed.), *Jacobitism and the '45* (Historical Association for Scotland 1995)

McKendrick, Neil, Brewer, John and Plumb, J. H., *The Birth of a Consumer Society. The Commercialization of Eighteenth Century England* (Europa 1980)

McLean, M., *The People of Glengarry: Highlanders in Transition, 1745–1820* (McGill-Queen's UP 1991)

McLynn, F., *The Jacobites* (Routledge and Kegan Paul 1985)

Mitchison, Rosalind, *Lordship to Patronage. Scotland 1603–1745* (Edward Arnold)

Parissien, S., *Adam Style* (Phaidon 1992)

Philipson, N. T., and Mitchison, Rosalind (eds.), *Scotland in the Age of Improvement* (1970)

Plumb, J. H., *Sir Robert Walpole*, 2 vols (Cresset Press 1956 and 1960)

Plumb, J. H., *The Growth of Political Stability in England, 1675–1725* (Penguin 1967)

Plumb, J. H., *The Making of a Historian: Collected Essays* (Harvester–Wheatsheaf 1988)

Porter, Roy, *Enlightenment: Britain and the Creation of the Modern World* (Penguin 2000)

Prebble, John, *The Darien Disaster* (1968)

Richards, E., *A History of the Highland Clearances*, 2 vols (Croom Helm 1982 and 1985)

Sanderson, M. H. B., *Robert Adam and Scotland* (HMSO 1992)

Scott, P. H., *Defoe in Edinburgh* (Tuckwell 1995)

Scott-Moncrieff, Lesley (ed.), *The '45: To Gather an Image Whole* (Mercat 1988)

Smart, A., *Allan Ramsay* (Yale UP 1992)

Smout, T. C., *A History of the Scottish People* (Penguin 1969)

Spadafora, David, *The Idea of Progress in Eighteenth Century Britain* (Yale 1990)

Speck, W. A., *Stability and Strife, England, 1714–1760* (Arnold 1977)

CHAPTER SIX

Anderson, Fred, *Crucible of War: The Seven Years' War and the Fate of Empire in British North America, 1754–1766* (Knopf 2000)

Armitage, David, *The Ideological Origins of the British Empire* (CUP 2000)

Ayling, Stanley, *The Elder Pitt*

Bailyn, Bernard, *The Ideological Origins of the American Revolution* (Harvard UP 1992)

Bailyn, Bernard, *The Ordeal of Thomas Hutchinson* (Harvard UP 1974)

Bailyn, Bernard, *Voyagers to the West. A Passage in the Peopling of America on the Eve of the Revolution* (Random House 1988)

Bayly, C. A., *Empire and Information: Intelligence Gathering and Social Communication in India, 1780–1870* (CUP 1997)

Bayly, C. A., *Imperial Meridian: The British Empire and the World, 1780–1830* (Longman 1989)

Bayly, C. A., *Rulers, Townsmen and Bazaars: North Indian Society in the Age of British Expansion, 1770–1870* (CUP 1983)

Bayly, C. A. *et al.* (eds.), *The Raj: India and the British, 1600–1947* (Nat. Portrait Gallery 1990)

Bayly, Susan, *Caste, Society and Politics in India from the Eighteenth Century to the Modern Age* (CUP 1999)

Beckles, Hilary, *A History of Barbados* (CUP 1990)

Blackburn, Robin, *The Making of New World Slavery. From the Baroque to the Modern 1492–1800* (Verso, 1997)

Butler, Jon, *Becoming America: The Revolution before 1776* (Harvard UP 2000)

Canny, N. (ed.), *The Origins of Empire: British Overseas Enterprise to the Close of the Seventeenth Century. The Oxford History of the British Empire, Vol. 1* (OUP 1998)

Chaudhuri, S. (ed.), *Calcutta: The Living City, Vol. 1: The Past* (OUP 1990)

Cohn, Bernard S., *Colonialism and Its Forms of Knowledge. The British in India* (Princeton 1996)

Conway, Stephen, *The British Isles and the War of American Independence* (OUP 2000)

Cook, Don, *The Long Fuse: How England Lost the American Colonies, 1760–1785* (Atlantic Monthly Press 1995)

Dickinson, H. T. (ed.), *Britain and the American Revolution* (Longman 1998)

Draper, T., *A Struggle for Power: The American Revolution* (Abacus 1997)

Dunn, Richard S., *Sugar and Slaves. The Rise of the Planter Class in the English West Indies 1625–1713* (Norton 1973)

Games, Alison, *Migration and the Origins of the English Atlantic World* (Harvard UP 1999)

George, Dorothy, M., *English Political Caricature to 1792* (Clarendon Press 1959)

Greene, Jack P., *The Intellectual Construction of America: Exceptionalism and Identity from 1492 to 1800* (University of North Carolina Press 1993)

Handler, J. S., and Lange, F. W., *Plantation Slavery in Barbados* (Harvard UP 1978)

Harvey, Robert, *Clive: The Life and Death of a British Emperor* (Hodder and Stoughton 1998)

Hibbert, C., *Redcoats and Rebels: The American Revolution through British Eyes* (Avon 1990)

Inikori, Joseph E., and Engerman, Stanley, L. (eds.), *The Atlantic Slave Trade: Effects on*

Economies, Societies and Peoples in Africa, the Americas and Europe (Duke UP 1992)

James, L., *Raj: The Making and Unmaking of British India* (Abacus 1997)

Keay, John, *The Honourable Company: A History of the English East India Company* (HarperCollins 1991)

Labarée, Benjamin Woods, *The Boston Tea Party* (OUP 1964)

Lawson, Philip, *The East India Company: A History* (Longman 1987)

Maier, Pauline, *American Scripture. Making the Declaration of Independence* (Random House 1997)

Maier, Pauline, *From Resistance to Revolution. Colonial Radicals and the Development of American Opposition to Britain, 1765–1776*

Marshall, P. J., *Bengal: The British Bridgehead, Eastern India, 1740–1828* (CUP 1987)

Marshall, P. J. (ed.), *The Eighteenth Century: The Oxford History of the British Empire, Vol 2* (OUP 1998)

Marshall, P. J., *Trade and Conquest: Studies on the Rise of British Dominance in India* (Variorum 1993)

Mintz, S. W., *Sweetness and Power: The Place of Sugar in Modern History* (Penguin 1985)

Mintz, S. W., *Tasting Food, Tasting Freedom. Excursions into Eating, Culture and the Past* (Beacon 1996)

Moorhouse, G., *Calcutta* (Weidenfeld and Nicolson 1971)

Padfield, P., *Maritime Supremacy and the Opening of the Western Mind* (Pimlico, 2000)

Pagden, Anthony, *Lords of All the World, Ideologies of Empire in Spain, Britain and France* c. *1500–1800* (Yale UP 1995)

Peters, Marie, *The Elder Pitt* (Longman 1998)

Pocock, Tom, *Battle for Empire: The Very First World War, 1756–63* (Michael O'Mara 1998)

Sandiford, Keith, A., *The Cultural Politics of Sugar. Caribbean Slavery and Narratives of Colonialism* (CUP 2000)

Sheridan, R. B. *Sugar and Slavery: An Economic History of the British West Indies, 1623–1775* (Caribbean UP 1974)

Sinha, N.K., *The Economic History of Bengal from Plassey to the Permanent Settlement*, 2 vols (Calcutta 1956 and 1962)

Spear, Percival, *The Nabobs: A Study of the Social Life of the English in Eighteenth-century India* (OUP 1998)

Walvin, James, *Black Ivory: A History of Slavery* (HarperCollins 1992)

Walvin, James, *Making the Black Atlantic: Britain and the African Diaspora* (Cassell 2000)

Walvin, James, *Questioning Slavery* (Routledge 1996)

Weller, Jac, *Wellington in India* (Longman 1972)

Wickwire, F. and M., *Cornwallis: The Imperial Years* (University of North Carolina Press 1980)

Wild, A., *The East India Company: Trade and Conquest from 1600* (HarperCollins 2000)

Young, Alfred F., *The Shoemaker and the Tea Party. Memory and the American Revolution* (Beacon 1999)

Zobel, Hiller, *The Boston Massacre* (Norton 1970)

ACKNOWLEDGEMENTS

'Epic' is a word that suffers from over-use these days, but the history of *A History of Britain* certainly has a long roll-call of heroes – other than its author – without whose unflagging labours neither television programmes nor book could possibly have got made.

At BBC Worldwide Sally Potter and my excellent editor Belinda Wilkinson have remained heroically undaunted by the prospect of what had been commissioned as one short book turning into three. In every important sense this work has been a collaboration between myself and an exceptionally gifted and devoted group of colleagues at BBC Television, in particular, Ian Bremner, Martin Davidson, Liz Hartford, and Mike Ibeji. Melisa Akdogan, Ben Ledden and Ashley Gethin were exceptionally resourceful both in the libraries and on location. Had I not had the tireless and invariably considerate help of Sara Fletcher, I would have come unglued in locations throughout the British Isles. Tanya Hethorn, Tim Sutton and Mark Walden-Mills have, in crucial ways, helped the presenter present. Susan Harvey in Factual Publicity has been the gentlest and friendliest of promoters. It's been a source of great happiness to work closely with John Harle on the music for the series. Laurence Rees, Glenwyn Benson and Janice Hadlow have all cast a benevolently critical eye on our work when it most mattered and have been our most generous supporters. Alan Yentob and Greg Dyke have both given us the sense of how much *A History of Britain* matters to the BBC.

I'm deeply grateful to a number of colleagues who were kind enough to read both scripts and chapters for errors, in particular, John Brewer, Ann Hughes, Holger Hoock, Peter Marshall, Steven Pincus and David Haycock. Any that remain are, of course, my own responsibility.

In a much larger and deeper sense, though, I owe an enormous debt of gratitude to the wisdom and erudition of teachers (including schoolteachers), from whom I first learned the great contentions of British and colonial history in the seventeenth and eighteenth centuries, and of friends and colleagues, whose scholarship and critical analysis is still a source of exhilarating illumination. Though they may well take exception to some (or many) of the views expressed in this book, I hope that the overdue thanks offered, in particular, to David Armitage, Roy Avery, Robert Baynes, Mark Kishlansky, Sir John Plumb, Roy Porter, Kevin Sharpe and Quentin Skinner, will not go amiss.

My agents at PFD – Michael Sissons and Rosemary Scoular – have been, as ever, towers of strength on whom I lean, and occasionally collapse. My thanks, too, to James Gill, Sophie Laurimore and Carol Macarthur. Provost Jonathan Cole at Columbia University has been exceptionally kind in allowing me the necessary leave to work on the series and I'm delighted to have played a part in pioneering the on-line seminar, produced jointly by BBC Education and Columbia in partnership with Fathom.Com, about the eighteenth-century British Empire. Jennifer Scott was an extraordinary colleague in the production of that innovative departure in popular historical education.

Shifting back and forth between book and script-writing is likely to make the head spin, and certain to make the writer-presenter generally impossible to be around. So I'm, as always, more grateful than I can say to my friends for submitting to recitations from the Schama book of lamentations – thank you, again – Clare Beavan, Lily Brett, John Brewer, Tina Brown, Jan Dalley, Alison Dominitz, Harry Evans, Amanda Foreman, Eliot Friedman, Mindy Engel Friedman, Andrew Motion, David Rankin, David Remnick, Anthony Silverstone, Beverly Silverstone, Jill Slotover, Stella Tillyard, Bing Taylor and Leon Wieseltier. To my nearest and dearest – Ginny, Chloe and Gabe – I give my heartfelt thanks for riding the storms of their unreasonably cranky Dad and husband, and for the calm waters and always-open harbour of their love.

INDEX

Page numbers in italics refer to illustrations

PICTURE CREDITS